The Western Tradition

The Western Tradition

Third Edition

EUGEN WEBER
University of California
Los Angeles

From the Ancient World to Louis XIV

D. C. HEATH AND COMPANY
Lexington, Massachusetts Toronto London

To the Mordlers

PREFACE

The passages gathered in this volume provide a reflection of the attitudes, ideas, or circumstances of the times which produced them. The choice was not an easy one, if only because every period is a complex collection of different attitudes, different tendencies, different problems, different men. The best one can do is to select documents that will throw light on the most typical or significant circumstances of an age. The selection must be arbitrary, and it is likely to slant in the direction of the editor's interests. In this case, I am trying to illustrate the developments and problems of Western Civilization from its remote origins to the present day. I can only hope that the following passages will put a little flesh on the bare bones of the textbook and give some body to the ghostly figures that parade too regularly through the pages of history books.

Readings are generally used in history courses as material for discussions complementing the lectures and as depositories for some of the great classic works or documents to which the courses refer. This book contains most of the classic texts to which teachers like to refer. It also contains passages which, in every section, lend themselves to discussion, argument, and various interpretations. In this connection, I have avoided cutting the ground from under the feet of teacher or student by the too copious introductions which, in some books, tend to furnish many ideas that the discussion itself should elicit and elucidate: my introductions *try* to be fairly noncommittal. In addition, the passages just mentioned are interspersed with more deliberately illustrative material, which throws an intimate light on the life and problems of a given time and place without necessarily lending itself to discussion. Thus, in his assignments, the teacher can pick and choose according to his purpose among passages that are illustrative or controversial, and I rather hope that such things as assignments omitted may catch the eye of the curious or the browsing, and lead, perhaps, to further reading.

This second revision of *The Western Tradition* has been undertaken in the wake of a book—*A Modern History of Europe*—which, roughly, deals with the last six centuries of European man. Inevitably, many passages reprinted here furnished fuel for those pages, while some of the things I read and thought while writing it are reflected here. There is always some risk in accumulations such as this—above all, the spiritual desiccation of the reader in a hurry, with little time to waste,

> And so the only books at which he looks
> Are books on books, and books on books on books.

Yet, even displaced, as if in a museum, these passages (or those of them that had it in them to begin with) still shine and still reflect their maker and their time. Acquaintance with them, even truncated, even compiled, is better than no acquaintance at all.

As with the second edition, the changes in the text consist more of addition than subtraction. Two figures make their entrance in the earlier part—St. Francis and Montaigne—without whom I cannot understand how the book thrived before. The most recent past (still very present) is reflected in sections on new orientations in the Christian churches and Christian belief; on the debates and tremors that living experience of communism has sparked among Marxists; and on the revolt of youth in different countries. Passages have been added here and there to show how people lived, as well as what they thought. Not least, an essay by Professor Trevor-Roper opens the discussion of what history is about, and what its relations are with social sciences. If the rest of the book offers the raw material of historical interpretation, Professor Trevor-Roper's essay shows what a lucid mind can do with it. In the ongoing argument of whether history is science or art, his pages prove that, however, "scientifically" approached, history *can* be an art.

Obviously, the same principles that went into this collection of readings and inspired its revisions must be applied in its use. This leaves me open to criticism for trying to cram in too much, ending with a grab bag difficult to cope with, let alone to read through in the space of an ordinary school year. But I would rather overrate than underrate my readers—rather ask too much than too little. It is bad enough that universities and colleges should devote so much time to what are in effect remedial courses designed to fill the gaps left in their students' schooling or, rather, to lay a groundwork which the schools have not bothered to provide. While this must be, there is yet no need to go overboard by trying to present the approach, and the understanding, of a vast, varied, and complex story as something easy and simple—leaving students with the impression that potted knowledge is as accessible and no more indigestible than potted shrimp.

CONTENTS

Introduction   xiii

The Past and the Present

Hugh Trevor-Roper: *History and Sociology*   xxi

The Ancient World

The First Great Empires

The Egyptians: *Hymn to the Nile*   3
    from The Book of the Dead   4
    Wenamon's Journey   6
    Hymn to the Aton   10
    Tut-Ankh-Amon's Restoration   12
The Babylonians: *The Code of Hammurabi*   15
The Assyrians: *Annals of Assur-Nasir-Pal*   21
    Annals of Ashurbanipal   26
The Sumerians: *Penitential Prayer to Every God*   31
    A Prayer to the Goddess Ishtar   32
    Extract from a Psalm   33

Ancient Israel

The Old Testament: *from Exodus*   34
    from The Psalms of David   39
    from Isaiah   40
    from Jeremiah   41
    from The Second Isaiah   42

Ancient Greece

Plutarch: *from The Life of Lykurgus*   46
Thucydides: *The Funeral Oration of Pericles*   50
    The Melian Dialogue   55
Sophocles: *Oedipus, King of Thebes*   61
Xenophon: *from the Memorabilia*   91
    from On Revenues   94
Plato: *from The Republic*   105
Aristotle: *from The Politics*   110
Lucretius: *from On the Nature of Things*   118
Epictetus: *from The Discourses*   128

Ancient Rome

Polybius: *The Roman Constitution*   131
Cicero: *from On the Commonwealth*   139
    from On the Laws   141
    Scipio's Dream   145
Petronius: *from Trimalchio's Dinner*   150
Seneca: *from The Epistles*   154

The Early Christian World

The New Testament: *from The Gospel According to St. Luke*   158
    from The Gospel According to St. Matthew   160
Pliny the Younger: *Letters*   164
Hadrian: *Letter to Minucius Fundanus*   166
Galerius: *Edict of Toleration*   166
Constantine: *Edict of Milan*   167
St. Augustine: *from The Confessions*   169
Church Councils: *The Nicene Creed*   178
    The Creed of Constantinople   178
    Definition of Faith by the Council of Chalcedon 178

Disintegration and Reconstruction

The Barbarians

Julius Caesar: *The Germans*   183
Ammianus Marcellinus: *Roman Policy Toward the Germans*   184
St. Jerome: *Letters*   186

Apollinaris Sidonius: *Letters*   188
Gregory of Tours: *History of the Franks*   194

Charlemagne

Charlemagne: *Letter to the Pope*   204
    from The Capitularies of the Army   205
    Letter to Abbot Fulrad   206
    Capitularies Relating to Education   206
    Admonitio Generalis   208
    General Capitulary for the Missi   208
Emperor's Missi: *A Letter*   210

Feudalism and Personal Dependence

An Anglo-Saxon Formula of Commendation   212
A Frankish Formula of Commendation   212
Acceptance of an Antrustion   213
Charter of Guardianship Granted by the King   213
Capitulary Concerning Freemen and Vassals   213
Capitulary of Mersen   214
Grant of a Fief   214
Grant of a Fief of Money   214
An Early Feudal Summons   215
Legal Rules for Military Service   215
Service of the Count of Champagne   215
Freeing of a Serf   216
Magna Charta   217
Covenant Between King John and the Barons   223

The Church in the Middle Ages

Innocent III: *Empire and Papacy*   225
Boniface VIII: *"Unam Sanctam"*   226
Monastic Rules: *Rule of St. Benedict*   227
    Rule of St. Francis   231
Thomas of Celano: *The Life of St. Francis*   233
St. Thomas Aquinas: *On the Existence of God*   240
Hinemar: *Description of the Cold Water Ordeal*   242
Raymond of Agiles: *Ordeal by Fire*   243
Report of Judicial Combat in Spain   244

The Crusades

Urban II: *Speech at Clermont*   247
Fulcher of Chartres: *Account of the First Crusade*   249
Anselme of Ribemont: *Letter to Archbishop of Reims*   250
Guy, a Knight: *Letter*   252

Medieval Life and Culture

Raoul Glaber: *Famine*   257
Galbert of Bruges: *A Good Prince Struggles Against Famine*   258
    Out with the Poor   259
Stories of the Troubadours: *from The Song of Roland*   259
    from Aucassin and Nicolette   264
Jacques De Vitry: *Life of the Students at Paris*   268
Geoffrey Chaucer: *from Canterbury Tales*   270

Economic Development of the Middle Ages

St. Thomas Aquinas: *On Fraud Committed in Buying and Selling*   280
    Of the Sin of Usury Which is Committed in Loans   283
Guild Ordinances: *Ordinance of the Gild Merchant of Southampton*   289
    Ordinance of the Gild Merchant of the Holy Trinity of Lynn Regis 291
    Articles of the Spurriers of London   293

The Making of the Modern World

Fresh Fields and Pastures New

Pico della Mirandola: *Oration on the Dignity of Man*   297
Niccolò Machiavelli: *from The Prince*   300
François Rabelais: *from Gargantua and Pantagruel*   313
Charles Dumoulin: *from On Contracts and Usury*   319
Paolo Toscanelli: *Letter to Columbus*   320
Christopher Columbus: *from The Journal*   323
Vasco da Gama: *from A Journal of the First Voyage*   325
John Cabot: *Report to the Duke of Milan*   329
Richard Hakluyt: *from Divers Voyages Touching the Discovery of America* 331
Space Theology   332

Reformation and Counter Reformation

John Wycliffe: *Conclusions*   335
    Reply to the Summons of the Pope   336
The Borgias: *from The Life and Times of Niccolò Machiavelli*   337
    from Cronaca della Citta di Perugia dal 1492 al 1503 339
    The Antiborgian Letter   340
Albert of Mainz: *Instructions Concerning Indulgences*   341
John Tetzel: *A Sermon on Indulgences*   343
Martin Luther: *The Ninety-five Theses*   345
    On the Babylonish Captivity of the Church   350
Peasant Revolt: *The Twelve Articles*   352
Thomas Bilney: *Letter to the Bishop of London*   355
John Calvin: *from The Institutes of the Christian Church*   358
Ignatius Loyola: *from Spiritual Exercises*   360
The Council of Trent: *Decrees*   363
Fr. Joachim Opser, S.J.: *Letter to the Abbot of Saint-Gall*   372
Papire Masson: *from Historie de Charles IX*   373

Political and Economic Changes

Report of Venetian Ambassador: *Power and Revenues of the States
    of Europe in 1423*   374
Henry VIII: *The Act of Supremacy*   377
    The Act of the Six Articles   378
Charles V: *The Abdication of Charles V*   379
The Library of Charles V at San Yuste   381
The Gold of the Indies   382
Revenues of the King of Spain   382
Henry VIII: *Beggars Act of 1531*   383
Elizabeth I: *Poor Relief Act*   386
Thomas More: *from Utopia*   390
Richard Hooker: *from Preface to the Laws of Ecclesiastical Policy*   394
Jean Bodin: *from La République*   399
Montaigne: *Of Managing One's Will*   402

The Seventeenth Century

Hans Jacob von Grimmelshausen: *from Simplicissimus*   417
Muscovy   423

General Patrick Gordon: *from The Diary of General Patrick Gordon of Auchleuchries*   430
Thomas Mun: *from England's Treasure by Foreign Trade*   433
Daniel Defoe: *from The Complete English Tradesman*   442
René Descartes: *from The Discourse Upon Method*   448
Isaac Newton: *from The Mathematical Principles of Natural Philosophy*   458
John Locke: *from An Essay Concerning Human Understanding*   460
Witch Hunting: *from The Witch-Persecutions at Trier*   463
    from The Witch-Persecution at Bamberg   464
    The Methods of Witch-Persecutions   468

The Political Debate

Jacques Bénigne Bossuet: *from On the Nature and Properties of Royal Authority*   473
Thomas Hobbes: *from The Leviathan*   476
John Locke: *from The Second Treatise on Government*   488

INTRODUCTION

The story outlined in these pages is manifold and, of course, unfinished as history itself. It does, however, possess a certain internal coherence, for it reflects the gradual progress of Western man to greater self-consciousness and self-control, his repeated attempts to master not only himself but the world around him—aims in the pursuit of which he was never more than partially successful. The forty centuries on which we touch in these two volumes led man through a wide gamut of experience and experiment. Several times—as in Egypt, Greece, or Rome—he achieved types of civilization that seemed supremely satisfactory, and several times these collapsed or were destroyed, though leaving behind them a fund of techniques and thought and values that were eventually incorporated into subsequent societies in the way in which the stones and the statues of ancient Rome were incorporated into the buildings of the Renaissance.

The latest of these cultural structures began to rise after the disintegration of the Roman Empire in the West, and upon its ruins. The notion of a middle age seems to be the invention of certain fifteenth-century humanists who felt that only two historical periods really counted: the long-lost golden age of classical antiquity and their own, modern, Renaissance. The intervening period, across which these men saw themselves continuing a great tradition, was dark and useless, a time of chaos and terror better forgotten now that it was past and deserving no name, unless to describe its character—dark or Gothic (i.e., barbarous)—or its position in the middle. Yet, neither the bubbling buoyancy of the humanists nor their intellectual snobbery would have been possible without the foundations—economic, political, and scholarly —laid by their predecessors' long struggle against chaos and unreason—enemies of man and of civilization as much in his mind as in the world around him. Hence, much of this book concerns the slow and self-conscious efforts of Europeans, like fallen angels, trying to recover the heights of order, knowledge, and sophistication upon which men were thought to have stood in Augustan days. By the time of Louis XIV men believed that this had been achieved, that the ground lost during the "dark ages" had been regained, and that the Great Century, the seventeenth, had reached a cultural level no whit inferior to that of the ancients. It had been a long haul, but modern man had made it: the latest times had nothing to envy the past.

While Louis XIV and many of his contemporaries viewed history—and particularly modern history—as a long campaign to recapture lost and ancient glories, we can see that it was much more than that. On his trek, back to past heights as a humanist might have it, forward to new heights as others were soon to claim, man had picked up, invented, developed many things the ancients had not known. The court of Louis XIV was not the court of Titus or Trajan, still less that of Darius or Alexander. For one thing, it was Christian. For another, it rested on a social and economic structure the ancients had not known. And then, quite simply, it was not the court of an ancient prince because such princes and such courts had had their day and were no more except in tales. It was different because it came later, because the intervening times had taught and untaught a great deal, had discovered vast unsuspected realms and changed the face of Europe and also of the world. In other words, whatever they thought, men had not come back to a coveted golden-age starting point, but had gone on to something which, better or worse, was altogether different. Though Louis the Great might look backward to Cyrus and Apollo, his regime pointed forward to the Enlightened Despot and the modern state.

Yet what seemed to matter at the time were the new confidence and the slowly dawning feeling in some quarters that, now that he had made up the lost ground, nothing would stop man from going forward. Here was the feeling that foreshadowed the great hopes of the eighteenth century:

> Go, wondrous creature! mount where science guides!
> Go, measure earth, weigh air, and state the tides;
> Instruct the planets in what orbs to run,
> Correct old Time and regulate the sun!

And behind it, ever present, was man himself, Homer's *Odysseus* or Swift's *Gulliver,* sly, enterprising, conceited, too clever by half and sometimes twice as foolhardy, taunting the Cyclops and sometimes the gods; feeling their wrath and surviving; hoisting himself, on the shoulders of his fellow men and too often at their expense, towards greater wisdom though never enough, towards his goal, though never attained.

First the eighteenth century, then the nineteenth, mark the high point of this optimism and the beginning of its decline. The nineteenth century opens with the echoes of 1789 still ringing in people's ears. To some they sound ominous; to others they carry promises of a better future. The twentieth century seems to realize both hopes and fears; as it advances through its second half there is expectation of discoveries greater than any before, yet much of the world lives in fear of the possibilities of a future grimly outlined in George Orwell's *1984* and already rendered almost out of date by later developments.

The latest moods and ideas always take time to percolate before they seriously affect public opinion. Long after scientists and scholars had begun to change their minds, ordinary men and women continued to believe that progress was inevitable—a law of nature and of history no less apparent in the long run than that of gravity. Thus the discovery that evil is part of the world order—

Even apparent successes were fraught with disillusion. One after another the panaceas from which so much had been expected in the past were tried or mistried, and found wanting: education and democracy, freedom of thought and of the press, parliamentary government, national self-determination, socialism and communism. All had been tried, and none had worked the miracles expected of them. Perhaps men had been mistaken in trusting to any formula to find perfection. At any rate, they felt increasingly nonplussed, disillusioned, disoriented. They had proved themselves capable of harnessing wind and water but not their own passions, and now they realized with horror not only that their improved techniques enabled them to inflict suffering and destruction upon themselves greater than ever before, but also that they lacked the standards or firm beliefs which might show how and to what purpose these vast and new-found powers should be used. They could not, indeed, decide whether tolerant indifference should be preferred to harsh, exclusive dogmas, or whether firm standards were better than none at all.

Most people, of course, live as they have always lived: from day to day, accepting without particular comment or examination whatever ideas happen to be entertained around them. Some can settle for this lowest common denominator and some cannot. They must investigate, question, criticize and, perhaps, hope. Between echoes of the past and echoes of the future, a future which is really the shadow which the present casts before it, the men of these centuries have lived and still live in very interesting times. But the Chinese have a saying that it were better if one's enemies alone lived in interesting times; for interesting times have a way of being uncomfortable times.

Certainly, there is no one way in which to read all this. The great French novelist Stendhal once suggested that the relationship between books and readers is like that between the bow and the violin it plays. The book is the bow; the violin that makes the sounds is the reader's soul, or, if you prefer, his personality. With certain reservations the same may be said about history and historical documents; and the most important of these reservations is bound to be that man could not, apparently, by the mere use of his reason and will, build the good life uncorrupted—came as a shock to many in the twentieth century.

Once upon a time evil had seemed an integral part of creation. Though they feared and, at least theoretically, abhorred it, men reckoned with it. But the eighteenth and still more the nineteenth century had exorcised the Devil together, only too often, with God and encouraged the belief that in time evil and corruption could and would be eradicated from the world and from human nature. More and more things could be explained, adjusted, and improved. Utopia grew less utopian and more like the pattern of the better life that awaited us or our near descendants—the forward projection of improvements already implicit in present techniques and present thought. And yet it was seen that as the twentieth century advanced the reason of man seemed unable to prevent wars and revolutions, while his improved techniques served to make such conflicts vaster and bloodier than ever. Nor was the new order that followed upon them, at least in the eyes of many, an improvement on the old.

the fact that while the reader of a novel can make out pretty well with a bit of native intelligence and some imagination, the reader of history, like the violinist, does better if he knows how to wield the bow and read the notes. But even for those who come to it without preparation, without particular knowledge, with nothing but curiosity, history can offer both pleasure and form. True, it is we who endow it with the latter. Order and coherence are artificial creations of the human mind; we introduce them to make complicated subjects easier to grasp, easier to understand. If we really want more we must go beyond this into the realm of a reality which is never simple and try to perceive the underlying complexity of the whole. So, perhaps it is not history that suggests a pattern or form but we who endow it with one or with many. When we speak of pleasure, however, the issue is simpler. Though history has its uses, these are less important and more controversial than its pleasures. And these last, however intellectually valid they might be, rely in the final analysis on the fundamental nature of history, which is a vast, many-sided, sometimes passionate, often commonplace, diverse, monotonous, exciting, depressing, exhilarating, terrifying, inspiring, disillusioning, unending story.

From this follows the commonplace, but perhaps still necessary, reminder that while history as it happens is only partly connected with man, history as we write it—that is, the tale and interpretation of these happenings—is altogether of our making. The study of history may be, indeed should be, as scientific and scrupulous as possible; its telling can never be more than a work of art and the fact that it is so often botched means only that men are clumsy. The study of history is, of course, discovery. It is also a matter of selection and interpretation for which facts, whatever they might be, are only the raw material. Above all, perhaps, it is part of our constant struggle to understand ourselves and what makes us tick. We are products, we are part, of our place, and time, and class, all of which are themselves determined, affected—*committed,* so to speak—by previous and contemporary developments which they cannot escape any more than we can. If "know thyself" has any meaning, then history is analysis on a very vast scale.

In one sense the documents that follow are evidence in the case of a Western Tradition and how it developed. In another sense this evidence has been rigged—rigged by the editor's selection, of course; but, besides, by our natural inclination, when looking over the past, to pick only horses that have won and to read a pattern into what was in its own time unpredictable confusion. The events of a time very often seem chaotic at the time. Later they seem clear enough; their general lines appear evident and so do the principles of their development. And this may be because we, as it were, *invent* them and invest them with coherence. But it may be, too, because there really is such a thing as a general trend, a dominant tendency or climate of opinion at any one time, and that this only becomes apparent in the perspective lent by distance. Still, invented or perceived, history remains an artifact, the work of man's mind and his imagination.

This should warn us as nothing will to remember always the unselfconscious character of so many historical developments, the remarkably unplanned, irrational fashion of human developments, the tremendous possibilities of alternative happenings, of things turning out differently. Naturally, we cannot stop again and again to consider what might have happened if Napoleon had failed to win the battle of Austerlitz, or if Luther had been burnt like Hus or allowed to die ineffectively like Wycliffe; our history is necessarily determined because it is the story of what has been, not of what might have been. And because the material with which we deal is so vast, we select what we know now are the significant developments, the ones with a future, the acts and the writings that are on the winning side, and we put them end to end to show just how coherently everything happened, that it was simply bound to happen, to create the world and the society we know, to shape countries like France or Spain within practically foreordained borders, and so forth.

It is because such thoughts are so tempting that it is healthy to remember that nothing, so far as we know, was foreordained; that men and countries and ideas fumbled for a long, long time against a background of reality that pointed to nowhere in particular or perhaps in the wrong direction as seen from today. In the fifteenth century the princess of Castile might have married the heir to the throne of Portugal instead of Ferdinand of Aragon, and the destinies of Spain, perhaps the destinies of the world, might have been different. And it is possible to argue in the same vein that for a long time the union of England, Scotland, Wales, and Ireland in one kingdom seemed no more natural and necessary than the union of Denmark, Iceland, Norway, and England in one kingdom under King Canute.

Thus, we ought to have some constant reminders of the unreality of deterministic history, in the same way as certain monastic Orders have constantly under their eyes the reminder that death lies at the end of life and to this purpose paint the words *Memento Mori*—Remember Death—on the walls of their refectories and on the doors of their cells. We ought to remember the infinite possibilities of what looks like sheer chance, or luck; and the fact that the patterns we see in history are conventions, artificially inserted like coat hangers, in what is really a shapeless garment—an otherwise shapeless mass of events. Such awareness is particularly important because we are forced to use these conventions—indeed, by the selective presentation of facts which we in particular consider significant, we have to *create* patterns in order to see our way through history at all. So there is nothing wrong with selective history, with deterministic history, with patterns of history like those that Toynbee, or Pirenne, or Marx, or the eschatology of Christian belief can present us with. They are, as a matter of fact, inescapable and necessary, and useful too, provided we remember that each offers one presentation of one aspect of a vaster truth which no one yet has managed to encompass and which it seems beyond the powers of a human being even to conceive.

Another thing worth bearing in mind is that documents of another age speak a language of their own, which may be understood at the price of great scholarship and self-exertion but which at the very least demands from us an effort of sympathy and imagination. A document, of course, does not have to be written on paper or parchment to serve the historian: a gravestone, a shield, a golden necklace, or a cathedral is as much a document as a twelfth-century charter or the text of the Treaty of Versailles. Each is the product of attitudes and preconceptions peculiar to its time; each can provide—not only in itself but through its position in place and time—information precious to the historian. But though, to take one example, we can gape at a Gothic cathedral, marvel at the strength of the sculpture or the embroidery of its ornament, enjoy or admire it, the cathedral no more speaks our language than a dogmatic Hindu does. It belongs to another world, with different conventions and different beliefs; the feelings it inspires in us are not necessarily, or even probably, the feelings it inspired in the men who built it or worshiped in it at the time when it dominated the life as well as the architecture of its city. The cathedral and ourselves, today, carry on two monologues, what the French call a *dialogue de sourds;* and however brilliant the interlocutors may be, there is nothing they can do about this unless one crosses into the opposite camp and learns, indeed accepts, the language of the other.

The same thing is true about written documents. The poets, the philosophers, and the politicians whose writings we may study speak to a world that is not our world, that is very far from us, and very difficult to imagine, let alone to comprehend. The kinds of motives they appeal to, the kinds of values they refer to, are at times so strange that they can become irritating or incomprehensible. The *Song of Roland* or the political philosophy of Bossuet are only two instances to be found below in which our acceptance of the values and the motives of an age, the cause-and-effect relationships which these people took for granted, may prove grudging and ill-natured.

And it is no good saying that a particular pattern of culture is that of a minority. Or, rather, it is important to know this, but also to know what it implies. Culture, after all, like all social influence, like political power in all ages, like belief, is the creation and often the preserve of a minority. Modern sociologists like to emphasize the obvious fact that the mass of people tends to follow and imitate certain "cultural" or "fashionable" leaders, whether individuals or groups. But one might say further that the character and climate of a society are set by the significant few, whether these are followed or not by the insignificant many. There is, after all, no need to actually share in the highest achievements of a form of art or thought in order to feel its influence. We can enjoy the works of Michelangelo or Beethoven even if we cannot perhaps soar as high as they, even if we cannot fully understand the conception behind them. More than that, the work of the men who pitched cathedral spires up into the skies just as much as that of the men who split the atom can be treated as a reflection—symbol or caricature—of certain important tendencies, moods, characteristics of a period, facets of it in which all men of that time must share even though they may be far from understanding, or appreciating, these works

—sometimes even from knowing them. Many of the documents that follow represent the ideas and the doings of a single man or a very few; such activities probably did not touch the great majority of people and perhaps still do not today. And yet quantitatively feeble, statistically unimpressive, they cast their influence like a great shadow far, far from the solid mass.

Too little, also, has been said about the extremely important fact that a work of the mind is naturally allusive. Even if the author wants to give the most complete account of the subject, it is never possible for him to tell absolutely everything. He always knows more than he tells; he takes certain things for granted as he assumes that his readers will know them already. To people of the same period, to the members of the same society, there is no need to write everything. They share certain key ideas, you might say key words, which automatically evoke other ideas, emotions, reactions, if they are used to the right audience. Ali Baba found this out when his magic "Open sesame!" proved useless except in a given circumstance, in front of the particular cave where it got results. In the same way, an appeal to Jesus Christ, Democracy, National Feeling, Class, or Race would be effective only upon minds and societies familiar with these concepts and ready to react to them. Thus every work of the mind carries within itself the image of the public for which it is meant. This is what makes it a historical document for us, but it is also what demands the effort of understanding needed to consider it in its proper context.

The Past and the Present

Born in 1914, Hugh Trevor-Roper, Regius Professor of Modern History at Oxford since 1957, made his first scholarly mark in his twenties with the publication of a study of *Archbishop Laud* (1940), now considered a classic of seventeenth-century English history. Within a few years, he would put his experience as Intelligence Officer in the British Army to use in writing *The Last Days of Hitler* (1947), probably the first book to treat the dead dictator with historical objectivity. Since then, numerous works have reaffirmed his mastery of a field that runs from *The Rise of Christian Europe* (1965) through to the present age.

The lecture that follows was delivered on December 5, 1968, as the Annual Oration at the London School of Economics. It allows us to witness one of the major historians of our day explaining and defending the uses of history, the persistent bond between past and present, the inescapable need of the present to understand itself in terms of its understanding of the past.

Hugh Trevor-Roper: *History and Sociology*

When the Director of the London School of Economics invited me to speak here, he left me free to choose my subject; but on such an occasion I think that a man should speak of the subject which he has studied and on which he may be presumed, sometimes, to have thought. A historian, like other men, lives in the present; but his study is of the past; and coming as I do from Oxford, where some vestiges of past habits still remain, to this institution, which places emphasis rather on the immediate present, I shall venture to consider the relation, if any, between the two.

"If any . . ." Some indeed, I know, would say that there is none. The great thing about the past, they tell us, is that it is past. Can we not then forget it and devote our limited span of time to the study of the present, in which we must live, or even of the future which, by our actions, however unconsciously, we determine? Historians, defending their own profession, may tell us that the historical process is continuous: that humanity is the same in all ages, and that therefore the lessons of the past may guide us even in the present. But even if this was true yesterday, is it necessarily true today? Is it not possible that, today, we live in a new age, a scientific, technological age, to which such lessons may be irrelevant —in which they may even be positively misleading? So we are told. Philosophers hitherto, said Marx, have sought to understand the world, but our task is to change it. History, said Mr. Henry Ford (who did change it), is bunk. "It is surely far more important," said our Minister of Education, addressing the Association of Education Committees last summer, "for young people to know all the facts about Vietnam than it is to know all the details of the Wars of the Roses." [1]

"All the facts about Vietnam . . ." This is a tall order. From whom are we to accept all these facts, how test them? Even to acquire these is an arduous task. Ought we not then to free our forward-looking minds for the purpose, to clear away the incubus of the past, or at least to transform that incubus, from a real nightmare, into the innocent goblin of a fairy tale? It is easy to do this. All we have to do is to remove the study of history from the serious world into the Disneyland of fantasy, in which truth and falsehood do not matter. The temptation, I admit, is very strong. Some distinguished historians, in the weekly press, assure us that it is right to do so: that history has no function but to entertain. Skillful writers also are eager to oblige, ready to dress up the Muse of History in more fashionable, more highly colored clothes for this new occasion. Then, when she has gone, when she has been pushed off into the Light Programme, other graver persons come and bid us turn our serious attention to the new queen of sciences, sociology.

I am afraid that I do not agree, and here, in this home of sociology, I shall venture to defend my disagreement. I venture to suggest that, whether it is en-

tertaining or not, the study of the past is, or can be, useful. Perhaps I would go further and maintain that it is necessary. To those who would say, with Marx, that it is more important to change than to understand the world, I would reply that, even so, without understanding we cannot rationally change it. To those who see the past as an incubus from which we must set ourselves free, I would reply, with Freud, that obsessions are purged only by understanding, not by repudiation. We cannot profitably look forward without also looking back.

Of course we must not be too ambitious. We must not expect too much from the study of history. The historical lens is not exact, and whether we look forward or backward through it, the image is quickly blurred, so that fine detail is often missed and precise parallels cannot be drawn. We cannot compare history with the exact sciences, like mathematics or engineering. Marxists indeed speak of "scientific history" and they have sometimes adjusted the recalcitrant details to fit the rules of their science. But I do not agree with them in this. If the phenomena do not obey the rules, I believe it is better to relax the rules in favour of the phenomena. History, I believe, has its rules, but they are not "scientific"; they are tentative and conditional, like the rules of life. There is an excellent historical periodical entitled, like this lecture, *Past and Present*. It began under Marxist control. The date of its escape from that control can be easily determined: it is the date (1959) when the sub-title was changed from "a journal of scientific history" to "a journal of historical studies."

But if the lessons of history elude easy

---

[1] For the text of Mr. Short's speech, which seems to me a fine example of educational philistinism, see *Education*, 5 July 1968.

formulation, they are none the less real, and they provide the reasons for its serious study. What then are these reasons?

First of all, I would suggest, there is a general reason: to avoid parochialism. We all agree that parochialism is a fault. By this we generally mean parochialism in space. But there is also parochialism in time. To understand our own country, we need to see it in its wider context of space, among other countries. Equally, to understand our own age, we need to see it in its wider context of time, among other ages. To study only our own time may seem, at first sight, proof of our modernity: it is a sign that we are concentrating on the real world. But in fact such concentration may easily be very superficial. It removes a whole dimension of thought, and so deprives us of the means of comparison. So much of our own contemporary history is hidden from us that we cannot hope to see it in full. It is so close to us that we cannot see it in correct proportion. It is not yet over, so that we cannot judge it by the result. Familiarity with the past can supply some of those defects. It can provide a standard of comparison. It can point to a known issue. By so doing, it can chasten our parochial arrogance.

Of course, to speak thus is to speak in generalities. To define is more difficult. Perhaps we can best define by opposition. In order to discover the advantages of studying history, we may consider the dangers of neglecting history. For both nations and individuals have sometimes made a virtue of neglecting history; and history has taken its revenge on them.

One instance of such historical revenge is the rise of nationalism in the nineteenth century. In many ways nationalism is the revolt of historically minded peoples against rulers who have thought in non-historical terms. In eighteenth-century Europe most enlightened men were cosmopolitan, international. They looked back at history and saw a "gothic" past from which they had emerged into the full light and freedom of the present; and they regarded "patriotism," national loyalty, national pride, as a vulgar relic of tribalism. How condescendingly the "enlightened" French Encyclopaedists looked at the literature of the past, of which one of them, D'Alembert, would have made a periodic bonfire! How contemptuously they dismissed the atavistic, irrational complaints of the bigoted, unenlightened Poles who squealed and squirmed in a most undignified fashion when their country was carved up and absorbed by the Enlightened Despots of Prussia, Russia and Austria! How impatiently, a generation later, the Bonapartist *afrancesados* of Spain looked down on the obscurantist bigots who resisted their rational reforms! But this triumph of Reason did not last. In the next century the nations revolted; and their revolt was nourished, everywhere, by history. It was the "historic nations," the nations which were conscious of their history—the Poles, Italians, Germans—which led the revolt; and all the nations in revolt began by discovering, or inventing, their history. No doubt the history which they discovered was not very good; the cosmopolitan historians of the eighteenth century were probably better as historians; but there was a large area of history which those historians had dangerously ignored and which now took its revenge.

We see the same process today in historic Asia and unhistoric Africa. In 1900 the colonial empires seemed "enlightened." Did they not bring material improvement, utility, modernity? The West was benevolent, cosmopolitan, the educator of the world. In 1940–41, Mr. Wendell Willkie, Franklin Roosevelt's defeated rival for the presidency of the United States, flew from country to country preaching the glowing message of "One World," and Vice-President Wallace afterwards further defined the new American ideal as "the century of the common man." I confess, I detest both these concepts of these two well-meaning men. I prefer variety and sophistication to such uniform banality. But quite apart from personal preference, such variety, I believe, is necessary. The variety of custom in the world is not merely the superficial diversity of a fundamentally uniform humanity. It has independent historic roots, and those roots will continue to thrust up shoots, after their kind: shoots which may be ignored, or cut, or fostered or distorted, but cannot be arbitrarily changed. This has been shown clearly in the past twenty years. Perhaps we would understand today's struggle in the Far East better if we knew less than "all the facts about Vietnam" and at least something about the Wars of the Roses.

This recrudescence of history, this periodic revenge of the past, which is my first reason for not forgetting it, is nowhere more obvious than in China today. Theoretically, the Chinese communist revolution is a repudiation of the millennial history of China. Communist China has broken decisively with its past, loudly and explicitly disowned its long and splendid history. The recent "cultural revolution" has emphasized and exaggerated that breach. The deposit of four thousand years has now been repudiated in its totality; everything that is old has been discarded; and all things, we are told, have been made new. But in fact, what has happened? The inheritance of the Kuomintang, of the Chinese Republic, has indeed been rejected, but the older inheritance of the Manchus, of the Chinese empire, has returned to fill the void. Today Peking is once again the capital of the Middle Kingdom. Chairman Mao, like the Son of Heaven, is to live for ten thousand years. The Europeans are again outer barbarians, whom the self-sufficient Celestial Empire has no need to know. The usages of international diplomacy, of the comity of nations, have been rejected; and foreign embassies provide the means not of negotiation but of tribute; of the enforced kowtow, of the sacked Legation, and of periodic humiliation by the officials of the vast, impervious, conformist bureaucracy.

Such is the revenge of history on those who ignore it. Expelled with a pitchfork, it nevertheless returns. How historical patterns thus reassert themselves, how historic continuity, even identity, persists below the apparent level of consciousness, is to me a mystery. Idealist historians speak of the spirit of a people, which they see no need to reduce into concrete terms. Perhaps the sociologists have some less airy formula. But in order to test any such formula, it must be studied against the dimension of time, that is, historically. No great political problem can be seen apart from its historical context. I well remember the debates that raged, in the 1930's, about the Spanish Civil War. To those who lived in their own time only, to the fashionable, ideologically committed commentators of the age, the Spanish Civil War was a war between international fascism and international communism, which was being fought out, almost by chance, in the Iberian peninsula. Superficially, of course, it was. But fundamentally, we all now realize, its causes lay deep in Spanish history. In that context alone could it be understood.

General Franco was seen by foreigners as the creature of Hitler and Mussolini. He saw himself, rather, as a hero of 1809. His opponents were seen, during the Civil War, as international communists. They were not. They were Spaniards, who looked back to an ancient peninsular tradition with which Marx had nothing whatever to do. The profoundest, most perceptive historian of that Civil War,— I refer to Mr. Gerald Brenan—once told me that he was provoked to write his account of it by the abysmal ignorance and folly of those Marxist crusaders who thought they could interpret, in the terms of twentieth-century international communism, a phenomenon which could only be understood in the terms of hitherto unstudied nineteenth—and pre-nineteenth —century Spain.

The same can be said, *mutatis mutandis,* of the Russian revolution, in which the Tsars have perhaps more longterm importance than Marx. The same can be said of modern Greece. And perhaps the War in the Far East would be better understood if it were interpreted with a little less of fashionable modern doctrine and a little more of unconsidered local history.

If past history—by whatever ducts and channels it flows—thus exercises a continuing force in human affairs, it is obvious that individuals also will greatly err who decline to consider its lessons. Once again I take an obvious instance from the 1930's. Neville Chamberlain, and those who supported him, were men of the twentieth century. They could not believe that Hitler, who was their contemporary, and who rose to power in a modern, highly industrial society, could be fundamentally different from themselves. He might be a vulgar demagogue; he might use extravagant language and violent methods; but at bottom his aims must surely be limited by the shared rationality of the twentieth century, as they knew it, and ultimately, if only one could see past the violence and the vulgarity, it must be possible to reach agreement. But Hitler was not a man of the twentieth century. No man who concentrates in himself the claims of a whole nation is a man of his own century only. Winston Churchill, out of office, writing, in those very years, a great historical study of the seventeenth century, was in a better position to understand the true character of Nazism than those who, from whatever side, understood, however well, only the immediate problems of their own time.

The same error, I suspect, was made by Franklin Roosevelt in his relations with Stalin. He believed, and at one time frankly stated,[2] that he could handle Stalin better than anyone else. At one time he would have constituted Stalin as an arbiter between Britain and America. He saw him, I suspect, as a political boss from another segment of Wendell Willkie's "one world": from Texas perhaps, or Huey Long's Louisiana, or Kentucky of the colonels: rough and ruthless, no doubt, but fundamentally "one of us." But Stalin was not one of us. Roosevelt and he might share, for a brief time, the responsibilities of a common war, just as Chamberlain and Hitler, for a brief time, held the balance of peace and war between them. But they did not, for that reason, live in the same context. Long years of Russian history, both conservative and revolutionary, formed the presuppositions and secret aims of Stalin, and those presuppositions and aims were

[2] See Winston Churchill, *The Second World War* (London, 1949–54), IV, p. 177.

not suspended by the war, or to be changed by personal diplomacy. Rather, the war was fought, by him, to secure those aims, and diplomacy consisted in temporarily concealing them.

But if past and present are thus continuous, so that the present cannot be fully understood in isolation from the past, can we be more particular? Can we use the past not merely to provide a general context within which the particular problems of the present may be better understood, but also to provide particular solutions to particular problems? Can we even, at least in theory—for this is logically entailed in that—use the past to predict the future?

Those who speak of "the science of history," "scientific history," would presumably answer yes. I would not go so far. Even if history were a science, I would remain basically sceptical: for there are sciences and sciences, and even in science we must never be too schematic, too quick to systematize: that is how sciences are not forwarded but arrested, frozen. And besides history, I believe, is not a science: it is an art in whose method several sciences are subsumed without making it thereby itself scientific.

At certain times, indeed, history itself has been declared scientific. It was scientific in the Middle Ages, and that scientific interpretation lasted, with the rest of the intellectual infrastructure of the Middle Ages, however damaged by heresy, until the mid-seventeenth century. In those centuries, History was understood to have both a beginning and an end. It began with the Creation and would end at the pre-ordained end of the world; and both dates could, theoretically at least, be scientifically determined with the perfection of astronomical tables and the clarification of sacred texts. Moreover, between those two terminal dates, which scientists were constantly making more precise, the events of history could—again in theory at least—be exactly predicted; for God had already, by His Providence, determined them all and by His prophets and His occasional direct revelations had exposed—cryptically indeed, fragmentarily indeed, but not insolubly to the ingenious believer—both the general outline and a basic quota of particular details, from which the rest might be deduced. At one period—in the first half of the seventeenth century, when the astronomers and mathematicians had established the measurement of time and the theologians were refining the exact meaning of the Apocalypse—it seemed as if the last remaining problems were solved and the few still unfulfilled events of history could be exactly predicted, just ahead of time, before all came to an end in 1666. . . .

How remote it all seems now! Why should we trouble ourselves now with these exploded fantasies? Why indeed except to show a lesson of history, and learn humility thereby. The past is littered with the *débris* of ambitious historical systems, in which some of the greatest minds of the time—a Scaliger, a Napier, a Newton—have been invested. And why should later systems be any more durable? Are the doctrines of linear progress, or the continuing dialectic of the class struggle, or the withering away of the state, or the Yin and Yang any less metaphysical in their foundations?

History, I believe, is dependent on several sciences in its detail. Since the Renaissance, one new science after another has been subordinated to it, and refined within it. Textual scholarship has corrected its sources, cryptography has increased them, *Quellenkritik* has interpreted them. Chronology has provided a new spinal cord on which we can reconnect the disjointed vertebrae of the remoter past. Sociology, authropology, have given new depth and breadth. But history itself, though resting on an ever more scientific base, remains itself too human a subject, too dependent on accident, too variable in the proportion even of its recurrent features, to be safely predictable. We may predict in detail, and conditionally, where we have the means of comparison, and such limited predictions may be scientifically, or at least empirically, tested and so justified and useful; but generally and absolutely there can be no prediction, only a guess; and a guess is, in the strict sense, worthless.

For instance, we may say that, according to the evidence of history, if there is a severe economic recession in a multi-racial society, there will be acute interracial tension, and we may say, according to the social pattern and ideological tendency of the time, what form that tension will take. We can use for this purpose the evidence of sixteenth- and seventeenth-century Spain, which will, I believe, be of more value than any purely modern sociological theory. But we cannot say unconditionally that, by the law of history, the next generation shall see the end of the world, or a "time of troubles," or the rise of a new empire, or universal peace, or indeed, in those absolute terms, anything else.

When people ask me whether historians should not be able, ideally, to prophesy the future, I ask them a simple question. Let them place themselves at any date in past history and say honestly whether any man could rationally have prophesied the course of the next fifty years. In 1900? Who could conceivably have forecast the convulsions of Europe or foreseen the total dissolution of the recently united German Reich? In 1950? Who would have supposed that America, the liberator of Europe, with its inherited cult of isolation and its public hatred of imperialism, would become the very type of imperialist power, fighting a long and bitter war in the Far East, and that a Democratic President would be denounced in Asia, however unjustly, as "the new Hitler"? I do not believe that any such prophecy would have been possible. If it had been made, it would have been not scientific but an inspired guess.

On the other hand, conditional prophecy is always possible, if the conditions are clearly understood, and the more we study history, and the more scientific its context becomes, and the more we respect its limits, the better we can prophesy. Jacob Burckhardt's prophecy, in the 1870's and 1880's, that the old monarchies would be pushed aside and a new race of *Gewaltmenschen* would rule as terrible dictators, beginning perhaps in Germany,[3] was a rational, limited prophecy based on historical understanding: he saw that the new industrial power, if it became political, would be quite different from the old, and that it was most likely to take root where industry was heaviest and old "liberal" forms weakest. Similarly Sir Halford Mackinder's prophecy, before the first World War, that the struggle for mastery in the world would center on Eastern Europe and that Tsarist Russia would be the great power of the

---

[3] Burckhardt's prophecies are in his letters to Friedrich von Preen. See Jacob Burckhardt, *Briefe,* ed. Felix Kaphahn (Leipzig, 1935), esp. pp. 348–9, 355–6, 484–7.

future,[4] was not invalidated by the total ruin of Tsarist Russia, first in war, then in revolution. Nor would it have been invalidated if Hitler had won his war. The essential condition was the control of the "Heartland." In fact, it was for that Heartland that Hitler and Stalin fought, and it was an ideological war, fought to the death, because both belligerents knew that the winner, whichever he was, would be the arbiter of Europe.

There are numerous such conditional laws of history; empirical rules which can be taken from a wide range of historical experience. Any of them may be applicable to the present, none of them provides a certain formula for the present. For one safe rule of history is that historical situations never exactly repeat themselves: there are too many variable ingredients in each situation for identical recurrence. Even if they should do so, the mere fact of repetition is a new ingredient which may alter the mixture.

I have often been asked, in the last twenty years, whether I could forecast an effective revival of Nazism in Germany. I have always answered, no; because I have never believed that the old doctrines could revive in the old form. They might survive, as a kind of dead deposit, in ageing minds. Elements of them would recur, here and there, in new situations: for some of the elements are permanent features of German history, and some are predictable responses to recurrent social pressures. But the fusion of all these elements in a particular dynamic pattern was caused, in the past, by the particular unrepeatable experience of one generation, and even if all the same circumstances should recur, in the same order (which is, inconceivable), the emotional content would not be communicable, unchanged, to another generation: the identical pattern of pressures and the same intellectual climate would not recur. For this reason, the new fascism, when it occurs, will occur with radical differences. Indeed, with such differences, it has already occurred. The arrogant cult of youth, the nihilism, the intolerance of dissent, the rejection of rational argument, the deliberate invocation of force to justify counter-force—all these have recently been resumed.[5] But they have been resumed in classes and circumstances very different from those of the 1920's and 1930's; and although a knowledge of the original fascism may help us to understand the new phenomenon, the precise form in which they have been resumed could not, I think, have been predicted.

This constant change of circumstance, and of "intellectual climate," is what makes the severance of the present from the past, in our studies, seem so dangerous. History is the empirical study of the past, which uses, or should use, all the sciences that are relevant to it. Sociology is the study—its advocates call it the scientific study: it is "social science"—of the present. Sociology entered historical study in the eighteenth century, with Montesquieu. It has remained within it, strengthening its position in it, ever since. Today, I cannot conceive of good history

---

[4] Halford Mackinder's views were finally presented in *Democratic Ideas and Reality* (London, 1919); but they had been formulated and expressed by him earlier.

[5] Since delivering this lecture, I have seen an issue of *The Beaver* (5 Dec. 1968), described as "The newspaper of the London School of Economics Union"; and I can add that the obscene and vindictive journalistic style of Julius Streicher's notorious anti-semitic periodical *der Stürmer* has also been resumed—though against other scapegoats.

without a sociological dimension. But if sociology is essential to history, history, I believe, is no less essential to sociology. Sociological models tend to be static. Unless they are tested, they are necessarily dogmatic. But the test of a model is the way it works, as the test of a car is the way it runs; and the running of the sociological model is history.

This, I suspect, is sometimes forgotten by "social scientists" who construct and admire their models in the workshop only and do not test them by running them through the dimension of time. For once they are running, we see that they are not mechanical models only; they are organisms, with a biology, a metabolism of their own. They respond to circumstances, even to the circumstances which they may create. They engage, as it were, in dialogue with other "models," which are also organisms, and those other models change too. The very dialogue generates change, and it is the sum of these changes which is history.

Once, in 1950, I had a provocative experience. I was at a Congress in Berlin. It was the time of the outbreak of the Korean War, and feelings in that vulnerable, isolated city were running high. The Congress was being run by the American C.I.A. As I sat there, one distinguished speaker after another rose to speak. All of them were Marxist social scientists in their original intellectual formation, though by now they had put their convictions into reverse. They now declared that communist society and western society were immutable models, absolutely incompatible with each other, and that one must destroy the other. There was no alternative. Therefore, he who was not for us was necessarily

against us in the holy war. As I listened to these remorseless speeches, historical analogies coursed through my head, and I saw, in past history, a very different lesson. I saw a succession of supposedly incompatible forms of society, sometimes indeed engaged in mutually destructive crusades, but sometimes also, behind their heavily fortified frontiers, competing with each other in less violent manner. Outmaneuvering each other, borrowing from each other, learning from each other, changing by contact with each other, until, with a change of generations, the crusading spirit (which was the product of a particular conjuncture) had evaporated, and the crusade itself, having been happily avoided, now seemed unnecessary. In order to expound my theme, I made several attempts to catch the chairman's eye, but somehow my attempts were never noticed; so I came home and wrote a short historical article which today, I hope, reads slightly better than those crusading speeches. It was an article on the co-existence of Christendom and the Turkish Empire; [6] but it could equally have been on other such ideological confrontations.

For instance, there is the ideological confrontation of Reformation and Counter-Reformation in sixteenth-century Europe. It is easy to construct abstract models of Protestant and Catholic societies, and having constructed them, to use them as permanent concepts. But although such models have their value, and at one particular time, or in one particular place, may even be true, we must always remember that they are abstractions, not realities: the historical reality is constantly changing. Some historians, misled by these abstractions, overlook the con-

[6] Reprinted in my *Historical Essays* (London, 1957), pp. 173–8.

tinual change, which caused the balance between the two societies to oscillate. Protestant or Marxist historians overlook the inhibiting ideological reaction in "reformed" societies and suppose that the intellectual supremacy of one period was necessarily, as part of the system, continued to another. Catholic historians similarly generalize from the temporary triumphs of the Counter-Reformation. But in fact intellectual or spiritual or economic superiority did not spring automatically from the "model," as applied. The reality was in constant process of adaptation. The very fact of competition quickened the process of adaptation—just as capitalist and communist society have transformed themselves out of recognition by their competition in the last forty years. Only a bigot of doctrine can fail, or refuse, to recognize this; and it is no doubt for that reason that, in communist countries today, history has been made to stand still and the social condition of England is permanently illustrated from the fossilized "model" supplied by the novels of Charles Dickens.

This debate between past and present, between history and "social science," is not new. It has an old ancestry. It is the debate between Machiavelli and the Churches in the sixteenth century, between Clarendon and Hobbes in the seventeenth, between Macaulay and the utilitarians in the nineteenth. Clarendon accused Hobbes of seeking to impose abstract "geometrical" models on society instead of taking advantage of the empirical lessons of history; and he urged him, though now at the advanced age of eighty-eight, to go into politics and sit in parlia-

ment, and thereby correct the illusions bred by "his solitary cogitations, how deep soever, and his too peremptory adhering to some philosophical notions, and even rules of geometry." [7] Macaulay even more rudely excoriated the mean and abject "sophisms," the "syllogisms," the scholastic deductions of James Mill, the illusion that "the science of government" could be derived "by short synthetical arguments" drawn from self-evident axioms about human nature. He extolled instead the empirical study of history whose best exponents, he too, like Clarendon, insisted, had been practical politicians—especially, of course, Whig politicians.[8] Much the same point was put, in terser form, by Mr. Quintin Hogg to an academic sociologist who had the misfortune to meet him, a few months ago, on television. Both Clarendon and Macaulay, it must be admitted, in their more extended arguments, made some mistakes—which, since I am on their side, I shall leave decently unexposed; for they were not fundamental: they do not affect the general argument. Instead, I shall conclude by asking how we can follow their advice and study history in such a way that, without adopting the extreme course of going into Parliament, we can profit from it in the present and so avoid the reproaches of Mr. Short. I believe that there are at least two golden rules which Macaulay himself would sometimes have been well advised to follow.

First, we must not force the pace of history or seek to extract from it more precise lessons than it will yield. The very value of history lies in its general lessons, its complexity, its suggestions and anal-

[7] Edward Hyde, Earl of Clarendon, *A Brief View of the Dangerous and Pernicious Errors* . . . *in Mr. Hobbes' book entitled Leviathan* (Oxford, 1676).

[8] Macaulay's views on Mill are expressed in his essays reviewing Mill's *Essay on Government* (1829) and Sir James Mackintosh's *History of the Revolution in England* (1835).

ogies, and the highly conditional nature of its parallels, not in concrete lessons or dogmatic conclusions. I know that people want such conclusions, and when historians will not give them such conclusions, they sometimes, in their disappointment, turn aside to the more positive (but not necessarily more helpful) assurances of the social scientists. But I insist that such precise conclusions are not warrantable, or valuable. All the greatest historians have refused to produce them, and those who have complied with the public demand by producing them, are quickly out of date. The great historians—Thucydides, Gibbon, Ranke—do not press an interpretation. The concessions that they make to the public are in form only: in style, in lucidity, in readability. They do not spell out crude lessons which can be neatly tabulated for busy readers by obliging epitomists. Therefore they are not always popular with those hasty students who wish to have their historical philosophy served up to them in a nutshell. The philosophy of the greatest historians cannot be quickly summarized. It is not crude. It is subtle; and in a long work it must be allowed gradually to emerge.

Secondly, we must, I believe, respect the independence of the past. All of us, living in our own time, tend to see the past on our own terms. We like to recognize, in past centuries, familiar problems, familiar faces: to see man looking towards us, not away from us. But this tendency, though natural, contains great dangers. It is right, I believe, to look for lessons in the past, to see its relevance to our own time, to observe the signs of continuity, connection and process. The past

is not to be studied for its own sake. That is mere antiquarianism. But it is anachronistic, distorting, to judge the past as if it were subject to the present, as if the men of the eighteenth or the sixteenth or the tenth century had no right to be independent of the twentieth. We exist in and for our own time: why should we judge our predecessors as if they were less self-sufficient: as if they existed for us and should be judged by us? Every age has its own intellectual climate, and takes it for granted, as we take ours. Because it was taken for granted, it is not explicitly expressed in the documents of the time: it has to be deduced and reconstructed. It also deserves respect. This is what the greatest of nineteenth-century historians, Leopold von Ranke, meant when he wrote that every age was "immediate to God," and implicitly blamed Macaulay for arraigning past ages before the tribunal of the present—the brief present of the mid-nineteenth century, which has now passed and may seem to us, in retrospect, a very partial tribunal.[9] To discern the intellectual climate of the past is one of the most difficult tasks of the historian but it is also one of the most necessary. To neglect it—to use terms like "rational," "superstitious," "Progressive," "reactionary," as if only that was rational which obeyed our rules of reason, only that progressive which pointed to us—is worse than wrong: it is vulgar.

Finally, in studying history, I believe that while we must always appreciate its extent and variety, we must always study one part of it in detail. To study on too narrow a front deprives us of the chance of analogy; but to study too generally is

---

[9] Ranke's implied criticism of Macaulay is in his *History of England* (Engl. transl., Oxford, 1875), IV., p. 364.

not to study at all. We cannot penetrate below the surface all the time, or we shall never come up for air, never rise above the subject to survey and compare. But if we do not, at some point, penetrate below the surface, we shall fall into the opposite error. We shall be obliged to take all our evidence at second-hand and shall end by believing, without testing, the fashionable orthodoxy of our time or place. Every age has its orthodoxy and no orthodoxy is ever right. It is changed, in due course, by those who approach the subject, whatever it is, with a certain humility and, above all, independence of mind. But those intellectual gifts need material on which to work, and that material, in history, must be raw material. In other words, the historian is amphibious: he must live some part of his time below the surface in order that, on emerging, he can usefully survey it from above. The historian who has specialized all his life may end as an antiquarian. The historian who has never specialized at all will end as a mere blower of froth. The antiquarian at least is useful to others.

I would have all historians specialize, for however short a space, on some part of their own history—for there they are at home: they can read the sources in their own language. This will prevent them from too easy generalization by showing upon what uncertain and controversial foundations received opinions are often based. But having done this, I would have them read the history of other countries, knowing that they will then do so with a double advantage. From their specialist study of their own history they will know how to reserve judgment on general history where they have not penetrated so deeply; and from their general study of foreign history, thus qualified, they will learn that comparative method which will prevent them from too readily accepting one formula of historical causation: from assuming (for instance) that parliamentary democracy, or trades unions, or liberal catchwords, or any catchwords, are the only way of salvation. By this double process they may make the study of the past not only interesting but useful. It will not prove to be a science. It will produce no ready-made answers. It will not enable them to prophesy. But it will enlarge their views. It may bring independence of judgment. And so it may enable them to understand, and by understanding, to improve, the present.

From the Ancient World to Louis XIV

The Ancient World

I. THE FIRST GREAT EMPIRES

II. ANCIENT ISRAEL

III. ANCIENT GREECE

IV. ANCIENT ROME

V. THE EARLY CHRISTIAN WORLD

*T*he roots of our Western tradition are to be found in the civilizations that developed round the eastern end of the Mediterranean during the two or three millennia before Christ. Practically every religious, philosophical, and social idea that the West has toyed with or tried out since, had been explored, adopted, and sometimes exploded before Augustus came to rule the Roman world in 31 B.C. Our diverse attitudes to law, to God, and to society arise from the discoveries and the decisions of this period.

In Sumeria, in Mesopotamia, and on the banks of the Nile, many societies developed and sometimes flourished. The records they have left are the earliest evidence of man's attempt to think through and organize his relationship with the circumambient world, with nature and supernatural forces, with other men in society, and with the omnipresent reality of death. We know the results of these attempts in religion and philosophy, political forms and laws—the forms of which we have inherited from Egypt, Babylon, and Assyria.

Somewhat later, an obscure people in the hills of Palestine, the Jews, in their turn contributed a new and revolutionary notion of man's relationship with God. Up to their time and for long after, man's attempt to live the good life—i.e., a life in accordance with the laws of nature and the will of supernatural powers—had been hampered by the apparent multitude, incoherence, and arbitrariness of gods and their will. Unable to know what the gods wanted or what they would do from one moment to the next, man lived in an unpredictable and arbitrary world, both on the moral and on the physical plane. The Jewish solution of the difficulty was the concept of a God, first all-powerful, later alone and exclusive, not devoid of arbitrariness but willing to indicate His general purpose and to lay down a law that men could follow. Here, for the future, was the basis of a firm and understandable relationship between mankind and divine authority.

But the most characteristic part of our heritage is that use of reason which, under the brilliant impulse of Greek thought and through the intermediary action of Rome, has come to mark the West. If there is anything peculiar to the Western tradition as opposed, say, to that of the East, it is the recurring appeal to reason, the assertion that our thought and the results it arrives at have real validity as against the irrational forces and unfathomable destinies of which men have always been aware. This belief in man, in man's reason and man's values, is by no means always in the ascendant; but it runs through the story of the Western world, and it is in the ancient world that we trace its beginnings.

I. The First Great Empires

The period represented here by thirty-three pages is in fact as long as the Christian era, which takes up almost the whole of the rest of this volume. It began some three thousand years before the birth of Christ, some five thousand before our own, and the civilizations it saw, the cities and empires that sprang up in the valleys of the Nile, the Tigris, and the Euphrates, have provided some of the most basic components of the Western tradition: writing, money, the wheel, the concept of an only god, the city, a written code of law, large-scale political organization.

The following passages afford only a glimpse of the two great intellectual elaborations of this time: Religion and Law, both closely connected. Neither was there, ready-made, for men to stumble upon; both had to be invented, thought out, introduced, before becoming part of the normal equipment of society. It requires a certain effort of historical understanding and imagination before we can shed preconceptions we have inherited from that time and, looking upon these prodigious inventions with fresh eyes, conceive their elaboration and evolution out of, and in response to, the circumstances and needs of the men and the societies which created them.

1. EGYPT

In a land which runs like a narrow corridor between vast stretches of desert, where the slender green ribbon of the river valley snakes its way through a black and ochre barrenness ever ready to encroach upon it, the river that provides the thread of life is dominant—a God today as it has been in the past and, indeed, a god perhaps not greater but certainly more important than all others.

Hymn to the Nile

Greetings, Oh Nile, who have manifested yourself on this earth and who comes in peace to give Egypt life; hidden god who guides the darkness, when he pleases to do so, irrigator of the meadows created by Ra to give all animals life; you feed the earth, uncreated; highway of the heavens, you descend, friend of bread and fruitfulness, benefactor of the grain, god Ptah who illumines every dwelling.

Lord of the fish, when the flood comes no bird invades useful belongings; you make the corn; you perpetuate the temples; rest of the fingers is your labor for the miserable thousands. If its level falls in the heavens, the gods fall on their faces, men waste away.

It opens the whole world to beasts,

Translated by Eugen Weber from Gaston Maspero, *Hymne au Nil* (Paris: 1868), pp. 19–31.

great and small find rest; men answer him with prayers. . . . When he shines, the world is filled with joy, all bodies are happy, every creature has been fed, every tooth can chew.

He brings fresh provisions, he creates all goods, the lord of pleasant and chosen nourishment; if there are offerings, it is thanks to him. It makes the grass grow for the cattle; it watches over the sacrifice of every god; the incense that comes from him is of the best. It takes hold of North and South, filling the warehouse, choking the barn, enriching the miserable. . . . During the flood, the people shows its joy; every heart is happy . . . , the divine cycle speaks through you. . . .

Rock of all justice, men implore you in flattering words that you may answer, and the answer comes in the flood. . . .

Oh Flood of the Nile, offerings are made to you, oxen sacrificed, birds immo-lated, the animals of the land taken for you, the sacrifice of fire offered to you; the offerings made to every God are as if made to the Nile . . . oxen, bulls, birds that one burns; the Nile has dug itself hiding places in the land of Thebes, but one ignores the name it bears in heaven; the god does not manifest his form, vain are the shapes attributed to him.

Men exalt and gods revere with awe the god who has made the terrors [or provisions], the god who has made his son Lord of the universe, to illuminate North and South. Rise and make yourself heard! Rise and make yourself heard, oh Nile! Rise and make yourself heard, oh Nile, you who give life to men by your herds, and to your herds by your meadows; rise and make yourself heard! Rise and make yourself heard, oh Nile! Rise and make yourself heard, oh Nile!

The Book of the Dead: The Negative Confession

Many of the texts which have come down to us from ancient Egypt are devoted to securing eternal happiness for a dead individual whom they accompanied into the grave and thence on his journey in the underworld. Such mortuary texts were gener-ally written on papyrus. They have been collected by modern scholars under the gen-eral title of *The Book of the Dead,* but this does not imply any unity except of pur-pose. The texts below are provided for the time when the deceased tries to justify himself and his deeds on earth before a posthumous court of the gods: a so-called negative confession, in which he denies having perpetrated any crimes, is followed by a series of positive claims. Taken together, they furnish us with a useful reflection of Egyptian social morality and ideas of right and wrong, at any rate during the sec-ond millennium B.C., from which these particular confessions seem to date. As in our own society, however, the Egyptians honored their laws more in the breach than in the observance: the dishonesty and corruption of Egyptian officials was notorious throughout the ancient East.

The following shall be said when the overseer of the palace, the chancellor-in-chief, Nu, triumphant, cometh forth into the Hall of Double Maati so that he may

From *The Book of the Dead According to the Theban Recension,* tr. E. A. Wallis Budge, in *Egyptian Literature,* ed. Epiphanius Wilson (London, 1901).

be separated from every sin which he hath done and may behold the faces of the gods. The Osiris Nu, triumphant, saith:

"Homage to thee, O Great God, Lord of Double Maati [Osiris, judge of the dead], I have come to thee, O my Lord, I have brought myself hither that I may behold thy beauties. I know thee, and I know thy name, and I know the names of the two and forty gods who exist with thee in this Hall of Double Maati, who live as warders of sinners and who feed upon their blood on the day when the lives of men are taken into account in the presence of the god Un-nefer [Osiris]: in truth, ['Lord of Justice'] is thy name. In truth I have come to thee, and I have brought Maat to thee, and I have destroyed wickedness for thee.

"I have not done evil to mankind. I have not oppressed the members of my family, I have not wrought evil in the place of right and truth. I have had no knowledge of worthless men. I have not wrought evil. I have not made to be the first consideration of each day that excessive labor should be performed for me. I have not brought forward my name for exaltation to honors. I have not ill-treated servants. I have not thought scorn of God. I have not defrauded the oppressed one of his property. I have not done that which is an abomination unto the gods. I have not caused harm to be done to the servant by his chief. I have not caused pain. I have made no man to suffer hunger. I have made no one to weep. I have done no murder. I have not given the order for murder to be done for me. I have not inflicted pain upon mankind. I have not defrauded the temples of their oblations. I have not purloined the cakes of the gods. I have not carried off the cakes offered to the *khus*. I have not committed fornication. I have not polluted myself [in the holy places of the god of my city]. I have neither added to nor filched away land. I have not encroached upon the fields of others. I have not added to the weights of the scales [to cheat the seller]. I have not misread the pointer of the scales [to cheat the buyer]. I have not carried away the milk from the mouths of children. I have not driven away the cattle which were upon their pastures. I have not snared the feathered fowl of the preserves of the gods. I have not caught fish [with bait made of] fish of their kind. I have not turned back water at the time [when it should flow]. I have not cut a cutting in a canal of running water. I have not extinguished a fire when it should burn. I have not violated the times of offering the chosen meat-offerings. I have not driven off the cattle from the property of the gods. I have not repulsed God in his manifestations. I am pure. I am pure. I am pure. I am pure.

"Homage to you, O gods, who dwell in the Broad Hall of the Two Justices, who are without deceit in your bodies, who live upon right and truth and who feed yourselves upon right and truth in the presence of Horus who dwells in his sun disc. Deliver me from Baba who feeds upon the entrails of the mighty on the day of the great judgment. Behold that I have come before you without sin, without guilt, without a witness against me, without anyone against whom I have borne false witness; therefore let nothing evil be done unto me. I live upon right and truth, and I feed upon right and truth. I have carried out the commandments of men as well as the things which please the gods. I have made the god satisfied with me by doing his will. I have given bread to the hungry man, and water to the thirsty man, and clothes to the naked man, and a boat to the marooned mariner. I have made holy offerings to the gods, and funeral offerings to the dead. Be you then my deliverers, be you then my protectors, and make no accusation against me in the presence of the great god. I am pure of mouth and pure of hands; therefore let it be said unto me by those who shall behold me, "Come in peace; come in peace."

Wenamon's Journey

The story of the voyage of Wenamon is the liveliest picture we have of the position of Egypt in the Eastern Mediterranean at the close of the Twentieth Dynasty, that is during or just after the reign of the last of the Ramses, about 1100 B.C.

Herihor, the High Priest of Amon, is *de facto* ruler at Thebes, in upper Egypt; Nesubenebded rules at Thanis in the Delta. The country is but a shadow of its former self, but even this shadow is a long one; and when Wenamon, an official of the temple of Amon at Karnak, sets off to seek timber for the god's ceremonial barge, the adventures he encounters on the way witness both Asiatic scepticism of remaining Egyptian power and an enduring respect for traditional Egyptian supremacy, even in its decline.

Year five, third month of the Harvest, the sixteenth, day of departure of Wenamon, eldest of the Hall, of the temple of Amon-Ra, king of gods, lord of Karnak, to bring the timber for the great and august barge of Amon-Ra, king of gods, which is on the Nile, called the Userhet of Amon.

The day I arrived at Tanis, abode of Smendes and Tentamon, I gave into their hands the writings of Amon-Ra, king of gods. They had them read in their presence and said: "Let it be done, let it be done, according to what Amon-Ra, king of gods, our master, sayeth!" I stayed in Tanis until the fourth month of the Harvest, then Smendes and Tentamon sent me with the ship-captain Mengebet and I embarked on the great Syrian sea, in the fourth month of the Harvest, on the first day. I arrived at Dor, a city of Thekel, and Bedel—its prince had much bread brought to me, a jug of wine and a joint of beef. Then a man of my ship ran away, having stolen a vessel of gold worth five *deben,* four vessels of silver worth twenty *deben* and a sack of eleven *deben* of silver. Total of what he stole, five *deben* of gold and thirty-one *deben* of silver [about 1.2 lbs of gold and 7.5 lbs of silver, presumably meant to be used in payment for the timber].

In the morning I rose and went to the abode of the prince and I said to him: "I have been robbed in your harbor. Since you are the prince of this land, you are its investigator, you should look for my money. For the money belongs to Amon-Ra, king of the gods, lord of the lands; it belongs to Nesubenebded; it belongs to Herihor, my lord, and the other magnates of Egypt! It belongs to you; it belongs to Weret; it belongs to Mekmel and to Zakar-Baal, the prince of Byblos!"

He said to me "To thy honor and thy excellence! Behold, I know nothing of

Adapted from Gaston Maspero, *Les Contes populaires de l'Egypte ancienne* (Paris: 1905), pp. 214–230, and James H. Breasted, *Ancient Records of Egypt* (Chicago: 1906), vol. IV, pp. 278–287.

this complaint that you have made to me. If the thief who went on your boat and stole your silver belonged to my land, I would repay it to you from my treasury, until he was found and identified. But the thief who robbed you belongs to your ship. Wait a few days here and I shall look for him."

When I had spent nine days moored in his harbor I went to call on him and said "Behold, you have not found my money. Therefore let me leave with the ship-captain and with those who go to sea!" He said to me "Be silent! . . . *Here the account breaks off, while Wenamon evidently leaves Dor, first for Tyre, then for Byblos. In Byblos he finds a Thekel ship.* In it I found thirty *deben* of silver and seized it, saying to the Thekel: "I will take your silver and it shall stay with me until you find my silver or the man who stole it. Though it was not you who stole it, I shall take it nevertheless. . . . They went away and I enjoyed my triumph in Byblos harbor. I made a place of concealment and I hid Amon-of-the-Way and I placed his things inside it.

The prince of Byblos sent to me saying "Get out of my harbor." I sent to him saying "Where should I go and why? Have the Thekel told you that I took their money? But see, the silver they had was my silver, which had been stolen from me in the harbor of Dor. But I am the messenger of Amon, whom Herihor, my master, has sent to you to bring the timber needed for the barge of Amon, and the ship that Smendes and Tentamon gave me has left. If you want me to leave your harbor, have a ship take me to Egypt." So I spent nineteen days in his harbor, and he sent to me daily saying "Get out of my harbor."

Now, while he was sacrificing to his gods, the god seized one of his youths and possessed him with a prophetic frenzy, so that he said "Bring up the god! Bring the messenger of Amon who has him! Amon made him come!"

Now, while the frenzied youth continued in his frenzy during the night, I had found a ship bound for Egypt and loaded all my belongings into it. Whilst I waited for the darkness thinking that when it fell I would load the god as well, so that no other eye may see him, the harbor master came to me saying "The prince bids you remain till morning." I said to him: "Aren't you the one who comes to me daily saying 'Get out of my harbor'? Aren't you bidding me wait tonight so that the ship I have found may leave and then you will come again telling me to go away?" He went and told this to the prince and the prince sent to the captain of the ship bidding him stay until morning.

When morning came, he sent and had me brought up in the fortress where he was, on the shore of the sea. I found him sitting in his upper room, with his back to a window, while the waves of the great Syrian sea beat against the rocks behind him.

I said to him "May Amon be kind to you!" He said to me "How long is it since you came away from the abode of Amon?" I said: "Five months and one day until now." And he said to me "If you are telling the truth, where is the writing of Amon which should be in your hand? Where is the letter of the High Priest of Amon which should be in your hand?" I said to him "I gave them to Nesubenebded and to Tentamon." Then he was very angry and he said to me "Now, see, neither letters nor credentials are in your hand. Where is the ship of cedar which Nesubenebded gave you? Where is its Syrian crew? Did he not entrust you to this foreign captain simply to have you killed and cast into the sea? . . ." But I said to him: "Wasn't it an Egyptian ship and an Egyptian crew sailing for Nesubenebded? He has no Syrian crews." He said to me: "There are surely twenty ships here in my harbor who trade with Nesubenebded and many more in Sidon that trade with Tanis [meaning Wenamon had had plenty of opportunities to send for fresh credentials]. And I was silent in this great hour.

He answered and said to me: "On what business have you come here?" I said: "I have come after the timber for the great and august barge of Amon-Ra, king of gods. Your father did it, your grandfather did it, and you will do it too!" He said to me: "True, they did it. And if you give me something for doing it, I will do it too! When my people carried out this mission, Pharaoh sent six ships full of Egyptian goods, and they unloaded them in our storehouses. You too must bring something for me." He had the journals of his fathers brought in, and had them read before me, and they found one thousand *deben* of silver and all kinds of things listed in the accounts.

So he said to me: "If the ruler of Egypt were the owner of my property, he would not send silver and gold, saying 'Carry out the mission of Amon.' It was not a royal order that was brought to my father. As for me, I am neither your servant nor the servant of him who sent you. If I cry out to the Lebanon, the heavens open up and the logs lie here on the shores of the sea. Give me the sails you have brought to propel your ships which will carry your logs to Egypt. Give me the ropes you have brought to lash the logs I fell for you. You cannot pay for the cedar you want. See, Amon founded all lands, having first

founded the land of Egypt, whence you come. For craftsmanship came forth from it to reach my land, and learning came forth from it to reach my land. What then are these miserable trips that they have had you make?"

I said to him: "That is not true! I am on no miserable journey! There is no ship upon the River that Amon does not own. For his is the sea, and his is the Lebanon you call your own. It is the nursery for the barge of Amon, lord of every ship. For Amon-Ra, king of gods, spoke to my master Herihor and said 'Send me,' and made me go forth, carrying this great god. But behold you have made this great god wait twenty-nine days in your harbor, although you did not know it. And isn't he still here while you stand and bargain for the Lebanon with Amon, its lord? As for what you say that former kings sent silver and gold, if they had given life and health they would not have sent the valuables; but they have sent the valuables to your fathers instead of life and health. Now, as for Amon-Ra, king of gods, he is the lord of life and health and he was the lord of your fathers who spent their lifetimes making offerings to Amon. And you too are the servant of Amon. If you say to Amon 'Yes I shall do it' and carry out his command, you shall live and be prosperous and healthy, and you will be good to your whole land and people. Wish not for yourself anything that belongs to Amon-Ra, king of gods. Why, a lion wants his own! And now let my scribe be brought to me, that I may send him to Nesubenebded and to Tentamon, the rulers whom Amon put in the north of his land, and they will send everything I ask them to send. . . ." So spake I to him.

So he gave my letter to his messenger [along with seven hewn logs]. His messenger went to Egypt and returned to me, to Syria, in the first month of the second season. Nesubenebded and Tentamon sent: four jars and one basin of gold; five jars of silver; ten garments of royal linen; five hundred rolls of papyrus; five hundred ox hides; five hundred coils of rope; twenty sacks of lentils; thirty baskets of dried fish. And Tentamon sent me personally five garments of royal linen, one sack of lentils and five baskets of fish.

The prince rejoiced and he detailed three hundred men and three hundred oxen, with overseers, to have the trees cut down. They felled them, and they spent the winter lying there. In the third month of the Harvest they dragged them to the seashore and the prince came out and stood by them.

He sent to me, saying: "Come!" Now, when I presented myself before him, the shadow of his sunshade fell upon me. Penamon, a butler, stepped between us, saying "The shadow of Pharaoh, life, prosperity, health, your lord, falls upon you." But the prince was angry with him, saying "Let him alone!" So I presented myself before him, and he answered and said to me: "See, the commission which my fathers formerly executed, I have executed, though you, for your part, have not done for me what your fathers would have done. See, the last of your timber has arrived and there it lies. Do according to my wish and come to load it, for they will give it to you. Do not start to contemplate the terror of the sea, for if you do you will also contemplate my own. Indeed, I do not know why I have not done to you what was done to the messengers of Khamwese [who came on a similar errand]. They spent seventeen years in the land and died here." And he said to his butler: "Take him and let him see their tomb, where they sleep."

I said to him: "Let me not see it! As for Khamwese, the messengers he sent you were mere men; there was no god among them And yet you say 'Go and see your peers.' You should rejoice and have an inscription made and say on it: 'Amon-Ra, king of gods, sent me Amon-of-the-Way, his divine messenger and Wenamon, his human messenger, after the timber for the great and august barge of Amon-Ra, king of gods. I felled it, I loaded it, I supplied him with my ships and crews, I had them brought to Egypt, to ask many years of life from Amon above that which was my fate.' Then in future days when a messenger comes from Egypt, who can write, and reads your name on the inscription, you shall receive water in the West like the gods who are there." . . .

I went to the seashore, to the place where the timbers lay, and I spied eleven Thekel ships coming in from the sea in order to say "Arrest him! Let not a ship of his pass to Egypt!" Then I sat down and began to weep. The letter scribe of the prince came out to me and said "What is the matter with you?" I said to him "Surely you have seen the birds go down to Egypt for a second time [another year had passed]. Behold: they travel to the cool pools, but how long shall I be here, forsaken? For you must surely see those who come to arrest me again."

He went and told it to the prince. The prince began to weep at these words, because they hurt him. He sent his letter scribe out to me, and he brought me two jugs of wine and a ram, and he sent me Tentuo, an Egyptian singer who was with him, saying "Eat, drink, do not let your heart feel apprehension, you shall hear what I have to say tomorrow."

Morning came and he had the Thekel called into his assembly. He stood in their midst and he said to the Thekel: "Why have you come?" They said to him: "We have come after the ships which you send to Egypt with our enemies." He said to them: "I cannot arrest the messenger of Amon in my land. Let me send him away and you shall pursue him to arrest him."

He loaded me on board and sent me away at the harbor of the sea. The wind drove me to the land of Alasa [Cyprus?]. And those of the city came out to kill me. I was brought among them to the place where was Heteb, princess of the town. I found her as she was going out of one of her houses and into another. I greeted her and said to the people who stood around her "There is surely one among you who understands Egyptian?" And one of them said "I understand it." I said to him: "Tell my lady that I have heard

as far as Thebes, the abode of Amon, that injustice is done in every city but not in the land of Alasa. Yet injustice is done here every day." She said "Indeed! What do you mean by this?" I said to her: "If the sea raged and the wind drove me to the land where you are, you should not let them take advantage of me to kill me. Yet, I being a messenger of Amon am one of those they will seek until the end of time. As for the crew of the prince of Byblos, whom they want to kill, their lord will surely find ten crews of yours and slay them in his town.

So she summoned the people and they stood before her and she said to me: "Spend the night . . ." *Here the account breaks off.*

The Amarna Revolution

The Pharaoh Amenhotep IV (1380–1362 B.C.) broke with the established religion of Egypt and instituted the worship of the Aton, the sun disc, as the source of life. The so-called Amarna Revolution attempted a distinct break with Egypt's traditional and static ways of life in religion, politics, art and literature. Pharaoh changed his name to Akhenaton, which might be translated as "He Who is Serviceable to the Aton," and moved his capital from Thebes to Tell el Amarna. Pharaoh's own attitude to the god is expressed in the famous hymn which follows. Beyond doubt, the hymn shows the universality and beneficence of the creating and recreating sun disc. A similarity of spirit and wording to the 104th Psalm has often been noted, and a direct relation between the two has been argued. Because Akhenaton was devoted to this god alone, the Amarna religion has been called monotheistic. This is a debatable question, and a reserved attitude would note that only Akhenaton and his family worshipped the Aton, Akhenaton's courtiers worshipped Akhenaton himself, and the great majority of Egyptians was ignorant of or hostile to the new faith.

Hymn to the Aton

Thou appearest beautifully on the horizon
    of heaven,
Thou living Aton, the beginning of life!
When thou art risen on the eastern horizon,

Thou hast filled every land with thy beauty.
Thou art gracious, great, glistening, and
    high over every land;

From *Ancient Near Eastern Texts Relating to the Old Testament,* 3rd ed., with Supplement, James B. Pritchard ed., and John A. Wilson trans. Copyright 1969 by Princeton University Press. Reprinted by permission of Princeton University Press.

Thy rays encompass the lands to the limit
of all that thou hast made:
As thou art Re, thou reachest to the end of
everything;
Thou subduest them for thy beloved son
[Akhenaton].
Though thou art far away, thy rays are on
earth;
Though thou art in their faces, no one
knows thy going.

When thou settest in the western horizon,
The land is in darkness, in the manner of
death.
They sleep in a room, with their heads
wrapped up,
Nor sees one eye the other.
All their goods which are under their heads
might be stolen,
But they would not perceive it.
Every lion is come forth from his den;
All creeping things, they sting.
Darkness is a shroud, and the earth is in
stillness,
For he who made them rests in his horizon.

At daybreak, when thou arisest on the ho-
rizon,
When thou shinest as the Aton by day,
Thou drivest away the darkness and givest
thy rays.
The Two Lands are in festivity every day,
Awake and standing upon their feet,
For thou hast raised them up.
Washing their bodies, taking their clothing,
Their arms are raised in praise at thy ap-
pearance.
All the world, they do their work.

All beasts are content with their pasturage;
Trees and plants are flourishing.
The birds which fly from their nests,
Their wings are stretched out in praise to
thy *ka*.

All beasts spring upon their feet.
Whatever flies and alights,
They live when thou hast risen for them.
The ships are sailing north and south as
well,
For every way is open at thy appearance.
The fish in the river dart before thy face;
Thy rays are in the midst of the great green
sea.

Creator of seed in women,
Thou who makest fluid into man,
Who maintainest the son in the womb of
his mother,
Who soothest him with that which stills his
weeping,
Thou nurse even in the womb,
Who givest breath to sustain all that he has
made!
When he descends from the womb to
breathe
On the day when he is born,
Thou openest his mouth completely,
Thou suppliest his necessities.
When the chick in the egg speaks within the
shell,
Thou givest him breath within it to main-
tain him.
When thou hast made him his fulfillment
within the egg, to break it,
He comes forth from the egg to speak at his
completed time;
He walks upon his legs when he comes forth
from it.

How manifold it is, what thou hast made!
They are hidden from the face of man.
O sole god, like whom there is no other!
Thou didst create the world according to
thy desire,
Whilst thou wert alone:
All men, cattle and wild beasts,
Whatever is on earth, going upon its feet,
And what is on high, flying with its wings.

The countries of Syria and Nubia, the land
  of Egypt,
Thou settest every man in his place,
Thou suppliest their necessities:
Everyone has his food, and his time of life
  is reckoned.
Their tongues are separate in speech,
And their natures as well;
Their skins are distinguished,
As thou distinguishest the foreign peoples.

Thou makest a Nile in the underworld,
Thou bringest it forth as thou desirest
To maintain the people of Egypt
According as thou madest them for thyself,
The lord of all of them, wearying himself
  with them,
The lord of every land, rising from them,
The Aton of the day, great of majesty.

All distant foreign countries, thou makest
  their life also,
For thou hast set a Nile in heaven,
That it may descend for them and make
  waves upon the mountains,
Like the great green sea,
To water their fields in their towns.
How effective they are, thy plans, O lord
  of eternity!
The Nile in heaven, it is for the foreign
  peoples
And for the beasts of every desert that go
  upon their feet;
While the true Nile comes from the under-
  world for Egypt.

Thy rays suckle every meadow.
When thou risest, they live, they grow for
  thee.
Thou makest the seasons in order to rear all
  that thou hast made,

The winter to cool them,
And the heat that they may taste thee.
Thou hast made the distant sky in order to
  rise therein,
In order to see all that thou dost make.
Whilst thou wert alone,
Rising in thy form as the living Aton,
Appearing, shining, withdrawing or ap-
  proaching,
Thou madest millions of forms of thyself
  alone.
Cities, towns, fields, road and river—
Every eye beholds thee over against them,
For thou art the Aton of the day over the
  earth. . . .

Thou art in my heart,
And there is no other that knows thee
Save thy son Nefer-kheperu-Re Wa-en-Re
  [Akhenaton],
For thou hast made him well-versed in thy
  plans and in thy strength.
The world came into being by thy hand,
According as thou hast made them.
When thou hast risen they live,
When thou settest they die.
Thou art lifetime thy own self,
For one lives only through thee.
Eyes are fixed on beauty until thou settest.
All work is laid aside when thou settest in
  the west.
But when thou risest again,
Everything is made to flourish for the king,
Since thou didst found the earth
And raise them up for thy son,
Who came forth from thy body:
the King of Upper and Lower Egypt, Akh-
  en-Aton,
and the Chief Wife of the King, Nefert-iti,
living and youthful forever and ever.

Tut-ankh-Amon's Restoration

The Amarna movement barely survived the reign of Akhenaton. His son-in-law,
Tut-ankh-Amon, was forced to come to terms with the representatives of the older

order—civil officials and priests. The heresy was crushed, the old gods reinstated and Amarna left to ruin. An inscription in the temple of Amon at Karnak tells of Tut-ankh-Amon's pious acts of restoration after the heresy. Clearly, the priests were doing well again. The country, however, was faring badly. So was the young king who soon disappeared from the throne, probably poisoned.

. . . The good ruler, performing benefactions for his father [Amon] and all the gods, for he has made what was ruined to endure as a monument for the ages of eternity and he has expelled deceit throughout the Two Lands, and justice was set up so that it might make lying to be an abomination of the land, as in its first time.

Now when his majesty appeared as king, the temples of the gods and goddesses from Elephantine down to the marshes of the Delta had gone to pieces. Their shrines had become desolate, had become mounds overgrown with weeds. Their sanctuaries were as if they had never been. Their halls were a footpath. The land was topsy-turvy and the gods turned their backs upon this land. If the army was sent to Djahi to extend the frontiers of Egypt, no success of theirs came at all. If one prayed to a god to seek counsel from him, he would never come at all. If one made supplication to a goddess similarly, she would never come at all. Their hearts were hurt in their bodies so that they did damage to that which had been made.

Now after days had passed by this, his majesty appeared upon the throne of his father. He ruled the regions of Horus; the Black Land [Egypt of the fertile black soil] and the Red Land [the desert] were under his authority, and every land was bowing down to the glory of him.

Now when his majesty was in his palace which is in the house of Aa-kepher-

ka-Re [Thutmose I, 1525–1495 B.C.], like Re in the heavens, then his majesty was conducting the affairs of this land and the daily needs of the Two Banks. So his majesty deliberated plans with his heart, searching for any beneficial deed, seeking out acts of service for his father Amon, and fashioning his august image of genuine fine gold. He surpassed what had been done previously. He fashioned his father Amon upon thirteen carrying-poles, his holy image being of fine gold, lapis lazuli, turquoise, and every august costly stone, whereas the majesty of this august god had formerly been upon eleven carrying-poles. He fashioned Ptah, South-of-His-Wall, Lord of Life of the Two Lands, his august image being of fine gold, upon eleven carrying-poles, his holy image being of fine gold, lapis lazuli, turquoise, and every august costly stone, whereas the majesty of this august god had formerly been on three carrying-poles.

Then his majesty made monuments for the gods, fashioning their cult-statues of genuine fine gold from the highlands, building their sanctuaries anew as monuments for the ages of eternity, established with possessions forever, setting for them divine offerings as a regular daily observance, and provisioning their food-offerings upon earth. He surpassed what had been previously, he went beyond what had been done since the time of the ancestors. He has inducted priests and prophets from the children of the nobles of their towns, each the son of a known man, whose own name is known. He has increased their property [that of the gods] in gold, silver, bronze and copper, without limit in any respect. He has filled their workhouses with male and female slaves, the product of his majesty's capturing in every foreign country. All the property of the temples has been doubled, tripled and quadrupled in silver, gold, lapis lazuli, turquoise, every kind of august costly stone, royal linen, white linen, fine linen, olive oil, gum, fat . . . incense, benzoin, and myrrh, without limit to any good thing. His majesty—life, prosperity, health!—has built their barques upon the river of new cedar from the terraces, of the choicest wood of Lebanon, worked with gold from the highlands. They make the river shine.

His majesty—life, prosperity, health! —has consecrated male and female slaves, women singers and dancers, who had been maidservants in the palace. Their work is charged against the palace and against the treasury of the Lord of the Two Lands. I cause that they be privileged and protected to the benefit of my fathers, all the gods, through a desire to satisfy them by doing what their *ka* wishes, so that they may protect Egypt.

The hearts of the gods and goddesses who are in this land are in joy; the possessors of the shrines are rejoicing; the regions are in jubilee and exultation throughout the entire land: the good times have come! The Ennead of gods who are in the Great House [Heliopolis] raise their arms in praise; their hands are filled with jubilees for ever and ever; all life and satisfaction are with them for the nose of the Horus who repeats births,* the beloved son of Amon, . . . for He fashioned him in order that He (Himself) might be fashioned.** . . .

* Pictorially, a god held the hieroglyph of life to the nose of the king.
** Amon made Tut-ankh-Amon the divine king in order that Amon might be advanced.

2. ASSYRIA AND BABYLONIA

Where the Egyptians had no codified secular laws, though they were made aware of the rules of social morality by custom and religion, the peoples of Mesopotamia, who knew little of the moral attitudes of their gods, were provided with definite laws—laws governing both private and public life, protected by terrifying curses, and generally enforced by powerful kings and dire penalties. The best-known collection of these laws is the Code of Hammurabi, who ruled in Babylon in the early seventeenth century B.C. But the various laws which he codified had been written up in Babylonia as early as 2250 B.C.

The code, with its magnificent prologue, is best read whole. The gods, explains Hammurabi, had named him "to promote the welfare of the people, cause justice to prevail in the land, destroy the wicked and the evil, that the strong might not oppress the weak"—at any rate, not beyond the ken and against the interests of the king himself. A code of laws "in the language of the land," as he put it, provided a pattern of order not only for the state but for the individual in his many activities, a pattern of unity and prosperity. The selections below give some idea of the varied situations this ancient society set itself to solve, the complex social gradations, the economic structure, the human problems, the business practices, and the frequent subtlety of which they showed themselves capable.

The *Code* of Hammurabi

1. If a man weave a spell and bring a charge of murder against another man and has not justified himself, the accuser shall be put to death.

2. If a man has put a spell upon another man, and has not justified himself, the one who is charged with sorcery shall go to the holy river, he shall plunge into the holy river, and if the holy river overcomes him, his accuser shall take his estate. If the holy river shows that man to be innocent and has saved him, he who charged him with sorcery shall be put to death and the man who plunged into the river shall take the estate of him who brought the charge against him.

8. If a man has stolen ox or sheep or ass or pig or ship, whether from the temple or from the palace, he shall pay thirtyfold; if he stole from a commoner, he shall render tenfold. If the thief cannot pay, he shall be put to death.

14. If a man has stolen the son of a freeman, he shall be put to death.

15. If a man has helped a male or female palace slave, or a commoner's male or female slave to escape out of the city gate, he shall be put to death.

16. If a man has harbored in his house a male or female slave fugitive from the palace or from a commoner, and has not produced them at the demand of the police, the owner of that house shall be put to death.

17. If a man has captured a fugitive male or female slave in the open country and driven him back to his master, the owner of the slave shall pay him two shekels of silver.

18. If that slave will not name his owner, he shall drive him to the palace and enquire into his record, and cause him to return to his owner.

19. If he keeps the slave in his house and afterwards the slave is seized in his possession, that man shall be put to death.

21. If a man has broken into a house, he shall be killed before the breach and walled in it.

22. If a man has robbed and has been captured, that man shall be put to death.

23. If the robber has not been caught, the man who has been despoiled shall recount before the god what he has lost, and the city and governor in whose territory the robbery took place shall make good to him his loss.

24. If a life was lost, the city and governor shall pay one mina of silver to his people.

25. If a fire broke out in a man's house and a man who has come to extinguish the fire has lifted up his eyes to the property of the householder and has taken the property of the householder, that man shall be thrown into the fire.

26. If a soldier or a constable, ordered on an errand of the king, goes not or hires a hireling and sends him in his place, that soldier or constable shall be put to death and his hireling shall take his estate.

27. If a soldier or a constable disappears whilst on military service and they have given his field and his orchard to another and he has carried on his obligations, if he returns and regains his city, they shall restore his field and his orchard

From *The Oldest Code of Laws in the World,* tr. C. H. W. Johns, Edinburgh, 1903.

and he shall fulfill his obligations himself.

32. If a soldier or a constable has been captured while on the service of the king and has been ransomed by a merchant and enabled to regain his city, if in his house there is means for his ransom, then he shall ransom himself; if in his house there is no means for his ransom, he shall be ransomed from the temple of his city; if in the temple of his city there is not means for his ransom, the palace shall ransom him. His field, his orchard and his house shall not be given for his ransom.

35. If a man has bought the cattle or sheep which the king has given to the soldier from the hand of the soldier, he shall be deprived of his money.

36. The field, orchard and house of a soldier, a constable or a tributary cannot be sold.

37. If a man has bought the field, orchard or house of a soldier, a constable or a tributary, his contract-tablet shall be broken and he shall forfeit his money. The field, orchard or house he shall return to its owner.

45. If a man has given his field for rent to a cultivator and has received the rent of his field, and afterwards a thunderstorm has ravaged the field or carried away the produce, the cultivator shall bear the loss.

48. If a man has a debt upon him and a thunderstorm ravaged his field or carried away the produce, or the corn has not grown for lack of water, in that year he shall make no return of corn to his creditor; he shall alter his contract-tablet and he shall not pay interest for that year.

53. If a man has neglected to strengthen the dyke of his canal, and a breach has opened in his dyke, and the waters have ravaged the meadow, the man in whose dyke the breach has been opened shall make good the corn that he caused to be lost.

54. If he is not able to make good the corn, they shall sell him and his goods for money, and the farmers of the meadow whose corn the water carried away shall share it.

104. If a merchant has lent a trader corn, wool, oil or any sort of goods to traffic with, the trader shall write down the price and pay it back; the trader shall take a sealed receipt of the price which he pays to the merchant.

105. If the trader has forgotten and has not taken a sealed receipt of the money he has given the merchant, money for which there is no sealed receipt shall not be put in his accounts.

106. If a trader has borrowed money from a merchant and then has disputed the fact, that merchant shall bring proof before god and witnesses concerning the money taken, and the trader shall give the merchant threefold the money he has borrowed.

107. If a merchant has wronged a trader and the trader has returned to the merchant whatever the merchant gave him, if the merchant disputed with the trader as to what the trader gave him, that trader shall bring proof before god and witnesses, and the merchant because he disputed the trader shall give the trader sixfold whatever he has taken.

108. If a wine merchant has not received corn as the price of drink, has received silver by the large weight and has made the price of drink less than the price of corn, they shall prove it against that wine merchant and throw her into the water.

109. If a wine merchant has collected outlaws in her house and has not seized

those outlaws and driven them to the palace, that wine merchant shall be put to death.

110. If a nun, a lady of god, who is not living in a convent, has opened the door of a wine shop or entered the wine shop for a drink, that woman shall be burned.

115. If a man holds a debt of corn or money against another man and levies a distraint, if the pledge dies a natural death in the house of his distrainer, that case has no penalty.

116. If the pledge has died in the house of his distrainer from blows or want, the owner of the pledge shall prove it against the merchant, and if it was the freeman's son who died, they shall put his son to death; and if it was a freeman's slave, he shall pay one third of a mina of silver and he shall lose whatever it was that he lent.

117. If a debt came due against a man, and he has given his wife, his son, his daughter for the money, or handed himself over to work off the debt, for three years they shall work in the house of their buyer or exploiter, in the fourth year they shall be set free.

122. If a man shall give silver, gold, or anything whatever to a man on deposit, whatever he gives he shall show to witnesses, arrange contracts, and give on deposit.

123. If he has given on deposit without witness and contract, and they deny receipt at the place of deposit, this case has no remedy.

124. If a man has given silver, gold, or anything whatever to a man on deposit before witnesses, and he has denied the fact, it shall be proved against that man and he shall pay double what he was to give.

125. If a man has given anything of his on deposit and where he gave it something of his has been lost along with something of the owner of the house, either by housebreaking or rebellion, the owner of the house who was careless shall make good the loss and shall seek out the lost property and take it from the thief.

126. If a man has lost nothing of his but has said that something of his is lost, since nothing of his is lost, the facts regarding this shall be recounted before god and whatever he has claimed he shall make up twofold and give to his loss.

127. If a man has caused the finger to be pointed against a nun or a man's wife, and has not justified himself, that man they shall throw down before the judge and brand his forehead.

128. If a man has married a wife and has not drawn up a contract, that woman is no wife.

129. If the wife of a man has been caught lying with another man, they shall bind them and throw them into the waters. If the owner of the wife would save his wife then in turn the king could save his servant.

130. If a man has forced the wife of a man, who has had no intercourse with a male and is dwelling in her father's house, and has lain in her bosom, and he has been caught, that man shall be killed, the woman will go free.

131. If a wife has been accused by her husband and she has not been caught lying with another male, she shall swear by god and shall return to her house.

132. If a wife has the finger pointed at her on account of another male but has not been caught lying with another male, for the sake of her husband she shall throw herself into the holy river.

133. If a man has been taken captive and in his house there is maintenance,

if his wife has gone out from her house and entered into the house of another, because that woman has not guarded her body and has entered the house of another, they shall prove it against that woman and throw her into the waters.

134. If a man has been taken captive and in his house there is no maintenance, and his wife has entered into the house of another, that woman has no blame.

135. If a man has been taken captive and in his house there is no maintenance, if his wife has entered the house of another and has borne children and afterwards her husband returns and regains his city, that woman shall return to her first husband, the children shall go after their father.

137. If a man has decided to put away his concubine who has borne him children or his wife who has granted him children, to that woman he shall return her marriage portion and shall give her half of the field, orchard and goods, and she shall bring up her children. From the time that her children are grown up, from whatever is given to her children they shall give her a share like that of one son, and she shall marry the husband of her choice.

138. If a man has put away his bride who has not borne him children, he shall return her dowry and pay her the marriage portion which she brought from her father's house, and shall put her away.

139. If there was no dowry, he shall give her one mina of silver for a divorce.

140. If he is a poor man, he shall give her one third of a mina of silver.

141. If the wife of a man who is living in the house of her husband has made up her mind to leave the house to engage in business and has acted the fool, neglecting the house and humiliating the husband, it shall be proved against her; and

if her husband has said "I put her away," he shall put her away and she shall go her way, and he shall not give her anything for her divorce.

142. If a woman hates her husband and has said "You shall not possess me," they shall inquire into her record and if she has been economical and has no vice and her husband has gone out and greatly belittled her, that woman has no blame, she will take her marriage portion and go off to her father's house.

143. If she has not been economical, a gadabout, has neglected her house and humiliated her husband, that woman they shall throw into the waters.

153. If a man's wife has caused her husband to be killed on account of another man, they shall impale that woman on a stake.

154. If a man has known his daughter, that man shall be expelled from the city.

155. If a man has betrothed a bride to his son and his son has known her, and the man afterwards has lain in her bosom and they have caught him, that man they shall bind and throw into the water.

157. If a man, after his father, has lain in the bosom of his mother, they shall burn both of them together.

175. If either a palace slave or a private slave has married the daughter of a free man and she has borne children, the owner of the slave shall have no claim on the children of the daughter of a free man for servitude.

176. And if a palace slave or a private slave has married the daughter of a free man and when they married she entered his house with a dowry from her father's house and they set up a household and acquired property, after the palace slave or the private slave has gone to his fate

the daughter of the free man shall take her dowry and whatever she and her husband have acquired shall be divided in two parts, and the owner of the slave shall take one half and the daughter of a free man shall take one half for her children. If she had no marriage portion, whatever her husband and she from the time they started have acquired shall be divided in two parts, half for the owner of the slave and half for her and her children.

195. If a man has struck his father, his hand shall be cut off.

196. If a man has caused the loss of a gentleman's eye, they shall cause him to lose one eye.

197. If he has shattered a gentleman's limb, they shall shatter his limb.

198. If he has caused a commoner to lose his eye or shattered a commoner's limb, he shall pay one mina of silver.

199. If he has caused the loss of an eye of a gentleman's servant or has shattered his limb, he shall pay half his price.

200. If a man has made the tooth of a man that is his equal fall out, they shall make his tooth fall out.

201. If he has made the tooth of a commoner fall out, he shall pay one third of a mina of silver.

202. If a man has struck the cheek of his superior, he shall be struck in the assembly with 60 strokes of a cowhide whip.

203. If a man of gentle birth has struck a man of gentle birth who is his equal, he shall pay one mina of silver.

204. If a poor man has struck a poor man, he shall pay ten shekels of silver.

205. If a slave has struck a free man, they shall cut off his ear.

206. If a man has struck a man in a quarrel and wounded him, he shall swear "I did not strike him deliberately" and shall answer for the doctor.

207. If he has died of his blows, he shall swear as before and, if he be of gentle birth, he shall pay half a mina of silver.

209. If a man has struck a gentleman's daughter and caused her to have a miscarriage, he shall pay ten shekels of silver for what was in her womb.

210. If that woman has died, they shall put to death his daughter.

211. If by his blows he has caused the daughter of a commoner to have a miscarriage, he shall pay five shekels of silver.

212. If that woman has died, he shall pay half a mina of silver.

213. If he has struck a gentleman's slave and caused a miscarriage, he shall pay two shekels of silver.

214. If that slave has died, he shall pay one third of a mina of silver.

215. If a doctor has treated a gentleman for a severe wound, with a bronze lancet and has cured him, or has opened an abcess of the eye for a gentleman with the bronze lancet and has cured the eye of the gentleman, he shall take ten shekels of silver.

218. If the doctor has treated a gentleman for a severe wound with a lancet of bronze and has caused the gentleman to die or has opened an abcess of the eye of a gentleman with the bronze lancet and has caused the loss of the gentleman's eye, they shall cut off his hands.

219. If the doctor has treated the severe wound of a commoner's slave and has caused his death, he shall render slave for slave.

226. If a brander has branded a slave with an indelible mark or has cut off the mark of a slave not his own without the owner's consent, they shall cut off his hands.

227. If a man has deceived the brander and has caused him to brand or cut off the mark of a slave not his own, that man shall be killed and immured in his own house, the brander shall swear "I did it unknowingly" and shall go free.

229. If a builder has built a house and not made his work strong and the house he built has fallen and so has caused the death of the owner of the house, that builder shall be put to death.

230. If he has caused the son of the owner of the house to die, they shall put to death the son of the builder.

231. If he has caused the slave of the owner of the house to die, he shall give slave for slave to the owner of the house.

232. If he has caused the loss of goods, he shall restore whatever losses he has caused, and because he did not make strong the house he built and it fell, he shall rebuild the house that fell at his own cost.

233. If a builder has built a house for a man and has not jointed his work, and the wall has fallen, that builder shall repair that wall at his own cost.

244. If a man has hired an ox or a sheep and a lion has killed it in the open field, that loss is for its owner.

245. If a man has hired an ox and caused it to die through neglect or by blows, he shall render ox for ox to the owner of the ox.

248. If a man has hired an ox and has crushed its horn, cut off its tail, or pierced its nostrils, he shall pay a quarter of its price.

249. If a man has hired an ox and god has struck it and it has died, that man shall swear before god and shall go free.

250. If a wild bull in his charge has gored a man, and caused him to die, that case has no remedy.

251. If a man's ox was inclined to gore and it was made known to him that this was so and he took no steps to tie him up or blunt his horns, and that ox has gored a man and caused him to die, he shall pay half a mina of silver for a gentleman, one third of a mina for a slave.

282. If a slave has said to his master "You are not my master," his master shall prove him to be his slave and his master shall cut off his ear.

The Wolf on the Fold

"The Assyrian came down like the wolf on the fold,
And his cohorts were gleaming in purple and gold;
And the sheen of their spears was like stars on the sea,
When the blue wave rolls nightly on deep Galilee." (Byron)

". . . and when they arose early in the morning, behold, they were all dead corpses."
(2 Kings 19:35)

Fiercest and most warlike among those Near Eastern peoples of whom history bears a tale were the Assyrians, northern neighbors of Babylon, whose greatest time lay between the ninth and the seventh centuries, B.C., a period characterized by constant and devastating warfare, like most others in history only more so. The realm of Assur was probably the first approximation of a world empire, showing the crude beginnings of large-scale political organization of many subject peoples in a great state. Mesopotamian culture followed in the wake of the Assyrian armies as it did in the trail of Babylonian caravans. There are many biblical references to Assyrian religion, and Manasseh of Juda, for one, seems to have fallen into Assyrian ways before he fell to Assyrian arms (2 Chronicles 33).

The annals of Assyrian kings have an almost hallucinatory quality in their repetition of rapine, destruction and death. The two quoted below are fascinating in their bloody monotony. Assurnasirpal was the first great conqueror of the ninth-century Assyrian revival; Ashurbanipal, the last of the great kings of prey whose power stretched from Kurdistan to the Nile. Their very conquests, however, were to bring them down. The victories of Ashurbanipal and his predecessors destroyed the power of those tribes that stood as a barrier against the Medes in the northeast and against the Persians in Elam, at the head of the Persian Gulf. After a Neo-Babylonian interlude, these new conquerors were going to take over.

Annals of Assur-nasir-Pal (885–860 B.C.)

I am a king, I am a lord, I am glorious, I am great, I am mighty, I have arisen, I am a chief, I am a prince, I am a warrior, I am great and I am glorious, Assur-nasir-habal, a mighty king of Assyria, proclaimer of the Moongod, worshipper of Anu, exalter of Yav, suppliant of the gods am I, servant unyielding, subduing the lands of his foes, a king mighty in battle, destroyer of cities and forests, chief over opponents, king of the four regions, expeller of his foes, prostrating all his enemies, prince of a multitude of lands and of all kings, even of all, a prince subduing those disobedient to him, who is ruling all the multitudes of men. These aspirations have gone up to the face of the great gods; on my destiny they have steadfastly determined; at the wishes of my heart and the uplifting of my hand, Istar, exalted lady, has favored me in my intentions, and has applied her heart to the conduct of my battles and warfare. In those days I Assur-nasir-pal, glorious prince, worshipper of the great gods, the wishes of whose heart Bel will cause him to attain, and who has conquered all kings who disobey him, and by his hand capturing his enemies, who in difficult places has beaten down assemblages of rebels; when Assur, mighty lord, proclaimer of my name, aggrandizer of my royalty over the kings of the four regions, has bountifully added his invincible power to the forces of my government putting me in possession of lands, and mighty forests for exploration has he given and urgently impelled me— by the might of Assur my lord, perplexed paths, difficult mountains by the impetuosity of my hosts I crossed and an equal there was not.

In the beginning of my reign and in my first campaign when the Sun-god, guider of the lands threw over me his beneficent protection, on the throne of my dominion I firmly seated myself; a sceptre, the dread of man, I took into my hands; my chariots and my armies I collected; I passed rugged paths, difficult mountains, ill-suited for the passage of chariots and armies and I went to the land of Nairi: Libie, their capital city, the cities Zurra and Abuqua, Arura, Aru-

Translated by J. M. Rodwell in *Babylonian and Assyrian Literature* (New York, 1901), pp. 168–85.

bie, situated within the limits of the land of Aruni and Etini, fortified cities, I took, their fighting men in numbers I slew; their spoil, their wealth, their cattle I spoiled; their soldiers were discouraged; they took possession of a difficult mountain, a mountain exceedingly difficult; after them I did not proceed, for it was a mountain ascending up like lofty points of iron, and the beautiful birds of heaven had not reached up into it: like nests of the young birds in the midst of the mountain they placed their defences into which none of the kings my fathers had ever penetrated . . . along the feet of that mountain I crept and hid: their nests, their tents I broke up; 200 of their warriors with weapons I destroyed; their spoil in abundance like the young of sheep I carried off; their corpses like rubbish on the mountains I heaped up; their relics in tangled hollows of the mountains I consumed; their cities I overthrew, demolished and burnt in fire. From the land of Nummi to the land of Kirruri I came down; the tribute of Kirruri . . . , horses, fish, oxen, horned sheep in numbers, copper as their tribute I received. An officer to guard boundaries over them I placed. While in the land of Kirruri they detained me, the fear of Assur my lord overwhelmed the lands of Gilzanai and Khubuskai; horses, silver, gold, tin, copper, *kams* of copper as their tribute they brought me. From the land of Kirruri I withdrew and passed to a territory close to the town Khulun in Kurdistan; their cities I occupied; their soldiers in numbers I slew; their spoil, their riches I carried off; their soldiers were discouraged; the summits rising over against the city of Nistun, which were menacing like the storms of heaven, I captured, into which none among the princes my sires had ever penetrated; my soldiers like birds

of prey rushed upon them; 260 of their warriors by the sword I smote down; their heads cut off in heaps I arranged; the rest of them like birds in a nest in the rocks of the mountains nestled; their spoil, their riches from the midst of the mountains I brought down; cities which were situated in the midst of vast forests I overthrew, destroyed, burned in fire; the rebellious soldiers fled from before my arms; they came down; my yoke they received; impost tribute and a Viceroy I set over them. Bubu, son of Bubua son of the Prefect of Nistun, in the city of Arbela I flayed; his skin I stretched in contempt upon the wall.

At that time an image of my person I made; a history of my supremacy upon it I wrote and on a mountain of the land of Ikin, in the city of Assur-nasir-pal I erected it. In my own eponym, in the month of July and the 24th day [probably 882 B.C.]. In honor of Assur and Istar the great gods my lords I quitted the city of Nineveh: to cities situated below Nipur and Pazate, powerful countries, I proceeded; Atkun, Nithu, Pilazi and 20 other cities in their environs I captured; many of their soldiers I slew; their spoil, their riches I carried off; the cities I burned with fire; the rebel soldiers fled before my arms, submitted and took my yoke; I left them in possession of their land. From the cities below Nipur and Pazate I withdrew; the Tigris I crossed; the land of Commagene I approached; the tribute of Commagene and of the Moschi in *kams* of copper, sheep and goats I received; whilst stationed in Commagene they brought me news that the city Suri in Bit-Khalupe had revolted. The people of Hamath had slain the governor. Ahiyababa the son of Lamamana they brought from Bit-Adini and made their king. By help of Assur and Yav, the great gods who aggrandize my royalty, chariots and an army I collected; the banks of the Chaboras I occupied; in my passage I collected tribute in abundance from Salman-haman-ilin from the city of Sunai [in the north of Mesopotamia]—silver, gold, tin, *kam* of copper, vestments of wool, vestments of linen. To Suri which is in Bit-Halupe I drew near; the fear of the approach of Assur my lord overwhelmed them; the great men and the multitudes of the city, coming up after me for the saving of their lives, submitted to my yoke; some slain, some living, some tongueless I made; Ahiyababa son of Lamamana whom from Bit-Adini they had fetched, I captured; in the valor of my heart and the steadfastness of my soldiers I besieged the city; the soldiers, rebels all, were taken prisoners; the nobles I had sent to the principal palace of his land; his silver, his gold, his treasure, his riches, his copper, tin, choice copper in abundance, alabaster and ironstone large in size, the treasures of his harem, his daughters and the wives of the rebels with their treasures, and the gods with their treasures, precious stones, his swift chariot, his horses, the harness, his chariot-yoke, trappings for horses, coverings for men, vestments of wool, vestments of linen, handsome altars of cedar, bowls of cedar-wood, beautiful black coverings, beautiful purple coverings, carpets, his oxen, his sheep, his abundant spoil, which like the stars of heaven could not be reckoned I carried off; Aziel as my lieutenant over them I placed; a trophy along the length of the great gate I erected. The rebellious nobles who had revolted against me and whose skins I had stripped off, I made into a trophy: some in the middle of the pile I left to decay; some on the top of the pile on stakes I impaled; some by the side of the pile I

placed in order on stakes; many within view of my land I flayed; their skins on the walls I arranged; of the officers of the King's officer, rebels, I cut off the limbs; I brought Ahiyababa to Nineveh; I flayed him and fastened his skin to the wall; laws and edicts over Lakie I established . . . to the land of Kasyari [near the modern Diarbekir] I proceeded, and to Kinabu, the fortified city of the province of Hulai. I drew near; with the impetuosity of my formidable attack I besieged and took the town; 600 of their fighting men with my arms I destroyed; 3000 of their captives I consigned to the flames; as hostages I left not one of them alive; Hulai the governor of the town I captured by my hand alive; their corpses into piles I built; their boys and maidens I dishonored; Hulai the governor of the city I flayed; his skin on the walls . . . I placed in contempt; the city I overthrew, demolished, burned with fire; the city of Mariru within their territory I took; 50 warriors by my weapons I destroyed; 200 of their captives in the flame I burned; the soldiers of the land of Nirbi I slew in fight in the desert; their spoil, their oxen, their sheep I brought away; Nirbu which is at the foot of mount Ukhira I boldly took; I then passed over to Tila their fortified city; from Khinabu I withdrew; to Tila I drew near; a strong city with three forts facing each other. The soldiers trusted to their strong forts and numerous army and would not submit; my yoke they would not accept; then with onset and attack I besieged the city; their fighting men with my weapons I destroyed; of their spoil, their riches, oxen and sheep I made plunder; much booty I burned with fire; many soldiers I captured alive; of some I chopped off the hands and feet; of others I cut off the noses and ears; of many I put out the eyes. One pile of bodies while yet alive and one pile of heads I reared up on the heights within their town; their heads in the midst I hoisted; their boys and their maidens I dishonored, the city I overthrew, razed and burned with fire. . . .

Nirbu which is in the land of Kasyari revolted; nine of their cities leagued themselves with Ispilipri, one of their fortified towns and trusted to a mountain difficult of access; but the heights of the hill I besieged and took; in the midst of the strong mountain their fighting men I slew; their corpses like rubbish on the hills I piled up; their common people in the tangled hollows of the mountains I consumed; their spoil, their property I carried off; the heads of their soldiers I cut off; a pile of them in the highest part of the city I built; their boys and maidens I dishonored; to the environs of the city Bliyani I passed; the banks of the river Lukia I took possession of; in my passage I occupied the towns of the land of Kirhi hard by; many of their warriors I slew; their spoil I spoiled; their cities with fire I burned. To the city of Ardupati I went. In those days the tribute of Ahiramu son of Yahiru of the land of Nilaai son of Bahiani of the land of the Hittites [here, roughly Syria] and of the Princes of the land of Hanirabi, silver, gold, tin, *kam* of copper, oxen, sheep, horses, as their tribute I received.

In the eponym of Assuridin [about 881 B.C.] they brought me news that Zab-Yav, prince of the land of Dagara, had revolted. The land of Zamua throughout its whole extent he boldly seized; near the city of Babite they constructed a fort; for combat and battle they marched forth. In the service of Assur, the great god my lord, and the great Merodach going before me, by the powerful aid which the lord Assur extended to my

people, my servants and my soldiers I called together; to the vicinity of Babite I marched. The soldiers trusted to the valor of their army and gave battle. But in the mighty force of the great Merodach going before me, I engaged in battle with them; I effected their overthrow; I broke them down; 1460 of their warriors in the environs I slew; their strong towns, with 100 towns within their territory I captured; their spoil, their youths, their oxen and sheep I carried off; Zab-Yav for the preservation of his life a rugged mountain ascended; 1200 of their soldiers I carried off; from the land of Dagara I withdrew; to the city of Bara I approached; the city of Bara I captured; 320 of their soldiers by my weapons I destroyed; their oxen, sheep and spoil in abundance I removed; 300 of their soldiers I took off . . . to the land of Nizir which they call Lulu-Kinaba I drew near; the city Bunasi one of their fortified cities belonging to Musazina and 20 cities nearby I captured; their soldiers were discouraged; they took refuge in a mountain difficult of access; I, Assur-nasir-pal swooped impetuously after them; their corpses lay thick on the hills of Nizir; 326 of their warriors I smote down; his horses I exacted of him; the common people in the tangled hollows I consumed; seven cities in Nizir among their fortresses I captured; their soldiers I slew; their riches, oxen, sheep I carried off; the cities themselves I burned; to my tents I returned for a halt; from those same tents I departed; to the cities of the land of Nizir whose site no one had ever seen I marched; the city of Larbusa, the fortified city of Kirtiara, and 8 cities of their territory I captured; the soldiers lost heart and took to a steep mountain, a mountain which rose high upward like sharp iron stakes; yet I ascended after them, in the midst of the mountain I scattered their corpses; 172 of their men I slew; soldiers in numbers in the hollows of the mountain I hunted down; their spoil, their cattle, their sheep I took away; their cities with fire I burned; their heads on the high places of the mountain I lifted up; their boys and maidens I dishonored; to the aforesaid tents I returned to halt; from those same tents I withdrew; 150 cities of the territory of Larbusai, Durlulumai, Bunisai and Barai I captured; their fighting men I slew; their spoil I spoiled; the city of Hasabtal I razed and burned with fire; 50 soldiers of Barai I slew in battle on the plain. In those days the princes of the entire land of Zamua were overwhelmed by the dread of the advance of Assur my lord and submitted to my yoke; horses, silver, gold, I received; the entire land under a Prefect I placed; horses, silver, gold, wheat, barley, submission, I imposed upon them.

[About 880 B.C.] when I was stationed in Nineveh they brought me news that Amaka and Arastua withheld the tribute and vassalage due to Assur my lord. In honor of Assur . . . I prepared for the third time an expedition against Zamua. . . . Near Zimaki I added my strong chariots and battering rams as major warlike implements to my stores; by night and daybreak I went down; the Turnat river on rafts I crossed; to Amali the strong city of Arastu I approached; with vigorous assault the city I besieged and took; 800 of their fighting men I destroyed by my weapons; I filled the streets of their city with corpses; their many houses I burned; many soldiers I took alive; their spoil in abundance I carried off; the city I overthrew, razed and burned with fire; the city Khudun and 20 cities in the neighborhood I took; their soldiers I slew; their booty in cattle and

sheep I carried off; their boys, their maidens I dishonored; the city of Kisirtu a fortified city of Zabini with ten neighboring cities I took; their soldiers I slew; their spoil I carried off; the cities of Barai and Kirtiara, Bunisai together with the province of Khasmar I overthrew, razed and burned with fire; I reduced the boundaries to a heap, and then from the cities of Arastua I withdrew; to the neighborhood of the territory of Laara and Bidirgi, rugged land, unsuited for the passage of chariots and an army I passed; to the royal city Zamri of Amika of Zamua I drew near; Amika fled in fear before the mighty prowess of my formidable attack and took refuge on a hill difficult of access; I brought forth the treasures of his palace and his chariot . . . from the city of Zamri I withdrew; to Lara, I cut through with axes of iron and with rollers of metal beat down the rugged hill country unfitted for the passage of chariots and armies . . . the kings of Zamua, all of them, drew back from the impetuousness of my servants and the greatness of my power and accepted my yoke; tribute of silver, gold, copper, *kam* of copper, vestments of wool, horses, oxen, sheep, goats, in addition to what I had settled before, I imposed upon them; a viceroy in Kalach I created . . . the rebel soldiers fled from before my arms; they fled to the mountains; I marched after them; within confines of the land of Aziru they settled and got ready the city of Mizu as their strong place; the land of Aziru I overthrew and destroyed; from Zimaki as far as Turnat I scattered their corpses; 500 of their fighting men I destroyed; their spoil in abundance I carried off.

The powerful chariots and battering-rams I put up in my stores; on rafts I passed the Tigris; all night I descended;

to Pitura a strong town of Dirrai I drew near—a very strong city: two forts facing each other, whose castle rose like the summit of a mountain. By the mighty hands of Assur my lord and the impetuosity of my army and my formidable attack I gave them battle; on two days before sunrise like Yav the inundator I rushed upon them; destruction upon them I rained with the might and prowess of my warriors; like the rush of birds coming upon them, the city I captured; 800 of their soldiers by my arms I destroyed; their heads I cut off; many soldiers I captured in my hand alive; their populace in the flames I burned; their spoil I carried off in abundance; a trophy of the living and of heads about the great gate I built; 700 soldiers I there impaled on stakes; the city I overthrew, razed and reduced to a heap of ruins all around; their boys, their maidens I dishonored; the city of Kukunu [on the upper Tigris] facing the mountain of Matni I captured; 700 of their fighting men I smote down with my weapons; their spoil in abundance I carried off; 50 cities of Dira I occupied; their soldiers I slew; I plundered them; 50 soldiers I took alive; the cities I overthrew, razed and burned; the approach of my royalty overcame them; from Pitura I withdrew and went down to Arbaki in Gilhi-Bitani; they quailed before the approach of my majesty and deserted their

towns and strong places. For the saving of their lives they went up mount Matni, a land of strength. I went after them in pursuit; 1000 of their warriors I left in the rugged hills; their corpses on a hill I piled up; with their bodies the tangled hollows of the mountains I filled; I captured 200 soldiers and cut off their hands; their spoil I carried away . . . the trees of their land I cut down; the wheat and the barley . . . I kept.

Ammiba'al the son of Zamani had been betrayed and slain by his nobles. To revenge Ammiba'al I marched; from before the vehemence of my arms and the greatness of my royalty they drew back. I took his swift chariots, trappings for men and horses one hundred in number, horses, harness, yokes, tribute of silver and gold with 100 talents in tin, 100 talents in copper, bowls of copper, vessels of copper, 1000 vestments of wool, *nui* wood, *eru* wood, horns, choice gold, the treasures of his palace, 2000 oxen, 5000 sheep, his wife, with large donations from her. The daughters of his chiefs with large donations from them I received. I, Assur-nasir-pal, great king, mighty king, king of legions, king of Assyria, son of Tuklat-Adar great and mighty king, king of legions, king of Assyria, noble warrior, walked in the strength of Assur his lord and found no equal among the kings of the four regions. . . .

Annals of Ashurbanipal (668–633 B.C.)

In my ninth campaign I mustered my troops and directed the march against Uaite, king of Arabia, who had broken my treaty and had not kept in mind the favors which I had shown him, but had thrown off the yoke of my lordship which

Assur had laid upon him in order that he should be tributary to me. He had refrained from asking after my welfare, and had withheld the gift of his heavy tribute. Like Elam, he heard of the rebellious plans of Akkad, and disregarded my

From Robert Francis Harper, ed., *Assyrian and Babylonian Literature,* D. Appleton and Company (New York: 1904), pp. 118–127.

treaty. Me—Ashurbanipal—the king, the pure priest, the pious chief, the product of the hands of Assur, he deserted and to Abiate and Aiamu, sons of Teri, he handed over his forces and sent them to the help of Shamash-shum-ukin, the hostile brother and made common cause with him. [*Shamash-shum-ukin had revolted against Ashurbanipal. He was eventually defeated.*] He, Shamash-shum-ukin, stirred up the Arabians to revolt along with himself and made plundering raids upon the people, dominion over whom Assur, Ishtar and the great gods had given to me to exercise and had entrusted to me. At the command of Assur and Ishtar I summoned my troops; on the way to Azarilu and Hirataqaçai in Edom, in the pass of Yabrud, in Beth-Ammon, in the districts of Hauran, in Moab, in Sa'arri, in Harge, and in the districts of Çubitu, a countless number of his men I killed and brought about his defeat. The Arabians, as many as had gone forth with him, I ran through with the sword, while he himself escaped from before Assur's mighty weapons and fled afar off. They set fire to the tents, their dwellings, and burned them up. Disaster overtook Uaite, and he fled alone to Nabataea.

As for Uaite, son of Hazael, cousin of Uaite, son of Birdadda, who had made himself king of Arabia—Assur, king of the gods, the great rock, changed his purpose, and he came into my presence. In order to exhibit the majesty of Assur and the great gods my lords, I laid heavy punishment upon him, in that I put him in a cage, and with wild beasts and dogs I bound him and set him to watch the city gate of Nineveh which is called "The Entrance to Temple Street."

Ammuladi also, king of Kedar, advanced in order to make war upon the kings of the West-land, whom Assur,

Ishtar and the great gods had entrusted to me. Under the protection of Assur, Sin, Shamash, Ramman, Bel, Nabu, Ishtar of Nineveh, Queen of Kidmuri, Ishtar of Arbela, Ninib, Nergal, and Nusku, I brought about his defeat. Him, together with Adyia, wife of Uaite, king of Arabia, they captured alive and brought before me. By the command of the great gods, my lords, I put a dog chain on him and set him to watch in a cage.

By the command of Assur, Ishtar and the great gods, my lords, I slew the ally of Abiate and Aiamu, sons of Teri, who had come to the help of Shamash-shum-ukin, the hostile brother, in order to enter into Babylon, and I brought about his defeat. The rest of them, who had entered into Babylon, through stress of famine ate one another's flesh. In order to save their lives they came forth from Babylon, and my army, which was besieging Shamash-shum-ukin, defeated him for the second time, while he himself fled alone, and in order to save his life threw himself at my feet. I granted him mercy, made him swear to the compacts by the great gods, and I made him king of Arabia instead of Uaite, son of Hazael.

However, he made common cause with the Nabataeans, and did not fear the oath by the great gods, but plundered the border of my land. Through the influence of Assur . . . , Natnu, King of Nabataea, a far-distant country, to whom Uaite had fled, heard of the power of Assur which emboldened me, and though never before had he sent his messengers to the kings, my fathers, and asked after their royal welfare, he was overcome by fear of the victorious arms of Assur, so that he asked after my royal welfare. But Abiate, son of Teri, unmindful of kindness, and regardless of the oath of the great gods, formed plans of revolt against me and made common cause with Natnu, King of Nabataea, and they mustered their forces for an attack upon my border. By the command of Assur . . . I mustered my troops and against Abiate I directed the march. The Tigris and the Euphrates at full flood they crossed over in safety; they marched by distant paths; they climbed high mountains; they made their way through dense forests; between high trees, thorns, briers, on a road full of brambles they marched uninjured. Through the land of Mash, a region of thirst and starvation, where the birds of the heavens do not fly, and where wild asses and gazelles do not pasture, a journey of 200 hours from Nineveh, the favorite city of Ishtar, the consort of Bel, after Uaite, king of Arabia, and Abiate, who had joined forces with the army of Nabataea, they marched.

In the month of Siwan, the month of Sin, the first and the most eminent son of Bel, on the 25th day of the procession of Beltis of Babylon, honored among the great gods, I set out from Hadatta. Near Laribda, a fortress of kunukke stone, by cisterns of water, I pitched my camp. My troops provided themselves with water for their thirst and marched on through the land of thirst, the region of starvation, as far as Hurarina. Between Yarku and Azalla, in the land of the Mash, a distant place, where wild animals do not live, and where the birds of the heavens do not make their nests, I brought about the defeat of the Isami, the tent-dwellers of Atarsamain and of Nabataea. Men, asses, camels, and sheep without number, I carried off as plunder. Sixteen hours' journey by land my troops marched on victoriously and returned in safety. In Azalla they drank their fill of water. From Azalla as far as Quraçiti, twelve hours' march through a land of thirst and starvation, they went on. I surrounded the tent-dwellers of Atarsamain and the Kedarenes of Uaite, son of Birdadda, king of Arabia. His gods, his mother, his sister, his wife, his family, the whole population of Kedar; the asses, the camels, and sheep, as many of them as my hands had captured under the protection of Assur and Ishtar, my lords, I set on the road to Damascus. In the month of Ab, the month of the Bow-star, the daughter of warlike Sin, on the third day, the festival of Marduk, king of the gods, I set out from Damascus; twelve hours' journey, all night long, I marched and came to Arbuliti. At Hukkurina, an impassable mountain, I came upon the tent-dwellers of Abiate, son of Teri, the Kedarene. I defeated him and carried away his spoil. Abiate and Aiamu, sons of Teri, by the command of Assur and Ishtar, my lords, my hands captured alive in battle. On their hands and feet I put iron chains, and along with the spoil of their land I took them to Assyria. The fugitives, who had fled from before my weapons, were afraid and took refuge on an impassable mountain. Over all places where there were cisterns and springs of water, as many as there were, I set watches, and I cut off the water necessary to their lives, allowing them only an occasional drink. They died of thirst and the rest cut open the camels of their herds, and to quench their thirst drank the blood and the liquid of the entrails. Of those who had gone out into the mountain, and had entered in and occupied a place of refuge, not one escaped, not a rebel escaped my hand; in their place of refuge my hand captured them: the people—male and female—the asses, camels, cattle and sheep, in countless numbers I carried away as spoils to Assyria. The whole of my land which Assur had given to me—all of it—throughout its whole extent they filled up. Camels, like sheep, I divided and distributed to the people of Assyria. In my land camels were worth from a half-shekel to a shekel of silver a piece at the auction gate. Tavernkeepers got camels, slaves received camels, brewers for a drink of beer and gardeners for a basket of fresh dates.

The warlike Pest-god overthrew Uaite, together with his troops, who had not kept my treaty and had escaped from before the weapons of Assur, my lord, and fled before them. Famine arose among them, and for their hunger they ate the flesh of their children. The curses, as many as were inscribed upon their treaty, Assur, Sin, Shamash, Ramman, Bel, Nabu, Ishtar of Nineveh, Queen of Kidmuri, Ishtar of Arbela, Ninib, Nergal and Nusku suddenly brought upon them. Young camels, asses, calves and lambs suckled their dams seven times each, and yet did not satisfy their stomachs with milk. The Arabians asked one another: "Why has such a calamity come upon Arabia?" and were answered: "Because we have not kept the great oaths of Assur, but have rebelled against the favors of Ashurbanipal, the king, the beloved of Bel." Beltis, the beloved of Bel, the strong one, honored of the goddesses, who sits enthroned with Anu and Bel, gored my enemy with their mighty horns. Ishtar who dwells in Arbela, clothed in flames and arrayed in brilliancy, rained down fire upon Arabia. The warlike Pest-god girded on war and overthrew my enemies. Ninib, the lance, the great warrior, the son of Bel, with his sharp arrows cut off my enemies. Nusku, the exalted messenger, who glorifies my lordship, who at the command of Assur walked by my side and protected my

sovereignty, placed himself at the head of my troops and overthrew my foes. The troops of Uaite heard of the attack of the weapons of Assur and Ishtar, the great gods, my lords, who came to my aid in battle, and they rebelled against him. He feared, fled from his house and went forth. Under the protection of Assur . . . my hands captured him and brought him to Assyria. In answer to my prayer which I had made for the overthrow of my enemies, by the command of Assur and Beltis, with the sharp-edged spear I held in my hand I pierced his jaw; through his cheek I put a rope, placed a dog-collar upon him and set him to watch in a cage at the east gate of Nineveh, which is called "The entrance to Temple-Street." In order to praise the glory of Assur, Ishtar and the great gods, my lords, I granted him mercy and let him live.

On my return march I conquered the city of Ushu, on the sea-coast. I killed the inhabitants of Ushu who had disobeyed their governors and refused to pay the tribute which they had to pay every year. Among the unsubmissive population I executed judgment; their gods and their men I carried as spoil to Assyria. The people of Akko who were rebellious I killed; hung their bodies upon stakes and surrounded the city with them. The rest of them I took to Assyria, formed them into a division and added them to my many troops, which Assur had given me. Aiamu, son of Teri, who had taken sides with Abiate, his brother, and had fought against my troops, I captured alive in battle with my own hands and in Nineveh, my capital, I flayed him.

Ummanaldash, King of Elam, whom from old Assur and Ishtar, my lords, had commanded to be my servant, and against whom by the command of their exalted deity, which is inflexible, his land afterwards rebelled, and who had fled alone from before the revolt ·of his servants which they had organized against him and had seized a mountain, from the mountain, the place of his refuge where he had fled, I brought forth like a falcon, and took to Assyria alive. Tammaritu, Pae and Ummanaldash, who one after another had exercised the lordship of Elam, and whom I had subjected to my yoke in the might of Assur and Ishtar, my lords, and Uaite, king of Arabia, whom I had defeated and taken from his own land to Assyria . . . I made them take the yoke of my state carriage and they drew it beneath me to the gate of the temple [of Beltis]. I threw myself upon my face and exalted their deity and praised their power in the midst of my hosts because Assur, Sin, Shamash, Ramman, Bel, Nabu, Ishtar of Nineveh, Queen of Kidmuri, Ishtar of Arbela, Ninib, Nergal and Nusku had subjected to my yoke those who were unsubmissive, and had placed me over my enemies with might and power.

At that time the harem, the resting-place of the palace which is in Nineveh, the lofty city which is beloved by Beltis, which Sennacherib my grandfather, king of Assyria, had built for his royal dwelling, that harem had become old with joy and gladness, and its walls had fallen. I, Ashurbanipal, the great king, the mighty king, the king of the world, the king of Assyria, the king of the four quarters of the world, because I had grown up in that harem, and Assur had preserved me therein as crown-prince and had extended his good protection and shelter of prosperity over me, and from the time when I took my seat upon the throne of my father and exercised lordship over widely extended lands and peoples had constantly sent me joyful tidings therein of victory over my enemies; and because my dreams on my bed at night were pleasant, and on that of the morning my fancies were bright; and because that dwelling brings prosperity to its lord, and the great gods have decreed a favorable fate for it, I tore down its ruins. In order to extend its area I tore it all down. I erected a building the site of whose structure was fifty *tikbi* in extent. I raised a terrace; but I was afraid before the shrines of the great gods, my lords, and did not raise that structure very high. In a good month, on a favorable day, I put in its foundation upon that terrace and laid its brickwork. I emptied sesame-wine and wine upon its cellar, and poured also upon its earthen wall. In order to build that harem the people of my land hauled its bricks there in wagons of Elam which I had carried away as spoil by the command of the gods. I made the kings of Arabia, who had violated their treaty with me and whom I had captured alive in battle with my own hands, carry baskets and wear workmen's caps in order to build that harem; and I imposed forced service upon them. They spent their days in moulding its bricks and performing forced service for it to the playing of music. With joy and rejoicing I built it from its foundation to its roof. I made more room in it than before, and made the work upon it splendid. I laid upon it long beams of cedars, which grew upon Sirara and Lebanon. I covered doors of liaru-wood, whose odor is pleasant, with a sheath of copper, and hung them in its doorways. I covered long beams with bright copper, and laid them as the frame of the doors of its porch. I completed that harem, my royal dwelling, in its entirety, and filled it with splendor. I planted around it a grove of all kinds of trees, and Sha-sa-sa fruits of every kind. I finished the work of its construction, offered splendid sacrifices to the gods, my lords, dedicated it with joy and rejoicing, and entered therein under a splendid canopy.

In days to come may that one among the kings, my sons, whose name Assur and Ishtar may proclaim for lordship over lands and peoples, when this harem becomes old and falls into decay, repair its damages; and may he see the inscription with my signature and those of my father and of my grandfather, the enduring royal race; and may he anoint it with ointment and offer sacrifices and set it up along with the inscription on which his own name is written; and may the great gods—as many as are written on these inscriptions—present him with power and might as they have me! But whoever destroys the inscription with my signature and those of my father and of my grandfather, and does not set it up along with his own inscription—him may Assur, Sin, Shamash, Ramman, Bel, Nabu, Ishtar of Nineveh, Queen of Kidmuri, Ishtar of Arbela, Ninib, Nergal and Nusku condemn by a judgment including the naming of my name!

3. MEN AND GODS

In their relations with the gods the peoples of Mesopotamia saw themselves as dealing with arbitrary and unfathomable powers whom they tried to placate without quite knowing how. These uneasy feelings were expressed in prayers and penitential psalms designed to appease the anger of the gods, to mitigate the result of their wrath, or simply to plead for a moment's pity.

The following prayer is addressed to all gods, even those who may be unknown. The penitent knows that his suffering is the result of his breaking some divine law but claims that he does not know just what he has done wrong or what god he may have offended. In any case, mankind is incapable of knowing the divine will, it lives in ignorance and constantly transgresses, and to single him out for punishment is unfair. This particular prayer, one of a series, was found on a tablet of the mid-seventh century B.C.; the original Sumerian composition is probably not much older than that. The prayer to Ishtar and the Psalm reflect the same perplexity of man disconcerted in an incomprehensible world.

Penitential Prayer to Every God

May the wrath of the heart of my god be pacified!

May the god who is unknown to me be pacified!

May the goddess who is unknown to me be pacified!

May the known and unknown god be pacified!

May the known and unknown goddess be pacified! . . .

The sin which I have committed I know not.

From "Penitential Psalms," tr. Robert F. Harper, in *Assyrian and Babylonian Literature,* ed. R. F. Harper (New York, 1901).

The misdeed which I have committed I know not.
A gracious name may my god announce!
A gracious name may my goddess announce!
A gracious name may my known and unknown god announce!
A gracious name may my known and unknown goddess annnounce!
Pure food have I not eaten,
Clear water have I not drunk.
An offence against my god I have unwittingly committed.
A transgression against my goddess I have unwittingly done.
O Lord, my sins are many, great are my iniquities!
My god, my sins are many, great are my iniquities! . . .
The sin, which I have committed, I know not.
The iniquity, which I have done, I know not.
The offence, which I have committed, I know not.
The transgression I have done, I know not.
The lord, in the anger of his heart, hath looked upon me.
The god, in the wrath of his heart, hath visited me.
The goddess hath become angry with me, and hath grievously stricken me.
The known or unknown god hath straitened me.
The known or unknown goddess hath brought affliction upon me.
I sought for help, but no one taketh my hand.
I wept, but no one came to my side.

I lamented, but no one hearkens to me.
I am afflicted, I am overcome, I cannot look up.
Unto my merciful god I turn, I make supplication.
I kiss the feet of my goddess and [crawl before her] . . .
How long, my god . . .
How long, my goddess, until thy face be turned toward me?
How long, known and unknown god, until the anger of thy heart be pacified?
How long, known and unknown goddess, until thy unfriendly heart be pacified?
Mankind is perverted and has no judgment.
Of all men who are alive, who knows anything?
They do not know whether they do good or evil.
O lord, do not cast aside thy servant!
He is cast into the mire; take his hand.
The sin which I have sinned, turn to mercy!
The iniquity which I have committed, let the wind carry away!
My many transgressions tear off like a garment!
My god, my sins are seven times seven; forgive my sins!
My goddess, my sins are seven times seven; forgive my sins!
Known and unknown god, my sins are seven times seven; forgive my sins!
Known or unknown goddess, my sins are seven times seven; forgive my sins!
Forgive my sins and I will humble myself before thee.

A Prayer to the Goddess Ishtar

How long, O my lady, shall my enemies persecute me?
How long shall they devise evil in rebellion and wickedness,

My persecutor, my pursuer, shall spy after me?
How long, O my lady, shall the crippled and diseased seek me?

He has prepared me a mourner's garment,
but I come joyfully before thee.
The weak have become strong, but I am
weak;
I am troubled like a flood which the evil
wind makes rage;
My heart has taken wing and has flown
away like a bird of the heavens;
I moan like a dove, night and day;
I am made desolate and I weep bitterly;
With grief and woe my soul is distressed.
What have I done, O my god and my god-
dess?
Is it because I feared not my god or my god-
dess that trouble has befallen me?
Sickness, headache, ruin and destruction
are come upon me;
Troubles, averted faces, and fulness of anger
are my lot;
Indignation, wrath, the rage of god and men.
I behold, O my lady, days of affliction,
months of sorrow, years of misfortune;
I behold, O my lady, judgment of disorder
and violence;
Death and misery make an end of me;

Desolate is my sanctuary, desolate is my
shrine,
Over my house, my gate and my fields afflic-
tion is poured forth.
As for my god, his face is turned elsewhere;
My family is scattered, my walls are broken
through;
But unto my lady do I give heed, my ear is
turned toward her;
My prayer is unto you, dissolve my punish-
ment;
Dissolve my sin, my fault, my mockery, and
my offence.
Forgive my mockery, accept my supplication,
Free my breast, send me comfort,
Guide my footsteps, that happily and proudly
among the living I may pursue my
way,
Speak the word, that at your command the
angry god may be favorable,
And that the goddess who is angry may be
gracious,
May my gloomy, smoking brazier shine,
May my quenched torch be relighted,
May my scattered family be collected.

Extract from a Psalm

Prayer was my rule, sacrificing my law,
The day of worship of my god my joy,
The day of devotion to my gods my profit
and gain.
What, however, seems good to one, to a
god may be displeasing;
What is spurned by oneself may find favor
with a god.
Who is there who can grasp the will of the
gods of heaven?
The plan of a god is full of mystery—who
can understand it?
How can mortals learn the ways of a god?
He who is still alive at evening is dead the
next morning;

In an instant he is cast into grief, of a sudden he is crushed;
This moment he sings and plays, in a twin-
kling he wails like a mourner.
Like day and night, mankind's spirit
changes:
If they hunger, they are like corpses.
If they have been satiated, they think themselves a rival to their god.
If things go well, they prate of mounting
to heaven.
If they are in distress, they speak of descending into the lower world.

From M. Jastrow, Jr., "Babylonian Parallels to Job," in *Journal of Biblical Literature*, XXV,
Part 2 (1906).

II. Ancient Israel

The pattern of the Hebrews' laws and religious observances is not very different from that of their neighbors. However, it embodies the original concept of a code of behavior, both religious and secular, laid down by God in a contract in which it is agreed that God will protect His people as long as they keep the commandments He has clearly laid down.

1. THE MAKING OF THE COVENANT

The exodus from Egypt probably took place in the thirteenth century B.C. and the Mosaic code dates back to some time before the year 1000 B.C. In the following passage we have the first statement of the rules laid down by God to govern the relations between Him and "His people." For the moment, God appears as a lawgiver not very different from other contemporary divinities whose authority was invoked to sanction laws, but He already shows the exclusive and intolerant characteristics that would lead to the development of monotheism.

Exodus

In the third month, when the children of Israel were gone forth out of the land of Egypt, the same day came they into the wilderness of Sinai. For they were departed from Rephidim, and were come to the desert of Sinai, and had pitched in the wilderness; and there Israel camped before the mount.

And Moses went up unto God, and the Lord called unto him out of the mountain, saying, Thus shalt thou say to the house of Jacob, and tell the children of Israel; You have seen what I did to the Egyptians, and how I carried you on eagle's wings, and brought you unto myself. Now, therefore, if you will really obey my voice and keep my covenant, then you shall be a peculiar treasure unto me above all people: for all the earth is mine. And you shall be unto me a kingdom of priests, and a holy nation. These are the words which you shall speak to the children of Israel.

And Moses came and called for the elders of the people, and laid before them all these words which the Lord commanded him. And all the people answered together, and said, All that the Lord has spoken we will do. And Moses returned the words of the people unto the Lord.

And the Lord said unto Moses, Lo, I come to you in a thick cloud, that the people may hear when I speak with you and believe you for ever. And Moses told the words of the people unto the Lord.

And the Lord said unto Moses, Go to the people, and purify them today and tomorrow, and let them wash their

All passages from the Old and New Testaments are adapted from the King James Version of the Bible.

34

clothes. And be ready for the third day: for the third day the Lord will come down in the sight of all the people upon mount Sinai. And you shall set bounds for the people round about the mount, saying, Take heed not to go up onto the mount or touch the border of it: whosoever touches the mount shall be surely put to death: not a hand shall touch it without being stoned or shot through; whether it be beast or man it shall not live. When the trumpet sounds a long blast, they shall come up to the mount.

And Moses went down from the mount unto the people, and purified the people; and they washed their clothes. And he said unto the people, Be ready for the third day: come not at your wives.

And it came to pass on the third day, in the morning, that there were thunders and lightnings, and a thick cloud upon the mount, and the voice of the trumpet exceeding loud; so that all the people that was in the camp trembled. And Moses brought forth the people out of the camp to meet with God; and they stood at the lower part of the mount. And mount Sinai was altogether on a smoke, because the Lord descended upon it in fire: and the smoke of the fire rose as the smoke of a furnace, and the whole mount quaked greatly. And when the voice of the trumpet sounded loud and long, and waxed louder and louder, Moses spoke and God answered him by a voice . . . and the Lord called Moses up to the top of the mount, and Moses went up.

And the Lord said unto Moses, Go down, warn the people, lest they break through unto the Lord to gaze and many of them perish. And let the priests also, which come near the Lord, purify themselves, lest the Lord break forth upon them. And Moses said unto the Lord, The people cannot come up to mount Sinai:

for you warned us, saying, Set bounds about the mount and sanctify it. And the Lord said unto him, Away, get down, and you shall come up, you and Aaron with you: but do not let the priests and the people break through to come up unto the Lord, lest he break forth upon them. So Moses went down to the people, and spoke unto them.

And God spoke all these words, saying: I am the Lord your God, which has brought you out of the land of Egypt, out of the house of bondage.

You shall have no other gods before me.

You shall not make for yourself any graven image, or any likeness of any thing that is in heaven above, or that is in the earth beneath, or that is in the water under the earth.

You shall not bow yourself down to them, nor serve them: for I the Lord your God am a jealous God, visiting the iniquity of the fathers upon the children unto the third and fourth generation of those that hate me; and showing mercy unto thousands of those that love me and keep my commandments.

You shall not take the name of the Lord your God in vain: for the Lord will not hold him guiltless that takes his name in vain.

Remember the sabbath day, to keep it holy. Six days shall you labor and do all your work, but the seventh day is the sabbath of the Lord your God: in it you shall not do any work, you, nor your son, nor your daughter, nor your man-servant, nor your maid-servant, nor your cattle, nor the stranger that is within your gates. For in six days the Lord made heaven and earth, the sea, and all that in them is, and rested the seventh day: wherefore the Lord blessed the sabbath day, and hallowed it.

Honor your father and your mother: that your days may be long upon the land which the Lord your God gives you.

You shall not kill.

You shall not commit adultery.

You shall not steal.

You shall not bear false witness against your neighbor.

You shall not covet your neighbor's house, you shall not covet your neighbor's wife, nor his man-servant, nor his maid-servant, nor his ox, nor his ass, nor anything that is your neighbor's.

And all the people saw the thunderings, and the lightnings, and the noise of the trumpet, and the mountain smoking; and when the people saw it they removed, and stood afar off. And they said unto Moses, You speak with us and we will hear: but do not let God speak with us, lest we die. And Moses said unto the people, Fear not: for God has come to prove you, and that his fear may be before your faces, that you should not sin. And the people stood afar off, and Moses drew near the thick darkness where God was.

And the Lord said unto Moses, Thus you shall say to the children of Israel: You have seen that I have talked with you from heaven. You shall not make with me gods of silver, neither shall you make to yourselves gods of gold. An altar of earth you shall make unto me, and shall sacrifice on it your burnt offerings, and your peace offerings, your sheep and your oxen. In all places where I record my name I will come unto you and I will bless you. And if you will make me an altar of stone, you shall not build it of hewn stone: for if you touch it with your tool you have polluted it. Neither shall you go up to my altar by steps, lest your nakedness should be visible thereon.

Now these are the judgments which you shall set before them: If you buy a Hebrew servant, six years shall he serve; and in the seventh he shall go out free for nothing. If he came in by himself, he shall go out by himself; if he was married, then his wife shall got out with him. If his master has given him a wife and she has borne him sons or daughters, the wife and her children shall be her master's, and he shall go out by himself. And if the servant shall plainly say, I love my master, my wife and my children; I will not go out free: then his master shall bring him to the judges; he shall also bring him to the door, or to the door post; and his master shall bore his ear through with an awl; and he shall serve him for ever.

And if a man sell his daughter to be a maid-servant, she shall not go out as the men-servants do. If she does not please her master who has betrothed her to himself, then he shall let her be redeemed: he has no power to sell her to a strange nation, seeing that he has dealt deceitfully with her. And if he has betrothed her to his son, he shall treat her after the manner of daughters. If he takes him another wife, her food, her raiment, and her duty of marriage he shall not diminish. And if he does not carry out these three obligations towards her, then she shall go out free without money.

He that smites a man so that he dies, shall be surely put to death. And if a man lies not in wait but God delivers his victim into his hand [i.e., unpremeditated crime], then I will appoint you a place to which he shall flee. But if a man come presumptuously upon his neighbor, to slay him with guile, you shall take him from my altar that he may die. And he that smites his father or his mother shall be surely put to death.

And he that steals a man and sells him, or if he is found holding him, he shall surely be put to death.

And he that curses his father or his mother shall surely be put to death.

And if men fight one another, and one hits another with a stone or with his fist, and he does not die but keeps to his bed: if he rises again and walks abroad with his staff [stick], then he that smote him shall be quit: he shall only pay for the loss of his time and see that he is thoroughly cured.

And if a man hits his servant or his maid with a rod and he dies under his hand, he shall be surely punished. Notwithstanding, if he stays alive a day or two, he shall not be punished: for he is his money.

If men fight and hurt a woman with child, so that she loses her fruit and yet no mischief follows, he shall surely be punished according to what the woman's husband demands; and he shall pay as the judges determine. And if any mischief follows, then you shall give life for life, eye for eye, tooth for tooth, hand for hand, foot for foot, burning for burning, wound for wound, stripe for stripe.

And if a man hits the eye of his servant or the eye of his maid so that it perishes, he shall let him go free for his eye's sake. And if he knocks out his servant's tooth or his maid-servant's tooth, he shall let him go free for his tooth's sake.

If an ox gores a man or a woman so that they die, then the ox shall be surely stoned, and his flesh shall not be eaten; but the owner of the ox shall be quit. But if the ox was wont to push with his horn before, and the owner had been informed of it and has not kept him in, and now it has killed a man or a woman, then the ox shall be stoned, and his owner shall also be put to death. If a sum of money should be laid on him, then he shall give for the ransom of his life whatsoever is laid upon him. Whether he has gored a son, or has gored a daughter, according to this judgment it shall be done unto him.

And if a man shall open a pit, or if a man shall dig a pit, and not cover it, and an ox or an ass should fall in it; the owner of the pit shall make it good and pay the owner, and the dead beast shall be his. And if one man's ox hurt another's so that it dies; then they shall sell the live ox, and divide the money of it; and the dead ox also they shall divide. Or if it is known that the ox used to push in times past and his owner has not kept him in, he shall surely pay ox for ox, and the dead beast shall be his in return. . . .

If a man should steal an ox, or a sheep, and kill it or sell it, he shall restore five oxen for an ox, and four sheep for a sheep. If a thief should be found breaking in and be smitten so that he dies, there shall be no blood shed for him. If he stays alive . . . he should make full restitution: if he has nothing, then he shall be sold for his theft. If the theft is definitely found in his hand alive, whether it is ox, ass or sheep, he shall restore double . . .

And if a man entices a maid that is not betrothed and lies with her, he shall surely endow her to be his wife. If her father utterly refuses to give her to him, he shall pay money according to the dowry of virgins.

You shall not suffer a witch to live.

Whosoever has intercourse with a beast shall be surely put to death.

He that sacrifices to any god, save only to the Lord, shall be utterly destroyed.

You will neither vex a stranger nor oppress him: for you were strangers in the land of Egypt. You shall not afflict any widow, or fatherless child. If you afflict them in any way, and they cry at all unto me, I will surely hear their cry; and my wrath shall wax hot, and I will kill you with the sword, and your wives shall be widows and your children fatherless.

If you lend money to any of my people that is poor . . . you shall not deal with him as if you were a usurer, nor shall you lay usury upon him. If you at all take your neighbor's raiment as a pledge, you shall return it to him by the time the sun goes down: for it is his only covering, and the raiment for his skin, and what else should he sleep in? And it shall come to pass, when he cries unto me, that I shall hear; for I am gracious. . . .

And in all things that I have said unto you be circumspect; and make no mention of the name of other gods—do not let it be heard out of your mouth . . .

The first of the firstfruits of your land you shall bring into the house of the Lord your God. You shall not seethe a kid in his mother's milk.

Behold, I send an Angel before you, to keep you in the way, and to bring you into the place which I have prepared. Beware of him, and obey his voice; provoke him not: for he will not pardon your transgressions, for my name is in him. But if you shall really obey his voice and do all that I tell you; then I will be an enemy to your enemies, and an adversary to your adversaries. For my Angel shall go before you, and bring you unto the Amorites, and the Hittites, and the Perizzites, and the Canaanites, the Hivites, and the Jebusites; and I will cut them down. You shall not bow down to their gods, nor serve them, nor follow their advice;

but you shall utterly overthrow them, and quite break down their images. And you shall serve the Lord your God, and he shall bless your bread and your water; and I will take sickness away from your midst.

There shall be no abortions in the land, nor barrenness: I will fulfil the number of your days. I will send my fear before you, and will destroy all the people to whom you shall come; and I will make all your enemies turn tail. And I will send hornets before you, which shall drive out the Hivite, the Canaanite, and the Hittite from your path. I will not drive them out from before you in one year, lest the land become desolate and the wild animals multiply against you. By little and little I will drive them out, until your numbers are increased and you inherit the land. And I will set your bounds from the Red Sea right up to the sea of the Philistines, and from the desert unto the river Jordan: for I will deliver the inhabitants of the land into your hand; and you shall drive them out before you. You shall make no covenant with them, nor with their gods. They shall not dwell in your land, lest they make you sin against me: for if you serve their gods, it will surely be a snare to you.

And Moses came and told the people all the words of the Lord, and all the judgments; and all the people answered with one voice, and said, All the words which the Lord has said will we do.

2. THE FALLING AWAY

The psalms of David date back to the tenth century. Already at this early date the Jews had been told to worship no other god, "for the Lord . . . is a jealous God" (*Exodus* 34:14); and a series of prophets reminded the people of this injunction and of their other misdeeds in breaking the law and the covenant with God. The eighth century prophecies of Isaiah enlisted the Assyrians in the service of God and early suggested the power of Jehovah over other peoples than the Jews; He could use this power to punish the unfaithful party to the covenant just as in other circumstances He could use it to help them. In this instance the punishment was not long awaited: a time of troubles—culminating in 586 B.C. with the fall of Jerusalem and the Babylonian captivity—ended only when Cyrus took Babylon, broke the Chaldaean power, and allowed the exiles to return home (538 B.C.).

The Psalms of David

PSALM 14.

The fool has said in his heart, There is no God. They are corrupt; they have done abominable works; there is none that does good. The Lord looked down from heaven upon the children of men to see if there were any that did understand and seek God. They are all gone aside, they are all together become filthy. There is none that does good, no, not one.

Have all the workers of iniquity no knowledge? who eat up my people as they eat bread, and call not upon the Lord. There were they in great fear, for God is in the generation of the righteous. You have shamed the counsel of the poor, because the Lord is his refuge. Oh that the salvation of Israel were come out of Zion! When the Lord brings back the captivity of his people, Jacob shall rejoice and Israel shall be glad.

PSALM 15.

Lord, who shall abide in your tabernacle? who shall dwell in your holy hill? He that walks uprightly, and works righteousness, and speaks the truth in his heart. He that backbites not with his tongue, nor does evil to his neighbor, nor takes up a reproach against his neighbor. In whose eyes a vile person is condemned; but he honors those that fear the Lord. He that swears to his own disadvantage, and keeps his word. He that does not put money out to usury, nor takes reward against the innocent. He that does these things shall never be moved.

PSALM 16.

Preserve me, O my God: for in you do I put my trust. O my soul, you have said unto the Lord, You are my Lord, my goodness cannot reach you, but it reaches towards the saints that are on the earth, and the excellent, in whom is all my delight. Their sorrows shall be multiplied that hasten after another god: their drink-offerings of blood will I not offer, nor take up their names into my lips. The Lord is my share of the inheritance, and my share of the cup: you maintain my lot. The lines are fallen unto me in pleasant places; truly, I have a goodly heritage.

I will bless the Lord who has given me counsel; . . . I have set the Lord always before me: because he is at my right hand, I shall not be moved. Therefore my heart is glad, and my glory rejoices; my flesh also shall rest in hope; for you will not leave my soul in hell; neither will you suffer your holy one to see corruption. You will show me the path of life: in your presence is fullness of joy; at your right hand there are pleasures for evermore.

Isaiah

Hear, O heavens, and give ear, O earth: for the Lord has spoken: I have nourished and brought up children, and they have rebelled against me. The ox knows his owner, and the ass his master's crib; but Israel does not know, my people does not consider.

Ah, sinful nation, a people laden with iniquity, a seed of evildoers, children that are corrupters! They have forsaken the Lord, they have provoked the Holy One of Israel unto anger, they are gone away backward.

Why should you be stricken any more? you will revolt more and more; the whole head is sick and the whole heart faint. From the sole of the foot right unto the head there is no soundness in it; but wounds, and bruises, and putrefying sores: they have not been closed, nor bound up, nor mollified with ointment. Your country is desolate, your cities are burned with fire: your land, strangers devour it in your presence, and it is desolate, as overthrown by strangers. And the daughter of Zion is left as a cottage in a vineyard, as a lodge in a garden of cucumbers, as a besieged city. Except the Lord of hosts has left us a very small remnant, we should have been as Sodom, we should have been like unto Gomorrah.

Hear the word of the Lord, you rulers of Sodom! Give ear unto the law of our God, you people of Gomorrah! To what purpose is the multitude of your sacrifices to me? says the Lord: I am full of the burnt offerings of rams, and the fat of fed beasts; and I delight not in the blood of bullocks, or of lambs, or of he-goats. When you come to appear before me, who has required this at your hand, in order to tread my court? Bring no more vain oblations; incense is an abomination unto me; the new moons and sabbaths, the calling of assemblies, I cannot away with; it is iniquity, even the solemn meeting. My soul hates your new moons and your appointed feasts: they are a trouble unto me; I am weary of bearing them. And when you spread out your hands I will hide my eyes from you: indeed, when you make your prayers I will not hear— your hands are full of blood. Wash yourselves, make yourselves clean, put away the evil of your doings from before my eyes, cease to do evil, learn to do good, seek judgment, relieve the oppressed, judge the fatherless, plead for the widow.

Come now, and let us reason together, says the Lord: though your sins be as scarlet, they shall be white as snow; though they be red like crimson, they shall be as wool. If you be willing and obedient, you shall eat the good of the land; but if you refuse and rebel, you shall be devoured with the sword— . . .

Woe unto them that decree unrighteous decrees, and that write grievousness which they have prescribed; to turn aside the needy from judgment, and to take away the right from the poor of my people, that widows may be their prey, and that they may rob the fatherless! And what will you do in the day of visitation, and in the desolation which shall come from afar? To whom will you flee for help? And where will you leave your glory? Without me they shall bow down under the prisoners, and they shall fall under the slain. For all this his anger is not turned away, but his hand is stretched out still.

O Assyrian, the rod of my anger, and the staff in their hand is my indignation. I will send him against a hypocritical nation, and against the people of my wrath will I give him a charge, to take the spoil, and to take the prey, and to tread them down like the mire of the streets. Howbeit he means not so, nor does his heart think so; yet it is in his heart to destroy and cut off nations not a few. For he says: "Are not my princes altogether kings? Is not Calno as Carchemish? Is not Hamath as Arpad? Is not Samaria as Damascus? As my hand has found the kingdoms of the idols, and whose graven images did excel them of Jerusalem and Samaria; shall I not, as I have done unto Samaria and her idols, so do to Jerusalem and her idols? . . . Behold, the name of the Lord comes from afar, burning with his anger, and the burden thereof is heavy; his lips are full of indignation, and his tongue is as a devouring fire. And his breath, as an overflowing stream, shall reach to the midst of the neck, to sift the nations with the sieve of vanity; and there shall be a bridle in the jaws of the people, causing them to err.

3. A PROMISE RENEWED

It was during the Babylonian exile of the sixth century B.C. that the Jews developed the idea of a sole God, who had made heaven and earth and who alone ruled the destinies of men and nations; and of a Messiah, the anointed of God, who would appear to replace the old, harsh covenant with a new, kindlier one. Such a development may be attributed, at least in part, to the need the exiles felt to find a reason for hope in what must have appeared a hopeless situation. The monotheistic and messianic results of this quest for hope may be seen in the passage from Jeremiah, who preached about 600 B.C., before the fall of Jerusalem; and also in the passage from the Second or Deutero-Isaiah, who wrote somewhat later.

Jeremiah

Behold, the days come, says the Lord, when I will sow the house of Israel and the house of Judah with the seed of man, and with the seed of beast. And it shall come to pass that just as I have watched over them to pluck up, and to break down, and to throw down and to destroy and to afflict, so I will watch over them to build and to plant, says the Lord.

In those days they shall say no more, The fathers have eaten sour grapes, and the children's teeth are set on edge. But every one shall die for his own iniquity: every man that eats the sour grape, his own teeth shall be set on edge.

Behold, the days come, says the Lord, when I will make a new covenant with the house of Israel, and with the house of Judah; not according to the covenant that I made with their fathers in the day when I took them by the hand to bring them out of the land of Egypt; which covenant they broke, although I was a husband unto them, says the Lord;—but this shall be the covenant that I will make with the house of Israel. After those days, says the Lord, I will put my law in their inward parts, and write it in their hearts; and will be their God and they shall be my people. And they shall teach no more every man his neighbor, and every man his brother, saying, Know the Lord. For they shall all know me, from the least of them right up to the greatest: for I will forgive their iniquity, and I will remember their sin no more.

The Second Isaiah

Take comfort, take comfort, my people, says your God. Speak encouragingly to Jerusalem, and cry unto her that her warfare is accomplished, that her iniquity is pardoned: for she has received from the Lord's hand double punishment for all her sins.

The voice of him that cries in the wilderness: Prepare the way of the Lord, make straight in the desert a highway for our God. . . . The voice said, Cry. And he said, What shall I cry?

All flesh is grass, and all the goodness thereof is like the flower of the field: the grass withers, the flower fades, because the spirit of the Lord blows not upon it. Surely the people is grass. The grass withers, the flower fades, but the word of our God shall stand for ever. . . .

Behold the Lord God will come with strong hand, and his arm shall rule for him: behold, his reward is with him, and his work before him. He shall feed his flock like a shepherd: he shall gather the lambs with his arm, and carry them in his bosom, and shall gently lead those that are with young.

Who has measured the waters in the hollow of his hand, and meted out heaven with the span, and comprehended the dust of the earth in a measure, and weighed the mountains in scales, and the hills in a balance? Who has directed the spirit of the Lord, or being his counsellor has taught him? With whom took he counsel, and who instructed him and taught him the path of judgment, and taught him knowledge, and showed him the way of understanding? Behold, the nations are as a drop in a bucket, and are counted as the small dust of the balance: behold he takes up the isles as a very little thing. And Lebanon is not sufficient to burn, nor the beasts of it sufficient for a burnt offering. All nations before him are as nothing; and they are counted to him less than nothing, and vanity. . . .

Have you not known? Have you not heard? Has it not been told you from the beginning? Have you not understood from the foundations of the earth? It is he that sits upon the circle of the earth, and the inhabitants of it are as grasshoppers; that stretches out the heavens as a curtain, and spreads them as a tent to dwell in; that brings the princes to nothing. He makes the judges of the earth as vanity. . . .

To whom, then, will you liken me—or shall I be equal? says the Holy One. Lift up your eyes on high, and behold who has created these things, that brings out their host by number: he calls them all by names by the greatness of his might, because he is strong in power, and not one fails. Why do you say, O Jacob, why do you speak, O Israel, My way is hid from the Lord, and my judgment is passed over from my God?

Have you not known? Have you not heard, that the everlasting God, the Lord, the Creator of the ends of the earth, faints not, neither is weary? There is no searching of his understanding. He gives power to the faint; and to those that have no might he increases strength. Even the youths shall faint and be weary, and the young men shall utterly fall: but those that wait upon the Lord shall renew their strength; they shall mount up with wings as eagles; they shall run and not be weary; and they shall walk and not be faint.

Thus says the Lord, your Redeemer and he that formed you from the womb, I am the Lord that makes all things; that stretches forth the heavens alone; that spreads out the earth by myself . . . that says to the deep be dry, and I will dry up your rivers; that says of Cyrus, He is my shepherd, and shall perform all my pleasure; even saying to Jerusalem, You shall be built; and to the temple, Your foundations shall be laid.

Thus says the Lord to his anointed, to Cyrus, whose right hand I have held, to subdue nations before him—I will go before you and make the crooked places straight. I will break in pieces the gates of brass, and cut asunder the bars of iron; and I will give you the treasures of darkness, and hidden riches of secret places, that you may know that I, the Lord who call you by your name, am the God of Israel. . . . I have surnamed you, though you have not known me. I am the Lord, and there is none else, there is no God beside me; I girded you, though you have not known me: that they may know from the rising of the sun, and from the west, that there is none beside me. I am the Lord, and there is none else. I form the light and create the darkness: I make peace, and create evil: I, the Lord, do all these things.

Thus says the Lord, the Holy One of Israel, and his Maker: Ask me of things to come concerning my sons, and concerning the work of my hands command me. I have made the earth, and created man upon it; I, even my hands, have stretched out the heavens, and all their host I have commanded. I have raised him up in righteousness, and I will direct all his ways; he shall build my city, and he shall let go my captives, not for price nor reward, says the Lord of hosts. . . .

Assemble yourselves and come; draw near together, you that are escaped of the nations: they have no knowledge that set up the wood of their graven image, and pray unto a god that cannot save. You must tell, and bring them near: indeed, let them take counsel together: who has declared this from ancient time? not I, the Lord? and there is no God else beside me; a just God, and a Saviour; there is none beside me.

Look towards me and be saved, all the ends of the earth; for I am God and there is none else. I have sworn by myself, the word is gone out of my mouth in righteousness, and shall not return, That unto me every knee shall bow, every tongue shall swear.

Who has believed our report? And to whom is the arm of the Lord revealed? For he shall grow up before him as a tender plant, and as a root out of dry ground: he has no form nor comeliness: and when we shall see him, there is no beauty that we should desire him. He is despised and rejected of men; a man of sorrows and acquainted with grief: and we hid as it were our faces from him; he was despised, and we esteemed him not. Surely, he has borne our griefs, and carried our sorrows: yet we did consider him stricken, smitten of God, and afflicted. But he was wounded for our transgressions, he was bruised for our iniquities: the chastisement of our peace was upon him; and with his stripes we are healed. All we like sheep have gone astray; we have turned every one to his own way; and the Lord has laid on him the iniquity of us all. He was oppressed, and he was afflicted, yet he opened not his mouth: he is brought as a lamb to the slaughter, and as a sheep before her shearers is dumb, so he opens not his mouth. He was taken from prison and from judgment: and who shall declare his generation? For he was cut off from the land of the living—for the transgression of my people was he stricken. And he made his grave with the wicked, and with the rich in his death; because he had done no violence, neither was any deceit in his mouth.

Yet it pleased the Lord to bruise him; he has put him to grief: when you shall make his soul an offering for sin, he shall see his seed, he shall prolong his days, and the pleasure of the Lord shall prosper in his hand. He shall see of the travail of his soul, and shall be satisfied: by his knowledge shall my righteous servant justify many; for he shall bear their iniquities. Therefore will I divide him a portion with the great, and he shall divide the spoil with the strong; because he has poured out his soul unto death: and he was numbered with the transgressors; and he bore the sin of many, and made intercession for the transgressors.

III. Ancient Greece

The dimly perceived beginnings of Greek history lie somewhere between 1300 and 1100 B.C., when Egypt was still a very great power under its Ramesside kings and the Assyrian empire was still a thing of the future. But the obscure and savage society of shepherds, fishermen, and pirate-traders which was developing unnoticed on the margins of the then civilized world was the forerunner of the most fruitful culture in the West. The earliest traces of this appear around 800 B.C., when the poems of Homer are already in existence and colonists swarm out from the Aegean to spread the area of Greek settlement from the Caucasus to Marseilles.

Between the eighth and fourth centuries B.C., the political history of Greece concerns the rise and fall of city-states—Miletus, Athens, Sparta, Thebes—but the mainland cities are overshadowed by the rich Ionian ports until the lead thrust upon them by the Persian wars and the victories they win therein endow them with glory, wealth, and supreme self-confidence. The fifth century is the great century of Greece and especially of Athens; but if it begins with Marathon and Salamis, it ends with the long-drawn-out agony of the Peloponnesian War. Subsequent political history, in spite of revivals, is a long tale of division and decay; but the thought and art of the later time, though different in form and content from that of the earlier period, are no less great. In the wake of wandering traders, of mercenaries, of conquerors like Alexander, even of slaves, Greek forms and values and ideas colored the civilizations of countries from India to the Channel, leading even their captors captive.

1. THE SPARTAN CONSTITUTION

It seems odd to begin a survey of Greek ways and purpose by introducing an anachronism—an article written in the first century of the Christian era about a semimythical person who is supposed to have given Sparta its laws some time in the ninth century B.C. But the essence of Spartan society was its stability, its deliberately arrested development; and it was held that the laws by which Spartans lived in the fifth and fourth centuries B.C. were much the same as those which Lykurgus instituted. In his biography of Lykurgus, Plutarch (c. 46–120 A.D.) describes a constitution which aimed at the complete subordination of the individual to the state. And the extracts below may well be contrasted with the attitudes we find reflected in the words of Pericles (see page 26) or even Xenophon (see page 67), representatives of a rival city-civilization.

45

80983

Plutarch: from the *Life of Lykurgus*

Of Lykurgus' many reforms, the first and most important was the establishment of the Council of Elders which, Plato says, by its admixture cooled the high fever of royalty, and, having an equal vote with the kings on vital points, gave caution and sobriety to their deliberations. For the state, which had hitherto been wildly oscillating between despotism on the one hand and democracy on the other, now, by the establishment of the Council of Elders, found a firm footing between these extremes, and was able to preserve a most equable balance, as the eight-and-twenty elders would lend the kings their support in the suppression of democracy, but would use the people to suppress any tendency to despotism. [He also instituted a popular assembly.]

When the people were assembled, he permitted no one to express an opinion; but the people was empowered to decide upon motions brought forward by the kings and elders. But in later times, as the people made additions and omissions, and so altered the sense of the motions before them, the kings, Polydorus and Theopompus, added these words to the [customary rules]: "and if the people shall decide crookedly, the chiefs and elders shall set it right." That is, they made the people no longer supreme, but practically excluded them from any voice in public affairs, on the ground that they judged wrongly. However, these kings persuaded the city that this also was ordained by the god [Apollo].

The second and boldest of Lykurgus' reforms was the redistribution of the land.

Great inequalities existed, many poor and needy people had become a burden to the state, while wealth had got into a very few hands. Lykurgus abolished all the mass of pride, envy, crime, and luxury which flowed from those old and more terrible evils of riches and poverty, by inducing all land-owners to offer their estates for redistribution, and prevailing upon them to live on equal terms one with another, and with equal incomes, striving only to surpass each other in courage and virtue, there being henceforth no social inequalities among them except such as praise or blame can create. [The lands were divided in such a way that every Spartan had a sufficient crop to live on: "enough food to maintain them in health, and they wanted nothing more."]

He desired to distribute furniture also, in order completely to do away with inequality; but, seeing that actually to take away these things would be a most unpopular measure, he managed by a different method to put an end to all ostentation in these matters. First of all, he abolished the use of gold and silver money, and made iron money alone legal; and this he made of great size and weight, and small value, so that the equivalent for ten minae required a great room for its stowage and a yoke of oxen to draw it. As soon as this was established, many sorts of crime became unknown in Lacedaemon. For who would steal or take as a bribe or deny that he possessed or take by force a mass of iron which he could not conceal, which no one envied him for possessing, which he could not even break up and make use of; for the iron when

From *Plutarch's Lives*, tr. Aubrey Stewart and George Long, 4 vols. (London, 1900), I, 71–95.

hot was, it is said, quenched into vinegar, so as to make it useless, by rendering it brittle and hard to work?

After this, he ordered a general expulsion of the workers in useless trades. Indeed, without this, most of them would have left the country when the ordinary currency came to an end, as they would not be able to sell their wares: for the iron money was not current among other Greeks, and had no value, being regarded as ridiculous; so that it could not be used for the purchase of foreign trumpery, and no cargo was shipped for a Laconian port, and there came into the country no sophists, no vagabond soothsayers, no panders, no goldsmiths or workers in silver plate, because there was no money to pay them with. Luxury, thus cut off from all encouragement, gradually became extinct; and the rich were on the same footing with other people, as they could find no means of display, but were forced to keep their money idle at home. For this reason such things as are useful and necessary, like couches and tables and chairs, were made there better than anywhere else, and the Laconian cup, we are told by Kritias, was especially valued for its use in the field. Its color prevented the drinker being disgusted by the look of the dirty water which it is sometimes necessary to drink, and it was contrived that the dirt was deposited inside the cup and stuck to the bottom, so as to make the drink cleaner than it would otherwise have been. These things were due to the lawgiver; for the workmen, who were not allowed to make useless things, devoted their best workmanship to useful ones.

Wishing still further to put down luxury and take away the desire for riches, he introduced the third and the most admirable of his reforms, that of the common dining table. At this the people were to meet and dine together upon a fixed allowance of food, and not to live in their own homes, lolling on expensive couches at rich tables, fattened like beasts in private by the hands of servants and cooks, and undermining their health by indulgence to excess in every bodily desire, long sleep, warm baths, and much repose, so that they required a sort of daily nursing like sick people. This was a great advantage, but it was a greater to render wealth valueless and, as Theophrastus says, to neutralize it by their common dining table and the simplicity of their habits. Wealth could not be used, nor enjoyed, nor indeed displayed at all in costly apparatus, when the poor man dined at the same table with the rich. . . . Men were not even allowed to dine previously at home, and then come to the public table, but the others, watching him who did not eat or drink with them, would reproach him as a sensual person, too effeminate to eat the rough, common fare.

Lykurgus did not establish any written laws; indeed, this is distinctly forbidden by one of the so-called [Customary Rules].

He thought that the principles of most importance for the prosperity and honor of the state would remain most securely fixed if implanted in the citizens by habit and training, as they would then be followed from choice rather than necessity; for his method of education made each of them into a lawgiver like himself. The trifling conventions of everyday life were best left undefined by hard-and-fast laws, so that they might from time to time receive corrections and additions from men educated in the spirit of the Lacedaemonian system. On this education the whole scheme of Lykurgus' laws depended.

Lykurgus did not view children as belonging to their parents but above all to the state; and therefore he wished his citizens to be born of the best possible parents; besides the inconsistency and folly which he noticed in the customs of the rest of mankind, who are willing to pay money, or use their influence with the owners of well-bred stock, to obtain a good breed of horses or dogs, while they lock up their women in seclusion and permit them to have children by none but themselves, even though they be mad, decrepit, or diseased; just as if the good or bad qualities of children did not depend entirely upon their parents, and did not affect their parents more than anyone else. [So, selective breeding was pursued to some extent.] But although men lent their wives in order to produce healthy and useful citizens, yet this was so far from the licence which was said to prevail in later times with respect to women, that adultery was regarded among them as an impossible crime.

A father had not the right of bringing up his offspring, but had to carry it to a certain place called Lesché where the elders of the tribe sat in judgment upon the child. If they thought it well-built and strong, they ordered the father to bring it up, and assigned one of the nine thousand plots of land to it; but if it was mean-looking or misshapen, they sent it away to a place called the Exposure . . . for they considered that if a child did not start in possession of health and strength, it was better both for itself and for the state that he should not live at all. . . . A certain supervision was exercised over the nurses. . . . Nor was each man allowed to bring up and educate his sons as he chose, but as soon as they were seven years of age he himself [Lykurgus] received them from their parents, and enrolled them in companies. Here they lived and messed in common, and were associated for play and for work. However, a superintendent of the boys was appointed, one of the best born and bravest men of the state, and they themselves in their troops chose as leader him who was wisest, and fiercest in fight. They looked to him for orders, obeyed his commands, and endured his punishments, so that even in childhood they learned to obey. . . . They learned their letters, because they are necessary, but all the rest of their education was meant to teach them to obey with cheerfulness, to endure labors, and to win battles. As they grew older, their training became more severe. They were closely shorn, and taught to walk unshod and to play naked. They wore no tunic after their twelfth year, but received one garment for all the year round. They were necessarily dirty, as they had no warm baths and ointments, except on certain days, as a luxury. They slept all together in troops and companies, on beds of rushes which they themselves had picked on the banks of the Eurotas, with their hands, for they were not allowed to use a knife. In winter they mixed the herb called lycophon with the rushes, as it is thought to possess some warmth.

Thus no time was left unemployed, and no place was left without someone to give good advice and punish wrong-doing. . . . [Stealing is part of their training and the boys' leader has them bring him] what they steal, which they do, some from the gardens, and some from the men's dining tables, where they rush in very cleverly and cautiously; for if one be taken, he is severely scourged for stealing carelessly and clumsily. They also steal what victuals they can, learning to take them from those who are asleep or off their guard. Whoever is caught is punished by stripes and starvation. Their meals are purposely made scanty, in order that they may exercise their ingenuity and daring in obtaining additions to them.

The lovers of the boys also shared their honor or disgrace; it is said that once when a boy in a fight let fall an unmanly word, his lover was fined by the magistrates. Thus was love understood among them; for even fair and honorable matrons loved young maidens, but none expected their feelings to be returned. Rather did those who loved the same person make it a reason for friendship with each other, and vie with one another in trying to improve in every way the object of their love.

The training of the Spartan youth continued till their manhood. No one was permitted to live according to his own pleasure, but they lived in the city as if in a camp, with a fixed diet and fixed public duties, thinking themselves to belong, not to themselves, but to their country. Those who had nothing else to do, either looked after the young and taught them what was useful, or themselves learned such things from the old. For ample leisure was one of the blessings with which Lykurgus provided his countrymen, seeing that they were utterly forbidden to practise any mechanical art, while money-making and business were unnecessary, because wealth was disregarded and despised. The Helots tilled the ground, and produced the regular crops for them. Indeed, a Spartan who was at Athens while the courts were sitting, and who learned that some man had been fined for idleness, and was leaving the court in sorrow accompanied by his griev-

ing friends, asked to be shown the man who had been punished for gentlemanly behavior. So slavish did they deem it to labor at trade and business. In Sparta, as was natural, lawsuits became extinct, together with money, as the people had neither excess nor deficiency, but all were equally well off, and enjoyed abundant leisure by reason of their simple habits. All their time was spent in dances, feasting, hunting, or gymnastic exercises and conversation, when they were not engaged in war.

He would not allow citizens to leave the country at pleasure, and to wander in foreign lands where they would contract outlandish habits, and learn to imitate the untrained lives and ill-regulated institutions to be found abroad. Also, he banished from Lacedaemon all strangers who were there for no useful purpose. . . . Strangers introduce strange ideas; and these lead to discussions of an unsuitable character, and political views which would jar with the established constitution, like a discord in music.

In all these acts of Lykurgus we cannot find any traces of the injustice and unfairness which some complain of in his laws, which they say are excellent to produce courage, but less so for justice. And the institution called *Krypteia,* if indeed it is one of the laws of Lykurgus as Aristotle tells us, would agree with the idea which Plato conceived about him and his system. The *Krypteia* was this: the leaders of the young men used at intervals to send the most discreet of them into different parts of the country, equipped with daggers and necessary food; in the daytime these men used to conceal themselves in unfrequented spots, and take their rest, but at night they would come down into the roads and murder any Helots they found. And often they would range about the fields, and make away with the strongest and bravest Helots they could find. Also, as Thucydides mentions in his History of the Peloponnesian War, those Helots who were especially honored by the Spartans for their valor were crowned as free men, and taken to the temples with rejoicings; but in a short time they all disappeared, to the number of more than two thousand, and in such a way that no man, either then or afterwards, could tell how they perished. Aristotle says that the Ephors, when they first take office, declare war against the Helots, in order that it may be lawful to destroy them. And much other harsh treatment used to be inflicted upon them;

and they were compelled to drink much unmixed wine, and then were brought into the public dining halls, to show the young what drunkenness is.

They were also forced to sing low songs, and to dance low dances, and not to meddle with those of a higher character. It is said that when the Thebans made their celebrated campaign in Lacedaemon, they ordered the Helots whom they captured to sing them the songs of Terpander and Alkman and Spendon the Laconian; but they begged to be excused, for, they said, "the masters do not like it." So it seems to have been well said that in Lacedaemon the free man was more free and the slave more a slave than anywhere else.

2. THUCYDIDES ON THE HISTORY OF THE PELOPONNESIAN WAR

Where Spartan conservatism represented, for better or worse, the element of stability in Greece, Athenian dynamism represented change—perhaps, depending on the point of view, progress. When Sparta and Athens eventually clashed, the Peloponnesian War overshadowed the life of Greece for the last third of the fifth century B.C. The best account of this bitter struggle between the major Greek land power and the newly forged maritime empire of the Athenians remains the contemporary one of the Athenian, Thucydides (himself a disgraced general in exile), which reflects the city-state both in her moments of greatness (as in the *Periclean Oration*) and when she is coldly self-assertive and cruel (as in the *Melian Dialogue*).

The Funeral Oration of Pericles

During the same winter [B.C. 431], in accordance with an old national custom, the funeral of those who first fell in this war was celebrated by the Athenians at the public charge. The ceremony is as follows: Three days before the celebration they erect a tent in which the bones

of the dead are laid out, and every one brings to his own dead any offering which he pleases. At the time of the funeral the bones are placed in chests of cypress wood, which are conveyed on hearses; there is one chest for each tribe. They also carry a single empty litter decked with

From *Thucydides,* tr. Benjamin Jowett, 2 vols., second ed., revised (Oxford, 1900).

a pall for all whose bodies are missing, and cannot be recovered after the battle. The procession is accompanied by any one who chooses, whether citizen or stranger, and the female relatives of the deceased are present at the place of interment and make lamentation. The public sepulchre is situated in the most beautiful spot outside the walls; there they always bury those who fall in war; only after the battle of Marathon the dead, in recognition of their pre-eminent valor, were interred on the field. When the remains have been laid in the earth, some man of known ability and high reputation, chosen by the city, delivers a suitable oration over them; after which the people depart. Such is the manner of interment; and the ceremony was repeated from time to time throughout the war. Over those who were the first buried Pericles was chosen to speak. At the fitting moment he advanced from the sepulchre to a lofty stage, which had been erected in order that he might he heard as far as possible by the multitude, and spoke as follows:

"Most of those who have spoken here before me have commended the lawgiver who added this oration to our other funeral customs; it seemed to them a worthy thing that such an honor should be given at their burial to the dead who have fallen on the field of battle. But I should have preferred that, when men's deeds have been brave, they should be honored in deed only, and with such an honor as this public funeral, which you are now witnessing. Then the reputation of many would not have been imperilled on the eloquence or want of eloquence of one, and their virtues believed or not as he spoke well or ill. For it is difficult to say neither too little nor too much; and even moderation is apt not to give the impression of truthfulness. The friend of the dead who knows the facts is likely to think that the words of the speaker fall short of his knowledge and of his wishes; another who is not so well informed, when he hears of anything which surpasses his own powers, will be envious and will suspect exaggeration. Mankind are tolerant of the praises of others so long as each hearer thinks that he can do as well or nearly as well himself, but, when the speaker rises above him, jealousy is aroused and he begins to be incredulous. However, since our ancestors have set the seal of their approval upon the practice, I must obey, and to the utmost of my power shall endeavor to satisfy the wishes and beliefs of all who hear me.

"I will speak first of our ancestors, for it is right and becoming that now, when we are lamenting the dead, a tribute should be paid to their memory. There has never been a time when they did not inhabit this land, which by their valor they have handed down from generation to generation, and we have received from them a free state. But if they were worthy of praise, still more were our fathers, who added to their inheritance, and after many a struggle transmitted to us their sons this great empire. And we ourselves assembled here to-day, who are still most of us in the vigor of life, have chiefly done the work of improvement, and have richly endowed our city with all things, so that she is sufficient for herself both in peace and war. Of the military exploits by which our various possessions were acquired, or of the energy with which we or our fathers drove back the tide of war, Hellenic or Barbarian, I will not speak; for the tale would be long and is familiar to you. But before I praise the dead, I should like to point out by what principles of action we rose to power, and under what institutions and through what manner of life our empire became great. For I conceive that such thoughts are not unsuited to the occasion, and that this numerous assembly of citizens and strangers may profitably listen to them.

"Our form of government does not enter into rivalry with the institutions of others. We do not copy our neighbors, but are an example to them. It is true that we are called a democracy, for the administration is in the hands of the many and not of the few. But while the law secures equal justice to all alike in their private disputes, the claim of excellence is also recognized; and when a citizen is in any way distinguished, he is preferred to the public service, not as a matter of privilege, but as the reward of merit. Neither is poverty a bar, but a man may benefit his country whatever be the obscurity of his condition. There is no exclusiveness in our public life, and in our private intercourse we are not suspicious of one another, nor angry with our neighbor if he does what he likes; we do not put on sour looks at him which, though harmless, are not pleasant. While we are thus unconstrained in our private intercourse, a spirit of reverence pervades our public acts; we are prevented from doing wrong by respect for authority and for the laws, having an especial regard to those which are ordained for the protection of the injured as well as to those unwritten laws which bring upon the transgressor of them the reprobation of the general sentiment.

"And we have not forgotten to provide for our weary spirits many relaxations from toil; we have regular games and sacrifices throughout the year; at home the style of our life is refined; and the delight which we daily feel in all these things helps to banish melancholy. Because of the greatness of our city the fruits of the whole earth flow in upon us; so that we enjoy the goods of other countries as freely as of our own.

"Then, again, our military training is in many respects superior to that of our adversaries. Our city is thrown open to the world, and we never expel a foreigner or prevent him from seeing or learning anything of which the secret if revealed to an enemy might profit him. We rely not upon management or trickery, but upon our own hearts and hands. And in the matter of education, whereas they from early youth are always undergoing laborious exercises which are to make them brave, we live at ease, and yet are equally ready to face the perils which they face. And here is the proof. The Lacedaemonians come into Attica not by themselves, but with their whole confederacy following; we go alone into a neighbor's country; and although our opponents are fighting for their homes and we on a foreign soil, we have seldom any difficulty in overcoming them. Our enemies have never yet felt our united strength; the care of a navy divides our attention, and on land we are obliged to send our own citizens everywhere. But they, if they meet and defeat a part of our army, are as proud as if they had routed us all, and when defeated they pretend to have been vanquished by us all.

"If then we prefer to meet danger with a light heart but without laborious training, and with a courage which is gained by habit and not enforced by law, are we not greatly the gainers? Since we do not anticipate the pain, although, when the hour comes, we can be as brave as those who never allow themselves to rest; and thus too our city is equally admirable in peace and in war. For we are lovers of the beautiful, yet simple in our tastes, and we cultivate the mind without loss of manliness. Wealth we employ, not for talk and ostentation, but when there is a real use for it. To avow poverty with us is not disgrace: the true disgrace is in doing nothing to avoid it. An Athenian citizen does not neglect the state because he takes care of his own household; and even those of us who are engaged in business have a very fair idea of politics. We alone regard a man who takes no interest in public affairs, not as a harmless, but as a useless character; and if few of us are originators, we are all sound judges of a policy. The great impediment to action is, in our opinion, not discussion, but the want of that knowledge which is gained by discussion preparatory to action. For we have a peculiar power of thinking before we act and of acting too, whereas other men are courageous from ignorance but hesitate upon reflection. And they are surely to be esteemed the bravest spirits who, having the clearest sense both of the pains and pleasures of life, do not on that account shrink from danger. In doing good, again, we are unlike others; we make our friends by conferring, not by receiving favors. Now he who confers a favor is the firmer friend, because he would fain by kindness keep alive the memory of an obligation; but the recipient is colder in his feelings, because he knows that in requiting another's generosity he will not be winning gratitude, but only paying a debt. We alone do good to our neighbors not upon a calculation of interest, but in the confidence of freedom and in a frank and fearless spirit. To sum up: I say that Athens is the school of Hellas, and that the individual Athenian in his own person seems to have the power of adapting himself to the most varied forms of action with the utmost versatility and grace. This is no passing

and idle word, but truth and fact; and the assertion is verified by the position to which these qualities have raised the state. For in the hour of trial Athens alone among her contemporaries is superior to the report of her. No enemy who comes against her is indignant at the reverses which he sustains at the hands of such a city; no subject complains that his masters are unworthy of him. And we shall assuredly not be without witnesses; there are mighty monuments of our power which will make us the wonder of this and of succeeding ages; we shall not need the praises of Homer or of any other panegyrist whose poetry may please for the moment, although his representation of the facts will not bear the light of day. For we have compelled every land and every sea to open a path for our valor, and have everywhere planted eternal memorials of our friendship and of our enmity. Such is the city for whose sake these men nobly fought and died; they could not bear the thought that she might be taken from them; and every one of us who survive should gladly toil on her behalf.

"I have dwelt upon the greatness of Athens because I want to show you that we are contending for a higher prize than those who enjoy none of these privileges, and to establish by manifest proof the merit of these men whom I am now commemorating. Their loftiest praise has been already spoken. For in magnifying the city I have magnified them, and men like them whose virtues made her glorious. And of how few Hellenes can it be said as of them, that their deeds when weighed in the balance have been found equal to their fame! Methinks that a death such as theirs has been gives the true measure of a man's worth; it may be the first revelation of his virtues, but is at any rate their final seal. For even those who come short in other ways may justly plead the valor with which they have fought for their country; they have blotted out the evil with the good, and have benefited the state more by their public services than they have injured her by their private actions. None of these men were enervated by wealth or hesitated to resign the pleasures of life; none of them put off the evil day in the hope, natural to poverty, that a man, though poor, may one day become rich. But, deeming that the punishment of their enemies was sweeter than any of these things, and that they could fall in no nobler cause, they determined at the hazard of their lives to be honorably avenged, and to leave the rest. They resigned to hope their unknown chance of happiness; but in the face of death they resolved to rely upon themselves alone. And when the moment came they were minded to resist and suffer, rather than to fly and save their lives; they ran away from the word of dishonor, but on the battle-field their feet stood fast, and in an instant, at the height of their fortune, they passed away from the scene, not of their fear, but of their glory.

"Such was the end of these men; they were worthy of Athens, and the living need not desire to have a more heroic spirit, although they may pray for a less fatal issue. The value of such a spirit is not to be expressed in words. Any one can discourse to you for ever about the advantages of a brave defence which you know already. But instead of listening to him I would have you day by day fix your eyes upon the greatness of Athens, until you become filled with the love of her; and when you are impressed by the spectacle of her glory, reflect that this empire has been acquired by men who knew their duty and had the courage to do it, who in the hour of conflict had the fear of dishonor always present to them, and who, if ever they failed in an enterprise, would not allow their virtues to be lost to their country, but freely gave their lives to her as the fairest offering which they could present at her feast. The sacrifice which they collectively made was individually repaid to them; for they received again each one for himself a praise which grows not old, and the noblest of all sepulchres—I speak not of that in which their remains are laid, but of that in which their glory survives, and is proclaimed always and on every fitting occasion both in word and deed. For the whole earth is the sepulchre of famous men; not only are they commemorated by columns and inscriptions in their own country, but in foreign lands there dwells also an unwritten memorial of them, graven not on stone but in the hearts of men. Make them your examples, and, esteeming courage to be freedom and freedom to be happiness, do not weigh too nicely the perils of war. The unfortunate who has no hope of a change for the better has less reason to throw away his life than the prosperous who, if he survive, is always liable to a change for the worse, and to whom any accidental fall makes the most serious difference. To a man of spirit, cowardice and disaster coming together are far more bitter than death, striking him unperceived at a time when he is full of courage and animated by the general hope.

"Wherefore I do not now commiserate the parents of the dead who stand here; I would rather comfort them. You know that your life has been passed amid manifold vicissitudes; and that they may be deemed fortunate who have gained most honor, whether an honorable death like theirs, or an honorable sorrow like yours and whose days have been so ordered that the term of their happiness is likewise the term of their life. I know how hard it is to make you feel this, when the good fortune of others will too often remind you of the gladness which once lightened your hearts. And sorrow is felt at the want of those blessings, not which a man never knew, but which were a part of his life before they were taken from him. Some of you are of an age at which they may hope to have other children, and they ought to bear their sorrow better; not only will the children who may hereafter be born make them forget their own lost ones, but the city will be doubly a gainer. She will not be left desolate, and she will be safer. For a man's counsel cannot have equal weight or worth, when he alone has no children to risk in the general danger. To those of you who have passed their prime, I say: 'Congratulate yourselves that you have been happy during the greater part of your days; remember that your life of sorrow will not last long, and be comforted by the glory of those who are gone. For the love of honor alone is ever young, and not riches, as some say, but honor is the delight of men when they are old and useless.'

"To you who are the sons and brothers of the departed, I say that the struggle to emulate them will be an arduous one.

For all men praise the dead, and, however pre-eminent your virtue may be, hardly will you be thought, I do not say to equal, but even to approach them. The living having their rivals and detractors, but when a man is out of the way, the honor and good-will which he receives is unalloyed. And, if I am to speak of womanly virtues to those of you who will henceforth be widows, let me sum them up in one short admonition: To a woman not to show more weakness than is natural to her sex is a great glory, and not to be talked about for good or for evil among men.

"I have paid the required tribute, in obedience to the law, making use of such fitting words as I had. The tribute of deeds has been paid in part; for the dead have been honorably interred, and it remains only that their children should be maintained at the public charge until they are grown up; this is the solid prize with which, as with a garland, Athens crowns her sons living and dead, after a struggle like theirs. For where the rewards of virtue are greatest, there the noblest citizens are enlisted in the service of the state. And now, when you have duly lamented, every one his own dead, you may depart."

The Melian Dialogue

In 416 B.C. the Athenians made an expedition against the island of Melos. As Thucydides explains, the Melians were colonists of the Spartans who would not submit to Athens like the other islanders. At first they were neutral and took no part. But when the Athenians tried to coerce them by ravaging their lands, they were driven into open hostilities. The generals encamped with the Athenian forces on the island. But before they did the country any harm, they sent envoys to negotiate with the Melians.

From *Thucydides*, tr. Benjamin Jowett, 2 vols., second ed., revised (Oxford, 1900).

One may expect that a certain amount of poetic license enters into the account that follows of the discussion between the two parties. Even so, the *Dialogue* remains an important statement of Greek statecraft: it reflects the Greek capacity to treat issues dispassionately, without irrelevant demagogy or emotion. By no means devoid of passion or unwilling to appeal to those "reasons of the heart that reason does not know," the Greek politician acknowledged that, in the end, politics are power politics. It was in such terms that he approached them, with businesslike arguments where the irrational found little place. They spoke as follows:

Ath. "We Athenians will use no fine words; we will not go out of our way to prove at length that we have a right to rule, because we overthrew the Persians; or that we attack you now because we are suffering any injury at your hands. We should not convince you if we did; nor must you expect to convince us by arguing that, although a colony of the Spartans, you have taken no part in their expeditions, or that you have never done us any wrong. But you and we should say what we really think, and aim only at what is possible, for we both alike know that into the discussion of human affairs the question of justice only enters where the pressure of necessity is equal, and that the powerful exact what they can, and the weak grant what they must."

Mel. "Well, then, since you set aside justice and invite us to speak of expediency, in our judgment it is certainly expedient that you should respect a principle which is for the common good; and that to every man when in peril a reasonable claim should be accounted a claim of right, and any plea which he is disposed to urge, even if failing of the point a little, should help his cause. Your interest in this principle is quite as great as ours, inasmuch as you, if you fall, will incur the heaviest vengeance, and will be the most terrible example to mankind."

Ath. "The fall of our empire, if it should fall, is not an event to which we look forward with dismay; for ruling states such as Lacedaemon are not cruel to their vanquished enemies. And we are fighting not so much against the Lacedaemonians as against our own subjects who may some day rise up and overcome their former masters. But this is a danger which you may leave to us. And we will now endeavor to show that we have come in the interests of our empire, and that in what we are about to say we are only seeking the preservation of your city. For we want to make you ours with the least trouble to ourselves, and it is for the interests of us both that you should not be destroyed."

Mel. "It may be your interest to be our masters, but how can it be ours to be your slaves?"

Ath. "To you the gain will be that by submission you will avert the worst; and we shall be all the richer for your preservation."

Mel. "But must we be your enemies? Will you not receive us as friends if we are neutral and remain at peace with you?"

Ath. "No, your enmity is not half so mischievous to us as your friendship; for the one is in the eyes of our subjects an argument of our power, the other of our weakness."

Mel. "But are your subjects really unable to distinguish between states in which you have no concern, and those which are chiefly your own colonies, and in some cases have revolted and been subdued by you?"

Ath. "Why, they do not doubt that both of them have a good deal to say for themselves on the score of justice, but they think that states like yours are left free because they are able to defend themselves, and that we do not attack them because we dare not. So that your subjection will give us an increase of security, as well as an extension of empire. For we are masters of the sea, and you who are islanders, and insignificant islanders too, must not be allowed to escape us."

Mel. "But do you not recognize another danger? For once more, since you drive us from the plea of justice and press upon us your doctrine of expediency, we must show you what is for our interest, and, if it be for yours also, may hope to convince you:—Will you not be making enemies of all who are now neutrals? When they see how you are treating us they will expect you some day to turn against them; and if so, are you not strengthening the enemies whom you already have, and bringing upon you others who, if they could help, would never dream of being your enemies at all?"

Ath. "We do not consider our really dangerous enemies to be any of the peoples inhabiting the mainland who, secure in their freedom, may defer indefinitely any measures of precaution which they take against us, but islanders who, like you, happen to be under no control, and all who may be already irritated by the necessity of submission to our empire—these are our real enemies, for they are the most reckless and most likely to bring themselves as well as us into a danger which they cannot but foresee."

Mel. "Surely, then, if you and your subjects will brave all this risk, you to preserve your empire and they to be quit of

it, how base and cowardly it would be in us, who retain our freedom, not to do and suffer anything rather than be your slaves."

Ath. "Not so, if you calmly reflect: for you are not fighting against equals to whom you cannot yield without disgrace, but you are taking counsel whether or not you shall resist an overwhelming force. The question is not one of honor but of prudence."

Mel. "But we know that the fortune of war is sometimes impartial, and not always on the side of numbers. If we yield now all is over; but if we fight there is yet a hope that we may stand upright."

Ath. "Hope is a good comforter in the hour of danger, and when men have something else to depend upon, although hurtful, she is not ruinous. But when her spendthrift nature has induced them to stake their all, they see her as she is in the moment of their fall, and not till then. While the knowledge of her might enable them to beware of her, she never fails. You are weak and a single turn of the scale might be your ruin. Do not you be thus deluded; avoid the error of which so many are guilty, who, although they might still be saved if they would take the natural means, when visible grounds of confidence forsake them, have recourse to the invisible, to prophecies and oracles and the like, which ruin men by the hopes which they inspire in them."

Mel. "We know only too well how hard the struggle must be against your power, and against fortune, if she does not mean to be impartial. Nevertheless we do not despair of fortune; for we hope to stand as high as you in the favor of heaven, because we are righteous, and you against whom we contend are unrighteous; and we are satisfied that our deficiency in power will be compensated by the aid of our allies the Spartans; they cannot refuse to help us, if only because we are their kinsmen, and for the sake of their own honor. And therefore our confidence is not so utterly blind as you suppose."

Ath. "As for the Gods, we expect to have quite as much of their favor as you: for are we not doing or claiming anything which goes beyond common opinion about divine or men's desires about human things? For of the Gods we believe, and of men we know, that by a law of their nature wherever they can rule they will. This law was not made by us, and we are not the first who have acted upon it; we did but inherit it, and shall bequeath it to all time, and we know that you and all mankind, if you were as strong as we are, would do as we do. So much for the Gods; we have told you why we expect to stand as high in their good opinion as you. And then as to the Lacedaemonians, when you imagine that out of very shame they will assist you, we admire the simplicity of your idea, but we do not envy you the folly of it. The Lacedaemonians are exceedingly virtuous among themselves, and according to their national standard of morality. But in respect of their dealings with others, although many things might be said, a word is enough to describe them—of all men whom we know they are the most notorious for identifying what is pleasant with what is honorable, and what is expedient with what is just. But how inconsistent is such a character with your present blind hope of deliverance!"

Mel. "That is the very reason why we trust them; they will look to their interest, and therefore will not be willing to betray the Melians, who are their own colonists, lest they should be distrusted by their friends in Hellas and play into the hands of their enemies."

Ath. "But do you not see that the path of expedience is safe, whereas justice and honor involve danger in practice, and such dangers the Spartans seldom care to face?"

Mel. "On the other hand, we think that whatever perils there may be, they will be ready to face them for our sakes, and will consider danger less dangerous where we are concerned. For if they need our aid we are close at hand, and they can better trust our loyal feeling because we are their kinsmen."

Ath. "Yes, but what encourages men who are invited to join in a conflict is clearly not the good-will of those who summon them to their side, but a decided superiority in real power. To this no men look more keenly than the Spartans; so little confidence have they in their own resources that they only attack their neighbors when they have numerous allies, and therefore they are not likely to find their way by themselves to an island, when we are masters of the sea."

Mel. "But they may send their allies: the Cretan sea is a large place; and the masters of the sea will have more difficulty in overtaking vessels which want to escape than the pursued in escaping. If the attempt should fail they may invade Attica itself; and then you will have to fight, not for the conquest of a land in which you have no concern, but nearer home, for the preservation of your confederacy and of your own territory."

Ath. "Help may come from Lacedaemon to you as it has come to others, and should you ever have actual experience of it, then you will know that never once have the Athenians retired from a siege through fear of a foe elsewhere. You told us that the safety of your city would be your first care, but we remark that, in this long discussion, not a word has been uttered by you which would give a reasonable man expectation of deliverance. Your strongest grounds are hopes deferred, and what power you have is, not to be compared with that which is already arrayed against you. Unless after we have withdrawn you mean to come, as even now you may, to a wiser conclusion, you are showing a great want of sense. For surely you cannot dream of flying to that false sense of honor which has been the ruin of so many when danger and dishonor were staring them in the face. Many men with their eyes still open to the consequences have found the word 'honor' too much for them, and have suffered a mere name to lure them on, until it has drawn down upon them real and irretrievable calamities; through their own folly they have incurred a worse dishonor than fortune would have inflicted upon them. If you are wise you will not run this risk; you ought to see that there can be no disgrace in yielding to a great city which invites you to become her ally on reasonable terms, keeping your own land, and merely paying tribute; and that you will certainly gain no honor if, having to choose between two alternatives, safety and war, you obstinately prefer the worse. To maintain our rights against equals, to be politic with superiors, and to be moderate towards inferiors is the path of safety. Reflect once more when we have withdrawn, and say to yourselves over and over again that you are deliberating about your one and only country, which may be saved or may be destroyed by a single decision."

The Athenians left the conference: the Melians, after consulting among themselves, resolved to persevere in their refusal, and made answer as follows:— "Men of Athens, our resolution is unchanged; and we will not in a moment surrender that liberty which our city, founded seven hundred years ago, still enjoys; we will trust to the good-fortune which by the favor of the Gods has hitherto preserved us, and for human help to the Lacedaemonians, and endeavor to save ourselves. We are ready however to be your friends, and the enemies neither of you nor of the Lacedaemonians, and we ask you to leave our country when you have made such a peace as may appear to be in the interest of both parties."

Such was the answer of the Melians; the Athenians, as they quitted the conference, spoke as follows:—"Well, we must say, judging from the decision at which you have arrived, that you are the only men who deem the future to be more certain than the present, and regard things unseen as already realized in your fond anticipation, and that the more you cast yourselves upon the Spartans and fortune, and hope, and trust them, the more complete will be your ruin."

The Athenian envoys returned to the army; and the generals when they found that the Melians would not yield, immediately commenced hostilities. . . . [Eventually] the Melians were induced to surrender at discretion. The Athenians thereupon put to death all who were of military age, and made slaves of the women and children. Then they colonized the island, sending thither five hundred settlers of their own.

3. GREEK TRAGEDY

Of the three very great tragic poets who lived in Athens in the fifth century B.C., Aeschylus (525–456 B.C.) is the earliest and least sophisticated and perhaps also the most powerful. His attitude is affirmative, heroic, clear-eyed. The theme of tragedy, the dramatic form which he invented, is the bond between man and a fate which he cannot understand or influence. Heroism consists in accepting this challenge and asserting one's will, like Prometheus, against overwhelming odds and the expectation of eventual defeat.

Sophocles (c. 496–406 B.C.) was the most philosophic and the most popular. If the world is unfathomable, he holds, this is something that must be accepted. Forgetfulness of our ultimate weakness, of our subjection to fate and to the will of the gods, exposes us to *hubris*—the pride which comes before a fall. The greater the *hubris,* the more terrible the fall, with tragedy lying not in heroic assertion but in defeat. Where Aeschylus's heroes triumph in defeat, those of Sophocles merely accept their fate.

Euripides (c. 484–406 B.C.) is the one whose art, least popular in his own lifetime though highly prized after his death, comes closest to the attitudes of our day. Where Sophocles advises us to accept and ask no questions, the younger man refuses anything so formless. He questions, doubts, and criticizes. His attitude is one of revolt against injustice and against the irrational, mixed with boundless pity for the folly and self-destructiveness of mankind. "If gods do evil, then they are not gods," he writes, implying that our rational standards of judgment are valid and that it is weakness to take refuge in talk of unfathomable powers. There are many things we cannot understand or control—our impulses among them—but they are not, for all that, either good or acceptable. And when we act, we must use the heads and hearts we have, not surrender to the blind and the unknown that ever stalks about us. There is much more to Euripides than this—much more to each of these men—too much to encompass here; but the play that follows, in the translation of Gilbert Murray, has been selected as showing one, and perhaps the most widespread, of the attitudes their works reflect.

It ought to be added that the dates of the three men's lives are only approximately known. An ancient story groups them round the battle of Salamis, the great sea victory of the Persian Wars in 480 B.C. Aeschylus fought among the hoplites, Sophocles danced in a young boys' choir to celebrate the victory, and Euripides was born on the day of the battle. So the story goes, illuminating the crowded richness of that extraordinary century.

Considering the wealth of alternatives that the output of these men presents, it has seemed best to include in this collection a play that is representative in three ways: (1) its author, Sophocles, was held by the Greeks themselves to be their greatest dramatic author; (2) Oedipus presents the dilemma of the self-reliant, would-be rational man faced by ineluctable fate in a manner that is as real for us today as it was for the contemporaries of Sophocles; (3) given here in its entirety and in the excellent translation of Gilbert Murray, the play offers an example of the classic form in which dramatists in all ages would find their inspiration.

Sophocles: *Oedipus, King of Thebes*

CHARACTERS IN THE PLAY

Oedipus, supposed son of Polybus, King of Corinth; now elected King of Thebes.

Jocasta, Queen of Thebes; widow of Laius, the late King, and now wife to Oedipus.

Creon, a Prince of Thebes, brother to Jocasta.

Tiresias, an old blind seer.

Priest of Zeus.

A Stranger from Corinth.

A Shepherd of King Laius.

A Messenger from the Palace.

Chorus of the Elders of Thebes.

A Crowd of Suppliants, men, women, and children.

ARGUMENT

While Thebes was under the rule of Laius and Jocasta there appeared a strange and monstrous creature, "the riddling Sphinx," "the She-Wolf of the woven song," who in some unexplained way sang riddles of death and slew the people of Thebes. Laius went to ask aid of the oracle of Delphi, but was slain mysteriously on the road. Soon afterwards there came to Thebes a young Prince of Corinth, Oedipus, who had left his home and was wandering. He faced the Sphinx and read her riddle, whereupon she flung herself from her rock and died. The throne being vacant was offered to Oedipus, and with it the hand of the Queen Jocasta.

Some ten or twelve years afterwards a pestilence has fallen on Thebes. At this point the play begins.

SCENE—*Before the Palace of Oedipus at Thebes. A crowd of suppliants of all ages are waiting by the altar in front and on the steps of the Palace; among them the Priest of Zeus. As the Palace door opens and Oedipus comes out all the suppliants with a cry move towards him in attitudes of prayer, holding out their olive branches, and then become still again as he speaks.*

Oedipus. My children, fruit of Cadmus' ancient tree
New springing, wherefore thus with bended knee
Press ye upon us, laden all with wreaths
And suppliant branches? And the city breathes
Heavy with incense, heavy with dim prayer
And shrieks to affright the Slayer.—Children, care
For this so moves me, I have scorned withal
Message or writing: seeing 'tis I ye call,
'Tis I am come, world-honoured Oedipus.
    Old Man, do thou declare—the rest have thus
Their champion—in what mood stand ye so still,
In dread or sure hope? Know ye not, my will
Is yours for aid 'gainst all? Stern were indeed
The heart that felt not for so dire a need.
    Priest. O Oedipus, who holdest in thy hand
My city, thou canst see what ages stand
At these thine altars; some whose little wing
Scarce flieth yet, and some with long living
O'erburdened; priests, as I of Zeus am priest,
And chosen youths: and wailing hath not ceased
Of thousands in the market-place, and by
Athena's two-fold temples and the dry
Ash of Ismenus' portent-breathing shore.
    For all our ship, thou see'st, is weak and sore

Shaken with storms, and no more lighteneth
Her head above the waves whose trough is
    death.
She wasteth in the fruitless buds of earth,
In parched herds and travail without birth
Of dying women: yea, and midst of it
A burning and a loathly god hath lit
Sudden, and sweeps our land, this Plague
    of power;
Till Cadmus' house grows empty, hour by
    hour,
And Hell's house rich with steam of tears
    and blood.
    O King, not God indeed nor peer to God
We deem thee, that we kneel before thine
    hearth,
Children and old men, praying; but of each
A thing consummate by thy star confessed
Thou walkest, and by converse with the
    blest;
Who came to Thebes so swift, and swept
    away
The Sphinx's song, the tribute of dismay,
That all were bowed beneath, and made us
    free.
A stranger, thou, naught knowing more than
    we,
Nor taught of any man, but by God's breath
Filled, thou didst raise our life. So the world
    saith;
So we say.
            Therefore now, O Lord and Chief,
We come to thee again; we lay our grief
On thy head, if thou find us not some aid.
Perchance thou hast heard Gods talking in
    the shade
Of night, or eke some man: to him that
    knows,
Men say, each chance that falls, each wind
    that blows
Hath life, when he seeks counsel. Up, O
    chief
Of men, and lift thy city from its grief;
Face thine own peril! All our land doth hold

Thee still our saviour, for that help of old:
Shall they that tell of thee hereafter tell
"By him was Thebes raised up, and after
    fell!"
Nay, lift us till we slip no more. Oh, let
That bird of old that made us fortunate
Wing back; be thou our Oedipus again.
And let thy kingdom be a land of men,
Not emptiness. Walls, towers, and ships,
    they all
Are nothing with no men to keep the wall.
    Oedipus. My poor, poor children! Surely
    long ago
I have read your trouble. Stricken, well I
    know,
Ye all are, stricken sore: yet verily
Not one so stricken to the heart as I.
Your grief, it cometh to each man apart
For his own loss, none other's; but this heart
For thee and me and all of us doth weep.
Wherefore it is not to one sunk in sleep
Ye come with waking. Many tears these days
For your sake I have wept, and many ways
Have wandered on the beating wings of
    thought.
And, finding but one hope, that I have
    sought
And followed. I have sent Menoikeus' son,
Creon, my own wife's brother, forth alone
To Apollo's House in Delphi, there to ask
What word, what deed of mine, what bitter
    task
May save my city.
            And the lapse of days
Reckoned, I can but marvel what delays
His journey. 'Tis beyond all thought that
    thus
He comes not, beyond need. But when he
    does,
Then call me false and traitor, if I flee
Back from whatever task God sheweth me.
    Priest. At point of time thou speakest.
Mark the cheer
Yonder. Is that not Creon drawing near?

They all crowd to gaze where Creon is approaching in the distance.

Oedipus. O Lord Apollo, help! And be the star
That guides him joyous as his seemings are!
   Priest. Oh! surely joyous! How else should he bear
That fruited laurel wreathed about his hair?
   Oedipus. We soon shall know.—'Tis not too far for one
Clear-voiced. (*Shouting*) Ho, brother! Prince! Menoikeus' son,
What message from the God?
   Creon (*from a distance*). Message of joy!

Enter Creon.

I tell thee, what is now our worst annoy,
If the right deed be done, shall turn to good.

The crowd, which has been full of excited hope, falls to doubt and disappointment.

Oedipus. Nay, but what is the message? For my blood
Runs neither hot nor cold for words like those.
   Creon. Shall I speak now, with all these pressing close,
Or pass within?—To me both ways are fair.
   Oedipus. Speak forth to all! The grief that these men bear
Is more than any fear for mine own death.
   Creon. I speak then what I heard from God.—Thus saith
Phoebus, our Lord and Seer, in clear command.
An unclean thing there is, hid in our land,
Eating the soil thereof: this ye shall cast
Out, and not foster till all help be past.
   Oedipus. How cast it out? What was the evil deed?
   Creon. Hunt the men out from Thebes, or make them bleed

Who slew. For blood it is that stirs to-day.
   Oedipus. Who was the man they killed? Doth Phoebus say?
   Creon. O King, there was of old King Laius
In Thebes, ere thou didst come to pilot us.
   Oedipus. I know: not that I ever saw his face.
   Creon. 'Twas he. And Loxias now bids us trace
And smite the unknown workers of his fall.
   Oedipus. Where in God's earth are they? Or how withal
Find the blurred trail of such an ancient stain?
   Creon. In Thebes, he said.—That which men seek amain
They find. 'Tis things forgotten that go by.
   Oedipus. And where did Laius meet them? Did he die
In Thebes, or in the hills, or some far land?
   Creon. To ask God's will in Delphi he had planned
His journey. Started and returned no more.
   Oedipus. And came there nothing back? No message, nor
None of his company, that ye might hear?
   Creon. They all were slain, save one man; blind with fear
He came, remembering naught—or almost naught.
   Oedipus. And what was that? One thing has often brought
Others, could we but catch one little clue.
   Creon. 'Twas not one man, 'twas robbers —that he knew—
Who barred the road and slew him: a great band.
   Oedipus. Robbers? What robber, save the work was planned
By treason here, would dare a risk so plain?
   Creon. So some men thought. But Laius lay slain,
And none to avenge him in his evil day.

Oedipus. And what strange mischief,
    when your master lay
Thus fallen, held you back from search and
    deed?
    Creon. The dark-songed Sphinx was here.
    We had no heed
Of distant sorrows, having death so near.
    Oedipus. It falls on me then. I will search
    and clear
This darkness.—Well hath Phoebus done,
    and thou
Too, to recall that dead king, even now,
And with you for the right I also stand,
To obey the God and succour this dear land.
Nor is it as for one that touches me
Far off; 'tis for mine own sake I must see
This sin cast out. Who'er it was that slew
Laius, the same wild hand may seek me too:
And caring thus for Laius, is but care
For mine own blood.—Up! Leave this altar-
    stair,
Children. Take from it every suppliant
    bough.
Then call the folk of Thebes. Say, 'tis my
    vow
To uphold them to the end. So God shall
    crown
Our greatness, or for ever cast us down.

        [*He goes in to the Palace.*

    Priest. My children, rise.—The King
    most lovingly
Hath promised all we came for. And may He
Who sent this answer, Phoebus, come con-
    fessed
Helper to Thebes, and strong to stay the
    pest.

*The suppliants gather up their boughs and
    stand at the side. The chorus of
    Theban elders enter.*

        Chorus.
(*They speak of the Oracle which they have
    not yet heard, and cry to Apollo by his
    special cry "I-ê."*)

A Voice, a Voice, that is borne on the
    Holy Way!
What art thou, O Heavenly One, O Word
    of the Houses of Gold?
Thebes is bright with thee, and my heart it
    leapeth; yet is it cold,
    And my spirit faints as I pray.
        I-ê! I-ê!
What task, O Affrighter of Evil, what task
    shall thy people essay?
    One new as our new-come affliction,
        Or an old toil returned with the years?
    Unveil thee, thou dread benediction,
        Hope's daughter and Fear's.
(*They pray to Athena, Artemis, and Apollo.*)
    Zeus-Child that knowest not death, to
    thee I pray,
O Pallas; next to thy Sister, who calleth
    Thebes her own
Artemis, named of Fair Voices, who sitteth
    her orbèd throne
In the throng of the market way:
        And I-ê! I-ê!
Apollo, the Pure, the Far-smiter; O Three
    that keep evil away,
    If of old for our city's desire,
        When the death-cloud hung close to
    her brow,
    Ye have banished the wound and the fire,
        Oh! come to us now!

(*They tell of the Pestilence.*)
Wounds beyond telling; my people sick unto
    death;
    And where is the counsellor, where is
    the sword of thought?
And Holy Earth in her increase perisheth:
    The child dies and the mother awaketh
    not.
        I-ê! I-ê!
We have seen them, one on another, gone
    as a bird is gone,
    Souls that are flame; yea, higher,
    Swifter they pass than fire,
        To the rocks of the dying Sun.

(They end by a prayer to Athena.)
Their city wasteth unnumbered; their chil-
 dren lie
 Where death hath cast them, unpitied,
 unwept upon.
The altars stand, as in seas of storm a high
 Rock standeth, and wives and mothers
 grey thereon
 Weep, weep and pray.
Lo, joy-cries to fright the Destroyer; a flash
 in the dark they rise,
 Then die by the sobs overladen.
 Send help, O heaven-born Maiden,
 Let us look on the light of her eyes!

(To Zeus, that he drive out the Slayer.)
 And Ares, the abhorred
 Slayer, who bears no sword,
But shrieking, wrapped in fire, stands over
 me,
 Make that he turn, yea, fly
 Broken, wind-wasted, high
Down the vexed hollow of the Vaster Sea;
 Or back to his own Thrace,
 To harbour shelterless.
Where Night hath spared, he bringeth end
 by day.
 Him, Him, O thou whose hand
 Beareth the lightning brand,
O Father Zeus, now with thy thunder, slay
 and slay!

(To Apollo, Artemis, and Dionysus.)
 Where is thy gold-strung bow,
 O Wolf-god, where the flow
Of living shafts unconquered, from all ills
 Our helpers? Where the white
 Spears of thy Sister's light,
Far-flashing as she walks the wolf-wild hills?
 And thou, O Golden-crown,
 Theban and named our own,
O Wine-gleam, Voice of Joy, for ever more
 Ringed with thy Maenads white,
 Bacchus, draw near and smite,
Smite with thy glad-eyed flame the God
 whom Gods abhor.

*During the last lines Oedipus has come out
from the Palace.*

Oedipus. Thou prayest: but my words if
 thou wilt hear
And bow thee to their judgement, strength
 is near
For help, and a great lightening of ill.
Thereof I come to speak, a stranger still
To all this tale, a stranger to the deed:
(Else, save that I were clueless, little need
Had I to cast my net so wide and far:)
Howbeit, I, being now as all ye are,
A Theban, to all Thebans high and low
Do make proclaim: if any here doth know
By what man's hand died Laius, your King,
Labdacus' son, I charge him that he bring
To me his knowledge. Let him feel no fear
If on a townsman's body he must clear
Our guilt: the man shall suffer no great ill,
But pass from Thebes, and live where else
 he will.

(No answer.)
Is it some alien from an alien shore
Ye know to have done the deed, screen him
 no more!
Good guerdon waits you now and a King's
 love
Hereafter.
 Ha! If still ye will not move
But, fearing for yourselves or some near
 friend,
Reject my charge, then hearken to what end
Ye drive me.—If in this place men there be
Who know and speak not, lo, I make decree
That, while in Thebes I bear the diadem,
No man shall greet, no man shall shelter
 them,
Nor give them water in their thirst, nor share
In sacrifice nor shrift nor dying prayer,
But thrust them from our doors, the thing
 they hide
Being this land's curse. Thus hath the God
 replied
This day to me from Delphi, and my sword

I draw thus for the dead and for God's
    word.
    And lastly for the murderer, be it one
Hiding alone or more in unison,
I speak on him this curse: even as his soul
Is foul within him let his days be foul,
And life unfriended grind him till he die.
More: if he ever tread my hearth and I
Know it, be every curse upon my head
That I have spoke this day.
                  All I have said
I charge ye strictly to fulfil and make
Perfect, for my sake, for Apollo's sake,
And this land's sake, deserted of her fruit
And cast out from her gods. Nay, were all
    mute
At Delphi, still 'twere strange to leave the
    thing
Unfollowed, when a true man and a King
Lay murdered. All should search. But I, as
    now
Our fortunes fall—his crown is on my brow,
His wife lies in my arms, and common fate,
Had but his issue been more fortunate,
Might well have joined our children—since
    this red
Chance hath so stamped its heel on Laius'
    head,
I am his champion left, and, as I would
For mine own father, choose for ill or good
This quest, to find the man who slew of yore
Labdacus' son, the son of Polydore,
Son of great Cadmus whom Agenor old
Begat, of Thebes first master. And, behold,
For them that aid me not, I pray no root
Nor seed in earth may bear them corn nor
    fruit,
No wife bear children, but this present curse
Cleave to them close and other woes yet
    worse.
    Enough: ye other people of the land,
Whose will is one with mine, may Justice
    stand
Your helper, and all gods for evermore.
                  [*The crowd disperses.*

Leader. O King, even while thy curse yet
    hovers o'er
My head, I answer thee. I slew him not,
Nor can I shew the slayer. But, God wot,
If Phoebus sends this charge, let Phoebus
    read
Its meaning and reveal who did the deed.
    Oedipus. Aye, that were just, if of his
      grace he would
Reveal it. How shall man compel his God?
    Leader. Second to that, methinks, 'twould
      help us most . . .
    Oedipus. Though it be third, speak!
      Nothing should be lost.
    Leader. To our High Seer on earth vision
      is given
Most like to that High Phoebus hath in
    heaven.
Ask of Tiresias: he could tell thee true.
    Oedipus. That also have I thought for.
      Aye, and two
Heralds have sent ere now. 'Twas Creon set
Me on.—I marvel that he comes not yet.
    Leader. Our other clues are weak, old
      signs and far.
    Oedipus. What signs? I needs must ques-
      tion all that are.
    Leader. Some travellers slew him, the tale
      used to be.
    Oedipus. The tale, yes: but the witness,
      where is he?
    Leader. The man hath heard thy curses.
      If he knows
The taste of fear, he will not long stay close.
    Oedipus. He fear my words, who never
      feared the deed?
    Leader. Well, there is one shall find him.
      —See, they lead
Hither our Lord Tiresias, in whose mind
All truth is born, alone of human kind.

*Enter Tiresias led by a young disciple. He
    is an old blind man in a prophet's robe,
    dark, unkempt and sinister in appear-
    ance.*

Oedipus. Tiresias, thou whose mind divineth well
All Truth, the spoken and the unspeakable,
The things of heaven and them that walk the earth;
Our city . . . thou canst see, for all thy dearth
Of outward eyes, what clouds are over her.
In which, O gracious Lord, no minister
Of help, no champion, can we find at all
Save thee. For Phoebus—thou hast heard withal
His message—to our envoy hath decreed
One only way of help in this great need:
To find and smite with death or banishing,
Him who smote Laius, our ancient King.
Oh, grudge us nothing! Question every cry
Of birds, and all roads else of prophecy
Thou knowest. Save our city: save thine own
Greatness: save me, save all that yet doth groan
Under the dead man's wrong! Lo, in thy hand
We lay us. And methinks, no work so grand
Hath man yet compassed, as, with all he can
Of chance or power, to help his fellow man.
   Tiresias (to himself). Ah me!
A fearful thing is knowledge, when to know
Helpeth no end. I knew this long ago,
But crushed it dead. Else had I never come.
   Oedipus. What means this? Comest thou so deep in gloom?
   Tiresias. Let me go back! Thy work shall weigh on thee
The less, if thou consent, and mine on me.
   Oedipus. Prophet, this is not lawful; nay, nor kind
To Thebes, who feeds thee, thus to veil thy mind.
   Tiresias. 'Tis that I like not thy mind, nor the way
It goeth. Therefore, lest I also stray . . .

He moves to go off Oedipus bars his road.

Oedipus. Thou shalt not, knowing, turn and leave us! See,
We all implore thee, all, on bended knee.
   Tiresias. Ye have no knowledge. What is mine I hold
For ever dumb, lest what is thine be told.
   Oedipus. What . wilt thou? Know and speak not? In my need
Be false to me, and let thy city bleed?
   Tiresias. I will not wound myself nor thee. Why seek
To trap and question me? I will not speak.
   Oedipus. Thou devil!

Movement of Leader to check him.

                              Nay; the wrath of any stone
Would rise at him. It lies with thee to have done
And speak. Is there no melting in thine eyes!
   Tiresias. Naught lies with me! With thee, with thee there lies,
I warrant, what thou ne'er hast seen nor guessed.
   Oedipus (to Leader, who tries to calm him). How can I hear such talk?—he maketh jest
Of the land's woe—and keep mine anger dumb?
   Tiresias. Howe'er I hold it back, 'twill come, 'twill come.
   Oedipus. The more shouldst thou declare it to thy King.
   Tiresias. I speak no more. For thee, if passioning
Doth comfort thee, on, passion to thy fill!

He moves to go.

Oedipus. 'Fore God, I am in wrath; and speak I will,
Nor stint what I see clear. 'Twas thou, 'twas thou,
Didst plan this murder; aye, and, save the blow,
Wrought it.—I know thou art blind; else I could swear

Thou, and thou only, art the murderer.

Tiresias (*returning*). So?—I command
    thee by thine own word's power,
To stand accurst, and never from this hour
Speak word to me, nor yet to these who ring
Thy throne. Thou art thyself the unclean
    thing.

Oedipus. Thou front of brass, to fling out
    injury
So wild! Dost think to bate me and go free?

Tiresias. I am free. The strong truth is in
    this heart.

Oedipus. What prompted thee? I swear
    'twas not thine art.

Tiresias. 'Twas thou. I spoke not, save for
    thy command.

Oedipus. Spoke what? What was it? Let
    me understand.

Tiresias. Dost tempt me? Were my words
    before not plain!

Oedipus. Scarce thy full meaning. Speak
    the words again.

Tiresias. Thou seek'st this man of blood:
    Thyself art he.

Oedipus. 'Twill cost thee dear, twice to
    have stabbed at me!

Tiresias. Shall I say more, to see thee rage
    again?

Oedipus. Oh, take thy fill of speech: 'twill
    all be vain.

Tiresias. Thou livest with those near to
    thee in shame
Most deadly, seeing not thyself nor them.

Oedipus. Thou think'st 'twill help thee,
    thus to speak and speak?

Tiresias. Surely, until the strength of
    Truth be weak.

Oedipus. 'Tis weak to none save thee.
    Thou hast no part
In truth, thou blind man, blind eyes, ears
    and heart.

Tiresias. More blind, more sad thy words
    of scorn, which none
Who hears but shall cast back on thee:
    soon, soon.

Oedipus. Thou spawn of Night, not I nor
    any free
And seeing man would hurt a thing like
    thee.

Tiresias. God is enough.—'Tis not my
    doom to fall
By thee. He knows and shall accomplish all.

Oedipus (*with a flash of discovery*). Ha!
    Creon!—Is it his or thine, this plot?

Tiresias. 'Tis thyself hates thee. Creon
    hates thee not.

Oedipus. O wealth and majesty, O skill
    all strife
Surpassing on the fevered roads of life,
What is your heart but bitterness, if now
For this poor crown Thebes bound upon my
    brow,
A gift, a thing I sought not—for this crown
Creon the stern and true, Creon mine own
Comrade, comes creeping in the dark to
    ban
And slay me; sending first this magic-man
And schemer, this false beggar-priest, whose
    eye
Is bright for gold and blind for prophecy.
Speak, thou. When hast thou ever shown
    thee strong
For aid? The She-Wolf of the woven song
Came, and thy art could find no word, no
    breath,
To save thy people from her riddling death.
'Twas scarce a secret, that, for common men
To unravel. There was need of Seer-craft
    then.
And thou hadst none to show. No fowl, no
    flame,
No God revealed it thee. 'Twas I that came,
Rude Oedipus, unlearned in wizard's lore,
And read her secret, and she spoke no more.
Whom now thou thinkest to hunt out, and
    stand
Foremost in honour at King Creon's hand.
I think ye will be sorry, thou and he
That shares thy sin-hunt. Thou dost look
    to me

An old man; else, I swear this day should bring
On thee the death thou plottest for thy King.
   Leader. Lord Oedipus, these be but words of wrath,
All thou hast spoke and all the Prophet hath.
Which skills not. We must join, for ill or well,
In search how best to obey God's oracle.
   Tiresias. King though thou art, thou needs must bear the right
Of equal answer. Even in me is might
For thus much, seeing I live no thrall of thine,
But Lord Apollo's; neither do I sign
Where Creon bids me.
               I am blind, and thou
Hast mocked my blindness. Yea, I will speak now.
Eyes hast thou, but thy deeds thou canst not see
Nor where thou art, nor what things dwell with thee.
Whence art thou born? Thou know'st not; and unknown,
On quick and dead, on all that were thine own,
Thou hast wrought hate. For that across thy path
Rising, a mother's and a father's wrath,
Two-handed, shod with fire, from the haunts of men
Shall scourge thee, in thine eyes now light, but then
Darkness. Aye, shriek! What harbour of the sea,
What wild Kithairon shall not cry to thee
In answer, when thou hear'st what bridal song,
What wind among the torches, bore thy strong
Sail to its haven, not of peace but blood.
Yea, ill things multitude on multitude
Thou seest not, which so soon shall lay thee low,

Low as thyself, low as thy children.—Go,
Heap scorn on Creon and my lips withal:
For this I tell thee, never was there fall
Of pride, nor shall be, like to thine this day.
   Oedipus. To brook such words from this thing? Out, I say!
Out to perdition! Aye, and quick, before . . .

      The Leader restrains him.

Enough then!—Turn and get thee from my door.
   Tiresias. I had not come hadst thou not called me here.
   Oedipus. I knew thee not so dark a fool. I swear
'Twere long before I called thee, had I known.
   Tiresias. Fool, say'st thou? Am I truly such an one?
The two who gave thee birth, they held me wise.
   Oedipus. Birth? . . . Stop! Who were they? Speak thy prophecies.
   Tiresias. This day shall give thee birth and blot thee out.
   Oedipus. Oh, riddles everywhere and words of doubt!
   Tiresias. Aye. Thou wast their best leader long ago.
   Oedipus. Laugh on. I swear thou still shalt find me so.
   Tiresias. That makes thy pride and thy calamity.
   Oedipus. I have saved this land, and care not if I die.
   Tiresias. Then I will go.—Give me thine arm, my child.
   Oedipus. Aye, help him quick.—To see him there makes wild
My heart. Once gone, he will not vex me more.
   Tiresias (*turning again as he goes*). I fear thee not; nor will I go before
That word be spoken which I came to speak.

How canst thou ever touch me?—Thou dost seek
With threats and loud proclaim the man whose hand
Slew Laius. Lo, I tell thee, he doth stand
Here. He is called a stranger, but these days
Shall prove him Theban true, nor shall he praise
His birthright. Blind, who once had seeing eyes,
Beggared, who once had riches, in strange guise,
His staff groping before him, he shall crawl
O'er unknown earth, and voices round him call:
"Behold the brother-father of his own
Children, the seed, the sower and the sown,
Shame to his mother's blood, and to his sire
Son, murderer, incest-worker."
                                                    Cool thine ire
With thought of these, and if thou find that aught
Faileth, then hold my craft a thing of naught.

[*He goes out. Oedipus returns to the Palace.*

Chorus.
(*They sing of the unknown murderer*)
What man, what man is he whom the voice of Delphi's cell
Hath named of the bloody hand, of the deed no tongue may tell?
    Let him fly, fly, for his need
    Hath found him; oh, where is the speed
That flew with the winds of old, the team of North-Wind's spell?
    For feet there be that follow. Yea, thunder-shod
    And girt with fire he cometh, the Child of God;
And with him are they that fail not, the Sin-Hounds risen from Hell.
For the mountain hath spoken, a voice hath flashed from amid the snows,

That the wrath of the world go seek for the man whom no man knows.
    Is he fled to the wild forest,
    To caves where the eagles nest?
O angry bull of the rocks, cast out from thy herd-fellows!
    Rage in his heart, and rage across his way,
    He toileth ever to beat from his ears away
The word that floateth about him, living, where'er he goes.

(*And of the Prophet's strange accusation.*)
Yet strange, passing strange, the wise augur and his lore;
    And my heart it cannot speak; I deny not nor assent,
But float, float in wonder at things after and before;
    Did there lie between their houses some old wrath unspent,
That Corinth against Cadmus should do murder by the way?
    No tale thereof they tell, nor no sign thereof they show;
Who dares to rise for vengeance and cast Oedipus away
    For a dark, dark death long ago!

Ah, Zeus knows, and Apollo, what is dark to mortal eyes;
    They are Gods. But a prophet, hath he vision more than mine?
Who hath seen? Who can answer? There be wise men and unwise.
    I will wait, I will wait, for the proving of the sign.
But I list not nor hearken when they speak Oedipus ill.
    We saw his face of yore, when the riddling singer passed;
And we knew him that he loved us, and we saw him great in skill.
    Oh, my heart shall uphold him to the last!

Enter Creon.

Creon. Good brother citizens, a frantic word
I hear is spoken by our chosen Lord
Oedipus against me, and here am come
Indignant. If he dreams, 'mid all this doom
That weighs upon us, he hath had from me
Or deed or lightest thought of injury, . . .
'Fore God, I have no care to see the sun
Longer with such a groaning name. Not one
Wound is it, but a multitude, if now
All Thebes must hold me guilty,—aye, and thou
And all who loved me—of a deed so foul.
   Leader. If words were spoken, it was scarce the soul
That spoke them: 'twas some sudden burst of wrath.
   Creon. The charge was made, then, that Tiresias hath
Made answer false, and that I bribed him, I?
   Leader. It was—perchance for jest. I know not why.
   Creon. His heart beat true, his eyes looked steadily
And fell not, laying such a charge on me?
   Leader. I know not. I have no eyes for the thing
My masters do.—But see, here comes the King.

   Enter Oedipus from the Palace.

   Oedipus. How now, assassin? Walking at my gate
With eye undimmed, thou plotter demonstrate
Against this life, and robber of my crown?
God help me! Me! What was it set me down
Thy butt? So dull a brain hast found in me
Aforetime, such a faint heart, not to see
Thy work betimes, or seeing not to smite?
Art thou not rash, this once! It needeth might
Of friends, it needeth gold, to make a throne
Thy quarry; and I fear me thou hast none.

   Creon. One thing alone I ask thee. Let me speak
As thou hast spoken; then, with knowledge, wreak
Thy judgment. I accept it without fear.
   Oedipus. More skill hast thou to speak than I to hear
Thee. There is peril found in thee and hate.
   Creon. That one thing let me answer ere too late.
   Oedipus. One thing be sure of, that thy plots are known.
   Creon. The man who thinks that bitter pride alone
Can guide him, without thought—his mind is sick.
   Oedipus. Who thinks to slay his brother with a trick
And suffer not himself, his eyes are blind.
   Creon. Thy words are more than just. But say what kind
Of wrong thou fanciest I have done thee. Speak.
   Oedipus. Didst urge me, or didst urge me not, to seek
A counsel from that man of prophecies?
   Creon. So judged I then, nor now judge otherwise.
   Oedipus (*suddenly seeing a mode of attack*). How many years have passed since Laius. . . .

   (*The words seem to choke him.*)
   Creon. Speak on. I cannot understand thee thus.
   Oedipus. (*With an effort.*) Passed in that bloody tempest from men's sight?
   Creon. Long years and old. I scarce can tell them right.
   Oedipus. At that time was this seer in Thebes, or how?
   Creon. He was; most wise and honoured, even as now.
   Oedipus. At that time did he ever speak my name?

Creon. No. To mine ear at least it never
  came.

Oedipus. Held you no search for those
  who slew your King?

Creon. For sure we did, but found not
  anything.

Oedipus. How came the all-knowing seer
  to leave it so?

Creon. Ask him! I speak not where I cannot know.

Oedipus. One thing thou canst, with
  knowledge full, I wot.

Creon. Speak it. If true, I will conceal it
  not.

Oedipus. This: that until he talked with
  thee, the seer

Ne'er spoke of me as Laius' murderer.

Creon. I know not if he hath so spoken
  now.

I heard him not.—But let me ask and thou
Answer me true, as I have answered thee.

Oedipus. Ask, ask! Thou shalt no murder
  find in me.

Creon. My sister is thy wife this many a
  day?

Oedipus. That charge it is not in me to
  gainsay.

Creon. Thou reignest, giving equal reign
  to her?

Oedipus. Always to her desire I minister.

Creon. Were we not all as one, she, thou
  and I?

Oedipus. Yes, thou false friend! There
  lies thy treachery.

Creon. Not so! Nay, do but follow me
  and scan

Thine own charge close. Think'st thou that
  any man
Would rather rule and be afraid, than rule
And sleep untroubled? Nay, where lives the
  fool—
I know them not, nor am I one of them—
Who careth more to bear a monarch's name
Than do a monarch's deeds? As now I stand
All my desire I compass at thy hand.

Were I the King, full half my deeds were
  done
To obey the will of others, not mine own.
Were that as sweet, when all the tale were
  told,
As this calm griefless princedom that I hold
And silent power? Am I so blind of brain
That ease with glory tires me, and I fain
Must change them? All men now give me
  God-speed,
All smile to greet me. If a man hath need
Of thee, 'tis me he calleth to the gate,
As knowing that on my word hangs the fate
Of half he craves. Is life like mine a thing
To cast aside and plot to be a King?
Doth a sane man turn villain in an hour?
  For me, I never lusted thus for power
Nor bore with any man who turned such
  lust
To doing.—But enough. I claim but just
Question. Go first to Pytho; find if well
And true I did report God's oracle.
Next, seek in Thebes for any plots entwined
Between this seer and me; which if ye find,
Then seize and strike me dead. Myself that
  day
Will sit with thee as judge and bid thee
  Slay!
But damn me not on one man's guess.—'Tis
  all
Unjust: to call a traitor true, to call
A true man traitor with no cause nor end!
And this I tell thee. He who plucks a friend
Out from his heart hath lost a treasured
  thing
Dear as his own dear life.
                    But Time shall bring
Truth back. 'Tis Time alone can make men
  know
What hearts are true; the false one day can
  show.

Leader. To one that fears to fall his words
  are wise,

O King; in thought the swift win not the
  prize.

Oedipus. When he is swift who steals against my reign
With plots, then swift am I to plot again.
Wait patient, and his work shall have prevailed
Before I move, and mine for ever failed.

    Creon. How then? To banish me is thy intent?

    Oedipus. Death is the doom I choose, not banishment.

    Creon. Wilt never soften, never trust thy friend?

    Oedipus. First I would see how traitors meet their end.

    Creon. I see thou wilt not think.

    Oedipus.   I think to save
My life.

    Creon.   Think, too, of mine.

    Oedipus.   Thine, thou born knave!

    Creon. Yes. . . . What, if thou art blind in everything?

    Oedipus. The King must be obeyed.

    Creon.   Not if the King
Does evil.

    Oedipus.   To your King! Ho, Thebes, mine own!

    Creon. Thebes is my country, not the King's alone.

Oedipus has drawn his sword; the Chorus shows signs of breaking into two parties to fight for Oedipus or for Creon, when the door opens and Jocasta appears on the steps.

    Leader. Stay, Princes, stay! See, on the Castle stair
The Queen Jocasta standeth. Show to her
Your strife. She will assuage it as is well.

    Jocasta. Vain men, what would ye with this angry swell
Of words heart-blinded? Is there in your eyes
No pity, thus, when all our city lies
Bleeding, to ply your privy hates? . . . Alack,

My lord, come in!—Thou, Creon, get thee back
To thine own house. And stir not to such stress
Of peril griefs that are but nothingness.

    Creon. Sister, it is the pleasure of thy lord,
Our King, to do me deadly wrong. His word
Is passed on me: 'tis banishment or death.

    Oedipus. I found him . . . I deny not what he saith,
My Queen . . . with craft and malice practising
Against my life.

    Creon.   Ye Gods, if such a thing
Hath once been in my thoughts, may I no more
See any health on earth, but, festered o'er
With curses, die!—Have done. There is mine oath.

    Jocasta. In God's name, Oedipus, believe him, both
For my sake, and for these whose hearts are all
Thine own, and for my brother's oath withal.
                  Strophe.

    Leader. Yield; consent; think! My Lord, I conjure thee!

    Oedipus. What would ye have me do?

    Leader. Reject not one who never failed his troth
Of old, and now is strong in his great oath.

    Oedipus. Dost know what this prayer means?

    Leader.   Yea, verily!

    Oedipus. Say then the meaning true.

    Leader. I would not have thee cast to infamy
Of guilt, where none is proved,
One who hath sworn and whom thou once hast loved.

    Oedipus. 'Tis that ye seek? For me, then . . . understand
Well . . . ye seek death or exile from the land.

Leader. No, by the God of Gods, the all-
seeing Sun!
May he desert me here, and every friend
With him, to death and utterest malison,
If e'er my heart could dream of such an
end!
But it bleedeth, it bleedeth sore,
In a land half slain,
If we join to the griefs of yore
Griefs of you twain.
Oedipus. Oh, let him go, though it be
utterly
My death, or flight from Thebes in beggary.
'Tis thy sad lips, not his, that make me know
Pity. Him I shall hate, where'er he go.
Creon. I see thy mercy moving full of
hate
And slow; thy wrath came swift and des-
perate.
Methinks, of all the pain that such a heart
Spreadeth, itself doth bear the bitterest part.
Oedipus. Oh, leave me and begone!
Creon.   I go, wronged sore
By thee. These friends will trust me as be-
fore.
[*Creon goes. Oedipus stands apart lost in
trouble of mind.*
Antistrophe.
Leader. Queen, wilt thou lead him to his
house again?
Jocasta. I will, when I have heard.
Leader. There fell some word, some blind
imagining
Between them. Things known foolish yet
can sting.
Jocasta. From both the twain it rose?
Leader.   From both the twain.
Jocasta. Aye, and what was the word?
Leader. Surely there is enough of evil
stirred,
And Thebes heaves on the swell
Of storm.—Oh, leave this lying where it
fell.
Oedipus. So be it, thou wise counsellor!
Make slight

My wrong, and blunt my purpose ere it
smite.
Leader. O King, not once I have an-
swered. Visibly
Mad were I, lost to all wise usages,
To seek to cast thee from us. 'Twas from
thee
We say of old blue sky and summer
seas,
When Thebes in the storm and rain
Reeled, like to die.
Oh, if thou canst, again
Blue sky, blue sky. . . . !
Jocasta. Husband, in God's name, say
what hath ensued
Of ill, that thou shouldst seek so dire a feud.
Oedipus. I will, wife. I have more regard
for thee
Than these.—Thy brother plots to murder
me.
Jocasta. Speak on. Make all thy charge.
Only be clear.
Oedipus. He says that I am Laius' mur-
derer.
Jocasta. Says it himself? Says he hath
witnesses?
Oedipus. Nay, of himself he ventures
nothing. 'Tis
This priest, this hellish seer, makes all the
tale.
Jocasta. The seer?—Then tear thy ter-
rors like a veil
And take free breath. A seer? No human
thing
Born on the earth hath power for conjuring
Truth from the dark of God.
                    Come, I will tell
An old tale. There came once an oracle
To Laius: I say not from the God
Himself, but from the priests and seers who
trod
His sanctuary: if ever son were bred
From him and me, by that son's hand, it
said,
Laius must die. And he, the tale yet stays

Among us, at the crossing of three ways
Was slain by robbers, strangers. And my
son—
God's mercy!—scarcely the third day was
gone
When Laius took, and by another's hand
Out on the desert mountain, where the land
Is rock, cast him to die. Through both his
feet
A blade of iron they drove. Thus did we
cheat
Apollo of his will. My child could slay
No father, and the King could cast away
The fear that dogged him, by his child to die
Murdered.—Behold the fruits of prophecy!
Which heed not thou! God needs not that
a seer
Help him, when he would make his dark
things clear.
  Oedipus. Woman, what turmoil hath thy
  story wrought
Within me! What up-stirring of old thought!
  Jocasta. What thought? It turns thee like
  a frightened thing.
  Oedipus. 'Twas at the crossing of three
  ways this King
Was murdered? So I heard or so I thought.
  Jocasta. That was the tale. It is not yet
  forgot.
  Oedipus. The crossing of three ways! And
  in what land?
  Jocasta. Phokis 'tis called. A road on
  either hand
From Delphi comes and Daulia, in a glen.
  Oedipus. How many years and months
  have passed since then?
  Jocasta. 'Twas but a little time before
  proclaim
Was made of thee for king, the tidings came.
  Oedipus. My God, what hast thou willed
  to do with me?
  Jocasta. Oedipus, speak! What is it trou-
  bles thee?
  Oedipus. Ask me not yet. But say, what
  build, what height

Had Laius? Rode he full of youth and
  might?
  Jocasta. Tall, with the white new-gleam-
  ing on his brow
He walked. In shape just such a man as
  thou.
  Oedipus. God help me! I much fear that
  I have wrought
A curse on mine own head, and knew it
  not.
  Jocasta. How sayst thou? O my King, I
  look on thee
And tremble.
  Oedipus (*to himself*). Horror, if the
  blind can see!
Answer but one thing and 'twill all be clear.
  Jocasta. Speak. I will answer though I
  shake with fear.
  Oedipus. Went he with scant array, or a
  great band
Of armed followers, like a lord of land?
  Jocasta. Four men were with him, one a
  herald; one
Chariot there was, where Laius rode alone.
  Oedipus. Aye me! 'Tis clear now.
                    Woman, who could bring
To Thebes the story of that manslaying?
  Jocasta. A house-thrall, the one man they
  failed to slay.
  Oedipus. The one man . . . ? Is he in
  the house to-day?
  Jocasta. Indeed no. When he came that
  day, and found
Thee on the throne where once sat Laius
  crowned,
He took my hand and prayed me earnestly
To send him to the mountain heights, to be
A herdsman, far from any sight or call
Of Thebes. And there I sent him. 'Twas a
  thrall
Good-hearted, worthy a far greater boon.
  Oedipus. Canst find him? I would see this
  herd, and soon.
  Jocasta. 'Tis easy. But what wouldst thou
  with the herd?

Oedipus. I fear mine own voice, lest it
spoke a word
Too much; whereof this man must tell me
true.
    Jocasta. The man shall come.—My lord,
methinks I too
Should know what fear doth work thee this
despite.
    Oedipus. Thou shalt. When I am tossed
to such an height
Of dark foreboding, woman, when my mind
Faceth such straits as these, where should
I find
A mightier love than thine?
                     My father—thus
I tell thee the whole tale—was Polybus,
In Corinth King; my mother Meropê
Of Dorian line. And I was held to be
The proudest in Corinthia, till one day
A thing befell: strange was it, but no way
Meet for such wonder and such rage as mine.
A feast it was, and some one flushed with
wine
Cried out at me that I was no true son
Of Polybus. Oh, I was wroth! That one
Day I kept silence, but the morrow morn
I sought my parents, told that tale of scorn
And claimed the truth; and they rose in
their pride
And smote the mocker . . . Aye, they satis-
fied
All my desire; yet still the cavil gnawed
My heart, and still the story crept abroad.
    At last I rose—my father knew not, nor
My mother—and went forth to Pytho's floor
To ask. And God in that for which I came
Rejected me, but round me, like a flame,
His voice flashed other answers, things of
woe,
Terror, and desolation. I must know
My mother's body and beget thereon
A race no mortal eye durst look upon,
And spill in murder mine own father's blood.
    I heard, and, hearing, straight from where
I stood,

No landmark but the stars to light my way,
Fled, fled from the dark south where Corinth
lay,
To lands far off, where never I might see
My doom of scorn fulfilled. On bitterly
I strode, and reached the region where, so
saith
Thy tale, that King of Thebes was struck to
death. . . .
Wife, I will tell thee true. As one in daze
I walked, till, at the crossing of three ways,
A herald, like thy tale, and o'er his head
A man behind strong horses charioted
Met me. And both would turn me from the
path,
He and a thrall in front. And I in wrath
Smote him that pushed me—'twas a groom
who led
The horses. Not a word the master said,
But watched, and as I passed him on the
road
Down on my head his iron-branchèd goad
Stabbed. But, by heaven, he rued it! In a
flash
I swung my staff and saw the old man crash
Back from his car in blood . . . Then all
of them
I slew.
        Oh, if that man's unspoken name
Had aught of Laius in him, in God's eye
What man doth move more miserable than I,
More dogged by the hate of heaven! No man,
kin
Nor stranger, any more may take me in;
No man may greet me with a word, but all
Cast me from out their houses. And withal
'Twas mine own self that laid upon my life
These curses.—And I hold the dead man's
wife
In these polluting arms that spilt his
soul . . .
Am I a thing born evil? Am I foul
In every vein? Thebes now doth banish me,
And never in this exile must I see
Mine ancient folk of Corinth, never tread

The land that bore me; else my mother's bed
Shall be defiled, and Polybus, my good
Father, who loved me well, be rolled in
    blood.
If one should dream that such a world began
In some slow devil's heart, that hated man,
Who should deny him?—God, as thou art
    clean,
Suffer not this, oh, suffer not this sin
To be, that e'er I look on such a day!
Out of all vision of mankind away
To darkness let me fall ere such a fate
Touch me, so unclean and so desolate!
    Leader. I tremble too, O King; but till
    thou hear
From him who saw, oh, let hope conquer
    fear.
    Oedipus. One shred of hope I still have,
    and therefore
Will wait the herdsman's coming. 'Tis no
    more.
    Jocasta. He shall come. But what further
    dost thou seek?
    Oedipus. This. If we mark him close and
    find him speak
As thou hast, then I am lifted from my
    dread.
    Jocasta. What mean'st thou? Was there
    something that I said . . . ?
    Oedipus. Thou said'st he spoke of rob-
    bers, a great band,
That slaughtered Laius' men. If still he
    stand
To the same tale, the guilt comes not my
    way.
One cannot be a band. But if he say
One lonely loin-girt man, then visibly
This is God's finger pointing toward me.
    Jocasta. Be sure of this. He told the story
    so
When first he came. All they that heard him
    know,
Not only I. He cannot change again
Now. And if change he should, O Lord of
    men,

No change of his can make the prophecy
Of Laius' death fall true. He was to die
Slain by my son. So Loxias spake . . . My
    son!
He slew no man, that poor deserted one
That died . . . And I will no more turn
    mine eyes
This way nor that for all their prophecies.
    Oedipus. Woman, thou counsellest well.
    Yet let it not
Escape thee. Send and have the herdsman
    brought.
    Jocasta. That will I.—Come. Thou know-
    est I ne'er would do
Nor think of aught, save thou wouldst have
    it so.

[*Jocasta and Oedipus go together into the
    Palace.*

        Chorus.
    (*They pray to be free from such great sins
       as they have just heard spoken of.*)
        Strophe.
Toward God's great mysteries, oh, let me
    move
    Unstained till I die
In speech or doing; for the Laws thereof
Are holy, walkers upon ways above,
    Born in the far blue sky;
Their father is Olympus uncreate;
    No man hath made nor told
Their being; neither shall Oblivion set
Sleep on their eyes, for in them lives a great
    Spirit and grows not old.

(*They wonder if these sins be all due to
    pride and if Creon has guilty am-
    bitions.*)
        Antistrophe.
'Tis Pride that breeds the tyrant; drunken
    deep
    With perilous things is she,
Which bring not peace: up, reeling, steep
    on steep

She climbs, till lo, the rock-edge, and the
    leap
    To that which needs must be,

The land where the strong foot is no more
    strong!
    Yet is there surely Pride
That saves a city; God preserve it long!
I judge not. Only through all maze of wrong
    Be God,, not man, my guide.

(*Or if Tiresias can really be a lying prophet
    with no fear of God; they feel that all
    faith in oracles and the things of God
    is shaken.*)
                    Strophe.
Is there a priest who moves amid the altars
    Ruthless in deed and word,
Fears not the presence of his god, nor falters
    Lest Right at last be heard?
If such there be, oh, let some doom be given
    Meet for his ill-starred pride,
Who will not gain his gain where Justice is,
Who will not hold his lips from blasphemies,
Who hurls rash hands amid the things of
    heaven
    From man's touch sanctified.

In a world where such things be,
    What spirit hath shield or lance
To ward him secretly
    From the arrow that slays askance?
If honour to such things be,
    Why should I dance my dance?

                    Antistrophe.
I go no more with prayers and adorations
    To Earth's deep Heart of Stone,
Nor yet the Abantes' floor, nor where the
    nations
    Kneel at Olympia's throne,
Till all this dark be lightened, for the finger
    Of man to touch and know,
O Thou that rulest—if men rightly call
Thy name on earth—O Zeus, thou Lord of
    all

And Strength undying, let not these things
    linger
    Unknown, tossed to and fro.

    For faint is the oracle,
        And they thrust it aside, away;
    And no more visible
        Apollo to save or slay;
    And the things of God, they fail
        As mist on the wind away.

*Jocasta comes out from the Palace followed
    by handmaids bearing incense and
    flowers.*

    Jocasta. Lord of the land, the ways my
        thought hath trod
Lead me in worship to these shrines of God
With flowers and incense flame. So dire a
    storm
Doth shake the King, sin, dread and every
    form
Of grief the world knows. 'Tis the wise
    man's way
To judge the morrow by the yester day;
Which he doth never, but gives eye and ear
To all who speak, will they but speak of
    fear.
    And seeing no word of mine hath power
        to heal
His torment, therefore forth to thee I steal,
O Slayer of the Wolf, O Lord of Light,
Apollo: thou art near us, and of right
Dost hold us thine: to thee in prayer I fall.

She kneels at the altar of Apollo Lukeios.

Oh, show us still some path that is not all
Unclean; for now our captain's eyes are dim
With dread, and the whole ship must follow
    him.

*While she prays a Stranger has entered and
    begins to accost the Chorus.*

    Stranger. Good masters, is there one of
        you could bring
My steps to the house of Oedipus, your
    King?

Or, better, to himself if that may be?
   Leader. This is the house and he within; and she
Thou seest, the mother of his royal seed.

Jocasta rises, anxious, from her prayer.

   Stranger. Being wife to such a man, happy indeed
And ringed with happy faces may she live!
   Jocasta. To one so fair of speech may the Gods give
Like blessing, courteous stranger; 'tis thy due.
But say what leads thee hither. Can we do
Thy wish in aught, or hast thou news to bring?
   Stranger. Good news, O Queen, for thee and for the King.
   Jocasta. What is it? And from what prince comest thou?
   Stranger. I come from Corinth.—And my tale, I trow,
Will give thee joy, yet haply also pain.
   Jocasta. What news can have that two-fold power? Be plain.
   Stranger. 'Tis spoke in Corinth that the gathering
Of folk will make thy lord our chosen King.
   Jocasta. How? Is old Polybus in power no more?
   Stranger. Death has a greater power. His reign is o'er.
   Jocasta. What say'st thou? Dead? . . . Oedipus' father dead?
   Stranger. If I speak false, let me die in his stead.
   Jocasta. Ho, maiden! To our master! Hie thee fast
And tell this tale.

               [The maiden goes.

           Where stand ye at the last
Ye oracles of God? For many a year
Oedipus fled before that man, in fear

To slay him. And behold we find him thus
Slain by a chance death, not by Oedipus.

Oedipus comes out from the Palace.

   Oedipus. Jocasta, thou I love to look upon,
Why call'st thou me from where I sat alone?
   Jocasta. Give ear, and ponder from what this man tells
How end these proud priests and their oracles.
   Oedipus. Whence comes he? And what word hath he for us?
   Jocasta. From Corinth; bearing news that Polybus
Thy father is no more. He has found his death.
   Oedipus. How?—stranger, speak thyself. This that she saith. . . .
   Stranger. Is sure. If that is the first news ye crave,
I tell thee, Polybus lieth in his grave.
   Oedipus. Not murdered? . . . How? Some passing of disease?
   Stranger. A slight thing turns an old life to its peace.
   Oedipus. Poor father! . . . 'tis by sickness he is dead?
   Stranger. The growing years lay heavy on his head.
   Oedipus. O wife, why then should man fear any more
The voice of Pytho's dome, or cower before
These birds that shriek above us? They foretold
Me for my father's murderer; and behold,
He lies in Corinth dead, and here am I
And never touched the sword . . . Or did he die
In grief for me who left him? In that way
I may have wrought his death . . . but come what may,
He sleepeth in his grave and with him all
This deadly seercraft, of no worth at all.
   Jocasta. Dear Lord, long since did I not show thee clear . . . ?

Oedipus. Indeed, yes. I was warped by
mine own fear.

Jocasta. Now thou wilt cast it from thee,
and forget.

Oedipus. Forget my mother? . . . It is
not over yet.

Jocasta. What should man do with fear,
who hath but Chance
Above him, and no sight nor governance
Of things to be? To live as life may run,
No fear, no fret, were wisest 'neath the sun.
And thou, fear not thy mother. Prophets
deem
A deed wrought that is wrought but in a
dream.
And he to whom these things are nothing,
best
Will bear his burden.

Oedipus.   All thou counsellest
Were good, save that my mother liveth still.
And, though thy words be wise, for good or
ill
Her I still fear.

Jocasta.   Think of thy father's tomb!
Like light across our darkness it hath come.

Oedipus. Great light; but while she lives
I fly from her.

Stranger. What woman, Prince, doth fill
thee so with fear?

Oedipus. Meropê, friend, who dwelt with
Polybus.

Stranger. What in Queen Meropê should
fright thee thus?

Oedipus. A voice of God, stranger, of dire
import.

Stranger. Meet for mine ears? Or of some
secret sort?

Oedipus. Nay, thou must hear, and Cor-
inth. Long ago
Apollo spake a doom, that I should know
My mother's flesh, and with mine own hand
spill
My father's blood—'Tis that, and not my
will,
Hath kept me always far from Corinth. So;

Life hath dealt kindly with me, yet men
know
On earth no comfort like a mother's face.

Stranger. 'Tis that, hath kept thee exiled
in this place?

Oedipus. That, and the fear too of my
father's blood.

Stranger. Then, surely, Lord . . . I
came but for thy good . . .
'Twere well if from that fear I set thee free.

Oedipus. Ah, couldst thou? There were
rich reward for thee.

Stranger. To say truth, I had hoped to
lead thee home
Now, and myself to get some good therefrom.

Oedipus. Nay; where my parents are I
will not go.

Stranger. My son, 'tis clear enough thou
dost not know
Thine own road.

Oedipus.   How? Old man, in God's
name, say.

Stranger. If this it is, keeps thee so long
away
From Corinth.

Oedipus.   'Tis the fear lest that word
break
One day upon me true.

Stranger.   Fear lest thou take
Defilement from the two that gave thee birth.

Oedipus. 'Tis that, old man, 'tis that doth
fill the earth
With terror.

Stranger.   Then thy terror all hath been
For nothing.

Oedipus.   How? Were not your King and
Queen
My parents?

Stranger.   Polybus was naught to thee
In blood.

Oedipus. How? He, my father!

Stranger.   That was he
As much as I, but no more.

Oedipus.   Thou art naught;

'Twas he begot me.

Stranger. 'Twas not I begot
Oedipus, neither was it he.

Oedipus. What wild
Fancy, then, made him name me for his
child?

Stranger. Thou wast his child—by gift.
Long years ago
Mine own hand brought thee to him.

Oedipus. Coming so,
From a strange hand, he gave me that great
love?

Stranger. He had no child, and the desire
thereof
Held him.

Oedipus. And thou didst find somewhere—or buy—
A child for him?

Stranger. I found it in a high
Glen of Kithairon.

*Movement of Jocasta, who stands riveted
with dread, unnoticed by the others.*

Oedipus. Yonder? To what end
Wast travelling in these parts?

Stranger. I came to tend
The flocks here on the mountain.

Oedipus. Thou wast one
That wandered, tending sheep for hire?

Stranger. My son,
That day I was the saviour of a King.

Oedipus. How saviour? Was I in some
suffering
Or peril?

Stranger. Thine own feet a tale could
speak

Oedipus. Ah me! What ancient pain stirs
half awake
Within me!

Stranger. 'Twas a spike through both
thy feet.
I set thee free.

Oedipus. A strange scorn that, to greet
A babe new on the earth!

Stranger. From that they fain

Must call thee Oedipus, *"Who-walks-in-
pain."*

Oedipus. Who called me so—father or
mother? Oh,
In God's name, speak!

Stranger. I know not. He should
know
Who brought thee.

Oedipus. So: I was not found by thee.
Thou hadst me from another?

Stranger. Aye; to me
One of the shepherds gave the babe, to bear
Far off.

Oedipus. What shepherd? Know'st thou
not? Declare
All that thou knowest.

Stranger. By my memory, then,
I think they called him one of Laius' men.

Oedipus. That Laius who was king in
Thebes of old?

Stranger. The same. My man did herding
in his fold.

Oedipus. Is he yet living? Can I see his
face?

Stranger (turning to the Chorus). Ye
will know that, being natives to the
place.

Oedipus. How?—Is there one of you
within my pale
Standing, that knows the shepherd of his
tale?
Ye have seen him on the hills? Or in this
town?
Speak! For the hour is come that all be
known.

Leader. I think 'twill be the Peasant Man,
the same,
Thou hast sought long time to see.—His
place and name
Our mistress, if she will, can tell most clear.

Jocasta remains as if she heard nothing.

Oedipus. Thou hear'st him, wife. The
herd whose presence here
We craved for, is it he this man would say?

Jocasta. He saith . . . what of it? Ask
not; only pray
Not to remember. . . . Tales are vainly
told.
   Oedipus. 'Tis mine own birth. How can
   I, when I hold
Such clues as these, refrain from knowing
all?
   Jocasta. For God's love, no! Not if thou
   car'st at all
For thine own life . . . My anguish is
enough.
   Oedipus (*bitterly*). Fear not! . . .
   Though I be thrice of slavish stuff
From my third grand-dam down, it shames
not thee.
   Jocasta. Ask no more. I beseech thee . . .
   Promise me!
   Oedipus. To leave the Truth half-found?
   'Tis not my mood.
   Jocasta. I understand; and tell thee what
   is good.
   Oedipus. Thy good doth weary me.
   Jocasta.   O child of woe,
I pray God, I pray God, thou never know!
   Oedipus (*turning from her*). Go, fetch
   the herdsman straight!—This Queen
   of mine
May walk alone to boast her royal line.
   Jocasta. (*She twice draws in her breath
   through her teeth, as if in some sharp
   pain.*)
Unhappy one, goodbye! Goodbye before
I go: this once, and never never more!

*She comes towards him, then turns and goes
into the palace.*

   Leader. King, what was that? She passed
   like one who flies
In very anguish. Dread is o'er mine eyes
Lest from this silence break some storm of
wrong.
   Oedipus. Break what break will! My mind
   abideth strong
To know the roots, how low soe'er they be,

Which grew to Oedipus. This woman, she
Is proud, methinks, and fears my birth and
name
Will mar her nobleness. But I, no shame
Can ever touch me. I am Fortune's child,
Not man's; her mother face hath ever smiled
Above me, and my brethren of the sky,
The changing Moons, have changed me low
and high.
There is my lineage true, which none shall
wrest
From me; who then am I to fear this quest?

Chorus.
(*They sing of Oedipus as the foundling of
their own Theban mountain, Kithai-
ron, and doubtless of divine birth.*)
Strophe.
If I, O Kithairon, some vision can borrow
   From seercraft, if still there is wit in the
   old,
Long, long, through the deep-orbed Moon
   of the morrow—
   So hear me, Olympus!—thy tale shall be
   told.
O mountain of Thebes, a new Theban shall
   praise thee,
   One born of thy bosom, one nursed at
   thy springs;
And the old men shall dance to thy glory,
   and raise thee
   To worship, O bearer of joy to my kings.
      And thou, we pray,
Look down in peace, O Apollo; I-ê, I-ê!

Antistrophe.
What Oread mother, unaging, unweeping,
   Did bear thee, O Babe, to the Crag-walker
   Pan;
Or perchance to Apollo? He loveth the leap-
   ing
   Of herds on the rock-ways unhaunted of
   man.
Or was it the lord of Cyllênê, who found
   thee,

Or glad Dionysus, whose home is the
height,
Who knew thee his own on the mountain,
as round thee
   The White Brides of Helicon laughed for
delight?
           'Tis there, 'tis there,
The joy most liveth of all his dance and
prayer.
   Oedipus. If I may judge, ye Elders, who
have ne'er
Seen him, methinks I see the shepherd there
Whom we have sought so long. His weight
of years
Fits well with our Corinthian messenger's;
And, more, I know the men who guide his
way,
Bondsmen of mine own house.
                Thou, friend, wilt say
Most surely, who hast known the man of old.
   Leader. I know him well. A shepherd of
the fold
Of Laius, one he trusted more than all.

The Shepherd comes in, led by two thralls.
He is an old man and seems terrified.

   Oedipus. Thou first, our guest from Corinth; say withal
Is this the man?
   Stranger. This is the man, O King.
   Oedipus. (*addressing the Shepherd*). Old
man! Look up, and answer everything I ask
thee.—Thou wast Laius' man of old?
   Shepherd. Born in his house I was, not
bought with gold.
   Oedipus. What kind of work, what way
of life, was thine?
   Shepherd. Most of my days I tended sheep
or kine.
   Oedipus. What was thy camping ground
at midsummer?
   Shepherd. Sometimes Kithairon, sometimes mountains near.
   Oedipus. Saw'st ever there this man thou
seest now?

   Shepherd. There, Lord? What doing?—
What man meanest thou?
   Oedipus (*pointing to the Stranger*). Look!
Hath he ever crossed thy path before?
   Shepherd. I call him not to mind, I must
think more.
   Stranger. Small wonder that, O King! But
I will throw
Light on his memories.—Right well I know
He knows the time when, all Kithairon
through,
I with one wandering herd and he with two,
Three times we neighboured one another,
clear
From spring to autumn stars, a good half-
year.
At winter's fall we parted; he drove down
To his master's fold, and I back to mine
own. . . .
Dost call it back, friend? Was it as I say?
   Shepherd. It was. It was. . . . 'Tis all
so far away.
   Stranger. Say then: thou gavest me once,
there in the wild,
A babe to rear far off as mine own child?
   Shepherd (*his terror returning*). What
does this mean? To what end askest thou?
   Stranger (*pointing to Oedipus*). That
babe has grown, friend. 'Tis our master
now.
   Shepherd. (*He slowly understands, then
stands for a moment horror-struck.*) No, in
the name of death! . . . Fool, hold thy
peace.

   He lifts his staff at the Stranger.

   Oedipus. Ha, greybeard! Wouldst thou
strike him?—'Tis not his
Offences, 'tis thine own we need to mend.
   Shepherd. Most gentle master, how do I
offend?
   Oedipus. Whence came that babe whereof
he questioneth?
   Shepherd. He doth not know . . . 'tis
folly . . . what he saith.

Oedipus. Thou wilt not speak for love;
but pain maybe . . .

Shepherd. I am very old. Ye would not
torture me.

Oedipus. Back with his arms, ye bond-
men! Hold him so.

*The thralls drag back the Shepherd's arms,
ready for torture.*

Shepherd. Woe's me! What have I done?
. . . What wouldst thou know?

Oedipus. Didst give this man the child,
as he doth say?

Shepherd. I did . . . Would God that
I had died this day!

Oedipus. 'Fore heaven, thou shalt yet, if
thou speak not true.

Shepherd. 'Tis more than death and
darker, if I do.

Oedipus. This dog, it seems, will keep us
waiting.

Shepherd.   Nay,
I said at first I gave it.

Oedipus.   In what way
Came it to thee? Was it thine own child, or
Another's?

Shepherd.   Nay, it never crossed my
door:
Another's.

Oedipus. Whose? What man, what
house, of these
About thee?

Shepherd.   In the name of God who
sees,
Ask me no more!

Oedipus.   If once I ask again,
Thou diest.

Shepherd.   From the folk of Laius, then,
It came.

Oedipus. A slave, or born of Laius'
blood?

Shepherd. There comes the word I dread
to speak, O God!

Oedipus. And I to hear: yet heard it
needs must be.

Shepherd. Know then, they said 'twas
Laius' child. But she
Within, thy wife, best knows its fathering.

Oedipus. 'Twas she that gave it?

Shepherd.   It was she, O King.

Oedipus. And bade you. . . what?

Shepherd.   Destroy it.

Oedipus.   Her own child?
Cruel!

Shepherd. Dark words of God had
made her wild.

Oedipus. What words?

Shepherd. The babe must slay his father;
so
'Twas written.

Oedipus.   Why didst thou, then, let him
go
With this old man?

Shepherd.   O King, my heart did bleed.
I thought the man would save him, past all
need
Of fear, to his own distant home . . . And
he
Did save him, to great evil. Verily
If thou art he whom this man telleth of,
Know, to affliction thou art born.

Oedipus.   Enough!
All will come true . . . Thou Light, never
again
May I behold thee, I in the eyes of men
Made naked, how from sin my being grew,
In sin I wedded and in sin I slew!

*He rushes into the Palace. The Shepherd is
led away by the thralls.*

Strophe.

Chorus. Nothingness, nothingness,
        Ye Children of Man, and less
            I count you, waking or dreaming!
        And none among mortals, none,
        Seeking to live, hath won
        More than to seem, and to cease
            Again from his seeming.
        While ever before mine eyes
        One fate, one example, lies—

Thine, thine, O Oedipus, sore
Of God oppressed—
What thing that is human more
Dare I call blessed?

Antistrophe.

Straight his archery flew
To the heart of living; he knew
    Joy and the fulness of power,
O Zeus, when the riddling breath
Was stayed and the Maid of Death
Slain, and we saw him through
    The death-cloud, a tower!

For that he was called my king;
Yea, every precious thing
Wherewith men are honoured, down
    We cast before him,
And great Thebes brought her crown
And kneeled to adore him.

Strophe.

But now, what man's story is such bitterness
    to speak?
What life hath Delusion so visited, and
    Pain,
    And swiftness of Disaster?
    O great King, our master,
How oped the one haven to the slayer and
    the slain?
And the furrows of thy father, did they turn
    not nor shriek,
Did they bear so long silent thy casting of
    the grain?

Antistrophe.

'Tis Time, Time, desireless, hath shown thee
    what thou art;
The long monstrous mating, it is judged
    and all its race.
    O child of him that sleepeth,
    Thy land weepeth, weepeth,
Unfathered. . . . Would God, I had
    never seen thy face!
From thee in great peril fell peace upon my
    heart,

In thee mine eye clouded and the dark is
    come apace.

A Messenger rushes out from the Palace.

Messenger. O ye above this land in
    honour old
Exalted, what a tale shall ye be told,
What sights shall see, and tears of horror
    shed,
If still your hearts be true to them that led
Your sires! There runs no river, well I ween,
Not Phasis nor great Ister, shall wash clean
This house of all within that hideth—nay,
Nor all that creepeth forth to front the day,
Of purposed horror. And in misery
That woundeth most which men have willed
    to be.
    Leader. No lack there was in what we
        knew before
Of food for heaviness. What bring'st thou
    more?
    Messenger. One thing I bring thee first
    . . . 'Tis quickly said.
Jocasta, our anointed queen, is dead.
    Leader. Unhappy woman! How came
        death to her?
    Messenger. By her own hand. . . . Oh,
        of what passed there
Ye have been spared the worst. Ye cannot
    see.
Howbeit, with that which still is left in me
Of mind and memory, ye shall hear her fate.
    Like one entranced with passion, through
        the gate
She passed, the white hands flashing o'er her
    head,
Like blades that tear, and fled, unswerving
    fled,
Toward her old bridal room, and disappeared
And the doors crashed behind her. But we
    heard
Her voice within, crying to him of old,
Her Laius, long dead; and things untold
Of the old kiss unforgotten, that should
    bring

The lover's death and leave the loved a thing
Of horror, yea, a field beneath the plough
For sire and son: then wailing bitter-low
Across that bed of births unreconciled,
Husband from husband born and child from
   child.
And, after that, I know not how her death
Found her. For sudden, with a roar of
   wrath,
Burst Oedipus upon us. Then, I ween,
We marked no more what passion held the
   Queen,
But him, as in the fury of his stride,
"A sword! A sword! And show me here," he
   cried,
"That wife, no wife, that field of blood-
   stained earth
Where husband, father, sin on sin, had
   birth,
Polluted generations!" While he thus
Raged on, some god—for sure 'twas none of
   us—
Showed where she was; and with a shout
   away,
As though some hand had pointed to the
   prey,
He dashed him on the chamber door. The
   straight
Door-bar of oak, it bent beneath his weight,
Shook from its sockets free, and in he burst
To the dark chamber.
                    There we saw her first
Hanged, swinging from a noose, like a dead
   bird.
He fell back when he saw her. Then we
   heard
A miserable groan, and straight he found
And loosed the strangling knot, and on the
   ground
Laid her.—Ah, then the sight of horror
   came!
The pin of gold, broad-beaten like a flame,
He tore from off her breast, and, left and
   right,
Down on the shuddering orbits of his sight

Dashed it: "Out! Out! Ye never more shall
   see
Me nor the anguish nor the sins of me.
Ye looked on lives whose like earth never
   bore,
Ye knew not those my spirit thirsted for:
Therefore be dark for ever!"
                    Like a song
His voice rose, and again, again, the strong
And stabbing hand fell, and the massacred
And bleeding eyeballs streamed upon his
   beard,
Wild rain, and gouts of hail amid the rain.
   Behold affliction, yea, afflictions twain
From man and woman broken, now made
   one
In downfall. All the riches yester sun
Saw in this house were rich in verity.
What call ye now our riches? Agony,
Delusion, Death, Shame, all that eye or ear
Hath ever dreamed of misery, is here.
   Leader. And now how fares he? Doth the
      storm abate?
   Messenger. He shouts for one to open
      wide the gate
And lead him forth, and to all Thebes dis-
   play
His father's murderer, his mother's . . .
   Nay,
Such words I will not speak. And his intent
Is set, to cast himself in banishment
Out to the wild, not walk 'mid human breed
Bearing the curse he bears. Yet sore his need
Of strength and of some guiding hand. For
   sure
He hath more burden now than man may
   endure.
   But see, the gates fall back, and that ap-
      pears
Which he who loathes shall pity—yea, with
   tears.

*Oedipus is led in, blinded and bleeding. The
   Old Men bow down and hide their
   faces; some of them weep.*

Chorus. Oh, terrible! Oh, sight of all
    This life hath crossed, most terrible!
    Thou man more wronged than
      tongue can tell,
  What madness took thee? Do there
    crawl
    Live Things of Evil from the deep
    To leap on man? Oh, what a leap
  Was His that flung thee to thy fall!

Leader. O fallen, fallen in ghastly case.
    I dare not raise mine eyes to thee;
    Fain would I look and ask and see,
  But shudder sickened from thy face.
Oedipus. Oh, pain; pain and woe!
    Whither? Whither?
  They lead me and I go;
    And my voice drifts on the air
    Far away.
  Where, Thing of Evil, where
  Endeth thy leaping hither?
Leader. In fearful ends, which none may
    hear nor say.
    Strophe.
Oedipus. Cloud of the dark, mine own
    For ever, horrible,
    Stealing, stealing, silent, uncon-
      querable,
    Cloud that no wind, no summer
      can dispel!
  Again, again I groan,
  As through my heart together crawl
    the strong
  Stabs of this pain and memories of
    old wrong.
Leader. Yea, twofold hosts of torment hast
    thou there,
  The stain to think on, and the pain to
    bear.

    Antistrophe.
Oedipus. O Friend, thou mine own
    Still faithful, minister
    Steadfast abiding alone of them that
      were,

Dost bear with me and give the
    blind man care?
Ah me! Not all unknown
Nor hid thou art. Deep in this dark a
    call
Comes, and I know thy voice in spite
    of all.
Leader. O fearful sufferer, and could'st
    thou kill
Thy living orbs? What God made blind
    thy will?
    Strophe.
Oedipus. 'Tis Apollo; all is Apollo,
  O ye that love me, 'tis he long time
    hath planned
    These things upon me evilly, evilly,
    Dark things and full of blood.
I knew not; I did but follow
    His way; but mine the hand
      And mine the anguish. What
      were mine eyes to me
      When naught to be seen was
      good?
Leader. 'Tis even so; and Truth doth
    speak in thee.
Oedipus. To see, to endure, to hear words
    kindly spoken,
  Should I have joy in such?
    Out, if ye love your breath,
  Cast me swift unto solitude, unbroken
    By work or touch.
      Am I not charged with death,
      Most charged and filled to the
      brim
      With curses? And what man
      saith
      God hath so hated him?
Leader. Thy bitter will, thy hard calamity,
  Would I had never known nor looked
    on thee!

    Antistrophe.
Oedipus. My curse, my curse upon him,
  That man whom pity held in the wil-
    derness,

Who saved the feet alive from the
    blood-fetter
And loosed the barb thereof!
That babe—what grace was done him,
    Had he died shelterless,
        He had not laid on himself this
           grief to bear,
        And all who gave him love.
Leader. I, too, O Friend, I had been hap-
    pier.
Oedipus. Found not the way to his fa-
    ther's blood, nor shaken
    The world's scorn on his mother,
        The child and the groom
        withal;
But now, of murderers born, of God
    forsaken,
    Mine own sons' brother;
        All this, and if aught can fall
        Upon man more perilous
        And elder in sin, lo, all
        Is the portion of Oedipus.
Leader. How shall I hold this counsel or
    thy mind
True? Thou wert better dead than living
    blind.
Oedipus. That this deed is not well and
    wisely wrought
Thou shalt not show me; therefore school
    me not.
Think, with what eyes hereafter in the place
Of shadows could I see my father's face,
Or my poor mother's? Both of whom this
    hand
Hath wronged too deep for man to under-
    stand.
Or children—born as mine were born, to see
Their shapes should bring me joy? Great
    God! To me
There is no joy in city nor in tower
Nor temple, from all whom, in this mine
    hour,
I that was chief in Thebes alone, and ate
The King's bread, I have made me separate
For ever. Mine own lips have bid the land

Cast from it one so evil, one whose hand
To sin was dedicate, whom God hath shown
Birth-branded . . . and my blood the dead
    King's own!
All this myself have proved. And can I then
Look with straight eyes into the eyes of men?
I trow not. Nay, if any stop there were
To dam this fount that welleth in mine ear
For hearing, I had never blenched nor
    stayed
Till this vile shell were all one dungeon
    made.
Dark, without sound. 'Tis thus the mind
    would fain
Find peace, self-prisoned from a world of
    pain.
    O wild Kithairon, why was it thy will
To save me? Why not take me quick and kill,
Kill, before ever I could make men know
The thing I am, the thing from which I
    grow?
Thou dead King, Polybus, thou city wall
Of Corinth, thou old castle I did call
My father's, what a life did ye begin,
What splendour rotted by the worm within,
When ye bred me! O Crossing of the Roads,
O secret glen and dusk of crowding woods,
O narrow footpath creeping to the brink
Where meet the Three! I gave you blood to
    drink.
Do ye remember? 'Twas my life-blood, hot
From my own father's heart. Have ye forgot
What deed I did among you, and what new
And direr deed I fled from you to do?
O flesh, horror of flesh! . . .
                But what is shame
To do should not be spoken. In God's name,
Take me somewhere far off and cover me
From sight, or slay, or cast me to the sea
Where never eye may see me any more.
    What? Do ye fear to touch a man so sore
Stricken? Nay, tremble not. My misery
Is mine, and shall be borne by none but me.
Leader. Lo, yonder comes for answer to
    thy prayer

Creon, to do and to decree. The care
Of all our land is his, now thou art weak.
    Oedipus. Alas, what word to Creon can I
    speak,
How make him trust me more? He hath
    seen of late
So vile a heart in me, so full of hate.

           Enter Creon

    Creon. Not to make laughter, Oedipus,
    nor cast
Against thee any evil of the past
I seek thee, but . . . Ah God! ye ministers,
Have ye no hearts? Or, if for man there stirs
No pity in you, fear at least to call
Stain on our Lord the Sun, who feedeth all;
Nor show in nakedness a horror such
As this, which never mother Earth may
    touch,
Nor God's clean rain nor sunlight. Quick
    within!
Guide him.—The ills that in a house have
    been
They of the house alone should know or
    hear.
    Oedipus. In God's name, since thou hast
    undone the fear
Within me, coming thus, all nobleness,
To one so vile, grant me one only grace.
For thy sake more I crave it than mine own.
    Creon. Let me first hear what grace thou
    wouldst be shown.
    Oedipus. Cast me from Thebes . . .
    now, quick . . . where none may
    see
My visage more, nor mingle words with me.
    Creon. That had I done, for sure, save
    that I still
Tremble, and fain would ask Apollo's will.
    Oedipus. His will was clear enough, to
    stamp the unclean
Thing out, the bloody hand, the heart of sin.
    Creon. 'Twas thus he seemed to speak;
    but in this sore

Strait we must needs learn surer than be-
    fore.
    Oedipus. Thou needs must trouble God
    for one so low?
    Creon. Surely; thyself will trust his an-
    swer now.
    Oedipus. I charge thee more . . . and,
    if thou fail, my sin
Shall cleave to thee . . . For her who lies
    within,
Make as thou wilt her burial. 'Tis thy task
To tend thine own. But me: let no man ask
This ancient city of my sires to give
Harbour in life to me. Set me to live
On the wild hills and leave my name to
    those
Deeps of Kithairon which my father chose,
And mother, for my vast and living tomb.
As they, my murderers, willed it, let my
    doom
Find me. For this my very heart doth know,
No sickness now, nor any mortal blow,
Shall slay this body. Never had my breath
Been thus kept burning in the midst of
    death,
Save for some frightful end. So, let my way
Go where it listeth.
               But my children—Nay,
Creon, my sons will ask thee for no care.
Men are they, and can find them everywhere
What life needs. But my two poor desolate
Maidens. . . . There was no table ever set
Apart for them, but whatso royal fare
I tasted, they were with me and had share
In all . . . Creon, I pray, forget them not.
And if it may be, go, bid them be brought,

Creon goes and presently returns with the
two princesses. Oedipus thinks he is
there all the time.

That I may touch their faces, and so
    weep . . .
Go, Prince. Go, noble heart! . . .
If I might touch them, I should seem to
    keep

And nōt to have lost them, now mine eyes
    are gone . . .
What say I?
In God's name, can it be I hear mine own
Beloved ones sobbing? Creon of his grace
Hath brought my two, my dearest, to this
    place.
Is it true?
    Creon. 'Tis true. I brought them, for in
      them I know
Thy joy is, the same now as long ago.
    Oedipus. God bless thee, and in this hard
      journey give
Some better guide than mine to help thee
    live.
    Children! Where are ye? Hither; come to
    these
Arms of your . . . brother, whose wild
    offices
Have brought much darkness on the once
    bright eyes
Of him who grew your garden; who, nowise
Seeing nor understanding, digged a ground
The world shall shudder at. Children, my
    wound
Is yours too, and I cannot meet your gaze
Now, as I think me what remaining days
Of bitter living the world hath for you.
What dance of damsels shall ye gather to,
What feast of Thebes, but quick ye shall
    turn home,
All tears, or ere the feast or dancers come?
And, children, when ye reach the years of
    love,
Who shall dare wed you, whose heart rise
    above
The peril, to take on him all the shame
That cleaves to my name and my children's
    name?
God knows, it is enough! . . .
My flowers, ye needs must die, waste things,
    bereft
And fruitless.
            Creon, thou alone art left
Their father now, since both of us are gone

Who cared for them. Oh, leave them not
    alone
To wander masterless, these thine own kin,
And beggared. Neither think of them such
    sin
As ye all know in me, but let their fate
Touch thee. So young they are, so desolate—
Of all save thee. True man, give me thine
    hand,
And promise.

Oedipus and Creon clasp hands.

        If your age could understand,
Children, full many counsels I could give.
But now I leave this one word: Pray to live
As life may suffer you, and find a road
To travel easier than your father trod.
    Creon. Enough thy heart hath poured its
      tears; now back into thine house re-
      pair.
    Oedipus. I dread the house, yet go I must.
    Creon. Fair season maketh all things fair.
    Oedipus. One oath then give me, and I go.
    Creon. Name it, and I will answer thee.
    Oedipus. To cast me from this land.
    Creon. A gift not mine but God's thou
      askest me.
    Oedipus. I am a thing of God abhorred.
    Creon. The more, then, will he grant thy
      prayer.
    Oedipus. Thou givest thine oath?
    Creon. I see no light; and, seeing not, I
      may not swear.
    Oedipus. Then take me hence. I care not.
    Creon. Go in peace, and give these chil-
      dren o'er.
    Oedipus. Ah no! Take not away my
      daughters!

They are taken from him.

    Creon. Seek not to be master more.
Did not thy masteries of old forsake thee
    when the end was near?
    Chorus. Ye citizens of Thebes, behold;
'tis Oedipus that passeth here.

Who read the riddle-word of Death, and
    mightiest stood of mortal men,
And Fortune loved him, and the folk that
    saw him turned and looked again.
Lo, he is fallen, and around great storms and
    the outreaching sea!
Therefore, O Man, beware, and look toward
    the end of things that be,

The last of sights, the last of days; and no
    man's life account as gain
Ere the full tale be finished, and the dark-
    ness find him without pain.

[*Oedipus is led into the house and the doors
close on him.*

4. GREEK POLITICAL THOUGHT

While the Peloponnesian War went on—on the mainland, in the islands, and on the sea—intellectual activity was by no means neglected. The most influential philosophical systems the Greeks have left us were forged in times of trouble, during the century that runs from Pericles to Alexander the Great, by Socrates, his pupil Plato, and Plato's pupil Aristotle. The *polis* provided no ivory towers for philosophers, nor was the pursuit of wisdom an occupation to set a man apart from his fellow citizens. The death of Socrates was due as much to political grudges as to his uncompromising temper. Plato, like Euripides, suffered political exile; Aristotle had to get out of Athens in a hurry when his patron, Alexander, died.

It is not surprising, therefore, that the main interests of these men—their search for the good, the true, and the beautiful—should be closely connected with politics: not only the science of government as such, but the discovery of the best way for men to live in society. Like that of his followers, Socrates's search for truth had an eminently practical purpose—discovering the rules by which man should conduct himself in the world—and to this he applied all the resources of a powerfully analytical mind. Indeed, it was the technique of persistent questioning and the refusal to accept anything without examination which he taught his pupils, that finally got him into trouble, as it is likely to get anyone trying to apply it today. Unfortunately, all his instruction was oral, and so we can approach him only through the work of pupils like Xenophon and Plato.

Xenophon: from the *Memorabilia*

Xenophon (about 434 to 355 B.C.) was a member of a well-to-do, conservative Athenian family, a contemporary of Plato and for a while a fellow student under Socrates. In his pages we find, instead of Plato's subtle brilliance, the matter-of-fact clarity and realism of the country squire. Banished from Athens, he operated for a while as a soldier of fortune and wrote mostly under Spartan patronage. His writings include the most fascinating true adventure story of antiquity, *The Anabasis,* and the *Memorabilia* of Socrates, in which the great philosopher is represented with almost photographic clarity though lacking in the depth which Plato imparts.

From *The Works of Xenophon,* tr. H. G. Dakyns, 4 vols. (London, 1897), III (Part 1).

BOOK I, CHAPTER II

The story is told of Alcibiades—how before the age of twenty he engaged his own guardian Pericles, at that time prime minister of the state, in a discussion concerning laws.

Alc. Please, Pericles, can you teach me what a law is?

Per. To be sure I can.

Alc. I should be so much obliged if you would do so. One so often hears the epithet "law-abiding" applied in a complimentary sense; yet, it strikes me, one hardly deserves the compliment if one does not know what a law is.

Per. Fortunately, there is a ready answer to your difficulty. You wish to know what a law is? Well, those are laws which the majority, being met together in conclave, approve and enact as to what it is right to do, and what it is right to abstain from doing.

Alc. Enact on the hypothesis that it is right to do what is good? or to do what is bad?

Per. What is good, to be sure, young sir, *not* what is bad.

Alc. Supposing it is not the majority, but, as in the case of an oligarchy, the minority, who meet and enact the rules of conduct, what are these?

Per. Whatever the ruling power of the state after deliberation enacts as our duty to do, goes by the name of *law*.

Alc. Then, if a tyrant, holding the chief power in the state, enacts rules of conduct for the citizens, are these enactments law?

Per. Yes, anything which a tyrant as head of the state enacts, also goes by the name of law.

Alc. But Pericles, violence and lawlessness—how do we define them? Is it not when a stronger man forces a weaker to do what seems right to him —not by persuasion but by compulsion?

Per. I should say so.

Alc. It would seem to follow that if a tyrant, without persuading the citizens, drives them by enactment to do certain things,—that is lawlessness?

Per. You are right; and I retract the statement that measures passed by a tyrant without persuasion of the citizens are law.

Alc. And what of the measures passed by a minority, not by persuasion of the majority, but in the exercise of its power only? Are we, or are we not, to apply the term violence to these?

Per. I think that anything which any one forces another to do without persuasion, whether by enactment or not, is violence rather than law.

Alc. It would seem then that everything which the majority, in the exercise of its power over the possessors of wealth, and without persuading them, chooses to enact, is of the nature of violence rather than of law.

To be sure (answered Pericles), adding: At your age we were clever hands at such quibbles ourselves. It was just such subtleties which we used to practice our wits upon; as you do now, if I mistake not.

To which Alcibiades replied: Ah, Pericles, I do wish we could have met in those days, when you were at your cleverest in such matters.

BOOK III, CHAPTER 8

Once when Aristippus set himself to subject Socrates to a cross examination, such as he had himself undergone at the hands of Socrates on a former occasion, Socrates, being minded to benefit those who were with him, gave his answers less in the style of a debater guarding against perversions of his argument, than of a man persuaded of the supreme importance of right conduct.

Aristippus asked him "if he knew of anything good," intending in case he assented and named any particular good thing, like food, or drink, or wealth, or health, or strength, or courage, to point out that the thing named was sometimes bad. But he, knowing that if a thing troubles us, we immediately want that which will put an end to our trouble, answered precisely as it was best to do.

Soc. Do I understand you to ask me whether I know anything good for fever?

Aristip. No (he replied), that is not my question.

Soc. Then for inflammation of the eyes?

Aristip. No, nor yet that.

Soc. Well then, for hunger?

Aristip. No, nor yet for hunger.

Well, but (answered Socrates) if you ask me whether I know of any good thing which is good for nothing, I neither know of it nor want to know. And when Aristippus, returning to the charge, asked him "if he knew of any thing beautiful," he answered: Yes, many things.

Aristip. Are they all like each other?

Soc. On the contrary, they are often as unlike as possible.

Aristip. How then (he asked) can that be beautiful which is unlike the beautiful?

Soc. Bless me! for the simple reason that it is possible for a man who is a beautiful runner to be quite unlike another man who is a beautiful boxer, or for a shield, which is a beautiful weapon for the purpose of defence, to be absolutely unlike a javelin, which is a beautiful weapon of swift and sure discharge.

Aristip. Your answers are no better now than when I asked you whether you knew any good thing. They are both of a pattern.

Soc. And so they should be. Do you imagine that one thing is good and another beautiful? Do not you know that relatively to the same standard all things are at once both beautiful and good? In the first place, virtue is not a good thing relatively to one standard and a beautiful thing relatively to another standard; and in the next place, human beings, on the same principle and relatively to the same standard, are called "beautiful and good"; and so the bodily frames of men relatively to the same standards are seen to be "beautiful and good," and in general all things capable of being used by man are regarded as at once beautiful and good relatively to the same standard— the standard being in each case what the things happen to be useful for.

Aristip. Then I presume even a basket for carrying dung is a beautiful thing?

Soc. To be sure. And a spear of gold is an ugly thing, if for their respective uses —the former is well and the latter ill adapted.

Aristip. Do you mean to assert that the same things may be beautiful and ugly?

Soc. Yes, to be sure; and by the same showing things may be good and bad: as, for instance, what is good for hunger may be bad for fever, and what is good for fever bad for hunger; or again, what is beautiful for wrestling is often ugly for running; and in general everything is good and beautiful when well adapted for the end in view, bad and ugly when ill adapted for the same.

CHAPTER 9

He said that *justice,* moreover, and all other *virtue* is *wisdom.* That is to say, things just, and everything else that is done with virtue, are "beautiful and good"; and neither will those who know these things deliberately choose anything else in their stead; nor will he who lacks the special knowledge of them be able to do them, but even if he makes the attempt will he miss the mark and fail. So the wise alone can perform the things which are "beautiful and good"; they that are unwise cannot, but even if they try they fail. Therefore, since all things just and generally all things "beautiful and good" are wrought with virtue, it is clear that justice and all other virtue is wisdom.

Xenophon on Revenues

Xenophon's pamphlet *On Revenues* was written in 355 B.C., one year after the birth of Alexander the Great, probably at Corinth. The old gentleman had been born in the days of Pericles, had grown up during the Peloponnesian War, had seen Sparta throw away the chance to exercise the leadership she had wrested from Athens, and Thebes lose the brief supremacy she had grasped in turn (371–362). He had lived through stirring times, much of his life an exile from Athens. But he remained an Athenian, and from the country estate that the Spartans had given him, in between hunting and estate management, between the memoirs and histories recalling earlier experiences—of Socrates or of Cyrus, the Persian prince whom he had served —he found time to enter the debates of everyday Athenian politics. It is from this point of view that the essay below deserves our interest, as throwing a useful light on the less exalted problems and circumstances of Greek life.

For myself I hold to the opinion that the qualities of the leading statesmen in a state, whatever they be, are reproduced in the character of the constitution itself.

As, however, it has been maintained by certain leading statesmen in Athens that the recognised standard of right and wrong is as high at Athens as elsewhere, but that, owing to the pressure of poverty on the masses, a certain measure of injustice in their dealing with the allied states could not be avoided; I set myself to discover whether by any manner of means it were possible for the citizens of Athens to be supported solely from the soil of Attica itself, which was obviously the most equitable solution. For if so,

herein lay, as I believed, the antidote at once to their own poverty and to the feeling of suspicion with which they are regarded by the rest of Hellas.

I had no sooner begun my investigation than one fact presented itself clearly to my mind, which is that the country itself is made by nature to provide the amplest resources. And with a view to establishing the truth of this initial proposition I will describe the physical features of Attica.

In the first place, the extraordinary mildness of the climate is proved by the actual products of the soil. Numerous plants which in many parts of the world appear as stunted leafless growths are here

From *The Works of Xenophon,* tr. H. G. Dakyns, 4 vols. (London, 1892) II.

fruit-bearing. And as with the soil so with the sea indenting our coasts, the varied productivity of which is exceptionally great. Again with regard to those kindly fruits of earth which Providence bestows on man season by season, one and all they commence earlier and end later in this land. Nor is the supremacy of Attica shown only in those products which year after year flourish and grow old, but the land contains treasures of a more perennial kind. Within its folds lies imbedded by nature an unstinted store of marble, out of which are chiselled temples and altars of rarest beauty and the glittering splendour of images sacred to the gods. This marble, moreover, is an object of desire to many foreigners, Hellenes and barbarians alike. Then there is land which, although it yields no fruit to the sower, needs only to be quarried in order to feed many times more mouths than it could as corn-land. Doubtless we owe it to a divine dispensation that our land is veined with silver; if we consider how many neighbouring states lie round us by land and sea and yet into none of them does a single thinnest vein of silver penetrate.

Indeed it would be scarcely irrational to maintain that the city of Athens lies at the navel, not of Hellas merely, but of the habitable world. So true is it, that the farther we remove from Athens the greater the extreme of heat or cold to be encountered; or to use another illustration, the traveller who desires to traverse the confines of Hellas from end to end will find that, whether he voyages by sea or by land, he is describing a circle, the centre of which is Athens.

Once more, this land though not literally sea-girt has all the advantages of an island, being accessible to every wind that blows, and can invite to its bosom or waft from its shore all products, since it is peninsular; whilst by land it is the emporium of many markets; as being a portion of the continent.

Lastly whilst the majority of states have barbarian neighbours, the source of many troubles, Athens has as her next-door neighbours civilised states which are themselves far remote from the barbarians.

All these advantages, to repeat what I have said, may, I believe, be traced primarily to the soil and position of Attica itself. But these natural blessings may be added to: in the first place, by a careful handling of our resident alien population. And, for my part, I can hardly conceive of a more splendid source of revenue than lies open in this direction. Here you have a self-supporting class of residents conferring large benefits upon the state, and instead of receiving payment themselves, contributing on the contrary to the gain of the exchequer by the sojourners' tax. Nor, under the term careful handling, do I demand more than the removal of obligations which, whilst they confer no benefit on the state, have an air of inflicting various disabilities on the resident aliens. And I would further relieve them from the obligation of serving as hoplites side by side with the citizen proper; since, beside the personal risk, which is great, the trouble of quitting trades and homesteads is no trifle. Incidentally the state itself would be benefited by this exemption, if the citizens were more in the habit of campaigning with one another, rather than shoulder to shoulder with Lydians, Phrygians, Syrians, and barbarians from all quarters of the world, who form the staple of our resident alien class. Besides the advantage (of so weeding the ranks), it would add a positive lustre to our city, were it admitted that the men of Athens, her sons, have reliance on themselves rather than on foreigners to fight her battles. And further, supposing we offered our resident aliens a share in various other honourable duties, including the cavalry service, I shall be surprised if we do not increase the goodwill of the aliens themselves, whilst at the same time we add distinctly to the strength and grandeur of our city.

In the next place, seeing that there are at present numerous building sites within the city walls as yet devoid of houses, supposing the state were to make free grants of such land to foreigners for building purposes in cases where there could be no doubt as to the respectability of the applicant, if I am not mistaken, the result of such a measure will be that a larger number of persons, and of a better class, will be attracted to Athens as a place of residence.

Lastly, if we could bring ourselves to appoint, as a new government office, a board of guardians of foreign residents like our Guardians of Orphans, with special privileges assigned to those guardians who should show on their books the greatest number of resident aliens,—such a measure would tend to improve the goodwill of the class in question, and in all probability all people without a city of their own would aspire to the status of foreign residents in Athens, and so further increase the revenues of the city.

At this point I propose to offer some remarks in proof of the attractions and advantages of Athens as a centre of commercial enterprise. In the first place, it will hardly be denied that we possess the finest and safest harbourage for shipping, where vessels of all sorts can come to moorings and be laid up in absolute se-

curity as far as stress of weather is concerned. But further than that, in most states the trader is under the necessity of loading his vessel with some merchandise or other in exchange for his cargo, since the current coin has no circulation beyond the frontier. But at Athens he has a choice: he can either in return for his wares export a variety of goods, such as human beings seek after, or, if he does not desire to take goods in exchange for goods, he has simply to export silver, and he cannot have a more excellent freight to export, since wherever he likes to sell it he may look to realise a large percentage on his capital.

Or again, supposing prizes were offered to the magistrates in charge of the market for equitable and speedy settlements of points in dispute to enable any one so wishing to proceed on his voyage without hindrance, the result would be that far more traders would trade with us and with greater satisfaction.

It would indeed be a good and noble institution to pay special marks of honour, such as the privilege of the front seat, to merchants and shipowners, and on occasion to invite to hospitable entertainment those who, through something notable in the quality of ship or merchandise, may claim to have done the state a service. The recipients of these honours will rush into our arms as friends, not only under the incentive of gain, but of distinction also.

Now the greater the number of people attracted to Athens either as visitors or as residents, clearly the greater the development of imports and exports. More goods will be sent out of the country, there will be more buying and selling, with a consequent influx of money in the shape of rents to individuals and dues and customs to the state exchequer. And to secure this augmentation of the revenues, mark you, not the outlay of one single penny; nothing needed beyond one or two philanthropic measures and certain details of supervision.

With regard to the other sources of revenue which I contemplate, I admit, it is different. For these I recognise the necessity of a capital to begin with. I am not, however, without good hope that the citizens of this state will contribute heartily to such an object, when I reflect on the large sums subscribed by the state on various late occasions, as, for instance, when reinforcements were sent to the Arcadians under the command of Lysistratus, and again at the date of the generalship of Hegesileos. I am well aware that ships of war are frequently despatched and that too although it is uncertain whether the venture will be for the better or for the worse, and the only certainty is that the contributor will not recover the sum subscribed nor have any further share in the object for which he gave his contribution.

But for a sound investment I know of nothing comparable with the initial outlay to form this fund. Any one whose contribution amounts to ten minae may look forward to a return as high as he would get on bottomry, of nearly one-fifth, as the recipient of three obols a day. The contributor of five minae will on the same principle get more than a third, while the majority of Athenians will get more than cent per cent on their contribution. That is to say, a subscription of one mina will put the subscriber in possession of nearly double that sum, and that, moreover, without setting foot outside Athens, which, as far as human affairs go, is as sound and durable a security as possible.

Moreover, I am of opinion that if the names of contributors were to be inscribed as benefactors for all time, many foreigners would be induced to contribute, and possibly not a few states, in their desire to obtain the right of inscription; indeed I anticipate that some kings, tyrants, and satraps will display a keen desire to share in such a favour.

To come to the point. Were such a capital once furnished, it would be a magnificent plan to build lodging-houses for the benefit of shipmasters in the neighbourhood of the harbours, in addition to those which exist; and again, on the same principle, suitable places of meeting for merchants, for the purposes of buying and selling; and thirdly, public lodging-houses for persons visiting the city. Again, supposing dwelling-houses and stores for vending goods were fitted up for retail dealers in Piraeus and the city, they would at once be an ornament to the state and a fertile source of revenue. Also it seems to me it would be a good thing to try to see if, on the principle on which at present the state possesses public warships, it would not be possible to secure public merchant vessels, to be let out on the security of guarantors just like any other public property. If the plan were found feasible this public merchant navy would be a large source of extra revenue.

I come to a new topic. I am persuaded that the establishment of the silver mines on a proper footing would be followed by a large increase of wealth apart from the other sources of revenue. And I would like, for the benefit of those who may be ignorant, to point out what the capacity of these mines really is. You will then be in a position to decide how to turn them to better account. It is clear, I presume, to every one that these mines have for a very long time been in active operation; at any rate no one will venture to fix the date at which they first began to be worked. Now in spite of the fact that the silver ore has been dug and carried out for so long a time, I would ask you to note that the mounds of rubbish so shovelled out are but a fractional portion of the series of hillocks containing veins of silver, and as yet unquarried. Nor is the silver-bearing region gradually becoming circumscribed. On the contrary it is evidently extending in wider area from year to year. That is to say, during the period in which thousands of workers have been employed within the mines no hand was ever stopped for want of work to do. Rather, at any given moment, the work to be done was more than enough for the hands employed. And so it is to-day with the owners of slaves working in the mines: no one dreams of reducing the number of his hands. On the contrary, the object is perpetually to acquire as many additional hands as the owner possibly can. The fact is that with few hands to dig and search, the find of treasure will be small, but with an increase of labour the discovery of the ore itself is more than proportionally increased. So much so, that of all operations with which I am acquainted, this is the only one in which no sort of jealousy is felt at a further development of the industry. I may go a step farther; every proprietor of a farm will be able to tell you exactly how many yoke of oxen are sufficient for the estate, and how many farm hands. To send into the field more than the exact number requisite every farmer would consider a dead loss. But in silver mining [operations] the universal complaint is the want of hands. Indeed there is no analogy between this and other industries. With an increase in the number of bronzeworkers articles of bronze may become so cheap that the bronze-worker has to re-

tire from the field. And so again with ironfounders. Or again, in a plethoric condition of the corn and wine market these fruits of the soil will be so depreciated in value that the particular husbandries cease to be remunerative, and many a farmer will give up his tillage of the soil and betake himself to the business of a merchant, or of a shopkeeper, to banking or money-lending. But the converse is the case in the working of silver; there the larger the quantity of ore discovered and the greater the amount of silver extracted, the greater the number of persons ready to engage in the operation. One more illustration: take the case of movable property. No one when he has got sufficient furniture for his house dreams of making further purchases on this head, but of silver no one ever yet possessed so much that he was forced to cry "enough." On the contrary, if ever anybody does become possessed of an immoderate amount he finds as much pleasure in digging a hole in the ground and hoarding it as in the actual employment of it. And from a wider point of view: when a state is prosperous there is nothing which people so much desire as silver. The men want money to expend on beautiful armour and fine horses, and houses, and sumptuous paraphernalia of all sorts. The women betake themselves to expensive apparel and ornaments of gold. Or when states are sick, either through barrenness of corn and other fruits, or through war, the demand for current coin is even more imperative (whilst the ground lies unproductive), to pay for necessaries or military aid.

And if it be asserted that gold is after all just as useful as silver, without gainsaying the proposition I may note this fact about gold, that, with a sudden influx of this metal, it is the gold itself which is depreciated whilst causing at the same time a rise in the value of silver.

The above facts are, I think, conclusive. They encourage us not only to introduce as much human labour as possible into the mines, but to extend the scale of operations within, by increase of plant, etc., in full assurance that there is no danger either of the ore itself being exhausted or of silver becoming depreciated. And in advancing these views I am merely following a precedent set me by the state herself. So it seems to me, since the state permits any foreigner who desires it to undertake mining operations on a footing of equality with her own citizens.

But, to make my meaning clearer on the question of maintenance, I will at this point explain in detail how the silver mines may be furnished and extended so as to render them much more useful to the state. Only I would premise that I claim no sort of admiration for anything which I am about to say, as though I had hit upon some recondite discovery. Since half of what I have to say is at the present moment still patent to the eyes of all of us, and as to what belongs to past history, if we are to believe the testimony of our fathers, things were then much of a piece with what is going on now. No, what is really marvellous is that the state, with the fact of so many private persons growing wealthy at her expense, and under her very eyes, should have failed to imitate them. It is an old story, trite enough to those of us who have cared to attend to it, how once on a time Nicias, the son of Niceratus, owned a thousand men in the silver mines, whom he let out to Sosias, a Thracian, on the following terms. Sosias was to pay him a net obol a day, without charge or deduction, for every slave of the thousand, and be responsible for keeping up the number perpetually at that figure.

So again Hipponicus had six hundred slaves let out on the same principle, which brought him in a net mina a day without charge or deduction. Then there was Philemonides, with three hundred, bringing him in half a mina, and others, I make no doubt there were, making profits in proportion to their respective resources and capital. But there is no need to revert to ancient history. At the present moment there are hundreds of human beings in the mines let out on the same principle. And given that my proposal were carried into effect, the only novelty in it is that, just as the individual in acquiring the ownership of a gang of slaves finds himself at once provided with a permanent source of income, so the state, in like fashion should possess herself of a body of public slaves, to the number, say, of three for every Athenian citizen. As to the feasibility of our proposals, I challenge any one whom it may concern to test the scheme point by point and to give his verdict.

With regard to the price then of the men themselves, it is obvious that the public treasury is in a better position to provide funds than any private individuals. What can be easier than for the Council to invite by public proclamation all whom it may concern to bring their slaves, and to buy up those produced? Assuming the purchase to be effected, is it credible that people will hesitate to hire from the state rather than from the private owner, and actually on the same terms? People have at all events no hesitation at present in hiring consecrated grounds, sacred victims, houses, etc., or in purchasing the right of farming taxes from the state. To ensure the preservation of the purchased property, the treasury can take the same securities precisely from the lessee as it does from those who purchase the right of farming its taxes. Indeed, fraudulent dealing is easier on the part of the man who has purchased such a right than of the man who hires slaves, since it is not easy to see how the exportation of public money is to be detected, when it differs in no way from private money. Whereas it will take a clever thief to make off with these slaves, marked as they will be with the public stamp, and in face of a heavy penalty attached at once to the sale and exportation of them. Up to this point then it would appear feasible enough for the state to acquire property in men and to keep a safe watch over them.

But with reference to an opposite objection which may present itself to the mind of some one: what guarantee is there that, along with the increase in the supply of labourers, there will be a corresponding demand for their services on the part of contractors? It may be reassuring to note, first of all, that many of those who have already embarked on mining operations will be anxious to increase their staff of labourers by hiring some of these public slaves (remember, they have a large capital at stake; and again, many of the actual labourers now engaged are growing old); and secondly, there are many others, Athenians and foreigners alike, who, though unwilling and indeed incapable of working physically in the mines, will be glad enough to earn a livelihood by their wits as superintendents.

Let it be granted, however, that at first a nucleus of twelve hundred slaves is formed. It is hardly too sanguine a supposition that out of the profits alone, within five or six years this number may be increased to at least six thousand. Again, out of that number of six thousand—supposing each slave to bring in an obol a day clear of all expenses—we get a revenue of sixty talents a year. And supposing twenty talents out of this sum laid out on the purchase of more slaves, there will be forty talents left for the state to apply to any other purpose it may find advisable. By the time the round number of ten thousand is reached the yearly income will amount to a hundred talents.

As a matter of fact, the state will receive much more than these figures represent, as any one here will bear me witness who can remember what the dues derived from slaves realised before the troubles at Decelea. Testimony to the same effect is borne by the fact, that in spite of the countless number of human beings employed in the silver mines within the whole period, the mines present exactly the same appearance to-day as they did within the recollection of our forefathers. And once more everything that is taking place to-day tends to prove that, whatever the number of slaves employed, you will never have more than the works can easily absorb. The miners find no limit of depth in sinking shafts or laterally in piercing galleries. To open cuttings in new directions to-day is just as possible as it was in former times. In fact no one can take on himself to say whether there is more ore in the regions already cut into, or in those where the pick has not yet struck. Well then, it may be asked, why is it that there is not the same rush to make new cuttings now as in former times? The answer is, because the people concerned with the mines are poorer nowadays. The attempt to restart operations, renew plant, etc., is of recent date, and any one who ventures to open up a new area runs a considerable risk. Supposing he hits upon a productive field, he becomes a rich man, but supposing he draws a blank, he loses the whole of his outlay; and that is a danger which people of the present time are shy of facing.

It is a difficulty, but it is one on which,

I believe, I can offer some practical advice. I have a plan to suggest, which will reduce the risk of opening up new cuttings to a minimum.

The citizens of Athens are divided, as we all know, into ten tribes. Let the state then assign to each of these ten tribes an equal number of slaves, and let the tribes agree to associate their fortunes and proceed to open new cuttings. What will happen? Any single tribe hitting upon a productive lode will be the means of discovering what is advantageous to all. Or, supposing two or three, or possibly the half of them, hit upon a lode, clearly these several operations will proportionately be more remunerative still. That the whole ten will fail is not at all in accordance with what we should expect from the history of the past. It is possible, of course, for private persons to combine in the same way, and share their fortunes and minimise their risks. Nor need you apprehend, sirs, that a state mining company, established on this principle, will prove a thorn in the side of the private owner, or the private owner prove injurious to the state. But rather like allies who render each other stronger the more they combine, so in these silver mines, the greater number of companies at work the larger the riches they will discover and disinter.

This then is a statement, as far as I can make it clear, of the method by which, with the proper state organisation, every Athenian may be supplied with ample maintenance at the public expense. Possibly some of you may be calculating that the capital requisite will be enormous. They may doubt if a sufficient sum will ever be subscribed to meet all the needs. All I can say is, even so, do not despond. It is not as if it were necessary that every feature of the scheme should be carried out at once, or else there is to be no ad-

vantage in it at all. On the contrary, whatever number of houses are erected, or ships built, or slaves purchased, etc., these portions will begin to pay at once. In fact, the bit-by-bit method of proceeding will be more advantageous than a simultaneous carrying into effect of the whole plan, to this extent: if we set about erecting buildings wholesale we shall make a more expensive and worse job of it than if we finish them off gradually. Again, if we set about bidding for hundreds of slaves at once we shall be forced to purchase an inferior type at a higher cost. Whereas, if we proceed tentatively, as we find ourselves able, we can complete any well-devised attempt at our leisure, and, in case of any obvious failure, take warning and not repeat it. Again, if everything were to be carried out at once, it is we, sirs, who must make the whole provision at our expense. Whereas, if part were proceeded with and part stood over, the portion of revenue in hand will help to furnish what is necessary to go on with. But to come now to what every one probably will regard as a really grave danger, lest the state may become possessed of an over large number of slaves, with the result that the works will be overstocked. That again is an apprehension which we may escape if we are careful not to put into the works more hands from year to year than the works themselves demand. Thus I am persuaded that the easiest method of carrying out this scheme, as a whole, is also the best. If, however, you are persuaded that, owing to the extraordinary property taxes to which you have been subjected during the present war, you will not be equal to any further contributions at present, what you should do is this: during the current year resolve to carry on the financial administration of the state within the limits of a sum equivalent to that which your dues realised before the peace. That done, you are at liberty to take any surplus sum, whether directly traceable to the peace itself, or to the more courteous treatment of our resident aliens and traders, or to the growth of the imports and exports, coincident with the collecting together of larger masses of human beings, or to an augmentation of harbour and market dues: this surplus, I say, however derived, you should take and invest so as to bring in the greatest revenue.

Again, if there is an apprehension on the part of any that the whole scheme will crumble into nothing on the first outbreak of war, I would only beg these alarmists to note that, under the condition of things which we propose to bring about, war will have more terrors for the attacking party than for this state. Since what possession I should like to know can be more serviceable for war than that of men? Think of the many ships which they will be capable of manning on public service. Think of the number who will serve on land as infantry (in the public service) and will bear hard upon the enemy. Only we must treat them with courtesy. For myself, my calculation is, that even in the event of war we shall be quite able to keep a firm hold of the silver mines. I may take it, we have in the neighbourhood of the mines certain fortresses —one on the southern slope in Anaphlystus; and we have another on the northern side in Thoricus, the two being about seven and a half miles apart. Suppose then a third breastwork were to be placed between these, on the highest point of Besa, that would enable the operatives to collect into one out of all the fortresses, and at the first perception of a hostile movement it would only be a short distance for each to retire into safety. In the event

of an enemy advancing in large numbers they might certainly make off with whatever corn or wine or cattle they found outside. But even if they did get hold of the silver ore, it would be little better to them than a heap of stones. But how is an enemy ever to march upon the mines in force? The nearest state, Megara, is distant, I take it, a good deal over sixty miles; and the next closest, Thebes, a good deal nearer seventy. Supposing then an enemy to advance from some such point to attack the mines, he cannot avoid passing Athens; and presuming his force to be small, we may expect him to be annihilated by our cavalry and frontier police. I say, presuming his force to be small, since to march with anything like a large force, and thereby leave his own territory denuded of troops, would be a startling achievement. Why, the fortified city of Athens will be much closer to the states of the attacking parties than they themselves will be by the time they have got to the mines. But, for the sake of argument, let us suppose an enemy to have arrived in the neighbourhood of Laurium; how is he going to stop there without provisions? To go out in search of supplies with a detachment of his force would imply risk, both for the foraging party and for those who have to do the fighting; whilst, if they are driven to do so in force each time, they may call themselves besiegers, but they will be practically in a state of siege themselves.

But it is not the income derived from the slaves alone to which we look to help the state towards the effective maintenance of her citizens, but with the growth and concentration of a thick population in the mining district various sources of revenue will accrue, whether from the market at Sunium, or from the various state buildings in connection with the silver mines, from furnaces and all the rest. Since we must expect a thickly populated city to spring up here, if organised in the way proposed, and plots of land will become as valuable to owners out there as they are to those who possess them in the neighbourhood of the capital.

If, at this point, I may assume my proposals to have been carried into effect, I think I can promise, not only that our city shall be relieved from a financial strain, but that she shall make a great stride in orderliness and in tactical organisation, she shall grow in martial spirit and readiness for war. I anticipate that those who are under orders to go through gymnastic training will devote themselves with a new zeal to the details of the training school, now that they will receive a larger maintenance whilst under the orders of the trainer in the torch race. So again those on garrison duty in the various fortresses, those enrolled as peltasts, or again as frontier police to protect the rural districts, one and all will carry out their respective duties more ardently when the maintenance appropriate to these several functions is duly forthcoming.

But now, if it is evident that, in order to get the full benefit of all these sources of revenue, peace is an indispensable condition,—if that is plain, I say the question suggests itself, would it not be worth while to appoint a board to act as guardians of peace? Since no doubt the election of such a magistracy would enhance the charm of this city in the eyes of the whole world, and add largely to the number of our visitors. But if any one is disposed to take the view, that by adopting a persistent peace policy, this city will be shorn of her power, that her glory will dwindle and her good name be forgotten throughout the length and breadth of Hellas, the view so taken by our friends here is in my poor judgment somewhat unreasonable. For they are surely the happy states, they, in popular language, are most fortune-favoured, which endure in peace the longest season. And of all states Athens is pre-eminently adapted by nature to flourish and wax strong in peace. The while she abides in peace she cannot fail to exercise an attractive force on all. From the mariner and the merchant upwards, all seek her, flocking they come; the wealthy dealers in corn and wine and oil, the owner of many cattle. And not these only, but the man who depends upon his wits, whose skill is to do business and make gain out of artificers of all sorts, artists and artisans, professors of wisdom [sophists], philosophers, and poets, with those who exhibit and popularise their works. And next a new train of pleasure-seekers, eager to feast on everything sacred or secular, which may captivate and charm eye and ear. Or once again, where are all those who seek to effect a rapid sale or purchase of a thousand commodities, to find what they want, if not at Athens?

But if there is no desire to gainsay these views—only that certain people, in their wish to recover that headship which was once the pride of our city, are persuaded that the accomplishment of their hopes is to be found, not in peace but in war, I beg them to reflect on some matters of history, and to begin at the beginning, the Median [war's]. Was it by high-handed violence, or as benefactors of Hellenes, that we obtained the headship of the naval forces, and the trusteeship of the treasury of Hellas? Again, when through the too cruel exercise of her presidency, as men thought, Athens was deprived of her empire, is it not the case that even in those days, as soon as we held aloof from injustice we were once more reinstated by the islanders, of their own free will, as presidents of the naval force? Nay, did not the very Thebans, in return for certain benefits, grant to us Athenians to exercise leadership over them? And at another date the Lacedaemonians suffered us Athenians to arrange the terms of hegemony at our discretion, not as driven to such submission, but in requital of kindly treatment. And to-day, owing to the chaos which reigns in Hellas, if I mistake not, an opportunity has fallen to this city of winning back our fellow-Hellenes without pain or peril or expense of any sort. It is given to us to try to harmonise states which are at war with one another: it is given to us to reconcile the differences of rival factions within those states themselves, wherever existing.

Make it but evident that we are minded to preserve the independence of the Delphic shrine in its primitive integrity, not by joining in any war but by the moral force of embassies throughout the length and breadth of Hellas,—and I for one shall not be astonished if you find our brother Hellenes of one sentiment; and eager under seal of solemn oaths to proceed against those, whoever they may be, who shall seek to step into the place vacated by the Phocians and to occupy the sacred shrine. Make it but evident that you intend to establish a general peace by land and sea, and, if I mistake not, your efforts will find a response in the hearts of all. There is no man but will pray for the salvation of Athens next to that of his own fatherland.

Again, is any one persuaded that, looking solely to riches and money-making, the state may find war more profitable than peace? If so, I cannot conceive a better method to decide that question than to allow the mind to revert to the past history of the state and to note well the sequence of events. He will discover that, in times long gone by, during a period of peace vast wealth was stored up in the acropolis, the whole of which was lavishly expended during a subsequent period of war. He will perceive, if he examines closely, that even at the present time we are suffering from its [war's] ill effects. Countless sources of revenues have failed, or if they have still flowed in, been lavishly expended on a multiplicity of things. Whereas, now that peace is established by sea, our revenues have expanded and the citizens of Athens have it in their power to turn these to account as they like best.

But if you turn on me with the question, "Do you really mean that even in the event of unjust attacks upon our city on the part of any, we are still resolutely to observe peace towards that offender?" I answer distinctly, No! But, on the contrary, I maintain that we shall all the more promptly retaliate on such aggression in proportion as we have done no wrong to any one ourselves, since that will be to rob the aggressor of his allies.

But now if none of these proposals be impracticable or even difficult of execution; if rather by giving them effect we may conciliate further the friendship of Hellas, whilst we strengthen our own administration and increase our fame; if by the same means the people shall be provided with the necessaries of life, and our rich men be relieved of expenditure on war; if with the large surplus to be counted on, we are in a position to conduct our festivals on an even grander scale than heretofore, to restore our temples, to rebuild our forts and docks, and to reinstate in their ancient privileges our priests, our senators, our magistrates, and our knights—surely it were but reasonable to enter upon this project speedily, so that we too, even in our own day, may witness the unclouded dawn of prosperity in store for our city.

But if you are agreed to carry out this plan, there is one further counsel which I would urge upon you. Send to Dodona and to Delphi, I would beg you, and consult the will of Heaven whether such provision and such a policy on our part be truly to the interest of Athens both for the present and for the time to come. If the consent of Heaven be thus obtained,

we ought then, I say, to put a further question: whose special favour among the gods shall we seek to secure with a view to the happier execution of these measures?

And in accordance with that answer, let us offer a sacrifice of happy omen to the deities so named, and commence the work; since if these transactions be so carried out with the will of God, have we not the right to prognosticate some further advance in the path of political progress for this whole state?

Plato: from *The Republic*

In a famous passage of *The Republic*, known as the Parable of the Cave, Plato makes Socrates try to explain something of the higher wisdom with which the ruler of the ideal state (the Republic) should be endowed. Socrates has already told his friend that "until philosophers are kings, or the kings and princes of this world have the spirit and the power of philosophy; until political power and wisdom meet in one, and those commoner natures who follow either to the exclusion of the other are compelled to stand aside, cities will get no rest from troubles and neither will mankind. Then only will this State of ours see the light of day with a good chance of survival."

After this, I said, here is a parable to illustrate the enlightenment or ignorance of our nature: —Imagine human beings living in a sort of underground den, which has a mouth open towards the light and reaching all across the den; they have been here from their childhood, and have their legs and necks chained so that they cannot move, and can only see before them; for the chains are arranged in such a manner as to prevent them from turning round their heads. At a distance above and behind them the light of a fire is blazing, and between the fire and the prisoners there is a track; and you will see, if you look, a low wall built along the track, like the screen which puppet players have

before them, over which they show the puppets.

I see, he said.

And do you see, I said, men passing along the wall carrying vessels, which appear over the wall; also figures of men and animals, made of wood and stone and various materials; and some of the passengers, as you would expect, are talking, and some of them are silent?

That is a strange image, he said, and they are strange prisoners.

Like ourselves, I replied; and they see only their own shadows, or the shadows of one another, which the fire throws on the opposite wall of the cave?

True, he said; how could they see any

From *The Republic of Plato*, tr. B. Jowett (Oxford, 1881).

thing but the shadows if they were never allowed to move their heads?

And of the objects which are being carried in like manner they would only see the shadows?

Yes, he said.

And if they were able to talk with one another, would they not suppose that they were naming what was actually before them?

Very true.

And suppose further that the prison had an echo which came from the other side, would they not be sure to fancy that the voice which they heard was that of a passing shadow?

No question, he replied.

There can be no question, I said, that the truth would be to them just nothing but the shadows of the images.

That is certain.

And now look again, and see how they are released and cured of their folly. At first, when any one of them is liberated and compelled suddenly to go up and turn his neck round and walk and look at the light, he will suffer sharp pains; the glare will distress him, and he will be unable to see the realities of which in his former state he had seen the shadows; and then imagine some one saying to him, that what he saw before was an illusion, but that now he is approaching real being and has a truer sight and vision of more real things,—what will be his reply? And you may further imagine that his instructor is pointing to the objects as they pass and requiring him to name them,—will he not be in a difficulty? Will he not fancy that the shadows which he formerly saw are truer than the objects which are now shown to him?

Far truer.

And if he is compelled to look at the light, will he not have a pain in his eyes which will make him turn away to take refuge in the objects of vision which he can see, and which he will conceive to be clearer than the things which are now being shown to him?

True, he said.

And suppose once more, that he is reluctantly dragged up a steep and rugged ascent, and held fast and forced into the presence of the sun himself, do you not think that he will be pained and irritated, and when he approaches the light he will have his eyes dazzled, and will not be able to see any of the realities which are now affirmed to be the truth?

Not all in a moment, he said.

He will require to get accustomed to the sight of the upper world. And first he will see the shadows best, next the reflections of men and other objects in the water, and then the objects themselves; next he will gaze upon the light of the moon and the stars; and he will see the sky and the stars by night, better than the sun, or the light of the sun, by day?

Certainly.

And at last he will be able to see the sun, and not mere reflections of him in the water, but he will see him as he is in his own proper place, and not in another; and he will contemplate his nature.

Certainly.

And after this he will reason that the sun is he who gives the seasons and the years, and is the guardian of all that is in the visible world, and in a certain way the cause of all things which he and his fellows have been accustomed to behold?

Clearly, he said, he would come to the other first and to this afterwards.

And when he remembered his old dwelling, and the wisdom of the den and his fellow-prisoners, do you not suppose that he would congratulate himself on the change, and pity them?

Certainly, he would.

And if they were in the habit of conferring honours on those who were quickest to observe and remember and foretell which of the shadows went before, and which followed after, and which were together, do you think that he would care for such honours and glories, or envy the possessors of them? Would he not say with Homer, "Better to be a poor man, and have a poor master," and endure anything, rather than to think and live after their manner?

Yes, he said, I think that he would rather suffer anything than live after their manner.

Imagine once more, I said, that such an one coming suddenly out of the sun were to be replaced in his old situation, is he not certain to have his eyes full of darkness?

Very true, he said.

And if there were a contest, and he had to compete in measuring the shadows with the prisoners who have never moved out of the den, during the time that his sight is weak, and before his eyes are steady (and the time which would be needed to acquire this new habit of sight might be very considerable), would he not be ridiculous? Men would say of him that up he went and down he comes without his eyes; and that there was no use in even thinking of ascending: and if any one tried to loose another and lead him up to the light, let them only catch the offender in the act, and they would put him to death.

No question, he said.

This allegory, I said, you may now consider in terms of the previous argument; the prison is the world of sight, the light of the fire is the sun, the ascent and vision of the things above you may truly regard as the upward progress of the soul into

the intellectual world; that is my poor belief, to which, at your desire, I have given expression. Whether I am right or not God only knows; but, whether true or false, my opinion is that in the world of knowledge the idea of good appears last of all, and is seen only with an effort; and, when seen, is also inferred to be the universal author of all things beautiful and right, parent of light and the lord of light in this world, and the source of truth and reason in the other: this is the first great cause which he who would act rationally either in public or private life must behold.

I agree, he said, as far as I am able to understand you.

I should like to have your agreement in another matter, I said. For I would not have you marvel that those who attain to this beatific vision are unwilling to descend to human affairs; but their souls are ever hastening into the upper world in which they desire to dwell; and this is very natural, if our allegory may be trusted.

Certainly, that is quite natural.

And is there anything surprising in one who passes from divine contemplations to human things, misbehaving himself in a ridiculous manner; if, while his eyes are dazzled and before he has become accustomed to the darkness visible, he is compelled to fight in courts of law, or in other places, about the images or shadows of images of justice, and is endeavouring to meet the conceptions of those who have never yet seen the absolute justice?

There is nothing surprising in that, he replied.

Any one who has common sense will remember that the bewilderments of the eyes are of two kinds, and arise from two causes, either from coming out of the light or from going into the light, which is true of the mind's eye, quite as much as of the bodily eye; and he who remembers this when he sees the soul of any one whose vision is perplexed and weak, will not be too ready to laugh; he will first ask whether that soul has come out of the brighter life, and is unable to see because unaccustomed to the dark, or having turned from darkness to the day is dazzled by excess of light. And then he will count the one happy in his condition and state of being, and he will pity the other; or, if he have a mind to laugh at the soul which comes from below into the light, there will be more reason in this than in the laugh which greets the other from the den.

That, he said, is a very just remark.

But if this is true, then certain professors of education must be mistaken in saying that they can put a knowledge into the soul which was not there before, like giving eyes to the blind.

Yes, that is what they say, he replied.

Whereas, I said, our argument shows that the power is already in the soul; and that as the eye cannot turn from darkness to light without the whole body, so too, when the eye of the soul is turned round, the whole soul must be turned from the world of generation into that of being, and become able to endure the sight of being, and of the brightest and best of being—that is to say, of the good.

Very true.

And this is conversion; and the art will be how to accomplish this as easily and completely as possible; not implanting eyes, for they exist already, but giving them a right direction, which they have not.

Yes, he said, that may be assumed.

And hence while the other qualities seem to be akin to the body, being infused by habit and exercise and not originally innate, the virtue of wisdom is part of a divine essence, and has a power which is everlasting, and by this conversion is rendered useful and profitable, and is also capable of becoming hurtful and useless. Did you never observe the narrow intelligence flashing from the keen eye of a clever rogue—how eager he is, how clearly his paltry soul sees the way to his end; he is the reverse of blind, but his keen eye-sight is taken into the service of evil, and he is dangerous in proportion to his intelligence?

Very true, he said.

But what if there had been a circumcision of such natures in the days of their youth; and they had been severed from the leaden weights, as I may call them, with which they are born into the world, which hang on to sensual pleasures, such as those of eating and drinking, and drag them down and turn the vision of their souls about the things that are below—if, I say, they had been released from them and turned round to the truth, the very same faculty in these very same persons would have seen the other as keenly as they now see that on which their eye is fixed.

That is very likely.

Yes, I said; and there is another thing which is likely, or rather a necessary inference from what has preceded, that neither the uneducated and uninformed of the truth, nor yet those who never make an end of their education, will be able ministers of State: not the former, because they have no single aim of duty which is the rule of their actions, private as well as public; nor the latter, because they will not act at all except upon compulsion, fancying that they are already in the islands of the blest.

Very true, he replied.

Then, I said, the business of us who

are the founders of the State will be to compel the best minds to attain that knowledge which has been already declared by us to be the greatest of all—to that eminence they must ascend and arrive at the good, and when they have ascended and seen enough we must not allow them to do as they do now.

What do you mean?

I mean that they remain in the upper world: but this must not be allowed; they must be made to descend again among the prisoners in the den, and partake of their labours and honours, whether they are worth having or not.

But is not this unjust? he said; ought we to give them an inferior life, when they might have a superior one?

You have again forgotten, my friend, I said, the intention of the legislator; he did not aim at making any one class in the State happy above the rest; the happiness was to be in the whole State, and he held the citizens together by persuasion and necessity, making them benefactors of the State, and therefore benefactors of one another; to this end he created them, not that they should please themselves, but they were to be his instruments in binding up the State.

True, he said, I had forgotten that.

Observe then, I said, Glaucon, that there will be no injustice in compelling our philosophers to have a care and providence of others; we shall explain to them that in other States, men of their class are not obliged to share in the toils of politics: and this is reasonable, for they grow up at their own sweet will, and the government would rather not have them. Now the wild plant which owes culture to nobody, has nothing to pay for culture; but we have brought you into the world expressly for this end, that you may be rulers of the hive, kings of yourselves and

of the other citizens. And you have been educated far better and more perfectly than they have, and are better able to share in the double duty. And therefore each of you, when his turn comes, must go down to the general underground abode, and get the habit of seeing in the dark; for all is habit; and when you are accustomed you will see ten thousand times better than those in the den, and you will know what the images are, and of what they are images, because you have seen the beautiful and just and good in their truth. And thus the order of our State will be a waking reality, and not a dream, as is commonly the manner of States; in most of them men are fighting with one another about shadows and are distracted in the struggle for power, which in their eyes is a great good. But the truth is, that the State in which the rulers are most reluctant to govern is best and most quietly governed, and that in which they are most willing, the worst.

Quite true, he replied.

And will our pupils, when they hear this, refuse to share in turn the toils of State, when they are allowed to spend the greater part of their time with one another in the heaven of ideas?

Impossible, he answered; for they are just men, and the commands which we impose upon them are just; there can be no doubt that every one of them will take office as a stern necessity, and not like our present ministers of State.

Yes, my friend, I said; and that is just the truth of the case. If you contrive for your future rulers another and a better life than that of a ruler, then you may have a well-ordered State; for only in the State which offers this will they rule who are truly rich, not in silver and gold, but in virtue and wisdom, which are the true blessings of life. Whereas if they go to the administration of public affairs, poor and hungering after their own private advantage, thinking that hence they are to snatch the good of life, order there can never be; for they will be fighting about office, and the civil and domestic broils which thus arise will be the ruin of the rulers themselves and of the whole State.

Aristotle: from *The Politics*

Aristotle (384–322 B.C.) was born in Stagira on the Thracian peninsula, son of a physician at the court of Macedon. He studied in Athens under Plato, spent some years as tutor to the future emperor, Alexander, and then returned to found his own school in Athens, the Lyceum. To Plato's concern with the ideal state, Aristotle added the idea of the possible based on examination of things as they are. *The Politics,* chapters from which are quoted below in the translation of J. E. C. Welldon, reflects this empirical approach, as it does the Greek attitude towards the *polis* in general.

THE PURPOSE OF THE STATE

Seeing that every state is a sort of association and every association is formed for the attainment of some Good—for some presumed Good is the end of all action—it is evident that, as some Good is the object of all associations, so in the highest degree is the supreme Good the object of that association which is supreme and embraces all the rest, in other words, of the State or political association.

Now it is wrong to confound, as some do, the functions of the constitutional statesman, king, householder and slavemaster. They hold that the difference between them is not one of kind, but depends simply upon the number of persons ruled, i.e. that a man is a slavemaster if he has but few subjects; if he has more, a householder; if still more, a constitutional statesman or king, there being no distinction between a large household and a small State; also that a man is either a king or a constitutional statesman according as he governs absolutely or in conformity to the laws of political science, being alternately ruler and subject. Such

an opinion is erroneous. Our meaning will be clear, however, if we follow our usual method of investigation. For as in other cases we have to analyse a compound whole into the uncompounded elements which are its least parts, so in examining the constituents of a State we shall incidentally best ascertain the points of difference between the above mentioned forms of government and the possibility of arriving at a scientific conclusion in regard to each of them.

Here, as elsewhere, the best system of examination will be to begin at the beginning and observe things in their growth.

There are certain primary essential combinations of those who cannot exist independently one of another. Thus male and female must combine in order to procreate children, nor is there anything deliberate or arbitrary in their so doing; on the contrary, the desire of leaving an offspring like oneself is natural to man as to the whole animal and vegetable world. Again, natural rulers and subjects combine for safety, and when I say "nat-

From *The Politics of Aristotle,* tr. J. E. C. Welldon (London, 1883), Book I, Chaps. 1, 2; Book III, Chap. 1; 6–9.

ural" I mean that there are some persons qualified intellectually to form projects, and these are natural rulers or natural masters; while there are others qualified physically to carry them out, and these are subjects or natural slaves, so that the interests of master and slave are coincident.

Now Nature has differentiated females from slaves. None of Nature's products wears a poverty-stricken look like the Delphian knife, as it is called, that cutlers make [a many-purpose knife, not very good for any]; each has a single definite object on the principle that any instrument admits of the highest finish, only if it subserves a single purpose rather than several. Among non Greek peoples on the other hand females and slaves stand on one and the same footing. The reason is that natural rulers do not exist among them, and the association they form consists of none but slaves male and female; hence the poet says: " 'Tis meet Greeks rule barbarians," implying the natural identity of barbarians or non Greeks and slaves.

But to resume: the associations of male and female, master and slave, constitute the primary form of household, and Hesiod was right when he wrote: "Get thee first house and wife and ox to plough withal," for an ox is to the poor what a servant is to the rich.

Thus the association naturally formed for the supply of everyday wants is a household; its members, according to Charondas, are "those who eat of the same store," or, according to the Cretan Epimenides, "those who sit around the same hearth."

Again, the simplest association of several households for something more than ephemeral purposes is a village. It seems that the village in its most natural form is derived from the household, including all the children of certain parents, and the children's children or, as the phrase sometimes is, "all who are suckled upon the same milk."

This is the reason why States were originally governed by kings, as is still the case with uncivilized peoples; they were composed of units accustomed to this form of government. For as each household is under the kingly government of its eldest member, so were also the offshoot-households as comprising none but blood relations. It is this condition of things that Homer means when he describes the Cyclops as "lawgivers each of his own wives and children," in allusion to their want of corporate life. This patriarchal government was universal in primitive times; in fact, the reason why all nations represent the polity of the Gods as monarchical is that such originally was, if it is not still, their own polity, and men assimilate the lives no less than the bodily form of the Gods to their own.

Lastly, the association composed of several villages in its complete form is the State, in which the goal of full independence may be said to be first attained. For as the State was formed to make life possible, so it exists to make life good. Consequently if it be allowed that the simple associations, i.e. the household and the village, have a natural existence, so has the State in all cases; for in the State they attain complete development, and Nature implies complete development, as the Nature of anything, e.g. of a man, a house, or a horse, may be defined to be conditioned when the process of production is complete. Or the naturalness of the State may be proved in another way: the object proposed or the complete development of a thing is its highest Good; but independence which is first attained in the State is a complete development or the highest Good and is therefore natural.

Thus we see that the State is a natural institution, that Man is naturally a political animal and that one who is not a citizen of any State, if the cause of his isolation be natural and not accidental, is either a superhuman being or low in the scale of civilization, as he stands alone like a blot "on the backgammon board." The "clanless, lawless, heartless" man so bitterly described by Homer is a case in point; for he is naturally a citizen of no State and a lover of war. Also that Man is a political animal in a higher sense than a bee or any other gregarious creature is evident from the fact that Nature, as we are fond of asserting, creates nothing without a purpose and Man is the only animal endowed with speech. Now mere sounds serve to indicate sensations of pain and pleasure and are therefore a sign to other animals as to Man; for their nature does not advance beyond the point of perceiving pain and pleasure and signifying these perceptions to one another. The object of speech on the other hand is to indicate advantage and disadvantage and therefore also justice and injustice. For it is a special characteristic which distinguishes Man from all other animals that he alone enjoys perception of good and evil, justice and injustice, and the like. But these are the principles of that association which constitutes a household or a State.

Again, in the order of Nature the State is prior to the household or the individual. For the whole must needs be prior to its parts. For instance, if you take away the body which is the whole, there will not remain any such thing as a foot or a hand, unless we use the same word in a different sense as when we speak of a stone hand as a hand. For a hand separated from the body will be a disabled hand; whereas it is the function or faculty of a thing which makes it what it is, and therefore when things lose their function or faculty it is not correct to call them the same things but rather homonymous, i.e. different things having the same name.

We see then that the State is a natural institution, and also that it is prior to the individual. For if the individual as a separate unit is not independent, he must be a part and must bear the same relation to the State as other parts to their wholes; and one who is incapable of associations with others, or is independent and has no need of such association, is no member of a State, in other words he is either a brute or a God. Now the impulse to political association is innate in all men. Nevertheless the author of the first combination, whoever he was, was a great benefactor of humankind. For Man, as in his condition of complete development, i.e. in the State, he is the noblest of all animals, so apart from law and justice he is the vilest of all. For justice is always most formidable when it is armed; and Nature has endowed Man with arms which are intended to subserve the purpose of prudence and virtue but are capable of being wholly turned to contrary ends. Hence if Man be devoid of virtue, no animal is so unscrupulous or savage, none so sensual, none so gluttonous. Just action, on the other hand, is bound up with the existence of a State; for the administration of justice is an ordinance of the political association and the administration of justice is nothing else than the decision of what is just.

THE NATURE OF THE STATE

In any inquiry into the nature and character of particular polities we may say that the first point to be considered is the nature of the State. At present there is often a difference of opinion, as one party asserts that it is the State which has done a certain action, and another that it is not the State but the Oligarchy, or the Tyrant, by whom it was governed. Also it is necessary to settle this point, as a State is the sphere in which all the activity of a statesman or legislator is displayed, and the polity itself is nothing more than a certain order of the inhabitants of the State. But as the State belongs to the category of compound things, like anything else which is a whole but composed of many parts, it is clear that we must first investigate the conception of the citizen; for the State is composed of a number of citizens. We have to inquire then to whom the title "citizen" belongs, or, in other words, what is the nature of a citizen. For the conception of the citizen as of the State is often disputed, nor is the world agreed in recognizing the same person as a citizen. Thus it often happens that one who is a citizen in a Democracy is not a citizen in an Oligarchy.

Now putting out of sight persons who acquire the title of citizen in some exceptional way, e.g. honorary citizens, we may lay it down that it is not residence which constitutes a citizen, as the qualification of residence belongs equally to aliens settled in the country and to slaves. Nor again does citizenship consist simply in the participation in legal rights to the extent of being party to an action as defendant or plaintiff, for this is a qualification possessed equally by the members of different States who associate on the basis of commercial treaties. (It may be observed that in many places resident aliens are not admitted to the full enjoyment even of these legal rights, but are obliged to put themselves under the protection of a pa-tron. It is only in a certain imperfect sense then that they are members of an association so constituted.) Such persons on the contrary are much in the same position as children who are too young to be entered upon the register of the deme or old men who are exempted from civil duties; for although these classes are to be called citizens in a certain sense, it is not in a sense quite absolute and unlimited, but with some such qualifying word as "immature" or "superannuated" or the like, it does not matter what. Our meaning at least is plain; we want a definition of the citizen in the absolute sense, one to whom no such exception can be taken as makes it necessary to correct our definition. For difficulties of a similar kind may be discussed and settled respecting persons who have been disfranchised or exiled. There is nothing whereby a citizen in the absolute sense is so well defined as by participation in judicial power and public office. But the offices of State are of two kinds. Some are determinate in point of time; thus there are certain offices which may never in any circumstances or may only after certain definite intervals be held a second time by the same person. Other officers again are perpetual, e.g. jurors and members of the Public Assembly. It will be objected perhaps that jurors and members of the Public Assembly are not officers of State at all and that their functions do not invest them with an official status; although it is ridiculous to deny the title of "officers" to the supreme authorities in the State. But this matter we may regard as unimportant; it is a mere question of name. The fact is that there is no word to express rightly the common function of a juror and a member of the Public Assembly. Let us call it for distinction's sake a perpetual office. Citizens, then, we may define as those who participate in judicial and deliberative office.

This is perhaps the definition of a citizen which is most appropriate to all who are so called. It is to be observed however that, where things included under a general head are specifically different and one is conceived of as first, another as second, and another as third, there is either no characteristic whatever in common to them all as such, or the common characteristic exists only in a slight degree. But polities, as we see, differ specifically from each other, some are later and others earlier; for the corrupt or perverted forms are necessarily later than the uncorrupted. What we mean by perverted forms will appear hereafter. It follows then that the citizen in each polity must also be different. Accordingly it is principally to the citizen in a Democracy that our definition applies; it is possibly true in the other polities, but not necessarily. For in some there is no democratical element, nor are there any regular public assemblies but only extraordinary ones, and the administration of justice is divided among various boards as, e.g. at Lacedaemon, where different civil cases are decided by different Ephors, cases of homicide by the Senate, and no doubt other cases by some other magistracy. It is the same at Carthage, where all suits are tried by certain magistrates. However, we need not give up our definition of citizen as it admits of correction. For in all polities except Democracy the right of voting in the Assembly and of acting as jurors belongs not to perpetual officers but to persons whose term of office is strictly defined; as it is either to such officers collectively or to some of them that judicial and deliberative functions, whether upon all or upon certain matters only, are assigned.

Thus we see clearly the nature of the citizen. One who enjoys the privilege of participation in deliberative or judicial office, he only is, according to our definition, a citizen of the State in question, and a State is in general terms such a number of persons thus qualified as is sufficient for an independent life.

DIFFERENT POLITIES

We have next to consider whether it is right to assume a single polity or several and, if several, what is the nature of each, and how many there are, and what are the points of distinction between them. A polity may be defined as an order of the State in respect of its offices generally, and especially of the supreme office. For the governing class is everywhere supreme in the State, and the nature of the polity is determined by the governing class. I mean, e.g. that it is the commons who are supreme in a Democracy, and the Few on the other hand in an Oligarchy, and accordingly we call their polities distinct. The same remark may be extended to all the rest; if the governing class is different, so is the polity.

We must begin by laying down (1) the object for which a State is framed and (2) the various kinds of rule which may be exercised over man in his social existence.

It has been stated at the very outset of our treatise . . . that Man is naturally a political animal, and consequently even where there is no need of mutual service, men are nonetheless anxious to live together. Still, it cannot be denied that the common advantage of all is also a motive of union, more or less operative according to the degree in which each individual is capable of the higher life. Although to the citizens, both collectively and individually, this higher life is emphatically the end proposed, yet life itself is also an object for which they unite and maintain the corporate political association; for it is probable that some degree of the higher life is necessarily implied in merely living, unless there is a great preponderance of hardship in the life. Certain it is that the majority of men endure much suffering without ceasing to cling to life, a proof that a certain happiness or natural sweetness resides in it.

It is because the object of political rule is the benefit of the subjects that in any State framed on the principle of equality and similarity among the citizens a claim is put forward for an alteration of rule. It was originally claimed, as is natural enough, that all should serve the State in turn, and that, as each citizen during his period of rule or office had already paid regard to the interest of another, so that other should in turn pay regard to his. But nowadays the profits derivable from the public service and an official status create a desire for perpetuity of office; it is as though the officers of State, being invalids, were to enjoy good health during all their term of power, in which case it is probable that they would be equally eager for office.

It is evident then that all such polities as regard the good of the community are really normal according to the principle of abstract justice, while such as regard the private good of the rulers are all corruptions or perversions of the normal polities; for the relations of rulers to the subjects in them are like the relations of a master to his slaves, whereas the State is properly a society of free persons.

Having now settled these points, we have next to consider the number of different polities and their nature. We will begin with the normal polities; for when they are determined the perverted forms will be evident at once.

As in any State the polity and the governing class are virtually the same, i.e. the polity is determined by the governing class, as the governing class is the supreme authority in a State, and as supreme power must be vested either in an individual or in a Few, or in the Many, it follows that when the rule of the individual, or the Few, or the Many, is exercised for the benefit of the community at large, the polities are normal, whereas the polities which subserve the private interest either of the individual or the Few or the masses are perversions; for either the members of the State do not deserve the name of citizens, or they ought to have a share in its advantages. The form of Monarchy in which regard is paid to the interest of the community is commonly known as Kingship, and the government of the Few, although of a number exceeding one, for the good of all, as Aristocracy, whether because the rule is in the hands of the best citizens or because they exercise it for the best interests of the State and all its members; while when it is the masses who direct public affairs for the interest of the community, the government is called by the name which is common to all the polities, viz. a Polity. The result in this case is such as might have been expected. For although it is possible to find an individual or a few persons of eminent virtue, it can hardly be the case that a large number are perfectly accomplished in every form of virtue; at the best they will only be accomplished only in military virtue, as it is the only one of which the masses are capable. The consequence is that in this polity, viz. the Polity proper, the military class is supreme, and all who bear arms enjoy full political privileges.

As perverted forms of the polities just mentioned we have Tyranny by the side of Kingship, Oligarchy of Aristocracy, and Democracy of Polity. For Tyranny is monarchical rule for the good of the Monarch; Oligarchy the rule of a Few for the good of the wealthy; and Democracy the rule of the Many for the good of the poor; none of them subserve the interest of the community at large. . . .

The really distinctive characteristics of Democracy and Oligarchy are poverty and wealth; and it is a necessary law that wherever wealth constitutes the title to rule, whether the rulers are a minority or a majority, the polity is an Oligarchy, whereas if the poor are rulers, it is a Democracy. But as a matter of fact, it happens, as we said, that in the one case the rulers are few, and in the other many; for there are only few people who are wealthy, whereas liberty is enjoyed by all alike, and wealth and liberty are the grounds upon which the two parties respectively base their claim to be masters of the polity.

In endeavoring to estimate the claims of the two parties, we must first ascertain what are the definitions they give of Oligarchy and Democracy, and what is the principle of justice characteristic of the one or the other. For Oligarchs and Democrats agree in this, that they both adhere to a certain principle of justice; but they do not advance beyond a certain point or put forward a full statement of justice in the proper sense of the word. Thus the one party, i.e. the Democrats, hold that justice is equality; and so it is, but not for all the world, but only for equals. The others, i.e. the Oligarchs, hold that in-equality is just, as indeed it is, but not for all the world, but only for unequals. Both put out of sight one side of the relation, viz. the persons who are to enjoy the equality or inequality, and consequently form a wrong judgment. The reason is that they are judging of matters which affect themselves, and we are all sorry judges when our personal interests are at stake. And thus whereas justice is a relative term and . . . implies that the ratio of distribution is constant in respect of the things distributed and the persons who receive them, the two parties, while they are of one mind about the equality of the thing, differ as to what constitutes equality in the recipients, principally for the reason just alleged, viz. that they are bad judges where their own interests are concerned, but secondly also because the fact that each maintains a certain principle of justice up to a certain point is one which itself leads them to suppose that they are maintaining a principle of justice in the absolute sense. For the Oligarchs, if they are superior in a particular point, viz. in money, assume themselves to be superior altogether; while the Democrats, if they are equal in a particular point, viz. in personal liberty, assume themselves to be equal altogether. But they omit the point of capital importance. If a multitude of possessions was the sole object of their association or union, then their share in the State is proportionate to their share in the property, and in this case there would seem to be no resisting the argument of the Oligarchical party that, where there is, e.g. a capital of one hundred *minae* the contributor of a single *mina* ought not, in justice, to enjoy the same share either of the principal or of the profits accruing as a person who has given the remaining ninety-nine. But the truth is that the object of their association is to live well, not merely to live; otherwise slaves and the lower animals might form a State, whereas this is in fact impossible, as they are incapable of happiness or of a life regulated by a definite moral purpose, i.e. of the conditions necessary to a State. Nor is the object military alliance and security against injury from any quarter. Nor again is the end proposed barter and intercommunion; for, if it were, the Tyrrhenians and Carthaginians and such nations as are connected by commercial treaties might be regarded as citizens of a single State. Among them there certainly exist contracts in regard to Customs, covenants against mutual injury, and formal articles of alliance. But there are no magistracies common to all the contracting parties instituted to secure these objects, but different magistracies exist in each of the States; nor do the members of the one feel concerned about the right character of members of the other or about the means of preserving all who come under the treaties from being unjust and harboring any kind of wickedness or indeed about any point whatever, except the prevention of mutually injurious actions. Virtue and vice on the other hand are matters of earnest consideration to all whose hearts are set upon good and orderly government. And from this fact it is evident that a State which is not merely nominally but in the true sense of the word a State should devote its attention to virtue. To neglect virtue is to convert the political association into an alliance differing in nothing except in the local contiguity of its members from the alliances formed between distant States, to convert the law into a mere covenant or, as the sophist Lycophron said, a mere surety for the mutual respect of rights, without any qualification for producing goodness or justice in the citizens. But it is clear that this is the true view of the State, i.e. that it promotes the virtue of its citizens. For if we were to combine different localities in one so that, e.g. the walls of Megara and Corinth were contiguous, yet the result would not be a single State. Nor again does the practice of intermarriage necessarily imply a single State, although intermarriage is one of the forms of association which are especially characteristic of States. So too if we suppose the case of certain persons living separately, although not so far apart as to prevent association, but under laws prohibitive of mutual injury in the exchange of goods, if we suppose, e.g. A to be a carpenter, B a husbandman, C a cobbler, D something else, and the total to amount to 10,000, but their association to be absolutely confined to such things as barter and military alliance, here again there would certainly not be a State. What then is the reason? It is assuredly not the absence of local contiguity in the association. For suppose the members were actually to form a union upon such terms of association as we have described, suppose at the same time that each individual were to use his own household as a separate State, and their intercourse were limited as under the condition of a defensive alliance to rendering mutual assistance against aggression, still the conception of a State in the strict view would not even then be realized, if their manner of social dealings after the union were to be precisely the same as when they lived apart.

It is clear then that the State is not merely a local association or an association existing to prevent mutual injury and to promote commercial exchange. So far is this from being the case that, although these are indispensable conditions, if a State is to exist, yet all these conditions do not necessarily imply a State. A State on the contrary is first realized when there is an association of households and families in living well, with a view to a complete and independent existence. . . . It is for this reason that there were established in different States matrimonial connections, clanships, common sacrifices, and such amusements as promote a common life. But all this is the work of friendship, for the choice of a common life implies no more than friendship. And thus while the end of a State is living well, these are only means to the end. A State, on the contrary, is the association of fami-

lies and villages in a complete and independent existence or in other words, according to our definition, in a life of felicity and nobleness. We must assume then that the object of the political association is not merely a common life but noble action. And from this it follows that they who contribute most to the association, as so conceived, possess a larger interest in the State than they who are equal or superior in personal liberty, or birth, but inferior in political virtue, or than they who have the superiority in wealth but the inferiority in virtue.

5. GREEK PHILOSOPHY: EPICUREANS AND STOICS

The great philosophic schools of the Hellenistic period grew out of the teaching of two contemporaries, Zeno and Epicurus. Zeno was a Phoenician born in Cyprus in the second half of the fourth century B.C., who made Socrates his chief inspiration and whose system found the supreme good in the effort to follow only reason, while remaining indifferent to external circumstances (chance, health, pain, etc.). Virtue is the only good and, since virtue depends upon will, everything really good or bad in a man's life depends upon himself. But virtue is a social characteristic, and it is a man's duty to do his best in public affairs. Stoicism had a long history, and Romans like Cicero, Seneca, and Marcus Aurelius were Stoics. But, by Seneca's time (*see· below*) the argument had been developed that the philosopher can be more socially useful by staying home, thinking and writing, than by public activity where his influence would, at best, be limited.

Epicurus was born in 342 B.C., son of a poor Athenian colonist on the island of Samos. He died in Athens in 270 B.C., having developed the principles of a philosophy designed chiefly to secure tranquillity. "Pleasure," he said, "is the beginning and the end of the blessed life"; and virtue is really "prudence in the pursuit of pleasure." The goal of man is personal satisfaction; above all, perhaps, that avoidance of pain which is the purest pleasure. Public life should be shunned.

Lucretius: from *On the Nature of Things*

The most eminent disciple of Epicurus was the poet Lucretius (96–55 B.C.), a contemporary of Julius Caesar. In his great poem, *On the Nature of Things,* he announced his purpose of freeing men from their superstitions, their fears of gods, and their terror of death by offering naturalistic explanations of all phenomena. Man

From Lucretius: *On the Nature of Things,* tr. Thomas Busby, Book V.

has come a long way from crude beginnings and is destined to go forward to even greater achievements. But he has to trust himself.

The great German historian Mommsen had this to say about Lucretius's work: "Of all the views of the world possible to a poetical mind in the Caesarean age this was the noblest and most ennobling, that it is a benefit for men to be released from a belief in the immortality of the soul, and thereby from the evil dread of death which steals over them like terror over children in a dark room." More positively, however, the great poem seems to reiterate the tough but somber philosophy of the ancient Hebrew sage: "Whatsoever thy hand findeth to do, do it with thy might; for there is no work, nor knowledge, nor wisdom in the grave, whither thou goest."

Huge the first race of men, their limbs well strung,
Hardy as hardy earth from which they sprung;
On strong and massy bones their structure rose,
Firm as the firmest oak that towering grows:
Nor heat nor cold they felt, nor weakness knew,
Nor from voluptuous feasts diseases drew;
Through long revolving years on nature thrived,
And, wildly bold, in savage freedom lived.
No sturdy husbandmen the land prepare,
Plant the young stocks, or guide the shining share:
For future crops the seed no sower throws,
Nor dresser clips the wild luxuriant boughs.
What earth spontaneous gave, and sun and showers,
Careless they took, and propt their nervid powers;
Their giant energies with acorns fed,
Wild summer apples, indurate and red:
Such in our wintry orchards sparing hang;
But larger theirs, and more abundant, sprang.
Earth in her primal strength these things bestowed,
With rich fecundity her bosom glowed;
O'er her broad surface various plenty reigned;
Her voluntary gifts man's race sustained.

Thus by her fruits the human race was nursed;
And springs and rivers slaked their parching thirst;
Called them, as now the fall from pouring heights
The thirst afflicted savage tribes invites.
For nightly roofs to hollow caves they hied,
Or with their gods in sylvan fanes reside;
Whence a sweet spring in silvery drops distills,
And rolls o'er polished stones, its bubbling rills;
O'er polished stones, and mossy greens they flow,
Meandering through the fertile vales below.
As yet, no fire their simple food prepared;
Nor spoils of beasts their hardened bodies shared:
Naked among the rocks and woods they ran,
And hollow mountains formed the abodes of man.
Shelter from winds and rains in groves they sought,
And nature's wants supplied as nature taught.
No common good they felt, no laws ordained,
Nor public justice private wrong restrained;
What power or fortune offered, no one spared;
Each his own welfare sought, nor further cared.

Then Venus' fire was all the lover's law,
And groves and woods the consummation
  saw;
Or mutual flames inspired the burning pair;
Or manhood's force compelled the unwilling
  fair;
Or softening presents taught her heart to
  yield;
Berries or acorns, fresh from bower or field.
  Bold in their native vigor, men pursued
With flying feet the fierce and savage brood;
With missile weapons urged the hardy chase;
And stones and clubs subdued the brutal
  race.
Some they hunt down, some their swift
  staves o'ertake,
Others they fled, and sought the sheltering
  brake,
When night o'ertook them with her sable
  shades,
Like bristly boars they pressed the grassy
  glades,
In leaves enwrapt; nor mourned the absent
  light,
Nor wandered through the darkness of the
  night;
But, in soft sleep dissolved, contented lay
Till rosy dawn proclaimed expected day:
For observation from their childhood taught
That day the night, and night the morning,
  brought.
Hence, they ne'er dreaded an eternal night,
But woke to hail the sure return of light:
Yet feared, lest prowling beasts that shun
  the day,
Should fall destructive on their human prey:
Roused from their sleep, and filled with
  timely dread
Of boars and lions, from their haunts they
  fled;
Trembling, resigned the leafy couch to those
Whom nature framed for their relentless
  foes.
  Yet, fewer, then, the call of death obeyed,
Left the sweet light of day for endless shade,

Than now; though, hapless, some were
  seized, o'erpowered,
Then by their fierce and savage foes de-
  voured:
These, as the brutes their reeking bowels
  rend,
See to a living grave their flesh descend;
Wake, with their piercing screams, the af-
  frighted skies
And fill the woods and mountains with their
  cries:
And those who fly, the cloud of fate sur-
  rounds;
Pressing with trembling hands their throb-
  bing wounds,
Death they implore, till gnawing worms
  consume
Their putrid flesh, and consummate their
  doom:
For then no healing science blessed mankind
No skilful hand the gushing wound could
  bind,
But then, fell war no thousands swept away.
Hurled to destruction in a single day:
In vain the raging ocean rolls and roars;
No ships were dashed upon the rocky
  shores:
Though calm again the sinking billows grew,
And all their awful violence withdrew,
Yet no smooth surface, no deceitful smile,
Could the fond, thoughtless mariner be-
  guile:
No dangerous art, then, traced the briny
  path,
No floating castles braved the ocean's wrath.
Grim Want o'er many urged his fatal power;
But now to ruin Plenty hurries more.
From noxious herbs some, thoughtless, drew
  their death;
Now studied poisons urge the fleeting breath.
  At length they bade the bough-built hut
  aspire,
And learned the luxury of skins and fire:
Then One to One in silken bondage held,
Raised man above the savage of the field;

Connubial love a purer bliss bestowed,
And with a chaste delight the bosom glowed;
While, pressing to the heart his smiling boy,
The ennobled father felt a father's joy.
Then, by indulgence softened, men no more
Braved the sharp cold, rude winds unin-
jured bore;
Hymen their fierceness tamed, and fondling
arts
Of darling children humanized their hearts.
Then neighborhoods grew and social com-
pacts rose;
To reason waked, no more they lived as
foes;
To women, children, kind protection yield;
The softer, weaker, from the stronger shield.
Though not yet all by order's voice were
swayed,
The greater part the laws of faith obeyed:
Man the approach of peace and union hailed,
And universal war no more prevailed:
Or gradual ravage, with its wide embrace,
Had, long ere this, suppressed the human
race.
Dumb motion now no longer things pro-
claimed;
By nature taught, the tongue each object
named;
As infants, ere they speak, by signs express
Their simple thoughts, and all their wants
confess.
. . . And is it wonderful that men, sup-
plied
With vocal organs, and in whom reside
The powers of intellect, should names de-
vise
For objects constantly before their eyes?
Would they of things the various nature
know,
Nor appellations on those things bestow;
Since e'en the mute creation signals find,
To speak the thoughts and feelings of their
mind;
Their love, their joy, their sorrow and their
ire,

And all the passions which their breasts
inspire?
When grim Molossian mastiffs are en-
raged,
And by no soothing art their wrath assuaged,
When fierce they snarl, they grin, their
fangs display.
From their deep throats gruff murmurs
break their way,
Unlike the sounds that rend our startled ears
When their loud clamorous voice the welkin
tears.
But view them when, with soft caressing
tongue,
Gently they lick their sprawling, playful
young;
Now feign to bite, now roll them o'er and
o'er,
Now, fondly gaping, threaten to devour;
But cautiously their harmless teeth employ,
And in soft whinings tell their tender joy:
Not as when left at home, they howl and
cry,
Or when with trembling fear they, crouch-
ing, eye
The uplifted whip, and whimper as they
lie . . .
Since, then, these creatures' dull percep-
tions cause
Their different notes, how clear that nature's
laws
Stronger must act on intellectual man!
That sounds have varied since the world
began;
And human speech was part of nature's
plan.
Let thirst of knowledge still thy mind
inspire:
Now sings the Muse the origin of fire.
Thunder this element to earth conveyed,
When loud it rattled, and its lightnings
played;
On their red wings the ardent vapors came,
And wrapped whole groves and forests in
their flame.

For now we see the same effect arise
When dart the flashing terrors of the skies:
Or, pressed by winds the laboring branches
    meet,
Strike, chafe and kindle to devouring heat;
From tree to tree it flies, from grove to
    grove
Climb the broad flames, and fire the realms
    above.
From friction, hence, or lightning's rage,
    might spring
The igniting cause, and fierce combustion
    bring.
    From the sun's heat men first acquired
    the art
Their viands to prepare; his rays that dart,
Ripening the yellow corn; that flowers un-
    fold,
Play on the fruits and change their green
    to gold,
The use of fire revealed: the wiser few
The lesson caught, and by example drew
Their fellow men; new habits were assumed
And savory meats the cloudy air perfumed.
    Then kings arose, fair cities then ap-
    peared,
Armies were formed, and citadels were
    reared;
Lands were divided, separate beeves as-
    signed,
As merit claimed, of body and of mind.
But chief the powers of body held the sway,
And strength and beauty bore the palm
    away.
Then gold was found, and men for riches
    burn,
And strength and beauty yielded in their
    turn;
The shining ore prevailed o'er old and
    young,
And gold was stronger than the brave and
    strong.
But once did reason rectify the mind
And chase the vain delusions of mankind;
The bliss of little with content and health,

This were their noblest boon, their truest
    wealth.
And, say, this little who should fear to
    want?
To whom this little would not fortune grant?
But for renown and power we every day
See mortals fling the sweets of life away:
These to their wealth a lasting base will
    give,
Then in soft ease and pleasure they will live.
But vain their labors, and absurd as vain,
Since those who anxiously aspire to gain
Nay, who secure, high honors and estate
(The greatest mid the wealthy and the
    great),
But journey haplessly; for Envy arms
Her hand with thunder, and their soul
    alarms;
Aims at their glory her destroying blow,
Their fame extinguishes and lays them low.
How happier they who peacefully obey,
Than those who struggle for imperial sway!
Who prostitute their anxious, wasted life
In sordid efforts and ambitious strife;
Climb the steep, thorny path, where perils
    wait,
And Envy urges with her deadly hate;
Arms with her bolts the candidates for power
And most delights to see her flames devour
The highest. These let pomp and pride ex-
    cite
And drive them struggling up the dangerous
    height;
Let Flattery's voice their eager ear beguile,
And stimulate their never ceasing toil.
This folly still behold, this ancient rage,
It maddens ours and will the latest age.
    Those monarchs slain, the glory of their
    throne
And sparkling diadem no longer shone.
The sceptre, emblem of their regal trust,
Stained with their blood and trodden in the
    dust,
Mourns its lost honors; while the rabble
    raise

Loud clamors, where they lately shouted
    praise;
Base in their power insult the mighty dead,
And triumph o'er whom living they would
    dread.
    Now to the mob the varying sway re-
      turned,
And vulgar breasts with wild ambition
    burned:
Fired by the thirst for power, for power they
    strain;
Empire's the dazzling prize, and all would
    reign.
Wearied with jarring interests, fierce dis-
    putes,
Where each man reasons, and where each
    refutes;
Tired of a state where all men all assailed,
Where equity nor polity prevailed;
Where the mad Many hold the Wise in awe
And violence usurps the throne of law;
All the fell power of anarchy deplore
And government and order would restore;
At length the sager few a code ordain;
And, future feuds and contests to restrain,
Rulers elect and check Contention's reign.
. . . Wretched the man who lives in lawless
    strife;
Who bursts the sacred bonds of social life:
Though Gods and men his cunning arts de-
    ceive,
In his own bosom fear and conscience live.
Hence, oft in slumber men their guilt be-
    tray;
Oft, when their fevered minds deliriums
    sway,
The plots discover long concealed by time
And tell in broken speech the secret crime.
    To Memmius now, inspiring Muse, dis-
    close
Whence of the Gods our first conceptions
    rose:
Whence altars towns adorned; whence sol-
    emn rites
And sacred festivals, divine delights,

And smoking hecatombs whose fumes arise
And roll in curling volumes to the skies:
Whence the sad terror that all earth per-
    vades,
Temples erects and plants the sacred shades.
Nor sure too high my ardent zeal aspires;
Obvious the course, nor keen research re-
    quires.
At first creation, forms divinely bright,
Radiant in beauty, burst upon the sight:
Men, e'en awake, the shadows wondering
    saw
Glowed as they gazed and felt a secret awe:
But to their dreams still grander visions
    came;
Visions of brighter, more gigantic, frame;
Whose active limbs astonishment excite,
Clothed in the glories of supernal night.
On these bright forms their fancy sense
    bestowed,
Language superb and worthy of a God.
Eternal, too, the shining phantoms seem,
Since on the sight descends a constant stream
Of images: and then what power can harm
Such mighty beings? What their fears alarm?
And those whom mortal terrors ne'er annoy
Peaceful must live, and perfect bliss enjoy.
Then, too, their shadowy wonders they
    display
With wondrous ease their limbs their will
    obey,
Nor ever dull fatigue or lassitude betray.
    In order, too, the rolling heavens ap-
    pear,
And varied seasons of the circling year:
But still the source of motion was concealed;
The Primum Mobile was unrevealed.
Hence, men to Gods creation's frame as-
    signed;
Themselves and all things to their will re-
    signed.
    Where glide the shining orbs for ever
    bright,
For ever rolling in refulgent light,
There they established the celestial bowers,

There fixed the mansions of the heavenly
    powers;
There, where the sun and moon their fires
    display,
The beam nocturnal and the flame of day;
The stars serene that shed their mingled
    rays,
The flying lightnings and the meteor's blaze;
The hail, the rain, the dews that float on
    high,
The thunder's awful bolts that threatening
    fly,
And all the dread commotions of the sky.
    Oh, hapless mortals! blindly pious race!
Why with such troublous rage the Gods dis-
    grace?
To your own age what idle fears ye taught!
On us what needless woes those fears have
    brought!
And still what griefs, what evils, shall supply
What floods of tears, to our posterity!
    Strange piety the crouching head to veil!
Fondly to sticks and stones to make appeal!
To every fane with spreading arms to fly,
Fall on the earth, and in dependence lie
Before the sacred shrines! with blood to stain
The sprinkled altars, and with praises vain
And vows on vows the heedless Gods obtest!
Calmly all things to view, be this confest
True piety. For, when the soul surveys
The grandeur heaven's illumined dome dis-
    plays;
The blue expanse, with sparkling stars o'er-
    spread,
And sun and moon that constant courses
    lead;
Then doubts that other evils had suppressed
Cloud the sad mind, and agitate the breast;
Doubts whether Gods the potent sinews
    claim
Yon orbs to wield, and heaven's stupendous
    frame.
To ignorance these evils mortals owe;
From doubts what terrors spring! what cease-
    less woe!

From ignorance we doubt Creation's birth;
The wandering stars and stationary earth;
How long the heavens great Nature will
    defend;
Whether their motion and their being end;
Or if, unfading, by the Gods they're framed
By everlasting energies inflamed;
In endless orbits formed to roll sublime
And triumph o'er the ravages of Time.
    Who calmly contemplates the blest
    abodes?
What heart but faints with terror of the
    Gods?
Whose limbs so nervid not to quake, when
    roll
The pealing thunders, and from pole to pole
Thick lightnings flash? What nations, free
    from fear,
Eye the blue fires, the loud explosions hear?
Proud tyrants tremble, fears their members
    thrill,
Forms of avenging gods their fancy fill;
Lest their foul crimes have armed the pow-
    ers on high
And the dread day of retribution's nigh.
And o'er the seas when winds and tempests
    roar
And heave the rolling mountains to the
    shore,
The gallant Admiral with legions armed,
And mighty elephants, with soul alarmed,
Falls he not prostrate to the powers above
To soothe their anger and their pity move?
Praying the blest Immortals to be kind
And make his peace with the reluctant
    wind;
Grant to his squadron soft, propitious gales,
And gently swell the bosom of his sails?
In vain! No prayers his tossing legions save;
Cold death awaits them and the Stygian
    wave.
Such the contempt some hidden power
    awards
To human greatness! Such its high regards
For rods and axes (glories of a day)

And all the ensigns of imperial sway!
With scornful sport it treats the gaudy
     things,
And on the proudly great its reckless venge-
     ance flings!
And then, when tremors seize this earthly
     ball,
And death and ruin threat to swallow all,
Should we, whilst all are trembling, feel
     surprise
If men their weakness see, themselves de-
     spise,
Give to the Gods omnipotence, and place
With them the government of being and
     of space?
     Now learn that Earth disclosed her var-
     ious ores
Lead, iron, silver, brass and golden stores
When to her hills fierce fires devouring came
And blazing forests fed the raging flame;
Whether from heaven the wasting fury
     spring,
Borne on the lightning's coruscating wing,
Or from fierce war the devastations flow
And woods were fired to scare the distant
     foe;
Or men, resolved to enlarge the fruitful soil,
Of their green pride the encumbered wilds
     despoil;
Or dauntlessly their savage tenants prest,
And with their shaggy hides themselves
     invest;
(For ere with nets and dogs they snared
     their prey,
With fire they drove them to the light of
     day . . .)
Whether from lurid heaven's ethereal flame
Or from mankind the wide destruction
     came;
Sprang the fierce fires from art or nature's
     power
That to their roots the crackling trees de-
     vour,
Spread unrestrained through wide extended
     woods,

Melt the burnt earth and boil the hissing
     floods;
Then from the earth's smoking veins red
     metals flow
Through delving channels, gliding as they
     glow:
When they to hardness cool, and men behold
The argent silver and the ruddy gold,
View the rich beauty of the shining ores
Thrown to the day from nature's latent
     stores;
See them the figures of their beds assume;
By fire if molten, aptly they presume
That various forms the fluid ores would take
And pointed instruments, or edged, might
     make;
To hew the woods, rough timbers smooth or
     cleave,
And the rude block a shapely figure
     give. . . .
. . . And now my Memmius will perceive
     the source
Whence the Rude Ages learned hard iron's
     force.
The earliest weapons hostile mortals tried,
Hands, teeth and nails and broken boughs
     supplied:
With chasing fire the foe they next assailed;
Then the tough brass, then iron's strength
     prevailed.
But brass, less stubborn and more plenteous
     found,
Claimed the first use: with brazen shares
     the ground
At first was ploughed, with brazen arms the
     field
Of battle blazed, brass taught the foe to
     yield;
Brass bade the suffering weak the strong
     obey,
Seized on their lands and bore their herds
     away.
Then hardier iron gradual use obtained
And brass, contemned, no more triumphant
     reigned:

The fertile glebe endured the iron share,
And iron gleamed in instruments of war.
　　To mount the war horse heroes first
　　　　aspired,
With the left hand to guide, the art acquired;
Full on the foe, with rushing force they
　　　sprung
And with the dexter hand the javelin they
　　　flung.
Ere with the flying car and mettled pair
They swept the field and crushed the ranks
　　of war.
First with a Pair, then Double Pair, they
　　strove;
Fixed the keen, cleaving scythe, and slaugh-
　　tering drove. . . .
These are of war the earliest arts; but who
Can think the inventors ne'er the effects
　　foreknew
So sure to follow; all the ills that rise?
Dread catalogue of human miseries!
Safer, perchance, to say these things had
　　birth
In various worlds, and not alone on earth:
Obtained throughout the Universal State,
Nor here, nor there, could claim their earli-
　　est date.
But not alone for victory brutes were
　　brought
Against the foe; but leaders chiefly sought
Vexatious combat—though, their numbers
　　small
And slightly skilled in arms, they saw their
　　certain fall.
Their vests the shaggy spoils of beasts sup-
　　plied,
And thorns inserted held the folding hide:
For Reason tells no weaving arts had birth
Till iron left the bosom of the earth:
Iron the chief, the grand material proved,
Iron the treadles, shuttles, spindles moved.
Had iron still been locked from human
　　sight,
Nor these, nor rattling beams, had sprung
　　to light.

But the first wheels and distaffs Men em-
　　ployed
Since more inventive powers their minds
　　enjoyed
Than those of women; more they claim of
　　arts,
And all that borrows mind, or mind imparts.
But the rough peasant mocked the slender
　　toil,
Called the male spinsters to the needy soil:
In softer hands the nimble shutters played
And the smooth treadles shapelier feet
　　obeyed.
Men to superior tasks their efforts turned;
For nobler arts and hardier labors burned.
　　Creative Nature (whence all things
　　began)
To sow, to plant, engraft, instructed man.
Berries and acorns as they fell to earth,
Giving, in season, kindred shoots to birth,
Taught him to plant; and bid the cultured
　　field
With fruitage teem, and fair abundance
　　yield;
Taught him to graft the tender slips, and
　　raise
In ordered rows, the suckling's blooming
　　sprays.
　　Then rising art to rising plenty led;
Improving earth enriching labor fed:
Wild fruits to ripeness swelled and, sweet as
　　fair,
With mellow juice repaid the peasant's
　　care.
The mountain woods a narrower bound as-
　　sumed,
And valleys waved with corn, with golden
　　produce bloomed.
Then cultivated Earth, no longer wild,
Her meadows, rivers, lakes and mountains
　　smiled!
Cornfields and vineyards waked to new
　　delight
The peasant's heart, and charmed his glad-
　　dened sight! . . .

. . . While the glad mind no higher good
    conceives,
The present good delight and pleasure gives:
But doth a more exalted bliss arise?
The joy that lived till then, that moment
    dies.
Hence acorns that could once the taste
    invite,
In time the pampered palate learned to
    slight.
The downy couch supplants the leafy bed
And glossy robes to shaggy skins succeed.
Yet the first man these savage spoils that
    wore
Such envy raised, his earth-born fellows tore
Quick from his back the vest his courage
    gained
And with his blood his shaggy honors
    stained;
Their murderous hands upon the victim
    laid;
And death the price of his invention paid.
    Then hides, now Gold and Purple, men
    delight;
No more for those, but fierce for these they
    fight;
And, sure, more folly we betray than those
Whose naked limbs the shivering winter
    froze;
While without gold and purple we, as well
Might all the rigors of the winds repel:
Since simplest habits will protection yield
And richest vestments but the body shield.
    How vain, then, all the troubles, cares
    and strife
That cheat weak mortals of the sweets of
    life!
No limits they assign to flattering wealth,
Nor know felicity is peace and health.
Ignorant of where the bounds of pleasure
    lie,
Into a sea of woes they anxious fly;

Evils unceasing court, and round the world
With maddening rage the flames of war are
    hurled.
    At length the Sun and Moon, that wake-
    ful roll
Their radiant orbs around the steady pole;
That to the circling skies their light display
To cheer the silent night or give the day;
Taught watchful man that Order governs
    all,
And wheels the seasons round this central
    ball.
    Now for defence arose embattled towers,
To castles chiefs withdrew their marshalled
    powers;
Lands were divided, spacious seas explored,
And civic union swayed the guardian sword;
Extending concord state with state com-
    bined
And held in welcome bondage humankind.
Then various arts appeared, then letters
    sprung,
Poets exploits divine in strains diviner sung:
But deeds of ages past were all unknown,
Or but by Reason's light obscurely shone.
Custom and slow Experience knowledge
    brought;
(Knowledge, with all the nobler blessings
    fraught;)
What life improves, or fosters Virtue's cause;
Fair Agriculture, Navigation, Laws,
Cities and Public Ways, rich Vestments,
    Arms,
Aspiring Temples, and the immortal charms
Of Painting, Sculpture, all that man refine;
Philosophy and Poesy divine.
    Thus Time with gradual light the mind
    illumes;
Thus new born energies the soul assumes;
From art to art the brightening radiance
    flies,
And to their full perfection all things rise.

Epictetus

Epictetus was a Stoic philosopher of the first century of our era. Born in Phrygia, in Asia Minor, he lived much of his life in Rome as the slave of one of Nero's favorites. The story goes that once, as his master was torturing him by twisting his leg, Epictetus remarked in a quiet voice, "You are going to break it." When the leg broke, he added only, "Haven't I told you so?" Stoics could be rather irritating.

We know so little of the details of his life that we cannot even fix precisely the dates of his birth and death. We do know that he somehow gained his freedom and began to teach in Rome until the Emperor Domitian purged the city of philosophers in 89 A.D. At that time Epictetus retired to Nicopolis in Epirus—a city Augustus had built to celebrate his victory at Actium—and there he taught until he was an old man. Since it seems that he never wrote anything himself, we know him, like Socrates, only through one of his pupils, Arrian, who published his lecture notes after his teacher's death.

Some things are under our control; yet others are not under our control. Thought, choice, desire, distaste are under our control, and, in a word, everything that is our own doing; our body, property, reputation, or function are not under our control, and, in a word, everything that is not our own doing. In addition, the things under our control are by their nature free, and cannot be hindered or thwarted; while the things which we do not control are weak, dependent, subject to interference, and not our own. Therefore it is well to remember that if you consider free what is naturally servile, and you think you own what is not your own, you will meet with hindrance and grief, you will be agitated and disturbed, and you will blame both gods and men; whereas if you only think your own to be your own, and what is not your own you think to be, as it really is, not your own, then no one will ever be able to compel you to anything, no one will hinder you, you will blame no one and find fault with no one, you will do absolutely nothing against your will, you will have no personal enemy, no one will be able to harm you, for there will be no harm that can touch you.

Men are disturbed not by things, but by the way in which they look at things. Thus, death is nothing terrible; otherwise Socrates would have thought it so. The terror of death consists in our own notion that death is terrible. Therefore, when we are hindered, or disturbed, or grieved, let us never attribute this to ourselves; that is, to our own attitude.

Do not demand that things (events) should happen as you wish, but wish them to happen as they do happen, and you will get on well.

All things serve and obey the laws of the universe: the earth, the sea, the sun, the stars, and the plants and animals of the earth. Our body also obeys these laws, when it is sick and well, young and old, and passes through all the other changes they decree. It is therefore reasonable that what depends on ourselves—that is, our own understanding—should not be the only rebel against the system. For the universal law is powerful and transcend-

From *The Discourses of Epictetus*, tr. by the editor.

ent, and it consults what is best for us by governing us in conjunction with the whole. And besides, opposition, apart from the fact that it is unreasonable, and produces nothing more than a useless struggle, throws us into pain and sorrows.

For all other pleasures it is best to substitute the consciousness that you are obeying God and performing, not in word but in deed, the duty of a man who is wise and good. It is a great thing to be able to say to yourself: "I practice the things that others are now solemnly arguing in the schools, and learning to state in paradoxes. I have made my own those qualities which in the schools are taught, debated and celebrated. Zeus has been pleased to let me recognise this within myself, to decide himself whether he has in me one that is fit for a soldier and a citizen, and to use me as a witness to oth-

er men about things that the will cannot control. See that your fears were vain, and your appetites vain. Do not seek your good outside yourselves—seek it within yourselves, else you will never find it. For this reason he now brings me here, now sends me there; he sets me before mankind, poor, powerless, and sick; he banishes me to Gyaros [1]; he leads me to prison; not that he hates me—Heaven forbid: for who hates the most faithful of his servants?—not that he neglects me, for he neglects not even the smallest things; but to try me, to temper me, and to use me as a witness to others. Appointed to such a service, to such a task, how can I still care where I am, or with whom, or what is said of me, instead of being wholly attentive to God, and to his orders and commands?"

---

[1] A wretched island in the Aegean to which criminals were sent at that time.

IV. Ancient Rome

The story of Rome, the great success story of the ancient world, lacks none of the familiar components. Part I shows frugal, hard-working beginnings on the land, gradual growth and prosperity based on fighting hard and keeping the given word, eventual success leading to corruption. In Part II we see the firm base on the land deserted, the frugality and hard work happily abandoned, the pledged word broken or conveniently forgotten, the incomparable fighting arm allowed to slip out of Roman grasp. It is a familiar morality tale, with the rake's progress beginning some time in the second century before the birth of Christ.

Yet, though decay of the virtues which had made Rome great set in so soon, the rules of behavior and the institutions forged during the tough first period survived for a long time. The code which we find reflected in the works of a Cicero or a Seneca may have been no more than an intellectual ideal even for them and their contemporaries of the first centuries, B.C. and A.D., but ideals have their importance, and these were honored at least in the breach if not in the observance. As long as they were honored (even though not followed) they continued, when invested with the prestige of even the memory of Roman greatness, to exert an important influence on the laws and the behavior of Western peoples and to furnish the basis of an educational system which only the twentieth century has begun to abandon.

1. THE REPUBLIC

In 167 B.C. Rome, interfering in the squabbles of Greece, took one thousand hostages from the Achaean League. One of these hostages was Polybius (c. 205–125 B.C.), member of a prominent family of Megalopolis in the Peloponnesus and a very great historian. In Rome, Polybius became a friend of the Scipios, was present at the fall of Numantia and Carthage, came to admire the new power, and set out in the *Histories* to tell its story. He proposed to explain "in what manner and under what kind of constitution it came about that nearly the whole world fell under the power of Rome in somewhat less than fifty-three years, an event certainly without precedent." The passages below are from the sixth book of the *Histories*, in the translation of Evelyn S. Shuckburgh.

Polybius: The Roman Constitution

As for the Roman constitution, it had three elements, each of them possessing sovereign powers: and their respective share of power in the whole state had been regulated with such a scrupulous regard to equality and equilibrium, that no one could say for certain, not even a native, whether the constitution as a whole were an aristocracy or democracy or despotism. And no wonder: for if we confine our observation to the power of the Consuls we should be inclined to regard it as despotic; if on that of the Senate, as aristocratic; and if finally one looks at the power possessed by the people it would seem a clear case of a democracy. What the exact powers of these several parts were and still, with slight modifications, are, I will now state.

The Consuls, before leading out the legions, remain in Rome and are the supreme masters of the administration. All other magistrates, except the Tribunes, are under them and take their orders. They introduce foreign ambassadors to the Senate; bring matters requiring deliberation before it; and see to the execution of the decrees. If, again, there are any matters of state which require the authorization of the people, it is their business to see to them, to summon the popular meetings, to bring the proposals before them, and to carry out the decrees of the majority. In the preparations for war also, and in a word in the entire administration of a campaign, they have all but absolute power. It is competent to them to impose on the allies such levies as they think good, to appoint the military tribunes, to make up the roll for soldiers and select those that are suitable. Besides they have absolute power of in-flicting punishment on all who are under their command while on active service: and they have authority to expend as much of the public money as they choose, being accompanied by a quaestor who is entirely at their orders. A survey of these powers would in fact justify our describing the constitution as despotic, a clear case of royal government. Nor will it affect the truth of my description if any of the institutions I have described are changed in our time or in that of our posterity: and the same remarks apply to what follows.

The Senate has first of all control of the treasury, and regulates the receipts and disbursements alike. For the Quaestors cannot issue any public money for the various departments of the state without a decree of the Senate, except for the service of the Consuls. The Senate controls also what is by far the largest and most important expenditure, that, namely, which is made by the censors every *lustrum* for the repair or construction of public buildings; this money cannot be obtained by the censors except by the grant of the Senate. Similarly all crimes committed in Italy requiring a public investigation, such as treason, conspiracy, poisoning, or wilful murder, are in the hands of the Senate. Besides, if any individual or state among the Italian allies requires a controversy to be settled, a penalty to be assessed, help or protection to be afforded, all this is the province of the Senate. Or again, outside Italy, if it is necessary to send an embassy to reconcile warring communities or to remind them of their duty, or sometimes to impose requisitions upon them, or to receive their submission, or finally to proclaim war

From *The Histories of Polybius*, tr. Evelyn S. Shuckburgh, 2 vols. (London, 1889).

against them, this too is the business of the Senate. In like manner, the reception to be given to foreign ambassadors in Rome and the answers to be returned to them, are decided by the Senate. With such business the people have nothing to do. Consequently, if one were staying at Rome when the Consuls were not in town, one would imagine the constitution to be a complete aristocracy: and this has been the idea entertained by many Greeks, and by many kings as well, from the fact that nearly all the business they had with Rome was settled by the Senate.

After this one would naturally be inclined to ask what part is left for the people in the constitution, when the Senate has these various functions, especially the control of the receipts and expenditure of the exchequer; and when the Consuls, again, have absolute power over the details of military preparation and an absolute authority in the field? There is, however, a part left the people, and it is a most important one. For the people is the sole fountain of honor and of punishment; and it is by these two things and these alone that dynasties and constitutions and, in a word, human society are held together: for where the distinction between them is not sharply drawn both in theory and practice, there no undertaking can be properly administered, as indeed we might expect when good and bad are held in exactly the same honor. The people then are the only court to decide matters of life and death; and even in cases where the penalty is money, if the sum to be assessed is sufficiently serious, and especially when the accused have held the higher magistracies. And in regard to this arrangement there is one point deserving especial commendation and record. Men who are on trial for their lives at Rome, while sentence is in

process of being voted, if even only one of the tribes whose votes are needed to ratify the sentence has not voted, have the privilege at Rome of openly departing and condemning themselves to a voluntary exile. Such men are safe at Naples, or Praeneste or at Tibur, and at other towns with which this arrangement has been duly ratified on oath.

Again, it is the people who bestow offices on the deserving, which are the most honorable rewards of virtue. It has also the absolute power of passing or repealing laws; and, most important of all, it is the people who deliberate on the question of peace or war. And when provisional terms are made for alliance, suspension of hostilities, or treaties, it is the people who ratify them or the reverse.

These considerations, again, would lead one to say that the chief power in the state was the people's, and that the constitution was a democracy.

Such, then, is the distribution of power between the several parts of the state. I must now show how each of these several parts can, when they choose, oppose or support each other.

The Consul, then, when he has started on an expedition with the powers I have described, is to all appearance absolute in the administration of the business in hand; still he has need of the support both of people and Senate, and, without them, is quite unable to bring the matter to a successful conclusion. For it is plain that he must have supplies sent to his legions from time to time; but without a decree of the Senate they can be supplied neither with grain, nor clothes, nor pay, so that all the plans of a commander must be futile if the Senate is resolved either to shrink from danger or hamper his plans. And, again, whether a Consul shall bring any undertaking to a conclusion or no depends entirely upon the Senate: for it has absolute authority at the end of a year to send another Consul to supersede him, or to continue the existing one in his command. Again, even to the successes of the generals the Senate has the power to add distinction and glory, and on the other hand to obscure their merits and lower their credit. For these high achievements are brought in tangible form before the eyes of the citizens by what are called "triumphs." But these triumphs the commanders cannot celebrate at all, unless the Senate concurs and grants the necessary money. As for the people, the Consuls are pre-eminently obliged to court their favor, however distant from home may be the field of their operations; for it is the people, as I have said before, that ratifies or refuses to ratify terms of peace and treaties; but most of all because when laying down their office they have to give an account of their administration before it. Therefore in no case is it safe for the Consuls to neglect either the Senate or the good will of the people.

As for the Senate, which possesses the immense power I have described, in the first place it is obliged in public affairs to take the multitude into account, and respect the wishes of the people; and it cannot put into execution the penalty for offences against the republic which are punishable with death, unless the people first ratify its decrees. Similarly, even in matters which directly affect the Senators, for instance in the case of a law diminishing the Senate's traditional authority, or depriving Senators of certain dignities and offices, or even actually cutting down their property, even in such cases the people have the sole power of passing or rejecting the law. But most important of all is the fact that, if the Trib-

unes interpose their veto, the Senate not only are unable to pass a decree, but cannot even hold a meeting at all, whether formal or informal. Now, the Tribunes are always bound to carry out the decree of the people, and above all things to have regard to their wishes: therefore, for all these reasons, the Senate stands in awe of the multitude and cannot neglect the feelings of the people.

In like manner the people on its part is far from being independent of the Senate, and is bound to take its wishes into account both collectively and individually. For contracts too numerous to count are given out by the censors in all parts of Italy for the repairs or construction of public buildings; there is also the collection of revenue from many rivers, harbors, gardens, mines, and land: everything, in a word, that comes under the control of the Roman government. And in all these the people at large are engaged; so that there is scarcely a man, so to speak, who is not interested either as a contractor or as being employed in the works. For some purchase the contracts from the censors for themselves; and others go partners with them; while others again go security for these contractors, or actually pledge their property to the treasury for them. Now over all these transactions the Senate has absolute control. It can grant an extension of time; and in case of unforeseen accident can relieve the contractors from a portion of their obligation, or release them from it altogether if they are absolutely unable to fulfill it. And there are many details in which the Senate can inflict great hardships, or, on the other hand, grant great indulgences to the contractors; for in every case the appeal is to it. But the most important point of all is that the judges are taken from its members in the majority of trials, whether public or private, in which the charges are heavy. Consequently, all citizens are much at its mercy; and being alarmed at the uncertainty as to when they may need its aid, are cautious about resisting or actively opposing its will. And for a similar reason men do not rashly resist the wishes of the Consuls, because one and all may become subject to their absolute authority on a campaign.

The result of this power of the several estates for mutual help or harm is a union sufficiently firm for all emergencies, and a constitution than which it is impossible to find a better. For whenever any danger from without compels them to unite and work together, the strength which is developed by the State is so extraordinary that everything required is unfailingly carried out by the eager rivalry shown by all classes to devote their whole minds to the need of the hour, and to secure that any determination come to should not fail for want of promptitude; while each individual works, privately and publicly alike, for the accomplishment of the business in hand. Accordingly, the peculiar constitution of the State makes it irresistible, and certain of obtaining whatever it determines to attempt. Nay, even when these external alarms are past, and the people are enjoying their good fortune and the fruits of their victories, and, as usually happens, growing corrupted by flattery and idleness, show a tendency to violence and arrogance—it is in these circumstances more than ever that the constitution is seen to possess within itself the power of correcting abuses. For when any one of the three classes becomes puffed up, and manifests an inclination to be contentious and unduly encroaching, the mutual interdependence of all the three and the possibility of the pre-

tensions of one being checked and thwarted by the others, must plainly check this tendency; and so the proper equilibrium is maintained by the impulsiveness of the one part being checked by its fear of the other. . . .

Nearly all historians have recorded as constitutions of eminent excellence those of Lacedaemonia, Crete, Mantinea, and Carthage. Some have also mentioned those of Athens and Thebes. The former I may allow to pass; but I am convinced that little need be said of the Athenian and Theban constitutions: their growth was abnormal, the period of their zenith brief, and the changes they experienced unusually violent. Their glory was a sudden and fortuitous flash, so to speak; and while they still thought themselves prosperous, and likely to remain so, they found themselves involved in circumstances completely the reverse. The Thebans got their reputation for valor among the Greeks by taking advantage of the senseless policy of the Lacedaemonians and the hatred of the allies toward them, owing to the valor of one or, at the most, two men who were wise enough to appreciate the situation; since fortune quickly made it evident that it was not the peculiarity of their constitution but the valor of their leaders that gave the Thebans their success. For the great power of Thebes notoriously took its rise, attained its zenith and fell to the ground with the lives of Epaminondas and Pelopidas. We must therefore conclude that it was not its constitution but its men that caused the high fortune which it then enjoyed.

A somewhat similar remark applies to the Athenian constitution also. For though it perhaps had more frequent interludes of excellence, yet its highest perfection was attained during the brilliant career of Themistocles; and having reached that point it quickly declined, owing to its essential instability. For the Athenian demos is always in the position of a ship without a commander. In such a ship, if fear of the enemy or the occurrence of a storm induce the crew to be of one mind and to obey the helmsman, everything goes well; but if they recover from this fear and begin to treat their officers with contempt and to quarrel with each other because they are no longer all of one mind, one party wishing to continue the voyage and the other urging the steersman to bring the ship to anchor; some letting out the sheets and others hauling them in and ordering the sails to be furled, their discord and quarrels make a sorry show to lookers on; and the position of affairs is full of risk to those on board engaged on the same voyage; and the result has often been that, after escaping the dangers of the widest seas, and the most violent storms, they wreck their ship in harbor and close to shore. And this is what has happened to the Athenian constitution. For, after repelling on various occasions the greatest and most formidable dangers by the valor of its people and their leaders, there have been times when, in periods of secure tranquility, it has gratuitously and recklessly encountered disaster. Therefore I need say no more about either it or the Theban constitution: in both of which a mob manages everything on its own unfettered impulse—a mob in the one city distinguished for headlong outbursts of fiery temper, in the other trained in long habits of violence and ferocity.

Now the Carthaginian constitution seems to me originally to have been well contrived in these most distinctively most important particulars. For they had kings, and the Gerusia had the powers of an aristocracy, and the multitude were supreme in such things as affected them; and on the whole the adjustment of its several parts was very like that of Rome and Sparta. But about the period of its entering on the Hannibalian war the political state of Carthage was on the decline, that of Rome improving. For whereas there is in every body, or polity, or business, a natural stage of growth, zenith and decay; and whereas everything in them is at its best at the zenith; we may thereby judge of the difference between these two constitutions as they existed at that period. For exactly so far as the strength and prosperity of Carthage preceded that of Rome in point of time, by so much was Carthage then past its prime, while Rome was exactly at its zenith, as far as its political constitution was concerned. In Carthage therefore the influence of the people in the policy of the state had already risen to be supreme, while at Rome the Senate was at the height of its power: and so, as in the one, measures were deliberated upon by the many, in the other by the best men, the policy of the Romans in all public undertakings proved the stronger; on which account though they met with capital disasters, by force of prudent counsels they finally conquered the Carthaginians in the war.

[Another reason for Roman success] is that the Carthaginians employ foreign mercenaries, the Romans native and citizen levies. It is in this point that the latter polity is preferable to the former. They have their hopes of freedom ever resting on the courage of mercenary troops; the Romans on the valor of their own citizens and the aid of their allies. The result is that even if the Romans have suffered a defeat at first, they renew the war with undiminished forces, which the Carthaginians cannot do. For, as the Romans are fighting for country and children, it is impossible for them to relax the fury of their struggle; but they persist with obstinate resolution until they have overcome their enemies. What has happened in regard to their navy is an instance in point. In skill the Romans are much behind the Carthaginians; yet the upshot of the whole naval war has been a decided triumph for the Romans, owing to the valor of their men. For although nautical science contributes largely to success in sea fights, still it is the courage of the mariners that turns the scale most decisively in favor of victory. The fact is that Italians as a nation are by nature superior to Phoenicians and Libyans both in physical strength and courage; but still their habits also do much to inspire the youth with enthusiasm for such exploits. One example will be sufficient of the pains taken by the Roman state to turn out men ready to endure anything to win a reputation in their country for valor.

Whenever one of their illustrious men dies, in the course of his funeral, the body with all its paraphernalia is carried into the forum to the Rostra, as a raised platform there is called, and sometimes is propped upright upon it so as to be conspicuous or, more rarely, is laid upon it. Then with all the people standing round, his son, if he has left one of full age and he is there, or failing him one of his relations, mounts the Rostra and delivers a speech concerning the virtues of the deceased and the successful exploits performed by him during his lifetime. By these means the people are reminded of what has been done, and made to see it with their own eyes (not only such as

were engaged in the actual transactions, but also those who were not) and their sympathies are so deeply moved that the loss appears not to be confined to the actual mourners but to be a public one affecting the whole people. After the burial and all the usual ceremonies have been performed, they place the likeness of the deceased in the most conspicuous spot in his house, surrounded by a wooden canopy or shrine. This likeness consists of a mask made to represent the deceased with extraordinary fidelity both in shape and color. These likenesses they display at public sacrifices adorned with much care. And when any illustrious member of the family dies, they carry these masks to the funeral, putting them on men whom they thought as like the originals as possible in height and other personal peculiarities. And these substitutes assume clothes according to the rank of the person represented: if he was a consul or praetor, a toga with purple stripes, if a censor, wholly purple; if he had also celebrated a triumph or performed any exploit of that kind, a toga embroidered with gold. These representatives also ride themselves in chariots, while the fasces and axes and all the other customary insignia of the particular offices lead the way according to the dignity of the rank in the state enjoyed by the deceased in his lifetime; and on arriving at the Rostra they all take their seats on ivory chairs in their order. There could not easily be a more inspiring spectacle than this for a young man of noble ambitions and virtuous aspirations. For can we conceive anyone to be unmoved at the sight of all these likenesses collected together of the men who have earned glory, all as it were living and breathing? Or what could be a more glorious spectacle?

Besides, the speaker over the body

about to be buried, after having finished the panegyric of this particular person, starts upon the others whose representatives are present, beginning with the most ancient, and recounts the successes and achievements of each. By this means the glorious memory of brave men is continually renewed; the fame of those who have performed any noble deed is never allowed to die; and the renown of those who have done good service to their country becomes a matter of common knowledge to the multitude, and part of the heritage of posterity. But the chief benefit of the ceremony is that it inspires young men to shrink from no exertion for the general welfare, in the hope of obtaining the glory which awaits the brave. And what I say is confirmed by this fact. Many Romans have volunteered to decide a whole battle by single combat; not a few have deliberately accepted certain death, some in time of war to secure the safety of the rest, some in time of peace to preserve the safety of the commonwealth. There have also been instances of men in office putting their own sons to death, in defiance of every custom and law, because they rated the interests of their country higher than those of natural ties even with their nearest and dearest.

Again the Roman customs and principles regarding money transactions are better than those of the Carthaginians. In the view of the latter, nothing is disgraceful that makes for gain; with the former, nothing is more disgraceful than to receive bribes and to make profit by improper means. For they regard wealth obtained from unlawful transactions to be as much a subject of reproach as a fair profit from the most unquestioned source is of commendation. A proof of the fact

is this. The Carthaginians obtain office by open bribery, but among Romans the penalty for this is death. With such a radical difference, therefore, between the rewards offered to virtue among the two peoples, it is natural that the ways adopted for obtaining them should be different also.

But the most important difference for the better which the Roman commonwealth appears to me to display is in their religious beliefs. For I conceive that what in other nations is looked upon as a reproach, I mean a scrupulous fear of the gods, is the very thing which keeps the Roman commonwealth together. To such an extraordinary height is this carried among them, both in private and in public business, that nothing could exceed it. Many people might think this unaccountable; but in my opinion their object is to use it as a check upon the common people. If it were possible to form a state wholly of philosophers, such a custom would perhaps be unnecessary. But seeing that every multitude is fickle and full of lawless desires, unreasoning anger, and violent passion, the only resource is to keep them in check by mysterious terrors and scenic effects of this sort. Wherefore, to my mind, the ancients were not acting without purpose or at random when they brought in among the vulgar those opinions about the gods, and the belief in the punishments in Hades: much rather do I think that men nowadays are acting rashly and foolishly in rejecting them. This is the reason why, apart from anything else, Greek statesmen, if entrusted with a single talent, though protected by ten accountants, yet cannot be induced to keep faith; whereas among the Romans, in their magistracies and embassies, men have the handling of a great amount of money, and yet from pure respect to their oath keep their faith intact. And, again, in other nations it is a rare thing to find a man who keeps his hands out of the public purse and is entirely pure in such matters. But among the Romans it is a rare thing to detect a man in the act of committing such a crime.

That to all things, then, which exist there is ordained decay and change, I think it requires no further arguments to show: for the inexorable course of nature is sufficient to convince us of it.

But in all polities we observe two sources of decay existing from natural causes, the one external, the other internal and self produced. The external admits of no certain or fixed definition, but the internal follows a definite order. What kind of polity, then, comes naturally first, and what second, I have already stated in such a way that those who are capable of taking in the whole drift of my argument can henceforth draw their own conclusions as to the future of the Roman polity. For it is quite clear, in my opinion. When a commonwealth, after warding off many great dangers, has arrived at a high pitch of prosperity and undisputed power, it is evident that, by the lengthened continuance of wealth within it, the manner of life of its citizens will become more extravagant; and that the rivalry for office and in other spheres of activity will become fiercer than it ought to be. And as this state of things goes on more and more, the desire of office and the shame of losing reputation, as well as the ostentation and extravagance of living, will prove the beginning of a deterioration. And of this change the people will be credited with being the authors, when they become convinced that they are being cheated by some from avarice, and are puffed up with flattery by others from love of office. For when that comes about, in their passionate resentment and acting under the dictates of anger, they will refuse to obey any longer or to be content with having equal powers with their leaders, but will demand to have all or far the greatest themselves. And when that comes to pass the constitution will receive a new name, which sounds better than any other in the world, liberty, or democracy; but, in fact, it will become that worst of all governments, mob-rule.

With this description of the formation, growth, zenith and present state of the Roman polity, and having discussed also its difference, for better and worse, from other polities, I will now at length bring my essay to its end.

Cicero and the Republic

Marcus Tullius Cicero was born in 106 B.C and died, at the hands of Marc Antony's men, in 43 B.C. The offspring of a respectable provincial family, he based a great political career leading to the Consulship on real ability and a highly articulate patriotism. In his writings we find Greek learning combined with the morality and practicality characteristic of Roman thought, a thought as aware of social responsibilities as that of the Greeks, but one which had progressed in Cicero's time from the concept of the city-state to a wider application.

From *The Treatises of Cicero,* tr. C. D. Yonge (London, 1853). "On the Commonwealth," Book I, chaps. 1–2; 25–29.

ON THE COMMONWEALTH, BOOK I

Without the virtue of patriotism, neither Caius Duilius nor Aulus Atilius, nor Lucius Metellus could have delivered Rome by their courage from the terror of Carthage; nor could the two Scipios, when the fire of the Second Punic War was kindled, have quenched it in their blood; nor, when it revived in greater force, could either Quintus Maximus have enervated it, or Marcus Marcellus have crushed it; nor, when it was repulsed from the gates of our own city, would Scipio have confined it within the walls of our enemies.

But Cato, at first a new and unknown man, whom all we who aspire to the same honors consider as a pattern to lead us on to industry and virtue, was undoubtedly at liberty to enjoy his repose at Tusculum, a most salubrious and convenient retreat. But he, mad as some people think him, though no necessity compelled him, preferred being tossed about amid the tempestuous waves of politics, even till extreme old age, to living with all imaginable luxury in that tranquility and relaxation. I omit innumerable men who have separately devoted themselves to the protection of our Commonwealth; and those whose lives are within the memory of the present generation I will not mention, lest any one should complain that I had invidiously forgotten himself or some one of his family. This only I insist on, that so great is the necessity of this virtue which nature has implanted in man, and so great is the desire to defend the common safety of our country, that its energy has continually overcome all the blandishments of pleasure and repose.

Nor is it sufficient to possess this virtue as if it were some kind of art, unless we put it into practice. An art, indeed, though not exercised, may still be retained in knowledge; but virtue consists wholly in its proper use and action. Now, the noblest use of virtue is the government of the Commonwealth, and the carrying out in real action, not in words only, of all those identical theories which those philosophers discuss at every corner. For nothing is spoken by philosophers so far as they speak correctly and honorably which has not been discovered and confirmed by those persons who have been the founders of the laws of states. For whence comes piety, or from whom has religion been derived? whence comes law, either that of nations, or that which is called the civil law? whence comes justice, faith, equity? whence modesty, continence, the horror of baseness, the desire of praise and renown? whence fortitude in labors and perils? Doubtless, from those who have instilled some of these moral principles in men by education, and confirmed others by custom, and sanctioned others by laws.

Moreover, it is reported of Xenocrates, one of the sublimest philosophers, that when someone asked him what his disciples learned, he replied, "To do that of their own accord which they might be compelled to do by law." That citizen, therefore, who obliges all men to those virtuous actions, by the authority of laws and penalties, to which the philosophers can scarce persuade a few by the force of their eloquence, is certainly to be preferred to the sagest of the doctors who spend their lives in such discussions. For which of their exquisite orations is so admirable as to be entitled to be preferred to a well constituted government, public justice, and good customs? Certainly, just as I think that magnificent and imperious cities are superior to castles and villages, so I imagine that those who regulate such cities by their counsel and authority are far preferable, with respect to real wisdom, to men who are unacquainted with any kind of political knowledge.

A commonwealth is a constitution of the entire people. But the people is not every association of men, however congregated, but the association of the entire number, bound together by the compact of justice, and the communication of utility. The first cause of this association is not so much the weakness of man, as a certain spirit of congregation which naturally belongs to him. For the human race is not a race of isolated individuals, wandering and solitary; but it is so constituted that even in the affluence of all things and without any need of reciprocal assistance it spontaneously seeks society.

It is necessary to presuppose these original seeds, as it were, since we cannot discover any primary establishment of the other virtues, or even of a commonwealth itself. These unions, then, formed by the principle which I have mentioned, established their headquarters originally in certain central positions, for the convenience of the whole population; and having fortified them by natural and artificial means, they called this collection of houses a city or town, distinguished by temples and public squares. Every people, therefore, which consists of such an association of the entire multitude as I have described, every city which consists of an assemblage of the people, and every commonwealth which embraces every member of these associations, must be regulated by a certain authority in order to be permanent.

This intelligent authority should always refer itself to that grand first principle which established the commonwealth. It must be deposited in the hands

of one supreme person, or entrusted to the administration of certain delegated rulers, or undertaken by the whole multitude. When the direction of all depends on one person, we call this individual a king; . . . when it is in the power of privileged delegates the state is said to be ruled by an aristocracy; and when the people are all in all, they call it a democracy or popular constitution. And if the tie of social affection which originally united men in political associations for the sake of public interest maintains its force, each of these forms of government is, I will not say perfect, nor in my opinion essentially good, but tolerable, and such that one may accidentally be better than another: either a just and wise king, or a selection of the most eminent citizens, or even the populace itself (though this is the least commendable form) may, if there be no interference of crime and cupidity, form a constitution sufficiently secure.

But in a monarchy, the other members of the state are often too much deprived of public counsel and jurisdiction; and under the rule of an aristocracy the multitude can hardly possess its due share of liberty, since it is allowed no share in the public deliberation and no power. And when all things are carried by a democracy, although it be just and moderate, yet its very equality is a culpable levelling, insomuch as it allows no gradations of rank. Therefore, even if Cyrus, the king of the Persians, was a most righteous and wise monarch, I should still think that the interest of the people (for this is, as I have said before, the same as the commonwealth) could not be very effectually promoted when all things depended on the beck and nod of one individual. And though at present the people of Marseille, our clients, are governed with the greatest justice by elected magistrates of the highest rank, still there is always in this condition of the people a certain appearance of servitude; and when the Athenians at a certain period, having demolished their Aeropagus, conducted all public affairs by the acts and decrees of the democracy alone, their state, as it no longer contained a distinct gradation of ranks, was no longer able to retain its original fair appearance.

The worst condition of things sometimes results from a confusion of those factious tyrannies into which kings, aristocrats, and democrats are apt to degenerate. For thus, from these diverse elements, there occasionally arises . . . a new kind of government. And wonderful indeed are the revolutions and periodic returns in natural constitutions of such alternations and vicissitudes; which it is the part of the wise politician to investigate with the closest attention. But to calculate their approach, and to join to this foresight the skill which moderates the course of events, and retains in a steady hand the reins of that authority which safely conducts the people through all the dangers to which they expose themselves, is the work of a most illustrious citizen, and of almost divine genius.

There is a fourth kind of government, therefore, which, in my opinion, is preferable to all these: it is that mixed and moderate government, which is composed of the three particular forms which I have already noticed.

THE LAWS, BOOK I

Of all the questions which are ever the subject of discussion among learned men,

there is none which is more important thoroughly to understand than this, that man is born for justice, and that law and equity have not been established by opinion, but by nature. This truth will become still more apparent if we investigate the nature of human association and society.

For there is not one thing so like or so equal to another, as in every instance man is to man. And if the corruption of customs, and the variation of opinions, did not induce an imbecility of minds, and turn them aside from the course of nature, no one would more nearly resemble himself than all men would resemble all men. Therefore, whatever definition we give of man will be applicable to the whole human race. And this is a good argument that there is no dissimilarity of kind among men. Because if this were the case, one definition could not include all men.

In fact, reason which alone gives us so many advantages over beasts, by means of which we conjecture, argue, refute, discourse, and accomplish and conclude our designs, is assuredly common to all men; for the faculty of acquiring knowledge is similar in all human minds, though the knowledge itself may be endlessly diversified. By the same senses we all perceive the same objects, and those things which move the senses at all, do move in the same way the senses of all men. And those first crude elements of intelligence which, as I before observed, are the earliest developments of thought, are similarly impressed upon all men; and that faculty of speech which is the interpreter of the mind, agrees in the ideas which it conveys, though it may differ in the words by which it expresses them.

From *The Treatises of Cicero,* tr. C. D. Yonge (London, 1853). "On the Laws," Book I, chaps. 10–16; Book II, chaps. 4–5.

And therefore there exists not a man in any nation, who, if he adopts nature for his guide, may not arrive at virtue.

Nor is this resemblance which all men bear to each other remarkable in those things only which are in accordance with the right reason, but also in errors. For all men alike are captivated by pleasure which, although it is a temptation to what is disgraceful, nevertheless bears some resemblance to natural good; for, as by its delicacy and sweetness it is delightful, it is through a mistake of the intellect adopted as something salutary.

And by an error scarcely less universal we shun death as if it were a dissolution of nature, and cling to life because it keeps us in that existence in which we were born. Thus, likewise, we consider pain as one of the greatest evils, not only on account of its present asperity, but also because it seems the precursor of mortality. Again, on account of the apparent resemblance between renown and honor, those men appear to us happy who are honored, and miserable who happen to be inglorious. In like manner our minds are all similarly susceptible of inquietudes, joys, desires, and fears; nor if different men have different opinions, does it follow that those who deify dogs and cats do not labor under superstition equally with other nations, though they may differ from them in the forms of its manifestation.

Again, what nation is there which has not a regard for kindness, benignity, gratitude and mindfulness of benefits? What nation is there in which arrogance, malice, cruelty, and unthankfulness are not reprobated and detested? And while this uniformity of opinion proves that the whole race of mankind is united together, the last point is that a system of living properly makes men better. . . .

It follows then that nature made us just that we might share our goods with each other and supply each other's wants. You observe in this discussion, whenever I speak of nature, I mean nature in its genuine purity, but that there is in fact such corruption, engendered by evil customs that the sparks, as it were, of virtue which have been given by nature are extinguished, and that antagonist vices arise around it and become strengthened.

But if, as nature prompts them to, men would with deliberate judgment, in the words of the poet "being men, hold nothing indifferent that concerns mankind" then would justice be cultivated equally by all. For to those to whom nature has given reason, she has also given right reason, and therefore also law, which is nothing else than right reason enjoining what is good, and forbidding what is evil. And if nature has given us law, she hath also given us right. But she has bestowed reason on all, therefore right has been bestowed on all. . . .

There is no expiation for the crimes and impieties of men. The guilty, therefore, must pay the penalty and bear the punishment; not so much those punishments inflicted by courts of justice, which were not always in being, do not exist at present in many places, and even where established are frequently biased and partial, but those of conscience; while the furies pursue and torment them, not with burning torches, as the poets feign, but with remorse of conscience and the tortures arising from guilt.

But were it the fear of punishment, and not the nature of the thing itself, that ought to restrain mankind from wickedness, what, I would ask, would give the villains the least uneasiness, abstracting from all fears of this kind? And yet none of them was ever so audaciously impotent but what he either denied that the action in question had been committed by him, or pretended some cause or other for his just indignation, or sought a defence of his deed in some right of nature. And if the wicked dare to appeal to those principles, with what respect ought not good men to treat them?

But if either direct punishment, or the fear of it, is what deters men from a vicious and criminal course of life, and not the turpitude of the thing itself, then none can be guilty of injustice, and the greatest offenders ought rather to be called imprudent than wicked.

On the other hand, those among us who are determined to the practice of goodness, not by its own intrinsic excellence, but for the sake of some private advantage, are cunning rather than good men. For what will not that man do in the dark who fears nothing but a witness and a judge? Should he meet a solitary individual in a desert place, whom he can rob of a large sum of money, and altogether unable to defend himself from being robbed, how will he behave? In such a case our man, who is just and honorable from principle and the nature of the thing itself, will converse with the stranger, assist him, and show him the way. But he who does nothing for the sake of another and measures everything by the advantage it brings, it is obvious, I suppose, how such a one will act; and should he deny that he would kill the man, or rob him of his treasure, his reason for this cannot be that he apprehends there is any moral turpitude in such actions, but only because he is afraid of a discovery, that is to say, that bad consequences will thence ensue, a sentiment this at which not only learned men but even clowns must blush.

It is therefore an absurd extravagance in some philosophers to assert that all things are necessarily just which are established by the civil laws and the institutions of nations. Are then the laws of tyrants just, simply because they are laws? . . . For my own part, I do not think such laws deserve any greater estimation than that passed during our own interregnum, which ordained that the dictator should be empowered to put to death with impunity whatever citizens he pleased, without hearing them in their own defence.

For there is but one essential justice which cements society, and one law which establishes this justice. This law is right reason, which is the true rule of all commandments and prohibitions. Whoever neglects this law, whether written or unwritten, is necessarily unjust and wicked.

But if justice consists in submission to written laws and national customs, and if, as the same school affirms, everything must be measured by utility alone, he who thinks that such conduct will be advantageous to him will neglect the laws, and break them if it is his power. And the consequence is that real justice has really no existence if it had not one by nature, and if that which was established as such on account of utility is overturned by some other utility.

But if nature does not ratify law, then all the virtues may lose their sway. For what becomes of generosity, patriotism and friendship? Where will the desire of benefiting our neighbors, or the gratitude that acknowledges kindness, be able to exist at all? For all these virtues proceed from our natural inclination to love mankind. And this is the true basis of justice, and without this not only the mutual charity of man, but the religious services of the gods, would be at an end; for these are preserved rather by the natural sympathy which subsists between divine and human beings, than by mere fear and humility.

But if the will of the people, the decrees of the senate, adjudications of magistrates, were sufficient to establish rights, then it might become right to rob, right to commit adultery, right to substitute forged wills, if such conduct were sanctioned by the votes or decrees of the multitude. But if the opinions and suffrages of foolish men had sufficient weight to outbalance the nature of things, then why should they not determine among them that what is essentially bad and pernicious should henceforth pass for good and beneficial? Or why, since law can make right out of injustice, should it not also be able to change evil into good?

But we have no other rule by which we may be capable of distinguishing between a good or a bad law than that of nature. Nor is it only right and wrong which are discriminated by nature, but generally all that is honorable is by this means distinguished from all that is shameful; for common sense has impressed in our minds the first principles of things, and has given us a general acquaintance with them, by which we connect with virtue every honorable quality, and with vice all that is disgraceful.

[The power of that law] is not only far more ancient than any existence of states and peoples, but is coequal with God himself, who beholds and governs both heaven and earth. For it is impossible that the divine mind can exist in a state devoid of reason; and divine reason must necessarily be possessed of a power to determine what is virtuous and what is vicious. Nor, because it was nowhere written that one man should maintain the pass of a bridge against the enemies' whole army, and that he should order the bridge behind him to be cut down, are we therefore to imagine that the valiant Cocles did not perform this great exploit agreeably to the laws of nature and the dictates of true bravery. Again, though in the reign of Tarquin there was no written law concerning adultery, it does not therefore follow that Sextus Tarquinius did not offend against the eternal law when he committed a rape on Lucretia, daughter of Tricipitinus. For, even then, he had the light of reason deduced from the nature of things, that incites to good actions and dissuades from evil ones; and which does not begin for the first time to be a law when it is drawn up in writing, but from the first moment that it exists. And this existence of moral obligation is coeternal with that of the divine mind. Therefore, the true and supreme law, whose commands and prohibitions are equally authoritative, is the right reason of the Sovereign Jupiter. . . .

Therefore as that divine mind, or reason, is the supreme law, so it exists in the mind of the sage, so far as it can be perfected in man. But with respect to civil laws, which are drawn up in various forms, and framed to meet the occasional requirements of the people, the name of law belongs to them not so much by right as by the favor of the people. For men prove by some such arguments as the following, that every law which deserves the name of a law, ought to be morally good and laudable. It is clear, say they, that laws were originally made for the security of the people, for the preservation of states, for the peace and happiness of society; and that they who first framed enactments of that time persuaded the people that they would write and publish such laws only as should conduce the general morality and happiness, if they would receive and obey them. And then such regulations, being thus settled and sanctioned, they were justly entitled laws. From which we may reasonably conclude that those who made unjustifiable and pernicious enactments for the people acted in a manner contrary to their own promises and professions, and established anything rather than laws, properly so called, since it is evident that the very signification of the word law comprehends the whole essence and energy of justice and equity. . . .

If then in the majority of nations, many pernicious and mischievous enactments are made, which have no more

right to the name of law than the mutual engagements of robbers, are we bound to call them laws? For as we cannot call the recipes of ignorant and unskilful empirics, who give poisons instead of medicines, the prescriptions of a physician, so likewise we cannot call that the true law of a people, of whatever kind it may be, if it enjoins what is injurious, let the people receive it as they will. For law is the just distinction between right and wrong, made conformable to that most ancient nature of all, the original and principal regulator of all things, by which the laws of men should be measured, whether they punish the guilty or protect and preserve the innocent.

The story of Scipio's dream, which follows, constitutes the last chapter of the treatise *On the Commonwealth*. It was the only fragment of that work known to Europe until 1822, when the librarian of the Vatican Library discovered other parts among the palimpsests in his collection. It is the most beautiful section of the book and was very much admired by scholars, especially those of the Renaissance, but it also offers an idea of the Roman conception of the world and of self-fulfillment. Cicero puts his ideas in the mouth of Scipio Africanus the Younger. Though written in 54 B.C., the scene is set in 129 B.C. when Scipio, in a dream, meets his illustrious ancestor who thus addresses him:

SCIPIO'S DREAM

Take courage, my Scipio, be not afraid, and carefully remember what I shall say to you.

Do you see that city Carthage, which, though brought under the Roman yoke by me, is now renewing former wars, and cannot live in peace (and he pointed to Carthage from a lofty spot, full of stars, and brilliant, and glittering)? To attack which city you are this day arrived in a station not much superior to that of a private soldier. Before two years, how-

ever, are elapsed, you shall be consul, and complete its overthrow; and you shall obtain by your own merit, the surname of Africanus which as yet belongs to you no otherwise than as derived from me. And when you have destroyed Carthage, and received the honor of a triumph, and been made censor, and in quality of ambassador visited Egypt, Syria, Asia and Greece, you shall be elected a second time consul in your absence and, by utterly destroying Numantia, put an end to a most dangerous war.

But when you have entered the Capi-

From *The Treatises of Cicero*, tr. C. D. Yonge (London, 1853), pp. 381–388. "On the Commonwealth," Book VI.

tol in your triumphal car, you shall find the Roman commonwealth all in a ferment, through the intrigues of my grandson, Tiberius Gracchus.

It is on this occasion, my dear Africanus, that you show your country the greatness of your understanding, capacity, and prudence. But I see that the destiny, however, of that time is, as it were, uncertain; for when your age shall have accomplished seven times eight revolutions of the sun, and your fatal hours shall be marked out by the natural product of these two numbers, each of which is esteemed a perfect one but for different reasons, then shall the whole city have recourse to you alone, and place its hopes in your auspicious name. On you the Senate, all good citizens, the allies, the people of Latium, shall cast their eyes; on you the preservation of the State shall entirely depend. In a word, if you escape the impious machinations of your relatives, you will, in quality of dictator, establish order and tranquility in the commonwealth. . . .

Now, in order to encourage you, my dear Africanus, continued the shade of my ancestor, to defend the state with the greater cheerfulness, be assured that for all those who have in any way conduced to the preservation, defence, and enlargement of their native country, there is a certain place in heaven where they shall enjoy an eternity of happiness. For nothing on earth is more agreeable to god, the supreme Governor of the universe, than the assemblies and societies of men united together by law, which are called states. It is from heaven that rulers and preservers came, and thither they return.

Though at these words I was extremely troubled, not so much at the fear of death, as at the perfidy of my own rela-

tions; yet I recollected myself enough to enquire whether he himself, my father Paulus, and others whom we look upon as dead were really living.

Yes, truly, replied he, they all enjoy life who have escaped from the chains of the body as from a prison. But as to what you call life on earth, that is no more than one form of death. But see, here comes your father, Paulus, towards you. And as soon as I observed him, my eyes burst out in a flood of tears; but he took me in his arms, embraced me, and bade me not weep.

When my first transports subsided and I regained the liberty of speech, I addressed my father thus: Thou best and most venerable of parents, since this, as I am informed by Africanus, is the only substantial life, why do I linger on earth, and not rather haste to come hither where you are?

That, replied he, is impossible; unless that God, whose temple is all that vast expanse you behold, shall free you from the fetters of the body, you can have no admission into this place. Mankind have received their being on this very condition, that they should labor for the preservation of that globe which is situated, as you see, in the midst of this temple and is called earth.

Men are likewise endowed with a soul which is a portion of the eternal fire which you call stars and constellations; and which, being round spherical bodies animated by divine intelligences, perform their circles and revolutions with amazing rapidity. It is your duty, therefore, my Publius, and that of all who have any veneration for the gods, to preserve this wonderful union of soul and body; nor without the express command of him who gave you a soul, should the least thought be entertained of quitting human life, lest you seem to desert the post assigned you by God himself.

But rather follow the examples of your grandfather here and of me your father, in paying a strict regard to justice and piety; which is due in a great degree to parents and relations, but most of all to our country. Such a life as this is the true way to heaven, and to the company of those who, after having lived on earth and escaped from the body, inhabit the place which you now behold.

This was the shining circle or zone whose remarkable brightness distinguishes it among the constellations, and which after the Greeks you call the Milky Way.

From thence, as I took a view of the universe, everything appeared beautiful and admirable; for there those stars are to be seen that are never visible from our globe, and everything appears of such magnitude as we could not have imagined. The least of all the stars was that removed furthest from heaven and situated next to the earth; I mean our moon, which shines from a borrowed light. Now the globes of the stars far surpass the magnitude of our earth, which at that distance appeared so exceedingly small, that I could not but be sensibly affected on seeing our whole empire no larger than if we touched the earth as it were at a single point.

And as I continued to observe the earth with great attention, How long, I pray you, said Africanus, will your mind be fixed on that object? Why do you not rather take a view of the magnificent temples among which you have arrived? The universe is composed of nine circles, or rather spheres, one of which is the heavenly one and is exterior to all the rest which it embraces; being itself the Supreme God, and bounding and containing the whole. In it are fixed those

stars which revolve with never varying courses. Below this are seven other spheres, which revolve in a contrary direction to that of the heavens. One of these is occupied by the globe which on earth they call Saturn. Next to that is the star of Jupiter, so benign and salutary to mankind. The third in order is that fiery and terrible planet called Mars. Below this again, almost in the middle region, is the Sun, the leader, governor and prince of the other luminaries; the soul of the world which it regulates and illumines, being of such vast size that it pervades and gives light to all places. Then follow Venus and Mercury, which attend as it were on the Sun. Lastly, the Moon, which shines only in the reflected beams of the Sun, moves in the lowest sphere of all. Below this, if we except that gift of the gods, the Soul, which has been given by the liberality of the gods to the human race, everything is mortal, and tends to dissolution; but above the Moon all is eternal. For the Earth, which is in the ninth globe, and occupies the centre, is immovable, and being the lowest all others gravitate towards it. When I had recovered myself from the astonishment occasioned by such a wonderful prospect, I thus addressed Africanus, "Pray, what is this sound that strikes my ears in so loud and agreeable a manner?" To which he replied: It is that which is called *the music of the spheres,* being produced by their motion and impulse; and being formed by unequal intervals, but such as are divided according to the justest proportion, it produces, by duly tempering acute with grave sounds, various concerts of harmony. For it is impossible that motions so great should be performed without any noise; and it is agreeable to nature that the extremes on one side should produce sharp, and on the other flat sounds. For which reason the sphere of the fixed stars, being the highest, and they being carried with a more rapid velocity, moves with a shrill and acute sound; whereas that of the Moon, being the lowest, moves with a very flat sound. As to the Earth, which makes the ninth sphere, it remains immovably fixed in the middle or lowest part of the universe. But those eight revolving circles in which both Mercury and Venus are moved with the same celerity, give out sounds that are divided by seven distinct intervals, which is generally the regulating number of all things.

This celestial harmony has been imitated by learned musicians, both on string instruments and with the voice, whereby they have opened to themselves a way to return to the celestial regions, as have likewise many others who have employed their sublime genius while on earth in cultivating the divine sciences.

By the amazing noise of this sound, the ears of mankind have been to some degree deafened. And indeed hearing is the dullest of the human senses. . . . And so inconceivably great is this sound which is produced by the rapid motion of the universe that the human ear is no more capable of receiving it than the eye is able to look steadfastly and directly on the sun . . .

While I was busy in admiring the scene of wonders, I could not help casting my eyes now and then on the earth. On which Africanus said: I perceive that you are still employed in contemplating the seat and residence of mankind. But if it appears to you so small, as in fact it really is, despise its vanities, and fix your attention forever on these heavenly objects. Is it possible that you should attain any human applause or glory that is worth the contending for? The earth, you

see, is peopled but in a very few places, and those too of small extent; and they appear like so many little spots of green scattered through vast uncultivated deserts. And those who inhabit the earth are not only so remote from each other as to be cut off from all mutual correspondence, but their situation being in oblique or contrary parts of the globe, or perhaps in those diametrically opposite to yours, all expectation of universal fame must fall to the ground.

You must likewise observe that the same globe of the earth is girt and surrounded with certain zones, whereof those two that are most remote from each other, and lie under the opposite poles of heaven, are congealed with frost; but that one in the middle which is far the largest is scorched with the intense heat of the sun. The other two are habitable, one towards the south, the inhabitants of which are your Antipodes with whom you have no connection; the other towards the north, is that which you inhabit, whereof a very small part, as you may see, falls to your share. For the whole extent of what you see is as it were but a little island, narrow at both ends and wide in the middle, which is surrounded by the sea which on earth you call the Great Atlantic Ocean, and which notwithstanding this magnificent name you see is very insignificant. And even in these cultivated and well known countries, has yours, or any of our names, ever passed the heights of the Caucasus or the currents of the Ganges? In what other parts to the north or to the south, or where the sun rises and sets, will your names ever be heard? And if we leave this out of the question, how small a space is there left for your glory to spread itself abroad? And how long will it remain in the memory of those whose minds are now full of it?

Besides all this, if the progeny of any future generation should wish to transmit to their posterity the traces of any one of us which they have heard from their forefathers, yet the deluges and combustions of the earth which must necessarily happen at their destined period will prevent our obtaining, not only an eternal, but even a durable glory. And after all, what does it signify whether those who shall hereafter be born talk of you, when those who have lived before you, whose number was perhaps not less, and whose merit certainly greater, were not so much as acquainted with your name? . . .

If, then, you wish to elevate your views to the contemplation of this eternal seat of splendor, you will not be satisfied with the praises of your fellow mortals, nor with any human rewards that your exploits can obtain; but VIRTUE herself must point out to you the true and only object worthy of your pursuit. . . . *Know, then that you are a god,* for a god it must be which flourishes and feels and recollects and foresees and governs, regulates and moves the body over which it is set as the Supreme Ruler does the world which is subject to him. For as that Eternal Being moves whatever is mortal in this world, so the immortal mind of man moves the frail body with which it is connected.

For whatever is always moving must be eternal. But that which derives its motion from a power which is foreign to itself, when that motion ceases must itself lose its animation. That alone, then, which moves itself can never cease to be moved, because it can never desert itself. Moreover, it must be the source and origin and principle of motion in all the rest. There can be nothing prior to a principle, for all things must originate from it ·and it cannot itself derive its existence

from any other source, for if it did it would no longer be a principle. And if it had no beginning it can have no end, for a beginning that is put an end to will neither be renewed by any other cause nor will it produce anything else but itself. All things, therefore, must originate from one source. Thus it follows that motion must have its source in something that is moved by itself, and which can neither have a beginning nor an end. Otherwise all the heavens and all nature must perish, for it is impossible that they can of themselves acquire any power of producing motion in themselves.

As, therefore, it is plain that what is moved by itself must be eternal, who will deny that this is the general condition and nature of minds? For, as everything is inanimate which is moved by an impulse exterior to itself, so what is animated is moved by an interior impulse of its own; for this is the peculiar nature and power of mind; and if that alone has the power of self motion, it can neither have had a beginning, nor can it have an end.

Do you, therefore, exercise this mind of yours in the best pursuits. And the best pursuits are those which consist in promoting the good of our country. Such employments will speed the flight of your mind to this its proper abode; and its flight will be still more rapid if, even while it is enclosed in the body, it will look abroad and disengage itself as much as possible from its bodily dwelling by the contemplation of things which are external to itself.

This it should do to the utmost of its power. For the minds of those who have given themselves up to the pleasures of the body, paying as it were a servile obedience to their lustful impulses, have violated the laws of god and man; and therefore, when they are separated from their bodies, flutter continually round the earth on which they lived, and are not allowed to return to this celestial region till they have been purified by the revolution of many ages.

Thus saying he vanished, and I awoke from my dream.

2. IMPERIAL ROME

The beginnings of the Roman Empire lie in the principate of Augustus (27 B.C.–14 A.D.), when the nephew of Julius Caesar became virtual monarch of what was still nominally a Republic. The end of the Empire in the west comes in the year 476, when the Herulian Odoacer, son of one of Attila's chieftains, deposed Romulus Augustulus, the last Western Emperor. But the Roman Empire continued to exist and Roman Emperors to rule in Constantinople or Nicaea until the last of them died in the ruins of his capital in 1453. Whether you count its life as lasting fifteen centuries or five, it endured for a very long time—long enough to leave an indelible impression on the memory of the world. The selections from Petronius and Seneca touch only on those aspects of the early Empire that provide a contrast with the preceding period and illustrate the changed *mores* of the time. They should not obscure the imposing outlines of the greatest power the world would know and remember for a very long while.

Petronius: from *Trimalchio's Dinner*

The family of Caius Petronius came from Gaul, but his career was made at the court of the Emperor Nero by whose favor he reigned for a while as the arbiter of taste and fashion, and by whose orders he eventually opened his veins in a warm bath in 66 A.D. In *Trimalchio's Dinner* the social satirist shows us a society dominated by the vulgar appetites and values of the new-rich, where the sobriety and the stern morals of an earlier age have given way to an overriding concern for conspicuous consumption.

Presently we took our places, and Alexandrian slaves poured water cooled with snow over our hands, while others approached our feet and with great skill began paring our corns; nor were they silent even over this rather disagreeable task, but kept singing all the time. I wanted to find out whether the whole household sang; and so I asked for something to drink; whereupon a slave served me, singing the while, like the others, a shrill ditty; and in fact, every slave who was asked for anything did exactly the same, so that you would have imagined yourself in the green-room of a comic opera troupe rather than in the dining-room of a private gentleman.

A very choice lot of hors d'oeuvres was then brought in; for we had already taken our places, all except Trimalchio himself for whom the seat of honor was reserved. Among the objects placed be-

From *Trimalchio's Dinner*, by Petronius Arbiter, tr. Harry Thurston Peck (New York, 1898).

fore us was a young ass made of Corinthian bronze and fitted with a sort of pack-saddle which contained on one side pale green olives and on the other side dark ones. Two dishes flanked this; and on the margin of them Trimalchio's name was engraved and the weight of the silver. Then there were little bridge-like structures of iron which held dormice seasoned with honey and poppy-seed; and smoking sausages were arranged over a silver grill which had underneath it dark Syrian plums to represent black coals, and scarlet pomegranate seeds to represent red hot ones.

In the midst of all this magnificence Trimalchio was brought in to the sound of music and propped up on a pile of well-stuffed cushions. The very sight of him almost made us laugh in spite of ourselves; for his shaven pate was thrust out of a scarlet robe, and around his neck he had tucked a long fringed napkin with a broad purple stripe running down the middle of it. On the little finger of his left hand he wore a huge gilt ring, and on the last joint of the next finger a ring that appeared to be of solid gold, but having little iron stars upon it. Moreover, lest we should fail to take in all his magnificence, he had bared his right arm, which was adorned with a golden bracelet and an ivory circle fastened by a glittering clasp.

As he sat there picking his teeth with a silver toothpick . . . a tray was brought in with a basket on which a wooden fowl was placed with its wings spread out in a circle after the fashion of setting hens. Immediately two slaves approached and amid a burst of music began to poke around in the straw, and having presently discovered there some pea-hens' eggs, they distributed them among the guests.

Trimalchio looked up during this operation and said, "Gentlemen, I had the hens' eggs placed under this fowl; but I'm rather afraid they have young chickens in them. Let's see whether they're still fit to suck."

So we took our spoons, which weighed not less than half a pound each, and broke the egg-shells, which were made of flour paste. As I did so, I was almost tempted to throw my egg on the floor, for it looked as though a chicken had just been formed inside; but when I heard an old diner-out by my side saying: "There's bound to be something good here," I thrust my finger through the shell and drew out a plump reed-bird, surrounded by yolk of egg well seasoned with pepper.

Trimalchio . . . called for the . . . dainties, inviting us with a loud voice to take a drink of honeyed wine also. Just then, however, at a signal given by music, all the dishes were swept off at once by a troop of slaves who sang over their work. Amid the bustle, a silver dish happened to fall on the floor, and when one of the servants started to pick it up, Trimalchio ordered him to be soundly cuffed, and told him to throw it down again; and presently there came in a servant, broom in hand, who swept up the silver dish along with the rest of the rubbish that lay on the floor. After this, there entered two long-haired Ethiopian slaves carrying little bags such as are used for sprinkling the sand in the amphitheatre, and from these they poured wine over our hands; for water was not good enough to wash in at that house.

The cook was rewarded with a drink, a silver crown, and a cup on a salver of Corinthian bronze. As Agamemnon began to examine this salver very closely, Trimalchio remarked:

"I'm the only person who has genuine Corinthian bronze."

I imagined that, in accordance with the rest of his conceit, he was going to say that his bronze had been brought to him from Corinth; but he gave the thing a better turn than that by saying:

"Perhaps you would like to know why I'm the only man who has true Corinthian bronze. Well, it's because the bronze-dealer from whom I buy is called Corinthus; for how can anything be Corinthian unless one has a Corinthus to make it? And lest you imagine that I'm an ignorant person, I'll let you know that I understand how Corinthian bronze first came to be made. When Troy was taken, Hannibal, a clever fellow and a sly dog, had all the bronze and silver statues heaped up into one pile and built a fire under them. The various metals all melted down into a single one, and then from the blended mass the artisans took metal and made dishes, and plates, and statuettes. That's the way that Corinthian bronze was first produced. . . . I'm a good deal of a connoisseur in silver too. I have a hundred large goblets, more or less, made out of that metal, on which Cassandra is represented as killing her sons, and the dead boys are depicted so vividly that you would think they were alive. I have also a thousand sacrificial bowls which Mummius left to my former owner, and on which is shown Dedalus shutting up Niobe in the Trojan Horse. I have, too, the battles of Hemeros and Petrais depicted on drinking cups, all of them very heavy. In fact, I wouldn't sell my special knowledge for any money."

A troupe [of Homeric actors] immediately came in, clattering their shields and spears. Trimalchio sat up on his couch, and while the Homeric actors in a pompous fashion began a dialogue in Greek verse, he read a book aloud in Latin, with a singsong tone of voice. Presently, when the rest had become silent, he said:

"Do you know what play they're acting? Diomede and Ganymede were two brothers. Their sister was Helen. Agamemnon carried her off and put a deer in her place for Diana, and so now Homer explains how the Trojans and the Parentines are waging war. Agamemnon, you must know, came off victor and gave his daughter Iphigenia to be the wife of Achilles. Thereupon Ajax went mad, and presently now will show us how it all ends."

As Trimalchio said this, the Homeric actors set up a shout, and while the slaves bustled about, a boiled calf was brought on in an enormous dish and with a helmet placed upon it. The actor who took the part of Ajax followed with a drawn sword, fell upon it as though he were mad, and hacking this way and that he cut up the calf and offered the bits to us on the point of his sword, to our great surprise.

We had no time to admire these elegant proceedings, for all of a sudden the ceiling of the room began to rumble and the whole dining-room shook. In consternation I jumped up, fearing lest some acrobat should come down through the roof; and all the other guests in surprise looked upward as though they expected some miracle from heaven. But, lo and behold, the panels of the ceiling slid apart, and suddenly a great hoop as though shaken off from a hogshead was let down, having gold crowns with jars of perfume hanging about its entire circumference. These things we were invited to accept as keepsakes, and presently a tray was set before us full of cakes with an image of Priapus as a centre piece made of confectionery and holding in its generous bosom apples of every sort and grapes, in the usual fashion, as being the god of gardens. We eagerly snatched at this magnificent display, and suddenly renewed our mirth at discovering a novel trick: for all the cakes and all the apples, when pressed the least bit, squirted saffron water into our faces.

Thinking that there was something of a religious turn to a course that was so suggestive of divine worship, we all rose up together and pronounced the formula, "Success to Augustus, Father of his Country!" But some of us, even after this solemn act, snatched up the apples and filled our napkins with them to carry away, a thing which I did myself, for I thought that I could not heap up enough presents in Giton's lap. [Giton was the narrator's slave.]

While this was going on, three slaves dressed in white tunics entered, two of whom placed images of the household gods upon the table, and the other one carrying around a bowl of wine called out "God bless us all!" Trimalchio told us that one image was the image of the God of Business, the second the image of the God of Luck, and the third the image of the God of Gain. There was a very striking bust of Trimalchio also, and as everybody else kissed it, I was ashamed not to do the same. . . .

[The company then moves off for a refresher in the bath house, where more food and drink are served, and the approach of dawn is ignored]

Soon after, for the first time, our mirth was checked: for when a young slave who was by no means bad looking had come in among the new servants, Trimalchio pounced upon him and began to kiss him for a long time. Whereupon

Fortunata [Trimalchio's wife] in order to prove her equal right in the household, began to abuse Trimalchio, styling him the scum of the earth and a disgraceful person. At last she called him a dog. Taking offence at this, Trimalchio threw a cup in her face, and she, as though she had lost an eye, shrieked and placed her trembling hands before her face. Scintilla also was very much disturbed and hid the cowering woman in her robe. A slave at once in an officious manner placed a cold jug against her cheek, leaning upon which Fortunata began to moan and cry.

On his side Trimalchio exclaimed: "How now? The jade doesn't remember that I took her off the stage and made an honest woman of her; she puffs herself up like a frog and fouls her own nest: a faggot not a lady. . . . Very well, now, I'll teach you to claw me, and just to show you on the spot what you've brought upon yourself, I order you, Habinnas, not to put her statue on my tomb, lest even after death I should be having scraps with her. In fact, to teach her how severe I can be, I forbid her to kiss me when I am dead."

After this thunderous blast, Habinnas fell to begging him not to be angry, saying: "None of us is perfect. We are men, you know, not gods." . . . On this Trimalchio could not keep back his tears and remarked: "I beg you, Habinnas, as you hope to be lucky, if I have done anything wrong, just spit in my face. I kissed this excellent young slave, not because of his good looks but because of his intelligence. He can say his multiplication table, he can read a book at sight, and he's saved up some money for himself out of his daily food allowance and bought a little stool and two ladles with his own money. So doesn't he deserve to have me keep my eye on him? But, of course, Fortunata won't have it. Isn't that so, you bandy legged creature? . . . But come, let's think of something more cheerful. I hope you're all comfortable, my friends. I used to be myself the same sort of person that you all are, but, by my own merits, I became what I am. It's brain that makes men, and everything else is all rot. One man'll tell you one rule of life, and another'll tell you another. But I say, "Buy cheap and sell dear," and so you see I'm just bursting with wealth. (Well, grunter, are you still crying? Pretty soon I'll give you something to cry for!) Well, as I was going on to say, my clever management brought me my present good fortune. When I came from Asia, I was about the height of this candle stick here and, in fact, I used to measure myself against it every day. And so as to get a beard on my mug I used to smear my lips with lamp oil. I was a great favorite with my master for fourteen years, and I was on pretty good terms with my master's wife. You understand what I mean. I'm not saying anything about it, because I'm not one of the boastful kind; but, as the gods would have it, I was really master in the house myself and I took his fancy greatly. Well, there's no need of a long story. He made me his residuary legatee, and I came into a fortune fit for a senator. But nobody ever gets enough. I became crazy to go into business; and, not to bore you, I had five ships built, loaded them with wine (and wine at that time

was worth its weight in gold) and sent them to Rome. You'd imagine that it had been actually planned that way, for every blessed ship was wrecked, and that's a fact not a fable. On one single day the sea swallowed down thirty million sesterces. Do you think I gave up? Not much! This loss just whetted my appetite as though it had been a mere nothing. I had other ships built, bigger and better, and they were luckier too, so that everybody said I was a plucky fellow. I loaded them with wine once more, with bacon, beans, ointment and slaves, and at that crisis Fortunata did a very nice thing, for she sold all her jewelry and even all her clothes, and put a hundred gold pieces in my hand. And this was really the germ of my good fortune. What the gods wish happens quickly. In a single round trip I piled up ten million sesterces, and immediately bought in all the lands that had belonged to my former owner. I built me a house and bought all the cattle that were offered for sale, and whatever I touched grew rich as a honey comb. After I began to have more money than my whole native land contains, then, says I, enough. I retired from business and began to lend money to freedmen. . . . But, believe me, a man is worth just as much as he has in his pocket; and according to what you hold in your hand so will you be held in esteem by others. That is what your friend has to say to you, a man who once, as they say, was a cat, but now is a king."

Seneca: from *The Epistles*

Another approach to life is revealed in the writings of a contemporary of Petronius, Lucius Annaeus Seneca, born in 4 B.C. at Cordova, in Spain, the son of a

Reprinted by permission of the publishers from Loeb Classical Library edition translated by R. M. Gummere, Seneca—*Epistulae Morales*, Volume I. Cambridge, Mass.: Harvard University Press.

talented father, Annaeus Seneca, the rhetorician, and member of a distinguished family. He was Nero's tutor, and a Stoic. His death, also by suicide, came shortly before that of Petronius. The two letters below were written by him between 63 and 65 A.D. to an Epicurean friend, the knight Lucilius.

ON THE PHILOSOPHER'S SECLUSION

"Do you bid me," you say, "to shun the throng and withdraw from men, and be content with my own conscience? Where are the counsels of your school, which order a man to die in the midst of active work?" As to the course which I seem to you to be urging on you now and then, my object in shutting myself up and locking the door is to be able to help a greater number. I never spend a day in idleness; I appropriate even a part of the night for study. I do not allow time for sleep but yield to it when I must, and when my eyes are wearied with waking and ready to fall shut, I keep them at their task. I have withdrawn not only from men, but from affairs, especially from my own affairs; I am working for later generations, writing down some ideas that may be of assistance to them. There are certain wholesome counsels, which may be compared to prescriptions of useful drugs; these I am putting into writing; for I have found them helpful in ministering to my own sores, which, if not wholly cured, have at any rate ceased to spread.

I point other men to the right path, which I have found late in life, when wearied with wandering. I cry out to them: "Avoid whatever pleases the throng: avoid the gifts of Chance! Halt before every good which Chance brings to you, in a spirit of doubt and fear; for it is the dumb animals and fish that are deceived by tempting hopes. Do you call these things the 'gifts' of Fortune? They are snares. And any man among you who wishes to live a life of safety will avoid,

to the utmost of his power, these limed twigs of her favor, by which we mortals, most wretched in this respect also, are deceived; for we think that we hold them in our grasp, but they hold us in theirs. Such a career leads us into precipitous ways, and life on such heights ends in a fall. Moreover, we cannot even stand up against prosperity when she begins to drive us to leeward; nor can we go down, either, 'with the ship at least on her course' or once for all; Fortune does not capsize us—she plunges our bows under and dashes us on the rocks.

Hold fast then to this sound and wholesome rule of life; that you indulge the body only so far as is needful for good health. The body should be treated more rigorously, that it may not be disobedient to the mind. Eat merely to relieve your hunger; drink merely to quench your thirst; dress merely to keep out the cold; house yourself merely as a protection against personal discomfort. It matters little whether the house be built of turf, or of variously colored imported marble; understand that a man is sheltered just as well by a thatch as by a roof of gold. Despise everything that useless toil creates as an ornament and an object of beauty. And reflect that nothing except the soul is worthy of wonder; for to the soul, if it be great, naught is great.

When I commune in such terms with myself and with future generations, do you not think that I am doing more good than when I appear as counsel in court, or stamp my seal upon a will, or lend my assistance in the senate, by word or action, to a candidate? Believe me, those who seem to be busied with nothing are busied with the greater tasks; they are dealing at the same time with writings mortal and things immortal.

But I must stop, and pay my customary contribution to balance this letter. The payment shall not be made from my own property; for I am still conning Epicurus. I read today in his works the following sentence: "If you would enjoy real freedom, you must be the slave of Philosophy." The man who submits and surrenders himself to her is not kept waiting; he is emancipated on the spot. For the very service of Philosophy is freedom. . . .

ON THE GOD WITHIN US

You are doing an excellent thing, one which will be wholesome for you, if, as you write me, you are persisting in your effort to attain a sound understanding; it is foolish to pray for this when you can acquire it from yourself. We do not need to uplift our hands towards heaven, or to beg the keeper of a temple to let us approach his idol's ear, as if in this way our prayers were more likely to be heard. God is near you, he is with you, he is within you. This is what I mean: a holy spirit indwells within us, one who marks our good and bad deeds, and is our guardian. As we treat this spirit, so are we treated by it. Indeed, no man can be good without the help of God. Can one rise superior to fortune unless God helps him to rise? He it is that gives noble and upright counsel. In each good man "A god doth dwell, but what god know we not."

If ever you have come upon a grove that is full of ancient trees which have grown to an unusual height, shutting out a view of the sky by a veil of pleached and intertwining branches, then the loftiness of the forest, the seclusion of the spot, and your marvel at the thick unbroken shade in the midst of the open spaces will prove to you the presence of deity. Or if a cave, made by the deep crumbling of the rocks, holds up a mountain on its arch, a place not built with human hands but hollowed out into such spaciousness by natural causes, your soul will be deeply moved by a certain intimation of the existence of god. We worship the sources of mighty rivers; we erect altars at places where great streams burst suddenly from hidden sources; we adore springs of hot water as divine, and consecrate certain pools because of their dark waters or their immeasurable depth. If you see a man who is unterrified in the midst of strangers, untouched by desire, happy in adversity, peaceful amid the storm, who looks down upon men from a higher plane, and views the gods on a footing of equality, will not a feeling of reverence for him steal over you? Will you not say: "This quality is too great and too lofty to be regarded as resembling this petty body in which it dwells? A divine power has descended upon that man." When a soul rises superior to other souls, when it is under control, when it passes through every experience as if it were of small account, when it smiles at our fears and at our prayers, it is stirred by a force from heaven. A thing like this cannot stand upright unless it be propped by the divine. Therefore, a greater part of it abides in that place from whence it came down to earth. Just as the rays of the sun do indeed touch the earth, but still abide at the source from which they are sent; even so the great and hallowed soul, which has come down in order that we may have a nearer knowledge of divinity, does indeed associate with us, but still cleaves to its origin; on that source it depends, thither it turns its gaze and strives to go, and it concerns itself with our doings only as a being superior to ourselves.

What, then, is such a soul? One which is resplendent with no external good, but only with its own. For what is more foolish than to praise in a man the qualities which come from without? And what is more insane than to marvel at characteristics which may at the next instant be passed on to someone else? A golden bit does not make a better horse. . . .

No man ought to glory except in that which is his own. We praise a vine if it makes the shoots teem with increase, if by its weight it bends to the ground the very poles which hold its fruit; would any man prefer to this vine one from which golden grapes and golden leaves hang down? In a vine the virtue peculiarly its own is fertility; in man also we should praise that which is his own. Suppose that he has a retinue of comely slaves and a beautiful house, that his farm is large and large his income; none of these things is in the man himself; they are all on the outside. Praise the quality in him which cannot be given or snatched away, that which is the peculiar property of the man. Do you ask what this is? It is soul, and reason brought to perfection in the soul. For man is a reasoning animal. Therefore, man's highest good is attained, if he has fulfilled the good for which nature designed him at first. And what is it which this reason demands of him? The easiest thing in the world,—to live in accordance with his own nature. But this is turned into a hard task by the general madness of mankind. We push one another into vice. And how can a man be recalled to salvation, when he has none to restrain him, and all mankind to urge him on? Farewell.

V. The Early Christian World

Jesus Christ was probably born in the year we now write paradoxically as 4 B.C., in the principate of Octavianus Augustus. The active years of his mission were probably between 26 and 30 A.D., in which year his crucifixion is usually placed, in the reign of the Emperor Tiberius. There can be no overstating the historical significance of this brief career but, immediately speaking, his followers were only a small and obscure sect among many—a Jewish sect offering one more of those mystery religions that were so popular in the Hellenistic world. In the age of the Empire, the influence of such Oriental cults was growing apace. When, in the second century, the secular power began to show signs of disintegration, men found encouragement in doctrines of a divine law independent of and superior to temporal law, doctrines which substituted spiritual authority for that of an increasingly oppressive and inefficient secular state. Along with the worshippers of Mithra, Isis, or the Invincible Sun, the followers of Jesus Christ benefited from this new mood to which they offered an authority and a consolation beyond the material world, and their faith was eventually rewarded by success—worldly success.

1. GOSPEL TEXTS

Insofar as the early Christians excited any notice outside the Jewish community which regarded them as heretics, it was through their ideas, which struck outsiders as decidedly odd. To us who have come to take them for granted to the extent of ignoring them, this may in turn seem odd. But a dispassionate reading of the passages below should show why (1) the Jewish community, (2) the Roman administrators, (3) the respectable property-owning man-in-the-street might read revolutionary threats in the new religion.

From: *The Gospel According to St. Luke*

Now in the fifteenth year of the reign of Tiberius Caesar, Pontius Pilate being governor of Judaea, and Herod being tetrarch of Galilee, and his brother Philip tetrarch of Ituraea and of the region of Trachonitis, and Lysanias the tetrarch of Abilene, Annas and Caiaphas being the high priests, the word of God came unto John the son of Zacharias in the wilderness. And he came into all the country about Jordan, preaching the baptism of repentance for the remission of sins; as it is written in the book of the words of Esaias the prophet, saying,

All passages from the New Testament are adapted from the King James version of the Bible.

158

The voice of one crying in the wilderness, Prepare ye the way of the Lord, Make his paths straight. Every valley shall be filled, and every mountain and hill shall be brought low; And the crooked shall be made straight, And the rough ways shall be made smooth; And all flesh shall see the salvation of God.

Then said he to the multitude that came forth to be baptized of him, O generation of vipers, who hath warned you to flee from the wrath to come? Bring forth therefore fruits worthy of repentance, and begin not to say within yourselves, We have Abraham to our father: for I say unto you, That God is able of these stones to raise up children unto Abraham. And now also the axe is laid unto the root of the trees: every tree therefore which bringeth not forth good fruit is hewn down, and cast into the fire. And the people asked him, saying, What shall we do then? He answereth and saith unto them, He that hath two coats, let him impart to him that hath none; and he that hath meat, let him do likewise. Then came also publicans to be baptized, and said unto him, Master, what shall we do? And he said unto them, Exact no more than that which is appointed you. And the soldiers likewise demanded of him, saying, And what shall we do? And he said unto them, Do violence to no man, neither accuse any falsely; and be content with your wages.

And as the people were in expectation, and all men mused in their hearts of John, whether he were the Christ, or not; John answered, saying unto them all, I indeed baptize you with water; but one mightier than I cometh, the latchet of whose shoes I am not worthy to unloose: he shall baptize you with the Holy Ghost and with fire: whose fan is in his hand, and he will thoroughly purge his floor,

and will gather the wheat into his garner; but the chaff he will burn with fire unquenchable.

And many other things in his exhortation preached he unto the people. But Herod the tetrarch, being reproved by him for Herodias his brother Philip's wife, and for all the evils which Herod had done, added yet this above all, that he shut up John in prison.

Now when all the people were baptized, it came to pass, that Jesus also being baptized, and praying, the heaven was opened, and the Holy Ghost descended in a bodily shape like a dove upon him, and a voice came from heaven, which said, Thou art my beloved Son; in thee I am well pleased.

And Jesus returned in the power of the Spirit into Galilee: and there went out a fame of him through all the region round about. And he taught in their synagogues, being glorified of all.

And he came to Nazareth, where he had been brought up: and, as his custom was, he went into the synagogue on the sabbath day, and stood up for to read. And there was delivered unto him the book of the prophet Esaias. And when he had opened the book, he found the place where it was written,

The Spirit of the Lord is upon me, Because he hath anointed me to preach the gospel to the poor; He hath sent me to heal the brokenhearted, to preach deliverance to the captives, And recovering of sight to the blind, To set at liberty them that are bruised, To preach the acceptable year of the Lord.

And he closed the book, and he gave it again to the minister, and sat down. And the eyes of all them that were in the synagogue were fastened on him. And he began to say unto them, This day is this scripture fulfilled in your ears. And all bare him witness, and wondered at the gracious words which proceeded out of his mouth. And they said, Is not this Joseph's son? And he said unto them, Ye will surely say unto me this proverb, Physician, heal thyself: whatsoever we have heard done in Capernaum, do also here in thy country. And he said, Verily I say unto you, No prophet is accepted in his own country. But I tell you of a truth, many widows were in Israel in the days of Elias, when the heaven was shut up three years and six months, when great famine was throughout all the land; but unto none of them was Elias sent, save unto Sarepta, a city of Sidon, unto a woman that was a widow. And many lepers were in Israel in the time of Eliseus the prophet; and none of them was cleansed, saving Naaman the Syrian. And all they in the synagogue, when they heard these things, were filled with wrath, and rose up, and thrust him out of the city, and led him unto the brow of the hill whereon their city was built, that they might cast him down head-long. But he passing through the midst of them went his way, and came down to Capernaum, a city of Galilee, and taught them on the sabbath days. And they were astonished at his doctrine: for his word was with power.

From: *The Gospel According to St. Matthew*

And seeing the multitudes, he went up into a mountain: and when he was set, his disciples came unto him: and he opened his mouth, and taught them, saying,

Blessed are the poor in spirit: for theirs is the kingdom of heaven.

Blessed are they that mourn: for they shall be comforted.

Blessed are the meek: for they shall inherit the earth.

Blessed are they which do hunger and thirst after righteousness: for they shall be filled.

Blessed are the merciful: for they shall obtain mercy.

Blessed are the pure in heart: for they shall see God.

Blessed are the peacemakers: for they shall be called the children of God.

Blessed are they which are persecuted for righteousness' sake: for theirs is the kingdom of heaven.

Blessed are ye, when men shall revile you, and persecute you, and shall say all manner of evil against you falsely, for my sake. Rejoice, and be exceeding glad: for great is your reward in heaven: for so persecuted they the prophets which were before you.

Ye are the salt of the earth: but if the salt have lost his savour, wherewith shall it be salted? It is thenceforth good for nothing, but to be cast out, and to be trodden under foot of men. Ye are the light of the world. A city that is set on an hill cannot be hid. Neither do men light a candle, and put it under a bushel, but on a candlestick; and it giveth light unto all that are in the house. Let your light so shine before men, that they may see your good works, and glorify your Father which is in heaven.

Think not that I am come to destroy the law, or the prophets: I am not come to destroy, but to fulfil. For verily I say unto you, Till heaven and earth pass, one jot or one tittle shall in no wise pass from the law, till all be fulfilled. Whosoever therefore shall break one of these least commandments, and shall teach men so, he shall be called the least in the kingdom of heaven: but whosoever shall do and teach them, the same shall be called great in the kingdom of heaven. For I say unto you, That except your righteousness shall exceed the righteousness of the scribes and Pharisees, ye shall in no case enter into the kingdom of heaven.

Ye have heard that it was said by them of old time, Thou shalt not kill; and whosoever shall kill shall be in danger of the judgment: but I say unto you, That whosoever is angry with his brother without a cause shall be in danger of the judgment: and whosoever shall say to his brother, Raca, shall be in danger of the council: but whosoever shall say, Thou fool, shall be in danger of hell fire. Therefore if thou bring thy gift to the altar, and there rememberest that thy brother hath aught against thee; leave there thy gift before the altar, and go thy way; first be reconciled to thy brother, and then come and offer thy gift. Agree with thine adversary quickly, whiles thou art in the way with him; lest at any time the adversary deliver thee to the judge, and the judge deliver thee to the officer, and thou be cast into prison. Verily I say unto thee, Thou shalt by no means come out thence, till thou hast paid the uttermost farthing.

Ye have heard that it was said by them of old time, Thou shalt not commit adultery: but I say unto you, That whosoever looketh on a woman to lust after her hath committed adultery with her already in his heart. And if thy right eye offend thee, pluck it out, and cast it from thee: for it is profitable for thee that one of thy members should perish, and not that thy whole body should be cast into hell. And

if thy right hand offend thee, cut it off, and cast it from thee: for it is profitable for thee that one of thy members should perish, and not that thy whole body should be cast into hell. It hath been said, Whosoever shall put away his wife, saving for the cause of fornication, causeth her to commit adultery: and whosoever shall marry her that is divorced committeth adultery.

Again, ye have heard that it hath been said by them of old time, Thou shalt not forswear thyself, but shalt perform unto the Lord thine oaths: but I say unto you, Swear not at all; neither by heaven; for it is God's throne: nor by the earth; for it is his footstool: neither by Jerusalem; for it is the city of the great King. Neither shalt thou swear by the head, because thou canst not make one hair white or black. But let your communication be, yea, yea; Nay, nay: for whatsoever is more than these cometh of evil.

Ye have heard that it hath been said, An eye for an eye, and a tooth for a tooth: but I say unto you, That ye resist not evil: but whosoever shall smite thee on thy right cheek, turn to him the other also. And if any man will sue thee at the law, and take away thy coat, let him have thy cloak also. And whosoever shall compel thee to go a mile, go with him twain. Give to him that asketh thee, and from him that would borrow of thee turn not thou away.

Ye have heard that it hath been said, Thou shalt love thy neighbour, and hate thine enemy. But I say unto you, Love your enemies, bless them that curse you, do good to them that hate you, and pray for them which despitefully use you, and persecute you; that ye may be the children of your Father which is in heaven: for he maketh his sun to rise on the evil and on the good, and sendeth rain on the just and on the unjust. For if ye love them which love you, what reward have ye? do not even the publicans the same? And if ye salute your brethren only, what do ye more than others? do not even the publicans so? Be ye therefore perfect, even as your Father which is in heaven is perfect.

Take heed that ye do not your alms before men, to be seen of them: otherwise ye have no reward of your Father which is in heaven.

Therefore when thou doest thine alms, do not sound a trumpet before thee, as the hypocrites do in the synagogues and in the streets, that they may have glory of men. Verily I say unto you, They have their reward. But when thou doest alms, let not thy left hand know what thy right hand doeth: that thine alms may be in secret: and thy Father which seeth in secret himself shall reward thee openly.

And when thou prayest, thou shalt not be as the hypocrites are: for they love to pray standing in the synagogues and in the corners of the streets, that they may be seen of men. Verily I say unto you, They have their reward. But thou, when thou prayest, enter into thy closet, and when thou hast shut thy door, pray to thy Father which is in secret; and thy Father which seeth in secret shall reward thee openly. But when ye pray, use not vain repetitions, as the heathen do: for they think that they shall be heard for their much speaking. Be not ye therefore like unto them: for your Father knoweth what things ye have need of, before ye ask him. After this manner therefore pray ye: Our Father which art in heaven, Hallowed be thy name. Thy kingdom come. Thy will be done in earth, as it is in heaven. Give us this day our daily bread. And forgive us our debts, as we forgive our

debtors. And lead us not into temptation, but deliver us from evil: For thine is the kingdom, and the power, and the glory, for ever. Amen. For if ye forgive men their trespasses, your heavenly Father will also forgive you: but if ye forgive not men their trespasses, neither will your Father forgive your trespasses.

Moreover when ye fast, be not, as the hypocrites, of a sad countenance: for they disfigure their faces, that they may appear unto men to fast. Verily I say unto you, They have their reward. But thou, when thou fastest, anoint thine head, and wash thy face; that thou appear not unto men to fast, but unto thy Father which is in secret: and thy Father, which seeth in secret, shall reward thee openly.

Lay not up for yourselves treasures upon earth, where moth and rust doth corrupt, and where thieves break through and steal: but lay up for yourselves treasures in heaven, where neither moth nor rust doth corrupt, and where thieves do not break through nor steal: for where your treasure is, there will your heart be also. The light of the body is the eye: if therefore thine eye be single, thy whole body shall be full of light. But if thine eye be evil, thy whole body shall be full of darkness. If therefore the light that is in thee be darkness, how great is that darkness! No man can serve two masters: for either he will hate the one, and love the other; or else he will hold to the one, and despise the other. Ye cannot serve God and mammon. Therefore I say unto you, Take no thought for your life, what ye shall eat, or what ye shall drink; nor yet for your body, what ye shall put on. Is not the life more than meat, and the body than raiment? Behold the fowls of the air: for they sow not, neither do they reap, nor gather into barns; yet your heavenly Father feedeth them. Are ye not much better than they? Which of you by taking thought can add one cubit unto his stature? And why take ye thought for raiment? Consider the lilies of the field, how they grow; they toil not, neither do they spin: and yet I say unto you, That even Solomon in all his glory was not arrayed like one of these. Wherefore, if God so clothe the grass of the field, which today is, and tomorrow is cast into the oven, shall he not much more clothe you, O ye of little faith? Therefore take no thought, saying, What shall we eat? or, What shall we drink? or, Wherewithal shall we be clothed? (For after all these things do the Gentiles seek:) for your heavenly Father knoweth that ye have need of all these things. But seek ye first the kingdom of God, and his righteousness; and all these things shall be added unto you. Take therefore no thought for the morrow: for the morrow shall take thought for the things of itself. Sufficient unto the day is the evil thereof.

Judge not, that ye be not judged. For with what judgment ye judge, ye shall be judged: and with what measure ye mete, it shall be measured to you again. And why beholdest thou the mote that is in thy brother's eye, but considerest not the beam that is in thine own eye? Or how wilt thou say to thy brother, Let me pull out the mote out of thine eye; and, behold, a beam is in thine own eye? Thou hypocrite, first cast out the beam out of thine own eye; and then shalt thou see clearly to cast out the mote out of thy brother's eye.

Give not that which is holy unto the dogs, neither cast ye your pearls before swine, lest they trample them under their feet, and turn again and rend you.

Ask, and it shall be given you; seek, and ye shall find; knock, and it shall be opened unto you: for every one that asketh receiveth; and he that seeketh findeth; and to him that knocketh it shall be opened. Or what man is there of you, whom if his son ask bread, will he give him a stone? Or if he ask a fish, will he give him a serpent? If ye then, being evil, know how to give good gifts unto your children, how much more shall your Father which is in heaven give good things to them that ask him? Therefore all things whatsoever ye would that men should do to you, do ye even so to them: for this is the law and the prophets.

Enter ye in at the strait gate: for wide is the gate, and broad is the way, that leadeth to destruction, and many there be which go in thereat: because strait is the gate, and narrow is the way, which leadeth unto life, and few there be that find it.

Beware of false prophets, which come to you in sheep's clothing, but inwardly they are ravening wolves. Ye shall know them by their fruits. Do men gather grapes of thorns, or figs of thistles? Even so every good tree bringeth forth good fruit; but a corrupt tree bringeth forth evil fruit. A good tree cannot bring forth evil fruit, neither can a corrupt tree bring forth good fruit. Every tree that bringeth not forth good fruit is hewn down, and cast into the fire. Wherefore by their fruits ye shall know them. Not every one that saith unto me, Lord, Lord, shall enter into the kingdom of heaven; but he that doeth the will of my Father which is in heaven. Many will say to me in that day, Lord, Lord, have we not prophesied in thy name? and in thy name have cast out devils? and in thy name done many wonderful works? And then will I profess unto them, I never knew you: depart from me, ye that work iniquity.

Therefore whosoever heareth these

sayings of mine, and doeth them, I will liken him unto a wise man, which built his house upon a rock; and the rain descended, and the floods came, and the winds blew, and beat upon that house; and it fell not: for it was founded upon a rock. And every one that heareth these sayings of mine, and doeth them not, shall be likened unto a foolish man, which built his house upon the sand: and the rain descended, and the floods came, and the winds blew, and beat upon that house; and it fell: and great was the fall of it.

And it came to pass, when Jesus had ended these sayings, the people were astonished at his doctrine: for he taught them as one having authority, and not as the scribes.

2. THE GROWTH OF CHRISTIANITY

During the years when rebellion and wars of succession were rending the Roman Empire, Christianity became a power to reckon with on the political as well as the religious plane, and contenders for the Imperial throne recognized this, first by granting it toleration, later by adopting it themselves, and lastly by proscribing paganism (in 378). In chapter XV of *The Decline and Fall of the Roman Empire,* Edward Gibbon assigns five causes for this success: (1) the inflexible and . . . intolerant zeal of the Christians, (2) the doctrine of a future life, (3) the miraculous powers ascribed to the primitive Church, (4) the pure and austere morals of the Christians, (5) the union and discipline of the Christian republic, which gradually formed an independent and increasing state in the heart of the Roman Empire.

Pliny the Younger: from *Letters*

Pliny the Younger, 62–120 A.D., Roman writer and friend of the emperor Trajan, was governor of the province of Bithynia about a hundred years after the death of Christ. In this capacity he had to face the problems created by the sect of Christians, who refused to worship gods and Emperor and who appeared to many as a dangerous subversive and antisocial group. The law was not too clear, and Pliny was a prudent man; so he sought the advice of his master. His letter, followed by Trajan's answer, is given below, translated from the tenth book of his *Letters* (96, 97).

PLINY TO TRAJAN

It is my rule, Master, to submit all my doubts to you: for who could better guide me when I hesitate, or instruct me in my ignorance? I have never been present at the trials of the Christians; I do not know therefore what method and what measure should be observed in pursuing or in punishing them. And not without grave doubt I wonder whether any difference is to be made according to age, or whether tender youth should be treated on the same footing as the adult; whether pardon can follow on repentance, whether a man who has once been a Christian gains nothing by recanting, whether the mere profession of Christianity is to be punished, though no crimes have been committed or only the crimes which the term implies.

In the meantime, this is the rule that I have followed toward those who have been denounced to me as Christians: I asked them whether they were Christians. To those who confessed, I repeated the question a second and then a third time, threatening them with capital punishment. Those who persisted were executed; for whatever the meaning of their admission, at least I felt sure that such stubbornness and such inflexible obstinacy had to be punished. Others, possessed with the same infatuation, I have directed to be sent to Rome as being Roman citizens. Soon, as usually happens in such cases, the accusation spreads with the spread of the investigation, and several different cases have come to light.

An unsigned placard was set up, accusing a large number of persons by name. Those who denied being or having been Christians, if they called upon the gods according to the formula that I dictated, and sacrificed with incense and wine before your image which I had ordered to be brought to this purpose with the statues of the gods, if finally they blasphemed Christ—all things which, it is said, cannot be obtained from those who are really Christians—these I thought it proper to release. Others, whose name had been given by an informer, began by saying they were Christians, then pretended that they were not, that they had been of that persuasion but were no more, some for three years, others for many more, some even for twenty. All of them also worshipped your image as well as the statues of the gods, and cursed Christ.

Anyway, they affirmed that the whole of their guilt or their error was that they were in the habit of meeting on certain definite days before sunrise, to sing a hymn to Christ as to a god, to swear by solemn oath not to commit some crime but to commit neither fraud, nor theft, nor adultery, never to break their word or to deny a trust when called upon to deliver it up. These rites accomplished, their custom was to separate and then to reassemble to take their food, which, whatever has been said about it, is ordinary and innocent. Even this practice they had given up after my edict by which I had forbidden political associations according to your orders. I thought it the more necessary to extract the truth from two slaves who were said to be deaconesses, even if they had to be tortured. I found only an unreasonable and excessive superstition.

Therefore I have suspended the proceedings to have recourse to your advice. The matter seemed to me well worth referring to you, especially because of the numbers of the accused. There is a multitude of persons of all ages, of all ranks, of both sexes too, who are or will be endangered. For it is not only throughout the cities, but also in the villages and the countryside that the contagion of this superstition has spread; however, I think it is possible to halt and cure it.

Certainly, there is no doubt that the temples which had been standing almost deserted begin to fill, that the sacred rites are taken up again after a long intermission, that the flesh of sacrificial animals is everywhere being sold which had only been finding very rare purchasers until recently. From which it is easy to believe what a lot of people could be cured from this error if room was left for repentance.

TRAJAN TO PLINY

My dear Pliny, you have followed exactly the right conduct in examining the cases of those who had been denounced to you as Christians. For it is impossible to set up a general rule which should have, so to speak, a fixed form of application. These people should not be pursued (searched for) automatically. If they are denounced and found guilty, they should be punished, but with the following restriction: the party that denies being a Christian and gives manifest proof that he is not, by his acts, I mean by sacrificing to our gods, even if he has incurred suspicion in the past, shall be pardoned as the price of his repentance.

As for anonymous denunciations, they must play no part as evidence in any accusation. It is a detestable procedure and does not belong in our age.

The problem continued to plague Roman rulers, beginning with Trajan's adopted son, Hadrian, who succeeded him in 117 A.D. and died in 138 A.D. Nor, as can be seen, did they in general think to solve the problem by persecution. At any rate, by the beginning of the fourth century the Christians had become too powerful and numerous to offend, and from now on they would be not only tolerated but wooed by the men who disputed control of the Empire. As the edict of Galerius shows, Constantine's proclamation was not the first official recognition of the right of Christians to their own beliefs.

RESCRIPT OF HADRIAN TO MINUCIUS FUNDANUS

I have received the letter written to me by your predecessor, Serenus Granianus, a most excellent man; and it does not seem well to pass over this report in silence, lest both the innocent be confounded and an occasion for robbery be given to false accusers. Accordingly, if the inhabitants are able to sustain their accusations openly against Christians, so as to charge them with something before the tribunal, I do not forbid them to do this. But I do not permit mere tumultuous cries and acclamations to be used, for it is much more equitable that if anyone wishes to make accusation, you should know the charges. If, therefore, anyone charges and proves that the men designated have done anything contrary to the laws, you are to fix penalties in proportion to their transgressions. By Hercules, you shall take special care, if, out of calumny, anyone prosecutes one of them, to inflict on the accuser a more severe punishment for his villainy.

EDICT OF TOLERATION BY GALERIUS, 311 A.D.

Among other arrangements which we are always accustomed to make for the prosperity and welfare of the republic, we had desired formerly to bring all things into harmony with the ancient laws and public order of the Romans, and to provide that even the Christians who had left the religion of their fathers should come back to reason; since, indeed, the Christians themselves, for some reason, had followed such a caprice and

From *Translations and Reprints from the Original Sources of European History* (henceforth to be cited as *Translations and Reprints*), Vol. 4, No. 1, D. C. Munro, Ed. (Philadelphia, 1897). Reprinted by permission of the University of Pennsylvania Press.

had fallen into such a folly that they would not obey the institutes of antiquity, which perchance their own ancestors had first established; but at their own will and pleasure, they would thus make laws unto themselves which they should observe and would collect various peoples in divers places in congregations. Finally, when our law had been promulgated to the effect that they should conform to the institutes of antiquity, many were subdued by the fear of danger, many even suffered death. And yet since most of them persevered in their determination, and we saw that they neither paid the reverence and awe due to the gods nor worshipped the God of the Christians, in view of our most mild clemency and the constant habit by which we are accustomed to grant indulgence to all, we thought that we ought to grant our most prompt indulgence also to these, so that they may again be Christians and may hold their conventicles, provided they do nothing contrary to good order. But we shall tell the magistrates in another letter what they ought to do.

Wherefore, for this our indulgence, they ought to pray to their God for our safety, for that of the republic, and for their own, that the republic may continue uninjured on every side, and that they may be able to live securely in their homes.

EDICT OF MILAN, 313 A.D.

When I, Constantine Augustus, as well as I, Licinius Augustus, had fortunately met near Mediolanum [Milan] and were considering everything that pertained to the public welfare and security, we thought that, among other things which we saw would be for the good of many, those regulations pertaining to the reverence of the Divinity ought certainly to be made first, so that we might grant to the Christians and to all others full authority to observe that religion which each preferred; whence any Divinity whatsoever in the seat of the heavens may be propitious and kindly disposed to us and all who are placed under our rule. And thus by this wholesome counsel and most upright provision we thought to arrange that no one whatsoever should be denied the opportunity to give his heart to the observance of the Christian religion, or of that religion which he should think best for himself, so that the supreme Deity, to whose worship we freely yield our hearts, may show in all things His usual favor and benevolence. Therefore, your Worship should know that it has pleased us to remove all conditions whatsoever, which were in the rescripts formerly given to you officially, concerning the Christians, and now any one of these who wishes to observe the Christian religion may do so freely and openly, without any disturbance or molestation. We thought it fit to commend these things most fully to your care that you may know that we have given to those Christians free and unrestricted opportunity of religious worship. When you see that this has been granted to them by us, your Worship will know that we have also conceded to other religions the right of open and free observance of their worship for the sake of the peace of our times, that each one may have the free opportunity to worship as he pleases; this regulation is made that we may not seem to detract aught from any dignity or any religion. Moreover, in the case of the Christians especially, we esteemed it best to order that if it happens that anyone heretofore has bought from our treasury or from anyone whatsoever, those places where they were previously accustomed to assemble, concerning which a certain decree had been made and a letter sent to you officially, the same shall be restored to the Christians without payment or any claim of recompense and without any kind of fraud or deception. Those, moreover, who have obtained the same by gift, are likewise to return them at once to the Christians. Besides, both those who have purchased and those who have secured them by gift, are to appeal to the vicar if they seek any recompense from our bounty, that they may be cared for through our clemency. All this property ought to be delivered at once to the community of the Christians through your intercession, and without delay. And since these Christians are known to have possessed not only those places in which they were accustomed to assemble, but also other property, namely the churches, belonging to them as a corporation and not as individuals, all these things which we have included under the above law, you will order to be restored, without any hesitation or controversy at all, to these Christians, that is to say to the corporations and their conventicles: —providing, of course, that the above arrangements be followed so that those who return the same without payment, as we have said, may hope for an indemnity from our bounty. In all these circumstances you ought to tender your most efficacious intervention to the community of the Christians, that our command may be carried into effect as quickly as possible, whereby, moreover, through our clemency, public order may be secured. Let this be done so that, as we have said above, Divine favor towards us, which, under the most important circumstances we have already experienced, may, for all time, preserve and prosper our successes together with the good of the state. Moreover, in order that the statement of this decree of our good will come to the notice of all, this rescript, published by your decree, shall be announced everywhere and brought to the knowledge of all, so that the decree of this, our benevolence, cannot be concealed.

3. THE EXPERIENCE OF CONVERSION

For a while after the edict of Milan, Christianity was only one among the many religions of the Empire; and though its power and prestige increased, they were not yet exclusive. The Church had to face the possibility of a reversal in imperial policy, such as was actually attempted during the brief but brilliant reign of Constantine's pagan nephew, Julian the Apostate (361–363). And it had to fight a host of heresies —i.e., opinions contrary to the orthodox doctrine—though to begin with it seemed difficult to predict which of the contending opinions would end as heretical and which as orthodox. As the years passed, however, conversions increased in number, and meanwhile the canons of faith were laid down more authoritatively.

We find an excellent account of the experience of conversion—an experience which many must have gone through—in the *Confessions of St. Augustine* (354–430), translated by C. Bigg.

The future bishop of Hippo and Doctor of the Church had started life as a mildly dissolute young man in the academic profession, had flirted with the Manicheans as well as with the orthodox Christians, but in spite of the pressure of his mother Monica (later St. Monica), who was herself a fervent Christian, the young intellectual had been unable to make up his mind for a long time. When he did, however, he plunged into his new faith with enthusiasm and passion which are reflected in the passages below.

From *The Confessions of Saint Augustine*

I desire to record all my past vileness and the carnal corruption of my soul: not that I love the retrospect, but that I may love Thee, O my God. For love of Thy love do I travel over again in the bitterness of my self-examination my most wicked ways; that Thou mayest be my joy, my never-failing joy, my blessed and fearless joy; that Thou mayest gather me again from the scattering wherein I was torn limb from limb; for, when I turned from the One, I melted away into the Many.

For in the time of youth I took my fill passionately among the wild beasts, and I dared to roam the woods and pursue my vagrant loves beneath the shade; and my beauty consumed away, and I was loathsome in Thy sight, pleasing myself and desiring to please the eyes of men.

God Is That True and Perfect Goodness, Whereof Temptation Is the Semblance

Alas, what was it then that I loved in thee, O my theft, thou midnight crime of my sixteenth year? How couldest thou be beautiful, seeing that thou wert a theft? Nay, art thou anything that I should thus apostrophise thee? Those pears that we stole were fair to look upon, because they were Thy creatures, O Thou Fairest of all and Creator of all, Thou good God, Thou Chief Good, my true Good. They were fair; but it was not for them that my wretched soul lusted. I had plenty of better pears; I gathered them only to steal. For I flung them away when gathered, and tasted no enjoyment but the wickedness, which gave me all my delight. For, if I did eat one of those pears, its flavour came from the sin. . . .

Thus doth the soul play the harlot, when she turns away, and seeks outside Thee those joys which she can only find in their purity by returning to Thee. He does but imitate Thee badly who flies from Thee, and lifts up his horn against Thee. Yet by that bad imitation he proves that Thou art the Creator of all nature, and that therefore it is not possible to fly from Thee. What was it then that I loved in that theft of mine? How was I imitating my Lord in my bad and vicious way? Was there a pleasure in defying the law, by fraud if not by force, in playing at freedom in the prison-house, in showing that I could do wrong with impunity, which might seem a phantom of omnipotence? Lo, such is the servant who runs away from his Lord and attains a shadow. O what corruption! What a horrible life, what a deep gulf of death! To think that one should love what is forbidden, just because it is forbidden!

From the *Confessions of St. Augustine,* tr. C. Bigg (London, 1897), (Book II, Chap. 1; Book II, Chap. 6; Book VIII, Chaps. 6, 7, 8, 9, 10, 11, 12.)

Pontitianus Describes the Life of Antony, the Egyptian Monk

And now will I tell and confess unto Thy Name, O Lord my Helper and my Redeemer, how Thou didst deliver me from the bond of the sexual desire by which I was so tightly held, and from the slavery of worldly affairs. I was pursuing my usual life, with ever-growing dissatisfaction, and daily was I sighing unto Thee. I attended Thy church, whenever there was a pause in that business under the burden whereof I groaned. With me was Alypius, now released from his legal duties after a third term of office as assessor, waiting to sell his experience to a new purchaser, as I was selling such faculty of speech as could be imparted by a teacher. Nebridius had proved his affection for us by accepting the post of lecturer under Verecundus, a citizen of Milan, professor of grammar, and one of our closest allies, who was in great need of a loyal colleague, and called, with the right of friendship, for the services of one of our company.

It was no desire of advancement, therefore, that had attracted Nebridius, for he might have obtained higher remuneration if he had chosen to keep to the teaching of literature, but he was too sweet and gentle a friend to refuse a request which appealed to his love. Yet he bore himself most discreetly, shunning the acquaintance of the great ones of this world, lest it should unsettle his mind; he wished to keep his freedom and reserve as many hours as possible of leisure for thought, or reading, or hearing lectures on philosophy.

On a certain day, then, when Nebridius for some reason was not present, it happened that Pontitianus paid a visit to Alypius and myself at our house. He was an African, and so a fellow-countryman, and held high rank in the household. He had some request to make, and we sat down and conversed. He noticed a volume lying on the draught table before us, picked it up, opened it, and to his great surprise found that it was the Apostle Paul, for what he expected to see was one of my wearisome rhetorical manuals. He looked at me with a smile, and told me how delighted he was to find so unexpectedly that book, and that alone on my table. For he was a faithful Christian, and often prostrated himself before Thee, our God, in church in long and frequent prayer. I replied that I spent much time over the scriptures, and this led him on to speak of Antony, the Egyptian monk, whose name was held in high honour by Thy servants, though I had never heard it till that hour. When he discovered my ignorance he enlarged his discourse, marvelling at our ignorance of so great a man, and gently showing us how great he was.

We listened with amazement to the tale of Thy wonders, so freshly wrought, almost in our own lifetime, so well attested, springing from the true faith and the bosom of the Catholic Church. We were all alike surprised, Alypius and I because the history was so extraordinary; he because we had never heard it. Thence he passed to speak of the crowded monasteries, and the ways of Thy sweetness, and the teeming solitudes of the desert, all strange news to us. There was a monastery at Milan, outside the city walls, full of good brothers, of whom Ambrose was foster-father; yet we had never heard of it. He went on talking, and we listened in silence. So he was led to tell us how once he and three of his comrades at Treves—the Emperor being detained at the afternoon games in the circus—went out for a stroll in the gardens beneath the city walls; how they parted company, two going off by themselves; how these two entered aimlessly into a house wherein dwelt certain of Thy servants, men poor in spirit, of whom is the kingdom of heaven, and found there a volume containing the life of Antony.

One of them began to read, and as he read his soul caught fire, so that then and there he began to think of plunging into the monastic life, and exchanging his worldly service for Thine. He was one of the officials of the Ministry of the Interior. Suddenly he was filled with holy love and sober shame, and, as if angered with himself, fixed his eyes upon his friend, saying, "Tell me, prithee, what goal are we seeking in all these toils of ours? What is it that we desire? What do we look to gain in the service? Can we hope in the palace to attain anything better than the friendship of the Emperor? How frail, how beset with perils is that prize! Through what dangers must we climb to a greater danger! And when shall we succeed? But, if I choose, I can be the friend of God from this moment."

He spoke, and, torn by the pangs of the new birth, returned to the book. As he read he was changed in the inner man, which Thou canst see, and his mind was alienated from the world, as soon appeared. For he read, with heart like a stormy sea; more than once he groaned, but he saw the better course, and made up his resolve. And so at last he said quite calmly to his friend, "I have broken with ambition, and determined to serve God. I am going to begin this moment, and here. If you do not care to follow my example, do not oppose me." "The service," replied the other, "is noble, and the wage is great; I will be your brother in arms." So both became Thine, and "built a tower

at their own cost," having determined to give up all and follow Thee. Shortly afterwards Pontitianus and his companions, who had been walking in a different part of the garden and looking for the lost couple, arrived at the house, where they found them, and pressed them to return, as the sun had already set. But the two friends told them of the resolve which had so wonderfully sprung up and taken shape in their minds, and begged them not to take it ill if they refused to go with them. "So we," said Pontitianus, "who could not change our course, shed tears, not for them but for ourselves; we congratulated them on their godly decision, commended ourselves to their prayers, and went back to the palace, dragging our hearts along the ground, while they remained in the house, with hearts uplifted to heaven." Both these men were betrothed, but their wives that should have been, followed the example of their lovers, and consecrated their virginity to Thee.

How the Narrative of Pontitianus Pricked Augustine to the Heart

Such was the story that Pontitianus told. But, whilst he was speaking, Thou, O Lord, didst turn me round into my own sight. I had set myself, as it were, upon my own back, because I was unwilling to see myself, and now Thou didst place me before my own eyes so that I beheld how ugly I was, how deformed, and filthy, and spotted, and ulcerous. I beheld and shuddered, yet whither could I flee from myself? And, if I strove not to look upon myself, the tale of Pontitianus caught me again, and again didst Thou hold up to me my own portrait, and forced my eyes to gaze upon my very features, so that I might discover and loathe my own iniquity. I knew it; but feigned ignorance, and winked at it, and forgot it. But at that moment the warmer my love for that pair of friends, whose wholesome resolve to give themselves up altogether into Thy healing hands was still ringing in my ears, the deeper was my hatred of myself. How many of my years—perhaps twelve whole years—had run to waste since the day when, as a youth of nineteen, I had read the Hortensius of Cicero, and heard the call to the study of wisdom. My plain duty was to scorn earthly delights and devote myself to the search after that happiness whereof the mere pursuit—not to speak of its attainment—is better than the possession of all the treasures and kingdoms of the world, better than all bodily pleasures, though they were to be had for a word. And yet I was wasting time.

Yea, wretched, O wretched youth that I had been, on the very threshold of my youth, I had even begged of Thee the gift of chastity; but I had said, "Give me chastity and self-control, but not just yet." For I was afraid lest Thou shouldest hear me in a moment, and in a moment heal that disease of lust, which I wanted to be sated, not eradicated. And I had wandered along the evil ways of godless superstition, not that I thought them right, only because I preferred them to others, which I angrily denounced without any serious reflection. And I flattered myself that the reason why, from day to day, I hesitated to cast off the world and its hopes and follow Thee alone, was that I could find no certain goal. And now the day had come when I was laid bare in my own sight, and the stern voice of conscience demanded, "Where is thy tongue? Wast thou not wont to say that thou wouldest not cast off the pack of thy vanity for an uncertain truth? Lo, the truth is certain, and thou art still bend-ing under thy pack, while others, who have not wearied themselves in research, nor spent a long ten years in study, are putting forth wings from free shoulders."

Thus did a horrible shame gnaw and confound my soul while Pontitianus was speaking. He ended his tale, despatched the business which had brought him to our house, and departed. But how did I reproach myself! With what sharp reasons did I flog my soul to make it follow me in my effort to follow Thee! And it would not; it refused and would not even make an excuse. All its arguments had been tried and found wanting, yet it resisted in sullen disquiet, fearing, as if it were death, the closing of that running sore of evil habit by which it was being wasted to death.

He Goes into the Garden. What Befell Him There

Disordered in look and mind by this desperate wrestle with my own soul in the secret chambers of my own heart, I fell upon Alypius, crying out, "What has come to us? What means this tale that thou hast heard? Simple men arise and take heaven by violence, and we with all our heartless learning—see how we are wallowing in flesh and blood. Shall we stand still because they have taken the lead? Shall we not follow if we could not lead?" I scarcely knew what I said, and flung away, leaving him staring in silent astonishment. For my voice was changed; my face, eyes, colour, tone expressed my meaning more clearly than my words.

There was a garden to our lodging, of which we were free, as indeed we were of the whole house. For our host, the master of the house, did not live there. Thither the tumult of my breast drove me, where no one could interrupt the duel into which I had entered with myself, until it should reach the issue which Thou alone couldest foresee. I was mad, unto salvation; I was dying, unto life; I knew what evil thing I was; what good thing I was soon to be I knew not. I fled then into the garden, and Alypius followed me step for step. For I had no secret wherein he did not share, and how could he leave me in such distress? We sat down, as far from the house as possible. I was groaning in spirit, shaken with a gust of indignation, because I could not enter into Thy Will and Covenant, O my God; yet all my bones were crying out that this was the way, the best of all ways, and no ship is needed for that way, nor chart, no, nor feet, for it is not so far as from the house to the spot where we were seated.

For to go along that road, aye, and to reach the goal, is all one with the will to go; but it must be a strong and single will, not a broken-winged wish fluttering hither and thither, rising with one pinion, struggling and falling with the other. In fine, in the midst of that passionate indecision, I was doing many things which men sometimes will, yet cannot perform, because they have lost a limb, because their limbs are bound with fetters, or enfeebled by disease, or incapacitated in some other way. If I tore my hair, or beat my brow, or clasped my hands about my knees, it was because I willed to do so. Yet I might have willed in vain, if the nerves had not obeyed my bidding. Many things then I did, in which will and power to do were not the same, yet did not that one thing which seemed to me infinitely more desirable, which, before long, I should have power to will, because, before long, I should certainly will to will it. For in this the power of willing is the power of doing, and yet I could not do it. And so my body lent a ready obedience to the slightest desire of the soul, moving its limbs in instant compliance, while my soul could not aid itself in carrying out its great resolve, which needed but resolve to accomplish it.

Why the Mind Is Not Obeyed When It Commands Itself

Now whence and why is this strange anomaly? Let Thy mercy shine as the light; and suffer me to ask, if perchance I may find an answer amid the dark places of human chastisement, and the midnight of the contrition of the sons of Adam. Whence is this anomaly and why? Mind commands body, and there is instant obedience; mind commands mind, and there is rebellion. Mind commands the hand to move, and so facile is the process that you can hardly distinguish the order from its fulfilment; now the mind is mind and the hand is body. Mind commands mind to will, and, though it is one, it will not hear. Whence and why is this anomaly? I say it commands to will; and it would not command unless it did will, and yet its command is inoperative.

But it does not will wholly, and therefore it does not command wholly. For it commands, in so far as it wills, and its command is not executed, in so far as it does not will. For the will commands that there should be a will, and not another will but itself. Certainly it is not the full will that commands, hence it is not the very thing that it commands. For if it were the full will, it would not even command itself to be, because it would be already. And so this "will and will not" is no anomaly, but a sickness of the mind, which is weighed down by evil habit, and cannot rise wholly when uplifted by truth. And so there are two wills, because one of them is not whole, and one of them possesses what the other lacks.

Let them perish from Thy presence, O God, yea, and they do perish, those vain talkers and seducers of the soul, who, because they have observed that in the act of deliberation there are two wills, maintain that there are two minds of differing natures, the one good and the other bad. They themselves are bad, while they hold these bad ideas, yet will they become good, if they see the truth and assent unto the truth, that Thy Apostle may say to them, "Ye were sometimes darkness, but now are ye light in the Lord." For these Manichees, wishing to be light not in the Lord but in themselves, imagining the essence of the soul to be the essence of God, have become thicker darkness than they were, for in their dread arrogance they have gone farther away from Thee, from Thee, the true Light which lighteth every man that cometh into the world. Mark what you say, and blush for shame. Draw near unto Him and be lightened, and your faces shall not be ashamed. Who was it that willed, who was it that could not will, when I was deliberating whether I should not at once serve the Lord my God, as I had long purposed to do? Was it not I, I myself? I could not fully will, I could not fully will not. And so I was at war with myself, and dragged asunder by myself. And the strife was against my will, yet it showed not the presence of a second mind, but the punishment of the one I had. Therefore it was no more I that wrought it, but sin that dwelt in me, the punishment of a sin that was more voluntary, because I was a son of Adam. For, if there are as many opposing natures as opposing wills, there will be not two but many more.

If a man deliberates whether he shall go to their conventicle or to the theatre they cry, "See, he has two natures; the good one draws him to us, the evil drags him back. For how else shall we account for this halting between conflicting wills?" But I say that both wills are bad, that which draws him to them, not less than that which drags him back to the theatre. They naturally think it a good will which pulls in their direction. But suppose one of our people is tossed about between two wills, to go to the theatre or to go to our church—will they not be puzzled what to say? Either they must reluctantly confess that the will which carries a man to our church is as good as that which carries their own professors and adherents to theirs, or they must allow that two evil natures and two evil minds are fighting in one man, and in this case their favourite doctrine that one is good and the other evil falls to the ground, or they must be converted to the truth, and cease to deny that, when a man deliberates, one soul is agitated by opposing wills. Let them then no longer maintain that, when two wills are contending in one man, two antagonistic minds, one good and one evil, are struggling over two antagonistic substances, created by two antagonistic principles.

For Thou, O God of truth, dost reprove and confute and convict them, for both wills may be bad, as when a man deliberates whether he shall murder by poison or by knife; whether he shall seize upon this field or the other, supposing that he cannot get both; whether he shall purchase pleasure by wantonness, or keep his money through covetousness; whether he shall go to the theatre or the circus, if there are shows at both on the same day; and there may be a third course open to him, for there may be a chance of robbing a house, and even a fourth, for there may be an opportunity of committing adultery as well.

Suppose that all these objects present themselves at the same time, and are all equally desired, yet cannot all be secured together, in this case they rend the mind with four conflicting wills, or even more, if there are more objects of desire. Yet they would not say that all these are different substances. The case is the same with good wills. For I ask them whether it is good to find sober delight in reading the Apostle, or in a psalm, or in discoursing upon the Gospel. They will say that each is good. What then if all are equally delightful, and all at the same time? Are not different wills distracting the heart, when we consider which we shall prefer? All are good, but they are in conflict, till one is chosen, and the will is no longer divided between many objects but poured in its full strength upon that one. So also, when eternity attracts us from above and the pleasure of earthly goods pulls us down from below, the soul does not will either the one or the other with all its force, but it is the same soul; and the reason why it is so vexed and torn is that truth forces it to love the better, while custom will not suffer it to cast away the worse.

The Flesh Wrestles with the Spirit in Augustine

Thus was I sick and tormented, reproaching myself more bitterly than ever, rolling and writhing in my chain till it should be wholly broken, for at present, though all but snapped, it still held me fast. And Thou, O Lord, wast urgent in my inmost heart, plying with austere mercy the scourges of fear and shame, lest I should fail once more, and the remnant of my worn and slender fetter, instead of breaking, should grow strong again, and bind me harder than ever. For I kept saying within myself, "O let it be now, let it be now"; and as I spoke the word I was on the verge of resolution. I was on the point of action, yet acted not; still I did not slip back into my former indifference, but stood close and took fresh breath. I tried again, and came a little nearer and a little nearer, I could all but touch and reach the goal, yet I did not quite reach or touch it, because I still shrank from dying unto death and living unto life, and the worse, which was ingrained, was stronger in me than the better, which was unstrained. And the moment, which was to make me different, affrighted me more the nearer it drew, but it no longer repelled or daunted, it only chilled me.

Trifles of trifles and vanities of vanities, my old mistresses, held me back; they caught hold of the garment of my flesh and whispered in my ear, "Can you let us go? and from that instant we shall see you no more for ever; and from that instant this and that will be forbidden you for ever." What did they mean, O my God, what did they mean by "this and that?" O let Thy mercy guard the soul of Thy servant from the vileness, the shame that they meant! As I heard them, they seemed to have shrunk to half their former size. No longer did they meet me face to face with open contradiction, but muttered behind my back, and, when I moved away, plucked stealthily at my coat to make me look back. Yet, such was my indecision, that they prevented me from breaking loose, and shaking myself free, and running after the voice that called me away; for strong habit supported them, asking me, "Do you think you can live without them?"

But the voice of Habit had lost its persuasion. For in that quarter to which I had set my face and was fain to fly, there dawned upon me the chaste dignity of Continence, calm and cheerful but not wanton, modestly alluring me to come and doubt not, holding out to welcome and embrace me her pious hands full of good examples. There might I see boys and girls, a goodly array of youth and of every age, grave widows and aged virgins, and in every one of them all was Continence herself, not barren but a fruitful mother of children, of joys born of Thee, her husband, O Lord. And she smiled upon me with a challenging smile, as if she would say, 'Canst not thou do what these have done? Was it their power, was it not that of the Lord their God, that gave them strength? The Lord their God gave me unto them. Thou standest on thyself, and therefore standest not. Cast thyself on Him; fear not; He will not flinch, and thou wilt not fall. Cast thyself boldly upon Him; He will sustain thee, and heal thee." And I blushed, for still I heard the whispers of the daughters of vanity, and still I hung in the wind. And again she seemed to say, "Stop thine ears against thy unclean members upon earth, that they may be mortified. They tell thee of delights, but not according to the law of the Lord thy God." Such was the debate that raged in my heart, myself battling against myself. Alypius kept close to my side and waited in silence to see the issue of my strange agitation.

How by a Voice and by the Words of the Apostle He Was Wholly Converted

Now, when deep reflection brought forth from its secret stores the whole cloud of my misery, and piled it up in the sight of my heart, there rose a whirlwind, carrying with it a violent burst of tears. And hereupon I rose and left Alypius, till my weeping and crying should be spent. For solitude seemed fitter for tears. So I went farther off, till I could feel that even his presence was no restraint upon me. Thus it was with me, and he guessed my feelings. I suppose I had said something before I started up; and he noticed that my voice was fraught with tears. So he remained upon the bench lost in wonder. I flung myself down under a fig tree, and gave my tears free course, and the floods of mine eyes broke forth, an acceptable sacrifice in Thy sight. And I cried unto Thee incessantly, not in these words, but to this purpose, "And Thou, O Lord, how long? How long, O Lord; wilt Thou be angry for ever? O remember not our iniquities of old times." For I felt that I was held fast by them, and I went on wailing, "How long, how long? to-morrow and to-morrow? Why not now? why not this hour make an end of my vileness?"

Thus I spoke, weeping in bitter contrition of heart, when, lo, I heard a voice from the neighbouring house. It seemed as if some boy or girl, I knew not which, was repeating in a kind of chant the words, "Take and read, take and read." Immediately, with changed countenance, I began to think intently whether there was any kind of game in which children sang those words; but I could not recollect that I had ever heard them. I stemmed the rush of tears, and rose to my feet; for I could not think but that it was a divine command to open the Bible, and read the first passage I lighted upon. For I had heard that Antony had happened to enter a church at the moment when this verse of the Gospel was being read,

"Go, sell all that thou hast and give to the poor, and thou shalt have treasure in heaven; and come and follow Me," that he had taken these words home to himself, and by this oracle been converted to Thee on the spot.

I ran back then to the place where Alypius was sitting; for, when I quitted him, I had left the volume of the Apostle lying there. I caught it up, opened it, and read in silence the passage on which my eyes first fell, "Not in rioting and drunkenness, not in chambering and wantonness, not in strife and envying: but put ye on the Lord Jesus Christ, and make not provision for the flesh to fulfil the lusts thereof." No further would I read, nor was it necessary. As I reached the end of the sentence, the light of peace seemed to be shed upon my heart, and every shadow of doubt melted away. I put my finger, or some other mark, between the leaves, closed the volume, and with calm countenance told Alypius. And then he revealed to me his own feelings, which were unknown to me. He asked to see what I had read. I showed him the text, and he read a little further than I had done, for I knew not what followed.

What followed was this: "Him that is weak in the faith receive." This he explained to me as applying to himself. These words of warning gave him strength, and with good purpose and resolve, following the bent of his moral character, which had always been much better than mine, without any painful hesitation, he cast in his lot with me. Immediately we went in to my mother, and to her great joy told her what had happened. But, when we explained to her how it had come to pass, she was filled with exultation and triumph, and blessed Thee, who art able to do above that we ask or think. For she saw that Thou hadst granted her far more than she had ever asked for me in all her tearful lamentations. For so completely didst Thou convert me to Thyself that I desired neither wife nor any hope of this world, but set my feet on the rule of faith, as she had seen me in her vision so many years ago. So Thou didst turn her mourning into joy, joy fuller by far than she had ventured to pray for, dearer and purer by far than that which she had hoped to find in the children of my flesh.

4. THE PROBLEMS OF FAITH

Even in the exalted account he gives of his conversion, St. Augustine had found time to get in a shot at the Manichean heretics. Preoccupation with this and other variants of the official interpretation of the Gospels is a constant theme in the history of the churches. Orthodox doctrine had to be established, the faithful had to be affirmed in it, and deviationists confuted. This task was carried out by a series of Councils, whose decrees would provide a firm base for Christian thought.

The main issues in every discussion were the nature of the Trinity and the doctrine of the Incarnation. Between the Council of Nicaea (325) and that of Chalcedon (451) it was finally decided that the Father and Son, though two distinct persons, were equal and of the same substance. But the doctrinal debates and decisions had political repercussions as well. Theology had become a matter of state. The Church itself had become a great worldly institution, concerned with worldly things;

and its unflagging attempts to bring about the City of God smacked increasingly of the methods used in the City of Man.

THE NICENE CREED AS FRAMED IN 325, ACCORDING TO THE TEXT CONTAINED IN THE ACTS OF THE COUNCIL OF CHALCEDON

We believe in one God, the FATHER, Almighty, Maker of all things visible and invisible. And in one Lord JESUS CHRIST, the Son of God, begotten of the Father, the only-begotten; that is, of the essence of the Father, God of God, Light of Light, very God of very God, begotten, not made, being of one essence with the Father; by whom all things were made, both in heaven and on earth; who for us men, and for our salvation, came down and was incarnate and was made man; he suffered, and the third day he rose again, ascended into heaven; and he shall come to judge the living and the dead. And in the HOLY GHOST. But those who say: "There was a time when he was not," and "He was not before he was made"; and "He was made out of nothing," or "He is of another substance or essence," or "The Son of God is created," or "changeable," or "alterable"— they are condemned by the holy catholic and apostolic church.

THE CREED AS REVISED BY THE COUNCIL OF CONSTANTINOPLE, ACCORDING TO THE TEXT CONTAINED IN THE ACTS OF THE COUNCIL OF CHALCEDON

We believe in one God, the FATHER Almighty, Maker of heaven and earth and of all things visible and invisible. And in one Lord JESUS CHRIST, the only-begotten Son of God, begotten of

the Father before all worlds, Light of Light, very God of very God, begotten, not made, being of one substance with the Father; by whom all things were made; who for us men and for our salvation came down from heaven, and was incarnate by the Holy Ghost of the Virgin Mary, and was made man; he was crucified for us under Pontius Pilate, and suffered, and was buried, and the third day he rose again, according to the Scriptures, and ascended into heaven, and sitteth on the right hand of the Father; and he shall come again, with glory, to judge the quick and the dead; whose kingdom shall have no end. And in the HOLY GHOST, the Lord and Giver of life, who proceedeth from the Father, who with the Father and the Son together is worshipped and glorified, who spake by the prophets. In one holy catholic and apostolic church. We acknowledge one baptism for the remission of sins; we look for the resurrection of the dead, and the life of the world to come. Amen.

DEFINITION OF FAITH BY THE COUNCIL OF CHALCEDON, A.D. 451

The holy and great and ecumenical Synod, which, by the grace of God and the command of our most pious and Christian Emperors, Marcian and Valentinian, Augusti, is convened in the metropolis, Chalcedon, of the province of Bithynia, in the chapel of the holy and pure martyr Euphemia, has decreed as follows:

Our Lord and Saviour Jesus Christ, when confirming the knowledge of the faith in his disciples, declared: 'Peace 1

All three Creeds from *Translations and Reprints,* IV, No. 2, E. K. Mitchell, Ed.

leave with you: my peace I give unto you,' so that no one might be in disagreement with his neighbor concerning the doctrines of religion, but that the proclamation of the truth might be made to all alike. Inasmuch, however, as the evil one ceases not to sow his tares among the seeds of religion, and is ever devising something new in opposition to the truth, therefore has our Lord, in his care as usual for the human race, raised up this pious, faithful and zealous Emperor and called together unto himself the heads of the priesthood from every quarter, so that the grace of Christ, the Lord of us all, being operative, we may remove every plague of falsehood from the sheep of Christ and nourish them with tender plants of truth. This we have accordingly done, expelling by a common vote the doctrines of error, renewing the unerring faith of the fathers, proclaiming the creed of the 318 to all, and adding as their compeers the fathers who accepted the same summary of religion. Such were those fathers who afterward gathered in the great Constantinople, 150 strong, and themselves ratified this same faith. While guarding in every respect the order and form of faith which was received by the holy Synod formerly held at Ephesus, of which Celestine of Rome and Cyril of Alexandria, sainted to memory, were the guides, we declare that the exposition of the right and unblemished faith made by the 318 holy and blessed fathers who gathered under the Emperor Constantine, of sainted memory, shall be pre-eminent; and affirm that those things are also valid which were decreed by the 150 holy fathers in Constantinople for the uprooting of the heresies which had then sprung up, and for the confirmation of the same catholic and apostolic faith. [Here follow the Creeds of Nicaea and Constantinople.] This wise and saving symbol of divine grace should indeed suffice for a complete knowledge and confirmation of religion, for it teaches the finalities concerning the Father and the Son and the Holy Spirit, and sets forth the incarnation of the Lord to those who faithfully receive it. However, since certain persons, attempting to make void the preaching of the truth, have through their individual heresies given rise to vain babbling, some daring indeed to destroy the mystery of the Lord's incarnation for us, and rejecting the designation God-bearer ["Mother of God"] as applied to the Virgin; while others, introducing an intermixture and fusion [of natures], imagine without reason that the nature of the flesh and the Godhead is all one, rashly maintaining that the divine nature of the Only-begotten by the mixture became passible. Wherefore, desiring to exclude every machination against the truth, the present holy, great, and ecumenical Synod, teaching the message unchanged from the beginning, decrees, in the first place, that the faith of the 318 holy fathers shall remain inviolate, and it confirms, on account of those that contend against the Holy Spirit, the doctrine concerning the essence of the Holy Spirit, afterwards promulgated by the 150 holy fathers gathered in the royal city. This they made known to all, not as though supplying any deficiency in preceding deliverances, but in order to make known in writing their deep conviction concerning the Holy Spirit, in opposition to such as seek to set aside his sovereignty. On account of those, however, who attempted to corrupt the mystery of the dispensation [incarnation], and shamelessly spoke of him who was born of the holy Mary as a mere man, the Synod has accepted the synodic letters of the blessed Cyril, pastor of the church of Alexandria, to Nestorius and the orientals, as well fitted to refute the wild ravings of Nestorius, and for the instruction of those seeking with holy zeal the meaning of the saving symbol; and it has rightly added to them the letter of the president of the great and ancient Rome, the blessed and holy archbishop Leo, written to the sainted archbishop Flavian for the overthrow of the errors of Eutyches, as agreeing with the confession of the great Peter, as a common pillar against all false believers, and for the confirmation of the orthodox dogmas. For it [the Synod] opposes those who attempt to resolve the sacred mystery of the dispensation [incarnation] into a duality of Sons; it excludes from the sacred fellowship those who dare to speak of the Godhead of the Only-begotten as passible; it withstands those who imagine a commixture or fusion of the two natures of Christ; it expels those who foolishly affirm that the 'form of a servant' which he assumed is of a heavenly or some other essence than that taken of us; and it anathematizes those who fancy that there were two natures of the Lord before the union, but make out that there was only one after the union. Following therefore the holy fathers, we together confess and unanimously teach that the Son and our Lord Jesus Christ is one and the same, perfect in Godhead, perfect in manhood; truly God and truly man; of a reasonable soul and [human] body, co-essential with the Father as regards his Godhead, also co-essential with us as regards his manhood, 'in all points like unto us, apart from sin'; before the ages begotten of the Father according to his Godhead, but in these last days, for us and for our salvation, [born] of Mary the Virgin, the Mother of God, according to his manhood; one and the same Christ,

Son, Lord, Only-begotten, he must be acknowledged as in two natures, without amalgamation, without change, indivisible, inseparable—the distinction of the natures not only not being destroyed by the union, but rather the peculiarity of each nature preserved, uniting indeed into one person and one subsistence [hypostasis]; not as though divided or separated into two persons, but as one and the same Son and Only-begotten, God the Logos, the Lord Jesus Christ; just as the prophets aforetime announced him and He himself, the Lord Jesus Christ, taught us, and the creed of the fathers has handed down to us. These things therefore having been defined by us with all possible exactness and care, the holy ecumenical Synod has decreed that no one shall advance, or write, or compose, or think, or teach others another faith; but those daring to compose, or bring forward, or teach, or deliver another symbol to such as desire to turn from heathenism, or Judaism, or any heresy whatsoever to a knowledge of the truth, they, if they be bishops or clerics, shall be deposed, the bishops from their bishoprics, the clerics from the clericate; but if they be monks or laymen, they shall be excommunicated.

Upon the reading of the definition all the most pious bishops were delighted and exclaimed: 'This is the faith of the fathers! The metropolitans must now subscribe while the imperial commissioners are here; definitions so good can allow of no delay; this is the faith of the apostles, we all agree to it, we all think thus!' The august and glorious commissioners said: 'These things having been defined by the holy fathers, and being agreeable to all, shall now go to his divine majesty, the Emperor.'

Disintegration and Reconstruction

I. THE BARBARIANS

II. CHARLEMAGNE (742–814)

III. FEUDALISM AND PERSONAL DEPENDENCE

IV. THE CHURCH IN THE MIDDLE AGES

V. THE CRUSADES

VI. MEDIEVAL LIFE AND CULTURE

VII. ECONOMIC DEVELOPMENT OF THE MIDDLE AGES

While Roman fought Roman to decide who should control an empire too vast for effective administration, the danger of invasion increased. Frontiers were left unguarded or undergarrisoned by generals who used their troops for political maneuvering. Across the border lay the barbarian, usually Germanic—an old enemy conquered or pressed back in the days of Roman power but still eager first to raid, later to take over, the rich provinces coveted for so long.

Yet eventually it was Rome that led its captors captive: the Church, which had evolved within the Empire, carried Latin order and organization through the chaotic years of disintegration, providing not only the new bond of a common religion but also a pattern for the embryonic authorities that developed in the place of the old. At the same time, the memory of Roman laws and institutions, above all of the Empire itself— a memory strengthened by the survival of the eastern portion ruled from Constantinople—served as an inspiration and a goad to the leaders of the new societies. A new Europe now arose, different in extent and in the solutions it proposed to the problem of relations between man and man, man and society, man and God. But while it is possible to see the new society as peculiar and isolated, the weight of evidence points to the constant influence of the Empire the barbarians had helped to destroy, only to find in it the vision they ceaselessly tried to recreate.

I. The Barbarians

The progressive barbarization of the western portion of the Empire (with the concomitant but much less obvious Romanization of the conquerors) was a slow and unsystematic process, in which the Romans tried to play one tribe against another and in which islands of Roman authority and culture survived even in areas long overrun by Germanic tribes. The following selections reflect some of the realities of this extended period of Roman-German interaction. There is a brief and superficial account of the Germans by Caesar, writing in the first century B.C.; a brisk description by Ammianus Marcellinus (who was a friend and comrade of the Emperor Julian the Apostate) of the methods used to cope with them some four centuries after Caesar; St. Jerome's comments on the failure to stem the barbarian tide, culminating in the shock of Alaric's sack of Rome in 410; and, lastly, some account of conditions in Gaul, where a few great Gallo-Roman nobles, like Apollinaris Sidonius or Gregory of Tours, carried on a waning cultural tradition amid the social and political anarchy of the fifth and sixth centuries.

1. JULIUS CAESAR: THE GERMANS, 53 B.C.

Two Roman historians have left us fairly lengthy descriptions of the Germans: Tacitus (c. 55–120 A.D.) and Caius Julius Caesar (101–44 B.C.). The latter was also one of the greatest military leaders of the ancient world. An able, not overly scrupulous politician, he began his career by pretending to serve the cause of the people against the all-powerful Pompey. This led to a deal that gave him the consulship in 59 B.C. and the governorship of Gaul over an extended period. Nine years of campaigning there established Roman power as far as the English Channel and the Rhine and won the successful general both glory and a devoted army. He used these advantages and his military skill to defeat Pompey and establish his own dictatorial power in Rome on a policy which favored the democratic party in the city. It was there, at this time, that he wrote his famous *Commentaries on the Gallic War* and it was there, too, that an aristocratic conspiracy put an end to his life on the ides of March.

The customs of the Germans differ much from those of the Gauls; for neither have they Druids to preside over religious services, nor do they care much for sacrifices. They count among the number of the gods those only whom they can see, and whose benign influence is manifest; namely, the Sun, Vulcan and the Moon. Of the others they have never even heard. Their whole life is made up of hunting and thoughts of war. From childhood they are exercised in labor and hardship. Those among them who remain longest in a state of celibacy are held in the high-

From *Translations and Reprints*, VI, No. 3, Arthur C. Howland, Ed.

est esteem, as they claim that thereby the stature of some is increased, while it adds to the strength and sinews of others. Indeed, to have had intercourse with a woman before twenty is considered a most disgraceful thing, nor is the concealment of such a matter possible, since they not only bathe together promiscuously in the streams, but use skins or small garments of reindeer hide for clothing, whereby a great part of the body is bare.

They are not devoted to agriculture, and the greater part of their food consists of milk, cheese and flesh; nor does anyone possess a particular piece of land as his own property, with fixed boundaries, but the magistrates and the chiefs assign every year to the clans and the bands of kinsmen who have assembled together as much land as they please in any locality they see fit, and on the following year compel them to move elsewhere. They offer many reasons for this custom; that the people may not lose their zeal for war through habits engendered by continued application to the cultivation of the soil; that they may not be eager to acquire large possessions, and that the more powerful may not drive the weaker from their property; that they may not build too carefully in order to avoid cold and heat; that the love of money may not spring up, from which come divisions and dissensions; that the common people may be held in contentment, since each one sees his own wealth kept equal to that of the most powerful.

It is a matter of the greatest pride to the tribes to lay waste the borders of their territory for as great a distance as possible and make them uninhabitable. They consider it a tribute to their valor when their neighbors are compelled to retire from those lands and when hardly any one dares set foot there; at the same time they think that they will thus be safer, since the fear of a sudden invasion is removed. When a tribe is either repelling an invasion or attacking a hostile territory, magistrates are chosen to lead them in the war, who have the power of life and death. In times of peace they have no general magistrate, but the chiefs of the districts and cantons exercise justice among their own people and settle controversies. Robbery, if done outside the borders of the tribe, carries with it no disgrace, and they declare that it is practiced for the sake of exercising the youth and preventing idleness. When any of the chiefs has said in an assembly that he is going to be the leader in a foray, and let those who wish to follow him hand in their names, they who approve of the raid and of the man rise up and promise their assistance, and are applauded by the masses. Those of the number who do not then follow him are considered deserters and traitors, and thereafter no faith whatever is placed in them.

To violate the rights of hospitality they hold to be a crime; whoever come to them for any reason whatever, they protect from injury, holding them sacred. Everybody's house is free to such, and they are furnished with food.

2. AMMIANUS MARCELLINUS: ROMAN POLICY TOWARD THE GERMANS, 370 A.D.

Ammianus Marcellinus, a Roman historian of the fourth century after Christ, was well qualified to write about warriors and military matters because he himself was above all a soldier. Born at Antioch, he began his career at an early age and campaigned both on the Rhine and on the Euphrates. When he had enough of fighting Persians and Alemanni, he settled down in Rome to write a history of the years between the reigns of Nero and Valens; in other words, from late in the first century to his own time. Written from the point of view of a pagan gentleman and severe moralist, the work is chiefly important for the light it throws on contemporary Roman society. The passage quoted below is evidence of the way in which Romans regarded the Germans and the methods which even high-minded soldiers approved for coping with them.

In the third consulate of the Emperor Valentinian a large band of Saxons came over the ocean and made an attack on the Roman boundary wall, laying waste the country with fire and sword. The first shock of this invasion was borne by Count Nannenus, the commander in that region, a careful and experienced veteran. But he had to do with a people who knew not the fear of death, and after he had lost a number of soldiers and had been himself wounded he had to admit himself unequal to carrying on the continuous strife. The Emperor having been informed of his necessity, Severus, the *magister peditum,* was allowed to come to his assistance. When he arrived with a force sufficient for the occasion and had drawn his troops up for battle the barbarians were so terrified that they did not dare risk an engagement, but awed by the splendor of the eagles and the battle standards, they sued for peace. Since this seemed to be for the best interests of the state, a treaty was agreed upon after a long discussion, whereby the Saxons were to furnish a large contingent of their warlike youth to serve under our standards while the remainder were allowed to depart, though without any plunder, and return whence they had come. And when their minds were now relieved of all anxiety and they were preparing to set out for home, a force of infantry was sent forward and quietly placed in ambush in a certain deep valley from which they were to make an attack on the barbarians as the latter passed by and so destroy them, as it was supposed, without difficulty. But it turned out very differently from what was hoped. For at the noise of their approach certain of the Romans in their excitement sprang forth too quickly, and no sooner were they seen than the barbarians with fearful whoops and yells made for them and overthrew them before they could form to resist the attack. Still our men drew quickly together in a circle and held their ground with the courage of despair. Many however were killed, and they would certainly have fallen to the last man had not the tumult been heard by a squadron of our heavy cuirassiers similarly placed at a fork of the road to attack the passing barbarians from the other side. These hastened to the rescue. Then the battle raged fiercely. The Romans with renewed courage rushed in on all sides, surrounded the enemy and cut them down with the sword. None of them ever saw again their native home. Not even a single one was allowed to survive the slaughter of his comrades. An upright judge might accuse us of baseness and perfidy in this affair, yet when one thinks the matter over one must admit that it was a just fate for a band of robbers to be thus destroyed when the opportunity was given us.

Though this affair had been so happily

carried out, Valentinian continued to feel much anxiety and solicitude, turning over many projects in his mind and planning with what stratagems he might break the pride of the Alemanni and their king Macrian, whose restlessness was bringing endless disturbance to the Roman state. For the remarkable thing about this people is that however great their losses through various causes from the very beginning on, yet they increase so fast that one would think that they had remained undisturbed for many ages. Finally after considering various plans it seemed best to the Emperor to weaken them by stirring up against them the Burgundians, a warlike people whose flourishing condition was due to the immense number of their young men, and who were therefore to be feared by all their neighbors.

3. ST. JEROME: LETTERS

St. Jerome was one of the great doctors of the Church. He spent most of his life (c. 331–420) in Jerusalem, where he translated the Bible into Latin, and where he conducted a busy and vigorous correspondence with all sorts of people. He lived through the disintegration of Roman power, and his letters reflect many of the more desperate moments of the time.

I shall now say a few words of our present miseries. A few of us have hitherto survived them, but this is due not to anything we have done ourselves but to the mercy of the Lord. Savage tribes in countless numbers have overrun all parts of Gaul. The whole country between the Alps and the Pyrenees, between the Rhine and the Ocean, has been laid waste by hordes of Quadi, Vandals, Sarmatians, Alans, Gepids, Herules, Saxons, Burgundians, Alemanni and—alas! for the commonweal!—even Pannonians. The once noble city of Mainz has been captured and destroyed. In its church many thousands have been massacred. The people of Worms after standing a long siege have been extirpated. The powerful city of Rheims, the Ambiani, the Altrebatae [tribes whose names survive in the cities Amiens and Arras], the Belgians on the outskirts of the world, Tournay, Spires, and Strasbourg have fallen to Germany: while the provinces of Aquitaine and of the Nine Nations, of Lyons and of Narbonne are, except for a few cities, one universal scene of desolation. And those whom the sword spares on the outside, famine ravages on the inside. I cannot speak without tears of Toulouse, which has been saved from falling until now through the valor of its reverend bishop Exuperius. Even the Spanish provinces are on the brink of ruin, and they tremble daily when they remember the Cimrian invasion; thus, whilst others suffer their misfortunes once in fact, they suffer them all the time in anticipation.

I say nothing of other places because I do not want to appear despondent of God's mercy. All that is ours now between the Black Sea and the Julian Alps, ceased to be ours for a while not long ago: thirty years long did the barbarians ignore the barrier of the Danube, and carry the fight into the heart of the Roman Empire. But long habit of this sort of thing has spent our tears. All but a few old people have now been born either in captivity or during a siege, and so none could miss a liberty they have never known. Yet who, in days to come, will credit the fact, and what chronicles will seriously discuss it, that Rome had to fight within her own borders for sheer survival; and that now she does not even fight, but buys the right to live by a tribute in gold and the gradual sacrifice of all her substance? This humiliation is not the fault of her Emperors [Arcadius and Honorius] who are both most religious men, but stems from the crime of a half-barbarian traitor [Stilicho] who has used our money to arm our foes against us [by a subsidy to the Göths' King Alaric]. In days gone by the Roman Empire was branded with eternal shame because, after routing the Romans at the battle of the Allia and laying waste the country, Brennus with his Gauls entered Rome itself [390 B.C.]. And this ancient disgrace could not be effaced until Gaul, whence the Gauls came, and Gaulish Greece [Galatia], where they had settled after their victories in East and West, were eventually defeated. Even Hannibal, who swept like a destructive storm from Spain right into Italy, did not dare lay siege to the city although he came within sight of it. Even Pyrrhus [King of Epirus] was so dominated by the prestige of the Roman name that, although he ravaged everything in his way, he nevertheless drew back from the city's neighborhood. Victor though he was, he did not presume to gaze upon what he had come to regard as a city of kings. Yet even for such insults—indeed, such presumptuous pride, they were still punished: Hannibal, banished from all the world (by our pursuit), found death at last by poison in Bithynia; and Pyrrhus, returning to his native land,

was slain in his own realm. The countries of both these men became tributaries of the Roman people. So it was once. But now, even if our arms were to meet with complete success, what can we win from our defeated foes? Nothing, except what we have already lost to them. The poet Lucan describes the erstwhile power of Rome in a glowing passage, and goes on to ask: "If Rome be weak, where shall we look for strength?" We might change the words to ask in turn: "If Rome be lost, where shall we look for help?" or, to quote the language of Virgil:

Were I to speak with hundred tongues
    from throat of bronze
The captives' woes here I could not relate
Or e'er recount the names of all the slain.

Even to say what I have said so far is charged with danger to myself who say it, and to those who hear it; for we are no longer free even to deplore our fate and are unwilling, indeed, we are afraid, to weep for our sufferings. . . .

While these things were happening . . . a terrible rumor came from the West. Rome had been besieged [by Alaric, 408] and its citizens had had to buy their lives with gold. Then, once they had been robbed in this fashion, they had been besieged again so that they should forfeit not only their wealth this time but their lives too. My voice sticks in my throat; and, as I dictate, sobs impair my speech. The city which had taken the whole world was itself taken [410]. In fact, famine went before the sword and only few citizens survived to be taken captive. In their panic and hunger the starving people fell back on horrible food: they even tore each other limb from limb so that they might get flesh to eat. Even the mother did not spare the nursling at her breast. In the night was Moab taken;

in the night did her wall fall down. "O God, the heathen have come into thine inheritance; thy holy temple they have defiled; Jerusalem they have made into an orchard. The dead bodies of thy servants they have given as meat to the fowls of the air, the flesh of thy saints to the beasts of the earth. Their blood they have shed like water round about Jerusalem; and there was none to bury them."

4. APOLLINARIS SIDONIUS: LETTERS

Caius Sollius Apollinaris Sidonius was born in Lyons about 430 of a senatorial family long settled in Gaul, and died bishop of Clermont, probably in 487. This was an extraordinarily rich period in the history of Europe, and Sidonius witnessed much of it. He was a younger contemporary of Attila and of Genseric the Vandal, and must have been about twenty when Aëtius with his Roman troops and German allies defeated Attila at Châlons. Soon after, the Vandals plundered a Rome already deflowered by the Visigoths forty-five years before. And before he died he was to hear that the last Western Emperor, Romulus Augustulus, had been deposed by his barbarian general, Odoacer (476). He himself, highly regarded as a poet and scholar, held office both in Gaul and at Rome, met or corresponded with almost every distinguished contemporary, dined with Majorian (Emperor of the West, 457–461), played backgammon with Theodoric II at the Visigothic court in Toulouse, married the daughter of the short-lived Emperor Avitus (454–456), and managed what not so many managed in his time—to live to a relatively ripe old age in comparative security and comfort. These were troubled times, and from his letters we get a glimpse of two worlds—that of the old Roman civilization in its decay and that of the new medieval circumstances in their beginnings.

TO HIS BROTHER-IN-LAW, AGRICOLA (454?)

You have often begged a description of Theodoric the Gothic king, whose gentle breeding fame commends to every nation. . . .

Well, he is a man worth knowing, even by those who cannot enjoy his close acquaintance, so happily have Providence and Nature joined to endow him with the perfect gifts of fortune; his way of life is such that not even the envy that lies in wait for kings can rob him of his proper praise. And first, as to his person. He is well set up, in height above the average man, but below the giant. His head is round, with curled hair retreating somewhat from the brow to the crown. His nervous neck is free from disfiguring knots. The eyebrows are bushy and arched; when the lids droop, the lashes reach almost half-way down the cheeks. The upper ears are buried under overlying locks, after the fashion of his race. The nose is finely aquiline; the lips are thin and not enlarged by undue distension of the mouth. Every day the hair springing from his nostrils is cut back; that on the face springs thick from the

From *Letters of Sidonius*, tr. O. M. Dalton, 2 vol. (Oxford: The Clarendon Press, 1915). Reprinted by permission of the publishers.

hollow of the temples, but the razor has not yet come upon his cheek, and his barber is assiduous in eradicating the rich growth on the lower part of the face. Chin, throat and neck are full, but not fat, and all of fair complexion; seen close, their color is fresh as that of youth; they often flush, but from modesty, and not from anger. His shoulders are smooth, the upper and fore-arms strong and hard; hands broad, breast prominent; waist receding. The spine dividing the broad expanse of the back does not project, and you can see the springing of the ribs; the sides swell with salient muscle, the well-girt flanks are full of vigor. His thighs are like hard horn; the knee-joints firm and masculine; the knees themselves the comeliest and least wrinkled in the world. A full ankle supports the leg, and the foot is small to bear such mighty limbs.

Now for the routine of his public life. Before daybreak he goes with a very small suite to attend the service of his [Arian] priests. He prays with assiduity, but, if I may speak in confidence, one may suspect more of habit than conviction in this piety. Administrative duties of the kingdom take up the rest of the morning. Armed nobles stand about the royal seat; the mass of guards in their garb of skins are admitted that they may be within call, but kept at the threshold for quiet's sake; only a murmur of them comes in from their post at the doors, between the curtain and the outer barrier. And now the foreign envoys are introduced. The king hears them out and says little. . . . The second hour arrives; he rises from the throne to inspect his treasure-chamber or stable. If the chase is the order of the day, he joins it, but never carries his bow at his side, considering this derogatory to the royal state. When a bird or beast is marked for him, or happens to cross his

path, he puts his hand behind his back and takes the bow from a page with the string all hanging loose; for as he deems it a boy's trick to bear it in a quiver, so he holds it effeminate to receive the weapon ready strung. When it is given him, he sometimes holds it in both hands and bends the extremities towards each other; at others he sets it, knot-end downward, against his lifted heel, and runs his finger up the slack and wavering string. After this, he takes his arrows, adjusts, and lets fly. He will ask you beforehand what you would like him to transfix; you choose, and he hits. If there is a miss through either's error, your vision will mostly be at fault, and not the archer's skill.

On ordinary days, his table resembles that of a private person. The board does not groan beneath a mass of dull and unpolished silver set on by panting servitors; the weight lies rather in the conversation than in the plate; there is either sensible talk or none. The hangings and draperies used on these occasions are sometimes of purple silk, sometimes only of linen; art, not costliness, commends the fare, as spotlessness rather than bulk the silver. Toasts are few, and you will oftener see a thirsty guest impatient, than a full one refusing cup or bowl. In short you will find . . . everywhere the discipline of a king's house. What need for me to describe the pomp of his feast days? No man is so unknown as not to know of them. But to my theme again. The siesta after dinner is always slight, and sometimes intermitted. When inclined for the board-game, he is quick to gather up the dice, examines them with care, shakes the box with expert hand, throws rapidly, humorously apostrophizes them, and patiently waits for the result. Silent at a good throw, he makes merry over a bad, annoyed by neither fortune, and always the philosopher. He is too proud to ask or to refuse a revenge; he disdains to avail himself of one if offered; and if it is opposed will quietly go on playing. . . . You see the strategist when he moves his pieces; his one thought is victory. Yet at play he puts off a little of his kingly rigor, inciting all to good fellowship and the freedom of the game: I think he is afraid of being feared. Vexation in the man whom he beats delights him; he will never believe that his opponents have not let him win unless their annoyance proves him really victor. You would be surprised how often the pleasure born of these little happenings may favor the march of great affairs. Petitions that some wrecked influence had left derelict come unexpectedly to port; I myself am gladly beaten by him when I have a favor to ask, since the loss of my game may mean the gaining of my cause. About the ninth hour the burden of government begins again. Back come the importunates, back the ushers to remove them; on all sides buzz the voices of petitioners, a sound which lasts till evening, and does not diminish till interrupted by the royal repast; even then they only disperse to attend their various patrons among the courtiers, and are astir till bedtime. Sometimes, though this is rare, supper is enlivened by the antics of mimes, but no guest is ever exposed to the wound of a biting tongue. Withal, there is no noise of hydraulic organ, or choir with its conductor intoning a set piece; you will hear no players of lyre or flute, no master of the music, no girls with cithara or tabor; the king cares for no strains but those which no less charm the mind with virtue than the ear with melody. When he rises to withdraw, the treasury watch begins its vigil; armed sentries stand on guard during the first hours of slumber.

But I am wandering from my subject. . . . My aim was to write a letter, not a history. Farewell.

TO HIS FRIEND DOMITIUS (461-7?)

You attack me for staying in the country; I might with greater reason complain of you for lingering in town. Spring already gives place to summer. . . . We are all perspiring in light silks or linens; but there you stay at Ameria all swathed up under your great gown, buried in a deep chair, and setting with yawns. . . . As you love your health, get away at once from your suffocating alleys, join our household as the most welcome of all guests, and in this most temperate of retreats evade the intemperate dog-star.

You may like to know the kind of place to which you are invited. We are at the estate known as Avitacum, a name of sweeter sound in my ears than my own patrimony because it came to me with my wife. . . .

On the west rises a big hill, pretty steep but not rocky, from which issue two lower spurs, like branches from a double trunk, extending over an area of about four *jugera*. But while the ground opens out enough to form a broad approach to the front door, the straight slopes on either side lead a valley right to the boundary of the villa, which faces north and south. On the south-west are the baths, which so closely adjoin a wooded rise that if timber is cut on the hill above, the piles of logs slide down almost by their own weight, and are brought up against the mouth of the furnace. At this point is the hot bath, which corresponds in size with the adjoining *unguentarium*, except that it has an apse with a semi-circular basin; here the hot water pressing through the sinuous lead pipes that pierce the wall issues with a sobbing sound. The chamber itself is well heated from beneath; it is full of day, and so overflowing with light that very modest bathers see themselves something more than naked. Next comes the spacious *frigidarium,* which may fairly challenge comparison with those in public baths. The roof is pyramidal, and the spaces between the converging ridges are covered with imbricated tiles; the architect has inserted two opposite windows about the junction of walls and dome, so that if you look up, you see the fine coffering displayed to the best advantage. The interior walls are unpretentiously covered with plain white stucco, and the apartment is designed by the nicest calculation of space to contain the same number of persons as the semi-circular bath holds bathers, while it yet allows the servants to move about without impeding one another. No frescoed scene obtrudes its comely nudities, gracing the art to the disgrace of the artist. . . . You will see upon these walls none of those things which it is nicer not to look upon. A few verses there are, harmless lines enough, since no one either regrets perusal or cares to peruse again. [Local marble is used and] though enriched by no cold splendor of foreign marble, my poor huts and hovels do not lack the coolness to which a plain citizen may aspire. . . . With this hall is connected on the eastern side an annexe, a piscina, or, if you prefer the Greek word, baptistery. . . . Into this the bathers pass from the hot room by three arched entrances in the dividing wall. The supports are not piers but columns, which your experienced architect calls the glory of buildings. Into this piscina, then, a stream lured from the brow of the hill is conducted in channels curving round the outside of the swim-

ming basin; it issues through six pipes ending in lions' heads. . . . When the master of the house stands here with his household or his guests about him, people have to shout in each other's ears, or the noise of falling water makes their words inaudible; the interference of this alien sound forces conversations which are quite public to assume an amusing air of secrecy. On leaving this chamber you see in front of you the withdrawing-room; adjoining it is the store-room, separated only by a movable partition from the place where our maids do our weaving.

On the east side a portico commands the lake, supported by simple wooden pillars instead of pretentious monumental columns. On the side of the front entrance is a long covered space unbroken by interior divisions [a long porch]. . . . At the end it is curtailed by a section cut off to form a delightfully cool bay, and here when we keep open house, the whole chattering chorus of nurses and dependents sounds a halt when the family retires for the siesta.

The winter dining-room is entered from this porch; a roaring fire on an arched hearth often fills this apartment with smoke and smuts. But that detail I may spare you; a glowing hearth is the last thing I am inviting you to enjoy just now. I pass instead to things which suit the season and your present need. From here one enters a smaller chamber or dining-room, all open to the lake and with almost the whole expanse of the lake in view. This chamber is furnished with a dining-couch and gleaming sideboard upon a raised area or dais to which you mount gradually, and not by abrupt or narrow steps from the portico below. Reclining at this table you can give the idle moments between the courses to the enjoyment of the prospect. If water of our famous springs is served and quickly poured into the cups, one sees snowy spots and cloudy patches form outside them; the sudden chill dulls the fugitive reflections of the surface almost as if it had been greased. . . . The thirstiest soul on earth . . . would set lip to the freezing brims with caution. From table you may watch the fisherman row his boat out to mid-lake, and spread his seine with cork-floats, or suspend his lines at marked intervals to lure the greedy trout on their nightly excursions through the lake. . . . The meal over, we pass into a drawing-room which its coolness makes a perfect place in summer. Facing north, it receives all the daylight but no direct sun: a very small intervening chamber accommodates the drowsy servants, large enough to allow them forty winks but not a regular sleep. It is delightful to sit here and listen to the shrill cicada at noon, the croak of frogs in the gloaming, the clangour of swans and geese in the earlier night or the crow of cocks in the dead of it, the ominous voice of rooks saluting the Dawn in chorus, or, in the half-light, nightingales fluting in the bushes and swallows twittering under the eaves. To this concert you may add the seven-stopped pipe of the pastoral Muse, on which the very wakeful shepherds of our hills will often vie with one another, while the herds about them low to the cow-bells as they graze along the pastures. All these tuneful songs and sounds will but charm you into deeper slumbers. If you leave the colonnade and go down to the little lakeside harbor, you come to a green lawn and hard by to a grove of trees. . . . There stand two great limes, with roots and trunks apart, but the boughs interwoven in one continuous canopy. In their dense shade we play at ball when my Ecdicius honors me with his company; but the mo-ment the shadow of the trees shrinks to the area covered by the branches we stop for want of ground, and repose our tired limbs at dice.

TO HIS FRIEND DOMNICIUS (470?)

You take such pleasure in the sight of arms and in those who wear them, that I can imagine your delight if you could have seen the young prince Sigismer on his way to the palace of his father-in-law in the guise of a bridegroom or suitor in all the pomp and bravery of the tribal fashion. [Sigismer was probably a Frankish prince out to wed a Burgundian princess.] His own steed with its caparisons, other steeds laden with flashing gems, paced before and after; but the conspicuous interest in the procession centered in the prince himself, as with a charming modesty he went afoot amid his bodyguard and footmen, in flame-red mantle, with much glint of ruddy gold, and gleam of snowy silken tunic, his fair hair, red cheeks, and white skin according with the three hues of his equipment. But the chiefs and allies who bore him company were dread of aspect, even thus on peace intent. Their feet were laced in boots of bristly hide reaching to the heels; ankles and legs were exposed. They wore high tight tunics of varied color hardly descending to their bare knees, the sleeves covering only the upper arm. Green mantles they had with crimson borders; baldrics supported swords hung from their shoulders, and pressed on sides covered with cloaks of skin secured by brooches. No small part of their adornment consisted of their arms; in their hands they grasped barbed spears and throwing axes; their left sides were guarded by shields, which flashed with tawny golden bosses and snowy silver borders, betraying at once their wealth and their good taste. Though the business at hand was wedlock, Mars was no whit less prominent in all this pomp than Venus. Why need I say more? Only your presence was wanting to the full enjoyment of so fine a spectacle.

TO THE LORD BISHOP PATIENS
(474)

One man deems happiness to consist in one thing, a second in another; my own belief is that he lives most to his own advantage who lives for others, and does heaven's work on earth by pitying the poverty and misfortune of the faithful. You may wonder at what I aim in these remarks. At yourself, most blessed father, for my sentiments refer especially to you, who are not content to succour only the distress which lies within your neighbourhood, but push your inquiries to the very frontiers of Gaul and, without respect of persons, consider each case of want upon its merits. . . . Your watchful eye ranges over other provinces than your own; the spreading tide of your benevolence bears consolation to the straitened, however far away. . . . I say nothing of your daily labor to relieve the need of your impoverished fellow-countrymen, of your unceasing vigils, your prayers, your charity. I pass over the tact with which you combine the hospitable and the ascetic virtues, so that the king [Chilperic the Burgundian, then ruling at Lyons] is never tired of praising your breakfasts and the queen your fasts. I omit your embellishment of the church committed to your care. . . . I do not mention the churches that rise in so many districts under your auspices, or the rich additions to their ornaments. I dismiss the fact that under your administration the faithful are increased and multiplied, while heretics alone diminish. I shall not tell how your apostolic chase for souls involves the wild Photinian heretics in the spiritual mesh of homily; or how barbarians once converted by your eloquence [follow your advice and are drawn] out of the profound gulfs of error. It may be true that some of these good deeds are not peculiar to you, and are shared by colleagues; but there is one which is yours peculiarly and which even your modesty cannot deny: it is this, that when the Gothic ravages were over, and the crops were all destroyed by fire, you distributed corn to the destitute throughout all the ruined land of Gaul at your own expense, though it would have been relief enough to our starving peoples if the grain had come to them, not as a free gift, but by the usual paths of commerce. We saw the roads encumbered with your grain-carts. Along the Saône and Rhône we saw more than one granary which you had entirely filled. The legends of the heathen are eclipsed; Triptolemus must yield his pride of place, whom his fatherland of Greece deified for his discovery of corn. . . . Your granaries filled not two paltry ships, as Triptolemus is said to have done, but the basins of two great rivers. If you disapprove as unsuited to your profession a comparison drawn from the Achaean superstition, I will recall instead the historic foresight of the patriarch Joseph. . . . I hold that man morally as great who copes with a similar disaster without any warning in advance. I cannot exactly tell the sum of gratitude which all the people owe you, inhabitants of Arles and Riez, Avignon, Orange, Viviers, Valence, and Trois Châteaux; it is beyond my powers to count the total thanks of men who were fed without having to count out a penny. But for the city of Clermont I can speak, and in its name I give you endless thanks; all the more that your help had no obvious inducement: we did not belong to your province, no convenient waterway led to us, we had no money to offer. . . . I would have you know that your glory travels over all Aquitaine: all pray for your welfare, their hearts go out to you in love and praise. . . . In these evil times you have proved yourself a good priest, a good father, and as good as a good year to men who would have starved but for your generosity. Deign to hold me in remembrance, my Lord Bishop.

5. GREGORY OF TOURS: HISTORY OF THE FRANKS

Georgius Florentius, the future bishop Gregory of Tours, was born at Clermont in the center of Gaul in 538 or 539 of an old Gallo-Roman senatorial family whose members had held high offices both in the Church and in the world. All but five of the incumbents of the see of Tours before he was elected to it had been, as he says with pride, of his kindred. His own pastorate was no more untroubled than any life or position could be in those disturbed Merovingian times; but he acquitted himself with courage and honesty, even when this brought him into serious danger from the resentment of the king. His *History of the Franks,* in which he traced the fortunes of the barbarians in Gaul up to the year 591, is marked by extreme credulousness and a rather clumsy style, both of which reflect the decline which had taken place in the cultural standards of Gaul since the days of Sidonius. It nevertheless remains a mine of information on the ways, the attitudes, and the superstitions of his time, as well as on the events he describes. Gregory died in 593 and was canonized shortly after.

At that time [491?] the king of the Burgundians was Gundioc. . . . He had four sons, Gundobad, Godigisel, Chilperic, and Gundomar. Gundobad put his brother Chilperic to the sword, and drowned his wife by tying a stone to her neck. Her two daughters he condemned to exile, the elder of whom, Chrona, had adopted the habit of a nun, while the younger was called Clotild. It happened that Clovis used often to send envoys into Burgundy, and they discovered the young Clotild. Observing her grace and understanding, and learning that she was of the blood royal, they spoke of these things to King Clovis who straightway sent an embassy to Gundobad, asking her in marriage. Gundobad was afraid to refuse, and handed her over to the men, who received her, and with all speed brought her before the king. At sight of her he greatly rejoiced and was united to her in wedlock, having already by a concubine one son named Theuderic.

Of Queen Clotild the king had a firstborn son whom the mother wished to be baptized; she therefore persistently urged Clovis to permit it, saying: "The gods whom ye worship are naught; they cannot aid either themselves or others, seeing that they are images carved of wood or stone or metal. Moreover the names which

From *The History of the Franks,* by Gregory of Tours, tr. O. M. Dalton, 2 vol. (Oxford: The Clarendon Press, 1927). Reprinted by permission of the publishers.

ye have given them are the names of men and not of gods. Saturn was a man, fabled to have escaped by flight from his son to avoid being thrust from his kingdom; Jupiter also, the lewdest practicer of all debaucheries and of unnatural vice, the abuser of the women of his own family, who could not even abstain from intercourse with his own sister, as she herself admitted in the words 'sister and spouse of Jove.' What power had Mars and Mercury? They may have been endowed with magical arts; they never had the power of the divine name. But ye should rather serve Him, who at His word created out of nothing the heaven and earth, the sea and all therein; who made the sun to shine and adorned the heaven with stars; who filled the waters with fish, the earth with animals, the air with birds; at whose nod the lands are made fair with fruits, the trees with apples, the vines with grapes; by whose hand the race of man was created; by whose largess every creature was made to render homage and service to the man whom he created." Though the queen ever argued thus, the king's mind was nowise moved towards belief, but he replied: "It is by command of our gods that all things are created and come forth; it is manifest that thy God avails in nothing; nay, more, He is not even proved to belong to the race of gods." But the queen, true to her faith, presented her son for baptism; she ordered the church to be adorned with hangings and curtains, that the king, whom no preaching could influence, might by this ceremony be persuaded to belief. The boy was baptized and named Ingomer, but died while yet clothed in the white raiment of his regeneration. Thereupon the king was moved to bitter wrath, nor was he slow to reproach the queen, saying: "If the child had been dedicated in the

name of my gods, surely he would have survived; but now, baptized in the name of thy God, he could not live a day." The queen replied: "I render thanks to the Almighty God, Creator of all things, who has not judged me all unworthy, and deigned to take into His kingdom this child born of my womb. My mind is untouched by grief at this event, since I know that they who are called from this world in the white robes of baptism shall be nurtured in the sight of God." Afterwards she bore another son, who was baptized with the name Chlodomer. When he too began to ail, the king said: "It cannot but befall that this infant like his brother shall straightway die, being baptized in the name of thy Christ." But the mother prayed, and God ordained that the child should recover.

Now the queen without ceasing urged the king to confess the true God, and forsake his idols; but in no wise could she move him to this belief, until at length he made war for a time against the Alamanni, when he was driven of necessity to confess what of his free will he had denied [496]. It befell that when the two hosts joined battle there was grievous slaughter, and the army of Clovis was being swept to utter ruin. When the king saw this, he lifted up his eyes to heaven, and knew compunction in his heart, and, moved to tears, cried aloud: "Jesus Christ, Thou that art proclaimed by Clotild Son of the living God, Thou that art said to give aid to those in stress, and to grant victory to those that hope in Thee I entreat from a devout heart the glory of Thy help. If Thou grant me victory over these enemies, and experience confirm that power which the people dedicated to Thy name claims to have proved, then will I also believe on Thee and be baptized in Thy name. I have called upon my gods, but they have withdrawn themselves from helping me; wherefore I believe that they have no power, since they come not to the help of their servants. Thee I now invoke, on Thee am I fain to believe, if but I may be plucked out of the hands of my enemies." And as he said this, lo, the Alamanni turned their backs and began to flee. And when they saw that their king was slain, they yielded themselves to Clovis, saying: "No longer, we entreat thee, let the people perish; we are now thy men." Then the king put an end to the war, and having admonished the people, returned in peace, relating to the queen how he had called upon the name of Christ and had been found worthy to obtain the victory. This happened in the fifteenth year of his reign.

Now King Lothar had seven sons by divers women: by Ingund he had Gunthar, Childeric, Charibert, Guntram, Sigibert, and a daughter Clothsind; by Aregund, sister of Ingund, Chilperic; by Chunsina he had Chramn. I will now tell how it was that he married his wife's sister. When he was already wedded to Ingund, and loved her with his whole heart, she made him the following suggestion: "My lord has done with his handmaid according to his pleasure, and taken her to his bed; now to make my reward complete, let my lord hear the proposal of his servant. I entreat him graciously to choose for his servant my sister an able and rich husband, that I be not humbled but exalted by her, and thus may give you yet more faithful service." On hearing this the king, who was most amorous by temperament, began to desire Aregund, and betaking himself to the domain where she lived, he married her. When she was his, he returned to Ingund and spoke as follows: "I have done my best to procure

for you the reward which your sweetness asked of me. I sought a man wealthy and of good wit, whom I might give in marriage to your sister, but I found none better than myself. Know therefore that I have taken her to wife, which I believe will not displease you." She answered: "Let my lord do that which seems good in his sight; only let his handmaid live in the enjoyment of his favor." Gunthar, Chramn, and Childeric died during their father's lifetime; the death of Chramn I shall tell in the sequel. Alboin, king of the Lombards, received as his bride Clothsind, the king's daughter.

Cautinus, after his succession to the see of Clermont, so demeaned himself as to be held in general loathing. He was given to wine beyond measure, and was often so far gone in drink that four men could hardly carry him from the table; the result was that at a later time he became epileptic. These excesses frequently occurred in public view. He reached, moreover, such a pitch of avarice that it seemed almost death to him if he failed to get at least some part of any lands marching with his own. If the owner was a person of standing, Cautinus picked a quarrel and robbed him with abuse; if he was of less account, he seized the property by force.

There was at this time a priest in Clermont named Anastasius, a man of free birth, who owned a property by grant of Queen Clotild of glorious memory. At several interviews the bishop had earnestly begged him to give him the queen's grant, and cede him the land. He was slow in yielding to the desire of the bishop, who sometimes sought to obtain his object by cajolery, at other times by threats; but at last ordered him to be brought to the city against his will, and there in the most shameless manner had him detained, commanding that if he refused to surrender the documents he should be roughly used and starved to death. Anastasius resisted like a man, and would not give up the deeds, affirming that he would rather himself waste away for want of food than leave his children destitute. He was then by the bishop's orders placed under guard to meet death by starvation unless he consented to produce the documents. Under the church of the holy martyr Cassius there was a most ancient crypt, far removed from sight; it contained a great sarcophagus of Parian marble in which lay the remains of some person dead long ago. The priest was buried alive above the dead man in this tomb, and the stone which had previously covered it was replaced; guards were then posted at the crypt door. But the men, satisfied that he was safe under the stone lid, lit a fire (for it was winter) and fell asleep under the influence of the wine which they warmed at it. Then the priest, like a new Jonah, from the confinement of his tomb, as from the bowels of hell, kept beseeching the mercy of the Lord. Now the sarcophagus, as I have said, was spacious; and though he was unable to turn his whole body, he was free to stretch his hands out at will. The remains of the dead man, as he used afterwards to relate, gave out a mortal stench. . . . As long as he could close his nostrils with his mantle he escaped the worst; but as soon as he moved the cloak a little, when he felt half stifled, the pestilential odor penetrated him through the mouth, through the nose, and, one might say, through the ears as well. To be brief, at the moment when, as I believe, the Lord had compassion on him, he stretched out his right hand to the border of the sarcophagus and found an iron crowbar

which, at the letting down of the lid, had remained between it and the rim of the tomb beneath. He moved this little by little [and eventually got out]. . . . It was dark, but Anastasius found another door of the crypt, secured by exceeding strong locks and by great nails, but so ill fitted together that he could see out between the planks. The priest bent his head between the chinks, perceived a man passing by, and called to him in a faint voice. The man heard him, and at once grasped his axe, cut through the planks to which the bolts were fixed, and opened a way out for the prisoner who, coming up out of darkness, proceeded home, first earnestly enjoining on the man to say nothing to any one of his adventure. He got the deeds given him by Queen Clotild and took them with him to King Lothar, to whom he told the story of his burial alive by the bishop. All present were astounded, declaring that not even Nero or Herod had perpetrated such a crime as to put a man alive into the grave. While they still spoke, Bishop Cautinus appeared before the king; but on the accusation of Anastasius he went away vanquished and confounded. Anastasius received diplomas from the king enabling him easily to defend his property, which he continued to possess, and bequeathed to his descendants. In Cautinus was neither piety nor consideration; he was wholly unversed in letters, whether sacred or profane. With the Jews, to whose influence he submitted, he was on familiar terms, not for their conversion, which should have been his care, but to buy of them precious objects. He was easily flattered, and they gave him gross adulation. Then they sold him the things at a higher price than they were worth.

At this time Chramn held his residence in Clermont; he was senseless in many of his acts, and these were the cause of his premature death. The people heaped curses on him. None capable of good or sound advice was favorite of his; he gathered round him persons of the baser sort. . . . For these only he cared, to their advice only he listened. Even the daughters of senatorial families were forcibly abducted by his orders. He drove Firminus from his office as count of the city with outrage, and appointed Salustius, son of Evodius, in his place. Firminus and his sister-in-law took sanctuary in the church. It was Lent, and Bishop Cautinus had made preparation to go in procession to the parish of Brioude. . . . He issued from the city with many a sigh, through fear of some mischance upon the way, for he, too, was menaced by King Chramn. While he was on the road, the king sent Imnachar and Scapthar, the chief of those about his person, with these instructions: "Go and drag Firminus with Caesaria his mother-in-law out of the church." When, therefore, the bishop had set out with singing of chants, as I have said above, these envoys of Chramn went into the church and did their best to soothe the fears of Firminus and Caesaria by various cajoleries. . . . Then Imnachar seized Firminus in his arms, and Scapthar Caesaria, and forced them out of the church, where their men were placed ready to seize them. They were at once sent into banishment. But on the second day their guards were heavy with sleep, and, finding themselves free, they fled to the church of the blessed Julian, thus saving themselves from exile, though their property was confiscated. But Bishop Cautinus, suspecting that he too might suffer outrage as he followed this very road to Brioude kept a saddled horse beside him; suddenly, looking round, he saw men riding behind to come up with him.

"Woe is me!" he cried; "these are the men sent by Chramn to take me." Thereupon he mounted the horse, left the procession, and plying both spurs managed alone and half dead to reach the porch of the church of the holy Julian. . . .

After the death of Theudebald [556 A.D.], Lothar succeeded to the land of the Franks, and was making his progress round it when he was informed by his people that the Saxons were once more in a mad ferment and in open rebellion against him; further, that they haughtily refused to pay the tribute which they had to bring every year. The king was angered at the news, and marched against them. But when he was almost at their boundaries, the Saxons sent envoys to him with this message: "It is not our will to presume against thee, nor would we refuse our usual tribute, which we have paid to your brothers and your nephews; if you demand it we will pay even more. One thing only we entreat, that there should be no conflict between our people and your army." At this King Lothar said to those about him: "These men speak well; let us not advance upon them, lest by chance we sin against God." But they answered: "We know that they are liars, and that they will in no way carry out their promise; let us therefore go and fall upon them." Again the Saxons sought peace, offering the half of their possessions. And Lothar said to his followers: "I entreat you, let these men be, lest the wrath of God be aroused against us." But they would not be satisfied. A third time the Saxons came, offering their raiment, their cattle, and all their movable property, saying: "Take all these things and the half of our land; only leave our wives and our children in freedom, and let there be no war between us." But even this would not satisfy the Franks. Then King

Lothar said: "Desist I pray you, desist from your purpose. The right is not on our side; do not set out on a war in which you will meet your ruin. But if go you will, I for my part shall not follow." Then, furious with the king, they rushed upon him, rending his tent and roughly abusing him; they even dragged him off by force, and would have killed him if he delayed in going off with them. King Lothar, seeing how matters stood, went with them against his will. When the battle was joined, the Franks were smitten by the enemy with great slaughter, and there fell so many upon both sides that hardly might the dead be reckoned up or numbered. Then Lothar, greatly troubled in spirit, entreated peace, declaring that he had attacked against his own desire. Peace was granted, and he returned home.

This year [570] there was question as to the day on which Easter fell. We in Tours, with many other cities, celebrated the holy paschal feast on the fourteenth day of the kalends of May [April 18]; others, with those of Spain, kept this feast on the twelfth day of the kalends of April [March 21]. It is said that, nevertheless, those springs in Spain which are filled by the will of God were full upon our Easter.

Now King Chilperic ordered heavy new tax-assessments to be made in all his kingdom [579–580?]. For which cause many left their cities and their own possessions, and sought other kingdoms, deeming it better to migrate than to remain exposed to such risk of oppression. For it was enacted that each proprietor should pay five gallons of wine for every half-acre of land. Further taxes were imposed on other lands and on serfs, which it was impossible to meet. The people of Limoges, perceiving with what a burden they were to be laden, assembled on the first of March and would have slain Mark the referendary, who had been ordered to carry out the plan; nor could they have been prevented, had not Bishop Ferreolus delivered him from his imminent peril. The mob seized the tax collector's lists and burned them all to ashes. Whereat the king was exceeding wroth, and dispatched thither men from about his person; through these he inflicted immense losses upon the people, crushed them with punishments, and freely inflicted the penalty of death. It is said that these envoys of the king falsely accused even priests and abbots of having incited the people to burn the lists during the riot, stretched them on posts, and subjected them to divers tortures. Afterwards yet severer tributes were imposed.

At Paris a certain woman fell under accusation, many asserting that she had forsaken her husband for another man. The husband's relatives went to her father, saying: "Either prove thy daughter innocent, or let her surely die, that her adultery be not suffered to bring disgrace upon our family." The woman's father answered: "I know that my daughter is wholly innocent, nor is there truth in this rumor spread by evil tongues. Yet in order that the charge may proceed no farther, I will establish her innocence by an oath." They answered: "If she be free from guile, affirm it with an oath over the tomb of the blessed martyr Dionysius [St. Denis]." "That I will do," said the father. On this understanding they met at the church of the holy martyr, where the father, lifting up his hands over the altar, swore that his daughter was without guilt. The husband's supporters, on the other hand, declared him perjured; thereupon an altercation arose, in which they un-sheathed their swords, and rushed upon each other, so that there was bloodshed before the very altar, though they were of high birth and among the first at the court of Chilperic. Many received sword-wounds; the holy church was splashed with blood of men; the doors were pierced by javelins and swords; the weapons of wickedness raged even at the sepulchre of the saint. As soon as the strife was with difficulty appeased, the celebration of holy offices in the church was suspended while the matter was brought to the king's cog-nizance. The parties hastened before the royal presence, but were not received into favor. The king ordered them to be sent back to the bishop of the city, that if they were found not guilty they might in due course be admitted to communion. They then made composition for their offences, and were again received into communion by Bishop Ragnemond, head of the church of Paris. A few days after, the woman, on being summoned to trial, strangled herself with a noose.

In this year [585] almost all Gaul was oppressed by famine. Multitudes were reduced to making a kind of bread by drying and pounding grape-seeds or hazel-blossom, and adding a little flour, while others did the same with fern roots. There were many who cut the green corn stalks and treated them in like manner; many others, who had no flour at all, plucked and ate various kinds of grass, whereupon their bodies swelled and they died. Great numbers languished and were starved to death. Then the merchants grievously robbed the people, so that a bushel of corn or half a measure of wine was hardly sold for a third of a gold piece. The poor sold themselves into slavery for the sake of a morsel of food.

A cruel feud now arose between citi-zens of Tours. While Sichar, the son of one John, deceased, was celebrating the feast of Christmas in the village of Man-thelan, with Austregisel and other people of the district, the local priest sent a serv-ant to invite several persons to drink wine with him at his house. When the servant came, one of the invited drew his sword and was brutal enough to strike, so that the man fell dead upon the spot. Sichar was bound by ties of friendship to the priest; and as soon as he heard of the servant's murder he seized his weapons and went to the church to wait for Austre-gisel. He in turn, hearing of this, took up his arms and equipment and went out against him. There was an encounter be-tween the two parties; in the general con-fusion Sichar was brought safely away by some clerics, and escaped to his coun-try estate, leaving behind in the priest's house money and raiment, with four wounded servants. After his flight, Austre-gisel burst into the house, slew the serv-ants, and carried off the gold and silver and other property. The two parties after-wards appeared before a tribunal of citi-zens, who found Austregisel guilty as a homicide who had murdered the servants, and without any right or sanction seized the property. A few days after the case had been before the court Sichar heard that the stolen effects were in the hands of Auno, his son, and his brother Eberulf. He set the tribunal at naught, and taking Audinus with him lawlessly attacked these men by night with an armed party. The house where they were sleeping was forced open, the father, brother and son were slain, the slaves murdered, and the movable property and herds carried off.

The matter coming to my ears I was sore troubled and, acting in conjunction with the judge, sent messengers bidding them come before us to see if the matter could be reasonably settled so that the parties might separate in amity and the quarrel go no farther. They came and the citizens assembled, whereupon I said: "Desist, O men, from further crime, lest the evil spread more widely. We have already lost sons of the Church, and now we fear that by this same feud we may be reft of others. Be ye peacemakers, I beseech you; let him who did the wrong make composition for the sake of brotherly love. . . . For Christ Himself has said: Blessed are the peacemakers, for they shall be called the children of God. And behold now, if he who is liable to the penalty has not the means of paying, the Church shall redeem the debt from her own funds; meanwhile, let no man's soul be lost." Speaking thus, I offered money belonging to the Church. But the party of Chramnesind [the son of the murdered Auno], who demanded justice for the death of his father and uncle, refused to accept it. When they were gone, Sichar made preparations for a journey, intending to proceed to the king, and with this in mind set out for Poitiers to see his wife first. But while he was there admonishing a slave to work, he struck him several times with a rod, whereupon the man drew the sword from his master's baldric and did not fear to wound him with it. He fell to the ground; but friends ran up and caught the slave, whom they first beat cruelly; then they cut off his hands and feet and condemned him to the gibbet. Meanwhile the rumor reached Tours that Sichar was dead. As soon as Chramnesind heard it, he warned his relations and friends, and went with all speed to Sichar's house. He plundered it and slew some of the slaves, burned down all the houses not only that of Sichar but also those belonging to other landholders on

the estate. He then took off with him the cattle, and all the movable effects. The parties were now summoned by the count to the city, and pleaded their own causes. The judges decided that he who had already refused a composition [i.e., Chramnesind] and then burned houses down should forfeit half of the sum formerly awarded to him, wherein they acted illegally, to ensure the restoration of peace. They further ordered that Sichar should pay the other moiety of the composition. The Church then provided the sum named in the judgment; the parties gave security, and the composition was paid, both sides promising each other upon oath that they would never make further trouble against each other. So the feud came to an end.

[In 587] the feud, which I above described as ended, broke out with revived fury. After the murder of the kinsfolk of Chramnesind, Sichar formed a great friendship with him; so fond of one another did they grow that often they shared each other's meals and slept in the same bed. One evening Chramnesind made ready a supper, and invited Sichar. His friend came, and they sat down together to the feast. But Sichar, letting the wine go to his head, kept making boastful remarks against Chramnesind, and is reported at last to have said: "Sweet brother, you owe me great thanks for killing your relations; for the composition you got after their death has filled your house with gold and silver. If it wasn't for that, which set you up, you would be poor and destitute today." Chramnesind heard these words with bitterness of heart and said within himself: "If I avenge not the death of my kinsmen, I deserve to lose the name of man, and to be called weak woman." And straightway he put out the lights and cleft the head of Sichar with his dagger. The man fell and died uttering but a faint sound as the last breath left him. The servants who had accompanied him fled away. Chramnesind stripped the body of its garments, and hung it from a post of his fence; he then rode away to the king [Childebert]. Entering the church, he prostrated himself at the king's feet and said: "I ask of you my life, most glorious king, for I have slain men who secretly did to death my kinsmen and plundered all their possessions." He then set forth the whole matter in due order. But Queen Brunhild took it exceeding ill that Sichar, who was under her protection, should have been slain thus, and broke into a fury against Chramnesind who, seeing that she was set against him, gained the village of Bouges in the territory of Bourges, where his kinsmen lived, because it counted to the kingdom of Guntram. Tranquilla, wife of Sichar, left her children and her husband's property in Tours and Poitiers and withdrew to her own kinsfolk in the village of Mauriopes, where she married again. Sichar was about twenty years of age when he died. In life he was a light fellow, a winebibber and man-slayer, who did violence to many in his drunkenness.

In Gaul the plague which I have so often named invaded the province of Marseilles, and a great famine afflicted Angers, Nantes, and Le Mans [591]. This was the beginning of sorrow, according as the Lord spake in the Gospels: "There shall be pestilence and famine, and earthquakes in divers places, and there shall arise false Christs and false prophets, and they shall give signs and wonders in the heaven, to mislead even the elect," as has befallen in this present time.

A certain man of Bourges, as he himself afterwards related, went into a glade to cut wood required to finish a certain work, when a swarm of flies encompassed him, in consequence whereof he was as one mad for the space of two years; from this it is evident that here was an evil device of the Devil. After this he traversed the neighboring towns and came to the province of Arles, where he clad himself in skins and gave himself to prayer like a holy man. The Enemy, to deceive him, gave him the power of divining the future. Next, to commit greater crimes, he left his place, and abandoning the aforesaid province, entered the country of Javols, giving himself out to be some great one, and not afraid to profess himself the Christ; he took with him a woman, supposed to be his sister, whom he caused to be called Mary. A multitude flocked to him, and brought their sick before him, whom, by laying on of hands, he restored to health. Those who thus came together to him bestowed upon him gold, silver, and raiment. But he, the more readily to beguile them, distributed these things among the poor, prostrating himself upon the earth, pouring forth prayers, together with the woman of whom I have spoken; he would then rise, and once more bid those who stood round about adore him. He foretold the future, and to some he announced coming sickness, to others losses; only to few did he promise good fortune to come. All these things he did by diabolical arts, and I know not what cunning tricks. And a vast multitude of the people was led astray by him, and not merely the uneducated, but even priests of the Church; more than three thousand persons followed him. In the meantime he began to rob and despoil many whom he met upon the road, making free gift of the spoil to those who had no possessions. Bishops and citizens he menaced with death if they refused to worship him. Entering the territory of Le Velay, he proceeded to the place called Anicium [Le Puy], and halted with his whole band near the neighboring churches, disposing his men like an army, as if to attack Aurelius, at that time bishop of the diocese. He then sent before him, as messengers to announce his arrival, naked men who leapt and performed antics as they went. The bishop, astounded at these doings, sent to him stout fellows to ask the meaning of his proceedings. One, who was foremost among them, first bowed down as if to kiss his knees, thus impeding his movements, and commanded him to be seized and stripped; he then in a trice drew his sword and cut him to pieces. So fell and died this Christ, who should rather be called Antichrist, and all his following were dispersed. The woman Mary was put to the torture, when she disclosed all his visionary schemes and his tricks. The men whose wits, by his devilish cunning, he had deranged so that they believed in him, never wholly recovered their senses, but ever professed him to be Christ, and this Mary to be partaker in his divinity. And throughout all the land of Gaul there arose many, attracting to themselves by such deceptions weak women who in a frenzy proclaimed them to be saints; and so they magnified themselves among the people. I myself saw many of them, whom by sharp reproof I strove to recall from their errors.

II. Charlemagne (742–814)

The first prince to re-establish a semblance of centralized authority and order on the Roman pattern was Charles, son of Pepin the Short, who succeeded his father as joint king of the Franks in 768. By 771 he had disposed of his brother and then reigned alone until his death in 814. He fought and conquered the Avars, the Bavarians, the Saxons, and the Lombards; he campaigned in Spain and left us the memory of the epic ambush of Roncevaux where Roland died; he exchanged embassies with Harun al-Rashid and with the Roman Emperor in Constantinople; he encouraged scholarship in the persons of Eginhard, Alcuin, and other clerics; and he invented a sort of royal inspectorate, the *missi dominici,* to keep in touch with a vast empire stretching from the North Sea to the Garigliano, from Bohemia to the Pyrenees.

When, in 800, Pope Leo III crowned him Emperor in Rome, he became the first barbarian to bear this dignity. Compared with the authority of earlier Roman Emperors or even of his fellow-Emperor in highly civilized Constantinople, that of Charlemagne was a makeshift thing, his attempted cultural revival threadbare, his vast domains held together more by personal allegiance than by effective administration. It is sufficiently impressive that he achieved what he did; but we cannot wonder that the structure he had built up by his energy and talent should fall to pieces after his death.

Letter to the Pope

The occasion of the first selection here cited was the death of Pope Hadrian I, in 795. The letter was written by Charles to the new Pope Leo III. In it the Carolingian monarch made his conception of the relation of Empire and Papacy clear in the following words.

I want to establish with Your Beatitude an inviolable pact of faith and charity by which . . . the Apostolic blessing can be with me everywhere and by which the very holy seat of the Roman Church can be constantly defended . . . by my devotion. . . . It is my part to defend everywhere the Holy Church of Christ by armed force, on the one hand against pagan raids and devastation of the unbelievers; on the other hand by the diffusion of the Catholic Faith. It is your part, most holy father, lifting your hands with Moses to help by your prayers the victory of our arms. Let Your Prudence attach itself in every way to the canonical laws and follow constantly the rules established by the holy fathers so that your life shall give in every manner the way of sanctity, so that your mouth will speak none but pious exhortations and that your light shall burn before all men.

[Charles' ideals were further defined in the instructions he gave to the messenger.] Make it clear to the Pope that he must live virtuously and above all that he must observe the holy canons. Tell him that he must piously govern the Holy Church of God according to the agreements which shall be made between yourselves and according to his conscience. Remind him often that the dignity to which he has acceded is a passing thing whilst the reward promised for good works is eternal. Persuade him to busy himself with the greatest diligence with uprooting the simoniac heresy which mars in any place the holy body of the Church. Let the Lord lead and guide his heart . . . so that he can usefully serve the Holy Church of God and intercede in our favor.

From the Capitularies on the Army

Naturally enough, the king's first and main concern was his army. This had to be regathered every year, and a great deal of thought and energy would be spent simply on getting *almost* all the men together at the same place at the same time before starting out on a campaign whose length was limited by the provisions the fighting men could carry and the time they could be kept away from their farms.

Capitularies were documents containing the ordinances or instructions of the Frankish kings. The name comes from the fact that they were divided into chapters; in Latin, *capitulae.*

Concerning going to the army; the count in his county under penalty of the ban, and each man under penalty of sixty solidi shall go to the army, so that they come to the appointed muster at that place where it is ordered. And the count himself shall see in what manner they are prepared, that is, each one shall have a lance, shield, bow with two strings, twelve arrows. And the bishops, counts, abbots shall oversee their own men and shall come on the day of the appointed muster and there show how they are prepared. Let them have breast-plates or helmets, and let them proceed to the army, that is, in the summer.

That the equipments of the king shall be carried in carts, also the equipments of the bishops, counts, abbots and nobles of the king; flour, wine, pork and victuals in abundance, mills, adzes, axes, augers, slings, and men who know how to use these well. And the marshals of the king shall add stones for these on twenty beasts of burden, if there is need. And each one shall be prepared for the army and shall have plenty of all utensils. And each count shall save two parts of the fodder in his county for the army's use, and he shall have good bridges, good boats.

From *Translations and Reprints,* VI, No. 5, D. C. Munro, Ed.

Abbots and bishops were not excluded by their cloth from Charles' warlike preparations. They, too, held fiefs and had military duties to fulfill. Nor is there any indication that such requirements were considered strange or unbecoming to a cleric.

Letter to Abbot Fulrad, 804–811

In the name of the Father, Son and Holy Ghost. Charles, most serene, august, crowned by God, great pacific Emperor, and also, by God's mercy, King of the Franks and Lombards, to Abbot Fulrad.

Be it known to you that we have decided to hold our general assembly this year in the eastern part of Saxony, on the river Bode, at the place which is called Stassfurt. Therefore, we have commanded you to come to the aforesaid place, with all your men well armed and prepared, on the fifteenth day before the Kalends of July, that is, seven days before the festival of St. John the Baptist. Come, accordingly, so equipped with your men to the aforesaid place that thence you may be able to go well prepared in any direction whither our summons shall direct; that is, with arms and gear also, and other equipment for war in food and clothing. So that each horseman shall have a shield, lance, sword, dagger, bow and quivers with arrows; and in your carts utensils of various kinds, that is, axes, planes, augers, boards, spades, iron shovels, and other utensils which are necessary in an army. In the carts also supplies of food for three months, dating from the time of the assembly, arms and clothing for a half-year. And we command this in general, that you cause it to be observed that you proceed peacefully to the aforesaid place, through whatever part of our realm your journey shall take you, that is, that you presume to take nothing except fodder, wood and water; and let the men of each one of your vassals march along with the carts and horsemen, and let the leader always be with them until they reach the aforesaid place, so that the absence of a lord may not give an opportunity to his men of doing evil.

Send your gifts, which you ought to present to us at our assembly in the middle of the month of May, to the place where we then shall be; if perchance your journey shall so shape itself that on your march you are able in person to present these gifts of yours to us, we greatly desire it. See that you show no negligence in the future if you desire to have our favor.

From *Translations and Reprints*, VI, No. 5, D. C. Munro, Ed.

Capitularies Relating to Education, 780–800

One of the Emperor's major aims was a revival of culture which, in the circumstances of the time, could only mean Christian culture. In pursuit of this objective he gathered at his court the most learned men of his time from every part of Western Europe, attempted to reform and improve clerical education throughout his lands, and in his own palace set up a center of higher studies where, for the first time in centuries, scholars and nobles, clerics and laymen, could meet on a common ground of letters and reason. The Emperor's deliberate purpose was to rebuild a Latin Christian civilization to go with the Latin Christian Empire he had in mind, and so his endeavors were not in the entirely disinterested pursuit of knowledge. But his interest was real and he did more for the rediscovery and preservation of cultural values than anyone within a range of centuries.

Alcuin wrote to him at one point: "If your intentions are carried out, it may be that a new Athens will arise in France and an Athens fairer than the old, for . . . ennobled by the teaching of Christ [it] will surpass the wisdom of the Academy." This makes rather pathetic reading when we know that a new tide of barbarism and destruction would soon be sweeping over Europe. Yet the ideal of a Christian culture that the Northumbrian monk and the illiterate barbarian king dreamed together did restore and preserve some of the inheritance of ancient civilization and literature. Partly because of these two men, this heritage was never quite lost again in the subsequent trials of the West and was eventually realized in the development of the Western tradition.

Charles, by the grace of God, King of the Franks and Lombards and Patrician of the Romans, to Abbot Baugulf and to all the congregation, also to the faithful committed to you, we have directed a loving greeting by our ambassadors in the name of omnipotent God.

Be it known, therefore, to your devotion pleasing to God, that we, together with our faithful, have considered it to be useful that the bishoprics and monasteries entrusted by the favor of Christ to our control, in addition to the order of monastic life and the intercourse of holy religion, in the culture of letters also ought to be zealous in teaching those who by the gift of God are able to learn, according to the capacity of each individual, so that just as the observance of the rule imparts order and grace to honesty of morals, so also zeal in teaching and learning may do the same for sentences, so that those who desire to please God by living rightly should not neglect to please him also by speaking correctly. For it is written: "Either from thy words thou shalt be justified or from thy words thou shalt be condemned." For although correct conduct may be better than knowledge, nevertheless knowledge precedes conduct. Therefore, each one ought to study what he desires to accomplish, so that so much the more fully the mind may know what

ought to be done, as the tongue hastens in the praises of omnipotent God without the hindrances of errors. For since errors should be shunned by all men, so much the more ought they to be avoided as far as possible by those who are chosen for this very purpose alone, so that they ought to be the especial servants of truth. For when in the years just passed letters were often written to us from several monasteries in which it was stated that the brethren who dwelt there offered up in our behalf sacred and pious prayers, we have recognized in most of these letters both correct thoughts and uncouth expressions; because what pious devotion dictated faithfully to the mind, the tongue, uneducated on account of the neglect of study, was not able to express in the letter without error. Whence it happened that we began to fear lest perchance, as the skill in writing was less, so also the wisdom for understanding the Holy Scriptures might be much less than it rightly ought to be. And we all know well that, although errors of speech are dangerous, far more dangerous are errors of the understanding. Therefore, we exhort you not only not to neglect the study of letters, but also with most humble mind, pleasing to God, to study earnestly in order that you may be able more easily and more correctly to penetrate the mys-

From *Translations and Reprints*, VI, No. 5, D. C. Munro, Ed.

teries of the divine Scriptures. Since, moreover, images, tropes and similar figures are found in the sacred pages, no one doubts that each one in reading these will understand the spiritual sense more quickly if previously he shall have been fully instructed in the mastery of letters. Such men truly are to be chosen for this work as have both the will and the ability to learn and a desire to instruct others. And may this be done with a zeal as great as the earnestness with which we command it. For we desire you to be, as it is fitting that soldiers of the church should be, devout in mind, learned in discourse, chaste in conduct and eloquent in speech,

so that whosoever shall seek to see you out of reverence of God, or on account of your reputation for holy conduct, just as he is edified by your appearance, may also be instructed by your wisdom, which he has learned from your reading or singing, and may go away joyfully giving thanks to omnipotent God. Do not neglect, therefore, if you wish to have our favor, to send copies of this letter to all your suffragans and fellow-bishops and to all the monasteries. [And let no monk hold courts outside of his monastery or go to the judicial and other public assemblies. Farewell.]

Admonitio Generalis, 789

And we also demand of your holiness that the ministers of the altar of God shall adorn their ministry by good manners, and likewise the other orders who observe a rule and the congregations of monks. We implore them to lead a just and fitting life, just as God Himself commanded in the Gospel. "Let your light so shine before men that they may see your good works and glorify your Father which is in heaven," so that by their example many may be led to serve God; and let them join and associate to themselves not only children of servile condition, but also

sons of free men. And let schools be established in which boys may learn to read. Correct carefully the Psalms, the signs in writing (*notas*), the songs, the calendar, the grammar, in each monastery or bishopric, and the catholic books; because often some desire to pray to God properly, but they pray badly because of the incorrect books. And do not permit your boys to corrupt them in reading or writing. If there is need of writing the Gospel, Psalter and Missal, let men of mature age do the writing with all diligence.

From *Translations and Reprints,* VI, No. 5, D. C. Munro, Ed.

General Capitulary for the *Missi*

One serious problem Charlemagne had to face was that of controlling his vast territories in an age of execrable or nonexistent communications, without the administrative and bureaucratic machinery we have come to take for granted. One of his solutions consisted in sending out itinerant officials, the *missi* or envoys (from the Latin *mittere,* to send) whose mission was to represent him, see that his orders were carried out, receive complaints, and, if necessary, administer justice in his name. The *missi* generally traveled in pairs composed of one cleric and one layman. The passage below contains their basic instructions.

From *Translations and Reprints,* VI, No. 5, D. C. Munro, Ed.

Concerning the embassy sent out by the lord emperor. Therefore, the most serene and most Christian lord emperor Charles has chosen from his nobles the wisest and most prudent men, both archbishops and some of the other bishops also, and venerable abbots and pious laymen, and has sent them throughout his whole kingdom, and through them by all the following chapters has allowed men to live in accordance with the correct law. Moreover, where anything which is not right and just has been enacted in the law, he has ordered them to inquire into this most diligently and to inform him of it; he desires, God granting, to reform it. And let no one, through his cleverness or astuteness, dare to oppose or thwart the written law, as many are wont to do, or the judicial sentence passed upon him, or to do injury to the churches of God or the poor or the widows or the wards or any Christian. But all shall live entirely in accordance with God's precept, justly and under a just rule, and each one shall be admonished to live in harmony with his fellows in his business or profession; the canonical clergy ought to observe in every respect a canonical life without heeding base gain, nuns ought to keep diligent watch over their lives, laymen and the secular clergy ought rightly to observe their laws without malicious fraud, and all ought to live in mutual charity and perfect peace. And let the *missi* themselves make a diligent investigation whenever any man claims that an injustice has been done to him by any one, just as they desire to deserve the grace of omnipotent God and to keep their fidelity promised to Him, so that entirely in all cases everywhere, in accordance with the will and fear of God, they shall administer the law fully and justly in the case of the holy churches of God and of the poor, of wards and widows and of the whole people. And if there shall be anything of such a nature that they, together with the provincial counts, are not able of themselves to correct it and to do justice concerning it, they shall, without any ambiguity, refer this, together with their reports, to the judgment of the emperor; and the straight path of justice shall not be impeded by any one on account of flattery or gifts from any one, or on account of any relationship, or from fear of the powerful.

Concerning the fidelity to be promised to the lord emperor. And he commanded that every man in his whole kingdom, whether ecclesiastic or layman, and each one according to his vow and occupation, should now promise to him as emperor the fidelity which he had previously promised to him as king; and all of those who had not yet made that promise should do likewise, down to those who were twelve years old. And that it shall be announced to all in public, so that each one might know, how great and how many things are comprehended in that oath; not merely, as many have thought hitherto, fidelity to the lord emperor as regards his life, and not introducing any enemy into his kingdom out of enmity, and not consenting to or concealing another's faithlessness to him; but that all may know that this oath contains in itself this meaning:

First, that each one voluntarily shall strive, in accordance with his knowledge and ability, to live wholly in the holy service of God in accordance with the precept of God and in accordance with his own promise, because the lord emperor is unable to give to all individually the necessary care and discipline.

Secondly, that no man, either through perjury or any other wile or fraud, on account of the flattery or gift of any one, shall refuse to give back or dare to abstract or conceal a serf of the lord emperor or a district or land or anything that belongs to him; and that no one shall presume, through perjury or other wile, to conceal or abstract his fugitive fiscaline serfs who unjustly and fraudulently say that they are free.

That no one shall presume to rob or do any injury fraudulently to the churches of God or widows or orphans or pilgrims; for the lord emperor himself, after God and His saints, has constituted himself their protector and defender.

That no one shall dare to lay waste a benefice of the lord emperor, or to make it his own property.

That no one shall presume to neglect a summons to war from the lord emperor; and that no one of the counts shall be so presumptuous as to dare to dismiss thence any one of those who owe military service, either on account of relationship or flattery or gifts from any one.

That no one shall presume to impede at all in any way a ban or command of the lord emperor, or to dally with his work or to impede or to lessen or in any way to act contrary to his will or commands. And that no one shall dare to neglect to pay his dues or tax.

That no one, for any reason, shall make a practice in court of defending another unjustly, either from any desire of gain when the cause is weak, or by impeding a just judgment by his skill in reasoning, or by a desire of oppressing when the cause is weak. But each one shall answer for his own cause or tax or debt unless any one is infirm or ignorant of pleading; for these the *missi* or the chiefs who are in the court or the judge who knows the case in question shall plead before the court; or if it is necessary, such a person may be allowed as is acceptable to all and knows the case well; but this shall be done wholly according to the convenience of the chiefs or *missi* who are present. But in every case it shall be done in accordance with justice and the law; and that no one shall have the power to impede justice by a gift, reward, or any kind of evil flattery or from any hindrance of relationship. And that no one shall unjustly consent to another in anything, but that with all zeal and goodwill all shall be prepared to carry out justice.

For all the above mentioned ought to be observed by the imperial oath.

A Letter of the Emperor's Missi

Armed with the Emperor's personal authority, his representatives tended to act as his watchdogs. They were well aware of the tricks that local lords were likely to attempt, aware too that only a firm hand could maintain a semblance of order in the vast barbarous society of Carolingian France. Nor were they professional administrators wallowing in jargon or repressions, but great lords themselves dealing with their social equals. Below is a letter of instructions addressed by four *missi dominici* to the counts in the region they were about to visit.

We address you this letter to order on the part of the Emperor and on our part to urge you most earnestly to make all efforts to fulfill all the obligations of your

From L. Halphen, *Empire Carolingien.*

charge concerning the worship of God, and the service of our master. He has ordered us, as well as all his other *missi*, to submit by the middle of April, a loyal report on the manner in which have been executed in his kingdom the orders which he has these last few years transmitted by his *missi*. He wished suitably to reward those who have conformed themselves to his order and to reprimand as they deserve those who have not. . . .

We urge you to reread your capitularies, to remember the verbal instructions which you have had and to show in their application such zeal as will deserve reward from God and from your master the great Emperor. Therefore we enjoin you to obey punctually and to expect of your subordinates and inferiors a punctual obedience to the orders of your bishop touching everything which concerns his ministry. Maintain all the rights of the Emperor such as have been defined in writing and orally, for you are accountable. Do justice in every way to the churches, to the widows, to the orphans, to everyone else without fraud, without corruption, without abusive delays, and watch that all your subordinates do likewise, if you want to be rewarded by God and our

master. If you come up against insubordination or disobedience, if anyone refuses to accept the decision which you have taken in conformity with law or justice, take note of it and let us know, either immediately if urgent or when we visit you, so that we may advise you according to the instructions which we have received from our master. Do not hesitate if you have a doubt on the meaning of a passage of this decree, to send us urgently one of your representatives capable of understanding our explanations so that you will be able yourselves to understand it all and with the help of God carry it all out. Above all be very careful not to be found, you and your subordinates, delaying or hindering justice or saying to the parties to a suit, "Just be quiet until the *missi* have gone by; we shall fix things between us afterwards." On the contrary do your best to hasten the judgment of cases pending before our arrival, for if you try out any such dirty trick, or if by negligence or malice you delay the course of justice until our coming, get it well into your heads that we shall give you a very bad report. Read and reread this letter and guard it well so that it will serve as witness between yourselves and us.

III. Feudalism and Personal Dependence

The centuries that follow the disintegration of Roman order know no strong central governments and lack the concept of absolute property in land, preferring the practical idea of use to the legalistic idea of ownership.

Feudalism is the name given to the system of organization in society which was based on a relationship between vassal and superior, arising from the surrender, the grant, and the holding of land in feud —i.e., as a benefice or holding. Early in the day, as the power of Rome had started to crack, both Romans and barbarians had learned to enter into voluntary agreements designed to secure protection or service, in which land (the only solid thing where everything was going up in smoke) served as a means of exchange. These relationships between lord and vassal, landlord and tenant, more or less arbitrary and undefined to start with, became more fixed and uniform with time. As western Europe began to settle down, feudal institutions became better defined. Land, too, was no longer the only benefice that counted: tolls, monopolies, and money payments began to count as much or more.

1. FEUDAL RELATIONSHIPS

Only a vast collection could begin to encompass the variety of arrangements and institutions by which the men of the Middle Ages sought to cope with problems of cooperation, political authority, social organization. A few documents are given below to illustrate some aspects of a process that can be followed from the seventh to the fourteenth century—by which time, of course, many nonfeudal institutions were already growing in strength.

AN ANGLO-SAXON FORMULA OF COMMENDATION

Thus shall one take the oath of fidelity:

By the Lord before whom this sanctuary is holy, I will to N. be true and faithful, and love all which he loves and shun all which he shuns, according to the laws of God and the order of the world. Nor will I ever with will or action, through word or deed, do anything which is unpleasing to him, on condition that he will hold to me as I shall deserve it, and that he will perform everything as it was in our agreement when I submitted myself to him and chose his will.

A FRANKISH FORMULA OF COMMENDATION, SEVENTH CENTURY

Who commends himself in the power of another:

This and the following seven documents are reprinted from *Translations and Reprints*, IV, No. 3, E. P. Cheyney, Ed.

To that magnificent lord *so and so,* I, *so and so.* Since it is known familiarly to all how little I have whence to feed and clothe myself, I have therefore petitioned your piety, and your good-will has decreed to me that I should hand myself over or commend myself to your guardianship, which I have thereupon done; that is to say in this way, that you should aid and succor me as well with food as with clothing, according as I shall be able to serve you and deserve it.

And so long as I shall live I ought to provide service and honor to you, suitably to my free condition; and I shall not during the time of my life have the ability to withdraw from your power or guardianship; but must remain during the days of my life under your power or defence. Wherefore it is proper that if either of us shall wish to withdraw himself from these agreements, he shall pay *so many* shillings to the other party (*pari suo*), and this agreement shall remain unbroken.

Wherefore it is fitting that they should make or confirm between themselves two letters drawn up in the same form on this matter; which they have thus done.

ACCEPTANCE OF AN ANTRUSTION,[1]
SEVENTH CENTURY

It is right that those who offer to us unbroken fidelity should be protected by our aid. And since *such and such* a faithful one of ours, by the favor of God, coming here in our palace with his arms, has seen fit to swear trust and fidelity to us in our hand, therefore we decree and command by the present precept that for the future *such and such* above mentioned be counted with the number of the antrustions. And if any one perchance

[1] A member of the bodyguard of Frankish princes.

should presume to kill him, let him know that he will be judged guilty of his wergild of 600 shillings.

CHARTER OF GUARDIANSHIP GRANTED BY THE KING, NINTH CENTURY

We wish it to be known to all our faithful, dwelling in the parts of Romania and Italy that certain men whose names are *such and such,* coming into our presence have begged and prayed us that on account of the injuries of evil men we should take them under the security of our protection, which we have done with willingness. On this account we have ordered this precept of our authority to be made and given to them; by which we require and command that no one of you take anything of their property from them against what is right, or presume to prosecute them in any cause unjustly; but it is allowed to them under our defence and protection and without opposition of any kind to live quietly on their own property. And if any causes shall have arisen against them which within their own country cannot be concluded without heavy and unreasonable expense, we will that these be suspended and reserved for our presence till they may receive a just and lawful final sentence, and let no one presume to deprive them of the opportunity of coming to us.

CAPITULARY CONCERNING FREEMEN AND VASSALS, 816

If any one shall wish to leave his lord (*seniorem*), and is able to prove against him one of these crimes, that is, in the first place, if the lord has wished to reduce him unjustly into servitude; in the second place, if he has taken counsel against his life; in the third place, if the lord has committed adultery with the wife of his vassal; in the fourth place, if he has wilfully attacked him with a drawn sword; in the fifth place, if the lord has been able to bring defence to his vassal after he has commended his hands to him, and has not done so; it is allowed to the vassal to leave him. If the lord has perpetrated anything against the vassal in these five points it is allowed the vassal to leave him.

CAPITULARY OF MERSEN, 847

We will moreover that each free man in our kingdom shall choose a lord, from us or our faithful, such a one as he wishes.

We command moreover that no man shall leave his lord without just cause, nor should any one receive him, except in such a way as was customary in the time of our predecessors.

GRANT OF A FIEF, 1200

I, Thiebault, count palatine of Troyes, make known to those present and to come that I have given in fee to Jocelyn d'Avalon and his heirs the manor which is called Gillencourt, which is of the castellanerie of La Ferté sur Aube; and whatever the same Jocelyn shall be able to acquire in the same manor I have granted to him and his heirs in augmentation of that fief. I have granted, moreover, to him that in no free manor of mine will I retain men who are of this gift. The same Jocelyn, moreover, on account of this has become my liege man, saving, however, his allegiance to Gerard d'Arcy, and to the lord duke of Burgundy, and to Peter, count of Auxerre. Done at Chouaude, by my own witness, in the year of the Incarnation of our Lord 1200 in the month of January. Given by the hand of Walter, my chancellor; note of Milo.

GRANT OF A FIEF OF MONEY, 1380

We, Regnault de Fauquemont, knight, lord of Bournes and of Sitter, make known to all by these presents, that we have become liege man of the king of France, our lord, and to him have made faith and homage because of 1000 livres of Tours of income which he has given to us during our life, to be drawn from his treasury at Paris. And we have promised to him and do promise by these presents to serve him loyally and well in his wars and otherwise against all who can live and die, in the form and manner in which a good and loyal subject ought to serve his sovereign lord. In testimony of which we have put our seal to these present letters. Given at Paris, the 15th day of June, the year 1380.

2. MILITARY SERVICE OF TENANTS

The vassal's obligation to serve his lord with horse and lance and sword, or anything else he might be able to scrape up, was the crux of the feudal bond; but it was an obligation which had to be clearly defined to prevent misunderstanding or undue exploitation. As with every contract, misunderstandings nevertheless occurred: vassals sought to evade their obligations, lords to exact more than their due, and this is particularly evident in the account of dirty doings in French high society which closes this section. A factor of additional interest about the same passage is its general incoherence and inconclusiveness: suggestions are made and apparently left hanging fire; all together the narrator does not seem to have progressed in cogency or power of coherent thought from the time of Gregory of Tours.

AN EARLY FEUDAL SUMMONS, PROBABLY 1072

W., king of the English, to Aethelwig, abbot of Evesham, greeting. I command you to summon all those who are under your charge and jurisdiction to have armed before me by the week after Whitsunday, at Clarendon, all the knights which are due to me. And do you also come to me on that day and bring with you armed those five knights which you owe to me from your abbey. Witness Eudo, the steward, at Winchester.

LEGAL RULES FOR MILITARY SERVICE, 1270

The baron and all vassals of the king are bound to appear before him when he shall summon them, and to serve him at their own expense for forty days and forty nights, with as many knights as each one owes; and he is able to exact from them these services when he wishes and when he has need of them. And if the king wishes to keep them more than forty days at their own expense, they are not bound to remain if they do not wish it. And if the king wishes to keep them at his expense for the defence of the realm, they are bound to remain. And if the king wishes to lead them outside of the kingdom, they need not go unless they wish to, for they have already served their forty days and forty nights.

SERVICE OF THE COUNT OF CHAMPAGNE

Then Louis, king of the French in order to escape from the pestilence, which was raging with great severity in the camp [before Avignon], betook himself to a certain abbey called Montpensier, which was not far distant from the siege works, till the city should be captured. There came to him at that place Henry, count of Champagne, who had passed forty days at the siege, asking license to return to his own possessions, according to the custom of France. When the king refused his permission the count replied that when his military service of forty days had been performed, he was not bound nor was he willing to remain longer. The king, however, was so inflamed by anger at this that he declared with an oath that if the count should withdraw then he would devastate his whole land with fire. Then the count, as the story goes, procured poison to be placed in the drink of the king, on account of his desire for the queen, for whom he had a guilty love, and was so impelled by the incentive of lust that he was not able to brook longer delay. When the count had thus gone away the king grew desperately sick, and the poison reaching his vital parts, he came to his end; although others say that it was not from poison but from dysentery that he died.

These three documents are quoted from *Translations and Reprints*, IV, No. 3, E. P. Cheyney, Ed.

3. FREEING OF A SERF

Like so many other medieval institutions, serfdom too can be traced back to Roman days—to the *villa*, where the land was worked both by slaves and by free *coloni*. But in the later centuries of the Roman Empire the freedom of the *coloni* became increasingly theoretical until, forbidden to leave the land on which they dwelt, they degenerated into serfs or, more correctly, villeins, tied by various obligations to the lord of the manor that had replaced the ancient *villa*, their service henceforth attached to the soil and transferred with it.

The rise of cities, the opportunities of warfare, depopulation, or new enterprises (e.g., putting more land to grass as the wool trade became more obviously profitable) all contributed to the gradual emancipation of the serfs in the later Middle Ages. But the act of manumission which follows seems superficially at least to be due to a different reason, and one by no means unrepresentative, either.

To all the faithful of Christ to whom the present writing shall come, Richard, by the divine permission, Abbot of Peterborough and of the Convent of the same place, eternal greeting in the Lord:

Let all know that we have manumitted and liberated from all yoke of servitude William, the son of Richard of Wythington, whom previously we have held as our born bondman, with his whole progeny and all his chattels, so that neither we nor our successors shall be able to require or exact any right or claim in the said William, his progeny, or his chattels. But the same William, with his whole progeny and all his chattels, shall remain free and quit and without disturbance, exaction, or any claim on the part of us or our successors by reason of any servitude forever.

We will, moreover, and concede that he and his heirs shall hold the messuages, land, rents and meadows in Wythington which his ancestors held from us and our predecessors, by giving and performing the fine which is called merchet for giving his daughter in marriage, and tallage from year to year according to our will, — that he shall have and hold these for the future from us and from our successors freely, quietly, peacefully, and hereditarily, by paying to us and our successors yearly 40s. sterling, at the four terms of the year, namely: at St. John the Baptist's day 10s., at Michaelmas 10s., at Christmas 10s., and at Easter 10s., for all service, exaction, custom, and secular demand; saving to us, nevertheless, attendance at our court of Castres every three weeks, wardship, and relief, and outside service of our lord the king, when they shall happen.

And if it shall happen that the said William or his heirs shall die at any time without an heir, the said messuage, land, rents, and meadows with their appurtenances shall return fully and completely to us and our successors. Nor will it be allowed to the said William or his heirs to give, sell, alienate, mortgage or encumber in any way, the said messuage, land, rents, and meadows, or any part of them, by which the said messuage, land, rents and meadows should not return to us and our successors in the form declared above. And if this should occur later, their deed shall be declared null, and what is thus alienated shall come to us and our successors.

From *Translations and Reprints,* III, No. 5, E. P. Cheyney, Ed.

Given at Borough, for the love of Lord Robert of good memory, once abbot, our predecessor and maternal uncle of the said William, and at the instance of the good man, Brother Hugh of Mutton, relative of the said abbot Robert, A.D. 1278, on the eve of Pentecost.

4. MAGNA CHARTA, GRANTED JUNE 15, 1215

Richard I, the Lion-Hearted, reigned over England but hardly in it (he spent nearly all his time warring abroad) from 1189 to 1199 and was succeeded by his brother John (1199–1216). John inherited the wars and debts that were the results of French enmity and Richard's spendthrift brawling, and he also blundered into more trouble of his own. Trouble with France, with the Pope, with the English Church and barons, eventually made his situation untenable until, at Runnymede, he was forced to sign an agreement with his rebellious vassals that granted most of their demands.

The Great Charter is still sometimes presented as a forward-looking document because it appears as the basis of English liberties. In effect, it looks back to a feudal situation that was already becoming obsolete and tries to restore the anarchic conditions existing before royal power had started to encroach on traditional feudal rights. There is little to show that any of the signatories believed the instrument would be effective. The barons mistrusted the king—and with good reason for he had no intention of keeping promises that tended to whittle away his power. It is this mutual suspicion that serves to explain the Covenant which follows on pages 199–200 as a form of reinsurance; and perhaps also the strange provisions of paragraph 61 (page 199), which deserve our attention.

And yet the Great Charter survives—not only as a prominent factor when interpreted or misinterpreted in the cause of further English liberties, but also as an illustration of its day, the forms and intentions and aspirations of an unfamiliar age.

John, by the Grace of God, King of England, Lord of Ireland, Duke of Normandy and Acquitaine, and Earl of Anjou, to his Archbishops, Bishops, Abbots, Earls, Barons, Justiciaries, Foresters, Sheriffs, Governors, Officers, and to all Bailiffs, and his faithful subjects, — Greeting. Know ye, that We, in the presence of God, and for the salvation of our own soul, and of the souls of all our ancestors, and of our heirs, to the honour of God, and the exaltation of the Holy Church and amendment of our Kingdom, by the counsel of our venerable fathers, Stephen, Archbishop of Canterbury, Primate of all England, and Cardinal of the Holy Roman Church, Henry, Archbishop of Dublin, William of London, Peter of Winchester, Joceline of Bath and Glastonbury, Hugh of Lincoln, Walter of Worcester, William of Coventry, and Benedict of Rochester, Bishops; Master Pandulph, our Lord the Pope's Subdeacon and familiar, Brother Almeric, Master of the Knights-Templars in England, and of these noble persons, William Mareschal

From Boyd C. Barrington: *The Magna Charta* (Philadelphia, 1900).

Earl of Pembroke, William Earl of Salisbury, William Earl of Warren, William Earl of Arundel, Alan de Galloway Constable of Scotland, Warin Fitz-Gerald, Hubert de Burgh Seneschal of Poictou, Peter Fitz-Herbert, Thomas Basset, Alan Basset, Philip de Albiniac, Robert de Roppel, John Mareschall, John-Fitz-Hugh, and others our liegemen; have in the first place granted to God, and by this our present Charter, have confirmed, for us and our heirs forever: —

1. That the English Church shall be free, and shall have her whole rights and her liberties inviolable; and we will this to be observed in such a manner, that it may appear from thence, that the freedom of elections, which was reputed most requisite to the English Church, which we granted, and by our Charter confirmed, and obtained the Confirmation of the same, from our Lord Pope Innocent the Third, before the rupture between us and our Barons, was of our own free will; which Charter we shall observe, and we will it to be observed with good faith, by our heirs forever.

We have also granted to all the freemen of our Kingdom, for us and our heirs, forever, all the underwritten Liberties, to be enjoyed and held by them and by their heirs, from us and from our heirs.

2. If any of our Earls or Barons, or others who hold of us in chief by military service, shall die, and at his death his heir shall be of full age, and shall owe a relief, he shall have his inheritance by the ancient relief; that is to say, the heir or heirs of an Earl, a whole Earl's Barony for one hundred pounds; the heir or heirs of a Knight, for a whole Knight's fee, by one hundred shillings at most; and he who owes less, shall give less, according to the ancient custom of fees.

3. But if the heir of any such be under age, and in wardship when he comes to age he shall have his inheritance without relief and without fine.

4. The warden of the land of such heir who shall be under age, shall not take from the lands of the heir any but reasonable issues, and reasonable customs, and reasonable services. . . . And if we shall give or sell to any one the custody of any such lands, and he shall make destruction or waste upon them, he shall lose the custody; and it shall be committed to two lawful and discreet men of that fee, who shall answer to us in like manner as it is said before.

5. But the warden, as long as he hath the custody of the lands, shall keep up and maintain the houses, parks, warrens, ponds, mills and other things belonging to them, out of their issues; and shall restore to the heir when he comes of full age his whole estate, provided with ploughs and other implements of husbandry, according as the time of wainage shall require, and the issues of the lands can reasonably afford.

6. Heirs shall be married without disparagement, so that before the marriage be contracted it shall be notified to the relations of the heir by consanguinity.

7. A widow after the death of her husband shall immediately, and without difficulty, have her marriage and her inheritance; nor shall she give anything for her dower, or for her marriage, or for her inheritance, which her husband and she held at the day of his death; and she may remain in her husband's house forty days after his death, within which time her dower shall be assigned.

8. No widow shall be distrained to marry herself, while she is willing to live without a husband; but yet she shall give security that she will not marry herself without our consent, if she hold of us, or

without the consent of the lord of whom she does hold, if she hold of another.

9. Neither we, nor our Bailiffs, will seize any land or rent for any debt, while the chattels of the debtor are sufficient for the payment of the debt; nor shall the sureties of the debtor be distrained, while the principal debtor is able to pay the debt; and if the principal debtor fail in payment of the debt, not having wherewith to discharge it, the sureties shall answer for the debt; and if they be willing, they shall have the lands and rents of the debtor, until satisfaction be made to them for the debt which they had before paid for him, unless the principal debtor can shew himself acquitted thereof against the said sureties.

10. If any one hath borrowed anything from the jews, more or less, and die before that debt be paid, the debt shall pay no interest so long as the heir shall be under age, of whomsoever he may hold; and if that debt shall fall into our hands, we will not take anything except the chattel contained in the bond.

11. And if any one shall die indebted to the jews, his wife shall have her dower and shall pay nothing of that debt; and if children of the deceased shall remain who are under age, necessaries shall be provided for them, according to the tenement which belonged to the deceased; and out of the residue the debts shall be paid, saving the rights of the lords [of whom the lands are held]. In like manner let it be with debts owing to others than jews.

12. No scutage nor aid shall be imposed in our kingdom, unless by the common council of our kingdom; excepting to redeem our person, to make our eldest son a knight, and once to marry our eldest daughter, and not for these, unless a reasonable aid shall be demanded.

¹ fined.

13. In like manner let it be concerning the aids of the City of London. And the City of London shall have all its ancient liberties, and its free customs, as well by land as by water. Furthermore, we will and grant that all other Cities, Burghs, and Towns, and Ports, should have all their liberties and free customs.

14. And also to have the common council of the kingdom, to assess and aid, otherwise than in the three cases aforesaid: and for the assessing of scutages, we will cause to be summoned the Archbishops, Bishops, Abbots, Earls, and great Barons, individually by our letters. And besides, we will cause to be summoned in general by our Sheriffs and Bailiffs, all those who hold of us in chief, at a certain day, that is to say at the distance of forty days (before their meeting), at the least, and to a certain place; and in all the letters of summons, we will express the cause of the summons; and the summons being thus made, the business shall proceed on the day appointed, according to the counsel of those who shall be present, although all who have been summoned have not come.

15. We will not give leave to any one, for the future, to take an aid of his own free men, except for redeeming his own body, and for making his eldest son a knight, and for marrying once his eldest daughter; and not that unless it be a reasonable aid.

16. None shall be distrained to do more service for a Knight's fee, nor for any other free tenement, than what is due from thence.

17. Common Pleas shall not follow our Court, but shall be held in any certain place.

20. A free-man shall not be amerced ¹ for a small offence, but only according to

the degree of the offence; and for a great delinquency, according to the magnitude of the delinquency, saving his contentment: a Merchant shall be amerced in the same manner, saving his merchandise, and a villein shall be amerced after the same manner, saving to him his Wainage, if he shall fall in to our mercy; and none of the aforesaid amerciaments shall be assessed, but by the oath of honest men of the vicinage.

21. Earls and Barons shall not be amerced but by their Peers, and that only according to the degree of their delinquency.

22. No Clerk shall be amerced for his lay holding, but according to the manner of the others as aforesaid, and not according to the quantity of his ecclesiastical benefice.

23. Neither a town nor any person shall be compelled to build bridges or embankments, excepting those which anciently and of right are bound to do it.

24. No Sheriff, Constable, Coroners, nor other of our Bailiffs shall hold pleas of our crown.

27. If any free-man shall die intestate, his chattels shall be distributed by the hands of his nearest relations and friends, under supervision of the Church, saving to every one the debts which the defunct owed.

28. No Constable nor other Bailiff of ours shall take the corn or other goods of any one without instantly paying money for them, unless he can obtain respite from the free-will of the seller.

29. No Constable [Governor of a Castle] shall compel any Knight to give money for castle-guard, if he be willing to perform it in his own person, or by another able man if he cannot perform it himself for a reasonable cause; and if we have carried or sent him into the army he shall be excused from castle-guard, according to the time that he shall be in the army by our command.

30. No Sheriff nor Bailiff of ours, nor any other person shall take the horses or carts of any free-man for the purpose of carriage, without the consent of the said free-man.

31. Neither we, nor our Bailiffs, will take another man's wood, for our castles or other uses, unless by the consent of him to whom the wood belongs.

32. We will not retain the lands of those who have been convicted of felony, excepting for one year and one day, and then they shall be given up to the lord of the fee.

35. There shall be one measure of wine throughout all our kingdom, and one measure of ale, and one measure of corn, namely, the quarter of London; and one breadth of dyed cloth, and of russets, and of halberjects, namely, two ells within the lists. Also it shall be the same with weights as with measures.

36. Nothing shall be given or taken for the future for the Writ of Inquisition of life or limb; but it shall be given without charge and not denied.

38. No Bailiffs, for the future, shall put any man to his law, upon his own simple affirmation, without credible witnesses produced for that purpose.

39. No free-man shall be seized, or imprisoned, or dispossessed, or outlawed, or in any way destroyed; nor will we condemn him, nor will we commit him to prison, excepting by the legal judgment of his peers, or by the laws of the land.

40. To none will we sell, to none will we deny, to none will we delay right or justice.

41. All Merchants shall have safety and security in coming into England, and

going out of England, and in staying and in traveling through England, as well by land as by water, to buy and sell, without any unjust exactions; according to ancient and right customs, excepting in the time of war, and if they be of a country at war against us: and if such are found in our land at the beginning of a war, they shall be apprehended without injury of their bodies and goods, until it be known to us, or to our Chief Justiciary, how the Merchants of our country are treated who are found in the country at war against us; and if ours be in safety there, the others shall be in safety in our land.

42. It shall be lawful to any person, for the future, to go out of our kingdom, and to return, safely and securely, by land or by water, saving his allegiance to us, unless it be in time of war, for some short space, for the common good of the kingdom: excepting prisoners and outlaws, according to the laws of the land, and of the people of the nation at war against us, and Merchants who shall be treated as it is said above.

45. We will not make Justiciaries, Constables, Sheriffs, or Bailiffs, excepting such as know the laws of the land, and are well disposed to observe them.

46. All Barons who have founded Abbeys, which they hold by Charters from the Kings of England, or by ancient tenure, shall have the custody of them when they become vacant, as they ought to have.

47. All Forests which have been made in our time shall be immediately disforested, and it shall be so done with waterbanks which have been taken or fenced in by us during our reign.

48. All evil customs of Forests and Warrens, and of Foresters and Warreners, Sheriffs, and their officers, Water-banks and their keepers, shall immediately be inquired into by twelve knights of the same county, upon oath, who shall be elected by good men of the same county; and within forty days after the inquisition is made they shall be altogether destroyed by them, never to be restored; provided that this be notified to us before it be done, or to our Justiciary, if we be not in England.

49. We will immediately restore all hostages and charters which have been delivered to us by the English in security of the peace and of their faithful service.

51. And immediately after the conclusion of the peace, we will remove out of the kingdom all foreign knights, crossbow-men, and stipendiary soldiers, who have come with horses and arms to the molestation of the kingdom.

52. If any have been disseised or dispossessed by us, without a legal verdict of their peers, of their lands, castles, liberties, or rights, we will immediately restore these things to them; and if any dispute shall arise on this head, then it shall be determined by the verdict of the twenty-five barons, of whom mention is made below, for the security of the peace. Concerning all those things of which any one hath been disseised or dispossessed, without the legal verdict of his peers by King Henry our father, or King Richard our brother, which we have in our hand, or others hold with our warrants, we shall have respite, until the common term of the Croisaders, excepting those concerning which a plea had been raised, or an inquisition taken, by our order, before our taking the Cross; but as soon as we shall return from our expedition, or if, by chance, we should not go upon our expedition, we will immediately do complete justice therein.

53. The same respite will we have,

and the same justice shall be done, concerning the disforestation of the forests, or the forests which remain to be disforested, which Henry, our father, or Richard, our brother, have afforested; and the same concerning the wardship of lands which are in another's fee, but the wardship of which we have hitherto had, occasioned by any of our fees held by Military Service; and for Abbeys founded in any other fee than our own, in which the Lord of the fee hath claimed a right; and when we shall have returned, or if we shall stay from our expedition, we shall immediately do complete justice in all these pleas.

54. No man shall be apprehended or imprisoned on the appeal of a woman for the death of any other man than her husband.

55. All fines that have been made by us unjustly, or contrary to the laws of the land, and all amerciaments that have been imposed unjustly, or contrary to the laws of the land, shall be wholly remitted, or ordered by the verdict of the twenty-five Barons, of whom mention is made below, for the security of the peace, or by the verdict of the greater part of them, together with the aforesaid Stephen, Archbishop of Canterbury, if he can be present, and others whom he may think fit to bring with him; and if he cannot be present, the business shall proceed, notwithstanding, without him; but so that if any one or more of the aforesaid twenty-five Barons have a similar plea, let them be removed from that particular trial, and others elected and sworn by the residue of the same twenty-five, be substituted in their room, only for that trial.

56. If we have disseised or dispossessed any Welshmen of their lands, or liberties, or other things, without a legal verdict of their peers; in England or in Wales, they shall be immediately restored to them; and if any dispute shall arise upon this head, then let it be determined in the Marches by the verdict of their peers: for a tenement of England, according to the law of England; for a tenement of Wales, according to the law of Wales; for a tenement of the Marches, according to the law of the Marches. The Welsh shall do the same to us and to our subjects.

58. We will immediately deliver up the son of Llewellyn, and all the hostages of Wales, and release them from their engagements which were made with us, for the security of the peace.

59. We shall do to Alexander, King of Scotland, concerning the restoration of his sisters and hostages, and his liberties and rights, according to the form in which we act to our other barons of England, unless it ought to be otherwise by the charters which we have from his father William, the late King of Scotland; and this shall be by the verdict of his peers in our court.

60. Also all these customs and liberties aforesaid, which we have granted to be held in our Kingdom, for so much of it as belongs to us, all our subjects, as well clergy as laity, shall observe towards their tenants as far as concerns them.

61. But since we have granted all these things aforesaid, for GOD and for the amendment of our kingdom, and for the better extinguishing the discord which has arisen between us and our Barons, we being desirous that these things should possess entire and unshaken stability forever, give and grant to them the security underwritten, namely, that the Barons may elect twenty-five Barons of the kingdom, whom they please, who shall with their whole power, observe, keep, and cause to be observed, the peace and liber-

ties which we have granted to them, and have confirmed by this, our present charter, in this manner; that is to say, if we, or our Justiciary, or our Bailiffs, or our officers, shall have injured any one in anything, or shall have violated any article of the peace or security, and the injury shall have been shown to four of the aforesaid twenty-five Barons, the said four Barons shall come to us, or to our Justiciary if we be out of the kingdom, and making known to us the excess [1] committed, petition that we cause that excess to be redressed without delay. And if we shall not have redressed the excess, or, if we have been out of the kingdom, our Justiciary shall not have redressed it within the term of forty days, computing from the time when it shall have been made known to us, or to our Justiciary, if we have been out of the kingdom, the aforesaid four Barons shall lay that cause before the residue of the twenty-five Barons; and they, the twenty-five Barons, with the community of the whole land, shall distress and harass us by all the ways in which they are able; that is to say, by the taking of our castles, lands and possessions, and by any other means in their power, until the excess shall have been redressed, according to their verdict, saving harmless our person and the persons of our Queen and children, and when it hath been redressed they shall behave to us as they have done before. And whoever of our land pleaseth may swear that he will obey the commands of the aforesaid twenty-five Barons in accomplishing all the things aforesaid, and that with them he will harass us to the utmost of his power; and we publicly and freely give leave to every one to swear who is willing to swear; and we will never forbid any to swear. Moreover, all those who are un-

[1] infringement.

willing to swear of their own accord to the twenty-five Barons, to distress and harass us together with them, we will compel them by our command to swear as aforesaid. . . . And we will obtain nothing from any one, by ourselves, nor by another, by which any of these concessions and liberties may be revoked or diminished. And if any such thing shall have been obtained, let it be void and null; and we will never use it, neither by ourselves nor by another.

63. Wherefore our will is, and we firmly command that the Church of England be free, and that the men in our kingdom have and hold the aforesaid liberties, rights and concessions, well and in peace, freely and quietly, fully and entirely, to them and their heirs, of us and our heirs, in all things and places forever, as is aforesaid. It is also sworn, both on our part and on that of the Barons, that all the aforesaid shall be observed in good faith and without any evil intention. Witnessed by the above and many others. Given by our hand in the Meadow which is called Runningmead, between Windsor and Staines, this 15th day of June, in the 17th year of our reign.

COVENANT MADE BETWEEN KING JOHN AND THE BARONS IMMEDIATELY AFTER THE EXECUTION OF THE MAGNA CHARTA

THIS is the Covenant made between our Lord John of England on the one part, and Robert Fitzwalter, elected Marshal of God and of the Holy Church of England, and Richard Earl of Clare, Geoffrey Earl of Essex and Gloucester, Roger Bigod Earl of Norfolk and Suffolk, Saher Earl of Winchester, Robert Earl of

Oxford, Henry Earl of Hereford, and the Barons underwritten: That is to say, William Marshall the younger, Eustace de Vescy, William de Mowbray, John Fitz Robert, Roger de Mont-Begun, William de Lanvalay, and other Earls and Barons, and Freemen of the whole Kingdom on the other part: Namely, That they the Earls and Barons and others before written, shall hold the custody of the City of London in bail from our Lord the King, saving that they shall clearly render all the debts and revenues within the same, to our Lord the King, until the term of the Assumption of the Blessed Virgin Mary, in the seventeenth year of his reign.

And the Lord of Canterbury shall hold in like manner of bail from our Lord the King, the custody of the Tower of London, to the aforesaid term, saving to the City of London, its liberties and free customs, and taking his oath in the keeping of the said Tower, that our Lord the King shall in the meanwhile not place a guard nor other forces in the aforesaid City, nor in the Tower of London.

And that also within the aforesaid term the oaths of the twenty-five Barons be tendered throughout all England, as it is contained in the Charter granted concerning the liberties and security of the kingdom; or to the attorneys of the twenty-five Barons as it is contained in the letters granted concerning the election of twelve knights for abolishing evil customs of the forests and others. And, moreover, within the said term, all the other demands which the Earls, Barons, or by the greater part of them, shall be judged proper to be granted, are to be given, according to the tenor of the said Charter. And if these things shall be done, or if our Lord the King, on his part shall agree to do them, within the term limited, then the City and Tower of London shall at the same term be delivered up to our Lord the King, saving always to the aforesaid City, its liberties and free customs as it is before written. And if these things shall not be done, and if our Lord the King shall not agree to do them within the period aforesaid, the Barons shall hold the aforesaid City and the Lord Archbishop the Tower of London, until the aforesaid deeds shall be completed. And in the meanwhile all of both parts shall recover the castles, lands, and towns which have been taken in the beginning of the war that has arisen between our Lord the King and the Barons.

IV. The Church in the Middle Ages

The one institution which preserved the Roman tradition of centralized authority, as well as a few of the cultural values of the past, was the Church. And, since it had fewer succession troubles, better laws and administration, and a more faithful body of followers than any of the temporal princes, the Church endured and waxed prosperous. Politically, the great problem it had to face was set by the relationship between spiritual and temporal powers. Things had changed since the time when Charlemagne had told Pope Leo III what he thought on that score. By the eleventh century we find popes telling emperors what is expected of them, and by the time of Innocent III (1198–1216) the claims of papal supremacy are clearly and authoritatively expressed.

Great assistance in carrying out the duties the Church had assumed in both the spiritual and the temporal spheres, was rendered by the regular clergy—organized in Orders, each with its own Rule and purpose. Every monastery that sprang up in the West after the sixth century provided a firm base for Christianity, sometimes in the wilderness, sometimes in enemy territory. The Western religious Orders did not show the slight degree of independence that many of their Eastern brethren did; on the contrary, where the secular clergy only too often accepted or preferred the protection of some local dignitary, the regular clergy looked to the Pope, on whom they always depended.

At first sight, both Christianity and monasticism seem rather ill adapted to an age of lawlessness and war and it may be argued that neither managed to carry out its original intentions or preserve the purity of its ideals. Yet, if they were affected by the nature of their times, they affected it in turn. The Christian Church of the Middle Ages is medieval, i.e., often brutal, violent, crude, and ignorant. On the other hand, the Middle Ages are Christian and thus a little less brutal, violent, crude, and ignorant than they might otherwise have been.

1. INNOCENT III ON EMPIRE AND PAPACY

Innocent III, a scion of the Roman nobility, was thirty-seven years old when he became Pope in 1198, and he reigned for eighteen years. He found the papacy weak and despised, restored papal power to its utmost limits, and left it highly organized and influential. Active and energetic, he took a hand in the upbringing of the young Frederic of Sicily, the future *Stupor Mundi*, clashed with Philip Augustus in France

Both of the following papal proclamations are reprinted from *Documents of the Christian Church,* H. Bettenson, Ed. (Oxford, 1950). Reprinted by permission of Oxford University Press and Geoffrey Cumberledge.

and John in England; initiated the Fourth Crusade, that resulted in the capture and sack of Constantinople; and preached and supported the Albigensian Crusade, which destroyed the flourishing culture of Languedoc. The limits or deformations of his successes showed up the limits of papal power, even when it had been reconstituted in strong hands. The papacy would remain a factor to reckon with, but the claims that Innocent put forward could never be realized.

The Creator of the universe set up two great luminaries in the firmament of heaven; the greater light to rule the day, the lesser light to rule the night. In the same way for the firmament of the universal Church, which is spoken of as heaven, he appointed two great dignities; the greater to bear rule over souls (these being, as it were, days), the lesser to bear rule over bodies (these being, as it were, nights). These dignities are the pontifical authority and the royal power. Furthermore, the moon derives her light from the sun, and is in truth inferior to the sun in both size and quality, in position as well as effect. In the same way the royal power derives its dignity from the pontifical authority: and the more closely it cleaves to the sphere of that authority the less is the light with which it is adorned; the further it is removed, the more it increases in splendour.

2. THE BULL "UNAM SANCTAM," 1302

[Pope Boniface, by his bull *Clericis Laicos* [1296], which tried to prevent taxing the clergy to get money for waging wars, offended not only Edward I of England but also Philip IV of France. Philip replied by prohibiting the export of money from France, which cut off French contributions to Rome. *Unam Sanctam* defined the papal claims. Philip was exasperated and sent an agent to seize Boniface at Anagni. The papal palace was plundered, the Pope's life was threatened, and he was imprisoned for some days. He died within a few weeks of the outrage.] [1303]

We are obliged by the faith to believe and hold—and we do firmly believe and sincerely confess—that there is one Holy Catholic and Apostolic Church, and that outside this Church there is neither salvation nor remission of sins. . . . In which Church there is one Lord, one faith, one baptism. At the time of the flood there was one ark of Noah, symbolizing the one Church; this was completed in one cubit and had one, namely Noah, as helmsman and captain; outside which all things on earth, we read, were destroyed. . . . Of this one and only Church there is one body and one head —not two heads, like a monster—namely Christ, and Christ's vicar is Peter, and Peter's successor, for the Lord said to Peter himself, "Feed My sheep." "My sheep," He said in general, not these or those sheep; wherefore He is understood to have committed them all to him. Therefore, if the Greeks or others say that they were not committed to Peter and his successors, they necessarily confess that they are not of Christ's sheep, for the Lord says in John, "There is one fold and one shepherd."

And we learn from the words of the Gospel that in this Church and in her power are two swords, the spiritual and the temporal. For when the apostles said, "Behold, here" (that is, in the Church, since it was the apostles who spoke) "are two swords"—the Lord did not reply, "It is too much," but "It is enough." Truly he who denies that the temporal sword is in the power of Peter, misunderstands the words of the Lord, "Put up thy sword into the sheath." Both are in the power of the Church, the spiritual sword and the material. But the latter is to be used for the Church, the former by her; the former by the priest, the latter by kings and captains but at the will and by the permission of the priest. The one sword, then, should be under the other, and temporal authority subject to spiritual. For when the apostle says "there is no power but of God, and the powers that be are ordained of God" they would not be so ordained were not one sword made subject to the other. . . .

Thus, concerning the Church and her power, is the prophecy of Jeremiah ful-

filled, "See, I have this day set thee over the nations and over the kingdoms," etc. If, therefore, the earthly power err, it shall be judged by the spiritual power; and if a lesser power err, it shall be judged by a greater. But if the supreme power err, it can only be judged by God, not by men; for the testimony of the apostle is "The spiritual man judgeth all things, yet he himself is judged of no man." For this authority, although given to a man and exercised by a man, is not human, but rather divine, given at God's mouth to Peter and established on a rock for him and his successors in Him whom he confessed, the Lord saying to Peter himself, "Whatsoever thou shalt bind," etc. Whoever therefore resists this power thus ordained of God, resists the ordinance of God. . . . Furthermore we declare, state, define and pronounce that it is altogether necessary to salvation for every human creature to be subject to the Roman pontiff.

3. MONASTIC RULES

Decay in monastic fervor and too flagrant departure from the Rules were eventually met by reforms, by the foundation of new houses and new Orders with stricter Rules, and, in due course, by the invention of itinerant missionaries, the friars, who were supposed to shun the property and creature comforts which had fattened and corrupted so many of their predecessors. It has seemed relevant to give below the Rule of the first monastic Order and that of a typical Order of friars. They illustrate what the Orders set out to do; history tells what they ended by doing.

Rule of St. Benedict

[Benedict of Nursia was born at Rome at the close of the fifth century. He renounced the world at the age of fourteen and finally settled at Monte Cassino, where he founded his monastery. He died in 543. By the ninth century his Rule had superseded all others; and it formed the basis of the new orders, such as the Cluniacs and Cistercians.]

From *Documents of the Christian Church*, H. Bettenson, Ed. By permission of the publishers and Geoffrey Cumberledge.

III. *Of Calling the Brethren to Counsel.* Whenever matters of importance have to be dealt with in the monastery, let the abbot summon the whole congregation and himself put forward the question that has arisen. Then, after hearing the advice of the brethren let him think it over by himself and do what he shall judge most advantageous. . . . But let the brethren give advice with all subjection of humility, so as not to presume obstinately to defend their own opinions; rather let the matter depend on the abbot's judgment, so that all should submit to whatever he decide to be best. Yet, just as it becomes the disciples to obey their master, so it behoves him to order all things with prudence and justice. And in all things let all follow the Rule as their guide: and let no one diverge from it without good reason. Let no one in the monastery follow his own inclinations, and let no one boldly presume to dispute with his abbot, whether within or without the monastery. The abbot, for his part, should do everything in the fear of the Lord and in observance of the Rule; knowing that he will surely have to give account to God for all his decisions, as to a most impartial judge. . . .

VIII. *Of the Divine Office at Night.* In the winter time, that is from the First of November until Easter, according to what is reasonable, they must rise at the eighth hour of the night, so that they rest a little more than half the night, and rise when they have had their full sleep. But let the time that remains after vigils be spent in study by those brothers who have still to learn any part of the psalter of lessons. From Easter, moreover, until the aforesaid First of November, let the hour of keeping vigils be so arranged that, after a short interval, in which the brethren may go out for the necessities of nature,

lauds, which are always to be said at break of day, may follow immediately.

XVI. *How Divine Office Shall Be Said in the Daytime.* As the prophet says: "Seven times in a day do I praise Thee." This sacred number seven will thus be fulfilled by us if, at lauds, at the first, third, sixth, ninth hours, at vesper time and at "completorium" we perform the duties of our service. . . . For, concerning the night hours, the same prophet says: "At midnight I arose to confess unto thee." Therefore, at these times, let us give thanks to our Creator concerning the judgements of his righteousness.

XXII. *How the Monks Are to Sleep.* Let them sleep in separate beds and let their beds be suitable to their manner of life, as the abbot shall appoint. If possible, let them all sleep in one room. But if there be too many for this, let them take their rest in groups of 10 or 20, with seniors in charge of each group. Let a candle be kept burning in the cell until morning. Let them sleep clothed, girdled with belts or cords—but without knives at their sides, lest they injure themselves in sleep. And thus let the monks be always ready; and, when the signal is given, let them rise without delay and rival one another in their haste to the service of God, yet with all reverence and modesty. Let not the younger brothers have bed by themselves, but dispersed among the seniors. And when they rise for the service of God let them gently encourage one another, because the sleepy ones are apt to make excuses.

XXIII. *Of Excommunication for Faults.* If a brother be found contumacious or disobedient, proud or a grumbler, or in any way acting contrary to the holy Rule and despising the orders of his seniors, let him, according to the Lord's commandment, be privately admonished once and twice by his seniors. If he do not then amend, let him be publicly rebuked before all. But if even then he do not correct himself, let him be subjected to excommunication, if he understand the gravity of this penalty. If, however, he is incorrigible, let him undergo corporal chastisement.

XXXIII. *Whether the Monks Should Have Anything of Their Own.* More than anything else is this vice of property to be cut off root and branch from the monastery. Let no one presume to give or receive anything without the leave of the abbot, or to retain anything as his own. He should have nothing at all: neither a book, nor tablets, nor a pen—nothing at all. For indeed it is not allowed to the monks to have bodies or wills in their own power. But for all things necessary they must look to the Father of the monastery. . . .

XXXIV. *Whether All Ought to Receive Necessaries Equally.* As it is written: "It was divided among them singly, according as each had need" (Acts iv. 35): whereby we do not say—far from it—that there should be respect of persons, but a consideration for infirmities. Wherefore he who needs less, let him thank God and not be grieved; but he who needs more, let him be humiliated on account of his weakness, and not made proud on account of the indulgence that is shown him. And thus all members will be in peace. Above all, let not the evil of grumbling appear, on any account, by the least word or sign whatever. But, if such a grumbler is discovered he shall be subjected to stricter discipline.

XXXV. *Of the Weekly Officers of the Kitchen.* The brothers shall wait on each other in turn that no one shall be excused from the kitchen work, unless he be prevented by sickness, or by preoccupation

with some matter of great necessity whereby is gained a greater reward and increase of charity. . . . An hour before each meal the weekly servers are to receive a cup of drink and a piece of bread over and above their ration, so that they may wait on their brethren without grumbling or undue fatigue. But on solemn days they shall fast till after Mass. . . .

XXXVIII. *Of the Weekly Reader.* At the meal times of the brothers there should always be reading; no one there may dare to take up the book at random and begin to read there; but he who is about to read for the whole week shall begin his duties on Sunday. And, entering upon his office after Mass and Communion, he shall ask all to pray for him, that God may avert from him the spirit of elation. And this verse shall be said in the oratory three times by all, he however beginning it: "O Lord, open Thou my lips, and my mouth shall show forth Thy praise." And thus, having received the benediction, he shall enter upon his duties as reader. And there shall be the greatest silence at table, so that no whispering or any voice save the reader's may be heard. And whatever is needed, in the way of food, the brethren should pass to each other in turn, so that no one need ask for anything. But if anything should be wanted let them ask for it by means of a sign rather than by speech.

XXXIX. *Of the Amount of Food.* We think it sufficient for the daily meal, either at the sixth or the ninth hour, that there be, at all seasons, two cooked dishes. And this because of the weaknesses of different people, so that he who happens not to be able to eat of one may make his meal of the other. Let two dishes, then, suffice for the brethren: or if fruits or fresh vegetables are obtainable, a third may be added. Let one pound of bread suffice for a day, whether there be one principal meal, or both dinner and supper. If there is to be supper, the cellarer must keep back a third of the pound, to be given out at supper. But if unusually heavy work has been done it shall be in the discretion and power of the abbot to make some addition; avoiding excess, above all things, that no monk be overtaken by indigestion. . . . All must abstain from the flesh of four-footed beasts, except the delicate and the sick.

XLII. *Of Silence after Compline.* Monks should practice silence at all times, but especially in the hours of night. Therefore on all days, whether fasting days or otherwise, let them sit together as soon as they have risen from supper (if it be not a fast day) and let one of them read the "Collations" ["Selections"] or "Lives of the Fathers," or something else which may edify the hearers. . . . At the end of the reading . . . let them say Compline and when that is over, let no one be allowed to speak to anyone. If anyone be found breaking this law of silence he shall undergo severe punishments. Unless the presence of guests should require speech, or the abbot should chance to issue some order. But, even so, let it be done with the utmost gravity and moderation.

XLVII. *Of the Daily Manual Labor.* Idleness is enemy of the soul. And therefore, at fixed times, the brothers ought to be occupied in manual labor; and again, at fixed times, in sacred reading. Therefore we believe that both those ought to be arranged thus: from Easter until the 1st of October, on coming out of Prime they shall do what labor may be necessary until the fourth hour. From the fourth hour until about the sixth, they shall apply themselves to reading. After the meal of the sixth hour, moreover, rising from

table, they shall rest in their beds in complete silence; or, perchance, he that wishes to read may read to himself in such a way as not to disturb any other. And None shall be said rather before the time, about the middle of the eighth hour; and again they shall work at their tasks until evening. But, if the needs of the place or poverty demand that they labor at the harvest, they shall not grieve at this: for then they are truly monks if they live by the labors of their hands; as did also our fathers and the apostles. Let all things be done with moderation, however, on account of the fainthearted. From the 1st of October, moreover, until the beginning of Lent they shall be free for reading until the end of the second hour. At the second hour Tierce shall be said, and all shall labor at the task which is enjoined upon them until the ninth. The first signal of None having been given, they shall each one leave off his work; and be ready when the second signal strikes. After the meal they shall be free for their readings or for psalms. . . . On Sunday all shall be occupied in reading, except those who are assigned to various duties. But if any is so negligent or slothful that he lacks the will or the ability to read, let some task within his capacity be given him, that he be not idle. For the weak or delicate brethren some work or craft must be found to keep them from idleness while not overwhelming them with such heavy labor as to drive them away. The abbot is to take their infirmity into consideration.

LIII. *Of the Reception of Guests.* All guests are to be received as Christ Himself; for He Himself said: "I was a stranger and ye took Me in." And to all, fitting honour shall be shown; but, most of all, to servants of the faith and to pilgrims. When, therefore, a guest is announced, the prior or the brothers shall run to meet him, with every service of love. And first they shall pray together; and thus they shall be joined together in peace. Which kiss of peace shall not first be offered, unless a prayer have preceded, on account of the wiles of the devil. In the salutation itself, moreover, all humility shall be shown. In the case of all guests arriving or departing: with inclined head, or with prostrating of the whole body upon the ground, Christ, who is also received in them, shall be adored. The guests moreover, having been received, shall be conducted to prayer; and afterwards the prior, or one whom he himself orders, shall sit with them. The law of God shall be read before the guest that he may be edified; and after this, every kindness shall be shown. A fast may be broken by the prior on account of a guest; unless, perchance, it be a special day of fast which cannot be violated. The brothers, moreover, shall continue their customary fasts. The abbot shall give water into the hands of his guests; and the abbot as well as the whole congregation shall wash the feet of all guests. . . .

LV. *Of Clothing.* Clothing shall be given to the brothers according to the nature of the places where they dwell, or the climate. For in cold regions more is required; but in warm, less. This is a matter for the abbot to decide. We nevertheless consider for temperate places a cowl and tunic apiece shall suffice—the cowl in winter hairy, in summer fine or worn —and a scapular for work. And for the feet, shoes and stockings. Concerning the color and size of all of which things the monks shall not talk; but they shall be such as can be found in the province where they are or as can be bought the most cheaply. The abbot, moreover, shall provide, as to the measure, that those vestments be not short for those using them; but of suitable length. And, when new ones are received, they shall always straightway return the old ones, to be kept in the wardrobe for the benefit of the poor. It is enough, moreover, for a monk to have two tunics and two cowls; a spare one for nights, and to permit to wash the things themselves. . . . And, in order that this vice of property may be cut off at the roots, all things which are necessary shall be given by the abbot: that is, a cowl, a tunic, shoes, stockings, girdle, a knife, a pen, a needle, a handkerchief, tablets: so that all excuse of necessity shall be removed.

LXVIII. *If Impossibilities Are Enjoined.* If it happen that any overwhelming or impossible task is set him, a brother should receive the command of one in authority with all meekness and obedience. But if he sees that the weight of the burden is utterly beyond his strength, let him, with patience and at a convenient time, suggest to his superior what makes it impossible—without presumption or obstinacy or answering back. If, after this suggestion, the command of the superior stand as it was first given, the subordinate shall realize that thus it is expedient for him: and he shall obey, with all charity and will trust in God's help.

Rule of St. Francis

The original rule of St. Francis consisted of a few precepts from the gospels. But the rapid expansion of the Order brought the need of more detailed regulations. This rule was approved by Pope Honorius III, in 1223. Bettenson's note.

From *Documents of the Christian Church,* H. Bettenson, Ed. By permission of the publishers and Geoffrey Cumberledge.

1. This is the Rule and way of life of the brothers minor; to observe the holy Gospel of our Lord Jesus Christ, living in obedience, without personal possessions, and in chastity. Brother Francis promises obedience and reverence to our Lord Pope Honorius, and to his canonical successors, and to the Roman Church. And the other brothers shall be bound to obey brother Francis and his successors.

2. If any wish to adopt this way of life, and shall come to our brothers, they shall send them to their provincial ministers; to whom alone, and to no others, permission is given to receive brothers. And the ministers shall carefully examine them in the Catholic faith and the sacraments of the Church. And if they believe all these, and will confess them faithfully and observe them steadfastly to the end; and if they have no wives, or if they have them and the wives have already entered a convent, or if with permission of the diocesan bishop they shall have given them permission to do so—they themselves having already taken a vow of continence, and their wives being of such age that no suspicion can arise in connection with them: the ministers shall tell them, in the words of the holy Gospel, to go and sell all that they have and carefully give it to the poor. But if they shall not be able to do this, their good will is enough. And the brothers and their ministers shall be careful not to concern themselves about their temporal goods; so that they may freely do with those goods exactly as God inspires them. But if advice is required, the ministers shall be allowed to send them to some God-fearing men by whose counsel they shall dispense their goods to the poor. After that they shall be given the garments of probation: namely two gowns without cowls and a belt, and hose and a cape down to the belt: unless to those same ministers something else may at some time seem to be preferable in the sight of God. And, when the year of probation is over, they shall be received into obedience; promising always to observe this way of life and Rule. And, according to the mandate of the lord pope, they shall never be allowed to break these bonds. For according to the holy Gospel, no one putting his hand to the plow and looking back is fit for the kingdom of God. And those who have now promised obedience shall have one gown with a cowl. And those who really need them may wear shoes. And all the brothers shall wear humble garments, and may repair them with sack cloth and other remnants, with God's blessing. And I warn and exhort them lest they despise or judge men whom they shall see clad in soft garments and in colors, enjoying delicate food and drink; but each one shall rather judge and despise himself.

4. I strictly command all the brothers never to receive coin or money either directly or through an intermediary. The ministers and guardians alone shall make provision, through spiritual friends, for the needs of the infirm and for other brothers who need clothing, according to the locality, season, or cold climate, at their discretion. . . .

5. Those brothers, to whom God has given the ability to work, shall work faithfully and devotedly and in such a way that, avoiding idleness, the enemy of the soul, they do not quench the spirit of holy prayer and devotion, to which other and temporal activities should be subordinate. . . .

6. The brothers shall possess nothing, neither a house, nor a place, nor anything. But, as pilgrims and strangers in this world, serving God in poverty and humility, they shall confidently seek alms, and

not be ashamed, for the Lord made Himself poor in this world for us. This is the highest degree of that sublime poverty, which has made you, my dearly beloved brethren, heirs and kings of the Kingdom of Heaven; which has made you poor in goods but exalted in virtues. . . .

8. All the brothers shall be bound always to have one of the brothers of the order as minister general and servant of the whole brotherhood, and shall be strictly bound to obey him. On his death the election of a successor shall be made by the provincial ministers and guardians in the chapter at Pentecost, at which the provincial ministers shall always be bound to assemble, wherever the minister general provides; and this once in three years or at a greater or less interval, according as is ordered by the aforesaid minister. . . .

11. I strictly charge all the brethren not to hold conversation with women so as to arouse suspicion, nor to take counsel with them. And, with the exception of those to whom special permission has been given by the Apostolic Chair, let them not enter nunneries. Neither may they become fellow godparents with men or women, lest from this cause a scandal may arise among the brethren or concerning brethren.

4. THE LIFE OF ST. FRANCIS

But the spirit of St. Francis (1182–1226) was more important than his rule, it was the personality of the little man who picked the worms out of the roadway so that they might not be crushed and had honey or wine put out in winter to keep the bees from starving that fascinated his contemporaries. Some of this personality appears in the life written in 1228/9 by one of his own friars, Thomas of Celano.

Thomas of Celano: *The Life of St. Francis*

36) Francis, therefore, Christ's valiant knight, went round the cities and fortresses proclaiming the Kingdom of God, preaching peace, teaching salvation and repentance for the remission of sins, not with plausible words of human wisdom, but with the learning and power of the Spirit. The Apostolic authority which had been granted him enabled him to act in all things with greater confidence, without using flattery or seducing blandishments. Incapable of showing favour to the lives of sinners, he could smite them with sharp reproof because he had first persuaded himself by practice of that which he endeavoured to commend to others by his words; and without fear of any reprover he uttered the truth most confidently, so that even the most learned men, mighty in renown and dignity, wondered at his discourses and were smitten by his presence with wholesome fear. Men ran, women too ran, clerks hastened, and Religious made speed to see and hear the Saint of God who seemed to all to be a man of another world. People of every age and either sex hastened to behold the wonders which the Lord was newly working in the world by His servant. Surely at that time, whether by holy Francis' pres-

From A. G. Ferrers Howell, *The Lives of S. Francis of Assisi by Brother Thomas of Celano* (London, 1908), pp. 36–42, 57–63, 78–81.

ence or by the fame [of him], it seemed that, as it were, a new light had been sent from heaven on earth, scattering the universal blackness of darkness which had so seized on well-nigh the whole of that region, that scarce any one knew whither he must go. For such depth of forgetfulness of God and such slumber of neglect of His commandments had oppressed almost all that they could scarce endure to be roused, even slightly, from their old and inveterate sins. . . .

38) But the chief matter of our discourse is the Order which as well from charity as by profession he took upon him and maintained. What then shall we say of it? He himself first planted the Order of Friars Minor (Lesser Brethren) and on that very occasion gave it that name; since (as is well known) it was written in the Rule: "And be they lesser": and in that hour, when those words were uttered, he said: "I will that this brotherhood be called the Order of Lesser Brethren" (Friars Minor). And truly they were "lesser," for, being subject to all, they ever sought for lowly dwellings, and for occupations in the discharge of which they might appear in some sort to suffer wrong, that they might deserve to be so founded on the solid basis of true humility that in happy disposition the spiritual building of all the virtues might arise in them. Verily on the foundation of stedfastness a noble structure of charity arose, wherein living stones heaped together from all parts of the world were built up into an habitation of the Holy Spirit. Oh, with what ardour of charity did Christ's new disciples burn! What love of their pious fellowship flourished among them! For whenever they came together in any place or met one another in the way (as is usual), there sprang up a shoot of spiritual love scattering over all love the seeds of true affection. What can

I say more? Their embraces were chaste, their feelings gentle, their kisses holy, their intercourse sweet, their laughter modest, their look cheerful, their eye single, their spirit submissive, their tongue peaceable, their answer soft, their purpose identical, their obedience ready, their hand untiring.

39) And for that they despised all earthly things, and never loved one another with private love, but poured forth their whole affection in common, the business of all alike was to give up themselves as the price of supplying their brethren's need. They came together with longing, they dwelt together with delight; but the parting of companions was grievous on both sides, a bitter divorce, a cruel separation. But these obedient knights durst put nothing before the orders of holy Obedience, and before the word of command was finished they were preparing to fulfil the order; not knowing how to distinguish between precept and precept, they ran, as it were, headlong to perform whatever was enjoined, all contradiction being put aside.

The followers of most holy Poverty, having nothing, loved nothing, and therefore had no fear of losing anything. They were content with a tunic only, patched sometimes within and without; no elegance was seen in it, but great abjectness and vileness, to the end they might wholly appear therein as crucified to the world. They were girt with a cord, and wore drawers of common stuff; and they were piously purposed to remain in that state, and to have nothing more. Everywhere, therefore, they were secure, nor kept in suspense by any fear; distracted by no care, they awaited the morrow without solicitude, nor, though oftentimes in great straits in their journeyings, were they ever in anxiety about a night's lodging. For when, as often happened, they lacked a lodging in the coldest weather, an oven sheltered them, or, at least, they lay hid by night humbly in underground places or in caves. And by day those who knew how to, worked with their hands, and they stayed in lepers' houses, or in other decent places, serving all with humility and devotion.

40) They would exercise no calling whence scandal might arise, but, by always doing holy, just, virtuous, and useful deeds, they provoked all with whom they lived to copy their humility and patience. The virtue of patience had so compassed them about that they rather sought to be where they might suffer persecution of their bodies than where they might be uplifted by the world's favour, if their holiness was acknowledged or praised. For many times when they were reviled, insulted, stripped naked, scourged, bound or imprisoned, they would not avail themselves of any one's protection, but bore all so bravely that the voice of praise and thanksgiving alone sounded in their mouth. Scarcely, or not at all, did they cease from praising God and from prayer; but, recalling by constant examination what they had done, they rendered thanks to God for what they had done well, and groans and tears for what they had neglected or unadvisedly committed. They deemed themselves forsaken by God unless they knew themselves to be constantly visited in their devotions by their wonted piety. And so when they would apply themselves to prayer they sought the support of certain appliances lest their prayer should be disturbed by sleep stealing over them. Some were held up by hanging ropes, some surrounded themselves with instruments of iron, while others shut themselves up in wooden cages. If ever their sobriety were disturbed (as commonly happens) by abundance of food or drink, or if, tired

by a journey, they overpassed, though but a little, the bounds of necessity, they tortured themselves most severely by many days' abstinence. In short they made it their business to keep down the promptings of the flesh with such maceration that they shrank not from often stripping themselves naked in the sharpest frost, and piercing their whole body with thorns so as to draw blood.

41) And so vigorously did they set at naught all earthly things that they scarce submitted to take the barest necessities of life, and shrank not from any hardships, having been parted from bodily comfort by such long usage. Amid all this they followed peace and gentleness with all men, and, ever behaving themselves modestly and peaceably, were most zealous in avoiding all occasions of scandal. For they scarcely spoke even in time of need, nor did any jesting or idle words proceed out of their mouth, in order that nothing immodest or unseemly might by any means be found in all their behavior and conversation. Their every act was disciplined, their every movement modest, all the senses had been so mortified in them that they scarce submitted to hear or see anything but what their purpose demanded; their eyes were fixed on the ground, their mind clave to Heaven. No envy, malice, rancour, evil-speaking, suspicion or bitterness had place in them, but great concord, continual quietness, thanksgiving, and the voice of praise were in them. Such were the teachings wherewith the tender father, not by word and tongue only, but above all in deed and truth, was fashioning his new sons. . . .

XXI. *Of his preaching to the birds and of the obedience of the creatures.*

58) During the time when (as has been said) many joined themselves to the

brethren, the most blessed father Francis was journeying through the valley of Spoleto, and came to a spot near Bevagna where a very great number of birds of different sorts were gathered together, viz., doves, rooks, and those other birds that are called in the vulgar tongue *monade*. When he saw them, being a man of the most fervent temper and also very tender and affectionate toward all the lower and irrational creatures, Francis the most blessed servant of God left his companions in the way and ran eagerly toward the birds. When he was come close to them and saw that they were awaiting him, he gave them his accustomed greeting. But, not a little surprised that the birds did not fly away (as they are wont to do) he was filled with exceeding joy and humbly begged them to hear the word of God: and, after saying many things to them he added: "My brother birds, much ought ye to praise your Creator, and ever to love Him who has given you feathers for clothing, wings for flight, and all that ye had need of. God has made you noble among His creatures, for He has given you a habitation in the purity of the air, and, whereas ye neither sow nor reap, He Himself doth still protect and govern you without any care of your own." On this (as he himself and the brethren who had been with him used to say) those little birds rejoicing in wondrous fashion, after their nature, began to stretch out their necks, to spread their wings, to open their beaks and to gaze on him. And then he went to and fro amidst them, touching their heads and bodies with his tunic. At length he blessed them, and, having made the sign of the cross, gave them leave to fly away to another place. But the blessed father went on his way with his companions, re-joicing and giving thanks to God Whom all creatures humbly acknowledge and revere. Being now, by grace become simple (though he was not so by nature) he began to charge himself with negligence for not having preached to the birds before, since they listened so reverently to God's word. And so it came to pass that from that day he diligently exhorted all winged creatures, all beasts, all reptiles and even creatures insensible, to praise and love the Creator, since daily, on his calling on the Saviour's name, he had knowledge of their obedience by his own experience.

59) One day (for instance) when he was come to the fortress called Alviano to set forth the word of God, he went up on an eminence where all could see him, and asked for silence. But though all the company held their peace and stood reverently by, a great number of swallows who were building their nests in that same place were chirping and chattering loudly. And, as Francis could not be heard by the men for their chirping, he spoke to the birds and said: "My sisters, the swallows, it is now time for me to speak too, because you have been saying enough all this time. Listen to the word of God and be in silence, and quiet, until the sermon is finished!" And those little birds (to the amazement and wonder of all the bystanders) kept silence forthwith, and did not move from that place till the preaching was ended. So those men, when they had seen the sign, were filled with the greatest admiration, and said: "Truly this man is a Saint, and a friend of the Most High.'" And with the utmost devotion they hastened at least to touch his clothes, praising and blessing God.

And it is certainly wonderful how even the irrational creatures recognized his tender affection towards them and perceived beforehand the sweetness of his love.

60) For once when he was staying at the fortress of Greccio, one of the brethren brought him a live leveret that had been caught in a snare; and when the blessed man saw it he was moved with compassion and said: "Brother leveret, come to me. Why didst thou let thyself be so deceived?" And forthwith the leveret, on being released by the brother who was holding him fled to the holy man, and, without being driven thither by any one, lay down in his bosom as being the safest place. When he had rested there a little while the holy father, caressing him with maternal affection, let him go, so that he might freely return to the woodland. At last, after the leveret had been put down on the ground many times, and had every time returned to the holy man's bosom, he bade the brethren carry it into a wood which was hard by. Something of the same kind happened with a rabbit (which is a very wild creature) when he was on the island in the lake of Perugia. He was also moved by the same feeling of pity towards fish, for if they had been caught, and he had the opportunity, he would throw them back alive into the water, bidding them beware of being caught a second time.

61) Once accordingly when he was sitting in a boat near a port on the lake of Rieti a fisherman caught a big fish called a tench, and respectfully offered it to him. He took it up joyfully and kindly, began to call it by the name of brother, and then putting it back out of the boat into the water he began devoutly to bless the name of the Lord. And while he continued thus for some time in prayer, the said fish played about in the water close

to the boat, and did not leave the place where Francis had put him, until, having finished his prayer, the holy man of God gave him leave to depart. Even so did the glorious father Francis, walking in the way of obedience, and taking upon him perfectly the yoke of Divine submission, acquire great dignity before God in that the creatures obeyed him. For water was even turned to wine for him when he was once in grievous sickness at the hermitage of Sant' Urbano; and when he had tasted it he got well so easily that all believed it to be a Divine miracle, as indeed it was. And truly he is a Saint whom the creatures thus obey and at whose nod the very elements are transmuted for other uses.

XXII. *Of his preaching at Ascoli; and how the sick were healed in his absence by things that his hand had touched.*

62) At the time when (as has been said) the venerable father Francis preached to the birds, as he went round about the cities and fortresses scattering seeds of blessing everywhere, he came to the city of Ascoli. Here, when according to his wont he was most fervently uttering the word of God, almost all the people, changed by the right hand of the Highest, were filled with such grace and devotion that in their eagerness to see and hear him they trod on one another. And at that time thirty men, clerks and lay people, received from him the habit of holy Religion. Such was the faith of men and women, such their devotion of mind toward God's Saint that he who could but touch his garment called himself happy. If he entered any city the clergy were joyful, the bells were rung, the men exulted, the women rejoiced together, the children clapped their hands and often took boughs

of trees and went in procession to meet him singing Psalms. Heretical wickedness was confounded, the Church's faith was magnified; and while the faithful shouted for joy, the heretics slunk away. For the tokens of holiness that appeared in him were such that no one durst speak against him; seeing that the crowds hung on him alone. Amidst and above all else he pronounced that the faith of the Holy Roman Church, wherein alone consists the salvation of all that are to be saved, must be kept, revered, and imitated. He revered the priests and embraced the whole hierarchy with exceeding affection.

63) The people would offer him loaves to bless, and would keep them for long after, and by tasting them they were healed of divers sicknesses. Many times also in their great faith in him they cut up his tunic so that he was left almost naked; and, what is more wonder, some even recovered their health by means of objects which the holy father had touched with his hand, as happened in the case of a woman who lived in a little village near Arezzo. She was with child, and when the time of her delivery came was in labour for several days and hung between life and death in incredible suffering. Her neighbours and kinsfolk had heard that the blessed Francis was going to a certain hermitage and would pass by that way. But while they were waiting for him it chanced that he went to the place by a different way, for he was riding because he was weak and ill. When he reached the place he sent back the horse to the man who had lent it him out of charity, by a certain brother named Peter. Brother Peter, in bringing the horse back passed through the place where the suffering woman was. The inhabitants on seeing him ran to him in haste, thinking he was the blessed Francis, but were exceedingly disappointed when they found

he was not. At length they began to inquire together if anything might be found which the blessed Francis had touched with his hand; and after spending a long time over this they at last hit upon the reins which he had held in his hand when riding: so they took the bit out of the mouth of the horse on which the holy father had sat, and laid the reins which he had touched with his own hands upon the woman: and forthwith her peril was removed and she brought forth her child with joy and in safety.

64) Gualfreduccio, who lived at Castel della Pieve, a religious man fearing and worshipping God with all his house, had by him a cord wherewith the blessed Francis had once been girded. Now it came to pass that in that place many men and not a few women were suffering from various sicknesses and fevers; and this man went through the houses of the sick, and, after dipping the cord in water or mixing with water some of the strands, made the sufferers drink of it, and so, in Christ's name, they all recovered. Now these things were done in blessed Francis' absence, besides many others which we could in nowise unfold in the longest discourse. But a few of those things which the Lord our God deigned to work by means of his presence we will briefly insert in this work. . . .

XXIX. *Of the love which he bore to all creatures for the Creator's sake. Description of his inner and outer man.*

80) It were exceeding long, and indeed impossible, to enumerate and collect all the things which the glorious father Francis did and taught while he lived in the flesh. For who could ever express the height of the affection by which he was carried away as concerning all the things that are God's? Who could tell the sweet-

ness which he enjoyed in contemplating in His creatures the wisdom, power and goodness of the Creator? Truly such thoughts often filled him with wondrous and unspeakable joy as he beheld the sun, or raised his eyes to the moon, or gazed on the stars, and the firmament. O simple piety! O pious simplicity! Even towards little worms he glowed with exceeding love, because he had read that word concerning the Saviour: "I am a worm, and no man." Wherefore he used to pick them up in the way and put them in a safe place, that they might not be crushed by the feet of passers-by. What shall I say of other lower creatures, when in winter he would cause honey or the best wine to be provided for bees, that they might not perish from cold? And he used to extol, to the glory of the Lord, the efficacy of their works and the excellence of their skill with such abundant utterance that many times he would pass a day in praise of them and of the other creatures. For as of old the three children placed in the burning fiery furnace invited all the elements to praise and glorify the Creator of the universe, so this man also, full of the spirit of God, ceased not to glorify, praise, and bless in all the elements and creatures the Creator and Governor of them all.

81) What gladness thinkest thou the beauty of flowers afforded to his mind as he observed the grace of their form and perceived the sweetness of their perfume? For he turned forthwith the eye of consideration to the beauty of that Flower which, brightly coming forth in springtime from the root of Jesse, has by its perfume raised up countless thousands of the dead. And when he came upon a great quantity of flowers he would preach to them and invite them to praise the Lord, just as if they had been gifted with reason. So also cornfields and vineyards, stones, woods, and all the beauties of the field, fountains of waters, all the verdure of gardens, earth and fire, air and wind would he with sincerest purity exhort to the love and willing service of God. In short he called all creatures by the name of brother, and in a surpassing manner, of which other men had no experience, he discerned the hidden things of creation with the eye of the heart, as one who had already escaped into the glorious liberty of the children of God.

Now, O good Jesus, in the heavens with the angels he is praising Thee as admirable who when on earth did surely preach Thee to all creatures as lovable.

82) For when he named Thy name, O holy Lord, his emotion passed man's understanding: he was all joy, filled with the purest gladness, and seemed in truth to be a new man and one of the other world. Accordingly, wherever he found any writing, Divine or human, whether by the way, in a house, or on the floor, he picked it up most reverently and placed it in some sacred or decent place, in case the name of the Lord or anything pertaining thereto should have been written on it. And one day, when one of the brethren asked him why he so diligently picked up even writings of pagans, and writings in which the name of the Lord was not traced, he gave this answer: "My son, it is because the letters are there whereof the most glorious name of the Lord God is composed. The good, therefore, that is in the writing belongs not to the pagans nor to any men, but to God alone, of whom is all good." And, what is not less to be wondered at, when he caused any letters of greeting or admonition to be written, he would not suffer a single letter or syllable to be cancelled, even though (as often happened) it were superfluous or misplaced.

83) O how fair, how bright, how glorious did he appear in innocency of

life, in simplicity of word, in purity of heart, in the love of God, in charity to the brethren, in ardent obedience, in willing submission, in angelic aspect! He was charming in his manners, of gentle disposition, easy in his talk; most apt in exhortation, most faithful in what he was put in trust with, far-seeing in counsel, effectual in business, gracious in all things; calm in mind, sweet in temper, sober in spirit, uplifted in contemplation, assiduous in prayer and fervent in all things. He was stedfast in purpose, firm in virtue, persevering in grace, and in all things the same. He was swift to pardon and slow to be angry. He was of ready wit, and had an excellent memory, he was subtle in discussion, circumspect in choice, and simple in all things; stern to himself, tender to others, in all things discreet. He was a man most eloquent, of cheerful countenance, of kindly aspect, free from cowardice, and destitute of arrogance. He was of middle height, inclining to shortness; his head was of moderate size, and round; his face somewhat long and prominent, his forehead smooth and small; his eyes were black, of moderate size, and with a candid look; his hair was dark, his eyebrows straight; his nose symmetrical, thin, and straight; his ears upright, but small; his temples smooth. His words were kindly, [but] fiery and penetrating; his voice was powerful, sweet-toned, clear and sonorous. His teeth were set close together, white, and even; his lips thin and fine, his beard black and rather scanty, his neck slender; his shoulders straight, his arms short, his hands attenuated, with long fingers and nails; his legs slight, his feet small, his skin fine, and his flesh very spare. His clothing was rough, his sleep very brief, his hand most bountiful. And, for that he was most humble, he showed all meekness to all men, adapting himself in profitable fashion to the behaviour of all. Among the saints, holier [than they], among the sinners he was like one of themselves. Help therefore the sinners, most holy father, thou lover of sinners, and deign, we pray thee, of thine abundant mercy, to raise up by thy most glorious advocacy those whom thou seest miserably lying in the defilement of their misdeeds.

5. ST. THOMAS AQUINAS: ON THE EXISTENCE OF GOD

St. Thomas Aquinas (1225–1274) is probably the leader among Catholic theologians. In a series of great works he based Catholic philosophy on the newly recovered ideas of the Greek philosopher Aristotle, insisted on the part of reason in religious thought, and tried to reconcile reason and traditional Catholic faith without falling into heresy as many others of this time seemed to be doing. He set down the lines on which the Catholic Church (at first suspicious of his new ideas) was to think and argue for a very long time.

On the Existence of God

The existence of God can be proved in five ways.

The first and more manifest way is the argument from motion. It is certain and

From the *Summa Theologica of St. Thomas Aquinas*, tr. by the Fathers of the English Dominican Province (New York, 1911), Part I, First Number Q. II, 19–27. Reprinted by permission of Benziger Brothers, Inc.

evident to our senses that some things are in motion. Whatever is in motion is moved by another, for nothing can be in motion except it have a potentiality for that towards which it is being moved; whereas a thing moves inasmuch as it is in act. By "motion" we mean nothing else than the reduction of something from a state of potentiality into a state of actuality. Nothing, however, can be reduced from a state of potentiality into a state of actuality, unless by something already in a state of actuality. Thus that which is actually hot as fire, makes wood, which is potentially hot, to be actually hot, and thereby moves and changes it. It is not possible that the same thing should be at once in a state of actuality and potentiality from the same point of view, but only from different points of view. What is actually hot cannot simultaneously be only potentially hot; still, it is simultaneously potentially cold. It is therefore impossible that from the same point of view and in the same way anything should be both moved and mover, or that it should move itself. Therefore, whatever is in motion must be put in motion by another, and that by another again. But this cannot go on to infinity, because then there would be no first mover; as the staff only moves because it is put in motion by the hand. Therefore it is necessary to arrive at a First Mover, put in motion by no other; and this everyone understands to be God.

The second way is from the formality of efficient causation. In the world of sense we find there is an order of efficient causation. There is no case known (neither is it, indeed, possible) in which a thing is found to be the efficient cause of itself; for so it would be prior to itself, which is impossible. In efficient causes it is not possible to go on to infinity, because

in all efficient causes following in order, the first is the cause of the intermediate cause, and the intermediate is the cause of the ultimate cause, whether the intermediate cause be several, or one only. To take away the cause is to take away the effect. Therefore, if there be no first cause among efficient causes, there will be no ultimate cause, nor any intermediate. If in efficient causes it is possible to go on to infinity, there will be no first efficient cause, neither will there be an ultimate effect, nor any intermediate efficient causes; all of which is plainly false. Therefore it is necessary to put forward a First Efficient Cause, to which everyone gives the name of God.

The third way is taken from possibility and necessity, and runs thus. We find in nature things that could either exist or not exist, since they are found to be generated, and to corrupt; and, consequently, they can exist, and then not exist. It is impossible for these always to exist, for that which can one day cease to exist must at some time have not existed. Therefore, if everything could cease to exist, then at one time there could have been nothing in existence. If this were true, even now there would be nothing in existence, because that which does not exist only begins to exist by something already existing. Therefore, if at one time nothing was in existence, it would have been impossible for anything to have begun to exist; and thus even now nothing would be in existence—which is absurd. Therefore, not all beings are merely possible, but there must exist something the existence of which is necessary. Every necessary thing either has its necessity caused by another, or not. It is impossible to go on to infinity in necessary things which have their necessity caused by another, as has been already proved in regard to efficient causes. Therefore we cannot but postulate the existence of some being having of itself its own necessity, and not receiving it from another, but rather causing in others their necessity. This all men speak of as God.

The fourth way is taken from the gradation to be found in things. Among beings there are some more and some less good, true, noble, and the like. But "more" and "less" are predicated of different things, according as they resemble in their different ways something which is in the degree of "most," as a thing is said to be hotter according as it more nearly resembles that which is hottest; so that there is something which is truest, something best, something noblest, and consequently, something which is uttermost being; for the truer things are, the more truly they exist. What is most complete in any genus is the cause of all in that genus; as fire, which is the most complete form

of heat, is the cause whereby all things are made hot. Therefore, there must also be something which is to all beings the cause of their being, goodness, and every other perfection; and this we call God.

The fifth way is taken from the governance of the world; for we see that things which lack intelligence, such as natural bodies, act for some purpose, which fact is evident from their acting always, or nearly always, in the same way, so as to obtain the best result. Hence it is plain that not fortuitously, but designedly, do they achieve their purpose. Whatever lacks intelligence cannot fulfil some purpose unless it be directed by some being endowed with intelligence and knowledge; as the arrow is shot to its mark by the archer. Therefore some intelligent being exists by whom all natural things are ordained towards a definite purpose; and this being we call God.

6. ORDEALS

While the theologians forged great and subtle systems of thought, at another level Christianity and barbarism, Christianity and paganism, mingled. The results affected the pattern of society, of worship, and of law. An instance of this can be seen in the practice of the ordeal.

The ordeal was an ancient Teutonic recipe for deciding the guilt or innocence of a suspected person by subjecting him to a severe physical test, such as grasping red hot metal or plunging a hand in boiling water. If he passed the test, this was taken as a proof that God had intervened on his behalf and he was shown to be innocent. For a long time the principle on which ordeals were based seemed eminently sensible. Most men found it more comprehensible than the conclusions of philosophers and more immediately useful.

Hincmar's Description of the Cold Water Ordeal

The following passage appears in the writings of a Carolingian prelate. Hincmar (806–882, Archbishop of Rheims) was the counsellor of Charles the Bald and

From *Translations and Reprints*, IV, No. 4, A. C. Howland, Ed.

his successors on the Frankish throne. He is the author of two treatises on Predestination and of a learned and disputatious discussion of King Lothar's divorce which seems a bit beside the point of a family and time whose divorces were the least of their pranks. But even dealing with the more concrete subject below Hincmar seems more interested in theory than in practice.

Now the one about to be examined is bound by a rope and cast into the water because, as it is written, each one shall be holden with the cords of his iniquity. And it is evident that he is bound for two reasons: to wit, that he may not be able to practice any fraud in connection with the judgment, and that he may be drawn out at the right time if the water should receive him as innocent, so that he perish not. For as we read that Lazarus, who had been dead four days (by whom is signified each one buried under a load of crimes), was buried wrapped in bandages and, bound by the same bands, came forth from the sepulchre at the word of the Lord and was loosed by the disciples at his command; so he who is to be examined by this judgment is cast into the water bound, and is drawn forth again bound, and is either immediately set free by the judgment of the judges, being purged, or remains bound till the time of his purgation and is then examined by the court. . . . And in this ordeal of cold water whoever, after the invocation of God, who is the Truth, seeks to hide the truth by a lie, cannot be submerged in the waters above which the voice of the Lord God has thundered; for the pure nature of the water recognizes as impure and therefore rejects as inconsistent with itself such human nature as has once been regenerated by the waters of baptism and is again infected by falsehood.

Raymond of Agiles: Ordeal by Fire

The siege of Antioch during the First Crusade (1096–1099) was long and hard. When the fortunes of the crusaders seemed lowest, however, a dream revealed that the lance with which a Roman soldier had cruelly pierced the side of Jesus Christ while He hung on the Cross was buried nearby. The discovery of the Holy Lance by Peter Bartholomew, to whom the revelation had been vouchsafed, bolstered morale enormously but also created an undercurrent of ugly insinuations. The genuineness of the relic was questioned by one of the leaders of the expedition, Count Bohemond, and by his followers. To silence their doubts, Peter was compelled to undergo the ordeal of fire, which would prove that his spear was indeed the holy one. Belief in the relic persisted, the siege continued, and Antioch eventually fell. Raymond of Agiles, whose account appears below, was a firm believer in the relic.

All these things were pleasing to us, and having enjoined on him [i.e., Peter Bartholomew] a fast, we declared that a fire should be prepared upon the day on which the Lord was beaten with stripes and put upon the cross for our salvation.

From *Translations and Reprints,* IV, No. 4, A. C. Howland, Ed.

And the fourth day thereafter was the day before the Sabbath. So when the appointed day came round a fire was prepared after the noon hour. The leaders and the people to the number of 60,000 came together; the priests were there also with bare feet, clothed in ecclesiastical garments. The fire was made of dry olive branches, covering a space thirteen feet long; and there were two piles with a space about a foot wide between them. The height of these piles was four feet. Now when the fire had been kindled so that it burned fiercely, I, Raimond, in presence of the whole multitude, spoke: "If Omnipotent God has spoken to this man face to face, and the blessed Andrew has shown him our Lord's lance while he was keeping his vigil, let him go through the fire unharmed. But if it is false let him be burned together with the lance which he is to carry in his hand." And all responded on bended knees, "Amen." The fire was growing so hot that the flames shot up thirty cubits high into the air and scarcely any one dared approach it. Then Peter Bartholomew clothed only in his tunic and kneeling before the bishop of Albar called to God to witness "that he had seen Him face to face on the cross, and that he had heard from Him those things above written. . . ." Then when the bishop had placed the lance in his hand, he knelt and made the sign of the cross and entered the fire with the lance, firm and unterrified. For an instant's time he paused in the midst of the flames, and then by the grace of God passed through. . . . But when Peter emerged from the fire so that neither his tunic was burned nor even the thin cloth with which the lance was wrapped up had shown any sign of damage, the whole people received him after that he had made over them the sign of the cross with the lance in his hand and had cried, "God aid us!" All the people, I say, threw themselves upon him and dragged him to the ground and trampled on him, each one wishing to touch him or to get a piece of his garment, and each thinking him near some one else. And so he received three or four wounds in the legs where the flesh was torn away, his back was injured and his sides bruised. Peter had died on the spot, as we believe, had not Raimond Pelet, a brave and noble soldier, broken through the wild crowd with a band of friends and rescued him at the peril of their lives. . . . After this Peter died in peace at the hour appointed to him by God, and journeyed to the Lord; and he was buried in the place where he had carried the lance of the Lord through the fire.

The Judicial Combat in Spain

The old Gothic or Mozarabic form of church service survived for a long time in the churches of Spain, but Gregory VII on his accession [1073] determined to substitute the Roman in place of the old national service in Castile and Leon. The supporters of the papal policy were not at first able to carry their point by means of argument, and resort was had to single combat between champions, one representing the Roman, the other the Gothic ritual. Howland's note.

From *Translations and Reprints*, IV, No. 4, A. C. Howland, Ed.

But before the recall [of the legate Richard] the clergy and people of all Spain were thrown into confusion by being compelled by the legate and the prince to accept the Gallic ritual. On an appointed day the king, the primate, the legate, the clergy, and a vast multitude of people came together and a long altercation took place, the clergy, soldiery and people firmly resisting a change in the service, the king, under the influence of the queen, supporting the change with threats and menaces. Finally the demands of the soldiers brought matters to such a crisis that it was decided to settle the dispute by a duel. When two soldiers had been selected, one by the king, who contended for the Gallic ritual, the other by the soldiery and people, who were equally zealous for the ritual of Toledo, the king's champion was defeated on the spot to the exultation of the people, because the victor was the champion of the Toledo service. But the king was so far persuaded by queen Constantia that he did not re-cede from his demands, adjudging the duel to be of no weight. . . . And when thereupon a great tumult arose among the soldiers and the people, it was finally decided that a copy of the Toledo ritual, and one of the Gallic should be placed in a great fire. When a fast had been imposed upon all by the primate, legate, and clergy, and all had devoutly prayed, the Gallic office was consumed by the fire, while the Gothic leaped up above the flames and was seen by all who stood there praising the Lord to be wholly uninjured and untouched by the fire. But since the king was obstinate and stiff-necked he would not turn aside either through fear of the miracle or through supplication of the people, but, threatening confiscation and death against those who resisted, he ordered the Gallic office to be adopted in all his dominions. Whence arose from the grief and sorrow of all the proverb, *Quo volunt Reges, vadunt Leges.*

V. The Crusades

The Crusades are sometimes cited as an impressive instance of the power of the Church and the influence of Christian motives during the Middle Ages. And indeed, it would be hard to imagine another purpose, another call, that could have mobilized Europe so thoroughly, carried so many men into faraway places with a feeling that they pursued not their own interest but a higher summons. This fundamental religious purpose must never be forgotten. However, once invented, the crusading concept could be used for all sorts of secular aims which might involve attacks on pagans, Jews, Muslims, and Christians in the bad books of the Church. So Jews were plundered, Albigensian heretics burnt, Baltic idol-worshipers enslaved, Greek Orthodox Constantinople taken by storm—all with the highest motives. Nor, after all, could a man be blamed for responding to appeals as enticing as that which the Saxon bishops and barons sent out early in the twelfth century to attract men for fighting and colonization in the Baltic lands:

> They [the natives] are an abominable people, but their land is very rich in flesh, honey, grain, birds, and abounding in all the products of the fertility of the earth when cultivated, so that none can be compared to it. So say they who know. Wherefore, O Saxons, Franks, Lotharingians, men of Flanders most famous—here you can both save your souls and, if it please you, acquire the best of land to live in.

But there is another aspect to the Crusades: when in 1095 Pope Urban II addressed the Council of Clermont, he knew, and his hearers knew, that there were too many fighting men abroad in the land, too many men and not enough land. It would not be a bad thing to direct their attention elsewhere, where the brutal valor of these potential troublemakers could be enlisted in a higher cause. Then, at worst, they would be burning and slaying Saracens, Wends, and Abodrites, ravaging other fields than those at home, plundering and perhaps, who knows, converting, strangers and not their kin. And so, between the eleventh and the fifteenth century, a long series of campaigns channeled off surplus manpower and energy into a Western counteroffensive in all the directions from which the West had formerly been hard pressed: up along the Baltic and south across the Pyrenees, east into the Balkans, into Syria, even into Egypt. And as the men poured out of Europe, riches began to pour in, both as loot and as merchandise. The Mediterranean, which for some centuries past had been a Muslim lake, turned into a great highway once more. Italy revived and so did European trade. And the world was given a first inkling of the trends of Western expansion.

1. URBAN'S SPEECH AT CLERMONT

As the eleventh century ran to a close, the papacy found itself faced with a complicated situation. In 1077 Gregory VII had compelled the Emperor Henry IV to do penance at Canossa, only to die in exile himself a few years later. Meanwhile the Italian balance of power and that of Europe as a whole was being modified by the appearance of a new factor—the Normans—who had imposed themselves in France, in Sicily and, of course, in England. At the same time the Middle East was being ravaged by the rising power of the Seljuk Turks, uncivilized, savage, threatening both the empire of Constantinople and the Western pilgrims whom their predecessors had tolerated.

It was against this background of events that an appeal for help from the Emperor of Constantinople, Alexius Comnenus, decided Urban II (1088–1099) to designate the reconquest of the Holy Places as the first and greatest target of Christian endeavors. The account which follows of the famous speech the Pope delivered at the Council of Clermont in 1095 is one of many differing versions among which the historian has to choose.

Oh, race of Franks, race from across the mountains, race chosen and beloved by God—as shines forth in very many of your works—set apart from all nations by the situation of your country, as well as by your catholic faith and the honor of the holy church! To you our discourse is addressed and for you our exhortation is intended. We wish you to know what a grievous cause has led us to your country, what peril threatening you and all the faithful has brought us.

From the confines of Jerusalem and the city of Constantinople a horrible tale has gone forth and very frequently has been brought to our ears, namely, that a race from the kingdom of the Persians, an accursed race, a race utterly alienated from God, a generation forsooth which has not directed its heart and has not entrusted its spirit to God, has invaded the lands of those Christians and has depopulated them by the sword, pillage and fire; it has led away a part of the captives into its own country, and a part it has

destroyed by cruel tortures; it has either entirely destroyed the churches of God or appropriated them for the rites of its own religion. They destroy the altars, after having defiled them with their uncleanness. They circumcise the Christians, and the blood of the circumcision they either spread upon the altars or pour into the vases of the baptismal font. When they wish to torture people by a base death, they perforate their navels, and dragging forth the extremity of the intestines, bind it to a stake; then with flogging they lead the victim around until the viscera having gushed forth the victim falls prostrate upon the ground. Others they bind to a post and pierce with arrows. Others they compel to extend their necks and then, attacking them with naked swords, attempt to cut through the neck with a single blow. What shall I say of the abominable rape of the women? To speak of it is worse than to be silent. The kingdom of the Greeks is now dismembered by them and

From *Translations and Reprints*, I, No. 2, D. C. Munro, Ed.

deprived of territory so vast in extent that it can not be traversed in a march of two months. On whom therefore is the labor of avenging these wrongs and of recovering this territory incumbent, if not upon you? You, upon whom above other nations God has conferred remarkable glory in arms, great courage, bodily activity, and strength to humble the hairy scalp of those who resist you.

Let the deeds of your ancestors move you and incite your minds to manly achievements; the glory and greatness of king Charles the Great, and of his son Louis, and of your other kings, who have destroyed the kingdoms of the pagans, and have extended in these lands the territory of the holy church. Let the holy sepulchre of the Lord our Saviour, which is possessed by unclean nations, especially incite you, and the holy places which are now treated with ignominy and irreverently polluted with their filthiness. Oh, most valiant soldiers and descendants of invincible ancestors, be not degenerate, but recall the valor of your progenitors.

But if you are hindered by love of children, parents and wives, remember what the Lord says in the Gospel, "He that loveth father or mother more than me, is not worthy of me." "Every one that hath forsaken houses, or brethren, or sisters, or father, or mother, or wife, or children, or lands for my name's sake shall receive an hundred-fold and shall inherit everlasting life." Let none of your possessions detain you, no solicitude for your family affairs, since this land which you inhabit, shut in on all sides by the seas and surrounded by the mountain peaks, is too narrow for your large population; nor does it abound in wealth; and it furnishes scarcely food enough for its cultivators. Hence it is that you murder and devour one another, that you wage war, and that frequently you perish by mutual wounds. Let therefore hatred depart from among you, let your quarrels end, let wars cease, and let all dissensions and controversies slumber. Enter upon the road to the Holy Sepulchre; wrest that land from the wicked race, and subject it to yourselves. That land which as the Scripture says "floweth with milk and honey," was given by God into the possession of the children of Israel.

Jerusalem is the navel of the world; the land is fruitful above others, like another paradise of delights. This the Redeemer of the human race has made illustrious by His advent, has beautified by residence, has consecrated by suffering, has redeemed by death, has glorified by burial. This royal city, therefore, situated at the centre of the world, is now held captive by His enemies, and is in subjection to those who do not know God, to the worship of the heathens. She seeks therefore and desires to be liberated, and does not cease to implore you to come to her aid. From you especially she asks succor, because, as we have already said, God has conferred upon you above all nations great glory in arms. Accordingly undertake this journey for the remission of your sins, with the assurance of the imperishable glory of the kingdom of heaven.

When Pope Urban had said these and very many similar things in his urbane discourse, he so influenced to one purpose the desires of all who were present, that they cried out, "It is the will of God! It is the will of God!" When the venerable Roman pontiff heard that, with eyes uplifted to heaven he gave thanks to God and, with his hand commanding silence, said:

Most beloved brethren, today is manifest in you what the Lord says in the

Gospel, "Where two or three are gathered together in my name there am I in the midst of them." Unless the Lord God had been present in your spirits, all of you would not have uttered the same cry. For, although the cry issued from numerous mouths, yet the origin of the cry was one. Therefore I say to you that God, who implanted this in your breasts, has drawn it forth from you. Let this then be your war-cry in combats, because this word is given to you by God. When an armed attack is made upon the enemy, let this one cry be raised by all the soldiers of God: It is the will of God! It is the will of God!

And we do not command or advise that the old or feeble, or those unfit for bearing arms, undertake this journey; nor ought women to set out at all, without their husbands or brothers or legal guardians. For such are more of a hindrance than aid, more of a burden than advantage. Let the rich aid the needy; and ac-cording to their wealth, let them take with them experienced soldiers. The priests and clerks of any order are not to go without the consent of their bishop; for this journey would profit them nothing if they went without permission of these. Also, it is not fitting that laymen should enter upon the pilgrimage without the blessing of their priests.

Whoever, therefore, shall determine upon this holy pilgrimage and shall make his vow to God to that effect and shall offer himself to Him as a living sacrifice, holy, acceptable unto God, shall wear the sign of the cross of the Lord on his forehead or on his breast. When, truly, having fulfilled his vow he wishes to return, let him place the cross on his back between his shoulders. Such, indeed, by the two-fold action will fulfill the precept of the Lord, as He commands in the Gospel, "He that taketh not his cross and followeth after me, is not worthy of me."

2. THE START OF THE FIRST CRUSADE, 1096

Fulcher of Chartres took part in the first crusade, and has left us many a vivid picture of the more important incidents. His account of the start has been translated in order to show the conflict of emotions in the breasts of the crusaders, and the motive which was strong enough to overcome the natural affections.

Fulcher of Chartres

Such then was the immense assemblage which set out from the West. Gradually along the march and from day to day this army grew by the addition of other armies, coming from every direction and composed of innumerable people. Thus one saw massed together an infinite multitude, speaking different languages and come from divers countries. All did not, however, melt into a single army until we had reached the city of Nicaea. What shall I add? The isles of the sea and the kingdoms of the whole earth were moved by God, so that one might believe that he saw the fulfillment of the prophecy of David, who said in his Psalms: "All nations whom Thou hast made shall come and worship before Thee, O Lord; and

From *Translations and Reprints*, I, No. 2, D. C. Munro, Ed.

shall glorify Thy name," and so that those who have reached the holy places may say justly: "We will worship where His feet have stood." Concerning this journey we read very many other predictions in the prophecies.

Oh, how great was the grief, how deep the sighs, what weeping, what lamentation among the friends when the husband left the wife so dear to him, his children also, and all his possessions of any kind; or his father, his mother, his brethren or his other kindred! And yet, in spite of these floods of tears which those who remained shed for their friends about to depart, and in their very presence, the latter did not suffer their courage to fail, and, out of love for the Lord, in no way hesitated to leave all that they held most precious, persuaded that they would gain a hundred-fold in receiving the recompense which God has promised to those who follow Him.

Then the husband announced to his wife the exact time of his return, assuring her that if he lived he would return to his country and to her at the end of three years. He commended her to the Lord, gave her a kiss and promised to come back to her. But the latter, who feared that she would never see him again, overcome with grief, was unable to stand, fell almost lifeless to the ground and wept over her dear one, whom she was losing in life, as if he were already dead. He then, as if he had no pity—and nevertheless he was filled with pity—and was not moved by lamentations of his wife or children or friends—and yet he was secretly moved—departed with mind firmly set upon his purpose. The sadness was for those who remained, and the joy for those who departed. What more can we say? "This is the Lord's doings; and it is marvelous in our eyes."

The letter which follows, written by a noble of Champagne to his feudal lord who also happens to be Archbishop of Reims, might serve to illustrate the conditions in which the Holy Lance was found (see above, p. 212) but also, and above all, the spirit in which the first crusaders viewed and undertook their task. Of the Lord of Ribemont we know no more, but Antioch was to fall some four months after his letter had been sealed, and Jerusalem in July of the following year.

ANSELME OF RIBEMONT TO MANASSES II, ARCHBISHOP OF REIMS, BEFORE ANTIOCH, ABOUT FEBRUARY 10, 1098

To his reverend lord M., by God's grace, Archbishop of Reims, A. of Ribemont, his vassal and humble servant—greeting.

Inasmuch as you are our lord and as the kingdom of France is especially dependent upon your care, we tell to you, our father, the events which have hap-

pened to us and the condition of the army of the Lord. Yet, in the first place, although we are not ignorant that the disciple is not above his master, nor the servant above his lord, we advise and beseech you in the name of our Lord Jesus to consider what you are and what the duty of a priest and bishop is. Provide therefore for our land, so that the lords may keep peace among themselves, the vassals may in safety work on their property, and the ministers of Christ may serve the Lord, leading quiet and tranquil lives. I also

From *Translations and Reprints*, I, No. 4, D. C. Munro, Ed.

pray you and the canons of the holy mother church of Reims, my fathers and lords, to be mindful of us, not only of me and of those who are now sweating in the service of God, but also of the members of the army of the Lord who have fallen in arms or died in peace.

But passing over these things, let us return to what we promised. Accordingly after the army had reached Nicomedia, which is situated at the entrance to the land of the Turks, we all, lords and vassals, cleansed by confession, fortified ourselves by partaking of the body and blood of our Lord, and proceeding thence beset Nicaea on the second day before the Nones of May. After we had for some days besieged the city with many machines and various engines of war, the craft of the Turks, as often before, deceived us greatly. For on the very day on which they had promised that they would surrender, Soliman and all the Turks, collected from neighboring and distant regions, suddenly fell upon us and attempted to capture our camp. However the count of St. Gilles, with the remaining Franks, made an attack upon them and killed an innumerable multitude. All the others fled in confusion. Our men, moreover, returning in victory and bearing many heads fixed upon pikes and spears, furnished a joyful spectacle for the people of God. This was on the seventeenth day before the Kalends of June.

Beset moreover and routed in attacks by night and day, they surrendered unwillingly on the thirteenth day before the Kalends of July. Then the Christians entering the walls with their crosses and imperial standards, reconciled the city to God, and both within the city and outside the gates cried out in Greek and Latin, "Glory to Thee, O God." Having accomplished this, the princes of the army met

the emperor who had come to offer tnem his thanks, and having received from him gifts of inestimable value, some withdrew, with kindly feelings, others with different emotions.

We moved our camp from Nicaea on the fourth day before the Kalends of July and proceeded on our journey for three days. On the fourth day the Turks, having collected their forces from all sides, again attacked the smaller portion of our army, killed many of our men and drove all the remainder back to their camps. Bohemond, count of the Normans, count Stephen, and the count of Flanders commanded this section. When these were thus terrified by fear, the standards of the larger army suddenly appeared. Hugh the Great and the duke of Lorraine were riding at the head, the count of St. Gilles and the venerable bishop of Puy followed. For they had heard of the battle and were hastening to our aid. The number of the Turks were estimated at 260,000. All of our army attacked them, killed many and routed the rest. On that day I returned from the emperor, to whom the princes had sent me on public business.

After that day our princes remained together and were not separated from one another. Therefore, in traversing the countries of Romania and Armenia we found no obstacle, except that after passing Iconium, we, who formed the advance guard, saw a few Turks. After routing these, on the twelfth day before the Kalends of November, we laid siege to Antioch, and now we captured the neighboring places, the cities of Tarsus and Laodicea and many others, by force. On a certain day, moreover, before we besieged the city, at the "Iron Bridge" we routed the Turks, who had set out to devastate the surrounding country, and we rescued many Christians. Moreover, we led back the horses and camels with very great booty.

While we were besieging the city, the Turks from the nearest redoubt daily killed those entering and leaving the army. The princes of our army seeing this, killed 400 of the Turks who were lying in wait, drove others into a certain river and led back some as captives. You may be assured that we are now besieging Antioch with all diligence, and hope soon to capture it. The city is supplied to an incredible extent with grain, wine, oil and all kinds of food. . . .

Again and again I beseech you, readers of this letter, to pray for us, and you, my lord archbishop, to order this to be done by your bishops. And know for certain that we have captured for the Lord 200 cities and fortresses. May our mother, the western Church, rejoice that she has begotten such men, who are acquiring for her so glorious a name and who are so wonderfully aiding the eastern Church. And in order that you may believe this, know that you have sent to me a tapestry by Raymond *"de Castello."* Farewell.

3. THE SEVENTH CRUSADE

In 1244 the Christian defeat at Gaza determined the final loss of the Holy Places in spite of the heroic struggle of Templars and Hospitalers, who held out for another half century in their remaining strongholds. After 1244 no more crusades would be directed to Palestine, but two attempts known as the Seventh Crusade (1248–1252) and the Eighth (1270) were made by Louis IX of France to outflank Muslim power, first in Egypt, then in Tunis. The letter below follows the opening of the Seventh Crusade which, after the landing at Damietta, was going to peter out rather sadly to the defeat inflicted upon the crusaders in the battle of Mansourah (1250) and their inglorious evacuation of Egypt. However, Louis IX, hardheaded enough in most respects, would not give up. While the remaining crusader holdings in Syria fell one by one into Saracen hands, the French king prepared an expedition to Tunis, whose ruler he hoped to convert. But once again luck was not with him and no sooner had he landed than he died of the plague before the walls of Carthage. He was canonized in 1297, which was the least he deserved for his troubles.

GUY, A KNIGHT, TO B. OF CHARTRES. FROM DAMIETTA, 1249

To his dear half-brother and well-beloved friend, master B. of Chartres, student at Paris, Guy, a knight of the household of the viscount of Melun, greeting and a ready will to do his pleasure.

Because we know that you are uneasy

about the state of the Holy Land and our lord, the king of France, and that you are interested in the general welfare of the church as well as the fate of many relatives and friends who are fighting for Christ under the king's orders, therefore, we think we ought to give you exact information as to the events of which a report has doubtless already reached you.

From *Translations and Reprints,* I, No. 4, D. C. Munro, Ed.

After a council held for that purpose, we departed from Cyprus for the East. The plan was to attack Alexandria, but after a few days a sudden tempest drove us over a wide expanse of the sea. Many of our vessels were driven apart and scattered. The sultan of Cairo and other Saracen princes, informed by spies that we intended to attack Alexandria, had assembled an infinite multitude of armed men from Cairo, Babylon, Damietta and Alexandria, and awaited us in order to put us, while exhausted, to the sword. One night we were borne over the waves by a violent tempest. Toward morning the sky cleared, the storm abated, and our scattered vessels came together safely. An experienced pilot who knew all the coast in this part of the sea and many idioms, and who was a faithful guide, was sent to the masthead, in order that he might tell us if he saw land and knew where we were. After he had carefully and sorrowfully examined all the surrounding country, he cried out terrified, "God help us, God help us, who alone is able; we are before Damietta."

Indeed all of us could see the land. Other pilots on other vessels had already made the same observation, and they began to approach each other. Our lord, the king, assured of our position, with undaunted spirit, endeavored to reanimate and console his men. "My friends and faithful soldiers," said he to them, "we shall be invincible if we are inseparable in our love of one another. It is not without the divine permission that we have been brought here so quickly. I am neither the king of France nor the holy church, you are both. I am only a man whose life will end like other men's when it shall please God. Everything is in our favor, whatever may happen to us. If we are conquered, we shall be mar-

tyrs; if we triumph, the glory of God will be exalted thereby—that of all France, yea, even of Christianity, will be exalted thereby. Certainly it would be foolish to believe that God, who foresees all, has incited me in vain. This is His cause, we shall conquer for Christ, He will triumph in us, He will give the glory, the honor and the blessing not unto us, but unto His name."

In the meantime our assembled vessels approached the land. The inhabitants of Damietta and of the neighboring shores could view our fleet of 1500 vessels, without counting those still at a distance and which numbered 150. In our times no one, we believe, had ever seen such a numerous fleet of vessels. The inhabitants of Damietta, astonished and frightened beyond expression, sent four good galleys, with well-skilled sailors, to examine and ascertain who we were and what we wanted. The latter having approached near enough to distinguish our vessels, hesitated, stopped, and, as if certain of what they had to report, made ready to return to their own party; but our galleys with the fast boats got behind them and hemmed them in, so that they were compelled, in spite of their unwillingness, to approach our ships.

Our men, seeing the firmness of the king and his immovable resolution, prepared, according to his orders, for a naval combat. The king commanded to seize these mariners and all whom they met, and ordered us afterward to land and take possession of the country. We then, by means of our mangonels which hurled from a distance five or six stones at once, began to discharge at them fire-darts, stones, and bottles filled with lime, made to be shot from a bow, or small sticks like arrows. The darts pierced the mariners and their vessels, the stones crushed them, the lime flying out of the broken bottles blinded them. Accordingly, three hostile galleys were soon sunk. We saved, however, a few enemies. The fourth galley got away very much damaged. By exquisite tortures we extracted the truth from the sailors who fell alive into our hands, and learned that the citizens of Damietta had left the city and awaited us at Alexandria. The enemies who succeeded in escaping and whose galley was put to flight, some mortally wounded, uttering frightful cries, went to tell the multitude of Saracens who were waiting on the shore, that the sea was covered with a fleet which was drawing near, that the king of France was coming in hostile guise with an infinite number of barons, that the Christians were 10,000 to one, and that they caused fire, stones, and clouds of dust to rain down. "However," they added, "while they are still fatigued from the labor of the sea, if your lives and your homes are dear to you, hasten to kill them, or at least to repulse them vigorously until our soldiers return. We alone have escaped with difficulty to warn you. We have recognized the ensigns of the enemy. See how furiously they rush upon us, equally ready to fight on land or sea."

In consequence of this speech, fear and distrust seized the enemy. All of our men, assured of the truth, conceived the greatest hopes. In emulation of one another they leaped from their vessels into the barks; the water was too shallow along the shore, the barks and the small vessels could not reach the land. Several warriors, by the express order of the king, cast themselves into the sea. The water was up to their waists. Immediately began a very cruel combat. The first crusaders were promptly followed by others and the whole force of infidels was scattered. We lost only a single man by the enemy's fire.

Two or three others, too eager for the combat, threw themselves into the water too quickly and owed their deaths to themselves rather than to others. The Saracens giving way, retired into their city, fleeing shamefully and with great loss. Great numbers of them were mutilated or mortally wounded.

We would have followed them closely, but our chiefs, fearing an ambuscade, held us back. While we were fighting, some slaves and captives broke their chains, for the gaolers had also gone out to fight us. Only the women, children and the sick had remained in the city. These slaves and captives, full of joy, rushed to meet us, applauding our king and his army, and crying "Blessed is he who cometh in the name of the Lord." These events happened on Friday the day of our Lord's Passion; we drew from it a favorable augury. The king disembarked joyfully and safely, as well as the rest of the Christian army. We rested until the next day, when, with the aid and under the guidance of slaves who knew the country and the roads, we got possession of what remained to be captured of the land and shore. But during the night the Saracens, who had discovered that the captives had escaped, had killed those who remained. They thus made of them glorious martyrs of Christ, to their own damnation.

In the darkness of the following night and on Sunday morning, as they lacked weapons and troops, the Saracens seeing the multitude of the Christians who were landing, their courage and firmness, and the sudden desolation of their own city, lacking leaders, superiors and persons to incite them, as well as destitute of strength and weapons for fighting, departed, taking their women and children and carrying off everything movable.

They fled from the other side of the city by little gates which they had made long before. Some escaped by land, others by sea, abandoning their city filled with supplies of all kinds. That same day at nine o'clock, two captives who escaped by chance from the hands of the Saracens, came to tell us what had happened. The king, no longer fearing an ambuscade, entered the city before three o'clock without hindrance and without shedding blood. Of all who entered only Hugo Brun, earl of March, was severely wounded. He lost too much blood from his wounds to survive, for he was careless of his life, because of the reproaches which had been inflicted upon him, and rashly rushed into the midst of the enemy. He had been stationed in the front rank, at his own request, because he knew that he was an object of suspicion.

I must not forget to say that the Saracens, after having determined to flee, hurled at us a great quantity of Greek fire, which was very injurious to us, because it was carried by a wind which blew from the city. But this wind, suddenly changing, carried the fire back upon Damietta, where it burned several persons and fortresses. It would have consumed more property, if the slaves who had been left had not extinguished it by a process which they knew, and by the will of God, who did not wish that we should take possession of a city which had been burnt to the ground.

The king, having then entered the city in the midst of cries of joy, went immediately into the temple of the Saracens to pray and thank God, whom he regarded as the author of what had taken place. Before eating, all the Christians, weeping sweet and sacred tears of joy, and led by the legate, solemnly sang that hymn of the angels, the Te Deum Laudamus.

Then the mass of the blessed Virgin was celebrated in the place where the Christians in ancient times had been wont to celebrate mass and to ring the bells, and which they had now cleansed and sprinkled with holy water. In this place, four days before, as the captives told us, the foul Mohammed had been worshiped with abominable sacrifices, loud shouts and the noise of trumpets. We found in the city an infinite quantity of food, arms, engines, precious clothing, vases, golden and silver utensils and other things. In addition we had our provisions, of which we had plenty, and other dear and necessary objects brought from our vessels.

By the divine goodness, the Christian army, like a pond which is greatly swollen by the torrents pouring in, was added to each day by some soldiers from the lands of lord Ville-Hardouin and some Templars and Hospitalers, besides pilgrims newly arrived, so that we were, by God's grace, largely reinforced. The Templars and Hospitalers did not want to believe in such a triumph. In fact, nothing that had happened was credible. All seemed miraculous, especially the Greek fire which the wind carried back onto the heads of those who hurled it against us. A similar miracle formerly took place in Antioch. A few infidels were converted to Jesus Christ and up to the present time have remained with us.

We, instructed by the past, will in the future exercise much prudence and circumspection in our actions. We have with us faithful Orientals upon whom we can count. They know all the country and the dangers which it offers; they have been baptized with true devotion. While we write, our chiefs are considering what it is necessary to do. The question is whether to proceed to Alexandria or Babylon and Cairo. We do not know what will be decided. We shall inform you of the result, if our lives are spared. The sultan of Babylon, having learned what has taken place, has proposed to us a general engagement for the morrow of St. John the Baptist's day, and in a place which the two armies shall choose, in order, as he says, that fortune may decide for the men of the East or the men of the West, that is between the Christians and themselves, and that the party to whom fate shall give the victory, may glory in it, and the conquered may humbly yield. The king replied that he did not fear the enemy of Christ one day more than another and that he offered no time for rest, but that he defied him to-morrow and every day of his life, until he should take pity on his own soul and should turn to the Lord who wishes the whole world to be saved, and who opens the bosom of His mercy to all those who turn to Him.

We tell you these things in this letter through our kinsman Guiscard. He seeks nothing else than that he may, at our expense, prepare himself for a professorship and have a fit lodging for at least two years.

We have learned nothing certain worth reporting about the Tartars. We can expect neither good faith from the perfidious, nor humanity from the inhuman, nor charity from dogs, unless God, to whom nothing is impossible, works this miracle. It is He who has purged the Holy Land from the wicked Charismians. He has destroyed them and caused them to disappear entirely from under heaven. When we learn anything certain or remarkable of the Tartars, or others, we will send you word either by letter or by Roger de Montefagi, who is to return to France in the spring, to the lands of our lord the viscount, to collect money for us.

VI. Medieval Life and Culture

It took a long time for Western man to work back to something like the level he had achieved at the beginning of the Christian era. The centuries that followed the barbarian invasions no longer look like a period of unrelieved darkness; but their twilight of ignorance, isolation, and insecurity is bad enough. Not until the twelfth century do we find the harsh pressures of the world relaxing and society developing the cultural forms and attitudes we associate with greater leisure, prosperity, and elbowroom. Intellectual activity shifts significantly from cathedral schools and other preserves of the Church to the new and revived universities. Artists, for their part, turn increasingly to the public of castles and courts. The rude and bloody warrior of an earlier day turns—at least ideally—into the Christian knight who lives according to an elevated code of chivalry. Love is exalted, first as a softening, civilizing influence, then as an end in itself. And the troubadour's hero passes through several stages, from Roland who is first and foremost a Christian champion, to Aucassin who is primarily a lover, to Chaucer's knight —a worthy professional soldier ready to fight even in the pay of the heathen—and lastly, though he is not to be found below, to the pathetic, leftover figure of Don Quixote. In this procession of heroes we can trace, among other things, a growing sophistication and also the ebb of attention paid to the rules and advice of the Church.

1. RAOUL GLABER: FAMINE

Where scarcity was the norm, famines were frequent occurrences, with their escort of epidemics, of vagrants and vagabonds, and of desperate attempts to keep alive, going as far as cannibalism. Here is the description which a Cluniac monk, Raoul Glaber, has left of the great hunger which covered most of Europe in the years 1032–1034.

The famine started to spread its ravages and one could fear the disappearance of the human race almost whole. The weather became so bad that none could find the right time for any sowing and that, especially because of the floods, there was no way of harvesting. . . . Continual rains had steeped the whole earth to the extent that during three years one could not dig furrows that would harbor the seed. By harvest time weeds and inauspicious tares had covered all the surface of the fields. In those parts where it gave the best results, a hogshead of seed would produce a harvest of about twelve bushels [that is, about one-fifth of the original seed], and this in turn produced hardly a handful. If by chance one found any food on sale, the seller could exact an excessive price at his will.

Meantime, when the savage beasts and the birds had been eaten, men began, under the empire of a devouring hunger, to gather in order to eat, all kinds of carrion and of things horrible to tell. Certain among them had recourse to escape from death to the roots of the forests and the weeds of the rivers. In the end one is seized by horror at the tale of perversions which then reigned over the human race. Alas! Oh, woe! A thing rarely heard of in the course of ages, a maddening hunger made that men devoured human flesh. Travellers were carried off by those stronger than they, their members cut up, cooked on the fire and devoured. Many of the people who were going from one place to another to flee the famine and who had found hospitality on the way, were slaughtered during the night and served as nourishment for those who had welcomed them. Many, by showing a fruit or an egg to children, lured them into isolated places, massacred and devoured

them. The bodies of the dead were in many places torn from the earth and served equally to appease hunger.

There was then tried in the region of Macon an experiment which had not, to our knowledge, yet been attempted anywhere else. Many people drew from the ground a white soil similar to clay, mixed it with what they had of wheat or bran, and made of this mixture bread, on which they relied so as not to die of hunger. However this practice brought merely the hope of salvation and the illusion of relief. One saw only pale and emaciated faces: many presented a skin distended by swellings; the human voice itself became shrill, similar to the little cries of dying birds. The corpses of the dead, whose multitude forced the living to abandon them here and there without burial, served as pasture to wolves who continued for a long time thereafter to seek their pittance among men. And as one could not, as we said, bury everyone individually because of the great number of dead, in certain places the men, fearing God, dug what was commonly known as charnel houses, in which the bodies of the dead were thrown by the five hundreds and more as long as room remained, pell mell, half naked or without any covering. The cross roads, the edges of the fields, also served as cemeteries. If some heard say that they would be better if they moved to other regions, many were those who perished on the way for want of food.

2. GALBERT OF BRUGES: A GOOD PRINCE STRUGGLES AGAINST FAMINE

The monk Galbert of Bruges tells how in 1125 Charles the Good, Count of Flanders, tried to take measures against the scarcity and want that seared his territories, like those of other princes. Clearly Charles combined charity with economic regulations designed to place more food on the market, especially at the worst period of the year: the months before the harvest.

But the good Count busied himself in supplying the needs of the poor by all means, by distributing alms, in the towns and villages dependent upon him, either in person or by his officers. Every day he fed one hundred poor at Bruges, allotting each one a large loaf of bread from before Lent until the new harvest. He took the same measures in his other cities. The same year the Lord Count decreed that at sowing time whoever sowed two measures of land had to sow one of beans and pease, for this kind of plant produced faster and earlier, which would permit to sustain the poor more quickly if the famine and scarcity did not cease in the course of the year. Similarly he had made recommendations in all his county to remedy in the future the needs of the poor to the extent that it was possible. He reproached the men of Ghent for their shameful behavior, who had left the poor to die of hunger before their doors instead of giving them to eat. He forbade the manufacture of beer, so that the poor would be better fed. He ordered in effect that bread should be made with oats so that the poor could at least subsist on bread and water. He taxed the price of wine at six pennies the quart, to put a stop to the speculations of the merchants who would thus be forced to exchange their stocks of wine for other merchandises, which would permit the poor to subsist more easily. Every day he had enough taken from his own table to nourish 130 poor.

3. OUT WITH THE POOR

Other communities and rulers were less merciful. The legend of the Pied Piper of Hameln reflects a great many attempts that communities made to get rid of their poor at times of scarcity. The Novellino of thirteenth-century Genoa gives an instance of such a case:

There was in Genoa a great rise in prices caused by a shortage of victuals, and there were there more vagabonds than in any other land. [The Council] hired several galleys and rowers who were paid, and then it proclaimed that all the poor must go to the shore and that they would receive bread from the commune. There came so many that it was a marvelous sight . . . all embarked on the ships. The captains were active. They forced the oars in the water and disembarked all these people in Sardinia. There, there was enough to live on. They abandoned them; and thus, in Genoa, there ceased this great rise in prices.

4. FROM: *THE SONG OF ROLAND*

Roland was a famous knight, one of the twelve peers of Charlemagne, who died in the valley of Roncevaux where he was covering the retreat of an army with which Charlemagne had attacked Spain. *The Song of Roland* is a much later production, and it is worth noting how the tough ninth-century warrior who, as far as we know,

From *The Song of Roland Done into English in the Original Measure,* tr. by C. Scott Moncrieff (London: Chapman & Hall, Ltd., 1919). By permission of the publishers and executors of the Estate of C. Scott Moncrieff.

fell in an ambush set by Christian tribes of the Pyrenees, is idealized and romantically presented as the valorous feudal knight with all the values of the courtly culture of the twelfth century.

CV

The count Rollanz, he canters through the field,
Holds Durendal, he well' can thrust and wield,
Right great damage he's done the Sarrazines
You'd seen them, one on other, dead in heaps,
Through all that place their blood was flowing clear!
In blood his arms were and his hauberk steeped,
And bloodied o'er, shoulders and neck, his steed.
And Oliver goes on to strike with speed;
No blame that way deserve the dozen peers,
For all the Franks they strike and slay with heat,
Pagans are slain, some swoon there in their seats,
Says the Archbishop: "Good baronage indeed!"
"Monjoie" he cries, the call of Charles repeats.

CVI

And Oliver has cantered through the crush;
Broken his spear, the truncheon still he thrusts;
Going to strike a pagan Malsarun;
Flowers and gold are on the shield, he cuts,
Out of the head both the two eyes have burst,
And all the brains are fallen in the dust;
He flings him dead, sev'n hundred else amongst.
Then has he slain Turgin and Esturgus;
Right to the hilt, his spear in flinders flew.

Then says Rollanz: "Companion, what do you?
In such a fight, there's little strength in wood,
Iron and steel should here their valour prove.
Where is your sword, that Halteclere I knew?
Golden its hilt, whereon a crystal grew."
Says Oliver: "I had not, if I drew,
Time left to strike enough good blows and true."

CVII

Then Oliver has drawn his mighty sword
As his comrade had bidden and implored,
In knightly wise the blade to him has shewed;
Justin he strikes, that Iron Valley's lord,
All of his head has down the middle shorn,
The carcass sliced, the broidered sark has torn,
The good saddle that was with gold adorned,
And through the spine has sliced that pagan's horse;
Dead in the field before his feet they fall.
Says Rollanz "Now my brother I you call;
He'll love us for such blows, our Emperor,"
On every side "Monjoie" you'ld hear them roar.

CXIX

Swift through the field Turpin the Archbishop passed;
Such shaven-crown has never else sung Mass
Who with his limbs such prowess might compass;

To th' pagan said: "God send thee all that's
bad!
One thou hast slain for whom my heart is
sad."
So his good horse forth at his bidding ran,
He's struck him then on his shield Toledan,
Until he flings him dead on the green grass.

CXXVI

That Archbishop begins the fight again,
Sitting the horse which he took from Gros-
saille;
That was a king he had in Denmark slain;
That charger is swift and of noble race;
Fine are his hooves, his legs are smooth and
straight,
Short are his thighs, broad crupper he dis-
plays,
Long are his ribs, aloft his spine is raised,
White is his tail and yellow is his mane,
Little his ears, and tawny all his face;
No beast is there, can match him in a race.
That Archbishop spurs on by vassalage,
He will not pause ere Abisme he assail;
So strikes that shield, is wonderfully arrayed,
Whereon are stones, amethyst and topaze,
Esterminals and carbuncles that blaze;
A devil's gift it was, in Val Metase,
Who handed it to the admiral Galafes;
So Turpin strikes, spares him not anyway;
After that blow, he's worth no penny wage;
The carcass he's sliced, rib from rib away,
So flings him down dead in an empty place.
Then say the Franks: "He has great vassal-
age,
With the Archbishop, surely the Cross is
safe."

CXXVII

The count Rollanz calls upon Oliver:
"Sir companion, witness you'll freely bear,
The Archbishop is a right good chevalier,
None better is neath Heaven anywhere;
Well can he strike with lance and well with
spear."

Answers that count: "Support to him we'll
bear!"
Upon that word the Franks again make yare;
Hard are the blows, slaughter and suffering
there,
For Christians too, most bitter grief and
care.
Who could have seen Rollanz and Oliver
With their good swords to strike and to
slaughter!
And the Archbishop lays on there with his
spear.
Those that are dead, men well may hold
them dear.
In charters and in briefs is written clear,
Four thousand fell, and more, the tales de-
clare.
Gainst four assaults easily did they fare,
But then the fifth brought heavy griefs to
bear.
They all are slain, those Frankish chevaliers;
Only three-score, whom God was pleased to
spare,
Before these die, they'll sell them very dear.

CXXX

Then says Rollanz: "Strong it is now, our
battle;
I'll wind my horn, so the King hears it,
Charlès."
Says Oliver: "That act were not a vassal's.
When I implored you, comrade, you were
wrathful.
Were the King here, we had not borne such
damage.
Nor should we blame those with him there,
his army."
Says Oliver: "Now by my beard, hereafter
If I may see my gentle sister Alde,
She in her arms, I swear, shall never clasp
you."

CXXXI

Then says Rollanz: "Wherefore so wroth
with me?"

He answers him: "Comrade, it was your
    deed:
Vassalage comes by sense, and not folly;
Prudence more worth is than stupidity.
Here are Franks dead, all for your trickery;
No more service to Carlun may we yield.
My lord were here now, had you trusted me,
And fought and won this battle then had
    we,
Taken or slain were the King Marsilie.
In your prowess, Rollanz, no good we've
    seen!
Charles the Great in vain your aid will
    seek—
None such as he till God His Judgement
    speak;—
Here must you die, and France in shame be
    steeped;
Here perishes our loyal company,
Before this night great severance and grief."

CXXXIII

Rollanz hath set the olifant to his mouth,
He grasps it well, and with great virtue
    sounds.
High are those peaks, afar it rings and loud,
Thirty great leagues they hear its echoes
    mount.
So Charlès heard, and all his comrades
    round;
Then said that King: "Battle they do, our
    counts."

CXXXV

The count Rollanz, though blood his mouth
    doth stain,
And burst are both the temples of his brain,
His olifant he sounds with grief and pain;
Charlès hath heard, listen the Franks again,
"That horn," the King says, "hath a mighty
    strain!"
Answers Duke Neimes: "A baron blows
    with pain!
Battle is there, indeed I see it plain.
Equip you, sir, cry out your old refrain,

That noble band, go succour them amain!
Enough you've heard how Rollanz doth com-
    plain."

CXXXVI

That Emperour hath bid them sound their
    horns.
The Franks dismount, and dress themselves
    for war,
Put hauberks on, helmets and golden swords;
Fine shields they have, and spears of length
    and force
Scarlet and blue and white their ensigns
    float.
His charger mounts each baron of the host;
They spur with haste as through the pass
    they go.
Nor was there one but thus to's neighbour
    spoke:
"Now, ere he die, may we see Rollanz, so
Ranged by his side we'll give some goodly
    blows."
But what avail? They've stayed too long
    below.

CLXIV

The count Rollanz, when dead he saw his
    peers,
And Oliver, he held so very dear,
Grew tender, and began to shed a tear;
Out of his face the colour disappeared;
No longer could he stand, for so much grief,
Will he or nill, he swooned upon the field.
Said the Archbishop: "Uulucky lord, in-
    deed!"

CLXV

When the Archbishop beheld him swoon,
    Rollanz,
Never before such bitter grief he'd had;
Stretching his hand, he took that olifant.
Through Rencesvals a little river ran;
He would go there, fetch water for Rollanz.
Went step by step, to stumble soon began,
So feeble he is, no further fare he can,

For too much blood he's lost, and no strength has;
Ere he has crossed an acre of the land,
His heart grown faint, he falls down forwards and
Death comes to him with very cruel pangs.

CLXVI

The count Rollanz wakes from his swoon once more,
Climbs to his feet; his pains are very sore;
Looks down the vale, looks to the hills above;
On the green grass, beyond his companions,
He sees him lie, that noble old baron;
'Tis the Archbishop, whom in His name wrought God;
There he proclaims his sins, and looks above;
Joins his two hands, to Heaven holds them forth,
And Paradise prays God to him to accord.
Dead is Turpin, the warrior of Charlon.
In battles great and very rare sermons
Against pagans ever a champion.
God grant him now His Benediction!

CLXVII

The count Rollanz sees the Archbishop lie dead,
Sees the bowels out of his body shed,
And sees the brains that surge from his forehead;
Between his two arm-pits, upon his breast,
Crossways he folds those hands so white and fair.
Then mourns aloud, as was the custom there:
"Thee, gentle sir, chevalier nobly bred,
To the Glorious Celestial I commend;
Ne'er shall man be, that will Him serve so well;
Since the Apostles was never such prophet,
To hold the laws and draw the hearts of men.
Now may your soul no pain nor sorrow ken,

Finding the gates of Paradise open!"

CLXXVI

The count Rollanz, beneath a pine he sits;
Turning his eyes towards Spain, he begins
Remembering so many divers things:
So many lands where he went conquering,
And France the Douce, the heroes of his kin,
And Charlemagne, his lord who nourished him.
Nor can we help but weep and sigh at this.
But his own self, he's not forgotten him,
He owns his faults, and God's forgiveness bids:
"Very Father, in Whom no falsehood is,
Saint Lazaron from death Thou didst remit,
And Daniel save from the lions' pit;
My soul in me preserve from all perils
And from the sins I did in life commit!"
His right-hand glove, to God he offers it
Saint Gabriel from's hand hath taken it.
Over his arms his head bows down and slips,
He joins his hands: and so is life finish'd.
God sent him down His angel cherubin,
And Saint Michael, we worship in peril;
And by their side Saint Gabriel alit;
So the count's soul they bare to Paradis.

CLXXVII

Rollanz is dead; his soul to heav'n God bare,
That Emperour to Rencesvals doth fare.
There was no path nor passage anywhere
Nor of waste ground no ell nor foot to spare
Without a Frank or pagan lying there.
Charles cries aloud: "Where are you, nephew fair?
Where's the Archbishop and that count Oliviers?
Where is Gerins and his comrade Gerers?
Otès the Duke, and the count Berengiers
And Ivorie, and Ive, so dear they were?
What is become of Gascon Engelier,

Sansun-the Duke and Anséis the fierce?
Where's old Gerard of Russillun; oh, where
The dozen peers I left behind me here?"
But what avail, since none can answer bear?
"God!" says the King, "Now well may I
    despair,
I was not here the first assault to share!"

Seeming enraged, his beard the King doth
    tear.
Weep from their eyes barons and chevaliers,
A thousand score, they swoon upon the
    earth;
Duke Neimes for them was moved with pity
    rare.

5. AUCASSIN AND NICOLETTE

Somewhere around the year 1200, somewhere in France, a troubadour invented and sang the series of tales that make up the love story of Aucassin and Nicolette, characteristic not only of the gentler habits and interests of a brutal age but of a new gallantry and a certain emancipation from the religious beliefs of a narrower, though only very slightly narrower, day. The present version is adapted from the English translation of F. W. Bourdillon (1887).

Now they tell how the Count Bougart of Valence made war on the Count Garin of Beaucaire, a war so great and wonderful and deadly that not a single day dawned but he was at the gates and the walls and the barriers of the town with a hundred knights and ten thousand soldiers on foot and on horseback; and he burned Garin's land and harried his country and killed his men.

Count Garin was old and feeble and had outlived his time. He had no heir, no son or daughter, except one boy. The young lord's name was Aucassin: he was fair and slim and tall, well made in legs and feet and body and arms. His hair was golden and in little curls; and his eyes were blue-gray and laughing; and his face was bright and oval; and his nose high and well set; and so full was he of good qualities that there were none bad in him, but only good. But he was so overcome by Love, who conquers all, that he did not want to be a knight, nor take arms, nor go to the tourney, nor do any of the things that he ought to have done. His father and his mother said to him:

"Son, now take your arms and mount your horse and fight for your land and help your men. If they see you among them, they will fight better for their lives and their goods, and for your land and mine."

"Father," said Aucassin, "what are you talking about? Let God never give me that which I ask of Him if I will be a knight, or mount a horse, or go into a battle, unless you give me Nicolette, my sweet friend, whom I love so much!"

"Son," said the father, "this cannot be. Let Nicolette alone! For she is a captive maid, who was brought from a foreign land; and the Viscount of this town bought her from the Saracens and brought her to this town and has reared her and baptized her and made her his god-daughter. And one of these days he will give her for husband a young bachelor who will earn bread for her honorably. You have nothing to do with this. And if you want to get a wife, I will give you the daughter of a King or of a Count. There is not a rich man in France whose daughter you cannot have if you will."

"Alas, father," said Aucassin, "where is there on earth position so high that Nicolette, my most sweet friend, if she had it, would not grace it? Were she Empress of Constantinople or of Allemaigne, Queen of England or of France, it would be little enough for her, so noble is she and gracious and debonair, and chockfull of good qualities."

When Count Garin of Beaucaire saw that he could not turn Aucassin, his son, from his love of Nicolette, he went to see the Viscount of the town who was his vassal, and said to him:

"Sir Viscount! You must get rid of Nicolette, your god-daughter! Accursed the land from which she was brought to this country! For through her I lose Aucassin; since he will not be a knight or do any of the things he ought to do. And you'd better know that if I can get hold of her I will burn her in a fire, and you too had better look out."

"Sir," said the Viscount, "it grieves me that he goes to her, or that he comes to her, or that he speaks to her. I had bought her with my money, and I have reared her and baptized her and made her my god-daughter, and I was planning to give her a young bachelor who would have earned bread for her honourably. And Aucassin, your son, would have had nothing to do with any of this. But since it is your will and your good pleasure, I will send her to such a land and to such a country that he shall nevermore see her with his eyes."

"You had better look to it," said Count Garin, "or you will have a great deal of trouble." And so they parted.

And the Viscount was a very rich man, with a palace overlooking a garden. In a chamber of this he put Nicolette, high on an upper floor, and an old woman with her to keep her company. He had bread carried there, and flesh, and wine, and whatever they might need. Then he had the door sealed up, so that there was no way to go in, nor to go out; there was only one little window overlooking the garden, through which they got a little fresh air.

So Nicolette was in prison in that chamber. And the cry and the noise went through all the land and through all the county that Nicolette was lost. Some said that Nicolette had fled; and some said that Count Garin had had her slain. Some rejoiced, but Aucassin did not. He went his way to the Viscount of the town and addressed him thus:

"Sir Viscount, what have you done with Nicolette, my most sweet friend, the thing that I loved best in all the world? Have you carried her off, or stolen her away from me? You had better know that if I die of this, you'll have to pay for it, and very right will it be. For you will have slain me with your two hands, since you have taken from me the thing that I loved best in the world."

"Fair sir," said the Viscount, "now let it be! Nicolette is a captive maid, whom I brought from a foreign land, and I bought her with my money from the Saracens. And I have reared her and baptized her and made her my god-daughter and have cherished her; and one of these days I should have given her a young bachelor who would have earned bread for her honourably. This is none of your business. Why do you not take the daughter of a king or a count? And moreover, what do you think you would have gained if you had made her your mistress, or taken her to your bed? Very little would you have won by that, for your soul would burn in Hell for it all the days of Eternity, since into Paradise you would never enter."

"What have I got to do in Paradise? I

seek not to enter there, provided I have Nicolette, my most sweet friend, whom I love so much. For none go to Paradise except such people as I will tell you. Those old priests go there, and old cripples and those maimed wretches that grovel all day and all night before the altars and in the old crypts; and those folk clad in old threadbare cloaks and in old rags and tatters, who are naked and barefoot and full of sores, who die of hunger and thirst and cold and miseries. These go to Paradise; with them I have nothing to do. But to Hell will I go. For to Hell go the fine clerks and the fine knights who have died in tourneys and in grand wars, and the brave soldiers and the noble men. With those will I go. And there too go the fair and gracious ladies who have friends two or three beside their husbands; and there go the gold and the silver and all the fine furs; and there too go the minstrels and the poets and the kings of the world. With those will I go, so that I have Nicolette, my most sweet friend, with me."

"Well," said the Viscount, "you're surely speaking of it in vain, since you will never see her again. And if you should speak to her and your father knew it, he would burn both me and her in a fire, and you yourself might have something to fear."

"This troubles me," said Aucassin. He leaves the Viscount, sad at heart, and goes to his room to mourn his fate and that of Nicolette.

Whilst Aucassin was in his chamber, and was bewailing Nicolette his friend, the Count Bougart of Valence, who had his war to carry on, did not forget it, but had summoned his men on foot and on horse, and advanced to attack the castle. The alarm is given with a great deal of noise; the knights and the soldiers arm themselves and rush to the gates and to

the walls to defend the castle; the townsfolk go up too and throw over arrows and sharpened stakes.

While the attack was in full blast, Count Garin came into the room where Aucassin was moaning and bewailing Nicolette, his most sweet friend, whom he loved so much. "Ah, son!" said he, "miserable lad: you see that they are attacking your castle, the best and the strongest of them all, and you had better know that if you lose it you lose all your inheritance. Son, take your arms and mount your horse and fight for your land and help your men. Even if you strike no one and no one strikes at you, if our men see you among them they will fight better for their goods and their lives, and your land and mine. And you are so tall and so strong that you are well able to do it, and do it you ought."

"Father," said Aucassin, "what are you saying? Let God never give me that which I ask of Him if I will be a knight, or mount a horse, or go into a battle, unless you give me Nicolette, my sweet friend, whom I love so much!"

"Son," said the father, "that cannot be. I would rather lose all that I have than to see you ever have her to woman or to wife."

He turned away. And when Aucassin saw him going away, he called him back. "Father," said Aucassin, "come here! I will make a fair covenant with you."

"And what is that, fair son?"

"I will take arms and go to the fight, on this understanding: that if God bring me back again safe and sound, you will let me see Nicolette, my sweet friend, long enough to speak two or three words to her and to kiss her once."

"I agree," said the father. He grants his wish, and Aucassin is glad.

Aucassin heard of the kiss

Which shall on return be his.
Had one given him pure gold
Marks a hundred thousand told,
Not so blithe of heart he were.
Rich array he bade them bear:
They made ready for his wear.
He put on a hauberk lined [1]
Helmet on his head did bind,
Girt his sword with hilt pure gold,
Mounted on his charger bold;
Spear and buckler then he took;
At his two feet cast a look:
They trod in the stirrups trim.
Wondrous proud he carried him.
His dear love he thought upon,
And his good horse spurred anon,
Who right eagerly went on.
Through the gate he rode straightway
Into the fray.

So, as you have listened and heard, Aucassin was in arms upon his horse. Heavens! how well his shield sat upon his shoulder, and his helmet on his head, and his swordbelt on his hip. And the boy was tall and strong and fair and slim and well made, and the horse on which he sat was eager and mettlesome, and the boy had ridden him well through the gateway. Now don't you suppose that he would have thought of taking spoils of oxen or cows or of goats, or of striking a knight or a knight striking him? Not at all! He did not think of it once; but he thought so much of Nicolette, his sweet friend, that he forgot his reins and whatever he ought to do. And the horse, who had felt the spurs, carried him on into the throng, and dashed right into the thick of his foes. And they laid hands upon him from every side, and stripped him of his shield and of his lance, and led him off prisoner then and there; and they were already discussing among themselves by what

death they should cause him to die. And when Aucassin heard it: "Oh, God!" says he. "Gentle Creature! Are these my mortal foes who are here leading me and who propose to cut off my head? And when my head has been cut off, nevermore shall I speak to Nicolette, my sweet friend whom I love so much! Yet I have here a good sword, and I sit on a good steed, still fresh. If I do not defend myself now, for her sake, let her love me no more or forsake the help of God!"

The boy was tall and strong, and the horse on which he sat was restive. And he puts his hand to the sword and begins to strike right and left, and cleaves helmets and nasals and fists and arms, and makes a havoc all around him, just as the wild boar does when the dogs set on him in the forest; so that he overthrew ten knights and wounded seven and dashed then and there out of the throng, and rode back again full gallop, sword in hand.

The Count Bougart of Valence had heard that they were about to hang Aucassin, his enemy, and he came that way. And Aucassin recognized him. The young man had his sword in hand, and he struck the count full on the helmet, so that he beat it in on his head. Quite stunned, the count fell to the ground; and Aucassin put out his hand and took him, and led him away by the nasal of his helmet and handed him over to his father.

"Father," said Aucassin, "see, here is your enemy who has made such war on you and done you so much harm. It is twenty years that this war has lasted and never was there a man could put an end to it."

"Fair son," said the father, "this is the sort of exploit for you, far better than dreaming after foolishness."

---

[1] A lined or twofold coat of mail was the special armor of the knight.

"Father," said Aucassin, "do not start preaching to me; better keep your word."

"Bah, what word, my son?"

"Alas, father! Have you forgotten? By my head, forget it who may, I will not forget it for it has got me by the heart. Did we not agree when I took my arms and went into the fray that, if God brought me back safe and sound, you would let me see Nicolette, my sweet friend, just long enough to speak two words or three to her and to kiss her only once? We made this agreement and I want you to keep it."

"I?" said the father. "Never help me God, if I ever keep this covenant with you. And if she was here now I would burn her in a fire, and you yourself had better look out."

"Is that all?" said Aucassin.

"So help me God," said his father. "Yes."

"I am surely very sorry when a man of your age lies," said Aucassin. "Count of Valence: I have made you prisoner."

"Verily you have!"

"Give me here your hand!"

"Willingly." He put his hand in his.

"Now you promise me," said Aucassin, "that in every one of your remaining days, if ever you find the means to hurt or molest my father in his person or his property, this you will do."

"Sir, in God's name!" says the Count of Valence, "do not mock me. Better set a ransom. You cannot ask gold or silver of me, steeds or palfreys, fine furs or hounds or hawks, that I will not give you."

"How is this?" says Aucassin. "Don't you recognize that you are my prisoner?"

"Yes, sire," said the Count Bougart.

"In that case, you had better promise what I ask, or else, may God never help me again, I'll have your head flying off in a trice."

"In God's name," says the Count Bougart, "I promise you whatever you want!" He promised him; and Aucassin made him get on a horse and he himself mounted another, and escorted him till he was in safety.

Which goes to show what can happen to fathers who do not keep their word. As for Aucassin and Nicolette, their adventures go on for quite a few more pages, through dungeons and forests, storms at sea, and captures by pirates, until they are reunited, she as a Princess of Carthage, he as Count of Beaucaire:

Soon as Aucassin beheld her
Both his arms to her he held,
Gently took her to his breast,
All her eyes and face caressed.
Long they lingered side by side;
And the next day by noontide
Aucassin her lord became;

Of Beaucaire he made her Dame.
After lived they many days,
And in pleasure went their ways.
Now has Aucassin his bliss,
Likewise Nicolette ywis.
Ends our song and story so;
For there is no more I know.

6. JACQUES DE VITRY: LIFE OF THE STUDENTS AT PARIS

The rise of the medieval city was accompanied by widespread changes in intellectual life and patterns of education. A time of troubles, when cultural values could only be hazardously preserved and handed on in a few isolated abbeys, was succeeded by a more settled period in which leadership in education centered around the great cathedral schools of northern France. By the twelfth century, however, the scholarship of the great cathedral schools as represented by Chartres was being challenged by other institutions, soon to be known as universities. Some were clerical like Paris—which the fame of Abelard had made the most popular teaching center in France—while others were chiefly lay, like Bologna, famed for its courses in Roman law.

This was a new, strange, and turbulent society where students would fight with townsmen or each other, using swords, cudgels, even bows and arrows; where teachers might become heroes or corpses with almost equal ease; and which excited the same disapproval from the moralists of the time as the milder versions of today seem to manage.

Jacques de Vitry, cardinal and historian, who died in 1240, preached the crusade against the Albigensians. The passage below suggests that this clever and censorious man may have considered a crusade against student wickedness to be almost as indicated.

Almost all the students at Paris, foreigners and natives, did absolutely nothing except learn or hear something new. Some studied merely to acquire knowledge, which is curiosity; others to acquire fame, which is vanity; others still for the sake of gain, which is cupidity and the vice of simony. Very few studied for their own edification, or that of others. They wrangled and disputed not merely about the various sects or about some discussions; but the differences between the countries also caused dissensions, hatreds and virulent animosities among them, and they impudently uttered all kinds of affronts and insults against one another.

They affirmed that the English were drunkards and had tails; the sons of France proud, effeminate and carefully adorned like women. They said that the Germans were furious and obscene at their feasts; the Normans, vain and boastful; the Poitevins, traitors and always adventurers. The Burgundians they considered vulgar and stupid. The Bretons were reputed to be fickle and changeable, and were often reproached for the death of Arthur. The Lombards were called avaricious, vicious and cowardly; the Romans, seditious, turbulent and slanderous; the Sicilians, tyrannical and cruel; the inhabitants of Brabant, men of blood, incendiaries, brigands and ravishers; the Flemish, fickle, prodigal, gluttonous, yielding as butter, and slothful. After such insults from words they often came to blows.

I will not speak of those logicians, before whose eyes flitted constantly "the lice of Egypt," that is to say, all the sophistical subtleties, so that no one could comprehend their eloquent discourses in which, as says Isaiah, "there is no wisdom." As to the doctors of theology, "seated in Moses' seat," they were swollen with learning, but their charity was not edifying. Teaching and not practicing, they have "become as sounding brass or a tinkling cymbal," or like a canal of stone, always dry, which ought to carry water to "the bed of spices." They not only hated one another, but by their flatteries

From *Translations and Reprints,* II, No. 3, D. C. Munro, Ed.

they enticed away the students of others; each one seeking his own glory, but caring not a whit about the welfare of souls.

Having listened intently to these words of the Apostle, "If a man desire the office of a bishop, he desireth a good work," they kept multiplying the prebends, and seeking after the offices; and yet they sought the work decidedly less than the preëminence, and they desired above all to have "the uppermost rooms at feasts and the chief seats in the synagogue, and greetings in the market." Although the

Apostle James said, "My brethren, be not many masters," they on the contrary were in such haste to become masters, that most of them were not able to have any students, except by entreaties and payments. Now it is safer to listen than to teach, and a humble listener is better than an ignorant and presumptuous doctor. In short, the Lord had reserved for Himself among them all, only a few honorable and timorous men who had not stood "in the way of sinners," nor sat down with the others in the envenomed seat.

7. FROM: CHAUCER'S CANTERBURY TALES

The *Canterbury Tales* were written by Geoffrey Chaucer (c. 1340–1400), who started the long poem in 1373 and kept at it for the rest of his life. It is rich and varied, just like Chaucer's own life. He fought in France before he was twenty, married (1366), which brought him a family connection with the powerful John of Gaunt, was employed on diplomatic missions (1369–1379), held various offices under the Crown, was elected to Parliament in 1386, found himself in disgrace for a few years when his patron could no longer protect him, but recovered royal favor and pensions from 1390 to his death about ten years later. No wonder he never completed the *Canterbury Tales,* which yet run to about eighteen thousand lines of verse, besides some passages in prose. His writing is delightful and he is really the first English poet.

GENERAL PROLOGUE

Here Begins the Book of the Tales of Canterbury: When April with its gentle showers has pierced the March drought to the root,—then folks long to go on pilgrimages, and palmers to visit foreign shores and distant shrines, known in various lands; and especially from every shire's end of England they travel to Canterbury, to seek the holy blessed martyr who helped them when they were sick.

One day in that season when I stopped at the Tabard in Southwark, ready to go on my pilgrimage to Canterbury with a

truly devout heart, it happened that a group of twenty-nine people came into that inn in the evening. They were people of various ranks who had come together by chance, and they were all pilgrims who planned to ride to Canterbury. The rooms and stables were large enough for each of us to be well lodged, and, shortly after the sun had gone down, I had talked with each of these pilgrims and had soon made myself one of their group. We made our plans to get up early in order to start our trip, which I am going to tell you about.

From *Chaucer's Canterbury Tales,* tr. by R. M. Lumiansky, ©, 1948, by Simon and Schuster, Inc. Reprinted by permission of Simon and Schuster, Publishers.

But, nevertheless, while I have time and space, before I go farther in this account, it seems reasonable to tell you all about each of the pilgrims, as they appeared to me; who they were, and of what rank, and also what sort of clothes they wore. And I shall begin with a Knight.

There was among us a brave KNIGHT who had loved chivalry, truth, and honor, generosity and courtesy, from the time of his first horseback rides. He had performed admirably in his lord's wars, during which he had traveled as widely as any man, in both Christendom and heathen countries, and he had always been cited for his bravery. He had been at Alexandria when it was conquered, and had sat at the head of the table many times in Prussia, above all the foreign knights. He had fought successfully in Lithuania and in Russia more frequently than any other Christian knight of similar rank. Also he had been in Grenada at the siege of Algeciras, and had fought in Benmarin. He had been at Ayas and Attalia when they were won, and had taken part in many an armed expedition in the Mediterranean. He had fought in fifteen large battles, in addition to the three times he had defended our faith in lists in Algeria, and each time he had killed his opponent. This same brave Knight had once been with the lord of Palathia to fight against another heathen in Turkey, and he had always been given valuable loot. But though he was brave, he was prudent, and as meek in his conduct as a maid. He had never yet in all his life spoken discourteously to anybody. He was a true and perfect gentle Knight. But let me tell you of his clothing and equipment: his horses were good, but he was not gaily dressed. He wore a thick cotton coat, which was all stained by his breast plates, for he had just returned from his travels and had set out at once on his pilgrimage.

With him there was his son, a young SQUIRE, a lover and a lusty bachelor, with hair as curly as if it had been set. He was about twenty years old, I would say, and he was of average height, remarkably agile, and very strong. He had already been on cavalry raids in Flanders, in Artois, and in Picardy, where he had borne himself well for one so young, in an effort to win favor with his lady. His clothes were as covered as a meadow with white and red flowers. All day he sang or played the flute; in fact, he was as joyful as the month of May. His cloak was short, with long, wide sleeves, and he sat his horse well and rode excellently. He could compose the words and music for songs, joust and also dance, and draw and write very well. So ardently did he love that he slept no more at night than a nightingale. He was courteous, humble, and helpful, and carved at the table for his father.

The Knight had brought along one servant, for he wished to travel that way, and this YEOMAN was dressed in a green coat and hood. He carefully carried a sheaf of bright, keen peacock arrows attached to his belt, and a strong bow in his hand. He knew very well how to care for his equipment, and the feathers on his arrows never drooped. His hair was cut short, and his complexion was brown. He understood all the tricks of woodcraft. He wore a bright leather wristguard, and carried a sword and a small shield on one side, and a fine ornamented dagger, as sharp as the point of a spear, on the other. A Christopher hung on his breast, and he had a hunter's horn with a green cord. In my opinion he was a real forester.

There was also a Nun, a PRIORESS, whose smile was very quiet and simple. Her harshest curse was "by St. Loy," and she was named Madam Eglantine. She sang the divine service very well, with excellent nasal intonation, and spoke French fluently and carefully with the accent of the school at Stratford-Bow, for the French of Paris was unknown to her. Her table manners were admirable: she allowed no crumb to fall from her lips, nor did she wet her fingers deeply in her sauce; she knew exactly how to carry the food to her mouth and made sure that no drops spilled upon her breast. She was very much interested in etiquette. So carefully did she wipe her lips that no trace of grease could be seen in her cup when she had drunk from it. She reached for her food very daintily, and truly she was very merry, with a pleasant disposition and an amiable manner. She took pains to imitate court behavior, to be dignified in bearing, and to be considered worthy of respect. But to tell you of her tender feelings: she was so kind and so full of pity that she would weep if she saw a dead or bleeding mouse caught in a trap. She had several small dogs which she fed with roasted meat or milk and fine bread; if one of her dogs died, or if someone beat it with a stick, she cried bitterly. Indeed, with her everything was tenderness and a soft heart. Her wimple was very neatly pleated, her nose shapely, her eyes blue, and her mouth very small, soft, and red. But, truly, she had a fair forehead; it was almost a hand's breadth wide, I swear, for, to tell the truth, she was not particularly small. I noticed that her cloak was very well made. On her arm she wore a coral rosary with large green beads for the Paternosters, from which hung a brightly shining golden brooch. And on this brooch was inscribed a capital A, surmounted by a crown, and after that *Amor vincit omnia*. This Prioress had another NUN, who was her chaplain, and three priests with her.

There was a MONK, an outstanding one, whose job it was to supervise the monastery's estates, and who loved hunting. He was a manly person, quite capable of serving as abbot. He had many excellent horses in his stable, and when he rode you could hear his bridle jingling in the whistling wind as clearly and also as loudly as the chapel bell at the subordinate monastery where the lord was prior. Because the rule of St. Maurus or of St. Benedict was old and somewhat stringent, this monk let old-fashioned things go and followed newfangled ideas. He didn't give a plucked hen for that text which says that hunters are not holy, and that a monk who is irresponsible is like a fish out of water—that is to say, a monk out of his cell. For he thought that text not worth an oyster; and I said his reasoning was good. Why should he study and drive himself crazy, always poring over a book in his cloister, or work and slave with his hands as St. Augustine orders? How shall that serve the world? Let Augustine have his labor for himself! Therefore this monk was a true hunter: he had greyhounds as swift as birds in flight; his greatest pleasure, for which he would spare no cost, was to ride and hunt the hare. I saw his sleeves edged at the wrist with fur, and that the finest in the land; and he had a very rare pin made of gold, with a love knot in the larger end, to fasten his hood under his chin. His head was bald and shone like glass, as did his face also, as if he had been anointed. He was a fine, fat lord, and in good shape. His protruding eyes rolled in his head and gleamed like coals under a pot. His boots were supple, and his horse richly equipped. Now surely he was a fair prelate; he was not pale as a tormented ghost. Of all roasts he loved a fat swan best. His horse was as brown as a berry.

There was a wanton, merry FRIAR, a licensed beggar and a very gay man. No member of all four orders knew so much of gossip and flattering talk. He had found husbands for many young women at his own expense. A noble representative he was of his order. Among the franklins all over his district, and also among the respectable women in the towns, he was well liked and intimate, for he had, as he said himself, more power of confession than a parish priest, since he was licensed by his order. He heard confession very agreeably, and his absolution was pleasant. When he thought he would get a good present, he was an easy man in giving penance. For to give a present to a poor order is a sign that a man is well shriven. He even boasted that he knew that a man who contributed was repentant, for there are many men with hearts so stern that they cannot weep, even when they are contrite. Therefore, instead of weeping and praying, people could give silver to the poor friars. His cloak was always stuffed full of knives and pins to be given to pretty women. And, certainly, he had a pleasant voice: he could sing and play the fiddle excellently. At ballad-singing he won the prize hands down. His neck was as white as the lily, but he was as strong as a champion wrestler. He knew the taverns well in every town, and cared more for every innkeeper and barmaid than for a leper or a beggar; it was not fitting, as far as he could see, for such an important man to be acquainted with lepers. It is not honest, and it will not advance a man, to deal with such poor folk; rather, he should deal with the rich and the food-merchants. And, above everything, wherever there was a chance for profit, this Friar was courteous and humbly helpful. There was no man anywhere more capable at this work. He was the best beggar in his order, and paid a certain sum for his grant so that none of his brethren came into his district. And even if a widow did not own a shoe, his greeting was so pleasant that before he left he would have got a coin. The money which he picked up on the sly amounted to more than his regular income. And he could frolic just like a puppy. During court meetings he could be of great help, for then he was not like a cloisterer with a coat as threadbare as a poor scholar's but like a master or a pope. His short coat was of double worsted, as neat as if it were freshly pressed. He intentionally lisped a bit in his joking, in order to make his English roll sweetly from his tongue, and when he played the harp after singing, his eyes twinkled in his head just like the stars on a frosty night. This worthy licensed beggar was named Hubert.

There was a MERCHANT with a forked beard, dressed in clothes of varied colors and sitting proudly on his horse; he wore a beaver hat from Flanders, and his boots were neatly fastened. He spoke his opinions very pompously, talking always about the increase in his profits. He wished the sea were kept open at all costs between Middleburg and Orwell, and was expert in selling money on the exchange. This responsible man kept his wits about him: so closemouthed was he about his dealings in bargaining and in borrowing and lending that no one knew when he was in debt. Nevertheless, he was really a worthy man; but, to tell the truth, I don't know what he was called.

There was also a CLERIC from Oxford, who had long ago applied himself to the study of logic. His horse was as thin as a rake, and he himself, I assure you, was by no means fat, but looked hollow and solemn. His overcoat was threadbare, for as yet he had found no benefice, and he was not worldly enough to hold a secular position. For he would rather have twenty books of Aristotle and his philosophy bound in red or black at the head of his bed than rich clothes, or a fiddle, or a gay psaltery. But though he was a philosopher, he still had but little gold in his chest, for he spent all he could get from his friends on books and on schooling, and prayed earnestly for the souls of those who gave him money with which to go to school. He was most concerned and occupied with studying. He spoke not one word more than was necessary, and that which he did say was correct and modest, brief and to the point, and filled with worth-while meaning. His talk centered on moral themes, and gladly would he learn and gladly teach.

A SERGEANT OF THE LAW, careful and wise, a most excellent man long practiced in legal discourse, was also there. He was discreet and well thought of—at least he seemed so, his words were so wise. Many times he had served as justice at assizes, appointed by letters from the King and also in the regular way. He had earned many large fees and presents of clothes as a result of his skill and his wide reputation. There was nowhere so able a buyer of land: he always sought unentailed ownership, and his papers were never invalidated. No man was so busy as he, and yet he seemed busier than he was. He had all the cases and decisions which had occurred since the time of King William at the tip of his tongue. He could compose and draw up a legal paper so that no one could complain about his phrasing, and he could recite every statute by heart. He rode unostentatiously in a coat of mixed color, with a silk belt on which there were small bars—I shall tell no more about his dress.

A FRANKLIN accompanied him. His beard was as white as a daisy, and he was sanguine by nature. Dearly did he love his bread dipped in wine in the morning. He had the habit of living for pleasure, for he was a true son of Epicurus, who held that pure pleasure was truly perfect bliss. He was a substantial landowner, St. Julian in his part of the country. Always his bread and ale were of the best, and nobody had a better cellar. His house was never without baked fish and meat in such quantity that it snowed food and drink, the choicest that you could imagine. His menus changed in accordance with the various seasons of the year. Many a fat bird was in his coop, and many a bream and pike in his fish pond. Woe to his cook unless the sauce were pungent and sharp and all the equipment in order. All day long his table stood ready laid in the hall. He was lord and sire of the sessions and had frequently served as member of parliament from his shire. A short dagger and a pouch of silk hung from his milk-white belt. He had served as administrator and as auditor for his shire. Nowhere was there such a worthy subvassal.

A HABERDASHER and a CARPENTER, a WEAVER, a DYER, and a TAPESTRYMAKER were with us, all clothed in the uniform of a great and important guild. Their equipment was all freshly and newly decorated: their knives were mounted with silver, not with brass; their belts and pouches were in every respect well and cleanly made. Indeed, each of them seemed suited to sit on a dais in the guildhall as burgess. Each, because of his wisdom, was able to serve as alderman. For they owned sufficient goods and money, as even their wives had to agree, or else they certainly would be blameworthy. It is a very fine thing to be called "Madam," to go in first to evening services, and to have a train carried like royalty.

These guildsmen had a COOK with

them for the trip to boil chickens with the bones and with the flavoring powder and the spice. He could easily recognize a draught of London ale, and could roast and boil, broil, fry, make stew, and bake good pies. But it was a shame, I thought, that he had a large sore on his shin. For he could make creamed capon with the best.

There was a SHIPMAN who lived far in the west; for all I know he was from Dartmouth. He rode upon a nag as best he could, in a coarse gown which came to his knees. Under his arm he had a dagger which hung down on a cord about his neck. The hot summer sun had tanned him heavily, and certainly he was a good fellow. Often while the wine-merchant slept, he had tapped the wine casks he brought from Bordeaux. He gave no heed to scruples. When he fought and had the upper hand, he made his prisoners walk the plank. But in his business—the correct reckoning of tides and streams; the handling of the ship's controls; the knowledge of the harbors, the moon, and the compass—there was none so good from Hull to Carthage. He was bold and wise in any undertaking. His beard had been shaken by many a tempest. He knew the condition of all the anchorages from Gotland Isle to Cape Finisterre, and every creek in Spain and Brittany. His ship was called the "Magdalen."

With us there was a PHYSICIAN; in all the world there was not another like him for talk of medicines and of surgery, for he was trained in astrology. He skillfully and carefully observed his patient through the astrological hours, and was quite able to place the waxen images of his patient so that a fortunate planet was ascendant. He knew the cause of every disease—whether hot, cold, moist, or dry—and how it developed, and of what humor. Indeed, he was the perfect practitioner: the cause and root of the disease determined, at once he gave the sick man his remedy. He had his apothecaries quite ready to send him drugs and sirups, for each of them worked to the other's profit—their friendship was not newly begun. This Physician knew well ancient Aesculapius and Dioscorides, and also Rufus, Hippocrates, Haly and Galen, Serapion, Rhazes, Avicenna, Averroes, Damascenus and Constantine, Bernard, Gatesden, and Gilbertine. His diet was moderate—not too much, but that little nourishing and digestible. But little time did he devote to the study of the Bible. He was dressed in red and blue cloth lined with taffeta and with silk; and yet he was not quick to spend his money. He held onto that which he gained during a plague. For, in medicine, gold is heathful in drinks; therefore, he especially loved gold.

There was a good WIFE from near Bath, but she was somewhat deaf, which was a shame. She had such skill in cloth-making that she surpassed the weavers of Ypres and Ghent. In all her parish there was no woman who could go before her to the offertory; and if someone did, the Wife of Bath was certainly so angry that she lost all charitable feeling. Her kerchiefs were of fine texture; those she wore upon her head on Sunday weighed, I swear, ten pounds. Her fine scarlet hose were carefully tied, and her shoes were uncracked and new. Her face was bold and red. All of her life she had had five husbands, not to mention other company in her youth—but of that we need not speak now. And three times she had been to Jerusalem; she had crossed many a foreign river; she had been to Rome, to Bologna, to St. James' shrine in Galicia, and to Cologne. About journeying through the country she knew a great deal. To tell the truth she was gap-toothed. She sat her gentle horse easily, and wore a fine headdress with a hat as broad as a buckler or a shield, a riding skirt about her large hips, and a pair of sharp spurs on her heels. She knew how to laugh and joke in company, and all the remedies of love, for her skill was great in that old game.

There was a good man of the church, a poor parish PARSON, but rich in holy thoughts and works. He was also a learned man, a clerk, ·who wished to preach Christ's gospel truly and to teach his parishioners devoutly. He was benign, wonderfully diligent, and extremely patient in .adversity, as he had proved many times. He did not at all like to have anyone excommunicated for non-payment of tithes; rather, he would give, without doubt, a portion of the offering and also of his salary to his poor parishioners. He needed little to fill his own needs. His parish was wide and the houses far apart, but he never failed, rain or shine, sick or well, to visit the farthest in his parish, be he rich or poor, traveling on foot with a staff in his hand. To his congregation he gave this noble example: first he practiced good deeds, and afterward he preached them. He took this idea from the gospels and added to it another: if gold rust, what shall iron do? For if a priest whom we trust is ·not worthy, it is no wonder that an ignorant man sins. And it is a shame, if a priest only realizes it, to see a wicked priest and a godly congregation. Surely a parson should set an example by his godliness as to how his parishioners should live. This Parson did not hire out his benefice and leave his people in difficulties while he ran off to St. Paul's in London to look for an endowment singing masses for the dead, or to be retained by a guild. He stayed at home and guarded his parish well so that evil did not corrupt it. He was a pastor and not a mercenary. And yet, though he himself was holy and virtuous, he was not contemptuous of sin-

ners, nor overbearing and proud in his talk; rather, he was discreet and kind in his teaching. His business was to draw folks to heaven by fairness and by setting a good example. But if any sinner, whether of high or low birth, was obstinate, this Parson would at once rebuke him for it sharply. I don't believe there is a better priest anywhere. He cared nothing for pomp and reverence, nor did he affect an overly nice conscience; he taught the lore of Christ and His twelve Apostles, but first he followed it himself.

With him there was a PLOWMAN, his brother, who had hauled many a load of manure. He was a good and true laborer, living in peace and perfect charity. With all his heart he loved God best at all times, whether it profited him or not, and next he loved his neighbor as himself. He would thresh and also ditch and dig free of charge, for the sake of Christ, to help a poor neighbor, if it were at all possible. He paid his tithes promptly and honestly both by working himself and with his goods. Dressed in a laborer's coat, he rode upon a mare.

There was also a Reeve, a Miller, a Summoner, and a Pardoner, a Manciple, and myself—there were no more.

The MILLER was a very husky fellow, tremendous in bone and in brawn which he used well to get the best of all comers; in wrestling he always won the prize. He was stocky, broad, and thickset. There was no door which he could not pull off its hinges or break by ramming it with his head. His beard was as red as any sow or fox, and as broad as a spade. At the right on top of his nose he had a wart, from which there grew a tuft of hairs red as the bristles of a sow's ears, and his nostrils were wide and black. A sword and a shield hung at his side. His mouth was as huge as a large furnace, and he was a jokester and a ribald clown, most of whose jests were of sin and scurrility. He knew quite well how to steal grain and charge thrice over, but yet he really remained reasonably honest. The coat he wore was white and the hood blue. He could play the bagpipe well and led us out of town to its music.

There was a friendly MANCIPLE of an Inn of Court whom other stewards might well imitate in order to buy provisions wisely. For no matter whether he bought for cash or on credit, he always watched his purchases so closely that he was constantly solvent and even ahead. Now isn't that a fine gift from God, that such an uneducated man can outwit a whole heap of learned men? He had more than thirty masters, who were expert and deep in legal matters; a full dozen of them were capable of serving as steward of the moneys and the lands of any lord in England, and of making that lord live within his own income and honorably out of debt (unless he were crazy), or just as sparingly as he wished. And these lawyers could take care of any emergency that occurred in the administration of a shire; and yet this Manciple made fools of them all.

The REEVE was a slender, choleric man. His beard was shaved as close as possible, and his hair was cut round by his ears and clipped short in front like a priest's. His legs were as long and lean as sticks, completely lacking calves. He knew fully how to keep a granary and a bin; there was no accountant who could get the best of him. From the drought and from the rainfall he could tell the expected yield of his seed and grain. His lord's sheep, cattle, dairy, swine, horses, equipment, and poultry were wholly under this Reeve's care, and his word had been accepted on the accounting ever since his lord was twenty years old. There was no one who could find him in arrears. There

was no bailiff, no sheepherder, nor any other laborer, whose petty tricks and stealings were not known to the Reeve; they were as afraid of him as of death. His house was well placed upon a heath and shadowed by green trees. He was better able to buy than was his lord. He had privately accumulated considerable money, for he knew very well how to please his lord subtly, to give and lend him money from the lord's own stock and therefore to receive thanks, plus a coat and hood. As a youth he had learned a good trade: he was a very fine woodworker, a carpenter. This Reeve rode upon a large, fine, dappled-gray horse called Scot. He wore a long blue topcoat, and carried a rusty sword by his side. This Reeve that I am telling about was from Norfolk, near a town called Bawdswell. His coat was tucked up like a friar's, and he always rode last in our procession.

There was a SUMMONER with us there who had a fiery-red babyish face, for he was leprous and had close-set eyes. He was as passionate and lecherous as a sparrow, and had black scabby brows and a scraggly beard. Children were frightened by his face. There was no quicksilver, litharge, or brimstone, borax, white lead, or any oil of tartar, or ointment which would rid him of his white pimples or of the bumps on his face. He really loved garlic, onions, and also leeks, and to drink strong wine, red as blood, after which he would speak and shout like a madman. Then, when he had drunk his fill of the wine, he would speak no word but Latin; he knew a few phrases, two or three, that he had learned out of some church paper—that is not unusual, for he heard Latin all day; and you know very well how a jay bird can say "Wat" as well as the Pope. But if anyone attempted to discuss other learned matter with the Summoner, it was at once evident that he had spent all of his philosophy; he would always cry: "The question is what is the law?" He was a friendly and a kind rascal; you couldn't find a better fellow. For a quart of wine, he would allow a good fellow to have his mistress for a year, and excuse him fully. And he could pull the same trick quite expertly on someone else. If he came across a good companion, he would teach him to have no fear of the archdeacon's excommunication, unless that man's soul was in his purse; for the punishment was sure to be in his purse, since, as the Summoner said, "The purse is the archdeacon's Hell." But I know very well that he certainly lied; every guilty man ought to be afraid of excommunication, which will as surely kill the soul as absolution will save it, and a man should also beware of a *Significavit.* This Summoner controlled all the young people of the diocese in his own way, and he knew their secrets and was their favorite adviser. He had placed a bouquet on his head, large enough to decorate an ale-house signpost. He had made himself a shield of a cake.

With him there rode an amiable PAR—DONER from Rouncivalle, his friend and colleague, who had just come from the court at Rome. Loudly he sang, "Come hither, Love, to me!" The Summoner, singing bass, harmonized with him; never was there a trumpet with half so loud a tone. This Pardoner had hair of a waxy yellow, but it hung as smoothly as strands of flax, and he wore what hair he had gathered into small bunches on top but then thinly spread out over his shoulders. But for sport he did not wear his hood, for it was tied up in his bag. He affected to ride all in the new fashion, uncovered except for his little cap. He had eyes which glared like those of a hare. A religious talisman was sewn to his cap. He

carried his bag, stuffed full of pardons hot from Rome, before him in his lap. His voice was small and goatlike. He had no beard, and never would have; his face was as smooth as if freshly shaven. I believe he was a eunuch. But in his business, there was not another such pardoner from Berwyck to Ware. For in his bag he had a pillowcase which he said had served as the veil of Our Lady; he claimed to have a piece of the sail with which St. Peter went to sea until Jesus Christ caught him. He had a metal cross embedded with stones, and also he had pig's bones in a jar. And with these same relics, when he found a poor parson living out in the country, he made more money in one day than the parson made in two months. And thus, with feigned flattery and tricks, he made monkeys of the parson and the people. But, finally, to tell the truth, he was in church a noble ecclesiastic. He could read a lesson or a parable very effectively, but best of all he could sing the offertory; for he knew very well that, when that service was over, he must sweeten his tongue and preach to make money as best he could. Therefore, he sang merrily and loud.

Now I have told you very briefly about the rank, the dress, and the number of these pilgrims, and also why this group was assembled in Southwark at this good inn called the Tabard, close to the Bell. But the time has come to tell you what we did that same night we arrived at the inn, and afterwards I shall tell you about our trip and all the rest of our pilgrimage. But, first, I beg you in your kindness not to consider me vulgar because I speak plainly in this account and give you the statements and the actions of these pilgrims, or if I repeat their exact words. For you know just as well as I that whosoever repeats a tale must include every word as nearly as he possibly can, if it is in the story, no matter how crude and low; otherwise, he tells an untrue tale, or makes up things, or finds new words. He cannot spare even his brother's feelings; he must say one word just as well as any other. Christ himself spoke quite crudely in Holy Writ, and you know very well that there is no vulgarity in that. Even Plato says, to those who can read him, that the words must be cousin to the deeds. Also I ask you to forgive me for not arranging the people in my tale by their rank as they should be. My wit is short, as you can well imagine.

Our Host made each of us very comfortable and soon sat us down to supper. He served us with the best food; the wine was strong, and we were glad to drink. Our Host was a seemly man, fit to serve as major-domo of a banquet hall. He was a large man with protruding eyes—no more impressive burgess is to be found in Cheapside—frank in his speech, wise, and well schooled, and nothing lacking in manliness. Also, he was a very merry man, and after supper began to play and told many jokes, among other things, after we had paid our bills. Then he said: "Now, ladies and gentlemen, truly you are heartily welcome here, for by my troth, if I do not lie, all this year I haven't seen so gay a group together in this inn as now. I would like to make you happy if I knew the way; in fact, I just now thought of a way to please you, and it shall cost you nothing.

"You are going to Canterbury—God speed you, and may the blessed martyr give you your reward! And I know very well that as you go along the road you plan to tell tales and to play, for truly, there's no fun or pleasure in riding along as dumb as a stone. Therefore, I shall make you a proposition, as I said before,

and do you a favor. And if you are unanimously agreed to stand by my judgment and to do as I shall suggest, tomorrow when you ride along the road, by the soul of my dead father, if you don't have fun I'll give you my head! Hold up your hands without more talk."

It didn't take us long to reach a decision. We didn't think the matter worth much careful discussion, and we voted his way without debate. Then we told him to explain his plan as he wished.

"Ladies and gentlemen," he said, "now listen carefully; but, I beg you, don't be contemptuous. Here is the point, to be brief, and plain: that each of you, to make our trip seem short, shall tell two tales of old adventures on the way to Canterbury—I mean it that way—and two more coming home. And the one of you who tells the best tales of all, that is to say, those greatest in moral teaching and in entertainment value, shall have a supper at the expense of all of us here in this inn, right by this column, when we come back from Canterbury. And, to make your trip more enjoyable, I will ride with you myself, at my own expense, and be your guide; and whoever will not accept my judgment along the way will have to bear the full expense of the trip for everybody. Now, if you agree to this plan, say so at once, without any more talk, and I shall immediately get myself ready."

We agreed, and gladly gave our oaths to obey; then we asked him also to agree to serve as our manager, and to judge and report our tales, and to arrange for a supper at a set price. Also, we agreed to be ruled in all things as he saw fit. Thus unanimously we accepted his suggestion, and at once the wine was fetched. We drank, and everyone went to bed without further loitering.

VII. Economic Development of the Middle Ages

The medieval Church, by prohibiting the lending of money at interest, made trade and business more difficult for the conscientious Christian. This mattered little while insecurity, poor means of communication, and uncertain means of exchange kept trade to a minimum; but it became awkward when, in a newly stabilized West, trade began to revive.

Meanwhile, merchants and craftsmen had organized their guilds and friendly societies, which were more than mere trade unions or monopolistic associations, though they were that too. They attained real political power in the prospering cities of the time, and a reading of their rules will show that they used their powers to regulate not only the market, production standards, and working conditions of their trade, but also the life, death, and social activities of their members. Yet we must not forget that these were originally religious associations, each under the aegis of its patron saint. The economic thought of the Middle Ages was religious thought; and, though orthodox doctrine turned out at times to be conveniently flexible, the day had not dawned when men would think of worldly matters as separate from spiritual ones and designed to operate by different rules.

1. ST. THOMAS AQUINAS: SUMMA THEOLOGICA

Thomas Aquinas, writing in the thirteenth century, expressed the accepted doctrine of the Church—a doctrine which must have put many economically active men in a painful quandary. It did serve, however, as the basis of the medieval business code and of a morality which, though honored more in the breach than the observance, set the standard to which people tried to adhere, which is the most that can be said of any standard.

Question LXXVII: On Fraud Committed in Buying and Selling

We next have to consider the sins which have to do with voluntary exchanges; first, fraud committed in buying and selling; second, usury taken on loans. For in the case of other forms of voluntary exchange, no kind of sin is noted which is to be distinguished from rapine or theft.

Under the first head there are four points to be considered: (1) sales unjust

Reprinted by permission of the publishers from Arthur Eli Monroe, editor *Early Economic Thought: Selections from Economic Literature Prior to Adam Smith*. Cambridge, Mass.: Harvard University Press, 1924.

with respect to price, that is, whether it is lawful to sell a thing for more than it is worth; (2) sales unjust with respect to the thing sold; (3) whether a seller is bound to point out a defect in the thing sold; (4) whether it is lawful to sell a thing in trade for more than was paid for it.

ARTICLE I: WHETHER A MAN MAY LAWFULLY SELL A THING FOR MORE THAN IT IS WORTH

The first article is analyzed as follows:

1. It seems that a man may lawfully sell a thing for more than it is worth. For in the exchanges of human life, justice is determined by the civil law. But according to this it is lawful for the buyer and seller to deceive each other, and this takes place when a seller sells a thing for more than it is worth, or the buyer pays less than it is worth. Therefore, it is lawful for a man to sell a thing for more than it is worth.

2. Furthermore, that which is common to all men seems to be natural and not sinful. But as Augustine relates, the saying of a certain actor was accepted by all: *you wish to buy cheap and sell dear;* which agrees with the saying in Proverbs xx, 14: *It is naught, it is naught, saith every buyer; and when he is gone away, then he will boast.* Therefore it is lawful to sell a thing for more and buy it for less than it is worth.

3. Furthermore, it does not seem to be unlawful to do by agreement what the claims of honor require. But according to the Philosopher,[1] in friendships based on utility recompense ought to be according to the advantage accruing to the beneficiary; and this sometimes exceeds the value of the thing given, as happens when a

[1] Aristotle.

man needs something very much, either to escape danger or to obtain some advantage. Therefore in contracts of buying and selling it is lawful to sell a thing for more than it is worth.

But opposed to this is the saying in Matthew vii, 12: *All things whatsoever you would that men should do unto you, do you also to them.* But no man wishes to have a thing sold to him for more than it is worth. Therefore no man should sell a thing to another for more than it is worth.

I answer that it is wholly sinful to practise fraud for the express purpose of selling a thing for more than its just price, inasmuch as a man deceives his neighbor to his loss. Hence Cicero says: *All deception should therefore be eliminated from contracts: the seller should not procure some one to bid up nor the buyer some one to bid down the price.*

If there is no fraud, we may speak of buying and selling in two ways: first, considering them in themselves, and in this respect buying and selling seem to have been instituted for the common advantage of both parties, since one needs something that belongs to the other, and conversely, as explained by the Philosopher. Now what has been instituted for the common advantage ought not to be more burdensome to one than to the other; hence a contract between them ought to be based on the equality of things. The value of a thing which is put to human use is measured by the price given; and for this purpose money was invented, as is explained in *Ethics,* V, 5. Hence, whether the price exceeds the value of a thing or conversely, the equality required by justice is lacking. Consequently, to sell dearer or to buy cheaper than a thing is worth is in itself unjust and unlawful.

We can speak of buying and selling in another sense, namely, the case where it accidentally turns out to the advantage of one and to the injury of the other; for example, when a man has great need of something, and another is injured if he is deprived of it; in such a case the just price will be one which not only takes into account the thing sold, but also the loss incurred by the seller in parting with it. And thus a thing may lawfully be sold for more than it is worth in itself, though not more than it is worth to its possessor. If, however, a man is greatly aided by something he has obtained from another, and the seller does not suffer any loss from doing without it, he ought not to charge more for it, since the advantage which accrues to the other is not due to the seller but to the condition of the buyer. Now no one has a right to sell to another what does not belong to him; though he may charge him for the loss he suffers. He, however, who derives great advantage from something received from another, may of his own accord pay the seller something in addition. This is a matter of honor.

In reply to the first argument above, it is to be said that, as explained earlier, human law is given to the people, among whom many are deficient in virtue, not to the virtuous alone. Hence human law could not prohibit whatever is contrary to virtue; it suffices for it to prohibit the things which destroy the intercourse of men, treating other things as lawful, not because it approves them, but because it does not punish them. Hence it treats as lawful, imposing no penalty, the case where a seller without deception obtains a higher price or a buyer pays a lower

price; unless the discrepancy is too great, since in that case even human law compels restitution to be made; for example, if a man were deceived as to the just price by more than half. But divine law leaves nothing unpunished which is contrary to virtue. Hence, according to divine law, it is considered unlawful if the equality required by justice is not observed in buying and selling; and he who has more is bound to recompense the one who suffers loss, if the loss is considerable. I say this, because the just price of things is not absolutely definite, but depends rather upon a kind of estimate; so that a slight increase or decrease does not seem to destroy the equality required by justice.

In reply to the second argument, it is to be said that, as Augustine remarks in the same passage: *that actor, either from looking into himself or from experience with others, believed that the desire to buy cheap and sell dear was common to all men. But since this is indeed wicked, each man can attain such justice as to resist and overcome this desire.* And he cites the example of a man who paid the just price for a book to one who, through ignorance, asked too little for it. Hence it is evident that this common desire is not natural but due to wickedness, and hence is common to many who travel the broad road of sin.

In reply to the third argument, it is to be said that in commercial justice the chief consideration is the equality of things; but in friendships based on utility the equality of advantage is considered; hence recompense ought to be according to the advantage derived; but in buying, according to the equality of things.

In Articles II and III, Aquinas argues that a sale is rendered unlawful by a defect in the thing sold, and that a seller is bound to declare a defect in the thing sold.

ARTICLE IV: WHETHER IN TRADING
IT IS LAWFUL TO SELL A THING
FOR MORE THAN WAS PAID FOR IT

The fourth point is analyzed as follows:

1. It seems that in trading it is not lawful to sell a thing for more than was paid for it. For Chrysostom says: *Whoever buys a thing in order to make a profit in selling it, whole and unchanged, is the trader who is cast out of God's temple;* and Cassiodorus writes to the same effect in commenting on a passage in Psalm lxx. *What else is trading, he says, but buying cheap and wishing to sell dear at retail?* and he adds: *Such traders the Lord cast out of the temple.* But nobody is cast out of the temple except on account of sin. Therefore such trading is sinful.

2. Furthermore, it is contrary to justice for a man to sell a thing for more than it is worth or to buy for less, as is shown in the first article of this question. But he who in trading sells a thing for more than he paid for it must have paid less than it was worth or be selling for more. Therefore this cannot be done without sin.

3. Furthermore, Jerome says: *Shun, as you would a pestilence, a trader cleric, who out of poverty has become rich, and out of obscurity famous.* Now trading seems to be forbidden to clerics for no reason except its sinfulness. Hence to buy a thing cheap and sell it dear in trade is a sin.

Opposed to this is Augustine's commentary on the passage in Psalm lxx: *The avaricious trader blasphemes over his loss, lies and perjures himself about the prices of his wares. But these are vices of the man, not of the craft which can be carried on without such vices.* Therefore, trading is not in itself unlawful.

I answer that it is the function of traders to devote themselves to exchanging goods. But, as the Philosopher says, there are two kinds of exchanges. One may be called natural and necessary, by means of which one thing is exchanged for another, or things for money to meet the needs of life, and this kind of trading is not the function of traders, but rather of household managers or of statesmen, who have to provide a family or a state with the necessaries of life. The other kind of exchange is that of money for money or of things for money, not to meet the needs of life, but to acquire gain; and this kind of trading seems to be the function of traders, according to the Philosopher. Now the first kind of exchange is praiseworthy, because it serves natural needs, but the second is justly condemned, because, in itself, it serves the desire for gain, which knows no limits but extends to infinity. Hence trading in itself is regarded as somewhat dishonorable, since it does not logically involve an honorable or necessary end.

Question LXXVIII: Of the Sin of Usury, Which Is Committed in Loans

ARTICLE I: WHETHER IT IS
SINFUL TO RECEIVE USURY
FOR MONEY LENT

To receive usury for money lent is, in itself, unjust, since it is a sale of what does not exist; whereby inequality obviously results, which is contrary to justice.

In proof of this, it should be noted that there are some things the use of which is the consumption of the things themselves; as we consume wine by using it to drink, and consume wheat by using it for food. Hence, in the case of such things, the use should not be reckoned apart from the thing itself; but when the use has been granted to a man, the thing is granted by this very fact; and therefore, in such cases, the act of lending involves a transfer of ownership. Therefore, if a man wished to sell wine and the use of the wine separately, he would be selling the same thing twice, or selling what does not exist; hence he would obviously be guilty of the sin of injustice. For analogous reasons, a man commits injustice who lends wine or wheat, expecting to receive two compensations, one as the restitution of an equivalent thing, the other as a price for the use, which is called *usury.*

There are some things, however, the use of which is not the consumption of the thing itself; thus the use of a house is living in it, not destroying it. Hence, in such cases, both may be granted separately, as in the case of a man who transfers the ownership of a house to another, reserving the use of it for himself for a time; or, conversely, when a man grants someone the use of a house, while retaining the ownership. Therefore a man may lawfully receive a price for the use of a house, and in addition expect to receive back the house lent, as happens in leasing and letting a house.

Now money, according to the Philosopher, was devised primarily for the purpose of effecting exchanges; and so the proper and principal use of money is the consumption or alienation of it, whereby it is expended in making purchases. Therefore, in itself, it is unlawful to receive a price for the use of money lent, which is called *usury;* and just as a man is bound to restore other things unjustly acquired, so he is bound to restore money received through usury.

He who is not bound to lend may receive compensation for what he has done: but he ought not to exact more. He is recompensed, however, according to the equality required by justice, if as much is returned to him as he lent. Hence if he exacts more for the use of a thing which has no use except the consumption of the substance, he exacts a price for what does not exist; and so it is an unjust exaction. . . .

ARTICLE II: WHETHER IT IS LAWFUL TO ASK FOR ANY OTHER CONSIDERATION FOR MONEY LENT

The second point is analyzed as follows:

1. It seems that a man may ask some other consideration for money lent. For every man may lawfully provide against his own loss. But sometimes a man suffers loss through lending money. Hence it is lawful for him to ask or exact something over and above the money lent, to make up for his loss.

2. Furthermore, every man is bound by a kind of requirement of honor to make some recompense to one who has done him a favor. But he who lends money to a man in need, does him a favor, for which some expression of gratitude is due. Hence he who receives is bound by natural duty to make some recompense. But it does not seem to be unlawful for a man to bind himself to something to which he is bound by natural law. Hence it does not seem to be unlawful for a man, in lending money to another, to contract for some compensation.

3. Furthermore, just as there are gifts by the hand, so there are gifts by the tongue and by service, as a gloss says on Isaiah xxxiii, 15: *Blessed is he that shak-*

eth his hands from all bribes. But it is lawful to receive service or even praise from one to whom money has been lent. Hence for analogous reasons it is lawful to receive some other gift.

4. Furthermore, there seems to be the same relation between gift and gift as between loan and loan. But it is lawful to receive money for other money given. Hence it is lawful to receive compensation in the form of another loan for money lent.

5. Furthermore, a man who transfers the ownership of money to another in a loan alienates it more than a man who entrusts it to a merchant or craftsman. But it is lawful to receive gain for money entrusted to a merchant or craftsman. Hence it is also lawful to receive gain from money lent.

6. Furthermore, a man may receive a pledge for money lent, the use of which may be sold for some price; as when the pledge is a field or a house which is inhabited. Hence it is lawful to make some gain from money lent.

7. Furthermore, it sometimes happens that a man sells his goods dearer in a sort of loan, or buys the property of another cheaper, or even increases the price in proportion to the delay in payment, or lowers it in proportion to the promptness; in all of which cases some compensation seems to be given as if for a loan of money. This, however, does not seem to be obviously unlawful. Hence it seems to be lawful to ask or exact some consideration for money lent.

Opposed to this is the mention of Ezechiel among other things required in a just man: *If he hath not taken usury and increase.*

I answer that, according to the Philosopher, everything is considered money of which the price can be measured by money. Hence, just as a man who, by a tacit or explicit agreement, receives money for the loan of money or anything else which is consumed by use, sins against justice as explained in the preceding article, so also anyone who, by tacit or explicit agreement, receives anything else, the price of which can be measured by money, is likewise guilty of sin. If, however, he receives something of this kind, not asking it and not according to any tacit or explicit obligation, but as a free gift, he does not sin; because even before he lent the money, he might lawfully receive a free gift, and he is not put at a disadvantage by the act of lending. Compensation in the form of things which are not measured by money may, however, be exacted lawfully, such as good will and love for the lender, or something similar.

In reply to the first argument, it is to be said that a lender may without sin contract with the borrower for compensation to cover the loss arising from the fact that he gives up something which belongs to him; for this is not selling the use of money, but avoiding loss; and it may be that the borrower avoids greater loss than the lender incurs; so that the borrower makes good the other's loss with advantage to himself. Compensation for loss, however, cannot be stipulated on the ground that the lender makes no profit on his money, because he should not sell what he does not yet possess, and which he may be prevented in various ways from getting.

In reply to the second argument, it is to be said that compensation for a favor may be made in two ways; first, as a requirement of justice, to which a man may be bound by definite agreement; and this obligation depends upon the amount of benefit received. Hence a man who receives a loan of money, or of something similar, the use of which is its consumption, is not bound to pay back more than he received in the loan: so that it is contrary to justice, if he is bound to return more. Secondly, a man is bound to make compensation for a favor as a requirement of friendship; in which more consideration is given to the spirit in which the benefit was conferred than to the extent of it; and to such a debt no civil obligation attaches, whereby a certain element of compulsion is introduced, making the compensation no longer spontaneous.

In reply to the third argument, it is to be said that if a man, by a sort of obligation tacitly or explicitly agreed to, expects or exacts compensation in the form of service or of words, it is just as if he exacted a gift from the hand; because both can be valued in money, as we see in the case of those who offer for hire the work they do with their hands or tongues. If, however, a gift of service or of language is not given as an obligation, but out of good will, which is not subject to valuation in money, it is lawful to receive, and exact, and expect this.

In reply to the fourth argument, it is to be said that money cannot be sold for more money than the amount lent, which is to be repaid. Nor is anything to be exacted or expected except a feeling of good will, which is not subject to valuation in money; from which a spontaneous loan may arise. The obligation to make a loan later is inconsistent with this, however, because such an obligation can also be valued in money. Hence, it is lawful for a lender to receive another loan in return, at the same time, but it is not lawful to bind the borrower to make a loan later.

In reply to the fifth argument, it is to be said that a lender of money transfers the ownership of the money to the borrower; so that the borrower holds it at his own risk, and is bound to restore it intact: hence the lender should not exact more. But he who entrusts his money to a merchant or craftsman, by means of some kind of partnership, does not transfer the ownership of his money to the latter, but it remains his; so that the merchant trades with it or the craftsman uses it at the owner's risk; hence he may lawfully claim a part of the gain arising therefrom, as being from his own property.

In reply to the sixth argument, it is to be said that if a man, in return for money lent to him, pledges something, the use of which can be valued at a price, the lender ought to count the use of this thing as part of the repayment of the loan; otherwise, if he wishes to have the use of that thing granted him without charge, it is just as if he received money for a loan, which is usury; unless the thing happened to be such as are usually lent without charge among friends, as in the case of a book.

In reply to the seventh argument, it is to be said that if a man wishes to sell his goods for more than their just price, expecting the buyer to pay later, it is plainly a case of usury, because such waiting for payment has the character of a loan. Hence whatever is exacted for such waiting, in excess of the just price, is a kind of price for a loan, which comes under the head of usury. And likewise, if a buyer wishes to buy for less than the just price, on the ground that he pays the money before the thing can be delivered to him, it is a sin of usury, because that paying of money in advance has the character of a loan, the price of which is the amount deducted from the just price of the thing bought. If, however, a man wishes to deduct from the just price, in order to obtain the money sooner, he is not guilty of a sin of usury.

ARTICLE III: WHETHER A MAN IS BOUND TO RESTORE ANYTHING HE MAY HAVE MADE OUT OF USURIOUS GAINS

It seems that a man is bound to restore anything he may have made out of usurious gains. . . . Opposed to this is the principle that a man may lawfully keep what he has legitimately acquired. But what is acquired with usurious gains is sometimes legitimately acquired: hence it may be lawfully retained.

I answer that, as stated above in the first article of this question, there are some things of which the use is the consumption of the things themselves, and which have no usufruct, according to the civil law. Hence, if such things were extorted by usury (for example, money, wheat, wine, or something similar), a man is not bound to make restitution beyond what he has received: because what is acquired by this means is not the fruit of such a thing but of human industry; unless perchance the other man suffer a loss through the withholding of such a good, losing a part of his property; for then he is bound to make compensation for the injury.

There are some things, however, of which the use is not their consumption; and such things have a usufruct; such as a house or a field or something of the kind. Hence, if a man has extorted the house or the field of another by usury, he is bound to restore not only the house or field but also the fruits obtained therefrom, because they are the fruits of the things of which another is the owner; and hence they belong to him.

Property acquired by means of usury does not belong to the same person as the usury, but to those who bought it; those from whom the usury was taken have some claims on it, however, as on the other property of the usurer. Hence it is not prescribed that such property be assigned to those from whom the usury was taken, because it may be worth more than the usury paid; but it is prescribed that the property be sold, and the price restored, that is, up to the amount of the usury received.

ARTICLE IV: WHETHER IT IS LAWFUL TO BORROW MONEY UPON USURY

1. It seems that it is not lawful to borrow money upon usury. For the Apostle says (Romans, i, 32) that *they are worthy of death, not only they that do these sins, but also they that consent to them that do them.* But he who borrows money upon usury consents to the usurer in his sin, and gives him an occasion for sin. Hence he also sins.

2. Furthermore, for no temporal advantage should one give another occasion for sin; for this is in the nature of active scandal, which is always sinful. . . . But he who seeks a loan from a usurer directly gives him an occasion for sin. Hence he is not excused by reason of any temporal advantage.

3. Furthermore, it seems to be no less necessary to deposit one's money sometimes with a usurer than to borrow from him. But depositing one's money with a usurer seems to be entirely unlawful, just as it would be unlawful to put a sword in the keeping of a madman, a maiden in the keeping of a libertine, or food in the keeping of a glutton. Hence it is not lawful to borrow from a usurer.

Opposed to this is the argument that a man who suffers an injury does not sin, according to the Philosopher; hence justice is not a mean between two vices, as stated in the same place. But the usurer sins, in doing injustice to the one who borrows upon usury. Hence the borrower upon usury does not sin.

I answer that it is in no way lawful to induce a man to commit sin; but it is lawful to use the sin of another for a good end; because even God uses all sins for some good end; for He draws some good out of every evil. . . . Hence when Publicola asked whether it was lawful to use the oath of a man swearing by false gods, in which he plainly sins, by paying them divine homage, Augustine answered that *he who uses the oath of one who swears by false gods, not for evil but for good, does not become a party to his sin in swearing by evil spirits, but to his good faith whereby he kept his word. If, however, he induced him to swear by false gods, he would sin.* So, in the present question, it is also to be said that it is in no way lawful to induce a man to lend upon usury; one may, however, borrow upon usury from a man who is ready to do it and practises usury, provided it be for some good purpose, such as helping oneself or somebody else out of difficulty; just as it is also lawful for one who falls among robbers to point out what goods he has, in order to save his life, though the robbers commit sin in plundering him.

In reply to the first argument, it is to be said that he who borrows money upon usury does not consent to the sin of the usurer, but uses it; nor does the taking of usury please him, but the loan, which is good.

In reply to the second argument, it is to be said that he who borrows money upon usury does not give the usurer occasion for taking usury, but for making a loan. The usurer himself, however, takes the occasion for sin from the malice of his heart. Hence, it is a passive scandal on his part, not an active one on the part of the borrower. Nor should the other, on account of such passive scandal, refrain from seeking a loan, if he is in need; because such passive scandal does not arise from infirmity or ignorance, but from malice.

In reply to the third argument, it is to be said that if a man deposited his money with a usurer who had no other with which to practise usury, or with the intention of making greater gains by way of usury, he would provide the material for sin; and so he himself would share the blame; but if a man deposits his money for safe-keeping with a usurer who has other money with which to practise usury, he does not commit a sin, but uses a sinful man for a good end.

2. THE GUILDS

The merchant guilds of western Europe generally developed as voluntary associations under religious protection. They combined the fellowship of the road, where traders had to travel in companies and caravans for safety's sake, with the "friendly society" in which men unite for charitable, sociable, or insurance purposes under the patronage of an appropriate saint.

In time, these voluntary merchant associations came to dominate the government of their cities and to develop into monopolistic bodies, protecting not only the safety of their members but also standards of trade and the membership's exclusive grip on the local market. In parts of Europe the guilds grew in wealth, numbers, and self-confidence to the point where they could carry on an independent existence apart from the organs of the feudal state; and they sometimes supplanted count, bishop, or state itself, as happened in certain *communes* of Italy, Germany, and northern France. In England they remained content with local government and economic power under the generally distant rule of the king. Even so, as the ordinances reprinted below go to show, the powers of English merchant guilds were extensive and their tendency was to regulate a member's life and conduct more or less from the cradle to the grave.

Ordinance of the Gild Merchant of Southampton

1. In the first place, there shall be elected from the gild merchant, and established, an alderman, a steward, a chaplain, four skevins [sheriffs or adjunct magistrates, from Latin *scabinus*, Fr. *échevin*], and an usher. And it is to be known that whosoever shall be alderman shall receive from each one entering into the Gild fourpence, the steward, twopence; the chaplain, twopence; and the usher, one penny. And the Gild shall meet twice a year: that is to say, on the Sunday next after St. John the Baptist's day, and on the Sunday next after St. Mary's day.

4. And when the Gild shall sit, the lepers of La Madeleine shall have of the alms of the Gild, two sesters [8 gallons] of ale, and the sick of God's House and of St. Julian shall have two sesters of ale. And the Friars Minor shall have two sesters of ale and one sester of wine. And four sesters of ale shall be given to the poor whenever the Gild shall meet.

6. And when the Gild sits, and any gildsman is outside of the city so that he does not know when it will happen, he shall have a gallon of wine, if his servants come to get it. And if a gildsman is ill and is in the city, wine shall be sent to him, two loaves of bread and a gallon of wine and a dish from the kitchen; and

two approved men of the Gild shall go to visit him and look after his condition.

7. And when a gildsman dies, all those who are of the Gild and are in the city shall attend the service of the dead, and gildsmen shall bear the body and bring it to the place of burial. And whoever will not do this shall pay according to his oath, two pence, to be given to the poor. And those of the ward where the dead man shall be ought to find a man to watch over the body the night that the dead shall lie in his house. And so long as the service of the dead shall last, that is to say the vigil and the mass, there ought to burn four candles of the Gild, each candle of two pounds weight or more, until the body be buried. And these four candles shall remain in the keeping of the steward of the Gild.

11. And if a gildsman shall be imprisoned in England in time of peace, the alderman with the steward and with one of the skevins, shall go at the cost of the Gild, to procure the deliverance of the one who is in prison.

12. And if any gildsman strikes another with his fist; and is convicted thereof, he shall lose the Gild until he shall have bought it back for ten shillings, and taken the oath of the Gild again like a

From *Translations and Reprints*, II, No. 1, E. P. Cheyney, Ed.

new member. And if a gildsman strikes another with a stick, or a knife, or any other weapon, whatever it may be, he shall lose the Gild and the franchise, and shall be held as a stranger until he shall have been reconciled to the good men of the Gild and has made recompense to the one whom he has injured, and has paid a fine to the Gild of twenty shillings; and this shall not be remitted.

15. And if a gildsman reviles or slanders another gildsman, and a complaint of it comes to the alderman, and if he is reasonably convicted thereof, he shall pay two shillings fine to the Gild, and if he is not able to pay he shall lose the Gild.

16. And if anyone who is of the franchise, speaks evil of a gildsman, and is convicted of this before the alderman, he shall pay five shillings for a fine or lose the franchise.

19. And no one of the city of Southampton shall buy anything to sell again in the same city, unless he is of the Gild merchant or of the franchise. And if anyone shall do so and is convicted of it, all which he has so bought shall be forfeited to the king; and no one shall be quit of custom unless he proves that he is in the Gild or in the franchise, and this from year to year.

20. And no one shall buy honey, fat, salt herrings, or any kind of oil, or millstones, or fresh hides, or any kind of fresh skins, unless he is a gildsman: nor keep a tavern for wine, nor sell cloth at retail, except on market or fair days; nor keep grain in his granary beyond five quarters, to sell at retail, if he is not a gildsman; and whoever shall do this and be convicted, shall forfeit all to the king.

21. No one of the Gild ought to be partner or joint dealer in any of the kinds of merchandise before mentioned with anyone who is not of the Gild, by any manner of coverture, or art, or contrivance, or collusion, or in any other manner. And whosoever shall do this and be convicted, the goods in such manner bought shall be forfeited to the king, and the gildsman shall lose the Gild.

22. If any gildsman falls into poverty and has not the wherewithal to live, and is not able to work or to provide for himself, he shall have one mark from the Gild to relieve his condition when the Gild shall sit. No one of the Gild nor of the franchise shall avow another's goods for his by which the custom of the city shall be injured. And if any one does so and is convicted, he shall lose the Gild and the franchise; and the merchandise so avowed shall be forfeited to the king.

23. And no private man nor stranger shall bargain for or buy any kind of merchandise coming into the city before a burgess of the Gild Merchant, so long as the gildsman is present and wishes to bargain for and buy this merchandise; and if anyone does so and is convicted, that which he buys shall be forfeited to the king.

24. And anyone who is of the Gild Merchant shall share in all merchandise which another gildsman shall buy or any other person, whosoever he is, if he comes and demands part and is there where the merchandise is bought, and also if he gives satisfaction to the seller and gives security for his part. But no one who is not a gildsman is able or ought to share with a gildsman, without the will of the gildsman.

25. And if any gildsman or other of the city refuse a part to the gildsman in the manner above said, he shall not buy or sell in that year in the town, except his victuals.

63. No one shall go out to meet a ship bringing wine or other merchandise com-

ing to the town, in order to buy anything, before the ship be arrived and come to anchor for unlading; and if any one does so and is convicted, the merchandise which he shall have bought shall be forfeited to the king.

Ordinance of the Gild Merchant of the Holy Trinity of Lynn Regis

4. The alderman to have on the day of Pentecost one sextary of wine, and the dean half a sextary, the clerk half and each of the skevins, the same day, half a sextary, and every day after, as long as the drinking shall continue, the alderman shall have half a sextary, the dean, clerk and each of the skevins one gallon, and each of the attendants half a gallon, at evening.

5. If any of the brethren shall disclose to any stranger the councils of the said Gild, to their detriment without the assent of the alderman and his brethren, he shall forfeit the sum of 32d.[1]

6. If any of the brethren shall fall into poverty or misery, all the brethren are to assist him by common consent out of the chattels of the house or fraternity, or of their proper own.

7. If any brother shall be impeached, either within Lynn or without, the brethren there present ought to assist him in their council, if they are called, to stand with him and counsel him without any costs; and if they do not they are to forfeit 32d.

8. None of the brethren is to come into the Gild before the alderman and his brethren with his cap or hood on, or barefoot, or in any rustic manner; if he does he is to be amerced [fined] 4d.

9. If any one should sleep at the Gild, either at the general meeting or at their feasts and drinking, he is to forfeit 4d.

10. If any one turns him rudely to his brother, or calls him by any rude name, he is to be amerced 4d.

11. If any is called and cited at a prime [regular meeting] and does not come before the issue of the first consult, he is to pay 1d. by order of the dean; and if he refuses and sits down he is to be amerced 4d.

12. If any one should be cited to the prime, and shall be found in the town or shall come late to the drinking, and the dean shall say to him to be there at the next prime, and he does not come before they begin to take judgments of defaults, he shall either make some reasonable excuse, or pay 12d., and if he comes before the faults are adjudged, and shall depart without leave he shall pay 12d.

13. If any one of this house shall buy anything and a brother shall come in unexpectedly before the agreement, or at it, he ought to be a partner with him that buys, and if the buyer refuses it, he is to be amerced half a mark.

16. If any poor brother shall die, the alderman and brethren shall see that his body be honorably buried, of the goods or chattels of the house, or out of alms, if he has not the wherewith to bury himself.

18. If any brother shall die, the dean is to summon all the brethren to make their offerings for the soul of the deceased; and if anyone is absent he is to give ½d. at the next prime following, for the soul of the defunct, and the dean is to have 4d. of the alms collected, for the citing of the brethren.

[1] pence—the d. stands for *denarius,* a small Roman coin.

From *Translations and Reprints,* II, No. 1, E. P. Cheyney, Ed.

20. No one shall intrude himself while the drinking continues.

21. If any brother shall offend another brother, in word or deed, he shall make no complaint but to the alderman first, and the mayor; if he does not he is to be amerced half a mark.

3. ARTICLES OF THE SPURRIERS OF LONDON, 1345

The articles of the spurmakers of London reflect the narrower economic interests of a craft guild that is not particularly concerned with the government of its city or even the conduct of its members outside business hours but rather with setting standards of production, regulating conditions of work and training, eliminating undercutting and unfair practices and, above all, the competition of nonmembers. It is worth considering the extent to which the new emphasis reflects the altered political and religious situation of the fourteenth century, the strength of royal power in England at the time, or simply the difference in nature between merchant and craft guilds.

Be it remembered, that on Tuesday, the morrow of St. Peter's Chains, in the nineteenth year of the reign of King Edward III, the articles underwritten were read before John Hammond, mayor, Roger de Depham, recorder, and the alderman; and seeing that the same were deemed befitting, they were accepted and enrolled in these words.

In the first place, — that no one of the trade of Spurriers shall work longer than from the beginning of the day until curfew rung out at the Church of St. Sepulchre, without Newgate; by reason that no man can work so neatly by night as by day. And many persons of the said trade, who compass how to practice deception in their work, desire to work by night rather than by day; and then they introduce false iron, and iron that has been cracked, for tin, and also they put gilt on false copper, and cracked. And further,—many of the said trade are wandering about all day, without working at all at their trade; and then, when they have become drunk and frantic, they take to their work, to the annoyance of the sick, and all their neighborhood, as well by reason of the broils that arise between them and the strange folks who are dwelling among them. And then they blow up their fires so vigorously, that their forges begin all at once to blaze to the great peril of themselves and of all the neighborhood around. And then, too, all the neighbors are much in dread of the sparks, which so vigorously issue forth in all directions from the mouths of the chimneys in their forges. By reason thereof it seems unto them that working by night should be put an end to, in order such false work and such perils to avoid: and therefore the mayor and the aldermen do will, by the assent of the good folks of the said trade, and for the common profit, that from henceforth such time for working, and such false work made in the trade, shall be forbidden. And if any person shall be found in the said trade to do the contrary hereof, let him be amerced, the first time in 40d., one-half thereof to go to the use of the Chamber of the Guildhall of London, and the other half to the use of the said trade; the second time, in half a mark, and the third time in 10s., to the use of the same Chamber and trade; and the fourth time, let him forswear the trade forever.

Also that no one of the said trade shall hang his spurs out on Sundays, or any other days that are double feasts; but only a sign indicating his business: and such spurs as they shall so sell, they are to show and sell within their shops, without exposing them without, or opening the doors or windows of their shops, on the pain aforesaid.

Also, that no one of the said trade shall keep a house or shop to carry on his business, unless he is free of the city; and that no one shall cause to be sold, or exposed for sale, any manner of old spurs for new ones, or shall garnish them or change them for new ones.

Also, that no one of the said trade shall take an apprentice for a less term than seven years, and such apprentice shall be enrolled according to the usages of the said city.

Also, that if any one of the said trade, who is not a freeman, shall take an apprentice for a term of years, he shall be amerced as aforesaid.

Also, that no one of the said trade shall receive the apprentice, serving-man or journeyman of another in the same trade, during the term agreed upon between his master and him; on the pain aforesaid.

Also, that no alien of another country, or foreigner of this country, shall follow or use the said trade, unless he is enfranchised before the mayor, alderman and chamberlain; and that by witness and surety of the good folks of the said trade, who will undertake for him as to his loyalty and his good behavior.

Also, that no one of the said trade shall work on Saturdays, after None [noon] has been rung out in the City; and not from that hour until the Monday morning following.

The Making of the Modern World

I. FRESH FIELDS AND PASTURES NEW

II. REFORMATION AND COUNTER REFORMATION

III. POLITICAL AND ECONOMIC CHANGES

IV. THE SEVENTEENTH CENTURY

V. THE POLITICAL DEBATE

There has been a great deal of debate as to the period to which the term Renaissance may legitimately be applied. Professor Haskins has pressed the claims of the twelfth century; Professor Butterfield has put forward those of the seventeenth. The case for each is strong; decision is difficult. A compromise between them would bring us back to the period favored by Michelet and Burckhardt; that is, to the fifteenth century. One point in favor of such an old-fashioned view is that the men of that time thought of themselves as living through a renaissance, a time of renewal which they contrasted with the dark and "gothic" barbarism of the past. They might well have written, with Shelley, that

> *The world's great age begins anew,*
> *The golden years return,*
> *The earth doth like a snake renew*
> *Her winter weeds outworn:*
> *Heaven smiles, and faiths and empires gleam*
> *Like wrecks of a dissolving dream.*

Certainly much that was new or, at least, refurbished, does seem to appear during this busy, bubbling period when in retrospect Heaven does seem to have smiled briefly upon Europe, even if the smile was only wryly ironical.

I. Fresh Fields and Pastures New

The documents that follow originated in the confused and busy period which we like to call the Renaissance. No period has only one aspect or mood, but in the long run every period can be defined in terms of the trend which proves to have been dominant or historically most significant. Thus, we can see these years as a time of questioning and re-affirmation, a rediscovery of forms and values which had been sub-merged since the barbarian invasions, a sense of emerging from the dark "gothic" ages into the sunlight of a new world—broadened by new dis-coveries, enriched by new enterprises, invested with a new significance. We may or may not agree, but to many intellectuals of the time—and to many nonintellectuals too—this seemed a better world to live in, a forward-looking world in which man, who had already accomplished so much, might be expected to accomplish yet more.

1. THE NEW MAN

Giovanni Pico della Mirandola (1463–1494) distinguished himself during his brief career by the precocity of his learning and the boldness of his ideas in philoso-phy and theology. His motto, *De omni re scibili* [Of all things that one can know], asserted that he knew all there was to be known; and though a doubt is permissible on that score, the claim itself seems to reflect a characteristic attitude of his time in which the borders between confidence and foolhardiness were very ill-defined.

Pico della Mirandola: *Oration on the Dignity of Man*

In the writings of the Arabs I have read, oh reverend Fathers [of the Church], that when someone asked the Saracen Abdalah what seemed to him the most wonderful thing in this theater of the world, he replied that nothing seemed more wonderful than man. The opinion of Mercury agrees with this: "What a miracle, oh Asclepius, is man!" As I was pondering the meaning of these words, the opinions which many had advanced about the greatness of human nature did not satisfy me—that man is the mediator of all creatures, the servant of superior beings, the lord of inferior ones, that he is the interpreter of nature by the keen-ness of his senses, by rational inquiry, by the light of his intellect; the intermediary between time and eternity, and, as the Persians say, the nexus of the world, its very wedding song; according to David a little lower than the angels. These are great reasons, to be sure, but they are not the most important. It is not those which give man the privilege of unlimited ad-miration to men. Indeed, why not, there-

From Pico della Mirandola, *Oration on the Dignity of Man* (1486), tr. Dr. D. Weinstein; reprinted by courtesy of the translator.

fore admire the angels and the blessed heavenly choirs even more?

But at last it seems that I have understood why man is the most fortunate of creatures and therefore worthy of all admiration, and what is the position which has been granted him in the universal order, so that not only the beasts but even the stars and the other worldly intelligences envy him. Incredible and marvelous! And why not, if it is indeed for that that he is considered to be a great miracle and a wonderful creature? But what this position is, listen, oh Fathers, if you please, to my discourse and grant it a favorable hearing.

The most high Father, God the Creator, had wrought this worldly home which we see, this august temple of divinity, according to the laws of his secret wisdom. He furnished the supercelestial region with intelligences, the celestial sphere he provided with eternal souls, the filthy and disgusting parts of the lower world he populated with a great assortment of creatures of every species. But, when the work was finished, the Creator wanted some one to reflect upon the reason behind such a great creation, who might love its beauty and marvel over its grandeur. And therefore, when everything was finished, as Moses and Timaeus attest, he thought at last of creating man. However, there was not one model left by which he might fashion a new offspring; there was nothing left in the treasury with which he could endow this new son. There was no station in all the world where this contemplator of the universe could sit. All were full; everything had been distributed to the highest, the middle and the lowest orders. But it was not fitting of the paternal power to have been worn out in the last act of creation. It was not worthy of his wisdom to have been left perplexed

over an important problem. Nor was it fitting to his provident love that the creature who was to have praised his divine liberality to others was compelled to complain of the lack of it to himself. At last that excellent creator decided that he to whom he was to give nothing for his own could share everything which had been given individually to the others. Thus he took man as the product of an undetermined nature and placed him in the middle of the world and said to him: "I have not given you, oh Adam, a definite seat or a special appearance, or any function of your own. The seat or the appearance or the function which you want, you may have and keep by your own desire and your own counsel.

"The other creatures have a defined nature which is fixed within limits prescribed by me. You, unhampered, may determine your own limits according to your own will, into whose power I have placed you. I have set you in the center of the world; from there you can better see whatever is in the world. I have made you neither heavenly nor terrestrial, neither mortal nor immortal, in order that, like a free and sovereign artificer, you can fashion your own form out of your own substance. You can degenerate to the lower orders of the brutes; you can, according to your own will, recreate yourself in those higher creatures which are divine."

Oh supreme generosity of God the Father! Oh supreme and wonderful felicity of man, to whom it is granted to have what he desires, to be what he wishes! The brutes receive all that they have from their mother's womb when they are born, as Lucullus says. The supreme spirits become either immediately or soon afterward that which they were destined to be for all eternity. At the time of man's birth the Father plants every kind of seed and the germs of every kind of existence; and the ones which each man cultivates are the ones which will grow, and they will bear their fruit in him. If they are vegetative, he will be a plant; if animal, he will be a brute; if they are rational, he will become a celestial creature; if intellectual, he will be an angel and the son of God. But if, not content with the lot of any kind of creature, he draws into the center of his own unity, his spirit will become one with God. In the solitary darkness of the Father he who has been set above all things will stand above all things. Who will not admire our chameleon? Or rather, who will admire anything more? Of him Asclepius the Athenian said, with justice, that, in religious rites, because of his versatility and his changeable nature, he symbolized Proteus. Hence those famous metamorphoses among the Hebrews and the Pythagoreans. In fact, the esoteric theology of the Jews at one moment transforms St. Enoch into an angel of divinity. Then, others into other divine spirits. The Pythagoreans changed wicked men into beasts and (if Empedocles is to be believed) even into plants. In imitation of that Mahomet frequently repeated, and rightly, that he who retreated from the sacred law became a brute. For it is not the bark which makes the tree but the stupid and insensitive nature; not the hide which makes the mule but the brutish and sensual soul. It is not separation from the body that makes an angel, but spiritual intelligence. If you see someone who is a slave of his stomach, crawling on the ground, it is a plant that you see, not a man. If you see someone blinded like Callypso by vain illusions of fantasy and emprisoned by dark allurements, the slave of his senses, he is a brute, not a man. If

he is a philosopher who looks at everything with reason, you will revere him: he is a heavenly creature, not an earthbound one. If he is a pure contemplative, unaware of his body, given over to mental perceptions, he is not an earthly nor a celestial creature, he is a more exalted spirit, surrounded by human flesh. And who would not admire the man who in the Old and New Testament is called, and rightly, first with the name of all flesh, then with the name of every creature, because he shapes, creates, and transforms himself into the appearance of every kind of flesh and into the nature of every kind of creature. So the Persian, Evantes writes, where he explains chaldaean theology, that man does not have any image of his very own but many exterior and foreign ones. Hence the saying of the Chaldeans that man is an animal of varying nature, multiform and inconstant. What of all this? It is that we may understand that from the time that we are born in this condition we are what we wish to be. We should take care that it be not said of us that, being honored, we did not realize we have become similar to brutes and foolish jackasses. Let rather the words of Asaph be repeated: "You are Gods, and you are all children of heaven," lest, abusing the indulgent generosity of the Father, we render harmful rather than salutary that choice liberty which he has given us. Let a sacred ambition enter our souls so that we do not satisfy ourselves with mediocre things, but aspire to the highest things, and strive with all our strength to reach them. From the moment that we wish it, we can. Let us despise earthly objects, let us disdain celestial ones, and leaving aside whatever is worldly, let us soar to that supramundane court which is close to the most high divinity. There, according to the sacred mysteries, the Seraphim, Cherubim, and Thrones have the primacy. Unable to give up, and impatient of second place, let us emulate their dignity and glory and, if we desire it, we shall be in no way inferior to them.

2. THE NEW STATE

Niccolò Machiavelli (1469–1527) is one of the most interesting writers of the Italian Renaissance and one of the most controversial. Born in Florence, he engaged in the politics and the diplomacy of the powerful republic, wrote its history, found himself in exile when his opponents, the Medici, returned to power. *The Prince* (1513) is not a work of advice so much as of observation. Machiavelli does not offer his ideas of what is good, but his impressions or conclusions of what seems to work. It is just this amoral quality of the essay that has shocked so many of his readers, though it fascinated others. (Catherine de Médicis, Francis Bacon, Richelieu, Spinoza, Napoleon, count among his admirers.)

Machiavelli: from *The Prince*

OF NEW PRINCEDOMS ACQUIRED BY THE AID OF OTHERS AND BY GOOD FORTUNE

They who from a private station become Princes by mere good fortune, do so with little trouble, but have much trouble to maintain themselves. They meet with no hindrance on their way, being carried as it were on wings, but all their difficulties arise when they arrive. Of this class are those on whom States are conferred either in return for money or through the favour of him who confers them; as it happened to many who were made Princes by Darius in the Greek cities of Ionia and the Hellespont, so that they might hold them for his security and glory; and as happened in the case of those Emperors who, from privacy, attained the Imperial dignity by corrupting the army. Such Princes are wholly dependent on the favour and fortunes of those who have made them great, though no supports could be less stable or less secure than these; and they lack both the knowledge and the power that would enable them to maintain their position. They lack the knowledge, because unless they have great parts and force of character, it is not to be expected that having always lived in a private station they should have learned how to command. They lack the power, since they cannot look for support from attached and faithful troops. Moreover, States suddenly acquired, like all else that is produced and grows up rapidly, can never have such root or hold as that the first storm that strikes them shall not overthrow them; unless, indeed, as I have said already, they who thus suddenly become Princes have a capacity for learning quickly how to defend what Fortune has placed in their lap, and can lay those foundations after their rise which by others are laid before.

Of each of these methods of becoming a Prince, namely by valour and by good

From Machiavelli, *The Prince,* adapted from the London edition of 1674.

fortune, I shall give you an example from times we can remember: the cases of Francesco Sforza and Cesare Borgia. By suitable measures and a great deal of ability, Francesco Sforza rose from privacy to be Duke of Milan, preserving with little trouble what it cost him infinite efforts to gain. On the other hand, Cesare Borgia, vulgarly spoken of as Duke Valentino, obtained his Princedom through the favourable fortunes of his father, and with these lost it, although, so far as in him lay, he used every effort and practised every expedient that a prudent and able man should, who desires to strike root in a State given him by the arms and fortune of another. For, as I have already said, he who does not lay his foundations at first, may if he be of great parts, succeed in laying them afterwards, though with inconvenience to the builder and risk to the building. And if we consider the various measures taken by Duke Valentino, we shall perceive how broad were the foundations he had laid whereon to rest his future power.

I do not think it superfluous to examine these, since I know not what lessons I could teach a new Prince more useful than the example of his actions. And if the measures taken by him did not profit him in the end, it was through no fault of his, but from the extraordinary and extreme malignity of Fortune.

In his efforts to aggrandize the Duke his son, Alexander VI had to face many difficulties, both immediate and remote. In the first place, he saw no way to make him Lord of any State which was not a State of the Church, while, if he sought to take for him a State belonging to the Church, he knew that the Duke of Milan and the Venetians would not consent: Faenza and Rimini being already under the protection of the latter. Further, he

saw that the arms of Italy, and those more especially whereof he might have availed himself, were in the hands of men who had reason to fear his aggrandizement, that is, of the Orsini, the Colonnesi, and their followers. These, therefore, he could not trust. It was consequently necessary that the existing order of things should be changed, and the States of Italy embroiled, in order that he might safely make himself master of some part of them; and this became easy for him when he found that the Venetians, moved by other causes, were plotting to bring the French once more into Italy. This design he accordingly did not oppose, but furthered by annulling the first marriage of the French King.

King Louis, therefore, came into Italy at the instance of the Venetians and with the consent of Pope Alexander, and no sooner was he in Milan than the Pope got troops from him to aid him in his enterprise against Romagna, which Province, moved by the reputation of the French arms, at once submitted. After thus obtaining possession of Romagna, and defeating the Colonnesi, Duke Valentino wanted to follow up and extend his conquests. Two causes, however, held him back, namely, the doubtful fidelity of his own forces, and the waywardness of France. For he feared that the Orsini, of whose arms he had made use, might let him down, and not merely prove a hindrance to further acquisitions, but take from him what he had gained, and that the King might do him the same turn. How little he could count on the Orsini was made plain when, after the capture of Faenza, he directed his arms against Bologna, and saw how reluctantly they took part in that enterprise. The King's mind he understood, when, after seizing on the Dukedom of Urbino, he was about to attack Tuscany; from which attempt Louis made him desist. Whereupon the Duke resolved to depend no longer on the arms or fortune of others. His first step, therefore, was to weaken the factions of the Orsini and Colonnesi in Rome. Those of their following who were of good birth, he gained over by making them his own gentlemen, assigning them a liberal provision, and conferring upon them commands and appointments suited to their quality; so that in a few months their old partisan attachments died out, and the hopes of all rested on the Duke alone.

He then waited for a chance to crush the chiefs of the Orsini, for those of the house of Colonna he had already scattered, and a good opportunity presenting itself, he turned it to the best account. For when the Orsini came at last to see that the greatness of the Duke and the Church involved their ruin, they assembled a council at Magione in the Perugian territory, whence resulted the revolt of Urbino, commotions in Romagna, and an infinity of dangers to the Duke, all of which he overcame with the help of France. His credit thus restored, the Duke, trusting no longer to the French or to other foreign aid, that he might not have to confront them openly, resorted to stratagem, and was so well able to dissemble his designs, that the Orsini, through the mediation of Signor Paolo (whom he failed not to secure by every friendly attention, furnishing him with clothes, money, and horses) were so won over as to be drawn in their simplicity into his hands at Sinigaglia.[1] The leaders thus disposed of, and their followers made his friends, the Duke had laid sufficiently good foundations for his future power, since he held all Romagna together with the Dukedom of Urbino, and had ingra-

[1] Where they were murdered.

tiated himself with the entire population of these States, more especially of Romagna, who now began to see that they were well off.

And since this part of his conduct merits both attention and imitation, I shall not pass it over in silence. After the Duke had taken Romagna, finding that it had been ruled by feeble Lords, who thought more of plundering than correcting their subjects, and gave them more cause for division than for union, so that the country was overrun with robbery, riot, and every kind of outrage, he judged it necessary, with a view to render it peaceful and obedient to his authority, to provide it with a good government. Accordingly he set over it Messer Remiro d'Orca, a stern and prompt ruler, who being entrusted with the fullest powers, in a very short time, and with much credit to himself, restored it to tranquillity and order. But afterwards apprehending that such unlimited authority might become odious, the Duke decided that it was no longer needed, and established in the centre of the Province a civil Tribunal, with an excellent President, in which every town was represented by its advocate. And knowing that past severities had created ill-feeling against himself, in order to purge the minds of the people and gain their goodwill, he tried to show them that any cruelty which had been done had not originated with him, but in the harsh character of his minister. Availing himself of the pretext this afforded, he one morning caused Remiro to be beheaded and exposed in the market place of Cesena with a block and bloody axe by his side—a savage spectacle which at once astounded and satisfied the populace.

But, returning to the point from which we diverged, I say that the Duke, finding himself fairly strong and in a measure secured against present dangers, being furnished with arms of his own choosing and having to a great extent got rid of those which, if left near him, might have caused him trouble, had to consider, if he desired to follow up his conquests, how he was to deal with France, since he saw he could expect no further support from King Louis, whose eyes were at last opened to his mistake. He therefore began to look about for new alliances, and to waver in his adherence to the French, then engaged in an expedition into the kingdom of Naples against the Spaniards, who were besieging Gaeta; his object being to secure himself against France; and in this he would soon have succeeded had Alexander lived.

Such was the line he took to meet present needs. As regards the future, he had to fear that a new Head of the Church might not be his friend, and might even seek to deprive him of what Alexander had given. This he thought to provide against in four ways. First, by exterminating all who were of kin to those Lords whom he had despoiled of their possessions, thereby leaving the new Pope no occasion for interference. Second, by gaining over all the Romans of good birth, so as to be able, as has been said, with their aid to hold the Pope in check. Third, by bringing the College of Cardinals, so far as possible, under his control. And fourth, by establishing his authority so firmly before his father's death, that he could by himself withstand the shock of a first onset.

Of these four objects, at the time when Alexander died, he had already effected three, and had almost carried out the fourth. For of the Lords whose possessions he had usurped, he had put to death all whom he could reach, and very few had escaped. He had gained over the Ro-

man nobility, and had the majority in the College of Cardinals on his side.

As to further acquisitions, his plan was to make himself master of Tuscany. He was already in possession of Perugia and Piombino, and had assumed the protectorate of Pisa, on which city he was about to spring, taking no heed of France, as indeed he no longer had occasion, since the French had been deprived of the kingdom of Naples by the Spaniards under conditions which made it necessary for both powers to buy his friendship. Pisa taken, Lucca and Siena must at once have yielded, partly through jealousy of Florence, partly through fear, and the position of the Florentines would then have been desperate.

If he had succeeded in these designs, as he was succeeding in that very year in which Alexander died, he would have won such power and reputation that he might afterwards have stood alone, relying on his own strength and resources, without being beholden to the forces and fortune of others. But Alexander died five years from the time he first unsheathed the sword, leaving his son with the State of Romagna alone consolidated, with all the rest unsettled, between two most powerful hostile armies, and sick almost to death. And yet such were the fire and courage of the Duke, he knew so well how men must either be conciliated or crushed, and so solid were the foundations he had laid in that brief period, that had these armies not been upon his back, or had he been in sound health, he must have surmounted every difficulty.

How strong his foundations were may be seen from this, that Romagna waited for him more than a month; and that although half dead, he remained in safety in Rome, where though the Baglioni, the Vitelli, and the Orsini came to attack him, they found no support. Moreover, since he was able if not to make whom he would Pope, at least to prevent the election of any whom he disliked, had he been in health at the time when Alexander died, all would have been easy for him. But he told me himself at the time when Julius II was created, that he had foreseen and provided for all else that could happen on his father's death, but had never anticipated that when his father died he too should be at death's door.

Taking all these actions of the Duke together, I can find no fault with him. It seems to me reasonable to put him forward, as I have done, as a pattern for all such as rise to power by good fortune and the help of others. For with his great spirit and high ambition he could not act otherwise than he did, and nothing but the shortness of his father's life and his own illness prevented the success of his designs. Whoever, therefore, on entering a new Princedom, judges it necessary to rid himself of enemies, to conciliate friends, to prevail by force or fraud, to make himself feared yet loved by his subjects, followed and revered by his soldiers, to crush those who can or ought to injure him, to introduce changes in the old order of things, to be at once severe and affable, magnanimous and liberal, to do away with a mutinous army and create a new one, to maintain relations with Kings and Princes on such a footing that they must see it is in their interest to aid him, and dangerous to offend, can find no brighter examples than in the actions of this Prince.

The one thing for which he may be blamed was the creation of Pope Julius II, in respect of whom he chose badly. Because, as I have said already, though he could not secure the election he desired, he could have prevented any other;
and he ought never to have consented to the creation of any one of those Cardinals whom he had injured, or who on becoming Pope would have reason to fear him; for fear is as dangerous an enemy as resentment. Those whom he had offended were, among others, San Pietro ad Vincula, Colonna, San Giorgio, and Ascanio; all the rest, excepting d'Amboise and the Spanish Cardinals (the latter from their being connected and under obligations, the former from the power he derived through his relations with the French Court), would on assuming the Pontificate have had reason to fear him. The Duke, therefore, ought, in the first place, to have laboured for the creation of a Spanish Pope; failing wherein, he should have agreed to the election of d'Amboise, but never to that of San Pietro ad Vincula. And he deceives himself who thinks that with the great, recent benefits cause old wrongs to be forgotten.

The Duke, therefore, erred in the part he took in this election; and his error was the cause of his ultimate downfall.

OF THOSE WHO BY CRIME COME TO BE PRINCES

But since from privacy a man may also rise to be a Prince in one or other of two ways, neither of which can be ascribed wholly either to valour or to fortune, it is fit that I note them here, though one of them may fail to be discussed more fully in treating of Republics.

The ways I speak of are, first, when the ascent to power is made by paths of wickedness and crime; and second, when a private person becomes ruler of his country by the favour of his fellow-citizens. The former method I shall make clear by two examples, one ancient the other modern, without entering further into the merits of the matter, for these, I think, should be enough for anyone who is constrained to follow them.

Agathocles the Sicilian came, not merely from a private station, but from the very dregs of the people, to be King of Syracuse. Son of a potter, through all the stages of his career he led an evil life. His vices, however, were conjoined with so much vigour both of mind and body, that enlisting as a common soldier, he rose through the various grades of the service to be Praetor of Syracuse. Established in that post, he resolved to make himself Prince, and to hold by violence and without obligation to others the authority which had been by consent entrusted to him. Accordingly, after imparting his design to Hamilcar, who with the Carthaginian armies was at that time waging war in Sicily, he one morning assembled the people and senate of Syracuse as though to consult with them on matters of public moment, and on a preconcerted signal caused his soldiers to put to death all the senators, and the wealthiest of the commons. These being thus disposed of, he seized and kept the sovereignty of the city without opposition from the people; and though twice defeated by the Carthaginians, and afterwards besieged, he was able not only to defend his city, but leaving a part of his forces for its protection, to invade Africa with the remainder, and so in a short time to raise the siege of Syracuse, reducing the Carthaginians to the utmost extremities, and forcing them to make terms whereby they resigned Sicily to him and confined themselves to Africa.

Whoever examines this man's actions and achievements will discover little or nothing in them that can be ascribed to chance, seeing, as has already been said,

that it was not through the favour of any one but by the regular steps of the military service, gained at the cost of a thousand hardships and hazards, he reached the Princedom which he afterwards maintained by so many daring and dangerous exploits. Still, to slaughter fellow-citizens, to betray friends, to be devoid of honour, pity, and religion, cannot be counted as merits, for these are means that may lead to power, but confer no glory. Wherefore, if in respect of the valour with which he encountered and extricated himself from dangers, and the constancy of his spirit in supporting and conquering adverse fortune, there seems no reason to judge him inferior to the greatest captains that have ever lived, his unbridled cruelty and inhumanity, together with his countless other crimes, forbid us to number him with the greatest men; but, at any rate, we cannot attribute to luck or to merit what he accomplished without either.

In our own times, during the papacy of Alexander VI, Oliverotto of Fermo, who, left an orphan some years before, had been brought up by his maternal uncle Giovanni Fogliani, was sent while still a lad to serve under Paolo Vitelli, in order that a thorough training under that commander might qualify him for high rank as a soldier. After the death of Paolo, he served under his brother, Vitellozzo, and in a very short time, being quick-witted, hardy, and resolute, he became one of the first soldiers of his company. But he thought it beneath him to serve under others; so, with the support of the Vitelleschi and the connivance of certain citizens of Fermo who preferred the slavery to the freedom of their country, he planned to seize on that town.

He accordingly wrote to Giovanni Fogliani that after many years of absence from home, he desired to see him and his native city once more and to look a little into the condition of his patrimony; and as his one endeavour had been to make himself a name, in order that his fellow-citizens might see his time had not been wasted, he proposed to return honourably attended by a hundred horsemen from among his own friends and followers; and he begged Giovanni graciously to arrange for his reception by the citizens of Fermo with corresponding marks of distinction, as this would be creditable not only to himself, but also to the uncle who had brought him up.

Giovanni, accordingly, did not fail in any proper attention to his nephew, but caused him to be splendidly received by his fellow-citizens, and lodged him in his house; where Oliverotto having passed some days, and made the necessary arrangements for carrying out his wickedness, gave a sumptuous banquet, to which he invited his uncle and all the first men of Fermo. When the repast and the other entertainment proper to such an occasion had come to an end, Oliverotto artfully turned the conversation to matters of grave interest, by speaking of the greatness of Pope Alexander and Cesare his son, and of their enterprises; and when Giovanni and the others were replying to what he said, he suddenly rose, observing that these were matters to be discussed in a more private place, and so moved to another room; whither his uncle and the other citizens followed him, and where they had no sooner seated themselves, than soldiers rushing out from places of concealment slew Giovanni and all the others.

After this butchery, Oliverotto mounting his horse, rode through the streets, and besieged the chief magistrate in the place, so that all were forced by fear to submit and accept a government of which he made himself the head. And all who from being disaffected, were likely to stand in his way, he put to death, while he strengthened himself with new ordinances, civil and military, to such effect, that for the space of a year during which he retained the Princedom, he not merely remained safe in Fermo, but grew formidable to all his neighbours. And it would have been as difficult to unseat him as to unseat Agathocles, had he not let himself be overreached by Cesare Borgia on the occasion when, as has already been told, the Orsini and Vitelli were entrapped at Sinigaglia; where he too being taken, one year after the commission of his parricidal crime, was strangled along with Vitellozzo, who had been his master in villainy as in valour.

It may be asked how it came that Agathocles and some like him, after numberless acts of treachery and cruelty, were able to live long in their own country in safety, and defend themselves from foreign enemies, without being conspired against by their fellow-citizens, whereas, many others, by reason of their cruelty, have failed to maintain their position even in peaceful times, not to speak of the perilous times of war. I believe that this results from cruelty being well or ill used. Those cruelties we may say are well used, if we may speak well of things evil, which are done once for all as necessary for your security, and are not afterwards persisted in, but so far as possible adapted to the advantage of the governed. Ill-used cruelties, on the other hand, are those which from small beginnings increase rather than diminish with time. Those who follow the first of these methods, may, by the grace of God and man, find, as Agathocles did, that their condition is not desperate; but by no possibility can the others maintain themselves.

Hence we may learn the lesson that on seizing a State, the usurper should plan ahead all the injuries he must inflict, and inflict them all at a stroke, that he may not have to renew them daily, but be enabled by their discontinuance to reassure men's minds and win them by benefits. Whosoever, either through timidity or from following bad counsels, acts otherwise, must keep the sword always drawn, and can put no trust in his subjects, who suffering from continued and constantly renewed severities can never feel sure of him. Injuries, therefore, should be inflicted all at once, that their ill savour being less lasting may less offend; whereas, benefits should be conferred little by little, that so they may be more fully relished.

But, before all things, a Prince should so live with his subjects that no vicissitude for better or worse shall cause him to alter his behaviour; for if the need to change come through adversity, it is too late to resort to severity; and any leniency you may then use will be wasted, since it will be seen to be compulsory and bring you no thanks.

OF THE QUALITIES FOR WHICH MEN, AND MOST OF ALL PRINCES, ARE PRAISED OR BLAMED

It now remains for us to consider what ought to be the conduct and bearing of a Prince in relation to his subjects and friends. And since I know that many have written on this subject, I fear it may be thought presumptuous in me to write of it also; the more so, because in my treatment of it, I depart widely from the views that others have taken.

But since it is my object to write what shall be useful to whosoever understands it, it seems to me better to follow the real truth of things than an imaginary view of them. For many Republics and Principalities have been imagined that were never seen or known to really exist. And the way in which we live, and that in which we ought to live, are things so wide apart, that he who leaves the one for the other is more likely to destroy than to save himself; since any one who would act up to a perfect standard of goodness in everything, must be ruined among so many who are not good. It is essential, therefore, for a Prince who would maintain his position, to have learned how to be other than good, and to use or not to use his goodness as necessity requires.

Laying aside, therefore, all fanciful notions concerning a Prince, and considering those only that are true, I say that all men when they are spoken of, and Princes more than others from their being set so high, are noted for certain of those qualities which attach either praise or blame. Thus one is accounted liberal, another miserly; one is generous, another greedy; one cruel, another tenderhearted; one is faithless, another true to his word; one effeminate and cowardly, another high-spirited and courageous; one is courteous, another haughty; one lewd, another chaste; one upright, another crafty; one firm, another facile; one grave, another frivolous; one devout, another unbelieving; and the like. Everyone, I know, will admit that it would be most laudable for a Prince to be endowed with all of the above qualities that are reckoned good; but since it is impossible for him to possess or constantly practise them all, the conditions of human nature not allowing it, he must be discreet enough to know how to avoid the reproach of those vices that would deprive him of his government, and, if possible, be on his guard also against those which might not deprive him of it. Though if he cannot wholly restrain himself, he may with less scruple indulge in the latter. But he need never hesitate to incur the reproach of those vices without which his authority can hardly be preserved; for if he well considers the whole matter, he will find that there may be a line of conduct that looks like virtue, but which would ruin him; and that there may be another course that looks like vice on which his safety and well-being may depend.

OF LIBERALITY AND MISERLINESS

Beginning, then, with the first of the qualities above noticed, I say that it may be well to be reputed liberal but that liberality without a reputation for it is bad; since, though it be worthily and rightly used, still if it be not known, you escape not the reproach of its opposite vice. Thus, to have credit for liberality with the world at large, you must neglect no circumstance of sumptuous display; the result being that a Prince who would be thought liberal will consume his whole substance in things of this sort and after all be obliged, if he would maintain his reputation for liberality, to burden his subjects with extraordinary taxes and resort to confiscations and all the other shifts whereby money is raised. But in this way he becomes hateful to his subjects, and growing impoverished is held in little esteem by any. So that in the end, having by his liberality offended many and obliged few, he is no better off than when he began, and exposed to all his original dangers. Recognizing this, and trying to retrace his steps, he at once incurs the reproach of miserliness.

A Prince, therefore, since he cannot without injury to himself practise this virtue of liberality so that it may be known, will not, if he is wise, greatly concern himself though he be called miserly. Because in time he will come to be regarded as more and more liberal, when it is seen that through his parsimony his revenues are sufficient; that he is able to defend himself against any who make war on him; that he can engage in enterprises against others without burdening his subjects; and thus exercise liberality towards all from whom he does not take, whose number is infinite, while he is miserly in respect of those only to whom he does not give, whose number is small.

In our own days we have seen no Princes accomplish great results save those who have been accounted miserly. All others have been ruined. Pope Julius II, after using his reputation for liberality to arrive at the Papacy, made no effort to preserve that reputation when making war on the King of France but carried on all his many campaigns without levying from his subjects a single extraordinary tax, providing for the increased expenditure out of his long-continued savings. Had the present King of Spain been accounted liberal, he never could have engaged or succeeded in so many enterprises.

A Prince, therefore, if he is enabled thereby to avoid plundering his subjects, to defend himself, to escape poverty and contempt and the necessity of becoming rapacious, ought to care little about the reproach of miserliness, for this is one of those vices which enable him to reign.

And should any object that Caesar by his liberality rose to power and that many others have been advanced to the highest dignities from their having been liberal and so reputed, I reply, "Either you are already a Prince or you seek to become one; in the former case liberality is hurtful, in the latter it is very necessary that you be thought liberal; Caesar was one of those who sought the sovereignty of Rome; but if after obtaining it he had lived on without retrenching his expenditure, he must have ruined the Empire." And if it be further urged that many Princes reputed to have been most liberal have achieved great things with their armies, I answer that a Prince spends either what belongs to himself and his subjects, or what belongs to others; and that in the former case he ought to be sparing but in the latter ought not to refrain from any kind of liberality. Because for a Prince who leads his armies in person and maintains them by plunder, pillage, and forced contributions, dealing as he does with the property of others, this liberality is necessary, since otherwise he would not be followed by his soldiers. "Of what does not belong to you or to your subjects you may, therefore, be a lavish giver, as were Cyrus, Caesar, and Alexander, for to be liberal with the property of others does not take from your reputation, but adds to it. What injures you is to give away what is your own." And there is no quality so self-destructive as liberality; for while you practise it you lose the means whereby it can be practised, and become poor and despised, or else, to avoid poverty, you become rapacious and hated. For liberality leads to one or other of these two results, against which, beyond all others, a Prince should guard.

And hence it is wiser to put up with the name of being miserly, which breeds ignominy, but without hate, than be obliged, from the desire to be reckoned liberal, to incur the reproach of rapacity, which breeds both hate and ignominy.

OF CRUELTY AND CLEMENCY, AND WHETHER IT IS BETTER TO BE LOVED OR FEARED

Passing to the other qualities above mentioned, I say that every Prince should desire to be accounted merciful and not cruel. Nevertheless, he should be careful not to abuse this quality of mercy. Cesare Borgia was reputed cruel, yet his cruelty restored Romagna, united it, and brought it to order and obedience; so that if we look at things in their true light, it will be seen that he was in reality far more merciful than the people of Florence, who, to avoid the imputation of cruelty, suffered Pistoja to be destroyed by factions.

A Prince should therefore disregard the reproach of cruelty where it enables him to keep his subjects united and faithful. For he who puts down disorder by a minimum of striking examples, will in the end be more merciful than he who from excessive leniency suffers things to take their course and so result in rapine and bloodshed; for these hurt the entire State, whereas the severities of the Prince injure individuals only.

And for a new Prince, above all others, it is impossible to escape a name for cruelty, since new States are full of dangers. . . .

Nevertheless, the new Prince should not be too ready of belief, nor too easily influenced. Nor should he himself be the first to raise alarms; but should so temper prudence with kindliness that too great confidence in others shall not throw him off his guard, nor groundless distrust render him insupportable.

And here comes in the question whether it is better to be loved rather than feared, or feared rather than loved. It might be answered that we should wish to be both; but since love and fear can hardly exist together, if we must choose between them, it is far safer to be feared than loved. For of men it may generally be said that they are thankless, fickle, false, studious to avoid danger, greedy of gain, devoted to you while you confer benefits upon them, and ready, as I said before, while the need is remote, to shed their blood and sacrifice their property, their lives, and their children for you; but when it comes near they turn against you. The Prince, therefore, who without otherwise securing himself builds wholly on what men say or promise is undone. For the friendships we buy with a price and not gain by greatness and nobility of character, though fairly earned, are not made good but fail us when we need them most.

Moreover, men are less careful how they offend him who makes himself loved than him who makes himself feared. For love is held by the tie of obligation, which, because men are a poor lot, is broken on every prompting of self-interest; but fear is bound by the apprehension of punishment which never loosens its grasp.

Nevertheless a Prince should inspire fear so that if he do not win love he may escape hate. For a man may very well be feared and yet not hated, as will always be the case so long as he does not intermeddle with the property or with the women of his citizens and subjects. And if forced to put any one to death, he should do so only when there is manifest cause or reasonable justification. But, above all, he must keep his hands off the property of others. For men will sooner forget the death of their father than the loss of their patrimony. Moreover, excuses for confiscation are never hard to find, and he who has once started to live by rapine always finds reasons for taking what is not his; whereas reasons for shed-

ding blood are fewer and sooner exhausted.

But when a Prince is with his army, and has many soldiers under his command, he must wholly disregard the reproach of cruelty, for without such a reputation in its Captain, you cannot hold an army together, ready for every emergency. Among other things remarkable in Hannibal this has been noted, that having a very great army, made up of men of many different nations and brought to serve in a foreign country, no dissension ever arose among the soldiers themselves, nor any mutiny against their leader, either in his good or in his evil fortunes. This we can only ascribe to the tremendous cruelty, which, joined with numberless great qualities, rendered him at once wonderful and terrible in the eyes of his soldiers; for without this reputation for cruelty his other virtues would not have had the results they did.

Unreflecting writers, indeed, while praising his achievements, have condemned the chief cause of them; but that his other merits would not by themselves have been so useful we may see from the case of Scipio, one of the greatest Captains of all times, whose armies rose against him in Spain from no other cause than his excessive leniency in allowing them freedoms inconsistent with military discipline. With which weakness Fabius Maximus taxed him in the Senate House, calling him the corrupter of the Roman soldiery. Again, when the Locrians were shamefully outraged by one of his lieutenants, he neither avenged them nor punished the insolence of his officer; and this because he was so easy-going. So that it was said in the Senate by one who tried to excuse him, that there were many who knew better how to refrain from doing wrong themselves than how to correct the wrong-doing of others. This temper, however, would in time have spoiled the name and fame even of Scipio, if he had continued in it, and retained his command. But living as he did under the control of the Senate, this hurtful quality was not merely veiled but came to be regarded as a glory.

Returning to the question of being loved or feared, I sum up by saying, that since his being loved depends upon his subjects, while his being feared depends upon himself, a wise Prince should build on what is his own and not on what rests with others. Only, as I have said, he must do his best to escape hatred.

HOW PRINCES SHOULD KEEP FAITH

Every one recognises how praiseworthy it is in a Prince to keep faith, and to act uprightly and not craftily. Nevertheless, we see from what has happened in our own days that Princes who have set little store by their word but have known how to overreach others by their cunning, have accomplished great things and in the end had the better of those who trusted to honest dealing.

It should be known, then, that there are two ways of acting, one in accordance with the laws, the other by force; the first of which is proper to men, the second to beasts. But since the first method is often ineffectual, it becomes necessary to resort to the second. A Prince should, therefore, understand how to use well both the man and the beast. And this lesson has been discreetly taught by the ancient writers, who relate how Achilles and many others of these old Princes were given over to be brought up and trained by Chiron the Centaur; since the only meaning of their having for teacher one who was half man

and half beast is, that it is necessary for a Prince to know how to use both natures and that the one without the other has no stability.

But since a Prince should know how to use the beast's nature wisely, he ought of beasts to choose both the lion and the fox; for the lion cannot guard himself from traps, nor the fox from wolves. He must therefore be a fox to discern traps, and a lion to drive off wolves.

To rely wholly on the lion is unwise; and for this reason a prudent Prince neither can nor ought to keep his word, when to keep it is hurtful to him and the causes which led him to give it are removed. If all men were good, this would not be good advice, but since they are dishonest and do not keep faith with you, you in return need not keep faith with them; and no Prince was ever at a loss for plausible reasons to cover a breach of faith. Of this infiniteness recent instances could be given, and it might be shown how many solemn treaties and engagements have been made empty and idle through want of faith in Princes and that he who has best known to play the fox has had the best success.

It is necessary, indeed, to put a good colour on this nature, and to be skillful in feigning and dissembling. But men are so simple and governed so absolutely by their present needs, that he who wishes to deceive will never fail in finding willing dupes. One recent example I will not omit. Pope Alexander VI had no care or thought but how to deceive, and always found material to work on. No man ever had a more effective manner of affirming things, or made promises with more solemn protestations, or observed them less. And yet, because he understood this side of human nature, his frauds always succeeded.

It is not essential, then, that a Prince should have all the good qualities I have enumerated above, but it is most essential that he should seem to have them. As a matter of fact I will venture to affirm that if he has and invariably practises them all, they are hurtful, whereas the appearance of having them is useful. Thus, it is well to seem merciful, faithful, humane, religious, and upright, and also to be so; but the mind should remain so balanced that were it needful not to be so, you should be able and know how to change to the contrary.

And you are to understand that a Prince, and most of all a new Prince, cannot observe all those rules of conduct in respect of which men are considered good; since he is often forced to act in opposition to good faith, charity, humanity, and religion in order to preserve his Princedom, he must therefore keep his mind ready to shift as the winds and tides of Fortune turn, and, as I have already said, ought not to leave good courses if he can help it but should know how to follow evil if he must.

A Prince should therefore be very careful that nothing ever escapes his lips which is not full of the five qualities above named, so that to see and hear him, one would think him the embodiment of mercy, good faith, integrity, kindliness, and religion. And there is no virtue which it is more necessary for him to seem to possess than this last; because men in general judge rather by the eye than by the hand, for all can see but few can touch. Every one sees what you seem, but few know what you are, and these few dare not oppose themselves to the opinion of the many who have the majesty of the State to back them up.

Moreover, in the actions of all men, and most of all of Princes, where there is no tribunal to which we can appeal, we look to results. Wherefore if a Prince succeeds in establishing and maintaining his authority, the means will always be judged honourable and be approved by every one. For the vulgar are always taken by appearances and by results, and the world is made up of the vulgar, the few only finding room when the many have no longer ground to stand on.

A certain Prince of our own days, whom it is as well not to name,[1] is always preaching peace and good faith, although he is the mortal enemy of both; and both, had he practised as he preaches, would, oftener than once, have lost him his kingdom and authority.

[1] Ferdinand of Aragon.

3. THE NEW EDUCATION

François Rabelais (1494–1553), Franciscan friar, Benedictine monk, doctor, professor of anatomy for a while, had a learned and inquisitive mind, representative of the best in French humanism. Quite a traveler, he was responsible for the introduction into western Europe of the Roman lettuce, but his surviving fame depends less on his medical studies or his culinary exploits than on the enduring popularity of the happy and lunatic world of giants and heroes he created in *Gargantua and Pantagruel*. The books describing their adventures have been banned repeatedly since the Sorbonne first placed *Pantagruel* on its *Index* in 1533. They are supposed to be coarse; they are certainly robust and rambunctious. But fundamentally Rabelais is a serious man and a critic of society, and the fun he makes of the pretensions of his day often applies just as well to ours. The selections that follow reflect the contemporary debate between the old-fashioned techniques of education and the new ideas of the humanists.

Rabelais: from *Gargantua and Pantagruel*

THE STUDY OF GARGANTUA, ACCORDING TO THE DISCIPLINE OF HIS SCHOOLMASTERS THE SOPHISTERS

The first day being thus spent and the bells put up again in their own place, the citizens of Paris, in acknowledgment of this courtesy, offered to maintain and feed his mare as long as he pleased, which Cargantua took in good part, and they sent her to graze in the forest of Bière. I think she is not there now. This done, he with all his heart submitted his study to the discretion of Ponocrates; who first of all appointed that he should do as he was accustomed, to the end it might be understood by what means, in so long time, his old masters had made him such a sot and puppy. He disposed therefore of his time in such fashion that ordinarily he did awake betwixt eight and nine o'clock, whether it was day or night (for so had his ancient governors ordained), alleging that which David saith, *Vanum est vobis ante lucem surgere.*[1] Then did he tumble and toss, wag his legs, and wallow in the bed some time, the better to stir up and rouse his vital spirits, and appareled himself according to the season; but willingly he would wear a great long gown of thick frieze, furred with fox skins. Afterwards he combed his head with a comb *de al-main,* which is the four fingers and the thumb, for his preceptors had said

[1] It is foolish to rise before light.

that to comb himself otherways, to wash and make himself neat, was to lose time in this world. Then he dunged, pissed, spued, belched, cracked, yawned, spitted, coughed, hawked, sneezed, and snotted himself like an archdeacon: and, to fortify against the fog and bad air, went to breakfast, having some good fried tripes, fair rashers on the coals, good gammons of bacon, store of good minced meat, and a great deal of sippet-brewis, made up of the fat of the beef-pot, laid upon bread, cheese, and chopped parsley strewed together.

Ponocrates showed him that he ought not to eat so soon after rising out of his bed, unless he had performed some exercise beforehand. Gargantua answered, "What! have not I sufficiently well exercised myself? I have wallowed and rolled myself six or seven turns in my bed, before I rose; is not that enough? Pope Alexander did so, by the advice of a Jew his physician, and lived till his dying day in despite of his enemies. My first masters have used me to it, saying, that to eat breakfast made a good memory; and therefore they drank first. I am very well after it, and dine but the better. And Master Tubal (who was the first licentiate at Paris) told me, that it was not enough to run apace, but to set forth betimes. So the total welfare of our humidity doth not depend upon drinking, switter-swatter like ducks, but in being at it early in the morning; hence the verse,

From Rabelais, *Gargantua and Pantagruel* (Chaps. XXI, XXIII), 1876.

To rise betimes is good for nothing,
To drink betimes is meat and clothing."

After a good breakfast he went to church, and they carried to him in a great basket a huge breviary, weighing, what in grease, clasps, parchment, and cover, little more or less than eleven hundred and six pounds. There he heard six and twenty or thirty masses. This while, to the same place came his matin-mumbler, muffled up about the chin, round as a hoop, and his breath pretty well antidoted with the vine-tree sirrup. With him he mumbled all his *kiriels,* which he so curiously thumbed and fingered that there fell not so much as one bead of them to the ground. As he went from the church, they brought him, upon a dray drawn with oxen, a confused heap of *patinotres* of Saint Claude, every one of the bigness of a hat-block; and sauntering along through the cloisters, galleries, or garden, he riddled over more of them than sixteen hermits would have done. Then did he study some paltry half hour with his eyes fixed upon his book; but (as the comedy has it) *his mind was in the kitchen.* Pissing then a whole potful, he sat down at table; and because he was naturally phlegmatic, he began his meal with some dozens of gammons, dried neats' tongues, botargos, sausages, and such other forerunners of wine; in the meanwhile, four of his folks did cast into his mouth, one after another continually, mustard by the whole shovels full. Immediately after that, he drank a horrible draught of white wine for the comfort of his kidneys. When that was done, he ate according to the season, meat agreeable to his appetite; and then left off eating when his belly was like to crack for fulness. As for his drinking, he had in that neither end nor

rule; for he was wont to say that the limits and bounds of drinking were, that a man might drink till the cork of his shoes swells up half a foot high.

HOW GARGANTUA WAS INSTRUCTED BY PONOCRATES, AND IN SUCH SORT DISCIPLINATED, THAT HE LOST NOT ONE HOUR OF THE DAY

When Ponocrates knew Gargantua's vicious manner of living, he resolved to bring him up in another way; but for a while bore with him, considering that Nature cannot endure a sudden change without great violence. Therefore, to begin his work the better he requested a learned physician of that time, called Master Theodore, seriously to ponder, if it were possible, how to bring Gargantua unto a better course; the said physician purged him canonically with Anticyrian hellebore, by which medicine he cleansed all that foulness and perverse habit of his brain. By this means, also, Ponocrates made him forget all that he had learned under his ancient preceptors, as Timotheus did to his scholars who had been instructed under other musicians: to do this the better they brought him into the company of learned men, who stirred in him an emulation and desire to whet his wit and improve his parts and to bend his study another way; so that the world might have a value for him. And afterwards he put himself into such a road, that he lost not any one hour in the day, but employed all his time in learning and honest knowledge. Gargantua awaked about four o'clock in the morning. Whilst they were rubbing him down, there was read unto him some chapter of the Holy

Scripture aloud and clearly, with a pronunciation fit for the matter; and hereunto was appointed a young page, born in Basche, named Anagnostes. According to the purpose and argument of that lesson, he oftentimes gave himself to worship, adore, pray, and send up his supplications to that good God, whose word did shew his majesty and marvellous judgment. Then went he unto the secret places to make excretion of his natural digestions; there his master repeated what had been read, expounding unto him the most obscure and difficult points. In returning, they considered the face of the sky, if it were such as they had observed it the night before, and into what signs the sun was entering, as also the moon for that day. This done he was appareled, combed, curled, trimmed, and perfumed, during which time they repeated to him the lessons of the day before; he himself said them by heart, and upon them would ground some practical cases concerning the estate of man, which he would prosecute sometimes two or three hours, but ordinarily they ceased as soon as he was fully clothed. Then for three good hours he had a lecture read unto him: this done, they went forth, still conferring on the substance of the lecture, either unto a field near the University, called the Brack, or unto the meadows, where they played at the ball, tennis, and at the pelitrigone, most gallantly exercising their bodies, as before they had done their minds; all their play was but in liberty, for they left off when they pleased, and that was commonly when they did sweat over all their body, or were otherwise weary. Then were they very well wiped and rubbed, changed their shirts, and walking soberly, went to see if dinner was ready. Whilst they stayed for that, they did clearly and eloquently pronounce some sentences that they had retained of the lecture. In the meantime Master Appetite came, and then very orderly sat they down at table. At the beginning of the meal, there was read some pleasant history of the warlike actions of former times, until he had taken a glass of wine. Then (if they thought good) they continued reading, or began to discourse merrily together; speaking first of the virtue, propriety, efficacy, and nature of all that was served at the table: of bread, of wine, of water, of salt, of fleshes, fishes, fruits, herbs, roots, and of their dressing; by means whereof he learned, in a little time, all the passages competent for this, that were to be found in Pliny, Athenaeus, Dioscorides, Julius Pollux, Galen, Porphyry, Oppian, Polybius, Heliodorus, Aristotle, Elian, and others. Whilst they talked of these things many times, to be more certain they caused the very books to be brought to the table. And so well and perfectly did he in his memory retain the things above said, that in those days there was not a physician that knew half so much as he did. Afterwards they conferred of the lessons read in the morning, and ending their repast with some conserve or marmalade of quinces, he picked his teeth with mastic toothpickers; washed his hands and eyes with fair fresh water, and gave thanks unto God in some neat hymn, made in the praise of the divine bounty and munificence. This done they brought in cards, not to play, but to learn a thousand pretty tricks and new inventions, which were all grounded upon arithmetic. By this means he fell in love with that numerical science, and every day after dinner and supper he passed his time in it as pleasantly as he was wont to do at cards and dice; so that at last he understood so well both the theory and practical part thereof, that Tunstall, the Englishman, who had written very largely to that purpose, confessed that verily, in comparison with him, he understood no more High Dutch.

And not only in that, but in the other mathematical science, as geometry, astronomy, and music. For, in waiting on the concoction, and attending the digestion of his food, they made a thousand pretty instruments and geometrical figures, and did in some measure practice the astronomical canons.

After this they recreated themselves with singing musically, in four or five parts, or upon a set theme or ground at random, as it best pleased them; in matter of musical instruments he learned to play upon the lute, the virginals, the harp, the all-man flute with nine holes, the viol, and the sackbut. This hour thus spent, and digestion finished, he did purge his body of natural excrements; then betook himself to his principal study for three hours together or more, as well to repeat his morning lectures, as to proceed in the book he had in hand, as also to write handsomely, to draw and form the antique and Roman letters. This being done they went abroad, and with them a young gentleman of Touraine, named the Esquire Gymnast, who taught him the art of riding. Changing then his clothes, he rode a Naples courser, a Dutch roussin, a Spanish gennet, a barded, or trapped steed, then a light fleet horse, unto whom he gave a hundred directions, made him try the high jumps, bounding in the air, clear the ditch with a skip, leap over a stile or pale, turn short in a ring both to the right and left hand. There he broke not his lance; for it is the greatest foolery in the world to say I have broken ten lances at tilt, or in fight; a carpenter can

do even as much; but it is a glorious and praiseworthy action, with one lance to break and overthrow ten enemies: therefore with a sharp, stiff, strong, and well-steeled lance would he usually force up a door, pierce a harness, beat down a tree, carry away the ring, lift up a cuirassier saddle, with the mail coat and gauntlet: all this he did in complete armour from head to foot. As for the prancing flourishes and smacking poppisms, for the better cherishing of the horse commonly used in riding, none did them better than he. The great vaulter of Ferrara was but an ape compared to him. He was singularly skilful in leaping nimbly from one horse to another, without putting foot to ground, and these horses were called desultories; he could likewise, from either side, with a lance in his hand, leap on horseback without stirrups, and rule the horse at his pleasure, without a bridle, for such things are useful in military engagements. Another day he exercised the battle-ax, which he so dexterously wielded both in the nimble, strong, and smooth management of that weapon, and in all the feats practisable by it, that he passed knight of arms in the field, and at all essays.

Then tossed he the pike, played with the two-handed sword, with the backsword, with the Spanish tuck, the dagger, poniard, armed or unarmed, with a buckler, with a cloak, with a target.

Then would he hunt the hart, the roebuck, the bear, the fallow deer, the wild boar, the hare, the pheasant, the partridge, and the bustard. He played at the baloon, and made it bound in the air, both with fist and foot.

He wrestled, ran, jumped, not at three steps and a leap, nor at the hare's leap, nor yet at the almanes; "for" said Gymnast, "these jumps are for the wars altogether unprofitable and of no use;" but at one leap he would skip over a ditch, spring over a hedge, mount six paces upon a wall, ramp and grapple after this fashion up against a window, of the full height of a lance. He did swim in deep waters on his belly, on his back, sideways, with all his body, with his feet only, with one hand in the air, wherein he held a book, crossing thus the breadth of the River Seine without wetting it, and dragged along his cloak with his teeth, as did Julius Caesar; then, with the help of one hand he entered forcibly into a boat, from whence he cast himself again headlong into the water, sounded the depths, hollowed the rocks, and plunged into the pits and gulphs. Then turned he the boat about, governed it, led it swiftly or slowly with the stream and against the stream, stopped it in its course, guided it with one hand, and with the other laid hard about him with a huge great oar, hoisted the sail, hied up along the mast by the shrouds, ran upon the edge of the decks, set the compass in order, tackled the bowlines, and steered the helm. Coming out of the water, he ran furiously up against a hill, and with the same alacrity and swiftness ran down again; he climbed up trees like a cat, and leaped from one to the other like a squirrel; he did pull down the great boughs and branches like another Milo; then with two sharp, well-steeled daggers and two tried bodkins, would he run up by the wall to the very top of a house, like a rat; then suddenly came down from the top to the bottom, with such an even composition of members, that by the fall he would catch no harm.

He did cast the dart, throw the bar, put the stone, practise the javelin, the boar-spear, or partisan, and the halbert; he broke the strongest bows in drawing, bended against his breast the greatest cross-bows of steel, took his aim by the eye with the hand-gun, and shot well, traversed, and planted the cannon, shot at butmarks, at the papgay from below upwards, from above downwards, then before him, sideways, and behind him, like the Parthians.

They tied a cable rope to the top of a high tower, by one end whereof hanging near the ground he wrought himself with his hands to the very top: then upon the same track came down so sturdily and firm that they could not, on a plain meadow, have run with more assurance. They set up a great pole, fixed upon two trees; there would he hang by his hands, and with them alone, his feet touching at nothing, would go back and forth along the aforesaid rope, with so great swiftness that hardly could one overtake him with running; and then, to exercise his breast and lungs, he would shout like all the devils in hell: I heard him once call Eudemon, from St. Victor's gate to Monmertre; Stentor had never such a voice at the siege of Troy.

Then, for the strengthening of his nerves or sinews, they made him two great sows of lead, each of them weighing eight thousand and seven hundred kintals, which they called *alteres;* those he took up from the ground, in each hand one, then lifted them up over his head, and held them without stirring three quarters of an hour or more, which was an inimitable force.

He fought at barriers with the stoutest and most vigorous champions; and when it came to the cope, he stood so sturdily on his feet that he abandoned himself to the strongest, in case they could remove him from his place, as Milo was wont to do of old; in whose imitation likewise he held a pomegranate in his hand, to give it unto him that could take it from him. The time being thus bestowed, and himself rubbed, cleansed, wiped, and refreshed with other clothes, he returned fair and softly, and passing through certain meadows, or other grassy places, beheld the trees and plants, comparing them with what is written of them in the books of the ancients, such as Theophrast, Dioscorides, Marinus, Pliny, Nicander, Macer, and Galen, and carried home to the house great handfuls of them, whereof a young page, called Rhizotomos, had charge; together with little mattocks, pickaxes, grubbing hooks, cabbies, pruning knives, and other instruments requisite for gardening. Being come to their lodging whilst supper was making ready, they repeated certain passages of that which had been read, and then sat down at table. Here remark, that his dinner was sober and thrifty, for he did then eat only to prevent the gnawings of his stomach, but his supper was copious and large, for he took then as much as was fit to maintain and nourish him; which, indeed, is the true diet prescribed by the art of good and sound physic; although a rabble of logger-headed physicians, nuzzeled in the brabbling shop of Sophisters, counsel the contrary. During that repast, was continued the lesson read at dinner, as long as they thought good; the rest was spent in good discourse, learned and profitable.

After they had given thanks, he set himself to sing vocally, and play upon harmonious instruments, or otherwise passed his time at some pretty sports, made with cards or dice, or in practising the feats of legerdemain, with cups and balls. There they stayed some nights in frolicking thus, and making themselves merry till it was time to go to bed; and, on other nights they would go make visits unto learned men, or to such as had been travellers in strange and remote countries. When it was full night, before they retired themselves, they went unto the most open place of the house, to see the face of the sky, and there beheld the comets, if any were, as likewise the figures, situations, aspects, opposition, and conjunctions of both fixed stars and planets.

Then with his master did he briefly recapitulate, after the manner of the Pythagoreans, that which he had read, seen, learned, done, and understood, in the whole course of that day.

Then prayed they unto God the Creator, in falling down before him, and strengthening their faith towards him, and glorifying him for his boundless bounty; and giving thanks to him for the time that was past, they recommended themselves to his divine clemency for the future, which being done they went to bed, and betook themselves to their repose.

4. THE NEW ECONOMICS

Carolus Molineus, or Charles Dumoulin (1500–1566), was one of the greatest jurists of his time. His life was stormy, his character somewhat difficult, plentifully endowed with the self-satisfaction current among the men of the Renaissance, calculated to influence people but not to make too many friends. The views he expressed in his treatise *On Contracts and Usury* (1546) met with a tempest of abuse from ecclesiastical quarters; but, compared with current doctrine, which was still that of Aquinas, they were much better suited to the realities of the time.

Charles Dumoulin: from *On Contracts and Usury*

Scholastic theologians, as well as canonists and jurists, considering the letter rather than the spirit or intent and purpose of the divine law, have believed there was something peculiarly and inherently vicious about usury or usurious gains, more than in unjust, deceitful sales, or other similar kinds of fraud. And this, not because one's neighbor is more harmed thereby; but because in a loan something more than the principal is received; as if usury *per se* were more detestable and more wicked, or *per se* more unlawful. Thus some hold that, although usury may sometimes not be contrary to charity, as if it were harmful, still there is always something rather dishonorable about it; or again, that the prohibition of usury is so strict according to divine law that it cannot be modified by legislation, even in cases where it is a question of public utility and the common good, and the civil amity which nature has established among men. Hence they have fallen into the infinite evasions and numerous errors and fallacies with which their very confused books are filled; all because they have not considered the purpose of the divine law, which is charity, as Christ himself testifies: *All things, therefore, whatsoever you would that men should do to you, do you also unto them. For this is the law and the prophets.* That is to say, this is its purpose. And St. Paul (I Timothy): *The end of the law is charity.* Also Romans 13 and Galatians 5: *He who loveth his neighbor hath fulfilled the law.* Therefore, usury is not forbidden and unlawful according to divine law, except insofar as it is contrary to charity. Since, however, usury is taken in many ways, that form alone is prohibited and condemned which offends against charity and love of one's neighbor. . . .

Suppose a merchant of means borrows money in order to make a profit from legitimate business, and promises to pay usury monthly or annually, instead of a portion of the expected profit: Should you say that the creditor, if unable to prove his claim to that much interest, or perhaps any interest at all, cannot lawfully contract for or receive such usury without injury to the debtor? Whatever all this crowd may have written, I see no harm in this, nothing contrary to divine or natural law; since nothing is done in it contrary to charity, but rather from mutual charity. It is plain that one grants the favor of a loan from his property; the other remunerates his benefactor with a part of the gain derived therefrom, without suffering any loss. Therefore the creditor lawfully receives more than his principal; and by the same reasoning, he may from the beginning covenant to this effect, within legitimate limits, however, and provided that the one who covenants does not plan any fraud against his neighbor, or demand usury unfairly. . . .

Just as the invention of money was necessary for the sake of exchange and the needs of men, so for a similar, though not so great, necessity, usury was invented and tolerated; for it is clear that people in business often need to use other people's money, nor is it expedient in all cases to arrange a partnership, a single man's industry being involved; and none are found who will lend for nothing. . . .

Reprinted by permission of the publishers from Arthur E. Monroe, editor *Early Economic Thought: Selections from Economic Literature Prior to Adam Smith.* Cambridge, Mass.: Harvard University Press, 1924.

Under these conditions [usury] is lawful, not only according to human law but also according to all law, divine and natural. . . .

5. THE NEW WORLD

Early in the fifteenth century the thought occurred to some of the traders, the sailors, and the princes of Europe that the Italo-Arab hold on the rich Eastern trade might be broken by the discovery of another route to the Indies. The need for new trade routes which would permit western Europe to break the Italian monopoly on trade with Egypt and the Levant went along with the interest shown by contemporary humanists in the nature of the physical world, an interest which served to provide better maps that took account of the data provided in the works of the ancient Ptolemy and of travelers like Marco Polo, and by the experience of other recent explorers on land or sea.

Though some of the greatest sailors involved in the new adventures were Italians like Columbus, Cabot, and Amerigo Vespucci, their first patrons were the rulers of the rising Iberian kingdoms: Portugal, Aragon, and Castile. While the latter were still chiefly concerned through much of the fifteenth century with the reconquest of the peninsula from its remaining Moorish masters, the Portuguese had early started to send vessels along the coast of Africa and into the South Atlantic. Thus the direction of Portuguese enterprises was mostly to the south and the east, and they eventually reached India by turning the Cape of Good Hope. This is partly why the later, Spanish, explorers sailed due west. On their heels came the vessels of other nations, interested in the vast possibilities of the new lands.

Paolo Toscanelli

In the summer of 1474, the Florentine scientist and astronomer, Paolo Toscanelli, found his advice in great demand on the subject of the resources of the Indies and the best way of getting there. Here is a letter he wrote in July of that year.

Paul, the Physician, to Cristobal Colombo, greeting. I perceive your magnificent and great desire to find a way to where the spices grow, and in reply to your letter I send you the copy of another letter which I wrote some days ago to a friend and favorite of the most serene King of Portugal, in reply to another which, by direction of his Highness he wrote to me on the said subject, and I send you another sea chart like the one I sent him, by which you will be satisfied respecting your enquiries: which copy is as follows:

"Paul the Physician, to Fernan Martins, Canon at Lisbon, greeting. It was pleasant to me to understand that your health was good, and that you are in the favor and intimacy with the most generous and most magnificent Prince, your King. I have already spoken with you respecting a shorter way to the places of

From *The Journal of Christopher Columbus,* tr. Clement R. Markham (London, 1893).

321

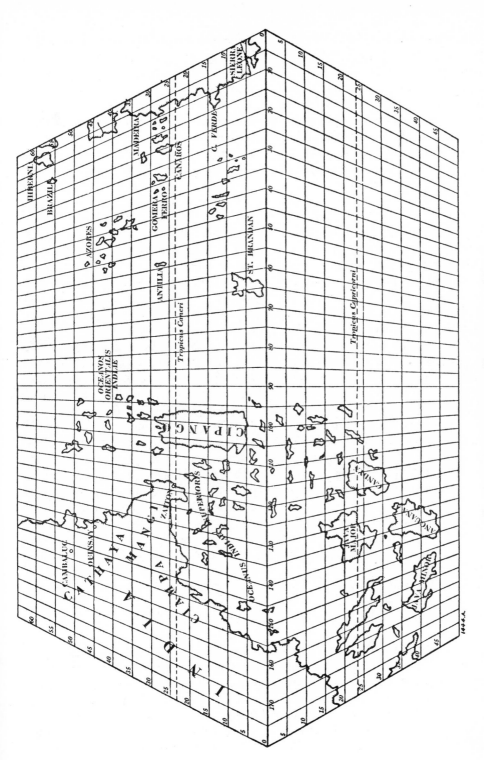

RESTORATION OF THE TOSCANELLI MAP

From *The Journal of Christopher Columbus*,
tr. Clement R. Markham (London, 1893).

spices than that which you take by Guinea, by means of maritime navigation. The most serene King now seeks from me some statement, or rather a demonstration to the eye, by which the slightly learned may take in and understand that way. I know this can be shown from the spherical shape of the earth, yet to make the comprehension of it easier, and to facilitate the work, I have determined to show that way by means of a sailing chart. I, therefore, send his Majesty a chart made by my own hands, on which are delineated your coasts and islands, whence you must begin to make your journey always westward, and the places at which you should arrive, and how far from the pole or the equinoctial line you ought to keep, and through how much space or over how many miles you should arrive at those most fertile places full of all sorts of spices and jewels. You must not be surprised if I call the parts where the spices are west, when they usually call them east, because to those always sailing west, those parts are found by navigation on the under side of the earth. But if by land and by the upper side, they will always be found to the east. . . . It is asserted that none but merchants live on the islands. For there the number of navigators with merchandize is so great that in all the rest of the world there are not so many as in the most noble port called Zaitun. For they affirm that a hundred ships laden with pepper discharge their cargoes in that port in a single year, besides other ships bringing other spices. That country is very populous and very rich, with a multitude of provinces and kingdoms, and with cities without number, under one prince who is called the Great Kan, which name signifies King of Kings, whose seat and residence is generally in the province of Katay. His ancestors desired intercourse with Christians now 200 years ago. They sent to the Pope [he refers to the journey of Nicolo and Maffeo Polo, who reached the court of Kublai Khan in 1260, returned as his envoys in 1269, started east again in 1271, taking their nephew Marco with them] and asked for several persons learned in the faith that they might be enlightened, but those who were sent, being impeded in their journey, went back. Also in the time of Eugenius [1] one of them came, who affirmed their great kindness towards Christians, and I had a long conversation with him on many subjects, about the magnitude of their rivers in length and breadth, and on the multitude of cities on the banks of the rivers. He said that on one river there were near 200 cities with marble bridges great in length and breadth, and everywhere adorned with columns. This country is worth seeking by the Latins, not only because great wealth may be obtained from it, gold and silver, all sorts of gems and spices, which never reach us; but also on account of its learned men, philosophers and expert astrologers, and by what skill and art so powerful and magnificent a province is governed, as well as how their wars are conducted. This is for some satisfaction to his request, so far as the shortness of time and my occupations admitted: being ready in future more fully to satisfy his royal Majesty as far as he may wish. Given at Florence, June 24th, 1474."

From the city of Lisbon due west there are 26 spaces marked on the map, each of which has 250 miles, as far as the most noble and very great city of Quinsay [which Marco Polo calls the City of Heaven]. For it is a hundred miles in circumference and has ten bridges, and its name signifies the city of Heaven; many won-

[1] Pope Eugenius IV, 1431–1447.

ders being related concerning it, touching the multitude of its handicrafts and its resources. This space is almost a third part of the whole sphere. That city is . . . near the province of Katay, in which land is the royal residence. But from the island Antilia, known to you [a fabulous island, after which the West Indian islands were first named around 1500] to the most noble island of Cipan-

go there are ten spaces. For that island is most fertile in gold, pearls, and precious stones, and they cover the temples and palaces with solid gold. Thus the spaces of the sea to be crossed in the unknown part are not great. Many things might perhaps have been declared more exactly, but a diligent thinker will be able to clear up the rest for himself. Farewell, most excellent one.

Christopher Columbus from *The Journal*

Christopher Columbus (1451–1506) was born in Genoa. His beginnings are still obscure. The ideas which led to his great project of reaching China by sailing west were based on the belief, going back to the Middle Ages, that there were lands in the Atlantic—lands he presumed to be Cipango and Cathay. Rebuffed by the Portuguese, who had other fish to fry, he entered the service of Spain and eventually persuaded Queen Isabella of Castile to grant him command of the three ships with which he would discover the new world. Leaving Spain on August 2, 1492, he returned eight months later having effected landings in San Salvador, Cuba, and Haiti. A second voyage brought him to Guadeloupe, Puerto Rico, and Jamaica; a third enabled him, after touching Trinidad, to reach the continent and sail along the South American coast from the mouth of the Orinoco River to Caracas. On his fourth and last trip he explored the coast of Central America from Honduras to the Gulf of Darien; but he had, by then, lost his credit at court and after his return (1504) was left to die in relative poverty and disgrace.

In the name of our Lord Jesus Christ.

Because, O most Christian, and very high, very excellent and puissant Princes, King and Queen of the Spains and of the islands of the Sea, our Lords, in this present year of 1492, after your Highnesses had given an end to the war with the Moors who reigned in Europe, and had finished it in the very great city of Granada, where in this present year, on the second day of the month of January, by force of arms, I saw the royal banners of your Highnesses placed on the towers of Alhambra,

which is the fortress of that city, and I saw the Moorish King come forth from the gates of the city and kiss the royal hands of your Highnesses, and of the Prince my Lord, and presently in that same month, acting on the information that I had given to your Highnesses touching the lands of India, and respecting a Prince who is called Gran Can, which means in our language King of Kings, how he and his ancestors had sent to Rome many times to ask for learned men of our holy faith to teach him, and how the Holy Father had never complied, insomuch that many people believing in

From *The Journal of Christopher Columbus,* tr. Clement R. Markham (London, 1893).

idolatries were lost by receiving doctrine of perdition: YOUR HIGHNESSES, as Catholic Christians and Princes who love the holy Christian faith, and the propagation of it, and who are enemies to the sect of Mahomet and to all idolatries and heresies, resolved to send me, Cristobal Colon, to the said parts of India to see the said princes, and the cities and lands, and their disposition, with a view that they might be converted to our holy faith; and ordered that I should not go by land to the eastward, as had been customary, but that I should go by way of the west, whither up to this day we do not know for certain that any one has gone.

Thus, after having turned out all the Jews from all your kingdoms and lordships, in the same month of January, your Highnesses gave orders to me that with a sufficient fleet I should go to the said parts of India. . . .

[The expedition left Palos on August 2, 1492; on October 12th,] at two hours after midnight, the land was sighted at a distance of two leagues. They shortened sail, and lay by under the mainsail without the bonnets. The vessels were hove to, waiting for daylight; and on Friday they arrived at a small island of the Lucayos [Columbus named it San Salvador; it is now Watling Island]. Presently they saw naked people. The Admiral went on shore in the armed boat, and Martin Alonzo Pinzon and Vicente Yañez, his brother, who was captain of the *Nina*. The Admiral took the royal standard, and the captains went with two banners of the green cross, which the Admiral took in all the ships as a sign, with an F and a Y and a crown over each letter, one on one side of the cross and the other on the other. Having landed, they saw trees very green, and much water, and fruits of diverse kinds. The Admiral called to the two captains and to the others who leaped on shore . . . and said that they should bear faithful testimony that he, in the presence of all, had taken, as he now took, possession of the said island for the King and for the Queen, his Lords making the declarations that are required. . . .

Presently many inhabitants of the island assembled. . . . I saw and knew (says the Admiral) that these people are without any religion, not idolaters but very gentle, not knowing what is evil, nor the sins of murder and theft, being without arms, and so timid that a hundred would fly before one Spaniard, although they joke with them. They, however, believe and know that there is a God in heaven, and say that we have come from heaven. At any prayer that we say, they repeat, and make the sign of the cross. Thus your Highnesses should resolve to make them Christians, for I believe that if the work was begun, in a little time the multitude of nations would be converted to our faith, with the acquisition of great lordships, peoples, and riches for Spain. Without doubt there is in this land a vast quantity of gold, and the Indians . . . do not speak without reason when they say that in these islands there are places where they dig out gold, and wear it on their necks, ears, arms and legs, the rings being very large. There are also precious stones, pearls, and an infinity of spices. . . . Here also there is a great quantity of cotton, and I believe it would have a good sale here without sending it to Spain, but to the cities of the Gran Can, which will be discovered without doubt, and many others ruled over by other lords, who will be pleased to serve your Highnesses, and whither will be brought other commodities of Spain and of the Eastern lands; but these are to the West as regards us.

They were to the west all right; but Columbus was never to enter into the land of Canaan that he had dreamed of for so long. Cuba was not Cipango; Katay he never found; and though the new world he discovered soon revealed other riches, it did not bring his masters the trade of the Indies. This was soon to fall into the hands of travelers following another route.

Vasco da Gama

The first half of the fifteenth century had seen the sailors of Portugal pushing south, along the African coast, in search of knowledge and gain. A series of expeditions, supported by the government, enabled Diego Cam to discover the Congo in 1484 and Bartholomeo Diaz to round the Cape of Good Hope in 1488. It was not for another ten years, however, that this discovery could be put to use by Vasco da Gama (c. 1469–1524) who set out in 1497 to reach India by rounding the Cape, and did actually reach Calecut, one of the chief trading ports of southern India, a year later. Vasco da Gama's voyage was the fount of Portugal's eastern empire, whose bases soon reached from Mozambique and the Persian Gulf to Canton; and the great explorer himself was appointed first Viceroy of the Indies.

In the year 1497 King Dom Manuel, the first of that name in Portugal, dispatched four vessels to make discoveries and go in search of spices. Vasco da Gama was the captain-major of these vessels.

FROM A JOURNAL OF THE FIRST VOYAGE OF VASCO DA GAMA

[On May 20, 1498] we anchored two leagues from the city of Calecut [in India]. The city . . . is inhabited by Christians. They are of a tawny complexion. Some of them have big beards and long hair, whilst others clip their hair short or shave the head, merely allowing a tuft to remain on the crown as a sign that they are Christians. They also wear mustaches. They pierce the ears and wear much gold in them. . . . The women of this country, as a rule, are ugly and of small stature. They wear many jewels of gold round the neck, numerous bracelets on their arms, and rings set with precious stones on their toes. All these people are well disposed and apparently mild of temper. At first sight they seem covetous and ignorant. . . . On the following morning . . . the captain-major set out to speak to the king, and took with him thirteen men, of whom I was one. We put on our best attire, placed bombards in our boats, and took with us trumpets and many flags. On landing, the captain-major was received by the alcalde, with whom were many men, armed and unarmed. The reception was friendly, as if the people were pleased to see us. . . . [On first arriving in Calecut] they took us to a large church [obviously a pagoda or temple] and this is what we saw: The body of the church is as large as a monastery, all built of stone and covered with tiles. . . . In the centre of the body of

From *A Journal of the First Voyage of Vasco da Gama* (London, 1898), E. J. Ravenstein, Ed.; from *The Three Voyages of Vasco da Gama and His Viceroyalty*, H. E. J. Stanley, Ed. 1869.

the church rose a chapel, all built of hewn stone, with a bronze door sufficiently wide for a man to pass, and stone steps leading up to it. Within this sanctuary stood a small image which they said represented Our Lady. Along the walls, by the main entrance, hung seven small bells. In this church the captain-major said his prayers, and we with him. . . . Many other saints were painted on the walls of the church, wearing crowns. They were painted variously, with teeth protruding an inch from the mouth, and four or five arms. . . .

The further we advanced in the direction of the king's palace, the more did the crowd increase in number. And when we arrived there, men of much distinction and great lords came out to meet the captain, and joined those who were already in attendance upon him. It was then an hour before sunset. When we reached the palace, we passed through a gate into a courtyard of great size and, before we arrived at where the king was, we passed four doors, through which we had to force our way, giving many blows to the people. When at last we reached the door where the king was, there came forth from it a little old man who holds a position resembling that of a bishop, and upon whose advice the king acts in all affairs of the church. This man embraced the captain when he entered the door. Several men were wounded at this door, and we only got in by the use of much force.

The king was in a small court, reclining upon a couch covered with a cloth of green velvet, above which was a good mattress, and upon this again a sheet of cotton stuff, very white and fine, more so than any linen. The cushions were after the same fashion. In his left hand the king held a very large golden spittoon, having a capacity of eight pints. At its

mouth this cup was 16 inches wide, and apparently it was massive. Into this cup the king threw the husks of a certain herb which is chewed by the people of this country for its soothing effects, and which they call betel nut. On the right side of the king stood a basin of gold, so large that a man might just encircle it with his arms: this contained the herbs. There were likewise many silver jugs. The canopy above the couch was all gilt. . . .

The king beckoned to the captain . . . to come nearer, but the captain did not approach him, for it is the custom of the country for no man to approach the king except only the servant who hands him the herbs, and when anyone addresses the king he holds his hand before his mouth, and remains at a distance. When the king beckoned to the captain he looked at us others, and ordered us to be seated on a stone bench near him, where he could see us. He ordered that water for our hands should be given us, also some fruit, one kind of which resembled a melon, except that its outside was rough and the inside sweet, whilst another kind of fruit resembled a fig and tasted very nice [apparently jack (a kind of breadfruit) and bananas].

And the captain told him he was the ambassador of a King of Portugal, who was Lord of many countries and the possessor of great wealth of every description, exceeding that of any king of these parts; that for a period of sixty years his ancestors had annually sent out vessels to make discoveries in the direction of India, as they knew that there were Christian kings like themselves. This, he said, was the reason which induced them to order this country to be discovered, not because they sought for gold or silver, for of this they had such an abundance that they needed not what was to be found in this country. . . . The captains sent out traveled for a year or two, until their provisions became exhausted, and then returned to Portugal, without having succeeded in making the desired discovery. There reigned a king now whose name was Dom Manuel, who had ordered him to build three vessels . . . and not to return to Portugal until he should have discovered this king of the Christians, on pain of having his head cut off. . . . And, finally, he had been instructed to say by word of mouth that the King of Portugal desired to be his friend and brother. . . .

On Tuesday [May 29, 1498] the captain got ready the following things to be sent to the king [of Calecut], viz., twelve pieces of striped cloth, four scarlet hoods, six hats, four strings of coral, a case containing six washstand basins, a case of sugar, two casks of oil and two of honey. And as it is the custom not to send anything to the king without the knowledge of the Moor, his factor, and of the *bale* [governor], the captain informed them of his intention. They came, and when they saw the present they laughed at it, saying that it was not a thing to offer to a king, that the poorest merchant from Mecca, or any other part of India, gave more, and that if he wanted to make a present it should be in gold, as the king would not accept such things. When the captain heard this he grew sad, and said that he had brought no gold; that, moreover, he was no merchant, but an ambassador; that he gave of that which he had, which was his own private gift, and not the king's; that if the king of Portugal ordered him to return he would intrust him with far richer presents. . . . Upon this they declared that they would not forward his presents, nor consent to his forwarding them himself. When they had gone, there came certain Moorish merchants and they all depreciated the present which the captain desired to be sent to the king. . . .

As a result of this and of other misunderstandings, relations between the Indians and the Portuguese got worse and worse. Nevertheless, the king of Calecut did let Vasco da Gama have a letter for his royal master, and the tenor of the letter was as follows:

Vasco da Gama, a gentleman of your household, came to my country, whereat I was pleased. My country is rich in cinnamon, cloves, ginger, pepper, and precious stones. That which I ask of you in exchange is gold, silver, corals, and scarlet cloth.

The survivors of the expedition reached Lisbon in July of 1499, and their reports greatly cheered the king; for that same month we find him writing to his neighbors, the King and Queen of Castile:

Most high and excellent Prince and Princess, most potent Lord and Lady!

Your Highnesses already know that we had ordered Vasco da Gama, a nobleman of our household, and his brother Paulo da Gama, with four vessels to make discoveries by sea, and that two years have now elapsed since their departure. And as the principal motive of this enterprise has been, with our predecessors, the service of God our Lord, and our own advantage, it pleased Him in His mercy to speed them on their route. From a message which has now been brought to this city by one of the captains, we learn that they did reach and discover India and other kingdoms and lordships bordering upon it; that they entered and navigated its sea, finding large cities, large edifices and rivers, and great populations, among whom is carried on all the trade in spices and precious stones, which are forwarded in ships . . . to Mecca, and thence to Cairo, whence they are dispersed throughout the world. Of these spices, etc., they have brought a quantity, including cinnamon, cloves, ginger, nutmeg, and pepper, as well as other kinds, together with the boughs and leaves of the same; also many fine stones of all sorts, such as rubies and others. And they also came to a country in which there are mines of gold, of which, as of the spices and precious stones, they did not bring as much as they could have done, for they took no merchandise with them.

As we are aware that your Highnesses will hear of these things with pleasure and satisfaction, we thought well to give this information. And your Highnesses may believe, in accordance with what we have learnt concerning the Christian people whom these explorers reached, that it will be possible, notwithstanding that they are not as yet strong in the faith nor

possessed of a thorough knowledge of it, to do much in the service of God and the exaltation of the Holy Faith, once they shall have been converted and fully fortified in it. And when they shall thus have been fortified in the faith, there will be an opportunity for destroying the Moors of those parts. Moreover, we hope, with the help of God, that the great trade which now enriches the Moors of those parts, through whose hands it passes without the intervention of other persons or peoples, shall, in consequence of our regulations, be diverted to the natives and the ships of our own kingdom, so that henceforth all Christendom, in this part of Europe, shall be able, in a large measure, to provide itself with those spices and precious stones. This, with the help of God, who in his mercy thus ordained it, will cause our designs and intentions to be pushed with more ardor, especially as concerns the war upon the Moors of the territories conquered by us in these parts, which your Highnesses are so firmly resolved upon, and in which we are equally zealous.

And we pray your Highnesses, in consideration of this great favor, which, with much gratitude, we received from our Lord, to cause to be addressed to Him those praises which are His due.

But, while Manuel had reason to regard the discovery of India as a favor of God, and while Ferdinand and Isabella probably gnashed their teeth to see the Portuguese finding spices and jewels to the east, where their ships had found mostly savages to the west, the Indians themselves had no cause to praise the God of these arrogant interlopers. Back in India, once more, we find Gama up to his old tricks

He then ordered the boats to go and plunder the small vessels, which were sixteen, and the two ships in which they found rice, and many jars of butter, and

many bales of stuffs. They then gathered all this together into the ships, with the crews of the two large ships, and he ordered the boats to get as much rice as they wanted, and they took that of four of the small vessels, which they emptied, for they did not want more. Then the captain-major commanded them to cut off the hands and noses of all the crews, and put all that into one of the small vessels, into which he ordered them to put the friar [a Brahmin envoy, dressed as a friar, who had come aboard under safe conduct], also without ears or nose or hands, which he had ordered to be strung up round his neck, with a palm leaf for the king, on which he told him to have a curry made to eat of what his friar brought with him. When all the Indians had been thus executed, he ordered their feet to be tied together, as they had no hands with which to untie them, and in order that they should not untie them with their teeth, he ordered men to strike upon their teeth with staves until they knocked them down their throats; and they were thus put on board, heaped up on top of each other, mixed up with the blood which streamed from them, and he ordered mats and dry leaves to be spread over them, and the sails to be set for the shore, and the vessel set on fire and there were more than eight hundred Moors. And the small vessel with the friar, with all the hands and ears, was also sent on shore under sail, without being fired. These vessels went at once on shore, where many people flocked together to put out the fire, and draw out those whom they found alive, upon which they made great lamentations.

John Cabot: *Report to the Duke of Milan*

In the meantime, the ruler of another Atlantic kingdom, the shrewd Henry VII of England, was taking a certain interest in the possibilities of the newly discovered lands and waters across the sea. The voyages of the Cabots, whom he sponsored in 1497 and 1498, reached Cape Breton Island, Newfoundland, Nova Scotia, and New England. Here is the account which a Milanese subject in England, Raimondo di Soncino, sent to the Duke of Milan in December 1497:

My most illustrious and most excellent Lord,

Perhaps amidst so many occupations of your Excellency it will not be unwelcome to learn how this Majesty has acquired a part of Asia without drawing his sword. In this kingdom there is a certain Venetian named Zoanne Caboto, of gentle disposition, very expert in navigation, who, seeing that the most serene Kings of Portugal and Spain had occupied unknown islands, meditated the achievement of a similar acquisition for the said Majesty. Having obtained royal privileges . . . he entrusted his fortune to a small vessel with a crew of 18 persons, and set out from Bristol, a port in the western part of this kingdom. Having passed Ibernia, which is still further to the west, and then shaped a northerly course, he began to navigate to the eastern part, leaving the North Star on the right hand; and having wandered thus for a long time, at length he hit upon land, where he hoisted the royal standard, and took possession for this Highness and, having obtained various proofs of his discovery he returned. The said Messer Zoanne, being a foreigner and poor, would not have been believed if the crew, who are nearly all English and who be-

From *The Journal of Christopher Columbus and Documents Relating to the Voyages of John Cabot and Gaspar Corte Real,* tr. Clement R. Markham (London, 1893).

long to Bristol, had not testified that what he said was the truth. This Messer Zoanne has the description of the world on a chart, and also on a solid sphere which he has constructed, and on which he shows where he has been. . . .

The said Englishmen, his companions, say that they took so many fish that this kingdom will no longer have need of Iceland, from which country there is an immense trade in fish. . . . But Messer Zoanne has set his mind on higher things, for he thinks that, when that place has been occupied, he will keep on still further towards the east, where he will be opposite to an island called Cipango . . . where he believes that all the spices of the world, as well as the jewels, are found. He further says that he was once at Mecca, whither the spices are brought by caravans from distant countries; and having inquired from whence they were brought and where they grow, they answered that they did not know, but that such merchandize was brought from distant countries by other caravans to their home; and they further say that they are also conveyed from other remote regions. And he adduced this argument, that if the eastern people tell those in the south that these things come from a far distance from them, presupposing the rotundity of the earth, it must be that the last turn would be by the north towards the west; and it is said that in this way the route would not cost more than it costs now, and also I believe it. And what is more, this Majesty, who is wise and not prodigal, reposes such trust in him because of what he has already achieved,

that he gives him a good maintenance, as Messer Zoanne himself told me. And it is said that before long his Majesty will arm some ships for him, and will give him all the malefactors to go to that country and form a colony, so that they hope to establish a greater depot of spices in London than there is in Alexandria.

The principal people in the enterprise belong to Bristol. They are great seamen, and now that they know where to go, they say that the trip there will not take more than 15 days after leaving Ibernia. I have also spoken to a Burgundian, who was a companion of Messer Zoanne, who affirms all this, and who wishes to return because the Admiral . . . has given him an island, and has given another to his barber of Castiglione, who is a Genoese, and both look upon themselves as Counts; nor do they look upon my Lord the Admiral as less than a Prince. I also believe that some poor Italian friars are going on this voyage, who have all had bishoprics promised to them. And if I had made friends with the Admiral when he was about to sail, I should have got an archbishopric at least; but I have thought that the benefits reserved for me by your Excellency will be more secure. I would venture to pray that, in the event of a vacancy taking place in my absence, I may be put in possession and that I may not be superseded by those who, being present, can be more diligent than I, who am reduced in this country to eating at each meal ten or twelve kinds of victuals, and to being three hours at table every day, two for love of your Excellency, to whom I humbly recommend myself.

Richard Hakluyt: from *Divers Voyages Touching the Discovery of America*

As the sixteenth century drew to a close, England had made little serious effort to colonize the new world. The Elizabethans were interested in discovery, pillage, and war, but few showed any enthusiasm for the hard, sustained work that would be involved in founding new communities on the North American shore. Sir Walter Raleigh was one of these few. Another was Richard Hakluyt (1553–1616), an Oxford man and preacher, whose *Principal Navigations, Voyages, Traffiques, and Discoveries of the English Nation* is, in H. A. L. Fisher's words, the prose epic of this age of adventures, though one devoted largely to recommending colonies as means of promoting trade and of ridding the country of its unprofitable members.

Hakluyt's propaganda led to the foundation in 1584 of a colony named, after the queen, Virginia; but the interest it generated was apparently insufficient to keep the new settlement alive. The colony was allowed to fade away without adequate support, and it had to be founded anew in 1607, under the succeeding reign of James I.

I marvel not a little (right worshipful) that since the first discovery of America (which is now full forescore and ten years), after so great conquests and plantings of the Spaniards and Portuguese there, that we of England could never have the grace to set fast footing in such fertile and temperate places as are left as yet unpossessed of them. But again, when I consider that there is a time for all men, and see the Portuguese time to be out of date, and that the nakedness of the Spaniards and their long hidden secrets are now at length espied, whereby they went about to delude the world, I conceive great hope that the time approaches and now is, that we of England may share and participate (if we will ourselves) both with the Spaniard and the Portuguese, in part of America and other regions, as yet undiscovered. And surely if there were in us that desire to advance the honor of our country which ought to be in every good man, we would not all this while have forborne [neglected] the possessing of those lands, which of equity and right appertain unto us, as by the discourses that follow shall appear most plainly. Yea, if we would behold with the eye of pity how all our Prisons are pestered and filled with able men to serve their Country, which for small robberies are daily hanged up in great numbers, even twenty at a clap, out of one jail (as was seen at the last assizes at Rochester), we would hasten and further every man to his power the deducting of [conveying] to some Colonies of our superfluous people into those temperate and fertile parts of America, which, being within six weeks sailing of England, are yet unpossessed by any Christians: and seem to offer themselves unto us, stretching nearer unto her Majesty's Dominions than to any other part of Europe. We read that the Bees when they grow to be too many in their own hives at home, are wont to be led out by their Captains to swarm abroad and seek themselves a new dwelling place. If the examples of the Grecians and Carthaginians of old time and the practice of our age may not move us yet

From *Divers Voyages Touching the Discovery of America* (London, 1850).

let us learn wisdom of these small weak and unreasonable creatures. It chanced very lately that upon occasion I had great conference in matters of Cosmography with an excellent learned man of Portugal most privy to all the discoveries of his nation, who wondered that those blessed countries from the point of Florida northward were all this while unplanted by Christians, protesting with great affection and zeal, that if he were now as young as I (for at present he is three score years of age) he would sell all he had, being a man of no small wealth and honor, to furnish a convenient number of ships to sea for the inhabiting of those countries, and reducing those gentle people to Christianity. . . .

Space Theology

The first Christians dealing with the inhabitants of the unexpected Western Hemisphere faced the problem of the humanity of these people who had not been mentioned in the Gospels. Were they part of the human family? Had Christ also died for them? Or were they really a nonhuman species, to be treated and exploited as animals?

A similar problem arises today, and, while religious attitudes are less influential on the world of today, we can glimpse in the problems of contemporary theologians some of the much more acute problems of the fifteenth century, when everything made sense in terms of religion and when the unity of man was much more a unity of Christian men.

The first interplanetary padre, confronted by an antennaed Martian or fly-eyed Venusian, will hardly know what to say about the Gospel. First he will have to find out how the space creature stands with God: Is he in an unfallen state like Adam and Eve before the apple? Is he fallen but redeemed and, if so, how? Is he under the Lordship of Christ, and should he be baptized?

Theological speculations along these lines, hotted up by space talk and Europe's recent rash of flying sauciness, are amusing continental Christian thinkers. Professor Eduard Stakemeier, Roman Catholic theologian at the Philosophical-Theological Academy at Paderborn, Germany, feels that planetary missionizing would be unwise.

"Christian teaching is indeed compatible with the assumption that there are extra-earthly rational creatures similar to human beings," he writes in the Dusseldorf daily, Rheinsche Post. "The supreme world aim is the glorification of God through rational beings. . . . Should we assume there to be nothing but deserts in all these [other] worlds?

"The inhabitants of other worlds could be like us, but they could also be much superior to us in sense and will. And perhaps they also surpass us in gratitude to the Creator and in goodness and love to all that demands love and kindness [but] in principle we must say that the Christian order of redemption was realized by God for this world. . . . Only we, who are descended from Adam, are born in original sin, and God became man to redeem us. . . . His church and His sacraments are [not] valid for . . . other planets."

Dr. Michael Schmaus, professor of Catholic dogma at the University of Munich, agrees that there is nothing in Christian teaching to deny the existence of unearthly rational beings. Christ, he writes, is certainly their head, for according to St. Paul, He is the head of the universe. But "the question remains open whether He also has the significance of Redeemer for them. That in turn depends on whether these rational creatures have sinned and whether, like mankind, they need redeeming. . . .

"If they, too, are to be redeemed through Christ, this does not mean that the heavenly Logos must appear amongst them as it did in the history of mankind. It could be that the redemption through Christ could be preached to them by some messenger of the faith without [Christ] making any visible appearance to them. But it is also possible that God did not give these creatures any supernatural goal and that He determined for them natural perfection. . . ."

Italian theologians have not yet entered into space theology with the same gusto as the Germans. Jesuit Father Antonio Messineo, contributing editor of the fortnightly *Civiltà Cattolica,* favors a wait-and-see attitude. "The question of an eventual missionary activity among the inhabitants of other planets," he said, "hinges on two fundamental questions: 1) is there spiritual and physical human life on planets, and 2) are the inhabitants still in the state of original grace, or have they fallen into sin?"

But Father Agostino Gemmelli, rector of Milan's Catholic University of the Sacred Heart, flatly denies the possibility of extraterrestrial life: the Scripture makes no mention of it. Says he: "If God had created other men on other planets, these men would not be derived from Adam and one would not be able to understand the logic of the Divine plan of man's salvation. . . . To admit that the divine plan of salvation is illogical is the same as not recognizing the infinite wisdom of God. It is fantastic to suppose that God would find place for such men on other planets. Remember that the world was created by God for God's glory. What glory would God derive from men deprived of supernatural gifts?"

In the face of the planetary emergency the Vatican maintained its calm. The whole question, said a spokesman, seemed as of this week "slightly premature."

II. Reformation and Counter Reformation

Movements for Church reform were nothing new in the Christian world. All through the Middle Ages the clergy were frequently attacked for failing to lead worthy lives; new doctrines were mooted; and attempts were made to replace the Latin Bible, incomprehensible to the vast majority of the laity and to a surprising number of the clergy, with translations in the local tongue. A look at the Wycliffite conclusions condemned by the Church, and at Wycliffe's letter to the Pope, shows defiance as rife in the fourteenth century as in the sixteenth.

When Luther tacked up his theses on the church door at Wittenberg, he did not think of himself as taking an original or revolutionary step. A feeling for Church reform was in the air, fostered by the studies and translations of Renaissance humanists like Erasmus and by the growth of a self-confident public opinion more critical of its religious leaders than of yore. But there was no need to think that reform would turn into revolt; nor would it have done so, perhaps, had German complaints been properly handled. However, once Luther and his supporters had been driven into open revolt, they benefited from economic and political circumstances which linked religious to political ideas. After 1521 there seems to have been no turning back; there would have to be reform, whether within the Church or outside it. In the event, there were both, with the "protestant" reform spurring the Church of Rome to put its house in order and reaffirm its doctrines. Thus, as the sixteenth century drew to a close, the unity of the Christian West had been shattered, but the divisions themselves created an intensity of religious concern and belief which had been unknown in Europe for a long time.

1. WYCLIFFE AND THE LOLLARDS

John Wycliffe (1324–1384) was born in Yorkshire, taught at Oxford and, on being expelled from the University in 1382, returned to his Leicestershire vicarage of Lutterworth where he lived quietly until his death. Wycliffe used his great knowledge and academic position at Oxford to attack the scandals and corruption in the Church of his time, protesting against much of its teaching and practice. He wanted preachers to preach in English, to base their preaching on the Scriptures, and to use an English Bible that would make the Scriptures available to all. The English Bible that bears his name was translated by his disciples, and preachers inspired by him spread the message throughout England. It also reached the University of Prague, where it led one of the professors, John Hus (1369–1415) to spread Wycliffe's doctrine that the Pope was to be obeyed only in so far as he acted in accordance with Scripture.

WYCLIFFITE CONCLUSIONS, TEN CONDEMNED AS HERETICAL AND FOURTEEN AS ERRONEOUS

I. That the material substance of bread and of wine remains, after the consecration, in the sacrament of the altar.

II. That the accidents do not remain without the subject, after the consecration, in the same sacrament.

III. That Christ is not in the sacrament of the altar identically, truly, and really in his proper corporal presence.

IV. That if a bishop or priest lives in mortal sin he does not ordain, or consecrate, or baptize.

V. That if a man has been truly repentant, all external confession is superfluous to him, or useless.

VI. Continually to assert that it is not founded in the gospel that Christ instituted the mass.

VII. That God ought to be obedient to the devil.

VIII. That if the Pope is foreordained to destruction and a wicked man, and therefore a member of the devil, no power has been given to him over the faithful of Christ by any one, unless perhaps by the Emperor.

IX. That since Urban the Sixth, no one is to be acknowledged as Pope; but all are to live, in the way of the Greeks, under their own laws.

X. To assert that it is against sacred scripture that men of the church should have temporal possessions.

XI. That no prelate ought to excommunicate any one unless he first knows that the man is excommunicated by God.

XII. That a person thus excommunicating is thereby a heretic or excommunicate.

XIII. That a prelate excommunicating a clerk who has appealed to the king, or to a council of the kingdom, on that very account is a traitor to God, the king, and the kingdom.

XIV. That those who neglect to preach, or to hear the word of God, or the gospel that is preached, because of the excommunication of men, are excommunicate, and in the day of judgment will be considered as traitors to God.

XV. To assert that it is allowed to any one, whether a deacon or a priest, to preach the word of God, without the authority of the apostolic see, or of a catholic bishop, or some other which is sufficiently acknowledged.

XVI. To assert that no one is a civil lord, no one is a bishop, no one is a prelate, so long as he is in mortal sin.

XVII. That temporal lords may, at their own judgment, take away temporal goods from churchmen who are habitually delinquent; or that the people may, at their own judgment, correct delinquent lords.

XVIII. That tithes are purely charity, and that parishioners may, on account of the sins of their curates, detain these and confer them on others at their will.

XIX. That special prayers applied to one person by prelates or religious persons, are of no more value to the same person than general prayers for others in a like position are to him.

XX. That the very fact that any one enters upon any private religion what-

From *Translations and Reprints,* Vol. 2, No. 5, E. P. Cheyney, Ed.

ever, renders him more unfitted and more incapable of observing the commandments of God.

XXI. That saints who have instituted any private religions whatever, as well of those having possessions as of mendicants, have sinned in thus instituting them.

XXII. That religious persons living in private religions are not of the Christian religion.

XXIII. That friars should be required to gain their living by the labor of their hands and not by mendicancy.

XXIV. That a person giving alms to friars, or to a preaching friar, is excommunicate; also the one receiving.

REPLY OF WYCLIFFE TO HIS SUMMONS BY THE POPE TO COME TO ROME, 1384

I have joyfully to tell what I hold, to all true men that believe and especially to the Pope; for I suppose that if my faith be rightful and given of God, the Pope will gladly confirm it; and if my faith be error, the Pope will wisely amend it.

I suppose over this that the gospel of Christ be heart of the corps of God's law; for I believe that Jesus Christ, that gave in his own person this gospel, is very God and very man, and by this heart passes all other laws.

I suppose over this that the Pope be most obliged to the keeping of the gospel among all men that live here; for the Pope is highest vicar that Christ has here in earth. For moreness of Christ's vicar is not measured by worldly moreness, but by this, that this vicar follows more Christ by virtuous living; for thus teacheth the gospel, that this is the sentence of Christ.

And of this gospel I take as believe, that Christ for time that he walked here, was most poor man of all, both in spirit and in having; for Christ says that he had nought for to rest his head on. And Paul says that he was made needy for our love. And more poor might no man be, neither bodily nor in spirit. And thus Christ put from him all manner of worldly lordship. For the gospel of John telleth that when they would have made Christ king, he fled and hid him from them, for he would none such worldly highness.

And over this I take it as believe, that no man should follow the Pope, nor no saint that now is in heaven, but in as much as he follows Christ. For John and James erred when they coveted worldly highness; and Peter and Paul sinned also when they denied and blasphemed in Christ; but men should not follow them in this, for then they went from Jesus Christ. And this I take as wholesome counsel, that the Pope leave his worldly lordship to worldly lords, as Christ gave them,—and move speedily all his clerks to do so. For thus did Christ, and taught thus his disciples, till the fiend had blinded this world. And it seems to some men that clerks that dwell lastingly in this error against God's law, and fail to follow Christ in this, been open heretics, and their fautors been partners.

And if I err in this sentence, I will meekly be amended, yea, by the death, if it be skilful, for that I hope were good to me. And if I might travel in mine own person, I would with good will go to the Pope. But God has needed me to the contrary, and taught me more obedience to God than to men. And I suppose of our Pope that he will not be Antichrist, and reverse Christ in this working, to the contrary of Christ's will; for if he summon against reason, by him or by any of his, and pursue this unskilful summoning, he is an open Antichrist. And merciful intent excused not Peter, that Christ should not call him Satan; so blind intent and wicked counsel excuses not the Pope here; but if he ask of true priests that they travel more than they may, he is not excused by reason of God, that he should not be Antichrist. For our belief teaches us that our blessed God suffers us not to be tempted more than we may; how should a man ask such service? And therefore pray we to God for our Pope Urban the Sixth, that his old holy intent be not quenched by his enemies. And Christ, that may not lie, says that the enemies of a man been especially his home family; and this is sooth of men and friends.

2. THE BORGIAS

The increasing worldliness of the Church and of its leading representatives sapped respect for the institution and spurred demands for reform. Among the most outrageous figures of Renaissance Italy were the Borgias, Pope Alexander VI (1492–1503) and his son Caesar (1475–1507), energetic and ruthless men whose efforts to break the power of the great Roman lords of the Orsini and Colonna clans and establish their power all over central Italy failed only after much bloodshed. Caesar, of course, is almost the hero of Machiavelli's *Prince;* but his father was just as unscrupulous and perhaps even more scandalous. And if none of his successors on the throne of St. Peter ever equalled his egregious performance, their political and financial activities continued to worry those who found them too worldly for the service of God.

The Predecessors

Sixtus IV, Innocent VIII, and Alexander VI are [the Popes] filling the most degraded period in papal history, and proving to what a state Italy was then reduced. The first of these men was a Genoese friar, who immediately after his election (1471) exhibited himself as a violent despot, devoid of all scruples and all decency. He needed money, and therefore put up to sale offices, benefices, and indulgences. He showed a downright mania for the advancement of his nephews, some of whom were, according to the general verdict, his own sons. One of these, Pietro Riario, was made Cardinal, with an income of sixty thousand crowns, and plunged so desperately into luxury, dissipation, and debauchery of all kinds, that he soon died, worn out by his vices, and overwhelmed with debts. The other brother, Girolamo, as zealously patronized, led the same sort of life. The Pope's whole policy was ruled by his greed of fresh acquisitions for his sons and nephews. It was solely because Lorenzo dei Medici had crossed these designs that the conspiracy of the Pazzi was hatched in the Vatican, and that on its failure the Pope made war upon Florence, and launched a sentence of excommunication against that

From Pasquale Villari, *The Life and Times of Niccolò Machiavelli,* trans. Mme. L. Villari (London, 1898), pp. 51–55.

city. Later, he joined the Venetians in their expedition against Ferrara, always with the same object of snatching some province for his family. A general war was the result, in which even the Neapolitans took part, by making an attack upon Rome, where fresh feuds among the nobility quickly broke out. . . .

The palaces of the Riario were being sacked, the Orsini and the Colonna in arms, when the Cardinals hurriedly assembling in conclave succeeded in patching up a truce. Then began a most scandalous traffic in votes for election to the Papal chair, which was sold to the highest bidder. The fortunate purchaser was Cardinal Cibo, who was proclaimed Pope on 29th August 1484, under the name of Innocent VIII. . . .

During all this confusion, anarchy had again broken loose in Rome, nor was any way found to restrain it: no morning passed without corpses being found in the streets. Malefactors who could pay, obtained safe conducts; those who could not were hung. Every crime had its price, and all sums over 150 ducats went to Franceschetto Cibo, the Pope's son; smaller amounts to the Chamber. Parricide, rape, any sort of crime, could obtain absolution for money. . . .

Meanwhile, Innocent VIII passed his time in festivities. He was the first Pope who openly acknowledged his own children, and celebrated their wedding feasts. Franceschetto espoused Maddalena, daughter of Lorenzo dei Medici (1487), and by way of recompense her brother, Giovanni, was made a Cardinal at the age of fourteen. . . . The Pope's sons and nephews made the town ring with the scandal of their daily life. Franceschetto Cibo lost 14,000 florins in a single night

at play with Cardinal Riario, whom he accused to the Pope of cheating at cards; the money, however, had already disappeared. The Eternal City had become a great market of offices and posts, often created only in order to be sold. And not only offices, but false bulls, indulgences to sinners, impunity for assassins could be had for money: a father, by payment of 800 ducats, obtained absolution for the murder of his two daughters. Every evening corpses found about the streets were thrown into the Tiber.

In the midst of these diabolical orgies, the Pope every now and then fell into a lethargy that was mistaken for death, and then his relations and his cardinals hurried to secure their treasures . . . and all Rome was in a tumult. The Pope would awake from his trance, and thereupon the merry-making went on as before, and assassination was once more the order of the day. At last a fresh attack of the Pope's malady left little room for hope. Anxious relations crowded round the bed of the dying man, who could take nothing but woman's milk; then, it was said, transfusion of blood was tried and three children sacrificed to the experiment.

But all was in vain and on the 25th of July, 1492—the same year in which Lorenzo dei Medici had died—Innocent VIII breathed his last at the age of sixty. At the death of Sixtus IV men had blessed the day that freed the world from so great a monster, and the following Pope was much worse than his predecessor. Nobody now believed that a worse than Innocent could be found, yet the infamy of the new Pope, Alexander VI, caused that of his predecessors to be totally forgotten.

The Son

Francesco Matarazzo, erudite philologist and secretary of the governor of Perugia, witnessed events which he later described in his *Cronaca della Citta di Perugia dal 1492 al 1503.*

[Cesare Borgia] was then the first captain of Italy, not so much by his great military science, but by treason and the power of gold; he had turned the art of war into the art of deception, which everybody learnt from him. After having destroyed all the lordships, he had the best of fighters on his side, all the most famous *condottieri.* Besides, wherever his soldiers went, he had them quartered free; thus they gained more in time of war than in time of peace and, thus, he had a great number of soldiers with him.

He was also one of the happiest of men; he had picked up a greater quantity of treasure and objects than anyone else in Italy. And nowhere in Italy were the soldiers so well provided with horses and fine clothing. Captain and *Gonfaloniere* of the Church, he was esteemed by all the lords. . . . Astrologers and necromancers declared him to be the very son of Fortune.

The Father

The jubilee of 1500 and the crowds it brought to Rome helped spread abroad the rumors concerning the private lives, debauchery and crimes of the Borgia clan. In his *Diaries* (Venice: 1871–82), Mario Sanuto, a Venetian historiographer and a contemporary of the Borgias, notes that "daily one finds in Rome men murdered, four or five every night, even bishops, prelates and others; everyone in Rome trembles in fear of being murdered by the Duke."

Among Machiavelli's many correspondents, Agostino Vespucci, the brother of Amerigo, reflected the general opinion concerning the death of a Cardinal, one among many, whose inheritance fell to the Pope.

Here everyone holds it to have been due to poison and to not having been on sufficiently good terms with the great *Gonfaloniere.* One hears often, very often in Rome of deaths of this sort. . . .

The Pope seems to me very worried by these rumors concerning the Great Turk, rumors that get ever stronger; he begins to say with many sighs, "Alas! in what land, on what seas shall I find a haven?" He doubles the guard at his palace, night and day, shows himself only with the greatest difficulty, and yet still plays Sylla with his proscriptions. In everybody's sight he deprives one of his property, another of his life, sends one into exile, another to forced labor, grabs the dwelling of another to install some rascal in it; and all this for the slightest motive, or for no motive at all. Besides, he lets his barons and his friends carry out every kind of outrage and crime, steal, ransack the shops and a thousand things of this sort. Here, benefices are for sale more readily than melons, waffles or drinking water in Florence. The courts of Rome are unemployed because all law rests in force and is in the hands of these rascals: to the point that the Turk seems necessary, since the Christians do not arise to extirpate this blackguard from the human conclave; such is the unanimous language of all decent men.

I have still to tell you that every night, between the Angelus and the first hour, one sees twenty-five women and more who are brought to the pontifical palace, behind a few riders—without speaking of the Pope who, for his part, keeps his illicit herd permanently on the premises —to the point that the whole palace has become the bawdy-house of every turpitude . . .

The Antiborgian Letter

In November 1501, an anonymous letter, probably written by a member of the Colonna family and resuming the tale of Borgia crimes, was intercepted on its way to the court of the Emperor Maximilian. It was transcribed by the papal Master of Ceremonies, Burchard, and is now known from its contents as the "Antiborgian letter."

The Emperor and the other princes of the Roman Empire must be informed of the infamies that this ignoble beast [Caesar] perpetrates in the Christian world. They must know the abominable crimes which are committed, crimes which tend to the despising of God and the overturning of religion, crimes so atrocious, so frightful that the best informed must be stupefied by them. These things must be told in the councils of the princes. . . . They must be told that the time of Antechrist, so often announced by the prophets, has arrived, for there has never been a worse enemy of our faith and our religion; it is impossible to imagine a more declared enemy of God, a more determined destroyer of the faith and religion of Christ. . . .

O frightful times! How far we are from the holiness of the Sovereign Pontiffs of old! How far we are from justice!

Posterity will find it hard to believe in the fire which devours the peoples. And yet the Christian princes still think of spreading the domain of religion! How shall we make war on Turk and on Arab as long as this internal scourge has not disappeared? Once upon a time, glorious princes made the vow to use their arms to increase the religion of Christ and recover Jerusalem; many and glorious martyrs shed their blood for this cause. Have all these labors been undertaken so that a Rodrigo Borgia, the greatest rogue of all times, should gain the pontificate by a criminal deal and make nonsense out of every human and divine right?

Let then the princes come to the aid of religion in distress, let them bring the ship of St. Peter into port, let them restore to Rome justice and peace, let them banish from Rome this pest engendered by the loss of Christianity . . .

The End

The Pope would live another two years, but the conditions of his death (August 18, 1503) and the stories it evoked seemed to confirm his living reputation. In the papal palace as in the Basilica of St. Peter, chaos prevailed. Lackeys and soldiers struggled with the clergy for pillows, vestments and torches, too precious to waste in burial. Soon, the corpse began to turn black, to decompose and to stink frightfully, developments to be expected in a Roman August but attributed at once to poison, to the devil, or to both. As the Marquis of Mantua wrote to his wife, Isabella d'Este: "After the death of Pope Innocent VIII, [his predecessor] during the conclave, [Borgia] made a pact with the devil, to whom he sold his soul in exchange for the papacy. . . . There are persons who affirm having seen, at the moment of death, seven devils in his room. After death, his body began to boil and the mouth to bubble like a cauldron on the fire. . . . He swelled so much that he had nothing of human form, and had become as broad as he was long. His burial was carried out with little ceremony. As everybody refused to touch him, a man dragged him by a rope tied to his feet, from his bed to a place where he was burnt."

3. THE MACHINERY OF INDULGENCES

The idea that the Pope could issue indulgences for the remission of sins was based on the theory that St. Peter and his successors had control of an inexhaustible treasury of merit which they could dispense to the faithful. This merit, due first to Christ and then to successive generations of good Christians, was seen as a store of spiritual wealth into which the Popes could dip at will for the benefit of the living and the dead. The Popes first began to use this power seriously as an inducement to pious activity, such as pilgrimages or crusades, but soon saw its pecuniary usefulness. As a rule, the administration of indulgences was accompanied by certain moral requirements—repentance, confession, etc. This is apparent in the instructions issued by the Archbishop of Mainz at the start of the great campaign of 1517, designed to raise money for the St. Peter's building fund. But such scrupulous instructions were not always obeyed.

Instructions Issued by Albert of Mainz

The first grace is the complete remission of all sins; and nothing greater than this can be named, since sinful man, deprived of the grace of God, obtains complete remission by these means and once more enjoys God's grace; moreover, through this remission of sins the punishment which one is obliged to undergo in purgatory on account of the affront to the Divine Majesty is all remitted, and the pains of purgatory completely blotted out. And although nothing is precious enough to be given in exchange for such a grace —since it is a free gift of God and grace is beyond price—yet in order that Christian believers may be the more easily induced to procure the same, we establish the following rules, to wit:

In the first place, every one who is contrite in heart and has made oral confession, shall visit at least the seven churches indicated for this purpose, to wit, those in which the papal arms are displayed, and in each church shall say five Paternosters and five Ave Marias in honour of the five wounds of our Lord Jesus Christ, whereby our salvation is won, or one Miserere, which psalm is particularly well

From *Documents of the Christian Church,* ed. Henry Bettenson (Oxford, 1943), pp. 257–260. Reprinted by permission of Oxford University Press and Geoffrey Cumberlege.

adapted for obtaining forgiveness of sins. . . .

The method of contributing to the chest, for the construction of the said fabric of the Chief of the Apostles.

Firstly, the penitentiaries and confessors, after they have explained to those making confession the greatness of this kind of plenary remission and of these privileges, shall ask them for how large a contribution, in money or in other temporal goods, they would wish, in good conscience, to be spared this method of full remission and privileges; and this is to be done that they may be more easily induced to contribute. And because the conditions of men, and their occupations, are so various and manifold, and we cannot consider and assess them individually, we have therefore decided that the rates can be determined thus, according to recognized classifications. . . .

Then follows a graded schedule of rates: kings and their families, bishops, etc., 25 Rhenish gold guilders; abbots, counts, barons, etc., 10; lesser nobles and ecclesiastics and others with incomes of 500, 6 guilders; citizens with their own income, 1 guilder; those with less, ½. Those with nothing shall supply their contribution with prayer and fasting, "for the kingdom of heaven should be open to the poor as much as the rich."

The second principal grace is a "confessional" [confessional letter] replete with the greatest, most important, and hitherto unheard of privileges. . . .

Firstly, the privilege of choosing a suitable confessor, even a regular of the mendicant orders. . . .

[The other privileges include the power given to this confessor to absolve in cases normally "reserved" for the Apostolic See.]

The third important grace is the participation in all the benefits of the Church universal; which consists in this, that contributors toward the said building, together with their deceased parents, who have departed this world in a state of grace, shall now and for eternity be partakers in all petitions, intercessions, alms, fastings, prayers, in each and every pilgrimage, even those to the Holy Land; furthermore, in the stations at Rome, in masses, canonical hours, mortifications, and all other spiritual benefits which have been, or shall be, brought forth by the universal, most holy Church militant or by any of its members. Believers who purchase confessional letters may also become participants in all these things. Preachers and confessors must insist with great perseverance upon these advantages, and persuade believers not to neglect to acquire these benefits along with their confessional letter.

We also declare that in order to obtain these two most important graces, it is not necessary to make confession, or to visit the churches and altars, but merely to procure the confessional letter. . . .

The fourth important grace is for those souls which are in purgatory, and is the complete remission of all sins, which remission the pope brings to pass through his intercession, to the advantage of said souls, in this wise: that the same contribution shall be placed in the chest by a living person as one would make for himself. It is our wish, however, that our sub-commissioners should modify the regulations regarding contributions of this kind which are given for the dead, and that they should use their judgment in all o*her cases where, in their opinion, modifications are desirable.

It is, furthermore, not necessary that the persons who place their contributions in the chest for the dead should be contrite in heart and have orally confessed, since this grace is based simply on the state of grace in which the dead departed, and on the contribution of the living, as is evident from the text of the bull. Moreover preachers shall exert themselves to make this grace more widely known, since through the same, help will surely come to departed souls, and the construction of the church of St. Peter will be abundantly promoted at the same time. . . .

4. JOHN TETZEL

John Tetzel (c. 1465–1519) was a German Dominican friar blessed with the art of salesmanship and evident oratorical talents whose sermons on Indulgences, when delivered not far from Wittenberg, were the cause of Luther's ninety-five Theses. In this way the sale of Indulgences and Tetzel's exaggerations may be said to have touched off the Reformation.

A Sermon on Indulgences

Venerable Sir, I pray you that in your utterances you may be pleased to make use of such words as shall serve to open the eyes of the mind and cause your hearers to consider how great a grace and gift they have had and now have at their very doors. Blessed eyes indeed, which see what they see, because already they possess letters of safe conduct by which they are able to lead their souls through that valley of tears, through that sea of the mad world, where storms and tempests and dangers lie in wait, to the blessed land of Paradise. Know that the life of man upon earth is a constant struggle. We have to fight against the flesh, the world and the devil, who are always seeking to destroy the soul. In sin we are conceived,—alas! what bonds of sin encompass us, and how difficult and almost impossible it is to attain to the gate of salvation without divine aid; since He causes us to be saved, not by virtue of the good works which we accomplish, but through His divine mercy; it is necessary then to put on the armour of God.

You may obtain letters of safe conduct from the vicar of our Lord Jesus Christ, by means of which you are able to liberate your soul from the hands of the enemy, and convey it by means of contrition and confession, safe and secure from all pains of Purgatory, into the happy kingdom. For we know that in these letters are stamped and engraven all the merits of Christ's passion there laid bare. Consider, that for each and every mortal sin it is necessary to undergo seven years of penitence after confession and contrition, either in this life or in Purgatory.

How many mortal sins are committed in a day, how many in a week, how many in a month, how many in a year, how many in the whole course of life! They

From *Translations and Reprints*, Vol. 2, No. 6, J. H. Robinson, Ed.

are well-nigh numberless, and those that commit them must needs suffer endless punishment in the burning pains of Purgatory.

But with these confessional letters you will be able at any time in life to obtain full indulgence for all penalties imposed upon you, in all cases except the four reserved to the Apostolic See. Therefore throughout your whole life, whenever you wish to make confession, you may receive the same remission, except in cases reserved to the Pope, and afterwards, at the hour of death, a full indulgence as to all penalties and sins, and your share of all spiritual blessings that exist in the church militant and all its members.

Do you not know that when it is necessary for anyone to go to Rome, or undertake any other dangerous journey, he takes his money to a broker and gives a certain percent—five or six or ten—in order that at Rome or elsewhere he may receive again his funds intact, by means of the letter of this same broker? Are you not willing, then, for the fourth part of a florin, to obtain these letters, by virtue of which you may bring, not your money, but your divine and immortal soul safe and sound into the land of Paradise?

Wherefore I counsel, order, and by virtue of my authority as shepherd, I command that they shall receive together with me and other priests, this precious treas-ure, especially those who were not confessed at the time of the holy Jubilee, that they may be able to obtain the same forever. For the time may come when you may desire, but yet be unable to obtain the least portion of the grace.

Also on the part of SS. D. N. the Pope and of the most Holy Apostolic See and of the most reverend sir, my legate, to each and every one who shall have profited by the sacred Jubilee and made confession, and to all who may profit by this present brief opportunity, and who shall have lent a helping hand to the construction of the aforesaid house of the Prince of the Apostles, they shall all be participants and sharers in all prayers, suffrages, alms, fasts, supplications, masses, canonical hours, disciplines, pilgrimages, papal stations, benedictions, and all other spiritual goods which now exist or may exist forever in the church militant, and in all of these, not only they themselves, but their relatives, kindred and benefactors who have passed away; and as they were moved by charity, so God, and SS. Peter and Paul, and all the saints whose bodies rest in Rome, shall guard them in peace in this vale, and conduct them through it to the heavenly kingdom. Give everlasting thanks in the aforesaid names and in mine to the reverend secular priests and prelates, etc.

5. MARTIN LUTHER

Martin Luther (1483–1546) was the son of a successful Saxon peasant-entrepreneur. He joined the order of Augustine friars to seek peace of mind and assurance of salvation—some kind of bridge between the wickedness of man and the goodness of God. Unable to visualize this bridge in the corrupt Church of his time, he found it at last in the faith that had also effected Augustine's salvation. If man had faith, he could be saved; in comparison to this supreme truth, "works" were of no avail, a priest's unction of no importance. Every baptized Christian was a priest.

These conclusions appear in the pamphlets he published (1520), all urging the laity to take a hand in the reformation of the Church. An excerpt of one is given below. But the success of such fighting works must be attributed in the first place to the original attack of 1517 upon those practical abuses of the Roman Church which most right-minded Germans regarded as shocking.

The Ninety-Five Theses

The theses were posted on the side door of the Castle church in Wittenberg on Halloween, 1517. Posting theses in a public place was the usual way of giving notice of the disputations which were a regular feature of academic life. So, there was nothing peculiar or revolutionary in the action. As a matter of fact, Luther thought the Pope would support his exposure of the evils of the indulgence trade.

In the desire and with the purpose of elucidating the truth, a disputation will be held on the underwritten propositions at Wittenberg, under the presidency of the Reverend Father Martin Luther, Monk of the Order of St. Augustine, Master of Arts and of Sacred Theology, and ordinary Reader of the same in that place. He therefore asks those who cannot be present and discuss the subject with us orally, to do so by letter in their absence. In the name of our Lord Jesus Christ. Amen.

1. Our Lord and Master Jesus Christ in saying "Repent ye" (*poenitentiam agite*), etc., intended that the whole life of believers should be penitence (*poenitentia*).

2. This word cannot be understood as sacramental penance (*poenitentia*), that is, of the confession and satisfaction which are performed under the ministry of priests.

3. It does not, however, refer solely to inward penitence (*poenitentia*); nay, such inward penitence is naught, unless it outwardly produces various mortifications of the flesh.

4. The penalty (*poena*) thus continues as long as the hatred of self (that is, true inward penitence); namely, till our entrance into the kingdom of heaven.

5. The pope has neither the will nor the power to remit any penalties except those which he has imposed by his own authority, or by that of the canons.

6. The Pope has no power to remit any guilt, except by declaring and warranting it to have been remitted by God; or at most by remitting cases reserved for himself; in which cases, if his power were despised, guilt would certainly remain.

7. Certainly God remits no man's guilt without at the same time subjecting him, humbled in all things, to the authority of his representative the priest.

8. The penitential canons are imposed only on the living, and no burden ought to be imposed on the dying, according to them.

9. Hence, the Holy Spirit acting in the Pope does well for us in that, in his decrees, he always makes exception of the article of death and of necessity.

10. Those priests act unlearnedly and wrongly who, in the case of the dying, reserve the canonical penances for Purgatory.

From *Translations and Reprints*, Vol. 2, No. 6, J. H. Robinson, Ed.

11. Those tares about changing the canonical penalty into the penalty of Purgatory seem surely to have been sown while the bishops were asleep.

12. Formerly the canonical penalties were imposed not after but before absolution, as tests of true contrition.

13. The dying pay all penalties by death, and are already dead to the canon laws, and are by right relieved from them.

14. The imperfect vigor or love of a dying person necessarily brings with it great fear, and the less it is, the greater the fear it brings.

15. This fear and horror is sufficient by itself, to say nothing of other things, to constitute the pains of Purgatory, since it is very near to the horror of despair.

16. Hell, Purgatory, and Heaven appear to differ as despair, almost despair, and peace of mind differ.

17. With souls in Purgatory it seems that it must needs be that as horror diminishes so love increases.

18. Nor does it seem to be proved by any reasoning or any Scriptures, that they are outside of the state of merit or of the increase of love.

19. Nor does this appear to be proved, that they are sure and confident of their own blessedness, at least all of them, though we may be very sure of it.

20. Therefore the Pope, when he speaks of the plenary remission of all penalties, does not mean really of all, but only of those imposed by himself.

21. Thus those preachers of indulgences are in error who say that by the indulgences of the Pope a man is freed and saved from all punishment.

22. For in fact he remits to souls in Purgatory no penalty which they would have had to pay in this life according to the canons.

23. If any entire remission of all penalties can be granted to any one it is certain that it is granted to none but the most perfect, that is to very few.

24. Hence, the greater part of the people must needs be deceived by this indiscriminate and high-sounding promise of release from penalties.

25. Such power over Purgatory as the Pope has in general, such has every bishop in his own diocese, and every parish priest in his own parish, in particular.

26. The Pope acts most rightly in granting remission to souls not by the power of the keys (which is of no avail in this case), but by the way of intercession.

27. They preach man who say that the soul flies out of Purgatory as soon as the money thrown into the chest rattles.

28. It is certain that, when the money rattles in the chest, avarice and gain may be increased, but the effect of the intercession of the Church depends on the will of God alone.

29. Who knows whether all the souls in Purgatory desire to be redeemed from it—witness the story told of Saints Severinus and Paschal?

30. No man is sure of the reality of his own contrition, much less of the attainment of plenary remission.

31. Rare as is a true penitent, so rare is one who truly buys indulgences—that is to say, most rare.

32. Those who believe that, through letters of pardon, they are made sure of their own salvation will be eternally damned along with their teachers.

33. We must especially beware of those who say that these pardons from the Pope are that inestimable gift of God by which man is reconciled to God.

34. For the grace conveyed by these pardons has respect only to the penalties

of sacramental satisfaction, which are of human appointment.

35. They preach no Christian doctrine who teach that contrition is not necessary for those who buy souls (out of Purgatory) or buy confessional licenses.

36. Every Christian who feels true compunction has of right plenary remission of punishment and guilt even without letters of pardon.

37. Every true Christian, whether living or dead, has a share in all the benefits of Christ and of the Church, given by God, even without letters of pardon.

38. The remission, however, imparted by the Pope is by no means to be despised, since it is, as I have said, a declaration of the divine remission.

39. It is a most difficult thing, even for the most learned theologians, to exalt at the same time in the eyes of the people the ample effect of pardons and the necessity of true contrition.

40. True contrition seeks and loves punishment; while the ampleness of pardons relaxes it, and causes men to hate it, or at least gives occasion for them to do so.

41. Apostolic pardons ought to be proclaimed with caution, lest the people should falsely suppose that they are placed before other good works of charity.

42. Christians should be taught that it is not the wish of the Pope that the buying of pardons should be in any way compared to works of mercy.

43. Christians should be taught that he who gives to a poor man, or lends to a needy man, does better than if he bought pardons.

44. Because by works of charity, charity increases, and the man becomes better; while by means of pardons, he does not become better, but only freer from punishment.

45. Christians should be taught that he who sees any one in need, and, passing him by, gives money for pardons, is not purchasing for himself the indulgences of the Pope but the anger of God.

46. Christians should be taught that, unless they have superfluous wealth, they are bound to keep what is necessary for the use of their own households, and by no means to lavish it on pardons.

47. Christians should be taught that while they are free to buy pardons they are not commanded to do so.

48. Christians should be taught that the Pope, in granting pardons, has both more need and more desire that devout prayer should be made for him than that the money should be readily paid.

49. Christians should be taught that the Pope's pardons are useful if they do not put their trust in them, but most hurtful if through them they lose the fear of God.

50. Christians should be taught that, if the Pope were acquainted with the exactions of the Preachers of pardons, he would prefer that the Basilica of St. Peter should be burnt to ashes rather than that it should be built up with the skin, flesh, and bones of his sheep.

51. Christians should be taught that as it would be the duty so would it be the wish of the Pope even to sell, if necessary, the Basilica of St. Peter, and to give of his own money to very many of those from whom the preachers of pardons extract money.

52. Vain is the hope of salvation through letters of pardon, even if a commissary—nay, the Pope himself—were to pledge his own soul for them.

53. They were enemies of Christ and of the Pope who, in order that the pardons may be preached, condemn the Word of God to utter silence in other churches.

54. Wrong is done to the Word of God when, in the same sermon, an equal or longer time is spent on pardons than on it.

55. The mind of the Pope necessarily is that, if pardons, which are a very small matter, are celebrated with single bells, single processions, and single ceremonies, the Gospel, which is a very great matter, should be preached with a hundred bells, a hundred processions, and a hundred ceremonies.

56. The treasures of the Church, whence the Pope grants indulgences, are neither sufficiently named nor known among the people of Christ.

57. It is clear that they are at least not temporal treasures, for these are not so readily lavished, but only accumulated, by means of the preachers.

58. Nor are they the merits of Christ and of the saints, for these, independently of the Pope, are always working grace to the inner man, and the cross, death, and hell to the outer man.

59. St. Lawrence said that the treasures of the Church are the poor of the Church, but he spoke according to the use of the term in his time.

60. We are not speaking rashly when we say that the keys of the Church, bestowed through the merits of Christ, are that treasure.

61. For it is clear that the power of the Pope is sufficient of itself for the remission of [canonical] penalties and of [reserved] cases.

62. The true treasure of the Church is the Holy Gospel of the glory and grace of God.

63. This treasure, however, is deservedly most hateful, because it makes the first to be last.

64. While the treasure of indulgences is deservedly most acceptable, because it makes the last to be first.

65. Hence the treasures of the Gospel are nets, wherewith of old they fished for the men of riches.

66. The treasures of indulgences are nets, wherewith they now fish for the riches of men.

67. Those indulgences, which the preachers loudly proclaim to be the greatest graces, are seen to be truly such as regards the promotion of gain.

68. Yet they are in reality most insignificant when compared to the grace of God and the piety of the cross.

69. Bishops and parish priests are bound to receive the commissaries of apostolical pardons with all reverence.

70. But they are still more bound to see to it with all their eyes, and take heed with all their ears, that these men do not preach their own dreams in place of the Pope's commission.

71. He who speaks against the truth of apostolical pardons, let him be anathema and accursed.

72. But he, on the other hand, who exerts himself against the wantonness and license of speech of the preachers of pardons, let him be blessed.

73. As the Pope justly thunders against those who use any kind of contrivance to the injury of the traffic in pardons.

74. Much more is it his intention to thunder against those who, under the pretext of pardons, use contrivances to the injury of holy charity and of truth.

75. To think that the Papal pardons have such power that they could absolve a man even if—by an impossibility—he had violated the Mother of God, is madness.

76. We affirm on the contrary that Papal pardons cannot take away even the least of venial sins, as regards its guilt.

77. The saying that, even if St. Peter were now Pope, he could grant no greater graces, is blasphemy against St. Peter and the Pope.

78. We affirm on the contrary that both he and any other Pope has greater graces to grant, namely, the Gospel, powers, gifts of healing, etc. (I Cor. XII).

79. To say that the cross set up among the insignia of the Papal arms is of equal power with the cross of Christ, is blasphemy.

80. Those bishops, priests and theologians who allow such discourses to have currency among the people will have to render an account.

81. This license in the preaching of pardons makes it no easy thing, even for learned men, to protect the reverence due to the Pope against the calumnies, or at all events, the keen questioning of the laity.

82. As for instance: Why does not the Pope empty Purgatory for the sake of most holy charity and of the supreme necessity of souls—this being the most just of all reasons—if he redeems an infinite number of souls for the sake of that most fatal thing, money, to be spent on building a basilica—this being a very slight reason?

83. Again; why do funeral masses and anniversary masses for the deceased continue, and why does not the Pope return, or permit the withdrawal of, the funds bequeathed for this purpose, since it is a wrong to pray for those who are already redeemed?

84. Again; what is this new kindness of God and the Pope, in that, for money's sake, they permit an impious man and an enemy of God to redeem a pious soul which loves God, and yet do not redeem that same pious and beloved soul out of free charity on account of its own need?

85. Again; why is it that the penitential canons, long since abrogated and dead in themselves, in very fact and not only by usage, are yet still redeemed with money, through the granting of indulgences, as if they were full of life?

86. Again; why does not the Pope, whose riches are at this day more ample than those of the wealthiest of the wealthy, build the single Basilica of St. Peter with his own money rather than with that of poor believers?

87. Again; what does the Pope remit or impart to those who through perfect contrition have a right to plenary remission and participation?

88. Again; what greater good could the Church receive than if the Pope, instead of once, as he does now, were to bestow these remissions and participations a hundred times a day on any one of the faithful?

89. Since it is the salvation of souls, rather than money, that the Pope seeks by his pardons, why does he suspend the letters and pardons granted long ago, since they are equally efficacious?

90. To repress these scruples and arguments of the laity by force alone, and not to resolve them by giving reasons, is to expose the Church and the Pope to the ridicule of their enemies, and to make Christian men unhappy.

91. If then pardons were preached according to the spirit and mind of the Pope, all these questions would be resolved with ease; nay, would not exist.

92. Away then with all those prophets

who say to the people of Christ: "Peace, peace," and there is no peace.

93. Blessed be all those prophets who say to the people of Christ: "The cross, the cross," and there is no cross.

94. Christians should be exhorted to strive to follow Christ their head through pains, deaths, and hells.

95. And thus trust to enter heaven through many tribulations, rather than in the security of peace.

On the Babylonish Captivity of the Church

OF ORDERS

Of this sacrament the Church of Christ knows nothing; it was invented by the church of the Pope. It not only has no promise of grace, anywhere declared, but not a word is said about it in the whole of the New Testament. Now it is ridiculous to set up as a sacrament of God that which can nowhere be proved to have been instituted by God. Not that I consider that a rite practised for so many ages is to be condemned; but I would not have human inventions established in sacred things, nor should it be allowed to bring in anything as divinely ordained, which has not been divinely ordained; lest we should be objects of ridicule to our adversaries. . . .

Which of the ancient Fathers has asserted that by these words priests were ordained? Whence then this new interpretation? It is because it has been sought by this device to set up a source of implacable discord, by which clergy and laity might be placed farther asunder than heaven and earth, to the incredible injury of baptismal grace and confusion of evangelical communion. Hence has originated that detestable tyranny of the clergy over the laity, in which, trusting to the corporal unction by which their hands are consecrated, to their tonsure, and to their vestments, they not only set themselves above the body of lay Christians, who have been anointed with the Holy Spirit, but almost look upon them as dogs, unworthy to be numbered in the Church along with themselves. Hence it is that they dare to command, exact, threaten, drive, and oppress, at their will. *In fine*, the sacrament of orders has been and is a most admirable engine for the establishment of all those monstrous evils which have hitherto been wrought, and are yet being wrought, in the Church. In this way Christian brotherhood has perished; in this way shepherds have been turned into wolves, servants into tyrants, and ecclesiastics into more than earthly beings.

How if they were compelled to admit that we all, so many as have been baptized, are equally priests? We are so in fact, and it is only a ministry which has been entrusted to them, and that with our consent. They would then know that they have no right to exercise command over us, except so far as we voluntarily allow of it. Thus it is said: "Ye are a chosen generation, a royal priesthood, a holy nation." (I Pet. ii. 9.) Thus all we who are Christians are priests; those whom we call priests are ministers chosen from among us to do all things in our name; and the priesthood is nothing else than a ministry. . . .

From *First Principles of the Reformation,* tr. H. Wace and C. A. Buchheim (Philadelphia: Lutheran Publication Society, 1885).

As far then as we are taught from the Scriptures, since what we call the priesthood is a ministry, I do not see at all for what reason a man who has once been made priest cannot become a layman again, since he differs in no wise from a layman, except by his ministerial office. But it is so far from impossible for a man to be set aside from the ministry, that even now this punishment is constantly inflicted on offending priests, who are either suspended for a time, or deprived for ever of their office. For that fiction of an indelible character has long ago become an object of derision. I grant that the Pope may impress this character, though Christ knows nothing of it, and for this very reason the priest thus consecrated is the lifelong servant and bondsman, not of Christ, but of the Pope, as it is at this day. But, unless I deceive myself, if at some future time this sacrament and figment fall to the ground, the Papacy itself will scarcely hold its ground, and we shall recover that joyful liberty in which we shall understand that we are all equal in every right, and shall shake off the yoke of tyranny and know that he who is a Christian has Christ, and he who has Christ has all things that are Christ's, and can do all things—on which I will write more fully and more vigorously when I find that what I have here said displeases my friends the papists.

6. THE PEASANT REVOLT, 1525

Once men had taken it upon themselves to interpret Scripture, it was only a matter of time before different interpretations would divide the reformers. Those who believed that ultimate sanction and authority were to be found in Scripture had no reason, besides their own judgment, to consider the authority of one interpreter superior to that of another. If Wittenberg was as good as Rome, then Zurich or Geneva, Münster, Canterbury, or Strasbourg need be no less. The ultimate appeal would always be to the Bible and to the believer's heart. But it is difficult to say in what proportion political motives mingled with religious ones in assuring the success of reformed ideas.

The serious peasant revolt which ravaged German lands in 1525 throws a lurid light on social and economic conditions in the area at the opening of the Reformation. The abuses against which the peasants rose were of long standing, and local revolts had punctuated the history of the Middle Ages. But the religious crisis helped fire the peasants' discontent into an explosion that threatened the princes, the cities, the whole social order, and even the Lutheran reform itself. As they rose, the peasants drafted their demands, of which there were many versions. The articles given below reflect the attitude of the least radical. Luther, who at first had appealed for peace, soon turned against the rebels and published his notorious plea to the German nobility, in which he asked them to "take pity on us poor people, and so kill, destroy, exterminate, drown in blood without mercy" the dangerous radicals.

The Twelve Articles of the Peasants

Peace to the Christian reader, and the Grace of God through Christ.

There are many evil writings put forth of late which take occasion on account of the assembling of the peasants, to cast scorn upon the Gospel, saying: Is this the fruit of the new teaching, that no one should obey but all should everywhere rise in revolt, and rush together to reform, or perhaps destroy entirely, the authorities, both ecclesiastical and lay? The articles below shall answer these godless and criminal fault-finders, and serve in the first place to remove the reproach from the word of God and, in the second place, to give a Christian excuse for the disobedience or even the revolt of the entire Peasantry. In the first place the Gospel is not the cause of revolt and disorder, since it is the message of Christ, the promised Messiah, the Word of Life, teaching only love, peace, patience and concord. Thus, all who believe in Christ should learn to be loving, peaceful, long-suffering and harmonious. This is the foundation of all the articles of the peasants (as will be seen) who accept the gospel and live according to it. How then can the evil reports declare the Gospel to be a cause of revolt and disobedience? That the authors of the evil reports and the enemies of the Gospel oppose themselves to these demands is due not to the Gospel but to the Devil, the worst enemy of the Gospel, who causes this opposition by raising doubts in the minds of his followers; and thus the word of God, which teaches love, peace and concord, is overcome. In the second place, it is clear that the peasants demand that this Gospel be taught them as a guide in life, and they ought not to be called disobedient or

disorderly. Whether God grant the peasants (earnestly wishing to live according to his word) their requests or no, who shall find fault with the will of the Most High? Who shall meddle in his judgments or oppose his majesty? Did he not hear the children of Israel when they called upon him and save them out of the hands of Pharaoh? Can he not save his own today? Yes, he will save them and that speedily. Therefore, Christian reader, read the following articles with care and then judge. Here follow the articles:

The First Article: First, it is our humble petition and desire, as also our will and resolution, that in the future we should have power and authority so that each community should choose and appoint a pastor, and that we should have the right to depose him should he conduct himself improperly. The pastor thus chosen should teach us the Gospel pure and simple, without any addition, doctrine or ordinance of man. For to teach us continually the true faith will lead us to pray God that through his grace this faith may increase within us and become a part of us. For if his grace work not within us we remain flesh and blood, which availeth nothing; since the Scripture clearly teaches that only through true faith can we come to God. Only through his mercy can we become holy. Hence such a guide and pastor is necessary, and in this fashion grounded upon the Scriptures.

The Second Article: According as the just tithe is established by the Old Testament and fulfilled in the New, we are ready and willing to pay the fair tithe of grain. The word of God plainly provides

From *Translations and Reprints*, Vol. II, No. 6, J. H. Robinson, Ed.

that in giving according to right to God and distributing to his people the services of a pastor are required. We will that for the future our church provost, whomsoever the community may appoint, shall gather and receive this tithe. From this he shall give to the pastor, elected by the whole community, a decent and sufficient maintenance for him and his [*im und den seynen*], as shall seem right to the whole community (or, with the knowledge of the community). What remains over shall be given to the poor of the place, as the circumstances and the general opinion demand. Should anything farther remain, let it be kept, lest anyone should have to leave the country from poverty. Provision should also be made from this surplus to avoid laying any land tax on the poor. In case one or more villages have themselves sold their tithes on account of want, and the village has taken action as a whole, the buyer should not suffer loss, but we will that some proper agreement be reached with him for the repayment of the sum by the village with due interest. But those who have tithes which they have not purchased from a village, but which were appropriated by their ancestors, should not, and ought not, to be paid anything farther by the village, which shall apply its tithes to the support of the pastors elected as above indicated, or to solace the poor, as is taught by the Scriptures. The small tithes, whether ecclesiastical or lay, we will not pay at all, for the Lord God created cattle for the free use of man. We will not, therefore, pay farther an unseemly tithe which is of man's invention.

The Third Article: It has been the custom hitherto for men to hold us as their own property, which is pitiable enough, considering that Christ has delivered and redeemed us all, without exception by the shedding of his precious blood, the lowly as well as the great. Accordingly, it is consistent with Scripture that we should be free and wish to be so. Not that we would wish to be absolutely free and under no authority. God does not teach us that we should lead a disorderly life in the lusts of the flesh, but that we should love the Lord our God and our neighbor. We would gladly observe all this as God has commanded us in the celebration of the communion. He has not commanded us not to obey the authorities, but rather that we should be humble, not only towards those in authority, but towards everyone. We are thus ready to yield obedience according to God's law to our elected and regular authorities in all proper things becoming to a Christian. We, therefore, take it for granted that you will release us from serfdom, as true Christians, unless it should be shown us from the Gospel that we are serfs.

The Fourth Article: In the fourth place it has been the custom heretofore, that no poor man should be allowed to touch venison or wild fowl, or fish in flowing water, which seems to us quite unseemly and unbrotherly, as well as selfish and not agreeable to the word of God. In some places the authorities preserve the game to our great annoyance and loss, recklessly permitting the unreasoning animals to destroy to no purpose our crops, which God suffers to grow for the use of man, and yet we must remain quiet. This is neither godly nor neighborly. For when God created man he gave him dominion over all the animals, over the birds of the air and over the fish in the water. Accordingly it is our desire if a man holds possession of waters that he should prove from satisfactory documents that his right has been unwittingly acquired by purchase. We do not wish to take it from him by force, but his rights should be exercised in a Christian and brotherly fashion. But whosoever cannot produce such evidence should surrender his claim with good grace.

The Fifth Article: In the fifth place we are aggrieved in the matter of woodcutting, for the noble folk have appropriated all the woods to themselves alone. If a poor man requires wood he must pay double for it, [or perhaps, two pieces of money]. It is our opinion in regard to a wood which has fallen into the hands of a lord, whether spiritual or temporal, that unless it was duly purchased it should revert again to the community. It should, moreover, be free to every member of the community to help himself to such firewood as he needs in his own home. Also, if a man requires wood for carpenter's purposes he should have it free, but with the knowledge of a person appointed by the community for that purpose. Should, however, no such forest be at the disposal of the community, let that which has been duly bought be administered in a brotherly and Christian manner. If the forest, although unfairly appropriated in the first instance, was later duly sold, let the matter be adjusted in a friendly spirit and according to the Scriptures.

The Sixth Article: Our sixth complaint is in regard to the excessive services demanded of us, which are increased from day to day. We ask that this matter be properly looked into so that we shall not continue to be oppressed in this way, and that some gracious consideration be given us, since our forefathers were required only to serve according to the word of God.

The Seventh Article: Seventh, we will not hereafter allow ourselves to be farther oppressed by our lords, but will let them demand only what is just and proper according to the word of the agreement between the lord and the peasant. The lord should no longer try to force more services or other dues from the peasant without payment, but permit the peasant to enjoy his holding in peace and quiet. The peasant should, however, help the lord when it is necessary, and at proper times, when it will not be disadvantageous to the peasant, and for a suitable payment.

The Eighth Article: In the eighth place, we are greatly burdened by holdings which cannot support the rent exacted from them. The peasants suffer loss in this way and are ruined; and we ask that the lords may appoint persons of honor to inspect these holdings, and fix a rent in accordance with justice, so that the peasant shall not work for nothing, since the laborer is worthy of his hire.

The Ninth Article: In the ninth place, we are burdened with a great evil in the constant making of new laws. We are not judged according to the offence, but sometimes with great ill will, and sometimes much too leniently. In our opinion we should be judged according to the old written law, so that the case shall be decided according to its merits, and not with partiality.

The Tenth Article: In the tenth place, we are aggrieved by the appropriation by individuals of meadows and fields which at one time belonged to a community. These we will take again into our own hands. It may, however, happen that the land was rightfully purchased, but when the land has unfortunately been purchased in this way, some brotherly arrangement should be made according to circumstances.

The Eleventh Article: In the eleventh place we will entirely abolish the due called *Todfall* [i.e., heriot], and will no longer endure it, nor allow widows and orphans to be thus shamefully robbed against God's will, and in violation of justice and right, as has been done in many places, and by those who should shield and protect them. These have disgraced and despoiled us, and although they had little authority they assumed it. God will suffer this no more, but it shall be wholly done away with, and for the future no man shall be bound to give little or much.

Conclusion: In the twelfth place it is our conclusion and final resolution, that if one or more of the articles here set forth should not be in agreement with the word of God, as we think they are, such article we will willingly recede from, when it is proved really to be against the word of God by a clear explanation of the Scripture. Or if articles should now be conceded to us that are hereafter discovered to be unjust, from that hour they shall be dead and null and without force. Likewise, if more complaints should be discovered which are based upon truth and the Scriptures, and relate to offences against God and our neighbor, we have determined to reserve the right to present these also, and to exercise ourselves in all Christian teaching. For this we shall pray God, since he can grant this, and he alone. The peace of Christ abide with us all.

6. REFORMATION ECHOES IN ENGLAND

Thomas Bilney was an English parson who underwent a powerful religious experience of the sort not uncommon among the new reformed sects. Here is an attempt he made to justify himself in a letter to the Bishop of London (1527). Tried and sent to the Tower for his beliefs, Bilney delivered himself by making submission, but soon fell back into "heresy" and was finally executed for it in 1531, only three years before the final break between the English Church and that of Rome, one witness more to the dangers of being prematurely right.

To the reverend father in Christ, Cuthbert, bishop of London, Thomas Bilney wisheth health in Christ, with all submission due unto such a prelate:

In this behalf, most reverend father in Christ, I think myself most happy that it is my chance to be called to examination before your reverence, for that you are of such wisdom and learning, of such integrity of life, which all men do confess to be in you, that even yourself cannot choose (if you do not too lightly esteem God's gifts in you), as often as you shall remember the great things which God hath done unto you, but straightways secretly in your heart, to his high praise say, "He that is mighty hath done great things unto me, and holy is his name." I rejoice, that I have now happened upon such a judge, and with all my heart give thanks unto God, who ruleth all things.

And albeit (God is my witness) I know not myself guilty of any error in my sermons, neither of any heresy or sedition, which divers do slander me of, seeking

From *The Acts and Monuments of John Foxe,* ed. Stephen R. Cattley, 7 vols. (London, 1837–1841), IV.

rather their own lucre and advantage, than the health of souls: notwithstanding I do exceedingly rejoice, that it is so foreseen by God's divine providence, that I should be brought before the tribunal seat of Tonstal, who knoweth as well as any other, that there will never be wanting a Jannes and a Jambres, who will resist the truth; that there shall never be lacking some Elymas, who will go about to subvert the straight ways of the Lord; and finally, that some Demetriuses, Pithonises, Balaams, Nicolaitans, Cains, and Ishmaels, will be always at hand, who will greedily hunt and seek after that which pertaineth unto themselves, and not that which pertaineth to Jesus Christ. . . .

But if any man seeketh to reduce those who were gone astray, into the fold of Christ, that is, the unity of faith, by and by there rise up certain against him, which are named pastors, but indeed are wolves; which seek no other thing of their flock, but the milk, wool, and fell, leaving both their own souls, and the souls of their flock, unto the devil.

These men, I say, rise up like unto Demetrius, crying out, "This heretic dissuadeth and seduceth much people every where, saying, that they are not gods, which are made with hands." These are they, these I say, most reverend father! are they, who, under the pretence of persecuting heretics, follow their own licentious lives; enemies unto the cross of Christ, who can suffer and bear anything rather than the sincere preaching of Christ crucified for our sins. These are they unto whom Christ threateneth eternal damnation, when he saith, "Wo be unto you scribes, Pharisees, and hypocrites! which shut up the kingdom of heaven before men, and you yourselves enter not in, neither suffer those which

would enter, to come in." These are they that have come in another way to the charge of souls, as it appeareth; "For if any man," saith Christ, "come in by me, he shall be saved; and shall come in, and go out, and find pasture." These men do not find pasture, for they never teach and draw others after them, that they should enter by Christ, who alone is the door whereby we must come unto the Father; but set before the people another way, persuading them to come unto God through good works, often times speaking nothing at all of Christ, thereby seeking rather their own gain and lucre, than the salvation of souls: in this point being worse than those who upon Christ (being the foundation) do build wood, hay, and straw. These men confess that they know Christ, but by their deeds they deny him.

These are those physicians upon whom that woman that was twelve years vexed with the bloody flux had consumed all that she had, and felt no help, but was still worse and worse, until such time as she came at last unto Christ; and after she had once touched the hem of his vesture, through faith she was so healed, that by and by she felt the same in her body. O mighty power of the most Highest! which I also, miserable sinner, have often tasted and felt, who, before I could come unto Christ, had even likewise spent all that I had upon those ignorant physicians, that is to say, unlearned hearers of confession; so that there was but small force of strength left in me (who of nature was but weak), small store of money, and very little wit or understanding; for they appointed me fastings, watching, buying of pardons and masses; in all things (as I now understand) they sought rather their own gain, than the salvation of my sick and languishing soul.

But at last I heard speak of Jesus, even

then when the New Testament was first set forth by Erasmus; which when I understood to be eloquently done by him, being allured rather by the Latin than by the word of God (for at that time I knew not what it meant), I bought it even by the providence of God, as I do now well understand and perceive: and at the first reading (as I well remember) I chanced upon this sentence of St. Paul (O most sweet and comfortable sentence to my soul!) in I Tim. i, "It is a true saying, and worthy of all men to be embraced, that Christ Jesus came into the world to save sinners: of whom I am the chief and principal." This one sentence, through God's instruction and inward working, which I did not then perceive, did so exhilarate my heart, being before wounded with the guilt of my sins, and being almost in despair, that immediately I felt a marvellous comfort and quietness, insomuch that my bruised bones leaped for joy.

After this, the Scripture began to be more pleasant unto me than the honey or the honey-comb; wherein I learned that all my travails, all my fasting and watching, all the redemption of masses and pardons, being done without trust in Christ, who only saveth people from their sins; these I say, I learned to be nothing else but even (as St. Augustine saith) a hasty and swift running out of the right way; or else much like to the vesture made of fig leaves, wherewithal Adam and Eve went about in vain to cover themselves, and could never before obtain quietness and rest, until they believed in the promise of God, that Christ, the seed of the woman, should tread upon the serpent's head: neither could I be relieved or eased of the sharp stings and bitings of my sins, before I was taught of God that lesson which Christ speaketh of in John

iii: "Even as Moses exalted the serpent in the desert, so shall the Son of Man be exalted, that all which believe on him, should not perish, but have life everlasting." . . .

And therefore, with all my whole power I teach, that all men should first acknowledge their sins, and condemn them, and afterwards hunger and thirst for that righteousness whereof St. Paul speaketh, "The righteousness of God, by faith in Jesus Christ, is upon all them which believe in him; for there is no difference: all have sinned, and lack the glory of God, and are justified freely through his grace, by the redemption which is in Jesus Christ:" which whosoever doth hunger or thirst for, without doubt they shall at length so be satisfied, that they shall not hunger and thirst for ever.

But, forasmuch as this hunger and thirst were wont to be quenched with the fulness of man's righteousness, which is wrought through the faith of our own elect and chosen works, as pilgrimages, buying of pardons, offering of candles, elect and chosen fasts, and oftentimes superstitions; and finally all kind of voluntary devotions (as they call them), against which God's word speaketh plainly in Deut. iv, v. 2, saying, "Thou shalt not do that which seemeth good unto thyself; but that which I command thee for to do, that do thou, neither adding to, neither diminishing any thing from it." Therefore, I say, often times I have spoke of those works, not condemning them (as I take God to my witness), but reproving their abuse; making the lawful use of them manifest even unto children; exhorting all men not so to cleave unto them, that they, being satisfied therewith, should loathe or wax weary of Christ, as many do: in whom I bid your fatherhood most prosperously well to fare.

And this is the whole sum. If you will appoint me to dilate more at large the things here touched, I will not refuse to do it, so that you will grant me time (for to do it out of hand I am not able for the weakness of my body); being ready always, if I have erred in anything, to be better instructed.

8. CALVINISM

John Calvin, born at Noyon in Picardy, 1509, died in 1564 at Geneva, where he had organized a Protestant republic. His religious system, known as Calvinism, has certain distinctive features: (1) the democratic origin which he attributes to religious authority; (2) the elimination of religious ceremonies; (3) the denial of any authority to tradition; (4) the dogma of predestination; (5) the reduction of the sacraments to two—baptism and communion. In France, the disciples of Calvin were also known as Huguenots, either after one of the Genevan leaders called Hugues or after the German word for fellows, *Eidgenossen.*

Founded upon very slender bases, Calvin's authority grew rapidly. A letter of the Venetian ambassador in Paris, written in 1561, informs the Doge: "Your Serenity will hardly believe the influence and power which the principal minister of Geneva, by name Calvin . . . possesses in this kingdom. He is a man of extraordinary authority, who by his mode of life, his doctrines, and his writings rises superior to all the rest." The French philosopher Renan explains this influence by saying that Calvin succeeded in an age and in a country that were hungry for Christianity, simply because he was the most Christian man of his generation. If Renan's reasoning is debatable, the prestige of Calvin and that which he reflected upon Geneva are not.

The Institutes of the Christian Church, 1559

The first edition of the *Institutio* was published in 1536, when Calvin was twenty-six. It was several times revised, but there was no development in Calvin's thought after the first edition. Calvin's genius was for organization rather than for theological speculation. (Bettenson's Note)

Book II. Chap. i. Therefore original sin is seen to be an hereditary depravity and corruption of our nature, diffused into all parts of the soul . . . wherefore those who have defined original sin as the lack of the original righteousness with which we should have been endowed, no doubt include, by implication, the whole fact of the matter, but they have not fully expressed the positive energy of this sin.

For our nature is not merely bereft of good, but is so productive of every kind of evil that it cannot be inactive. Those who have called it concupiscence have used a word by no means wide of the mark, if it were added (and this is what many do not concede) that whatever is in man, from intellect to will, from the soul to the flesh, is all defiled and crammed with concupiscence; or, to sum it up brief-

From *Documents of the Christian Church,* ed. Henry Bettenson (London, 1950). Reprinted by permission of Oxford University Press and Geoffrey Cumberlege.

ly, that the whole man is in himself nothing but concupiscence. . . .

Chap. iv. The old writers often shrink from the straight-forward acknowledgement of the truth in this matter, from motives of piety. They are afraid of opening to the blasphemers a window for their slanders concerning the works of God. While I salute their restraint, I consider that there is very little danger of this if we simply hold to the teaching of Scripture. Even Augustine is not always emancipated from that superstitious fear; as when he says (Of Predestination and Grace ss 4, 5) that "hardening" and "blinding" refer not to the operation of God, but to His foreknowledge. But there are so many sayings of Scripture which will not admit of such fine distinctions; for they clearly indicate that God's intervention consists in something more than His foreknowledge. . . . In the same way their suggestions as to God's "permission" are too weak to stand. It is very often said that God blinded and hardened the reprobate, that he turned, inclined, or drove on their hearts . . . And no explanation of such statements is given by taking refuge in "foreknowledge" or "permission." We therefore reply that this [process of hardening or blinding] comes about in two ways. When His light is removed, nothing remains but darkness and blindness; when His Spirit is taken away, our hearts harden into stone; when His guidance ceases, we are turned from the straight path. And so He is rightly said to blind, to harden, to turn, those from whom He takes away the ability to see, to obey, to keep on the straight path. But the second way is much nearer the proper meaning of the words; that to carry out his judgements he directs their councils and excites their wills, in the direction which he has decided upon, through the agency of Satan, the minister of his wrath. . . .

Book III. chap xxi. No one who wishes to be thought religious dares outright to deny predestination, by which God chooses some for the hope of life, and condemns others to eternal death. But men entangle it with captious quibbles; and especially those who make foreknowledge the ground of it. We indeed attribute to God both predestination and foreknowledge; but we call it absurd to subordinate one to the other. When we attribute foreknowledge to God we mean that all things have ever been, and eternally remain, before his eyes; so that to his knowledge nothing is future or past, but all things are present; and present not in the sense that they are reproduced in imagination (as we are aware of past events which are retained in our memory), but present in the sense that He really sees and observes them placed, as it were, before His eyes. And this foreknowledge extends over the whole universe and over every creature. By predestination we mean the eternal decree of God, by which He has decided in His own mind what He wishes to happen in the case of each individual. For all men are not created on an equal footing, but for some eternal life is pre-ordained, for others eternal damnation. . . .

Book IV. chap xiv. *Concerning Sacraments.* . . . It is convenient first of all to notice what a Sacrament is. Now the following seems to me to be a simple and proper definition of a Sacrament. An external symbol by which the Lord attests in our consciences His promises of goodwill towards us to sustain the inferiority of our faith, and we on our part testify to our piety towards Him as well as in His presence and before the angels as in the sight of men. Another way of putting it, more condensed but equally valid, would be: A testimony of God's grace to us confirmed by an external sign, with our answering witness of piety towards Him. . . .

Chap. xvii. *Concerning the Sacred Supper of Christ.* That sacred communication of his own flesh and blood by which Christ pours his life into us, just as if he were to penetrate into the marrow of our bones, he witnesses and attests in the Supper. And that he does not by putting before us a vain or empty sign, but offering there the efficacy of his Spirit, by which he fulfils his promise. And in truth he offers and displays the thing there signified to all who share that spiritual feast; though only by the faithful is it perceived and its fruits enjoyed. . . . If it is true that the visible sign is offered to us to attest the granting of the invisible reality, then, on receiving the symbol of the body, we may be confident that the body itself is no less given to us.

9. THE COUNTEROFFENSIVE

The Protestant Revolution was spreading over northwestern Europe: in 1534 the English church broke from Rome; in 1536 Calvin began his work in Geneva; in 1537 Denmark, in 1539 Saxony and Brandenburg, in 1541 the Palatinate, turned toward reform. Meanwhile, in 1541 John Knox, the enthusiastic follower of Calvin, introduced the reform in Scotland. During this time, however, the Church had not remained inactive. New militant orders had been founded—Jesuits and Capuchins— to carry the fight into the enemy camp. The Inquisition had been reorganized on the Spanish model. For a few years after 1553 England had been reconciled to Rome. But above all, in the long-drawn-out Council of Trent (1545–1563) the Church put its own house in order and reaffirmed the fundamentals of Catholic doctrine.

The Jesuits

The Society of Jesus, founded by Ignatius Loyola (1491–1556), was skillfully organized into a great force for the conservation and propagation of the Roman Church. The Society started with six friends, in 1534, but it was not until 1540 that Pope Paul III could be induced to give his approval. The following extracts are given to show the spirit of obedience which served to make the Society such a mighty influence of propaganda. (Bettenson's Note)

Ignatius Loyola: *Spiritual Exercises*

A. RULES FOR THINKING WITH
THE CHURCH

1. Always to be ready to obey with mind and heart, setting aside all judgment of one's own, the true spouse of Jesus Christ, our holy mother, our infallible and orthodox mistress, the Catholic Church, whose authority is exercised over us by the hierarchy.

2. To commend the confession of sins to a priest as it is practiced in the Church;

From *Documents of the Christian Church,* ed. Henry Bettenson (London, 1950). Reprinted by permission of Oxford University Press and Geoffrey Cumberlege.

the reception of the Holy Eucharist once a year, or better still every week, or at least every month, with the necessary preparation.

3. To commend to the faithful frequent and devout assistance at the holy sacrifice of the Mass, the ecclesiastical hymns, the divine office, and in general the prayers and devotions practiced at stated times, whether in public in the churches or in private.

4. To have a great esteem for the religious orders, and to give the preference to celibacy or virginity over the married state.

5. To approve of the religious vows of chastity, poverty, perpetual obedience, as well as the other works of perfection and supererogation. Let us remark in passing, that we must never engage by vow to take a state (such e.g. as marriage) that would be an impediment to one more perfect. . . .

6. To praise relics, the veneration and invocation of Saints: also the stations, and pious pilgrimages, indulgences, jubilees, the custom of lighting candles in the Churches, and other such aids to piety and devotion.

7. To praise the use of abstinence and fasts as those of Lent, of Ember Days, of Vigils, of Friday, of Saturday, and of others undertaken out of pure devotion: also voluntary mortifications, which we call penances, not merely interior, but exterior also.

8. To commend moreover the construction of Churches and ornaments; also images, to be venerated with the fullest right, for the sake of what they represent.

9. To uphold especially all the precepts of the Church, and not censure them in any manner; but, on the contrary, to defend them promptly, with reasons drawn from all sources, against those who criticize them.

10. To be eager to commend the decrees, mandates, traditions, rites and customs of the Fathers in the Faith or our superiors. As to their conduct; although there may not always be the uprightness of conduct that there ought to be, yet to attack or revile them in private or in public tends to scandal and disorder. Such attacks set the people against their princes and pastors; we must avoid such reproaches and never attack superiors before inferiors. The best course is to make private approach to those who have power to remedy the evil.

11. To value most highly the sacred teaching, both the Positive and the scholastic, as they are commonly called. . . .

12. It is a thing to be blamed and avoided to compare men who are still living on the earth (however worthy of praise) with the Saints and Blessed, saying: This man is more learned than St. Augustine, etc. . . .

13. That we may be altogether of the same mind and in conformity with the Church herself, if she shall have defined anything to be black which to our eyes appears to be white, we ought in like manner to pronounce it to be black. For we must undoubtingly believe, that the spirit of our Lord Jesus Christ, and the Spirit of the Orthodox Church His Spouse, by which Spirit we are governed and directed to Salvation, is the same; . . .

14. It must also be borne in mind, that although it be most true, that no one is saved but he that is predestinated, yet we must speak with circumspection concerning this matter, lest perchance, stressing too much the grace or predestination of God, we should seem to wish to shut out the force of free will and the merits of good works; or on the other hand, at-

tributing to these latter more than belongs to them, we derogate meanwhile from the power of grace.

15. For the like reason we should not speak on the subject of predestination frequently; if by chance we do so speak, we ought so to temper what we say as to give the people who hear no occasion of erring and saying, "If my salvation or damnation is already decreed, my good or evil actions are predetermined"; whence many are wont to neglect good works, and the means of salvation.

16. It also happens not unfrequently, that from immoderate preaching and praise of faith, without distinction or explanation added, the people seize a pretext for being lazy with regard to any good works, which precede faith, or follow it when it has been formed by the bond of charity.

17. Nor any more must we push to such a point the preaching and inculcating of the grace of God, as that there may creep thence into the minds of the hearers the deadly error of denying our faculty of free will. We must speak of it as the glory of God requires . . . that we may not raise doubts as to liberty and the efficacy of good works.

18. Although it is very praiseworthy and useful to serve God through the motive of pure charity, yet we must also recommend the fear of God; and not only filial fear, but servile fear, which is very useful and often even necessary to raise man from sin. . . . Once risen from the state, and free from the affection of mortal sin, we may then speak of that filial fear which is truly worthy of God, and which gives and preserves the union of pure love.

B. OBEDIENCE OF THE JESUITS

Let us with the utmost pains strain every nerve of our strength to exhibit this virtue of obedience, firstly to the Highest Pontiff, then to the Superiors of the Society; so that in all things, to which obedience can be extended with charity, we may be most ready to obey his voice, just as if it issued from Christ our Lord . . . , leaving any work, even a letter, that we have begun and have not yet finished; by directing to this goal all our strength and intention in the Lord, that holy obedience may be made perfect in us in every respect, in performance, in will, in intellect; by submitting to whatever may be enjoined on us with great readiness, with spiritual joy and perseverance; by persuading ourselves that all things (commanded) are just; by rejecting with a kind of blind obedience all opposing opinion or judgment of our own; and that in all things which are ordained by the Superior where it cannot be clearly held (*definiri*) that any kind of sin intervenes. And let each one persuade himself that they that live under obedience ought to allow themselves to be borne and ruled by divine providence working through their Superiors exactly as if they were a corpse which suffers itself to be borne and handled in any way whatsoever; or just as an old man's stick which serves him who holds it in his hand wherever and for whatever purpose he wish to use it.

The Council of Trent

The chief act of the Counter Reformation issued from the Alpine city of Trent where, in three meetings held in 1545–1549, 1551–1552, and 1562–1563, the Church tackled the problems of Protestantism, the need for a more precise definition of Catholic faith, and ultimately the need for a new internal discipline. The loss of many Catholics who had left Rome for rival churches was thus compensated by raising the standards of religious life and by the reorganization and systematization of both doctrine and administration.

DECREE TOUCHING THE OPENING OF THE COUNCIL

Doth it please you,—unto the praise and glory of the holy and undivided Trinity, Father, and Son, and Holy Ghost; for the increase and exaltation of the Christian faith and religion; for the extirpation of heresies; for the peace and union of the Church; for the reformation of the Clergy and Christian people; for the depression and extinction of the enemies of the Christian name,—to decree and declare that the sacred and general council of Trent do begin, and hath begun?

They answered: It pleaseth us.

DECREE CONCERNING THE EDITION, AND THE USE OF THE SACRED BOOKS

Moreover, the same sacred and holy Synod,—considering that no small utility may accrue to the Church of God, if it be made known which out of all the Latin editions, now in circulation, of the sacred books, is to be held as authentic,—ordains and declares, that the said old and vulgate edition, which, by the lengthened usage of so many ages, has been approved of in the Church, be, in public lectures, disputations, sermons and expositions, held as authentic; and that no one is to dare, or presume to reject it under any pretext whatever.

Furthermore, in order to restrain petulant spirits. It decrees, that no one, relying on his own skill, shall,—in matters of faith, and of morals pertaining to the edification of Christian doctrine,—wrestling the sacred Scripture to his own senses, presume to interpret the said sacred Scripture contrary to that sense which holy mother Church,—whose it is to judge of the true sense and interpretation of the holy Scriptures,—hath held and doth hold; or even contrary to the unanimous consent of the Fathers; even though such interpretations were never (intended) to be at any time published. Contraveners shall be made known by their Ordinaries, and be punished with the penalties by law established.

DECREE CONCERNING ORIGINAL SIN

That our Catholic *faith, without which it is impossible to please God,* may, errors being purged away, continue in its own perfect and spotless integrity, and that the Christian people may not *be carried about with every wind of doctrine;* whereas that old serpent, the perpetual enemy of mankind, amongst the very many evils

From *The Canons and Decrees of the Sacred and Oecumenical Council of Trent*, tr. J. Waterworth (London, 1848).

with which the Church of God is in these our times troubled, has also stirred up not only new, but even old, dissensions touching original sin, and the remedy thereof; the sacred and holy, oecumenical and general Synod of Trent,—lawfully assembled in the Holy Ghost, the three same legates of the Apostolic See presiding therein,—wishing now to come to the reclaiming of the erring, and the confirming of the wavering,—following the testimonies of the sacred Scriptures, of the holy Fathers, of the most approved councils, and the judgment and consent of the Church itself, ordains, confesses, and declares these things touching the said original sin:

1. If any one does not confess that the first man, Adam, when he had transgressed the commandment of God in Paradise, immediately lost the holiness and justice wherein he had been constituted; and that he incurred, through the offense of that prevarication, the wrath and indignation of God, and consequently death, with which God had previously threatened him, and, together with death, captivity under his power who thenceforth *had the empire of death, that is to say, the devil,* and that the entire Adam, through that offense of prevarication, was changed, in body and soul, for the worse; let him be anathema.

2. If any one asserts, that the prevarication of Adam injured himself alone, and not his posterity; and that the holiness and justice, received of God, which he lost, he lost for himself alone, and not for us also; or that he, being defiled by the sin of disobedience, has only transfused death, and pains of the body, into the whole human race, but not sin also, which is the death of the soul; let him be anathema:—whereas he contradicts the apostle who says: *By one man sin entered*

into the world, and by sin death, and so death passed upon all men, in whom all have sinned.

3. If any one asserts, that this sin of Adam,—which in its origin is one, and being transfused into all by propagation, not by imitation, is in each one as his own,—is taken away either by the powers of human nature, or by any other remedy than the merit of the *one mediator, our Lord Jesus Christ, who hath reconciled us to God in his own blood, made unto us justice, sanctification, and redemption;* or if he denies that the said merit of Jesus Christ is applied, both to adults and to infants, by the sacrament of baptism rightly administered in the form of the Church; let him be anathema: *For there is no other name under heaven given to men, whereby we must be saved.* Whence that voice: *Behold the lamb of God, behold him who taketh away the sins of the world;* and that other: *As many as have been baptized have put on Christ.*

DECREE ON JUSTIFICATION

. . . No one, moreover, so long as he is in this mortal life, ought so far to presume as regards the secret mystery of divine predestination, as to determine for certain that he is assuredly in the number of the predestinate; as if it were true, that he that is justified, either cannot sin any more, or, if he do sin, that he ought to promise himself an assured repentance; for except by special revelation, it cannot be known whom God hath chosen unto Himself. . . .

DECREE ON THE SACRAMENTS IN GENERAL

Canon I. If any one saith, that the sacraments of the New Law were not all instituted by Jesus Christ, our Lord; or, that they are more, or less, than seven, to wit, Baptism, Confirmation, the Eucharist, Penance, Extreme Unction, Holy Orders, and Matrimony; or even that any one of these seven is not truly and properly a sacrament; let him be anathema.

Canon IV. If any one saith, that the sacraments of the New Law are not necessary unto salvation, but superfluous; and that, without them, or without the desire thereof, men obtain of God, through faith alone, the grace of justification;—though all (the sacraments) are not indeed necessary for every individual; let him be anathema.

Canon V. If any one saith that these sacraments were instituted for the sake of nourishing faith alone; let him be anathema.

Canon VI. If any one saith, that the sacraments of the New Law do not contain the grace which they signify; or, that they do not confer that grace on those who do not place an obstacle thereunto; as though they were merely outward signs of grace or justice received through faith, and certain marks of the Christian profession, whereby believers are distinguished amongst men from unbelievers; let him be anathema.

Canon VII. If any one saith, that grace, as far as God's part is concerned, is not given through the said sacraments, always, and to all men, even though they receive them rightly, but (only) sometimes, and to some persons; let him be anathema.

Canon VIII. If any one saith, that by the said sacraments of the New Law grace is not conferred through the act performed, but that faith alone in the divine promise suffices for the obtaining of grace; let him be anathema.

Canon IX. If any one saith, that, in the three sacraments, Baptism, to wit, Confirmation, and Order, there is not imprinted in the soul a character, that is, a certain spiritual and indelible sign, on account of which they cannot be repeated; let him be anathema.

Canon X. If any one saith, that all Christians have power to administer the word, and all the sacraments; let him be anathema.

Canon XI. If any one saith, that, in ministers, when they effect, and confer the sacraments, there is not required the intention at least of doing what the Church does; let him be anathema.

Canon XII. If any one saith, that a minister, being in mortal sin,—if so be that he observe all the essentials which belong to the effecting, or conferring of, the sacrament,—neither effects, nor confers the sacrament; let him be anathema. . . .

DECREE CONCERNING THE MOST HOLY SACRAMENT OF THE EUCHARIST

. . . And because that Christ, our Redeemer, declared that which He offered under the species of bread to be truly His own body, therefore has it ever been a firm belief in the Church of God, and this holy Synod doth now declare it anew, that, by the consecration of the bread and of the wine, a conversion is made of the whole substance of the body of Christ our Lord, and of the whole substance of the wine into the substance of His blood; which conversion is, by the holy Catholic Church, suitably and properly called Transubstantiation.

ON THE MOST HOLY SACRAMENT OF THE EUCHARIST

Canon I. If any one denieth, that, in the sacrament of the most holy Eucharist, are contained truly, really and substantially, the body and blood together with the soul and divinity of our Lord Jesus Christ, and consequently the whole Christ; but saith that He is only therein as in a sign, or in figure, or virtue; let him be anathema.

Canon II. If any one saith, that, in the sacred and holy sacrament of the Eucharist, the substance of the bread and wine remains conjointly with the body and blood of our Lord Jesus Christ, and denieth that wonderful and singular conversion of the whole substance of the bread into the Body, and of the whole substance of the wine into the Blood— the species only of the bread and wine remaining—which conversion indeed the Catholic Church most aptly calls Transubstantiation; let him be anathema.

Canon III. If any one denieth, that, in the venerable sacrament of the Eucharist, the whole Christ is contained under each species, and under every part of each species, when separated; let him be anathema.

Canon IV. If any one saith, that, after the consecration is completed, the body and blood of our Lord Jesus Christ are not in the admirable sacrament of the Eucharist, but (are there) only during the use, whilst it is being taken, and not either before or after; and that, in the hosts, or consecrated particles, which are reserved or which remain after communion, the true Body of the Lord remaineth not; let him be anathema.

Canon V. If any one saith, either that the principal fruit of the most holy Eucharist is the remission of sins, or, that other effects do not result therefrom; let him be anathema.

Canon VI. If any one saith, that, in the holy sacrament of the Eucharist, Christ, the only-begotten Son of God, is not to be adored with the worship, even external of latria; and is, consequently, neither to be venerated with a special festive solemnity, nor to be solemnly borne about in processions, according to the laudable and universal rite and custom of holy church; or, is not to be proposed publicly to the people to be adored, and that the adorers thereof are idolators; let him be anathema.

Canon VII. If any one saith, that it is not lawful for the sacred Eucharist to be reserved in the *sacrarium*, but that, immediately after consecration, it must necessarily be distributed amongst those present; or, that it is not lawful that it be carried with honour to the sick; let him be anathema.

Canon VIII. If any one saith, that Christ, given in the Eucharist, is eaten spiritually only, and not also sacramentally and really; let him be anathema.

Canon IX. If any one denieth, that all and each of Christ's faithful of both sexes are bound, when they have attained to years of discretion, to communicate every year, at least at Easter, in accordance with the precept of holy Mother Church; let him be anathema.

Canon X. If any one saith, that it is not lawful for the celebrating priest to communicate himself; let him be anathema.

Canon XI. If any one saith, that faith alone is a sufficient preparation for receiving the sacrament of the most holy Eucharist; let him be anathema. And for fear lest so great a sacrament may be received unworthily, and so unto death and condemnation, this holy Synod ordains and declares, that sacramental confession, when a confessor may be had, is of necessity to be made beforehand, by those whose conscience is burdened with mortal sin, how contrite even soever they may think themselves. But if any one shall presume to teach, preach, or obstinately to assert, or even in public disputation to defend the contrary, he shall be thereupon excommunicated.

ON THE SACRIFICE OF THE MASS

. . . . Canon I. If any one saith, that in the mass a true and proper sacrifice is not offered to God; or, that to be offered is nothing else but that Christ is given us to eat; let him be anathema.

Canon II. If any one saith, that by those words, *Do this for the commemoration of me* . . . Christ did not institute the apostles priests, or, did not ordain that they, and other priests should offer His own body and blood; let him be anathema.

Canon III. If any one saith, that the sacrifice of the mass is only a sacrifice of praise and of thanksgiving; or, that it is a bare commemoration of the sacrifice consummated on the cross, but not a propitiatory sacrifice; or, that it profits him only who receives; and that it ought not to be offered for the living and the dead for sins, pains, satisfactions, and other necessities; let him be anathema.

DECREE ON REFORMATION

And forasmuch as, though the habit does not make the monk, it is nevertheless needful that clerics always wear a dress suitable to their proper order, that by the decency of their outward apparel they may show forth the inward correctness of their morals; but to such a pitch, in these days, have the contempt of religion and the rashness of some grown, as that, making but little account of their own dignity, and of the clerical honour, they even wear in public the dress of laymen—setting their feet in different paths, one of God, the other of the flesh;—for this cause, all ecclesiastical persons, howsoever exempted, who are either in sacred orders or in possession of any manner of dignities, personates, or other offices, or benefices ecclesiastical; if, after having been admonished by their own bishop, even by a public edict, they shall not wear a becoming clerical dress, suitable to their order and dignity, and in conformity with the ordinance and mandate of the said bishop, they may, and ought to be, compelled thereunto, by suspension from their orders, office, benefice, and from the fruits, revenues, and proceeds of the said benefices; and also, if, after having been once rebuked, they offend again herein [they are to be coerced] even by deprivation of the said offices and benefices. . . .

Whereas too, *he who has killed his neighbour on set purpose and by lying in wait for him, is to be taken away from the altar,* because he has voluntarily commited a homicide; even though that crime have neither been proved by ordinary process of law, nor be otherwise public, but is secret, such a one can never be promoted to sacred orders; nor shall it be lawful to confer upon him any ecclesiastical benefices, even though they have no cure of souls; but he shall be forever excluded from every ecclesiastical order, benefice, and office. . . .

There is nothing that continually *instructs others unto piety,* and the service of God, more than the life and example of those who have dedicated themselves to the divine ministry. For as they are seen to be raised to a higher position, above the things of this world, others fix their eyes upon them as upon a mirror, and derive from them what they are to imitate. Wherefore clerics called to have the Lord for their portion, ought by all means so to regulate their whole life and conversation, as that in their dress, comportment, gait, discourse, and all things else, nothing appear but what is grave, regulated, and replete with religiousness; avoiding even slight faults, which in them would be most grievous; that so their actions may impress all with veneration. Whereas, therefore, the more useful and decorous these things are for the Church of God, the more carefully also are they to be attended to; the holy Synod ordains, that those things which have been heretofore copiously and wholesomely enacted by sovereign pontiffs and sacred councils, —relative to the life, propriety of conduct, dress, and learning of clerics, and also touching the luxuriousness, feastings, dances, gambling, sports, and all sorts of crime whatever, as also the secular employments, to be by them shunned,—the same shall be henceforth observed, under the same penalties, or greater, to be imposed at the discretion of the Ordinary; nor shall any appeal suspend the execution hereof, as relating to the correction of manners. But if anything of the above shall be found to have fallen into desuetude, they shall make it their care that it be brought again into use as soon as possible, and be accurately observed by all, any customs to the contrary notwithstanding; lest they themselves may have, God being the avenger, to pay the penalty deserved by their neglect of the correction of those subject to them . . .

ON REFORMATION

. . . How shameful a thing, and how unworthy it is of the name of clerics who have devoted themselves to the service of God, to live in the filth of impurity, and unclean bondage, the thing itself doth testify, in the common scandal of all the faithful, and the extreme disgrace entailed on the clerical order. To the end, therefore, that the ministers of the Church may be recalled to that continency and integrity of life which becomes them; and that the people may hence learn to reverence them the more, that they know them to be more pure of life: the holy Synod forbids all clerics whatsoever to dare to keep concubines, or any other woman of whom any suspicion can exist, either in their own houses, or elsewhere, or to presume to have any intercourse with them: otherwise they shall be punished with the penalties imposed by the sacred canons, or by the statutes of the (several) churches. But if, after being admonished by their superiors, they shall not abstain from these women, they shall be *ipso facto* deprived of the third part of the fruits, rents, and proceeds of all their benefices whatsoever, and pensions; which third part shall be applied to the fabric of the church, or to some other pious place, at the discretion of the bishop. If, however, persisting in the same crime, with the same or some other woman, they shall not even yet have obeyed upon a second admonition, not only shall they thereupon forfeit all the fruits and proceeds of their benefices and pensions, which shall be applied to the places aforesaid, but they shall also be suspended from the administration of the benefices themselves, for as long a period as shall seem fit to the Ordinary, even as the delegate of the Apostolic See. And if, having been thus suspended, they nevertheless shall not put away those women, or even if they shall have intercourse with them, then shall they be for ever deprived of their ecclesiastical benefices, portions, offices, and pensions of whatsoever kind, and be rendered thenceforth incapable and unworthy of any manner of honours, dignities, benefices and offices, until, after a manifest amendment of life, it shall seem good to their superiors, for a cause, to grant them a dispensation. But if, after having once put them away, they shall have dared to renew the interrupted connexion, or to take to themselves other scandalous women of this sort, they shall, in addition to the penalties aforesaid, be smitten with the sword of excommunication. Nor shall any appeal, or exemption, hinder or suspend the execution of the aforesaid; and the cognizance of all the matters above-named shall not belong to arch-deacons, or deans, *or* other inferiors, but to the bishops themselves, who may proceed without the noise and the formalities of justice, and by the sole investigation of the truth of the fact. . . .

ON THE SACRAMENT OF ORDER

Canon I. If any one saith, that there is not in the New Testament a visible and external priesthood; or that there is not any power of consecrating and offering the true body and blood of the Lord, and of forgiving and retaining sins; but only an office and bare ministry of preaching the Gospel; or, that those who do not preach are not priests at all; let him be anathema.

Canon II. If any one saith, that, besides the priesthood, there are not in the Catholic Church other orders, both greater and minor, by which, as by certain steps, advance is made unto the priesthood; let him be anathema.

Canon III. If any one saith, that order, or sacred ordination, is not truly and properly a sacrament instituted by Christ the Lord; or, that it is a kind of human figment devised by men unskilled in ecclesiastical matters; or, that it is only a kind of rite for choosing ministers of the word of God and of the sacraments; let him be anathema.

Canon IV. If any one saith, that, by sacred ordination, the Holy Ghost is not given; and that vainly therefore do the bishops say, *Receive ye the Holy Ghost;* or, that a character is not imprinted by that ordination; or, that he who has once been a priest, can again become a layman; let him be anathema.

Canon V. If any one saith, that the sacred unction which the Church uses in holy ordination, is not only not required, but is to be despised and is pernicious, as likewise are the other ceremonies of Order; let him be anathema.

Canon VI. If any one saith, that in the Catholic Church there is not a hierarchy by divine ordination instituted, consisting of bishops, priests, and ministers; let him be anathema.

Canon VII. If any one saith, that bishops are not superior to priests; or, that they have not the power of confirming and ordaining; or, that the power which they possess is common to them and to priests; or, that orders, conferred by them, without the consent, or vocation of the people, or of the secular power, are invalid; or, that those who have neither been rightly ordained, nor sent, by ecclesiastical and canonical power, but come from elsewhere, are lawful ministers of the word and of the sacraments; let him be anathema.

Canon VIII. If any one saith, that the bishops, who are assumed by authority of the Roman Pontiff, are not legitimate and true bishops, but are a human figment; let him be anathema.

ON THE SACRAMENT
OF MATRIMONY

Canon IX. If any one saith, that clerics constituted in sacred orders, or Regulars, who have solemnly professed chastity, are able to contract marriage, and that being contracted it is valid, notwithstanding the ecclesiastical law or vow; and that the contrary is nothing else than to condemn marriage; and, that all who do not feel that they have the gift of chastity, even though they have made a vow thereof, may contract marriage; let him be anathema: seeing that God refuses not that gift to those who ask for it rightly, neither does *He suffer us to be tempted above that which we are able.*

ON THE INVOCATION, VENERATION,
AND RELICS OF SAINTS
AND ON SACRED IMAGES

The holy Synod enjoins on all bishops, and others who sustain the office and charge of teaching, that, agreeably to the usage of the Catholic and Apostolic Church, received from the primitive times of the Christian religion, and agreeably to the consent of the holy Fathers, and to the decrees of sacred Councils, they especially instruct the faithful diligently concerning the intercession and invocation of saints; the honour (paid) to relics; and the legitimate use of images: teaching them, that the saints, who reign together with Christ, offer up their own prayers to God for men; that it is good and useful suppliantly to invoke them, and to have recourse to their prayers, aid, (and) help for obtaining benefits from God, through

His Son, Jesus Christ our Lord, who is alone our Redeemer and Saviour; but that they think impiously, who deny that the saints, who enjoy eternal happiness in heaven, are to be invocated; or who assert either that they do not pray for men; or, that the invocation of them to pray for each of us even in particular, is idolatry; or, that it is repugnant to the word of God; and is opposed to the honour of the *one mediator of God and men, Christ Jesus;* or, that it is foolish to supplicate, vocally, or mentally, those who reign in heaven. Also, that the holy bodies of holy martyrs, and of others now living with Christ,—which bodies were the living members of Christ, and *the temple of the Holy Ghost,* and which are by Him to be raised unto eternal life, and to be glorified,—are to be venerated by the faithful; through which (bodies) many benefits are bestowed by God on men; so that they who affirm that veneration and honour are not due to the relics of saints; or, that these, and other sacred monuments, are uselessly honoured by the faithful; and that the places dedicated to the memories of the saints are in vain visited with the view of obtaining their aid; are wholly to be condemned, as the Church has already long since condemned, and now also condemns them.

Moreover, that the images of Christ, of the Virgin Mother of God, and of the other saints, are to be had and retained particularly in temples, and that due honour and veneration are to be given them; not that any divinity, or virtue, is believed to be in them, on account of which they are to be worshipped; or that anything is to be asked of them; or, that trust is to be reposed in images, as was of old done by the Gentiles who placed their hope in idols; but because the honour which is shown them is referred to the prototypes which those images represent; in such wise that by the images which we kiss, and before which we uncover the head and prostrate ourselves, we adore Christ; and we venerate the saints, whose similitude they bear; as, by the decrees of Councils, and especially of the second Synod of Nicaea, has been defined against the opponents of images. . . .

DECREE CONCERNING INDULGENCES

Whereas the power of conferring Indulgences was granted by Christ to the Church; and she has, even in the most ancient times, used the said power, delivered unto her of God; the sacred holy Synod teaches, and enjoins, that the use of Indulgences, for the Christian people most salutary, and approved of by the authority of sacred Councils, is to be retained in the Church; and It condemns with anathema those who either assert, that they are useless; or who deny that there is in the Church the power of granting them. In granting them, however, It desires that, in accordance with the ancient and approved custom in the Church, moderation be observed; lest, by excessive facility, ecclesiastical discipline be ener-

vated. And being desirous that the abuses which have crept therein, and by occasion of which this honourable name of Indulgences is blasphemed by heretics, be amended and corrected, It ordains generally by this decree, that all evil gains for the obtaining thereof,—whence a most prolific cause of abuses amongst the Christian people has been derived,—be wholly abolished. But as regards the other abuses which have proceeded from superstition, ignorance, irreverence, or from whatever other source, since by reason of the manifold corruptions in the places and provinces where the said abuses are committed, they cannot conveniently be specially prohibited; It commands all bishops, diligently to collect, each in his own church, all abuses of this nature, and to report them in the first provincial Synod; that, after having been reviewed by the opinions of the other bishops also, they may forthwith be referred to the Sovereign Roman Pontiff, by whose authority and prudence that which may be expedient for the universal Church will be ordained; that thus the gift of holy Indulgences may be dispensed to all the faithful, piously, holily, and incorruptly. . . .
Amen.

10. THE MASSACRE OF ST. BARTHOLOMEW

The clash of two or more opposing views of truth, each claiming to be ultimate, each intolerant of every other view, would have been bitter enough. Matters were not improved when religious confession was enlisted in the service of rival political interests as it was, for instance, in France where protestantism became identified with the struggle of a section of the nobility against the growing power of central government. Throughout the second half of the sixteenth century, France was ravaged by savage struggles, the Wars of Religion, marked by a long series of plots and counterplots, murders, massacres and actual open warfare. The Catholic party was headed by the Lorraine family of Guise, the protestants by the Bourbons, supported by Admiral de Coligny. Both sides tried to secure control of the royal government which was in the hands of a widow-queen, Catherine de Médicis, and of her rather unimpressive sons. In 1572, the marriage of Henri de Bourbon, King of Navarre, a protestant, to Catherine's daughter Margaret, a ceremony for which the flower of protestant nobility had gathered in Paris, seemed to offer the Catholic party a chance to decapitate the enemy by one master stroke. The result was the massacre of St. Bartholomew's night, which, ordered by the King and enthusiastically carried out by the ultra-Catholic population of Paris, made some 3000 victims in the capital—as well as a good many in the provinces.

Philip II of Spain and the Court of Rome rejoiced greatly. It is said that the news of the massacre made Philip laugh for the only time in his life. The Pope, for his part, ordered a *Te Deum,* declaring that the news pleased him more than fifty victories of Lepanto (against the Turks). Such joy, however, proved somewhat premature and the massacre only one more bloody incident in a conflict which dragged out another twenty years. France would remain Catholic, though tolerant of protestants, but Henri of Navarre became its king—first of the Bourbons who were to rule the country for two centuries. More important, far from declining as its opponents had hoped, royal power grew, the anarchy of half a century's civil war bringing grist to the mill of central authority.

Letter of Fr. Joachim Opser, S.J., sub-prior of Clermont College to the Abbot of Saint-Gall, August 26, 1572.

I think I shall not bore you if I mention in detail an event as unexpected as it is useful to our cause, and which not only delights the Christian world with admiration, but brings it to a peak of rejoicing. Concerning this you will hear what the Captain has to say [the Captain commanding the detachment of the King's Swiss Mercenaries that broke into the house of the Huguenot leader, Admiral Coligny, and murdered the Admiral]. Rejoice in advance, but do not for that disdain or reject as superfluous the lines I write with more satisfaction perhaps than seems quite proper, for I affirm nothing I have not got from authoritative sources.

The Admiral has perished miserably on August 24, with all the heretical French nobility. (One can say it without exaggeration.) What immense car-

nage! I shuddered at the sight of this river [the Seine] full of naked and horribly mutilated corpses. Up to the present, the King has spared none but the King of Navarre [the future Henry IV]. In effect, today August 26, towards one o'clock, the King of Navarre attended Mass with the King Charles, so that all conceive the greatest hopes of seeing him change his religion. . . . Everyone agrees in praising the prudence and magnanimity of the King who, after having by his kindness and indulgence fattened, as it were, the heretics like cattle, has suddenly had them slaughtered by his soldiers. . . . All heretical book-sellers that one could find have been massacred and cast naked into the river. Ramus, who had jumped out of his bedroom, quite high up, still lies naked on the river bank, pierced by numerous dagger-

From *Bulletin de la Société de l'Histoire du Protestantisme français,* Vol. XIII (Paris, 1882), pp. 243–247.

blows. In a word, there is no one (even women not excepted) who has not been either killed or wounded.

One more thing as concerns the massacre of the Admiral; I hold these details from the man who gave him the third blow with his battle axe, from that Conrad Burg who used to be groom at Steward Joachim Waldemann's at Wyl. When the Swiss, under the orders of the Duc d'Anjou, had broken in the doors, Conrad, followed by Leonhard Grunenfelder of Glaris and Martin Koch of Fribourg, reached the Admiral's room which was the third in the house. The servant was killed first. The Admiral was in a dressing gown and none at first wanted to lay hands on him; but Martin Koch, more daring than the others, struck the wretch with his halberd; Conrad gave him the third blow, and at the seventh at last he fell dead against the chimney of his room. By order of the Duc de Guise his corpse was thrown out of the window and, after tying a rope round his neck as is the way with criminals, he was offered in display for all the people by dragging him to the Seine. Such was the end of that pernicious man, who not only brought a great many to the brink [of perdition] in his lifetime, but who, dying, swept a crowd of heretical nobles into hell with him.

Papire Masson, the King's Historiographer, notes in his *Histoire de Charles IX:*

This carnage arrived in the sight of the King, who watched it from the Louvre with much pleasure. Few days later, he went himself to the gallows of Montfaucon to see the corpse of Coligny which was hanging by its feet; and as some of his suite feigned reluctance to step near because of the corpse's stink: "The smell of a dead foe," said he, "is sweet and pleasant."

On September 8, 1572, Rome celebrated the massacre's success with a Mass of Thanks in the Church of Saint-Louis-des-Français, "for the great grace received of God."

All-powerful God, who stands against the proud and grants grace to the humble, we offer you the tribute of our most fervent praise for that, caring for the faith of your servants, you have granted them a brilliant triumph over the perfidious opponents of the Catholic people and we humbly beseech you to continue in your mercy that which you have begun in your constancy, for the glory of your name which is invoked in our midst. In the name of Christ, grant us our prayer!

III. Political and Economic Changes

Cultural developments take place against a political and economic background. The fifteenth and sixteenth centuries witnessed very profound changes in the political and economic structure of the West. New worlds had been discovered, new powers had risen, old powers had waned, the trickle of goods and bullion from overseas was growing into a stream. The Muslims, expelled from the Iberian Peninsula, had made great strides at the other end of Europe, where Hungary had fallen in 1526 and Vienna itself was for the first time besieged in 1529.

Hard pressed by changing realities, the old feudal order of society had decayed but had not yet been replaced by a new order. Hence, this is a period of transition, with all the suffering and the disorder that follow social changes as yet uncomprehended and, therefore, unmastered. The Reformation too had created political problems which princes and statesmen strove to handle as best they could: what should be the relationship between church and state, whence comes the prince's right to rule, can more than one religious belief be tolerated in the state? These issues were to be threshed out in the course of the sixteenth century, and the answers proposed would be very different in tenor from those which the prereformation world might have found acceptable.

1. THE POWER AND REVENUES OF THE STATES OF EUROPE IN 1423

The document below is given in order to facilitate comparison with later developments. It appears in a fifteenth-century life of the Venetian Doge, Mocenigo. The Venetian Ambassadors were the best intelligence agents of their time and kept their government informed as to the doings of foreign powers by a system of regular reports.

Income of all the Christian powers and what they are able to do. The king of France with all his force and the feudal services of princes, dukes, marquises, counts, barons, knights, bishops, abbots, canons, priests, and citizens, can in his own country raise 30,000 horsemen skilled in arms. If desiring to send them out of the country the said realm could not, since the costs would be doubled, send more than 15,000 horse. Before the war with their own countrymen, it could have raised 100,000, for that war destroyed both Church and revenues. In the total therefore 15,000 horse. The king of England with the power of his revenues, and the feudal services of princes and others as above could, paying them every month, raise at home 30,000 horsemen skilled in arms. In making the test of war

From *Translations and Reprints,* Vol. 3, No. 2, R. P. Falkner, Ed.

these powers are equal. They have always been powerful in their undertakings. And if one of these forces had been greater than the other, one would have been destroyed. The English were overcome, after the division occurred in England, and they could not make provision for their forces. This was before 1414. They had 40,000 horse. Wars have weakened these countries, their men and their revenues, so that now wishing to send a force out of the country it is agreed that they have the half, i.e., 15,000 horsemen. The king of Scotland is lord of a great country, and of a people of so great poverty that he would not be able to maintain with his revenues and the taxes and dues of the clergy and laity, 10,000 horsemen skilled in arms in his own country; outside of the country on account of the great cost, 5000 horse. The king of Norway who is lord of a great country, and a people equally poor could not maintain at home with his revenues and the taxes and dues of clergy and laity 10,000 horsemen skilled in arms, abroad 5000 horse. The king of Spain with all his revenues and feudal dues of clergy and laity, with all his forces 30,000 horsemen skilled in arms. In 1414 he paid for 20,000. Wishing to maintain them out of the country at double cost they would be 15,000 horsemen. The king of Portugal with all his revenues from clergy and laity, with all his force, would have, if he paid every month, at home 6000 horsemen skilled in arms, abroad 3000 horse. The king of Brittany with all his revenues and feudal dues of clergy and laity, paying every month could maintain at home 8000 horsemen skilled in arms, abroad 4000. The master of St. James with all his force of men skilled in arms, at home 4000 horsemen, abroad 2000. The duke of Burgundy with all his force as above at home 3000 cav-

alry. In 1414 he held 1000. But war has destroyed the country. Abroad 5000 men. The king René (of Provence) with all his revenues would be able to raise at home 6000 horse, abroad 3000. The duke of Savoy with all his revenues would be able to raise at home 8000 horse, abroad 4000. The marquis of Montferrat would be able to hold 2000 horse at home, 1000 abroad. The count Francesco Sforza, duke of Milan, with all his force could hold as mercenaries 10,000 horse at home and 5000 abroad. The signory of Venice can, with all its force pay for 10,000 horsemen skilled in arms at home, and 5000 abroad. The marquis of Ferrara at home 2000 horsemen, abroad 1000. The marquis of Mantua, at home 2000, abroad 1000. The signory of Bologna 2000 at home, 1000 abroad. The community of Siena at home 2000, abroad 1000. The Signory of Florence with all its revenues of 1414 could place 1000. At present through the wars it can place 4000 horsemen at home and 2000 abroad.

The Pope with all his revenues of his States of the Church, and with the profits of churches which he receives, was able in 1414 to raise 8000 horsemen; at present at home 6000 horsemen, abroad 3000. The king of Aragon in the Realm of Naples can raise with all his revenues 12,000 horsemen at home and 6000 abroad. The princes of the Realm are able with all their revenues to raise 4000 horsemen at home, 2000 abroad. The Community of Genoa were able in 1414 to maintain 5000 horsemen. But through their present dissension and the wars they are only able to maintain at present 2000. The Barcelonians with all the community and the lord of Catalonia, counting citizens and knights, can at home every month maintain 12,000 horsemen, and abroad 6000. All Germany with the lords temporal and spiritual, the free and the other cities, north and south Germany, and the Emperor who is German, can raise with all their resources and revenues 60,000 horsemen at home and 30,000 abroad. The king of Hungary, with all the dukes, lords, princes, barons, prelates, clergy and laity, and with all his resources and revenues can raise at home 80,000 horsemen, abroad 40,000. The grand master of Prussia with all his revenues, 30,000 horsemen. In 1414 he had 50,-000. But war has weakened him. Abroad 15,000 horsemen. The king of Poland with all his revenues, with dukes, marquises, barons, cities and boroughs can raise at home 50,000 horsemen, abroad 25,000. The Wallachians with all their revenues and feudal service, at home 20,-000 horsemen, abroad 10,000. Morea with its resources of 1414 could raise 50,-000 horsemen. War has weakened them. At present at home 20,000, abroad 10,-000. All Albania, Croatia, Slavonia, Servia, Russia, and Bosnia with all their revenues at home 30,000, abroad 15,000. The king of Cyprus with all his revenues can raise in the Island 2000, abroad 1000. The duke of Nicea in the Archipelago with all his power can pay for 2000 horsemen at home, 1000 abroad. The grand master of Rhodes with all his revenues and feudal dues of his liegemen, clergy and laity of the island, would be able to raise 4000 horsemen at home, 2000 abroad. The lord of Mitylene 2000 horsemen, abroad 1000. The emperor of Trebizonde with all his power could raise at home 25,000 horsemen, abroad 15,000. The king of Georgia with his revenues of 1414 could raise 30,000 horsemen. At present he can raise at home 10,000 horsemen, abroad 5000.

Power of the Infidel Monarchs. The Turk can in all his dominions raise 40,-000 horsemen, valiant men to defend him against the Christians. The Caraman with all his power can raise at home 60,000 horsemen, abroad 30,000. Ussun Cassan with all his power can raise at home 20,000 horsemen in the service of Mahomet, abroad 10,000. The Caraifan with all his resources at home 20,000, abroad 10,000. Tamerlane with all his Tartar power can raise at home 1,000,-000 horsemen, abroad 500,000. The king of Tunis, of Granada and the other cities of Barbary who have galleys and boats to the injury of Christians, at home are 100,000 horsemen, abroad 50,000.

Revenues of some Christian princes in the year 1423. The king of France in the year 1414 had 2,000,000 ducats ordinary revenues. But the wars which have continued for forty years have reduced the ordinary revenues to 1,000,000 ducats. The king of England had 2,000,000 ducats ordinary revenue. The continued wars have desolated the island. At the present time he has 700,000 ducats revenue. The king of Spain had in 1410, 3,-000,000 ducats ordinary revenue, but the continued wars have reduced it to 800,000 ducats. The king of Portugal had in 1410, 200,000 ducats revenue. By the wars it is reduced to 140,000 ducats. The king of Brittany in 1414 had 200,000 ducats revenue. By the wars it is reduced to 140,000 ducats. The duke of Burgundy had in 1400, 3,000,000 ducats. By the wars it is reduced to 900,-000 ducats. The duke of Savoy as a free country has 150,000 ducats revenue. The marquis of Montferrat as a free country has 150,000 ducats revenue. Count Francesco, duke of Milan [in 1423 duke Filippo Maria Visconti of Milan had

1,000,000 ducats revenue] Count Francesco has at present on account of the wars only 500,000 ducats. The signory of Venice had in 1423, 1,100,000 ducats ordinary revenue. By reason of great wars which have destroyed commerce it has 800,000 ducats ordinary revenue. The marquis of Ferrara had in 1423, 70,-000 ducats ordinary revenue. Through the Italian wars he has by remaining at peace 150,000 ducats. The Marquis of Montferrat had in 1423, 150,000 ducats, to-day 60,000 ducats. The Bolognese

had in 1423, 400,000 ducats ordinary revenue. But by the wars it has come to 200,000 ducats. Florence in 1423 had a revenue of 400,000 ducats. But since then, through the great wars it is reduced to 200,000 ducats. The pope, though formerly he had none, has 400,000 ducats ordinary revenue. The Genoese through the great division among them are reduced to 130,000 ducats. The king of Aragon, in all his realm with Sicily, though at first he had considerably more, has a revenue of 310,000 ducats.

2. HENRY VIII

In an age of forceful figures, Henry VIII stands out as one of the most conspicuous. His popular fame seems to rest primarily on half a dozen wives, but the historian sees him as the central figure and dominating force in England during the whole of his long reign (1509–1547)—fighting hard to establish a secure succession for the Tudor dynasty that his father, Henry VII, had founded on Bosworth Field (1485); beginning the English Reformation; and gathering in his hands powers and loyalties for which Church and Crown had vied a long time.

The Act of Supremacy, 1534

An Act concernynge the Kynges Highness to be supreme heed of the Churche of Englande and to have auctoryte to reforme and redresse all errours, heresyes and abuses yn the same.

Albeit the Kynges Majestie justely and rightfully is and oweth to be the supreme heed of the Churche of England, and so is recognysed by the clergy of this Realme in theyr convocacions; yet neverthelesse for corroboracion and confirmacion thereof, and for increase of vertue in Cristis Religion within this Realme of England, and to represse and extirpe all errours, heresies and other enormyties and abuses heretofore used in the same. Be it enacted by auctority of this present Parliament

that the Kyng our Soveraign Lorde, his heires and successours Kynges of this Realme shall be takyn, acceptyd, and reputed the onely supreme heed in erthe of the Churche of England callyd Anglicana Ecclesia, and shall have and enjoye annexed and unyted to the Ymperyall Crowne of this Realme as well the title and style thereof, as all Honours Dignyties prehemynences jurisdiccions privileges auctorities ymunyties profitis and commodities to the said dignyties of supreme heed of the same Churche belongyng and apperteyning: And that our said Soveraigne Lorde his heires and successours Kynges of this Realme shall have full power and auctorite from tyme to

From *Translations and Reprints*, Vol. 1, No. 1, E. P. Cheyney, Ed.

tyme to visite represse redresse reforme order correct restrayne and amende all suche errours heresies abuses offences contemptes and enormyties whatsoever they be whiche by any maner spirituall auctoryte or juristiccion ought or maie lawfullye be reformyd repressyd ordred redressyd correctyd restrayned or amendyd,

most to the pleasure of almyghtie God the increase of vertue yn Chrystis Religion and for the conservacy of the peace unyte and tranquylyte of this Realme: Any usage custome foreyne laws foreyne auctoryte prescripcion or anye other thinge or thinges to the contrarie hereof notwithstandinge.

The Act of the Six Articles, 1539

AN ACT ABOLISHING DIVERSITY IN OPYNIONS

Where the Kinges most excellent Majestie is by Gods lawe supreme head ymmediately under him of this hole churche and congregation of Englande intendinge the conservacion of the same Churche and congregation in a true syncere and unyforme doctrine of Christ's Religion.

Forasmuche as in the saide parliament synode and convacacion there were certen articles, matters and questions proponed and set forth touchinge Christen Religion.

The Kinges most Royal Majestie most prudently ponderinge and consideringe that by occasion of variable and sundrie opinions and judgements of the saide articles, greate discorde and variance hathe arisen as well amongest the clergie of this his Realme as amongest a great number of vulgar people his lovinge subjects of the same, and beinge in a full hope and truste that a full and perfect resolucion of the saide articles shoulde make a perfecte concorde and unyte generally amonge all his lovinge and obedient subjects; of his most excellent goodness not only commanded that the saide articles shoulde deliberately and advisedly by his saide Archbisshops Bishopps and other

lerned men of his clergie be debated argued and reasoned, and their opinions therein to be understood declared and knowne, but also most graciously vouchsaved in his owne princelie person to discend and come into his said highe Courte of Parliament and Counsaile and there like a Prince of most highe Prudence and noe lesse lernynge opened and declared many things of highe lerning and great knowledge touchinge the said articles matters and questions, for an unytye to be had in the same; whereupon, after a greate and longe deliberate and advised disputacion and consultacion had and made concerning the saide articles, as well by the consent of the Kinges Highness as by the assent of the Lordes spirituall and temporall and other lerned men of his clergie in their convacacion, and by the consent of the Commons in this present parliament assembled, it was and is fynally resolved accorded and agreed in manner and forme following, that is to say: First, that in the most blessed Sacrament of the aulter, by the strengthe and efficacy of Christs myghtie worde, it beinge spoken by the prest, is present really, under the forme of bread and wyne, the naturale bodye and bloode of our Saviour Jesu Crist, conceyved of the Virgin Marie, and after the consecracion there remayneth noe substance of

From *Translations and Reprints*, Vol. 1, No. 1, E. P. Cheyney, Ed.

bread or wyne, nor any other substance but the substance of Criste, God and man; secondly, that Comunion in bothe kinds is not necessarie *ad salutem* [for salvation] by the lawe of God to all persons; and that it is to be believed and not doubted of, but that in the fleshe under forme of bread is the verie blode, and withe the blode under forme of wyne is the verie fleshe, as well aparte as thoughe they were bothe together; thirdly, that Priests after the order of Presthode receyved as afore may not marye by the lawe of God; fourthlye, that vowes of chastitye and wydowhood by man or woman made to God advisedly

ought to be observed by the lawe of God, and that it exempteth them from other libertyes of Cristen people, which without that they myght enjoye; fyftly, that it is mete and necessarie that private masses be contynued and admytted in this the Kings English Churche and congregacion as whereby good Cristen people orderinge them selfes accordingly doe receyve bothe godly and goodly consolacions and benefyttes and it is agreable also to Gods lawe; sixtly, that auricular confession is expedient and necessarie to be retayned and contynued used and frequented in the Churche of God.

3. CHARLES V

Where Henry VIII appears as the type of the new king of the new nation-state, his contemporary, Charles V (1500–1558), may almost be said to close the medieval tradition in which the prince's authority, derived from God, was not necessarily connected with local or national attachments. The Emperor tried to be a "parfit, gentil," and, of course, Christian knight; but, though his revenues were very great and though his writ ran from Bohemia to the Indies, he met with disappointment and in the weariness of failure retired to the Spanish monastery of San Yuste to end his life in relative peace. But perhaps it is the anachronism he represents which explains the frustration of his attempts to hold together his vast and disconnected realm—the failure Charles expressed in his abdication speech below.

The Abdication of Charles V, Brussels, 1555

Although Philibert has fully explained to you, my friends, the causes which have determined me to surrender these states and leave them to my son Don Philip, in order that he may possess and rule them, yet I wish to say certain things with my own mouth. You will remember that upon the 5th of February of this year there had elapsed forty years since my grandfather the emperor Maximilian, in the same place and at the same hour declared my majority at the age of fifteen, withdrew

me from the guardianship under which I had remained up to that time and made me master of myself. The following year, which was my sixteenth, king Ferdinand died, my mother's father and my grandfather, in the kingdom over which I then commenced to reign, because my beloved mother, who has but lately died, was left, after the death of my father, with disordered judgment and never sufficiently recovered her health to become mistress of herself.

At that time I went to Spain, by way of the sea. Soon came the death of my grandfather Maximilian, in my 19th year, and although I was still young they conferred upon me in his stead the imperial dignity. I had no inordinate ambition to rule a multitude of kingdoms, but merely sought to secure the welfare of Germany, to provide for the defence of Flanders, to consecrate my forces to the safety of Christianity against the Turk and to labor for the extension of the Christian religion. But although such zeal was mine, I was unable to show so much of it as I might have wished, on account of the troubles raised by the heresies of Luther and the other innovators of Germany, and on account of serious war into which the hostility and envy of neighboring princes had driven me, and from which I have safely emerged, thanks to the favor of God.

This is the fourth time that I go to Spain, there to bury myself. I wish to say to you that nothing I have ever experienced has given me so much pain or rested so heavily upon my soul as that which I experience in parting from you to-day, without leaving behind me that peace and quiet which I so much desired. My sister Mary, who in my absence has governed you so wisely and defended you so well, has explained to you, in the last assembly, the reasons for my determination. I am no longer able to attend to my affairs without great bodily fatigue and consequent detriment to the affairs of the state. The cares which so great a responsibility involves; the extreme dejection which it causes; my health already ruined; all these leave me no longer the strength sufficient for governing the states which God has confided to me. The little strength that remains to me is rapidly disappearing. So I should long ago have put down the burden, if my son's immaturity and my moth-

er's incapacity had not forced both my spirit and my body to sustain its weight until this hour.

The last time that I went to Germany I had determined to do what you see me do to-day, but I could not bring myself to do it when I saw the wretched condition of the Christian state, a prey to such a multitude of disturbances, of innovations, of singular opinions as to faith, of worse than civil wars, and fallen finally into so many lamentable disorders. I was turned from my purpose because my ills were not yet so great, and I hoped to make an end of all these things and restore the peace. In order that I might not be wanting in my duty I risked my strength, my goods, my repose and my life for the safety of Christianity and the defence of my subjects. From this struggle I emerged with a portion of the things I desired. But the king of France and certain Germans, failing to preserve the peace and amity they had sworn, marched against me and were upon the point of seizing my person. The king of France took the city of Metz, and I, in the dead of winter, exposed to intense cold, in the midst of snow and blood, advanced with a powerful army raised at my own expense to retake the city and restore the Empire. The Germans saw that I had not yet laid aside the imperial crown and had no disposition to allow its majesty to be diminished.

I have carried out what God has permitted, since the outcome of our efforts depends upon the will of God. We human beings act according to our powers, our strength, our spirit, and God awards the victory and permits defeat. I have ever done as I was able, and God has aided me. I return to Him boundless thanks for having succored me in my greatest trials and in all my dangers.

To-day I feel so exhausted that I should not be of any aid to you, as you see yourselves. In my present state of dejection and weakness, I should have to render a great and serious account to God and man, if I did not lay aside authority, as I have resolved to do, since my son, king Philip, is of an age sufficiently advanced to be able to govern you, and he will be, I hope, a good prince to all my beloved subjects.

I am determined then to retire to Spain, to yield to my son Philip the possession of all my states, and to my brother, the king of the Romans, the Empire. I particularly commend to you my son, and I ask you only in remembrance of me, that you extend to him the love which you have always borne towards me; moreover I ask you to preserve among yourselves the same affection and harmony. Be obedient towards justice, zealous in the observance of the laws, preserve respect for all that merits it, and do not refuse to grant to authority the support of which it stands in need.

Above all, beware of infection from the sects of neighboring lands. Extirpate at once the germs, if they appear in your midst, for fear lest they may spread abroad and utterly overthrow your state, and lest you may fall into the direst calamities. As to the manner in which I have governed you I confess that I have been more than once deceived, led astray by the inexperience of youth, by the hasty conclusions of young manhood, or by some other fault of human weakness. Nevertheless I make bold to assert, that never of my knowledge or by my will has wrong or violence been done to any of my subjects. If any can complain of having suffered such, I aver that it is unknown to me and against my will: I declare before all the world that I regret it from the bottom of my heart, and I beseech all present, and those who are not here as well, to wish me well and to pardon me.

The Library of Charles V at San Yuste (1555–1558)

The Almagestus, the great astronomical work of Ptolemy.

The Imperial Astronomy, by Santa Cruz, who had given lessons in mathematics to Charles V.

Caesar's Commentaries, in Italian (Tuscan).

History of Spain, ancient and mediaeval, edited by Florian de Ocampo.

The Consolations of Boethius, of which there were several copies, in French, Italian and Latin.

Commentaries upon the German War, by the Grand Commander of Alcantara.

Caballero Determinado, a poetical romance.

Meditations of St. Augustine and two other books of pious meditations.

The works of Doctor Constantin Ponce de la Fuente, and of Father Pedro de Soto upon Christian Doctrine.

Sum of Christian Mysteries, by Tilleman.

Two breviaries, a missal, two illuminated psalters, the commentary of Father Thomas de Portocarrero upon the Psalm: "In te, Domine, speravi."

Selected prayers from the Bible.

Though after 1855 the Imperial crown passed to the German branch of the Habsburg family, Philip II (1527–1598) was probably the most powerful prince of his time. For his policy and his almost continuous wars he could draw upon the resources of a vast realm upon which the sun never set. Not the least part of his wealth derived from Spain's American colonies where important silver deposits were discovered in Mexico and Peru, the most famous, at Cerro de Potosi, being opened in 1545. Yet it would appear that, even so, the king lived well beyond his income. A great and growing amount of bullion found its way into Europe, to pay the king's debts to foreign bankers and the wages of his soldiers. War and mismanagement drained Spain of its wealth, decimated its manpower, and contributed to the inflation so characteristic of the period. In 1617, we shall find the Castilian Cortes complaining that the treasure from America "immediately goes to foreign kingdoms, leaving this one in extreme poverty."

The Gold of the Indies, 1559

From New Spain are obtained gold and silver, cochineal [little insects like flies], from which crimson dye is made, leather, cotton, sugar and other things; but from Peru nothing is obtained except minerals. The fifth part of all that is produced goes to the king, but since the gold and silver is brought to Spain and he has a tenth part of that which goes to the mint and is refined and coined, he eventually gets one-fourth of the whole sum, which fourth does not exceed in all four or five hundred thousand ducats, although it is reckoned not alone at millions, but at millions of pounds. Nor is it likely that it will long remain at this figure, because great quantities of gold and silver are no longer found upon the surface of the earth, as they have been in past years;

and to penetrate into the bowels of the earth requires greater effort, skill and outlay, and the Spaniards are not willing to do the work themselves, and the natives cannot be forced to do so, because the Emperor has freed them from all obligation of service as soon as they accept the Christian religion. Wherefore it is necessary to acquire negro slaves, who are brought from the coasts of Africa, both within and without the Straits, and these are selling dearer every day, because on account of their natural lack of strength and the change of climate, added to the lack of discretion upon the part of their masters in making them work too hard and giving them too little to eat, they fall sick and the greater part of them die.

Revenues of the King of Spain, 1559

From these his realms his majesty receives every year an income of five millions of gold in times of peace: one and one-half millions from Spain; a half-million from the Indies; one from Naples and Sicily, and another from Flanders and the Low Countries. But his expenses are six millions, and this excess is covered by extraordinary taxes according to his pleasure, whence it appears that he could control only a small amount of

money for special undertakings, since he consumes for his ordinary needs everything that he derives from his realms. But looked at from another point of view, the Emperor, his father, although he had the same burdens, was nevertheless able to carry on extensive wars and enterprises in Italy and outside of Italy, both by land and sea, and the same king was able in these later years to maintain great armies in Flanders, in Piedmont, in Lombardy and in the kingdom, and many soldiers in Africa against the Turk. So that we may calculate that he spent more than ten millions of gold; wherefore it may be put down as a fact that although expenses may exceed income, yet a way is not wanting to great princes, whereby they may find large sums of money in times of great need, particularly in the case of the king of Spain, not so much on account of the mines which are found in Spain and the Indies, of which the Spanish nation, according to its custom, makes no great account, as from the fact that he has so many states and so many subjects and nearly all are rich, and from them he has had so much aid, not through force or violence, but for the most part with common consent of the people, persuaded that public and private interest demanded such a policy.

It would appear that the great results which the Spaniards have accomplished are not to be ascribed to the financial strength derived from the mines, because you see on one side France and the Turk, extremely rich without mines, and on the other the Emperor, with more mines in his realms than all the rest of Europe possesses, always in need.

4. HENRY VIII: BEGGARS ACT OF 1531

One of the first tasks the rulers of the new nation-states had to face was the establishment of order in their territories. Prosperity meant power, but order meant prosperity; and to that end new legislation was needed and it had to be enforced. Throughout Europe the problem of beggars, rogues, and vagabonds was one of the first that princes had to tackle. Ignoring the economic causes of the evils that plagued them, they did their best to cope with them by means of laws and decrees which sought to cauterize ills they could neither prevent nor cure. Yet one law was never enough, for law enforcement was difficult and unemployment even then turned numbers of unsettled and often violent men and women into potential sources of trouble.

An Act Concerning Punishment of Beggars and Vagabonds (1531)

Where in all places throughout this realm of England vagabonds and beggars have of long time increased and daily do increase in great and excessive numbers, by the occasion of idleness, mother and root of all vices, whereby hath insurged and sprung and daily insurgeth and springeth continual thefts, murders, and other heinous offences and great enormities, to the high displeasure of God, the inquietation and damage of the King's people, and to the marvellous disturbance of the common weal of this realm. And whereas many and sundry good laws, strait statutes and ordinances, have been before this time devised and made, as well by the King our Sovereign Lord as also by divers his most noble progenitors, kings of England, for the most necessary and due reformation of the premises, yet that, notwithstanding, the said numbers of vagabonds and beggars be not seen in any party to be diminished, but rather daily augmented and increased into great routs and companies, as evidently and manifestly it doth and may appear; be it

From *Statutes of the Realm*, III, 328.

therefore enacted. . . . That the Justices of the Peace . . . shall from time to time, as often as need shall require, by their discretions divide themselves within the said shires (etc. . . .) and so being divided shall make diligent search and enquiry of all aged, poor, and impotent persons which live or of necessity be compelled to live by alms of the charity of the people that be or shall be hereafter abiding . . . within the limits of their division, and after and upon such search made the said Justices of Peace . . . shall have power and authority by their discretions to enable to beg, within such . . . limits as they shall appoint, such of the said impotent persons which they shall find and think most convenient within the limits of their division to live of the charity and alms of the people, and to give in commandment to every such aged and impotent beggar (by them enabled) that none of them shall beg without the limits to them so appointed, and shall also register and write the names of every such impotent beggar (by them appointed) in a bill or roll indented, the one part thereof to remain with themselves and the other part by them to be certified before the Justices of Peace at the next Sessions . . . there to remain under the keeping of the Custos Rotulorum; And that the said Justices of Peace . . . shall make and deliver to every such impotent person by them enabled to beg, a letter containing the name of such impotent person and witnessing that he is authorized to beg and the limits within which he is appointed to beg, the same letter to be sealed within such . . . seals as shall be engraved with the name of the limit wherein such impotent person so authorized to beg do beg in any other place than within such limits that he shall be assigned unto, that then the Justices of

Peace . . . shall by their discretions punish all such persons by imprisonment in the stocks by the space of 2 days and 2 nights, giving them but only bread and water, and after that cause every such impotent person to be sworn to return again without delay to the (limits . . .) where they be authorized to beg in.

II. And be it enacted, that no such impotent person (as is above said) . . . shall beg within any part of this realm except he be authorized by writing under seal as is above said. And if any such impotent person . . . be vagrant and go a-begging having no such letter under seal as is above specified, that then the constables and all other inhabitants within such town or parish where such person shall beg shall cause every such beggar to be taken and brought to the next Justice of Peace or High Constable of the Hundred; and thereupon the said Justice of Peace or High Constable shall command the said constables and other inhabitants of the town or parish which shall bring before him any such beggar that they shall strip him naked from the middle upward and cause him to be whipped within the town where he was taken, or within some other town where the same Justice or High Constable shall appoint . . . ; And if not, then to command such beggar to be set in the stocks in the same town or parish where he was taken by the space of 3 days and 3 nights, there to have only bread and water; and thereupon the said Justice or High Constable afore whom such beggar shall be brought shall limit to him a place to beg in, and give to him a letter under seal in form above remembered, and swear him to depart and repair thither immediately after his punishment to him executed.

III. And be it further enacted . . . That if any person or persons being whole and mighty in body and able to labour, . . . or if any man or woman being whole and mighty in body and able to labour having no land, master, nor using any lawful merchandise, craft, or mystery, whereby he might get his living . . . be vagrant and can give none reckoning how he doth lawfully get his living, that then it shall be lawful to the constables and all other the King's officers, ministers, and subjects of every town, parish and hamlet to arrest the said vagabonds and idle persons and them to bring to any of the Justices of Peace of the same shire or liberty . . . and that every such Justice of Peace . . . shall cause every such idle person so to him brought to be had to the next market town or other place where the said Justices of Peace . . . shall think most convenient, . . . and there to be tied to the end of a cart naked and be beaten with whips throughout the same market town or other place till his body be bloody by reason of such whipping; and after such punishment and whipping had, the person so punished . . . shall be enjoined upon his oath to return forthwith without delay in the next and straight way to the place where he was born, or where he last dwelled before the same punishment by the space of 3 years, and there put himself to labour like as a true man oweth to do; and after that done, every such person so punished and ordered shall have a letter sealed with the seal of the hundred, rape, wapentake, city, borough, town, liberty, or franchise wherein he shall be punished, witnessing that he hath been punished according to this Estatute, and containing the day and place of his punishment, and the place whereunto he is limited to go, and by what time he is limited to come thither, within which time he may lawfully beg by the way, shewing the same letter, and otherwise not; And if he do not accomplish the order to him appointed by the said letter, then to be eftsoons taken and whipped till he be repaired where he was born or where he last dwelled by the space of three years, and there put his body to labour for his living or otherwise truly get his living without begging as long as he is able so to do; And if the person so whipped be an idle person and no common beggar, then after such whipping he shall be kept in the stocks till he hath found surety to go to service or else to labour after the discretion of the said Justice of Peace . . . afore whom any such idle person being no common beggar shall be brought, . . . or else to be ordered and sworn to repair to the place where he was born or where he last dwelled by the space of three years, and to have like letter and such further punishment, if he eftsoons offend this Estatute as is above appointed to and for the common, strong, and able beggars, and so from time to time to be ordered and punished till he put his body to labour or otherwise gets his living truly according to the law: And that the Justices of the Peace of every shire . . . shall have power and authority within the limits of their Commissions to enquire of all majors, bailiffs, constables, and other officers and persons that shall be negligent in executing of this Act: And if the constables and inhabitants within any town or parish . . . be negligent . . . that then the township or parish . . . shall lose and forfeit for every such impotent beggar . . . 3s. 4d., and for every strong beggar, . . . 6s. 8d. . . . And that all Justices of Peace . . . shall have full power and authority as well to hear and determine every such default by presentment as by such bill of information, and upon every presentment afore them and upon every such bill of information to make process by distress against the inhabitants of every such town and parish. . . .

IV. And be it enacted . . . that scholars of the Universities of Oxford and Cambridge that go about begging, not being authorized under the seal of the said Universities by the Commissary, Chancellor, or Vice-Chancellor of the same, and all and singular shipmen pretending losses of their ships and goods of the sea going about the country begging without sufficient authority witnessing the same, shall be punished and ordered in manner and form as is above rehearsed of strong beggars; and that all proctors and pardoners going about in any country or countries or abiding in any city, borough, or town, some of them using divers and subtile crafty and unlawful games and plays, and some of them feigning themselves to have knowledge of physic, faces, palmistry, or other crafty sciences, whereby they delude people that they can tell their destinies, deceases, and fortunes, and such other like fantastical imaginations, to the great deceit of the King's subjects, shall upon examination had before two Justices of Peace, whereof the one shall be of the Quorum, if he by provable witness be found guilty of any such deceits, be punished by whipping at two days together after the manner above rehersed: And if he eftsoons offend in the said offence or any like offence, then to be scourged two days and the third day to be put upon the pillory from 9 of the clock till 11 before noon of the same day, and to have one of his ears cut off; and if he offend the third time, to have like punishment with whipping, standing on the pillory, and to have his other ear cut off; and that Justices of Peace have like authority in every liberty and franchise within their shires where they be Justices of Peace for the execution of this Act in every part thereof as they shall have without the liberty or franchise.

5. ELIZABETH I: POOR RELIEF ACT OF 1598

The first English statute specifically directed "for the provision and relief of the poor" dates back to 1552; this sort of legislation was strengthened in 1563 by introducing the principle of compulsion to the collection of funds for poor relief. The English Poor Law reached its final stages with the Acts of 1598 and 1601, the second patterned on the first, whose main features obtained until the nineteenth century. In the Act of 1598, given below, we find the principle of poor relief recognized as a public concern and put to the charge of the community.

An Act for the Relief of the Poor (1598)

Be it enacted by the authority of this present Parliament, That the Churchwardens of every parish, and four substantial householders there . . . who shall be nominated yearly in Easter week, under the hand and seal of two or more Justices of the Peace in the same county, whereof one to be of the Quorum, dwelling in or near the same parish, shall be called Overseers of the Poor of the same parish; and they or the greater part of them shall take order from time to time

From *Statutes of the Realm*, IV, 896.

by and with the consent of two or more Justices of Peace for setting to work of the children of all such whose parents shall not by the said persons be thought able to keep and maintain their children. And also all such persons married or unmarried as having no means to maintain them use no ordinary and daily trade of life to get their living by; and also to raise weekly or otherwise (by taxation of every inhabitant and every occupier of lands in the said parish in such competent sum and sums of money as they shall think fit) a convenient stock of flax, hemp, wool, thread, iron, and other necessary ware and stuff to set the poor on work, and also competent sums of money for and towards the necessary relief of the lame, impotent, old, blind, and such other among them being poor and not able to work, and also for the putting out of such children to be apprentices, to be gathered out of the same parish according to the ability of the said parish; and to do and execute all other things, as well for disposing of the said stock as otherwise concerning the premises, as to them shall seem convenient: Which said Churchwardens, and Overseers so to be nominated, or such of them as shall not be prevented by sickness or other just excuse to be allowed by such two Justices of Peace or more, shall meet together at the least once every month in the church of the said parish, upon the Sunday in the afternoon after divine service, there to consider of some good course to be taken and of some meet orders to be set down in the premises; and shall within four days after the end of their year, and after other overseers nominated as aforesaid, make and yield up to such two Justices of Peace a true and perfect account of all sums of money by them received, or rated and cessed and not received, and also of such stock as shall be in their hands or in the hands of any of the poor to work, and of all other things concerning their said office, and such sum or sums of money as shall be in their hands shall pay and deliver over to the said Churchwardens and Overseers newly nominated and appointed as aforesaid: upon pain that every one of them absenting themselves without lawful cause as aforesaid from such monthly meeting for the purpose aforesaid, or being negligent in their office or in the execution of the orders aforesaid being made by and with the assent of the said Justices of Peace, to forfeit for every such default twenty shillings.

II. And be it also enacted, That if the said Justices of Peace do perceive the inhabitants of any parish are not able to levy among themselves sufficient sums of money for the purposes aforesaid, That then the said Justices shall and may tax, rate, and assess as aforesaid any other of other parishes, or out of any parish within the hundred where the said parish is, to pay such sum and sums of money to the Churchwardens and Overseers of the said poor parish for the said purposes as the said Justices shall think fit, according to the intent of this law; And if the said hundred shall not be thought to the said Justices able and fit to relieve the said several parishes nor able to provide for themselves as aforesaid, then the Justices of Peace at their general Quarter Sessions, or the greater number of them, shall rate and assess as aforesaid, . . . other parishes . . . as in their discretion shall seem fit.

III. And that it shall be lawful for the said Churchwardens and Overseers or any of them, by warrant from any such two Justices of Peace, to levy as well the said sums of money of every one that shall refuse to contribute according as they shall be assessed, by distress and sale of the offender's goods, as the sums of money or stock which shall be behind upon any account to be made as aforesaid, rendering to the party the overplus; and in defect of such distress, it shall be lawful for any such two Justices of the Peace to commit him to prison, there to remain without bail or mainprize till payment of the said sum or stock; and the said Justices of Peace or any one of them to send to the House of Correction such as shall not employ themselves to work being appointed thereunto as aforesaid; And also any two such Justices of Peace to commit to prison every one of the said Churchwardens and Overseers which shall refuse to account, there to remain without bail or mainprize till he have made a true account and satisfied and paid so much as upon the said account shall be remaining in his hands.

IV. And be it further enacted, That it shall be lawful for the said Churchwardens and Overseers or the greater part of them, by the assent of any two Justices of the Peace, to bind any such children as aforesaid to be apprentices where they shall see convenient, till such man-child shall come to the age of four and twenty years, and such woman-child to the age of one and twenty years; the same to be as effectual to all purposes as if such child were of full age and by indenture of covenant bound him or herself.

V. And to the intent that necessary places of habitation may more conveniently be provided for such poor impotent people, Be it enacted by the authority aforesaid, That it shall and may be lawful for the said Churchwardens and Overseers or the greater part of them, by the leave of the lord or lords of the manor whereof any waste or common within their parish is or shall be parcel . . . to erect, build, and set up in fit and convenient places of

habitation in such waste or common, at the general charges of the parish or otherwise of the hundred or county as aforesaid, to be taxed, rated, and gathered in manner before expressed, convenient Houses of Dwelling for the said impotent poor; And also to place inmates or more families than one in one cottage or house. . . .

VI. Provided always, That if any person or persons shall find themselves grieved with any cess or tax or other act done by the said Churchwardens and other persons or by the said Justices of Peace, that then it shall be lawful for the Justices of Peace at their general Quarter Sessions, or the greater number of them, to take such order therein as to them shall be thought convenient, and the same to conclude and bind all the said parties.

VII. And be it further enacted, That the parents or children of every poor, old, blind, lame, and impotent person, or other poor person not able to work, being of sufficient ability, shall at their own charges relieve and maintain every such poor person in that manner and according to that rate as by the Justices of Peace of that county where such sufficient persons dwell, or the greater number of them, at their general Quarter Sessions shall be assessed; upon pain that every one of them forfeit 20s. for every month which they shall fail therein.

X. And be it further enacted by the authority aforesaid, That . . . no person or persons whatsoever shall go wandering abroad and beg in any place whatsoever, by licence or without, upon pain to be esteemed, taken, and punished as a rogue: Provided always, That this present Act shall not extend to any poor people which shall ask relief of victuals only in the same parish where such poor people do dwell . . .

XII. And forasmuch as all begging is forbidden by this present Act; Be it further enacted by the authority aforesaid, That the Justices of Peace of every county or place corporate, or the more part of them, in their general Sessions to be holden next after the end of this session of Parliament, or in default thereof at the Quarter Sessions to be holden about the Feast of Easter next, shall rate every parish to such a weekly sum of money as they shall think convenient, so as no parish be rated above the sum of 6 pence nor under the sum of an halfpenny weekly to be paid, and so as the total sum of such taxation of the parishes in the said county; which sums so taxed shall be yearly assessed by the agreement of the parishioners within themselves, or in default thereof by the Churchwardens and Constables of the same parish or the more part of them, or in default of their agreement by the order of such Justice or Justices of Peace as shall dwell in the same parish or (if none be there dwelling) in the parts next adjoining; And if any person shall refuse or neglect to pay any such portion of money so taxed, it shall be lawful for the said Churchwardens and Constables, or in their default for the Justices of the Peace, to levy the same by sale of the goods of the party so refusing or neglecting or to commit such person to prison, there to abide without bail till he have paid the same.

XIII. And be it also enacted, That the said Justices of the Peace at their general Quarter Sessions to be holden at the time of such taxation, shall set down what competent sum of money shall be sent quarterly out of every county or place corporate for the relief of the poor prisoners of the King's Bench and Marshalsea, and also of such hospitals and alms-houses as shall be in the said county, . . .

XVI. Provided always nevertheless, That every soldier being discharged of his service or otherwise lawfully licensed to pass into his country, and not having wherewith to relieve himself in his travel homewards, and every seafaring man landing from sea not having wherewith to relieve himself in his travel homewards. having a testimonial under the hand of some one Justice of Peace of or near the place where he was landed or was discharged, setting down therein the place and time where and when he landed or was discharged, and the place of the party's dwellingplace or birth unto which he is to pass, and a convenient time to be limited therein for his passage, shall and may, without incurring the danger or penalty of this Act, in the usual ways directly to the place unto which he is directed to pass and within the time in such his testimonial limited for his passage, ask and receive such relief as shall be necessary in and for his passage; This Act or anything therein contained to the contrary notwithstanding.

XVII. Provided always, That this Act shall endure no longer than to the end of the next Session of Parliament.

6. THOMAS MORE

Sir Thomas More was born in London (1478), the son of a Justice of the King's Bench. At sixteen he was placed, according to the custom of his time, in the household of the Archbishop of Canterbury, there to learn the ways of a gentleman by serving a gentleman. The Archbishop thought highly of the lad, for whom he predicted a great future; More in turn never lost his early respect for his first master, whom he brings into the passage below. The young man's education was perfected at Oxford, where he became the friend of men like Erasmus and John Colet and drank deep of the new learning of the time. Brilliant lawyer and parliament man, he was much against his will appointed Lord Chancellor of England after Wolsey's fall, disapproved of Henry VIII's ecclesiastical policy, and finally resigned his office in 1532. His conscience forcing him to refuse the Oath of Supremacy, he was imprisoned in the Tower and beheaded in 1535, to the shock and indignation of all Catholic Europe. He had written a number of works of controversy and two histories; but his reputation rests on the *Utopia,* two books written in Latin—the first in 1515, the second in 1516—which were immediately popular and soon translated (into German, 1524; French, 1530; Italian, 1548; English, 1551). In the following passage from Book I, the speaker presents some views on the England of his day.

From *Utopia*

I pray you, Sir (quoth I) have you been in our country?

Yes, indeed (quoth he) and there I tarried for four or five months not long after the Cornish insurrection of 1497. In the meantime, I was much indebted to the right reverend father, John Morton, Archbishop and Cardinal of Canterbury, and at that time also Lord Chancellor of England: a man, Master Peter (for Master More already knows what I will say) not more honorable for his authority than for his prudence and virtue. He was of small stature, and though stricken in age yet carried his body upright. In his face there shone such amiable reverence as was pleasant to behold; he was gentle in his talk, and yet earnest and sage. Often he enjoyed speaking sharply to those about him, to find out, but without harm, what prompt wit and what bold spirit were in every man. He took great delight in these, as being virtues much agreeing with his own inclinations, provided they were not combined with impudence. And those who lived up to such standards he would lovingly embrace as able and deserving of a post in the public service. In his speech he was fine, eloquent and pithy. In the law he had profound knowledge, in wit he was incomparable, and in memory wonderfully excellent. These qualities which were inborn to him, he had made perfect by learning and practice. The king put much trust in his counsel, and when I was there you might say that in a sense the public weal depended upon him. He had been taken from school into the court while still very young, and there he had passed all his time in much trouble and business, being continually tumbled and tossed in the waves of diverse misfortunes and adversities. And so, through many and great dangers, he had learned the experience of the world, something that cannot be easily forgotten when it has been learned in this manner.

It happened on a certain day, when I sat at his table, there was present a certain layman, well versed in the laws of your country. I cannot tell how the occasion arose, but this man began diligently and earnestly to praise that strict and rigorous justice which at that time was being executed upon felons who, as he said, were mostly being hanged twenty at a time upon one gallows. And, seeing that so few escaped punishment, he said he could not help but greatly wonder and marvel how, and by what evil luck, it should be that in spite of this thieves were nevertheless so rife and rank everywhere. Nay, Sir, quoth I (for I dared boldly speak my mind before the Cardinal) do not marvel at this: for this punishment of thieves passes the limits of justice, and is also very hurtful to the public weal. For it is too extreme and cruel a punishment for theft, and yet not sufficient to refrain and withhold men from theft. For simple theft is not so great an offence that it ought to be punished with death. Neither is there any punishment so horrible that it can keep men from stealing who have no other skill or craft by which to earn their living. Therefore on this point, not you alone but also most people in the world are like bad schoolmasters who are readier to beat than to teach their pupils. For great and horrible punishments are appointed for thieves, whereas much rather provision should have been made that there should be some means by which they could get their living, so that no man should be driven to this extreme necessity, first to steal, then to die.

Yes (quoth he) but for this there is quite enough provision already. There are handicrafts, there is husbandry for people to get their living by if they would not willingly be nought. No, I said, you cannot get away with this: for first of all, I shall say nothing of those that return from the wars, maimed and lame—as not long ago out of Blackheath Field [where the Cornishmen's rebellion was crushed], and a little before that out of the wars in France: such, I say, as put their lives in jeopardy for the public weal or for the king's sake, and then by reason of weak-

ness or lameness are not able to take up their old crafts anew, and too old to learn new ones—of them I will say nothing, forasmuch as this is all we can expect from wars. But let us consider those things that happen daily before our eyes.

First there is a great number of gentlemen, who cannot be content to live idle themselves on that which others have labored for: I mean their tenants whom they squeeze and shave to the quick, by raising their rents (for this is the only point of frugality they use, to bring other men to beggary through their lavishness and prodigal spending). These gentlemen, I say, do not only live in idleness themselves, but also carry about with them at their tails a great flock or train of idle and loitering servingmen who never learned any craft whereby to get their living. These men, as soon as their master is dead, or they themselves fall ill, are at once thrust out of doors. For gentlemen would rather keep idlers than sick men, and many times the dead man's heir is not able to maintain as great a house and keep as many servingmen as his father did. Then, in the meantime, those who are thus out of work either starve or else manfully play the thieves. For what would you have them do? When they have wandered about so long that they have worn their clothing threadbare and also impaired their health, then gentlemen, because of their pale and sickly faces and their patched coats, will not take them into their service. And farmers do not dare to give them a job, knowing well enough that the sort of man who has been idly and daintily pampered up in idleness and pleasure, who used to swagger through the street with a bragging look, a sword and buckler by his side, and think himself too good to be any man's mate, is not fit to do true and faithful service to a poor man with a spade and a mattock, for small wages and hard fare.

Nay, by Saint Mary, Sir (quoth the lawyer) that is not so. For this kind of men we must make the most of. For in them, as men of stouter stomachs, bolder spirits, and manlier courage than handicraftsmen and ploughmen are, in them consists the whole power and strength of our army when we must fight in battle.

Forsooth, Sir, you might as well say (quoth I) that for war's sake you must cherish thieves. For surely you shall never lack thieves whilst you have them. And thieves are far from being the most false and fainthearted soldiers, and soldiers are far from being the most cowardly of thieves: so well do these two crafts agree together. But faulty argument, though it is much used among you, in England, yet is not peculiar to you only, but common almost to all nations. Yet France, besides this, is troubled and infected with a much sorer plague. The whole kingdom is filled and besieged with hired soldiers in peacetime (if that be peace) which are brought in under the same color and pretence that has persuaded you to keep these idle servingmen. For these wise fools and very arch-dolts thought that the wealth of their country depended on there always being in readiness a strong and sure garrison, especially of old practised soldiers—for they put no trust at all in untrained men. And therefore they are forced to look for war, so that they may always have trained soldiers and cunning manslayers, lest their hands and their minds should wax dull through idleness or lack of exercise. But how pernicious and pestilent a thing it is to maintain such beasts, the Frenchmen have learnt from their own sufferings, and the examples of the Romans, Carthaginians,

Syrians, and many other countries do manifestly declare. For not only the empire, but also the fields and the cities of all these, on different occasions have been overrun and destroyed by their own army which they had been keeping up. Now how unnecessary a thing [this sort of standing army] is, may be seen from this: that the French soldiers who from their youth have been trained and inured to feats of arms, do not flatter themselves to have often got the upper hand and mastery over your new made and untrained soldiers.

But I will not talk too much on this point, lest I should seem to flatter you. But you can also argue that these same handicraftsmen in your cities, or the rude and uplandish ploughmen of the country, are not supposed to be greatly afraid of your gentlemen's idle servingmen, unless their stature does not correspond to their courage, or their bold stomachs have been discouraged through poverty. Thus you may see that it is not to be feared lest they should be effeminated if those whose stout and sturdy bodies (for gentlemen bother to corrupt and spoil only picked and chosen men) have been weakened by rest and idleness were brought up in good crafts and laborsome works. Truly, howsoever the case stands, I do not think it is much to the public weal that you should, for the sake of war—which you never have but when you will yourselves—keep and maintain an innumerable flock of that sort of men, that are so troublesome and useless in the peacetime of which you ought to have a thousand times more regard than of war. But yet this is not the only cause of stealing. There is another, which, I suppose, is proper and peculiar to Englishmen alone.

What is that? quoth the Cardinal. Forsooth, my lord, quoth I, your sheep that used to be so meek and tame, and such small eaters, now, as I hear say, have become such great devourers and so wild that they eat up and swallow up the very men themselves. They consume, destroy and devour whole fields, houses and cities. For notice that in those parts of the realm whence comes the finest and therefore the dearest wool, there noblemen and gentlemen, and indeed certain abbots, holy men no doubt, not contenting themselves with the yearly revenues and profits that their lands gave their forefathers and predecessors, nor being content that they live in peace and pleasure contributing nothing to the public weal but rather hurting it, leave no ground for tillage. They enclose all pastures; they pull down the houses, they pluck down towns, and leave nothing standing except for the church to be made into a sheephouse. And, as though you lost no small quantity of ground by forests, chases, lands and parks, those good holy men turn all dwelling places and all glebe land into desolation and wilderness.

Therefore in order that one covetous and insatiable cormorant and very plague of his native country may compass about and enclose many thousand acres of ground together within one pale or hedge, the farmers are thrust out of their own, or else by constraint and fraud, or by violent oppression they are done out of it, or by wrongs and injuries they are so wearied that they are compelled to sell everything. Therefore, by one means or by another, by hook or by crook, they are forced to move away, poor, silly, wretched souls, men, women, husbands, wives, fatherless children, widows, woefull mothers with their young babes and their

whole household, small in substance but great in numbers as farming requires many hands. Away they trudge, I say, out of their known and accustomed houses, finding no place to rest in. All their household stuff is worth very little, though there is no reason why it need be sold: yet, being suddenly thrust out, they are constrained to sell it for almost nothing. And when they have wandered about until that has been spent, what else can they do then but steal, and then, by God, be justly hanged, or go about a-begging? And yet even in that case they are cast into prison as vagabonds, because they wander and work not: yet no man will put them to work, though they may offer themselves to do it ever so willingly.

For one shepherd or herdsman is enough to eat up with his cattle that ground for which many hands were need ed when it was used for farming. And this is also the cause why foodstuffs are now dearer in many places. And besides this, the price of wool has risen so that poor folks, who used to work it and make cloth thereof, are no longer able to buy any at all. And by this means very many are forced to give up working and give themselves to idleness. For after so much ground had been enclosed for pasture, a great number of sheep died of the sheep-rot that God would have done better to send upon the sheepmasters' own heads. And though the number of sheep is once more increasing fast, yet the price does not fall one mite, because there are so few sellers. For the sheep have almost all come into a few rich men's hands, who have no need to sell before they want, and they do not want before they can sell as dear as they want.

7. RICHARD HOOKER

As the sixteenth century drew to a close, it became increasingly clear in western Europe that concern for the spiritual welfare and unity of a nation might well harm its political welfare and unity. Long-drawn-out religious conflicts had torn France and had traced their bloody marks across the face of England. Statesmen and philosophers began to suggest that tolerance is not necessarily sin and that an uncompromising religious attitude might be more hindrance than help in the politics of this world. These men who put the visible welfare of the community above its spiritual salvation were known as the *Politiques*.

Richard Hooker (1554–1600) was an English theologian who undertook to show that religious extremism, either Catholic or Puritan, was undesirable. His fundamental idea is that law is the manifestation of the divine order of the universe, and the sovereign who administers the law must preserve and enforce this divine order.

Preface to the Laws of Ecclesiastical Policy

One example herein may serve for many, to shew that false opinions, touching the will of God to have things done, are wont to bring forth mighty and violent practices against the hinderances of them; and those practices new opinions more pernicious than the first, yea most extremely sometimes opposite to that which the first did seem to intend. Where the people took upon them the reformation of the Church by casting out popish superstition, they having received from their pastors a general instruction "that whatsoever the heavenly Father hath not planted must be rooted out," proceeded in some foreign places so far that down went oratories and the very temples of God themselves. For as they chanced to take the compass of their commission stricter or larger, so their dealings were accordingly more or less moderate. Amongst others there sprang up presently one kind of men, with whose zeal and forwardness the rest being compared were thought to be marvellous cold and dull. These grounding themselves on rules more general; that whatsoever the law of Christ commandeth not, thereof Antichrist is the author: and that whatsoever Antichrist or his adherents did in the world, the true professors of Christ are to undo; found out many things more than others had done, the extirpation whereof was in their conceit as necessary as of any thing before removed. Hereupon they secretly made their doleful complaints everywhere as they went, that albeit the world did begin to profess some dislike of that which was evil in the kingdom of darkness, yet fruits worthy of a true repentance were not seen; and that if men did repent as they ought, they must endeavor to purge the earth of all manner of evil, to the end there might follow a new world afterward, wherein righteousness only should dwell. Private repentance they said must appear by every man's fashioning his own life contrary unto the customs and orders of this present world, both in greater things and in less. To this purpose they had always in their mouths those greater things, charity, faith, the true fear of God, the cross, the mortification of the flesh. All their exhortations were to set

From R. Hooker, *Works*, 3 vols., 7th ed. (Oxford, 1888).

light of the things in this world, to count riches and honours vanity, and in token thereof not only to seek neither, but if men were possessors of both, even to cast away the one and resign the other, that all men might see their unfeigned conversion unto Christ. They were solicitors of men to fasts, too often meditations of heavenly things, as it were conferences in secret with God by prayers, not framed according to the frozen manner of the world, but expressing such fervent desires as might even force God to hearken unto them. Where they found men in diet, attire, furniture of house, or any other way, observers of civility and decent order, such they reproved as being carnally and earthly minded. Every word otherwise than severely and sadly uttered seemed to pierce like a sword through them. If any man were pleasant, their manner was presently with deep sighs to repeat those words of our Saviour Christ, "Woe be to you which now laugh, for ye shall lament." So great was their delight to be always in trouble, that such as did quietly lead their lives, they judged of all other men to be in most dangerous case. They so much affected to cross the ordinary custom in every thing, that when other men's use was to put on better attire, they would be sure to shew themselves openly abroad in worse: the ordinary names of the days in the week they thought it a kind of profaneness to use, and therefore accustomed themselves to make no other distinction than by numbers, the First, Second, Third day.

From this they proceeded unto public reformation, first ecclesiastical, and then civil. Touching the former, they boldly avouched that themselves only had the truth, which thing upon peril of their lives they would at all times defend; and that since the Apostles lived, the same

was never before in all points sincerely taught. Wherefore that things might again be brought to that ancient integrity which Jesus Christ by his word requireth, they began to control the ministers of the gospel for attributing so much force and virtue unto the scriptures of God. . . . The Book of God they notwithstanding for the most part so admired, that other disputation against their opinions than only by allegation of Scripture they would not hear; besides it they thought no other writings in the world should be studied; insomuch as one of their great prophets exhorting them to cast away all respects unto human writings, so far to his motion they condescended, that as many as had any books save the Holy Bible in their custody, they brought and set them publicly on fire. When they and their Bibles were alone together, what strange fantastical opinion soever at any time entered into their heads, their use was to think the Spirit taught it them. Their phrenesies concerning our Saviour's incarnation, the state of souls departed, and such-like, are things needless to be rehersed. And forasmuch as they were of the same suite with those of whom the Apostle speaketh, saying, "They are still learning, but never attain to the knowledge of truth," it was no marvel to see them every day broach some new thing, not heard of before. Which restless levity they did interpret to be their growing to spiritual perfection, and a proceeding from faith to faith. The differences amongst them grew by this mean in a manner infinite, so that scarcely was there found any one of them, the forge of whose brain was not possessed with some special mystery. Whereupon, although their mutual contentions were most fiercely prosecuted amongst themselves, yet when they came to defend the cause common to them all against the adversaries of their faction, they had ways to lick one another whole; the sounder in his own persuasion excusing *the dear brethren,* which were not so far enlightened, and professing a charitable hope of the mercy of God towards them notwithstanding their swerving from him in some things. Their own ministers they highly magnified as men whose vocation was from God; the rest their manner was to term disdainfully Scribes and Pharisees, to account their calling a human creature, and to detain the people as much as might be from hearing them. . . .

The pretended end of their civil reformation was that Christ might have dominion over all; that all crowns and sceptres might be thrown down at his feet; that no other might reign over Christian men but he, no regiment keep them in awe but his discipline, amongst them no sword at all be carried besides his, the sword of spiritual excommunication. For this cause they laboured with all their might in overturning the seats of magistracy, because Christ hath said, "Kings of nations"; in abolishing the execution of justice, because Christ hath said, "Resist not evil"; in forbidding oaths, the necessary means of judicial trial, because Christ hath said, "Swear not at all": finally, in bringing in community of goods, because Christ by his Apostles hath given the world such example, to the end that men might excel one another not in wealth the pillar of secular authority, but in virtue.

These men at the first were only pitied in their error, and not much withstood by any; the great humility, zeal, and devotion, which appeared to be in them, was in all men's opinion a pledge of their harmless meaning. . . . Luther made request unto Frederick duke of Saxony, that within his dominion they might be

favourably dealt with and spared, for that (their error exempted) they seemed otherwise right good men. By means of which merciful toleration they gathered strength, much more than was safe for the state of the commonwealth wherein they lived. They had their secret corner-meetings and assemblies in the night, the people flocked unto them by thousands. . . .

In all these things being fully persuaded, that what they did, it was obedience to the will of God, and that all men should do the like; there remained, after speculation, practice, whereby the whole world thereunto (if it were possible) might be framed. This they saw could not be done but with mighty opposition and resistance; against which to strengthen themselves, they secretly entered into league of association. And peradventure considering, that although they were many, yet long wars would in time waste them out; they began to think whether it might not be that God would have them do, for their speedy and mighty increase, the same which sometime God's own chosen people, the people of Israel, did. Glad and fain they were to have it so; which very desire was itself apt so to breed both an opinion of possibility, and a willingness to gather arguments of likelihood, that so God Himself would have it. Nothing more clear unto their seeming, than that a new Jerusalem being often spoken of in Scripture, they undoubtedly were themselves that new Jerusalem, and the old did by way of a certain figurative resemblance signify what they should both be and do. Here they drew in a sea of matter, by applying all things unto their own company, which are any where spoken concerning divine favours and benefits bestowed upon the old commonwealth of Israel: concluding that as Israel was delivered out of Egypt, so they spiritually out of the Egypt of this world's servile thraldom unto sin and superstition; as Israel was to root out the idolatrous nations, and to plant instead of them a people which feared God; so the same Lord's good will and pleasure was now, that these new Israelites should, under the conduct of other Joshuas, Samsons, and Gideons, perform a work no less miraculous in casting out violently the wicked from the earth, and establishing the kingdom of Christ with perfect liberty: and therefore, as the cause why the children of Israel took unto one man many wives, might be lest the casualties of war should any way hinder the promise of God concerning their multitude from taking effect in them; so it was not unlike that for the necessary propagation of Christ's kingdom under the Gospel the Lord was content to allow as much.

Now whatsoever they did in such sort collect out of Scripture, when they came to justify or persuade it unto others, all was the heavenly Father's appointment, his commandment, his will and charge. Which thing is the very point, in regard whereof I have gathered this declaration. For my purpose herein is to show, that when the minds of men are once erroneously persuaded that it is the will of God to have those things done which they fancy, their opinions are as thorns in their sides, never suffering them to take rest till they have brought their speculations into practice. The lets and impediments of which practice their restless desire and study to remove leadeth them every day forth by the hand into other more dangerous opinions, sometimes quite and clean contrary to their first pretended meanings; so what will grow out of such errors as go masked under the cloak of divine authority, impossible it is that ever the wit of man should imagine, till time have

brought forth the fruits of them; for which cause it behoveth wisdom to fear the sequels thereof, even beyond all apparent cause of fear. These men, in whose mouths at the first sounded nothing but only mortification of the flesh, were come at the length to think they might lawfully have their six or seven wives apiece; they which at the first thought judgment and justice itself to be merciless cruelty, accounted at the length their own hands sanctified with being embrued in Christian blood; they who at the first were wont to beat down all dominion, and to urge against poor constables, "Kings of nations;" had at the length both consuls and kings of their own erection amongst themselves: finally, they which could not brook at the first that any man should see, no not by law, the recovery of goods injuriously taken or withheld from him, were grown at the last to think they could not offer unto God more acceptable sacrifice, than by turning their adversaries clean out of house and home, and by enriching themselves with all kinds of spoil and pillage; which thing being laid to their charge, they had in a readiness their answer, that now the time was come, when according to our Saviour's promise, "the meek ones must inherit the earth"; and that their title hereunto was the same which the righteous Israelites had unto the goods of the wicked Egyptians. . . .

Wherefore if we anything respect their error, who being persuaded even as you are have gone further upon that persuasion than you allow; if we regard the present state of the highest governor placed over us, if the quality and disposition of our nobles, if the orders and laws of our famous universities, if the profession of the civil or the practice of the common law amongst us, if the mischiefs whereinto even before our eyes so many others have fallen headlong from no less plausible and fair beginnings than yours are: there is in every of these considerations most just cause to fear lest our hastiness to embrace a thing of so perilous consequence should cause posterity to feel those evils, which as yet are more easy for us to prevent than they would be for them to remedy.

The best and safest way for you therefore, my dear brethren, is, to call your deeds past to a new reckoning, to reexamine the cause ye have taken in hand, and to try it even point by point, argument by argument, with all the diligent exactness ye can; to lay aside the gall of that bitterness wherein your minds have hitherto over-abounded, and with meekness to search the truth. Think ye are men, deem it not impossible for you to err; sift unpartially your own hearts, whether it be force of reason or vehemency of affection, which hath bred and still doth feed these opinions in you. If truth do any where manifest itself, seek not to smother it with glosing delusions, acknowledge the greatness thereof, and think it your best victory when the same doth prevail over you. . . .

Far more comfort it were for us (so small is the joy we take in these strifes) to labour under the same yoke, as men that look for the same eternal reward of their labours, to be joined with you in bands of indissoluble love and amity, to live as if our persons being many our souls were but one, rather than in such dismembered sort to spend our few and wretched days in a tedious prosecuting of wearisome contentions: the end whereof, if they have not some speedy end,

will be heavy even on both sides. Brought already we are even to that estate . . . whereby all parts are entered into a deadly war amongst themselves, and that little remnant of love which was, is now consumed to nothing. The only godliness we glory in, is to find out somewhat whereby we may judge others to be ungodly. Each other's faults we observe as matter of exprobration and not of grief. . . . With the better sort of our own our fame and credit is clean lost. The less we are to marvel if they judge vilely of us, who although we did well would hardly allow thereof. On our backs they also build that are lewd, and what we object one against another, the same they use to the utter scorn and disgrace of us all. This we have gained by our mutual home-dissensions. This we are worthily rewarded with, which are more forward to strive than becometh men of virtuous and mild disposition.

But our trust in the Almighty is, that with us contentions are now at their highest float, and that the day will come (for what cause of despair is there?) when the passions of former enmity being allayed, we shall with ten times redoubled tokens of our unfeignedly reconciled love, shew ourselves each towards other the same which Joseph and the brethren of Joseph were at the time of their interview in Egypt. Our comfortable expectation and most thirsty desire whereof what man soever amongst you shall any way help to satisfy (as we truly hope there is no one amongst you but some way or other will) the blessings of the God of peace, both in this world and in the world to come, be upon him more than the stars of the firmament in number.

8. JEAN BODIN

Jean Bodin (1530–1596) was a French magistrate and political writer. Concerned with the waste and destruction brought to France by the religious struggles between Huguenots and Catholics, he put his faith in a central power that would be a monarchy tempered by the popular will as expressed by the States-General. His great work on the *Republic,* published in 1576, only four years after the Massacre of Saint Bartholomew, with the deliberate purpose of strengthening the position of the king as a source of national unity above rival sects and political parties, achieved a great reputation in its own day especially in those moderate circles which, wanting to separate politics from theology, saw in the royal power a mainstay of peace and order.

From *La République*, 1576

Since an impetuous tempest has tormented the ship of our Republic with such violence that the captain himself and the pilots are engaged in continual labor, it is needful that the passengers themselves lend a hand with the sails, with the ropes, and with the anchor; as well as to those who have not enough strength. [It is needful] that they give some good advice or that they present their suggestions plainly to those who can command the weather and appease the tempests, because all together run the same danger, one which does not affect our enemies which are on certain ground and who take a singular pleasure at the wreck of our Republic; who run amongst the debris and who enrich themselves by the precious things which are constantly manufactured in order to save the kingdom. [The kingdom] which once upon a time possessed all the empires of Germany, of Hungary, of Spain and of Italy and all the possessions of the Gauls just until the Rhine and which were under the rule of its laws. . . .

That is why for myself, not being able to do anything better, I have undertaken to talk of the Republic in popular language because the sources of the Latin language have practically dried up . . . [since Plato] those who have written speak of the affairs of the world without any knowledge of the laws, and even of public law, which has been forgotten beneath conclusions which one has drawn especially out of the profound and sacred mysteries of political philosophy a thing which has given occasion of trouble and tribulation [for] good states. We have, for example, Machiavelli, who has been the vogue amongst tyrants, and whom Paul Iove, having put him among the outstanding men, nevertheless calls an atheist and ignorant of all literature. As to atheism, he has glorified it by his writings. As to knowledge, I think that those who are in the know [and] who talk softly and learnedly and resolve subtly the high affairs of state are in agreement that he has never gotten to the bottom of political science which does not lie in the tricks of tyrants which he has brought together from all the corners of Italy and which like a soft poison run through his book on the Prince. . . .

From Bodin, *Les six livres de la république* (Lyon, 1593), tr. George L. Mosse in *Europe in Review* (New York, 1957), pp. 67–69; by permission of Rand McNally & Co.

Sovereignty is the absolute and perpetual power of a republic which the Romans called *majestas* . . . the Republic is a legal government of several families and that which they have in common with sovereignty added. I have said that this [sovereign] power is perpetual. . . . It is possible to give sovereign power to one or to many for a limited time. . . . [such men] are nothing better than subjects, and when they are in power they cannot call themselves sovereign princes because they are nothing but administrators and trustees of that power until it pleases the people or the prince to revoke it . . . The People are continually invested of it [the power]. They can give power and authority to judge or to command for a certain time, or for so long and so much a time as pleases them. . . . That is why the law says that the governor of a province . . . after his time has expired, gives the power back to those depositories.

Let us perceive now another part of our definition and see what the words "absolute power" actually mean. The people are the rulers of a Republic. [They can] give pure and simple perpetual power to someone to dispose of their goods and persons, or of all the state at his pleasure, and to let him do as he likes, just as the property owner can give his goods pure and simple without any other reason than his liberality. That is a true gift which has no strings attached once it has been made and accepted, in contrast with other gifts which have conditions and qualifications and which [therefore] are not true gifts . . . So the sovereignty or absolute power. It must be that the conditions imposed in the creation of a prince conform, however, to the laws of God and of nature. . . .

In this we can recognize the power and majesty of a true sovereign prince: When the estates of the people are assembled, persons request and supplicate to their prince in all humility without [however having any power to command, disclaim, or to deliberate, [or] to declare laws, edicts and ordinances [unless] it pleases the king to consent or to dissent, to command or to defend. And those . . . who have written of the duty of magistrates and others have gone out of their way to argue that the estates of the people are more illustrious than the prince; a thing which revolts true subjects in the obedience which they owe to their sovereign monarch. There is neither reason nor any foundation whatsoever for such an opinion. . . .

The prince is not held to ordinances and edicts unless these edicts and ordinances coincide with natural justice. . . . It is divine and natural law to obey the edicts and ordinances of him to whom God has given the power over us, if these edicts are not directly opposed to the rule of God who is above all princes. . . . The subject owes obedience to his sovereign prince against all, saving the majesty of God who is the absolute ruler of all the princes of the world. From this axiom we can draw a rule of state: that is to know that the sovereign prince is held to the contracts which he has made, be it with his subjects [or] be it with strangers, because he is the guardian for the subjects of [those] mutual conventions and obligations which they have made one with the other. . . .

There is no crime more detestable in a prince [than] perjury. . . . Also, it is badly spoken to say that the sovereign prince has the power to steal the goods of anyone and to do evil . . . because that connotes weakness, feebleness and laxness of heart. Moreover, the sovereign prince does not have the power to infringe the law of nature which God, of Whom it is the image, has instituted. He [the prince] cannot, therefore, take the goods of anyone without just and reasonable cause, be it by buying or exchange, or legitimate confiscation, or [by] making a treaty with the enemy which he cannot conclude otherwise than by taking the goods of particular or private persons for the preservation of the state. . . . For natural law decrees that the public good is above all individuals and that subjects surrender not only their injuries and vengeances, but also their goods for the well being of the republic. . . . Because there is nothing higher on earth after God than sovereign princes, and as they are established by Him as His lieutenants to command men, it is necessary to be aware of their station, to respect them and to revere their majesty in all obedience, to talk to them with all honor; because he who abuses his sovereign prince abuses God of Whom he is the image on earth. . . . In order that one can recognize him who is . . . the sovereign prince, one has to know his qualities which are not common to other subjects; because if they were common they could not be any part of a sovereign prince. . . .

He who has no [earthly] sovereign is he who gives law to all his subjects, who makes peace and war, who gives power to all the offices and magistrates of his country, who levies taxes, [who] enfranchises him who seems worthy, and who gives pardon to him who had deserved death: What more power could one desire in a sovereign prince? These are always the marks of sovereign power. . . . Just as the great sovereign God cannot create a god who is His equal because He is infinite, so we can say that the princes whom we have described as the image of God cannot elevate a subject to his station because then his [the prince's] power would no longer exist. . . .

Because this is so, it follows that the prime mark of sovereignty is not to give justice, because that is common to the prince and to the subjects, just as is [the power] to institute or to abolish offices, because the prince and the subject [both] may share that power—especially as respects the officers serving justice or the police, or war or finance . . . [nor] is it the prime mark of sovereignty to give rewards to them who have merited them, because that is common to the prince and the magistrates, because the magistrates may receive that power from the prince; also, it is not a prime mark of sovereignty to take counsel of the affairs of a state, because that may be the charge of the privy council or the senate of the Republic. . . . We might say the same thing as regards the law [which] the magistrates can give to them who are within the power of their jurisdiction, but he [the magistrate] can do nothing against the edicts and ordinances of his sovereign prince and to make this point clearer, we must presuppose that the word of the law signifies the right command of him, or of those who have power over all others without exception of person; and to go further, . . . there is no one but the sovereign prince who can give law to all his subjects without exception, be it in general or in particular.

9. MONTAIGNE

"If you can keep your head, when all about you are losing theirs . . ." Michel Eyquem de Montaigne (1533–1592) was one of the few who did. Counsellor in the *Parlement* (High Court) of Bordeaux, near which his estate lay; eventually mayor of the great port; he soon left the public life to which his rank had led him for the peace of his manor at Montaigne, where he read books and composed the *Essays* whose publication, beginning in 1580, would make him famous. Unusual in trying to take no side in the religious wars then tearing France apart, Montaigne was more unusual still in that he felt no hatred for his enemies—at least, no more than circumstances required. His humorous scepticism and his detachment would be recognized as subversive when his book was placed on the *Index* in 1676. In his own lifetime, though, he lived as a conformist and died as a Catholic, appreciated by his king (Henry IV), by his neighbors and, even, by his (sometimes nagging) wife.

"We are great fools. 'He has spent his life in idleness,' we say. 'I have done nothing today.' What, have you not lived? That is not only the fundamental but the most illustrious of your occupations. 'If I had been placed in a position to manage great affairs, I would have shown what I could do.' Have you been able to think out and to manage your own life? You have done the greatest task of all. . . . Our great and glorious masterpiece is to live appropriately. All other things—ruling, building, hoarding up treasure—are only little appendages and props, at most." We can consider this a fitting epitaph for the man whose tomb now stands in the hallway of what was once the University of Bordeaux.

The following essay, one of his most famous, reflects the wide reading of a Renaissance man, greedy like many of his contemporaries for the wisdom of the ancients, ready to quote them at the drop of a quill, but also ready to assimilate this wisdom into a stoic epicureanism of his own: moderate, good-humored, and philosophical in the best sense of that word.

Of Managing One's Will

Few things, in comparison of what commonly affect other men, move, or, to say better, possess me; for 'tis but reason they should concern a man, provided they do not take possession of him. I am very solicitous, both by study and reasoning, to enlarge this privilege of insensibility, which is naturally raised to a pretty high degree in me; so that consequently I espouse or am very much moved with very few things. I have my sight clear enough, but I fix it upon very few objects; my sense delicate and tender enough, but an apprehension and application stubborn and negligent. I am very unwilling to engage myself; as much as in me lies, I employ myself wholly upon myself; and in this very subject should rather choose to curb and restrain my affection from plunging itself over head

From William Hazlitt, ed. and trans., *The Complete Works of Michael de Montaigne* (Philadelphia, 1879), pp. 490–501.

and ears into it, it being a subject that I possess at the mercy of others, and over which fortune has more right than I; so that even so much as to health, which I so much value, it were necessary for me not so passionately to cover and desire it as to find diseases insupportable. A man ought to moderate himself betwixt the hatred of pain and the love of pleasure, and Plato sets down a middle path of life betwixt both. But against such affections as wholly carry me away from myself and fix me elsewhere, against these, I say, I oppose myself with my utmost force and power. 'Tis my opinion that a man should lend himself to others, and only give himself to himself. Were my will easy to lend itself out, and to be swayed, I should not stick there; I am too tender, both by nature and custom:

Born and bred up in negligence and ease,
I fly from business as from disease.

(Ovid)

The hot and obstinate disputes wherein my adversary would at last have the better, the issue that would render my heat and obstinacy disgraceful, would perhaps vex me to the last degree. Should I set myself to it at the rate that others do, my soul would never have the force to bear the emotions and alarms that attend those who pursue and grasp at so much; it would immediately be disordered by this inward agitation. If sometimes I have been put upon the management of other men's affairs, I have promised to take them in hand, but not into my lungs and liver; to take them upon me, not to incorporate them; to take pains for, but not to be impassioned about, them. I have a care of them, but I will not brood upon them. I have enough to do to order and govern the domestic tumults that I have in my own veins and bowels, without introducing a crowd of other men's affairs, and am sufficiently concerned about my own proper and natural business, without meddling with the concerns of others. Those who know how much they owe to themselves, and how many offices they are bound to of their own, find that nature has given them this commission, full enough to keep them from being ever idle: "Thou hast business enough at home, look to that."

Men let themselves out to hire; their faculties are not for themselves, but to be employed for those to whom they have enslaved themselves: their hirers are in their houses, not themselves. This common humour pleases not me. We must be thrifty of the liberty of our souls, and never let them out but upon just occasions, which are very few, if we judge aright. Do but observe such as have accustomed themselves to be at every one's call, they do it indifferently upon all, as well upon little as upon great occasions, in that which nothing concerns them, as much as in what imports them most; they intrude themselves indifferently wherever there is business and obligation, and are without life, when not in the bustle of affairs: "they only seek business for business sake" (Seneca). It is not so much that they will go, as that they cannot stand still: like a rolling stone that does not stop till it can go no farther. Business, by a certain sort of men, is thought a mark of capacity and honour; their souls seek repose in motion, as children do by being rocked in a cradle; they may pronounce themselves as serviceable to their friends, as troublesome to themselves. No one distributes his money to others, but every one distributes his time and his life. There is nothing of which we are so prodigal as of these two things, of which to be thrifty would be both commendable and useful. I am of a quite contrary humour; I look to myself, and commonly covet with no great ardour what I do desire, and desire little, and employ and busy myself but rarely and temperately in the same way. Whatever they take in hand, they do it with their utmost power and vehemence. There are so many dangerous steps, that, for the more safety, we must a little lightly and superficially slide through the world, and not rush through it. Pleasure itself is painful in its depth:

> Thou upon glowing coals dost tread,
> Under deceitful ashes hid.
>
> (Horace)

The citizens of Bordeaux chose me mayor of their city at a time when I was at a distance from France, and still more remote from any such thought. I begged to be excused, but I was told that I had committed an error in so doing, and the greater because the king had moreover interposed his command in the affair. 'Tis an office that ought to be looked upon so much more honourable, as it has no other pay nor advantage than the bare honour of its execution. It continues two years but may be extended by a second election, which very rarely happens. It was so to me, and had never been so but twice before, some years ago to Monsieur Lanssac, and lately to Monsieur de Biron, marshal of France, in which place I succeeded, and left mine to Monsieur de Matignon, marshal of France also. Proud of so noble a fraternity,

> Both fit for governing in peace and war.
>
> (Virgil)

Fortune would have a hand in my promotion, by this particular circumstance, which she put in of her own, not altogether vain; for Alexander disdained the ambassadors of Corinth, who came to make him a tender of the burgess-ship of their city; but when they proceeded to lay before him that Bacchus and Hercules were also in the register, he thankfully accepted the offer.

At my arrival, I faithfully and conscientiously represented myself to them for such as I find myself to be; a man without memory, without vigilance, without experience, and without vigour; but withal without hatred, without ambition, without avarice, and without violence. That they might be informed and know what they were to expect from my service, and being that the knowledge they had had of my father, and the honour they had for his memory, had been the only motives to confer this upon me, I plainly told them that I should be very sorry any thing should make so great an impression upon me, as their affairs and the concerns of their city had done upon him, whilst he had the same government to which they had preferred me. I very well remember, when a boy, to have seen him in his old age, tormented with and solicitous about the public affairs, neglecting the soft repose of his own house, to which the declension of his age had attached him for several years before, the management of his own affairs, and his health, and certainly despising his own life, which was in great danger of being lost, by being engaged in long and painful journeys on their behalf. Such was he, and this humour of his proceeded from a marvelous goodness of nature. Never was there a more charitable and popular spirited man. Yet this which I commend in others, I do not love to follow myself, and am not without excuse.

He had heard that a man must forget himself for his neighbour, and that particular individuals were in no manner of consideration in comparison with the general concern. Most of the rules and precepts of this world run this way, to drive us out of ourselves into the world, for the benefit of public society: they thought to do a great feat, to divert us from ourselves, presuming we were but too much fixed at home, and by a too natural inclination, and have said all they could to that purpose; for 'tis no new thing for wise men to preach things as they serve, not as they are. Truth has its obstructions, inconveniences, and incompatibilities with us: we must be often deceived, that we may not deceive ourselves, and shut our eyes, and stupefy our understandings, to redress and amend them: "For the ignorant judge, and therefore are oft to be deceived, lest they should err" (Quintilian). When they prescribe us to love three, four, fifty degrees of things above ourselves, they do like archers who, to hit the mark, take their aim a great deal higher than the butt: to set a crooked stick straight, we bend it the contrary way. . . .

The principal charge we have is, to every one his own conduct, and 'tis for this that we are here. As he who should forget to live a virtuous and holy life, and should think he acquitted himself of his duty in instructing and training up others to it, would be a fool; even so he who abandons his own particular healthful and pleasant living to serve others, takes, in my opinion, a wrong and an unnatural course.

I would not that men should refuse, in the employments they take upon them, their attention, pains, their eloquence, and their sweat and blood, in time of need . . . but 'tis only as a loan, and incidentally; his mind being always in repose and in health not without action, but without vexation, without passion.

To be simply doing costs him so little that he acts even sleeping; but he must set on the motion with discretion; for the body receives the offices imposed upon it, just according to what they are; the mind often extends, and makes them heavier at its own expense, giving them what measure it pleases. Men perform like things with several sorts of endeavour, and different contentions of the will: the one does well enough without the other; for how many people hazard themselves every day in war, without any concern which way it goes, and thrust themselves into the dangers of battles, the loss of which will not break their next night's sleep? And such a man may be at home, out of danger, which he durst not have looked upon, who is more passionately concerned for the issue of this war, and whose soul is more anxious about events, than the soldier who stakes his life and blood in the quarrel. I could have engaged myself in public employments, without quitting myself a nail's breadth, and have given myself to others without abandoning myself. This sharpness and violence of desires more hinders than it advances the execution of what we undertake, fills us with impatience against slow or contrary events, and with heat and suspicion against those with whom we have to do. We never carry on that thing well by which we are prepossessed and led:

For overheat doth carry on things ill.

He who therein employs only his judgment and address proceeds more cheerfully: he counterfeits, he gives way, he defers all things at his ease, according to the necessities of occasions; he fails in his attempts, without trouble and affliction, ready and entire for a new effort; he always rides bridle in hand. In him who is drunk with violent and tyrannic intention, we see of necessity much imprudence and injustice: the impetuosity of his desire carries him away; these are rash motions, and, if fortune does not very much assist, of very little fruit. Philosophy wills that in the revenge of injuries received we should strip ourselves of choler, not that the chastisement should be less, but, on the contrary, that the revenge may be the better and more heavy, which it conceives will be by this impetuosity hindered. For anger does not only trouble, but of itself does also weary, the arm of those who chastise; this fire benumbs and wastes their force: as in precipitation, "haste fetters itself." For example, according to what I commonly see, avarice has no greater impediment than itself; the more bent and vigorous it is, the less it rakes together, and commonly sooner grows rich, when disguised in a vizor of liberality. . . .

Do but consider that, even in vain and frivolous actions, as at chess, tennis, and the like, this eager and ardent engaging with an impetuous desire immediately throws the mind and members into indirection and disorder; a man confounds and hinders himself; he that carries himself the most moderately, both towards gain and loss, has always his wits about him; the less peevish and passionate he is at play, he plays much more advantageously and surely.

As to the rest, we hinder the mind's seizure and hold, in giving it so many things to seize upon: some things we are only to offer to it, to tie others to it, and others to incorporate with it: it can feel and discern all things, but ought to feed on nothing but itself, and should be instructed in what properly concerns itself, that is properly of its own having and substance. The laws of nature teach us ex-

actly what we need. After the sages have told us that, according to nature, no one is indigent, and that every one is so according to opinion, they very subtly distinguish betwixt the desires that proceed from her and those that proceed from the disorder of our own fancy: those of which we can see the end are hers; those that fly before us, and of which we can see no end, are our own. Want of goods is easily repaired; poverty of soul is irreparable:

If what's for man enough enough could be
It were enough: but as we plainly see
That won't suffice, how can I e'er believe
That any wealth my mind content can give?
(Lucilius)

Socrates seeing a great quantity of riches, jewels, and furniture of great value, carried in pomp through the city: "How many things," said he, "do I not desire!" Metrodorus lived on twelve ounces a day; Epicurus upon less; Metrocles slept in winter abroad among sheep; in summer in the cloisters of churches. Cleanthes lived by the labour of his own hands, and boasted, "That Cleanthes, if he would, could maintain yet another Cleanthes."

If that which nature exactly and originally requires of us for the conservation of our being be too little, let us dispense with a little more; let us call every one of our habits and conditions nature; let us tax and treat ourselves by this measure; let us stretch our appurtenances and accounts so far; for so far I fancy we have some excuse. Custom is a second nature, and no less powerful. What is wanting to my custom I hold to be wanting to me; and I should be almost as well content that they took away my life, as take me far from the way wherein I have so long lived. I am no more in a condition for any great change, nor to put myself into a new and unwonted course, though never so much to my advantage. 'Tis past the time for me to become other than what I am; and as I should complain of any great adventure that should now befall me, that it came not in time to be enjoyed:

For what are fortune's gifts, if I'm denied
Their cheerful use?   (Horace)

so should I complain of any inward acquest. It were almost better never, than so late, to become an honest man, and well understanding in living, when a man has no longer to live. I, who am going, would readily resign to any new-comer all the wisdom I have acquired for the world's commerce: "after meat comes mustard." I want no goods of which I can make no use; of what use is knowledge to him that has lost his head? 'Tis adding insult to injury for fortune to offer us presents that will only inspire us with a just despite that we had them not in their due season. Guide me no more, I can no longer go. Of so many parts as make a perfect man, patience suffices. Give an excellent treble to a chorister that has rotten lungs, and eloquence to a hermit exiled in the deserts of Arabia. There needs no art to further a fall; the end finds itself of itself, at the conclusion of every affair. My world is at an end, my form expired; I belong to the past, and am bound to authorise it, and to conform my end to it. I will here mention, by way of example, that the recent eclipse by the pope of ten days,* has taken me so low that I cannot well get used to it; I belong to the years wherein we kept another kind of account. So ancient and so long a custom challenges and calls me back to it; I am constrained to be somewhat

heretical in this point: impatient of any even though a corrective innovation. My imagination, in spite of my teeth, always pushes me ten days forward or backward, and is ever murmuring in my ears, "This rule concerns those who are going to be." If health itself, sweet as it is, returns to me by fits, 'tis rather to give me cause of regret than fruition of itself; I have no place left to keep it in. Time leaves me, without which nothing can be possessed. Oh, what little account should I make of those great elective dignities that I see in such esteem in the world, that are never conferred but upon men who are taking leave of it, in whom they do not so much regard how well he will discharge his trust, as how short his administration will be; from the very entry they look at the exit. In short, I am about to finish this man, and not to rebuild another. By long habit this form is, in me, turned into substance, and fortune into nature.

I say, therefore, that every one of us feeble creatures is excusable in thinking that to be his own which is comprised under this measure; but withal, beyond these limits, 'tis nothing but confusion; 'tis the largest extent we can grant to our own claim. The more business we create ourselves, the more we amplify our possession, so much more do we expose ourselves to the blows and adversities of fortune. The career of our desires ought to be circumscribed, and restrained to a short limit of near and contiguous conveniences; and ought moreover, to perform their course, not in a right line, that ends elsewhere, but in a circle, of which the two points by a short wheel meet and terminate in ourselves. Actions that are carried on without this reflection (a near

* The introduction of the Gregorian calendar, 1582.

and essential reflection I mean), such as those of ambitious and avaricious men, and many more who run point blank, and whose career always carries them before themselves, such actions, I say, are erroneous and sickly.

Most of our business is farce: "All the world's a stage, and all the men and women merely players" (Petronius). We must play our part well, but withal as the part of a borrowed personage; we must not make a real essence of a mask and outward appearance, nor of a strange person our own; we cannot distinguish the skin from the shirt; 'tis enough to meal the face without mealing the breast. I see some who transform and transubstantiate themselves into as many new shapes and new beings as they undertake employments, and who prelate themselves even to the heart and liver, and carry their office along with them, even to the close stool; I cannot make them distinguish the salutations that are made to them from those made to their commission, their train, or their mule: "They so much give themselves up to fortune as even to forget nature" (Petronius); they swell and puff up their souls and their natural way of speaking, according to the height of their magisterial place. The mayor of Bordeaux and Montaigne have ever been two by very manifest separation. To be an advocate or a treasurer, a man must not be ignorant of the knavery of such callings; an honest man is not accountable for the vice or folly of his business, and yet ought not to refuse to take the calling upon him; 'tis the custom of his country, and there is money to be got by it; a man must live by the world, and make his best of it, such as it is. But the judgment of an emperor ought to be above his empire, and view and consider it as an accident; and he ought to know how to enjoy himself apart from it, and to communicate himself as James and Peter, to himself at least.

I cannot engage myself so deep and so entire; when my will gives me to a party, 'tis not with so violent an obligation that my judgment is infected with it. In the present broils of this kingdom, my interest in the one side has not made me forget either the laudable qualities of some of our adversaries, nor those that are reproachable in my own party. People generally adore all of their own side; for my part I do not so much as excuse most things in those of mine; a good book has never the worse grace for being written against me. The knot of the controversy excepted, I have always kept myself in equanimity and pure indifference: "And have no express hatred beyond the necessity of war" (Quintus Curtius); for which I am pleased with myself, and the more, because I see others commonly fail in the contrary way. Such as extend their anger and hatred beyond the dispute in question, as most men do, show that they spring from some other occasion and particular cause; like one who, being cured of an ulcer, has yet a fever remaining, by which it appears that the ulcer had another more concealed beginning. It is because they are not concerned in the common cause, because it is wounding to the state and common interest, but are only nettled by reason of their private and particular concern: this is why they are so especially animated, beyond justice and public reason: "Every one was not so much angry against things in general as against those that particularly concerned himself" (Livy). I would have matters go well on our side; but if they do not, I shall not run mad. I am heartily for the right party; but I do not affect to be taken notice of for an especial enemy to others, and beyond the general quarrel. I am a mortal enemy to this vicious form of censure: "He is of the league because he admires the Duke of Guise. He is astonished at the king of Navarre's valour and diligence, and therefore he is a Huguenot. He finds such and such faults in the king, and therefore he is seditious in his heart;" and I would not grant to the magistrate that he did well in condemning a book, because it had placed a heretic among the best poets of the time. Shall we not dare to say of a thief that he has a handsome leg? Because a woman is a strumpet, must it needs follow that she has a stinking breath? . . . If they take a hatred against an advocate, he will not be allowed the next day to be eloquent. I have elsewhere spoken of the zeal that pushes on worthy men to the like faults. For my part I can say: "such an one does this ill, and that well and virtuously." So, in the prognostics or sinister events of affairs, they will have every one, in his own party, blind or a blockhead; and our persuasion and judgment be subservient, not to truth, but to the project of our desires. I should rather incline towards the other extreme, so much do I fear being suborned by my desire; to which may be added, that I am a little tenderly distrustful of things that I wish.

I have in my time seen wonders in the way of an indiscreet and prodigious facility in people to suffer their hopes and belief to be led and governed which way has best pleased and served their leaders, through a hundred mistakes one upon another, and through dreams and phantasms. I no more wonder at those who have been blinded and led by the nose by the ape's tricks of Apollonius and Mahomet. Their sense and understanding is absolutely taken away by their passion: their discretion has no longer any other

choice than that which smiles upon them, and supports their cause. I principally observed that in the beginning of our intestine distempers: this other, which is sprung up since, in imitation, has surpassed it: by which I am satisfied that it is a quality inseparable from popular errors; after the first that sets out, opinions drive on one another like waves with the wind; you are not part of the body, if you utter a word of objection, and do not follow the common run. But doubtless they wrong the just side, when they go about to assist it with fraud; I have ever been against that practice: 'tis only fit to work upon weak heads; for the sound, there are surer and more honest ways to keep up their courage, and to excuse adverse accidents. . . .

We must not precipitate ourselves so headlong after our affections and interest. As, when I was young, I opposed the progress of love, which I perceived to advance too fast upon me, and had a care lest it should at last become so pleasing as to force, captivate, and wholly reduce me to its mercy, so I do the same upon all other occasions, where my will is running on with too warm an appetite; I lean opposite to the side it inclines to, as I find it going to plunge and make itself drunk with its own wine: I evade nourishing its pleasure so far, that I cannot recover it without infinite loss. Souls that, through their own stupidity, only discern things by halves, have this happiness, that they smart the less with hurtful things: 'tis a spiritual leprosy that has some show of health, and such a health as philosophy does not altogether contemn; but yet we have no reason to call it wisdom, as we often do. And after this manner a man mocked Diogenes, who, in the depth of winter, and stark naked, went hugging an image of snow for a trial of his patience;

seeing him in this exercise: "Art thou very cold?" said he; "Not at all," replied Diogenes; "Why, then," said the other, "what great and exemplary thing dost thou think thou art doing now?" To estimate a man's firmness, we must know what his suffering is.

But souls that are to meet with adverse events, and the injuries of fortune in their depth and sharpness, that are to weigh and taste them according to their natural weight and sharpness, let such show their skill in avoiding the causes and diverting the blow. What did King Cotys do? He paid liberally for the rich and beautiful service of porcelain that had been brought him; but, seeing it was exceedingly brittle he immediately broke it, in order to prevent so easy a matter of displeasure against his servants. In like manner, I have willingly avoided all confusion in my affairs, and never coveted to have my estate contiguous to those of my relations, and those with whom I desired a strict friendship; whence matter of unkindness and fallings-out often proceed. I formerly loved cards and dice, but have long since left them off, only for this reason, that though I carry my losses as handsomely as another, I was not quiet within. Let a man of honour, who ought to be sensible of the lie, and who will not take a scurvy excuse for satisfaction, avoid occasions of dispute. I shun melancholic and sour-natured men as I would the plague; and in matters I cannot talk of without emotion and concern, I never meddle, if not compelled by duty: " 'Tis better not to begin, than to desist" (Seneca). The surest way, then, is to prepare one's-self before the occasion.

I know very well that some wise men have taken another way, and have not feared to grapple and engage to the utmost upon several subjects: these are confident of their own strength, under cover of which they protect themselves in all ill successes, making their patience wrestle and contend with disaster. . . . Let us never attempt these examples; we shall never come up to them. They set themselves resolutely, and without trouble, to behold the ruin of their country, to which all the good they can contrive or perform is due: this is too much and too rude for our common souls to undergo. Cato gave up the noblest life that ever was upon this account; but it is for us smaller men to fly from the storm as far as we can; we ought to shun pain, instead of cultivating patience, and dip under the blows we cannot parry. Zeno seeing Chremonides, a young man whom he loved, draw near to sit down by him, suddenly started up, and Cleanthes asking the reason why he did so: "I hear," said he, "that physicians especially order repose, and forbid emotion, in all excitements." Socrates does not say: "Do not surrender to the charms of beauty; stand your ground, and do your utmost to oppose it." "Fly it," says he, "shun the sight and encounter of it, as of a powerful poison, that darts and wounds at a distance" (Xenophon). And the Holy Spirit, in like manner: "Lead us not into temptation" (Matt. 6:13). We do not pray that our reason may not be combated and overcome by concupiscence, but that it should not be so much as tried by it; that we should not be brought into a state wherein we should have so much as to suffer the approaches, solicitations, and temptations of sin; and we beg of Almighty God to keep our consciences quiet, fully and perfectly delivered from all commerce of evil.

Such as say that they have reason for their avenging passion, or any other sort of troublesome agitation of mind, do often say true, as things now are, but not as they were; they speak to us when the causes of their error are nourished and advanced by themselves: but look back, recall these causes to their beginning, and there you will put them to a nonplus. Will they have their fault less, for being of longer continuance; think they of an unjust beginning the sequel can be just? Whoever desires the good of his country, as I do, without fretting and pining, will be troubled, but will not swoon to see it threatened either with its own ruin, or a not less ruinous continuance: poor vessel, that the waves, the wind, and the pilot toss and steer to so contrary designs! He who does not gape after the favour of princes, as after a thing he cannot live without, does not much concern himself at the coldness of their reception and countenance, nor at the inconstancy of their wills. He who does not brood over his children or his honours with a slavish propension, ceases not to live commodiously enough after their loss. He who does good principally for his own satisfaction will not be much troubled to see men judge of his actions contrary to his merit. A quarter of an ounce of patience will provide sufficiently against such inconveniences. I find ease in this receipt, redeeming myself in the beginning as cheap as I can; and find that by this means I have escaped much trouble and many difficulties. With very little effort I stop the first sally of my emotions, and quit the subject that begins to be troublesome, before it carries one away. He who stops not the start will hardly ever be able to stop the career: he who cannot keep them out will never get them out, when they are once in; he who cannot crush them at the beginning, will never do it after; nor ever keep himself from falling, if he cannot recover himself when first he begins to totter. . . .

How often have I done myself a manifest injustice, to avoid the hazard of having yet a worse done me by the judges, after an age of vexations, dirty and vile practices, more enemies to my nature than fire or the rack? "A man should be an enemy to all contention as much as he lawfully may, and I know not whether or not something more: for 'tis not only handsome, but sometimes also advantageous too, a little to recede from one's right" (Cicero). Were we wise, we ought to rejoice and boast, as I one day heard a young gentleman of a good family very innocently do, that his mother had lost her suit, as if it had been a cough, a fever, or something very troublesome to keep. Even the favours that fortune might have given me through relationship, or acquaintance with those who have sovereign authority in our affairs, I have conscientiously waived, and very carefully avoided employing them to the prejudice of others, and of advancing my pretensions above their true right. In fine, I have so much prevailed by my endeavours (happy 'tis for me I can say), that I am to this day a virgin from all suits at law, though they have made me very fair offers, and with very just ground, would I have hearkened to them; and a virgin from quarrels too; I have almost passed over a long life without any offence of moment, either active or passive, or without ever hearing myself called by a worse word than my own name; a rare favour of heaven!

Our greatest agitations have ridiculous motives and causes; and I have in my time seen the wisest heads in this kingdom assembled with great ceremony, and at the public expense, about treaties and agreements, of which the real decision in the mean time absolutely depended upon the ladies' cabinet council, and the inclination of some woman body. The poets very well understood this, when they put all Greece and Asia to fire and sword for an apple. Enquire why that man hazards his life and honour upon the fortune of his rapier and dagger: let him acquaint you with the occasion of the quarrel; he cannot do it without blushing, 'tis so idle and frivolous!

A little thing will engage you in't, but being once embarked, all cords draw; greater considerations are then required, more hard and more important. How much easier is it not to enter in, than it is to get out? We should proceed contrary to the reed, which at its first spring produces a long and straight shoot, but afterwards, as if tired and out of breath, runs into thick and frequent joints and knots, as so many pauses, which demonstrate that it has no more its first vigour and constancy: 'twere better to begin fair and calmly, and to keep a man's breath and vigour for the weight and stress of the business. We guide and govern affairs in their beginnings, and have them then in our own power; but afterwards, when they are once at work, 'tis they that guide and govern us, and we have to follow them.

Yet do I not pretend by this to say that this plan has relieved me of all difficulty, and that I have not often had enough to do to curb and restrain my passions; they are not always to be governed according to the measure of occasions, and often have their entries very sharp and violent. Yet good fruit and profit may thence be reaped, except by those who in well-doing are not satisfied with any benefit, if reputation be wanting; for, in truth, such an effect is of no account, but by every one in himself; you are better contented, but no more esteemed, seeing you reformed yourself before you came into play, or that any vice was discovered in you. Yet

not in this only, but in all other duties of life also, the way of those who aim at honour is very different from that they proceed by, who propose to themselves order and reason. I find some who rashly and furiously rush into the lists, and cool in the race. As Plutarch says, that as those who, through awkwardness, are soft and facile to grant whatever is desired of them, are afterwards as frail to break their word and to recant; so likewise he who enters lightly into a quarrel, is subject to run as lightly out of it. The same difficulty that keeps me from entering into it would, when once hot and engaged in it, incite me to maintain it with resolution. 'Tis, perhaps, wrong; but when a man is once engaged, he must go through with it or die. "Undertake coldly," said Bias, "but pursue with ardour" (Laertius). For want of prudence, men fall into want of courage, which is still more intolerable.

Most accommodations of our quarrels now-a-days are discreditable and false: we only seek to save appearances, and in the mean time betray and disavow our true intentions; we salve over the fact. We know very well how we said the thing, and in what sense we spoke it, and all the company, and all our friends with whom we would appear to have the advantage, understand it well enough too; 'tis at the expense of our frankness, and the honour of our courage, that we disown our thoughts, and seek subterfuge in falsehood to make friends; we give ourselves the lie, to excuse the lie we have given another. You are not to consider whether your word or action may admit of another interpretation; 'tis your own real and sincere interpretation, your real meaning, that you are thenceforward to maintain, whatever it cost you. Men address themselves to your virtue and your conscience, which are neither of them to be disguised:

let us leave these pitiful ways and expedients to the tricksters of the law. The excuses and satisfactions that I see every day made and given to repair indiscretion, seem to me more scandalous than the indiscretion itself. It were better to affront your adversary a second time, than to offend yourself by giving him such satisfaction. You have braved him in your heat and anger and you go to appease him in your cooler and better sense; and by that means lay yourself lower, and at his feet, whom before you pretended to overtop. I do not find anything a gentleman can say so rude and vicious in him, as unsaying what he has said is infamous, when that unsaying is authoritatively extracted from him; forasmuch as obstinacy is more excusable in him than pusillanimity. Passions are as easy for me to evade, as they are hard for me to moderate: " 'Tis easier to tear them altogether from the mind, than to moderate them" (Seneca). He who cannot attain unto that noble stocial impassibility, let him secure himself in the bosom of this popular stupidity of mine: what those great souls performed by their virtue, I inure myself to do by complexion. The middle region harbours storms and tempests; the two extremes of philosophers and rustics concur in tranquillity and happiness:

How blest the sage! whose mind can pierce
  each cause
Of changeful nature, and her wond'rous
  laws;
Who tramples fear beneath his foot, and
  braves
Fate, and stern death, and hell's resounding
  waves!
Blest too, who knows each god that guards
  the swain,
Pan, old Sylvanus, and the Dryad train.
                              (Virgil)

The birth of all things is weak and ten-

der; and therefore we are to have an eye to beginnings; for as then, in their infancy, the danger is not perceived, so, when it is grown up, neither is the remedy to be found. I had every day encountered a million of crosses, harder to digest, in the progress of ambition, than it has been difficult for me to curb the natural propension that inclined me to it:

For well might I be shy,
To raise my head so high.
                    (Horace)

All public actions are subject to various and uncertain interpretations, for too many heads judge of them. Some say of this city employment of mine (and I am willing to say a word of it, not that it is worth so much, but to exhibit my conduct in such things), that I have behaved myself in it like a man not easy to be moved, and with a languishing affection; and they have some colour for what they say. I endeavour to keep my mind and my thoughts in repose: "As being always quiet by nature, so also now by age" (Cicero); and if they sometimes lash out on some rude and sensible impression, 'tis in truth, without my advice. Yet, from this natural heaviness of mine, men ought not to conclude a total inability in me (for want of care and want of sense are two very different things), and much less any ingratitude towards that city, who employed the utmost means they had in their power to oblige me, both before they knew me and after, and did much more for me in choosing me anew, than conferring that honour upon me at first. I wish them all the good that can befall them, and certainly had occasion offered, there is nothing I would have spared for their service. I did for them as I would have done for myself. 'Tis a good, warlike, and generous people, but capable of obedience and discipline, and of whom the best use may be made, if well guided. They say also that my administration was passed over without mark or thing worthy of record. Very good! They accuse my cessation in a time when every body almost was convicted of doing too much. I am impatient to be doing where my will spurs me on; but this point is an enemy to perseverance. Let whoever will make use of me according to my own way, employ me in affairs where vigour and liberty are required; where a direct, short, and moreover a hazardous conduct is necessary; I may do something: but if it must be long, subtle, laborious, artificial, and intricate, they would do better to call in somebody else. All important offices are not hard: I came prepared to work a little more, had there been great occasion; for it is in my power to do something more than I do, or than I love to do; I did not to my knowledge omit any thing that my duty really required. I easily forget those offices that ambition mixes with duty, and shelters under that title; these are they that, for the most part, fill the eyes and ears, and give men the most satisfaction: not the thing, but the appearance contents them; they think men sleep, if they hear no noise. My humour is no friend to tumult; I could appease a riot without emotion, and chastise a disorder without alteration. If I stand in need of anger and inflammation, I borrow it and put it on; my manners are heavy, rather faint than sharp. I do not condemn a magistrate that sleeps, provided the people under his charge sleep as well as he: the laws in that case sleep too. For my part I commend a gliding, quiet, and silent life, "neither abject nor overbearing:" my fortune will have it so. I am descended from a family that has lived without lustre or tumult, and time out of mind, particularly ambitious

of the character of truth and honesty.

Our people now-a-days are so bred up to bustle and ostentation, that goodness, moderation, equability, and such quiet and obscure qualities, are no more regarded: rough bodies make themselves felt, the smooth are imperceptibly handled; sickness is felt; health little, or not at all; no more than the oils that foment us, in comparison of the pain for which we are fomented. 'Tis acting for a man's reputation and particular profit, not for the public good, to refer that to be done in the public place which a man may as well do in the council-chamber, and to noon-day what might have been done the night before; and to be jealous to do that himself which his colleague can do as well as he. So some surgeons of Greece used to perform their operations upon scaffolds, in the sight of the people, to draw more practice and profit. They think that good orders cannot be understood but by the sound of trumpet. Ambition is not a vice of little people and of so mean abilities as ours. One said to Alexander: "Your father will leave you a great dominion, easy and pacific," but this youth was envious of his father's victories, and the justice of his government, and would not have enjoyed the empire of the world in ease and peace. Alcibiades, in Plato, had rather die young, beautiful, rich, noble, and learned, and all this par excellence, than stop in the state of such a condition; this disease is perhaps excusable in so strong and so full a soul. When these wretched and dwarfish little souls gull and deceive themselves, and think to spread their fame, for having given right judgment in some affair, or kept up the discipline of the guard of the city gate, the more they think to exalt their heads, the more they show their tails. This little well-doing has neither body nor life; it vanishes in the first month, and goes no farther than from one street to another. Talk of it, in God's name, to your son or your servant; like that old fellow who, having no other auditor of his praises, nor approver of his valour, boasted to his chambermaid, crying out: "O, Peretta, what a brave man hast thou as thy master!" At the worst, talk of it to yourself; like a counsellor of my acquaintance, who, having disgorged a whole cart-load of paragraphs with great heat, and as great folly, coming out of the council-chamber to make water, was heard very conscientiously to mutter betwixt his teeth: "Not unto us, O Lord, not unto us, but unto thy name, be the glory" (*Psalm* 113). He who can get it of nobody else, let him pay himself out of his own purse.

Fame is not prostituted at so cheap a rate; rare and exemplary actions, to which it is due, would not endure the company of this prodigious crowd of little every-day performances. Marble may exalt your titles as much as you please, for having repaired a rod of a ruinous wall, or cleansed a public sewer, but not men of sense. Renown does not follow all good deeds, if novelty and difficulty be not conjoined; nay, so much as mere estimation, according to the Stoics, is not due to every action that proceeds from virtue; neither will they allow him bare thanks who, out of temperance, forbears to meddle with any old blear-eyed hag. We have pleasures suitable to our fortunes; let us not usurp those of grandeur. Our own are more natural, and by so much more solid and sure, as they are more low. If not for that of conscience, yet at least for ambition's sake, let us reject ambition; let us disdain that thirst of honour and renown, so low and mendicant, that it makes us beg it of all sorts of people. "What praise is that which is to be got in the market, by abject means, and at what cheap rate soever" (Cicero)? 'Tis dishonour to be so honoured. Let us learn to be no more greedy of honour than we are capable of it. To be puffed up with every action that is innocent, or of use, is only for such with whom such things are extraordinary and rare; they will value it as it costs them. How much the more a good effect makes a noise, so much I abate of the goodness of it, as I enter into suspicion that it was more performed for notice than upon the account of goodness: being exposed upon the stall, it is half sold. Those actions have much more grace and lustre that slip from the hand of him that does them negligently and without noise, and that some honest man after chooses out and raises from the shade, to produce it to the light upon its own account: "All things, truly, seem more laudable to me that are performed without ostentation and without testimony of the people," says the most vainglorious man in the world (Cicero).

I had no care but to conserve and to continue, which are silent and insensible effects. Innovation is of great lustre, but 'tis interdicted in this time, when we are pressed upon, and have nothing to defend ourselves from but novelties. To forbear doing is often as noble as to do; but 'tis less in the light: and the little good I have in me is almost all of this kind. In fine, occasions in this employment of mine have been confederate with my humour, and I thank them for it. Is there any one who desires to be sick that he may see his physician at work? And would not that physician deserve to be whipped who should wish the plague amongst us, that he might put his art in practice? I have never been of that wicked, though common enough, humour, to desire that the trouble and disorders of this city should elevate and honour my government: I have ever willingly contributed all I could to their tranquillity and ease. He who will not thank me for the order, gentle and silent calm, that has accompanied my administration, cannot, however, deprive me of the share that belongs to me by the title of my good fortune. And I am of such a composition that I would as willingly be happy as wise; and had rather owe my successes purely to the favour of Almighty God than to any industry or operation of my own. I had sufficiently published to the world my unfitness for such public offices. But I have something in me yet worse than incapacity, which is that I am not much displeased at it, and that I do not much go about to cure it, considering the course of life that I have proposed to myself. Neither have I satisfied myself in this employment, but I have very near arrived at what I expected from myself, and have much surpassed what I promised them with whom I had to do; for I am apt to promise something less than what I am able to do, and than what I hope to make good. I am sure that I have left no impressions of offence or hatred behind me; and as to leaving regret or desire of me amongst them, I at least know very well that I never much affected it:

Wouldst thou I should a quiet sea believe,
To this inconstant monster credit give?
(Virgil)

IV. The Seventeenth Century

War, economic activity, and a far-reaching revolution in scientific thought characterized the seventeenth century. It is worth insisting on the last two, since the economic activity ensured the rise of a newly significant social class which owed its position to trade rather than to traditional rank or prowess and which left its mark on the political thought of the time when it introduced the notion of contract into the search for social authority. At the same time, the new scientific activity stressed a rational approach which had been somewhat ignored for centuries past. But just because the seventeenth century was a time of scientific revolution, this does not mean that superstition was dead. On the contrary, this was the golden age of witches, when witch-hunters lit their pyres all over Europe and the shadow of the Black Mass hung even over the court of Louis XIV.

1. THE THIRTY YEARS' WAR: SIMPLICISSIMUS

Hans Jacob Christopher von Grimmelshausen was a German writer (c. 1620–1676) who spent part of his life soldiering on various sides during the Thirty Years' War. In the picaresque novel which he published in 1668, he has left us fascinating descriptions of German life during this period and also a document concerning some of the directions taken during these years by the speculations of some. For most of Germany they were difficult years, in which towns and countryside were occupied successively by Catholics and Protestants, Danes, Swedes, French and Saxons, mercenaries of Wallenstein or Tilly, devastated by men, famines and epidemics, all seeming to vie with each other in their destructiveness. This was the country over which the young Grimmelshausen marched, now with the Imperial soldiers, now with the Swedes, and over which he carries his hero.

THE FATE OF A FARM

When these horsemen took over my father's smoky house, the first thing they did was to bring in their horses; then each one started to destroy everything and tear everything to pieces. Some were killing the cattle, and broiling or roasting the carcasses; others were going through the house, determined not to miss any thing good there might be for them to find; even the privy was not safe from their investigations, as if we had hidden there Jason's Golden Fleece. Others were making great bundles of linen and clothes and all sorts of stuff, as if they were going to open a flea market someplace, and what they weren't going to carry away

Tr. by the editor from chaps. 4, 15, 16 of Simplicius *Simplicissimus* (1669).

417

with them they pulled to pieces. Some shoved their swords through the piles of straw or hay as if they hadn't had enough pigs to kill; others shook the feathers out of the mattresses and filled them with bacon and salt meat and other things as if they expected to sleep on them better that way. Others were breaking down the stoves and the window panes, as if they thought that summer was going to last forever. They were smashing the tableware and carrying away with them these useless pieces of copper or pottery or pewter. They burnt beds, and the tables, and the chairs, and the benches, when they could have found plenty of dry fire-wood in the yard. Of pots and of pans they shattered the lot; either because they didn't want to eat anything but roast meat any more, or because they only planned to stay with us for one single meal. Our maid underwent such treatment in the stables that she could hardly walk coming out. Is it not shameful to have such things happening? As for the groom, they laid him on the ground, they put a funnel into his mouth, and they poured in a whole tubful of foul matter. They called this "a little drink in the Swedish manner"; but he didn't find it at all to his taste. They also forced him to guide them on another raid, where they captured both people and cattle whom they brought into our yard. Among them they got my father, and my mother, and my sister Ursula.

Then they started to take the flints out of the cocks of the pistols in order to use them as thumbscrews, and to torture the poor beggars as if they were sorcerers who needed to be punished before being burnt. As a matter of fact, the soldiers had already shoved one of the captured peasants into the oven and they were trying to keep him warm in there (so he would tell them the hiding place of his little hoard). They had tied a cord around the head of another, and they were tightening the cord with a garrot, so that with every turn they gave it, the blood gushed out of his mouth, his nose and his ears. In short, each man was busy working out some new kind of torture for the peasants and so each victim had his own particular kind of torment.

However it seemed to me at the time that my father was the luckiest of them all, because he admitted with roars of laughter what the others were forced to reveal in the midst of sufferings and fearful plaints.

This kind of honor was his, no doubt, because he was the head of the family. The soldiers put him before a great fire, they tied him so that he couldn't move his arms or his legs, and they rubbed the soles of his feet with damp salt; then they had our old goat lick it off. He was so tickled by this that he nearly died of laughter. It all seemed to me so pleasant and so silly—I had never seen nor heard my father laugh so long—that, either because his laughter was contagious, or else because I couldn't understand what was going on, I had to laugh too. That is how my father told the raiders what they wanted to know, and revealed the hiding place of his treasure which consisted of gold and pearls and jewels; a much richer hoard than one would have expected a peasant to own.

I cannot say anything about the treatment of the women, the maids, and the young girls who had been captured, because the soldiers didn't let me see what they were doing to them. I know only that one heard sighs and groans in various corners, and I thought that my mother and my sister Ursula were probably no better off than the others.

THE DREAM OF SIMPLICISSIMUS

Lost in these thoughts, discouraged, shivering, hunger hugging my stomach, I went to sleep. In my dream I thought I saw that all the trees which surrounded my dwelling place had suddenly changed, and taken on another aspect. On top of each tree there was a gentleman, and the branches were covered, instead of leaves, by all sorts of people: Some had their long lances, others had muskets, carbines, halberds, standards, and also fifes and drums. It was an amusing sight, for all these people were arranged in an orderly manner, each one in his proper place according to his rank. The roots of the tree were made of little people, artisans, workmen, and especially peasants and other unimportant folk. And yet it was they who lent the tree its strength and its life, and who renewed its vitality as it ran out. They also replaced the fallen leaves and they furnished others in their place from among their numbers, not without loss and inconvenience for themselves. You could hear them groaning under the weight of those who were sitting on the tree; because everything rested on them, and pressed them so hard that they sweated even the silver from their purses. And when the silver was not forthcoming, the quartermasters knocked them about so harshly, with great broomsticks, that they drew great sighs from their hearts, tears from their eyes, blood from under their nails, and the marrow from their bones. In spite of this there were a certain number of jolly fellows amongst them who didn't seem to care and who accepted everything with a smile; overwhelmed by oppression, they sought and found consolation in their merriment.

So the roots of these trees were resigned to spending their lives in pain and in sighing, but the people who sat on the lowest branches had to endure even worse trouble and torments. And yet they were always gayer than the first. They were also insolent, tyrannical, impious for the most part, and for the roots they made a load so heavy as to be almost unbearable. As the wind passed through them you could hear them singing the following song:

To endure horror, thirst, and pain and
    strife;
To work or to starve as things might be;
To be violent and unjust; that is our life,
For fighting men at arms are we.

And these words were perfectly true and conformed to their activities. In effect, the life and the pastime of these men consisted in eating and drinking too much, enduring hunger and thirst, living in debauchery, rattling the dice and gambling, killing and being killed, shooting and being shot, torturing and being tortured, hunting and being hunted, terrorizing and being terrorized, robbing and being robbed, frightening and being frightened, sowing evil and desolation wherever they went; in one word, of carrying everywhere destruction, ruin and death, while being themselves exposed to these evils. Neither the winter nor the summer, neither snow nor ice, neither heat nor cold, neither wind nor rain, nor the mountains, nor the valleys, or the fields or the marshes, or the mountain passes or the sea, or great walls or waters, or fire or ramparts, or the dangers that threaten body, soul, or conscience; not the laws of their life or heaven, or anything else whatever its reason, whatever its name—none of these could stop them. They continued with great enthusiasm to carry out all their villainies until in some battle or siege or assault, or even in billets (which we know are a soldier's paradise, especially if he can get himself quartered on some nice fat peasant whom he can exploit) they end by finding their death. Only a few could survive such a life and they, if they had not been successful in their thefts and rapine, became beggars and miserable vagabonds in their old age.

Immediately above these miserable beings there sat a number of old chicken thieves, who had been living on the lower branches for several years but who now, by dint of the greatest risks, had made a success of their thievery, and were living on its proceeds. These looked like serious, solid people and rather more honest than those below them, if only because they overtopped them.

Above them yet again you could find the people who were rather better off, but who also had rather higher pretensions because they commanded those of inferior degree. These carried the title of lickspittles: they bustled about among the lowest of the lancers and cursed them, and beat them with sticks to make them go forward. They furnished the musketeers with the oil they needed to grease their weapons, but carried neither weapons nor themselves into battle.

Above them there was an empty space on the trunk of the tree, a breach in continuity. It was a piece of trunk without any branches, and greased with a soap of disfavor. This was there so that no soldier, unless he should be of noble birth, could climb higher, either by his courage or by his merit or by his wisdom, whatever his skill in climbing might be. This part was more slippery than a column of polished marble or a mirror of steel.

Above it the ensigns were set; some were young, others were already middle-aged. The young had risen by nepotism; the old had got there themselves, either by climbing the golden ladder of corruption, or by some other means offered them by chance.

Yet higher in a more elevated position I saw others who had also their troubles, their worries and their tribulations; but they had the advantage of being able to grease their skillets and their purses with bacon which they cut out of the roots with a knife they called "war contribution." They showed their particular skill whenever a commissary arrived who emptied a barrelful of silver over the tree in order to give it new life. Sitting on top as they did, the ensigns caught most of the silver and let hardly any of it get by them to the lower reaches of the tree, so that those on the lower branches died rather of hunger than by the enemy's blows, while those on top seemed to be safe from both these dangers. This is why I could see everybody in ceaseless movement trying to get up the tree; for each one wanted to conquer for himself a place in the happy, higher regions. Only a few ne'er-do-wells, lazy and debauched, unworthy even of the rations they were drawing, didn't care about rising higher. They reckoned they had enough trouble where they were.

The ambitious ones below looked forward to the fall of their leaders in order to take their places, but when one in ten thousand actually managed to obtain so lofty a place, he only reached it at that miserable age when one is better off sitting by the fire, than fighting against the enemy.

If some man, in any position, honestly carried out his task and bore himself bravely in the midst of danger, he only roused the jealousy of others, or else some deadly or unexpected blow of fate deprived him at the same time of his post and of his life.

Nowhere was the pressure greater than at this particular part of the tree trunk: whoever had a good sergeant or a good quarter-master would not want to lose him and he would necessarily be lost once he got a commission. That is why the old experienced soldiers always lacked preferment and the ones who got on were the paperscratchers, the potmen, the old page-boys, the ruined nobles, the poor relations, the parasites or starvelings, who kept the bread out of the mouths of the men who really deserved promotions. These were the ones who could aspire to an ensign's commission.

Such injustice so discontented an old sergeant major that he started grumbling furiously; but Adelhold, representative of the nobility, addressed him thus:

"Don't you know that everywhere and always military command is entrusted to nobles, because they are better fitted to such functions than anybody else? It is not the old graybeards who defeat the enemy—otherwise we could enroll a company of billygoats. Tell me, my veteran friend, are not the officers of noble birth more respected by the soldiery than those who started out in the ranks? And what kind of military discipline can you get that isn't based on respect? Can not a general more legitimately trust a gentleman than the son of a peasant who has deserted the plow of his father, and never rendered his own parents any service? A nobleman of integrity would rather die than soil his name by treason, desertion, or any other crime. All preference is due to the nobility. . . . Even if one of you is a good soldier, unafraid of the smell of gun powder, able always to strike great blows, he is not able, just because of that, to command others and act with prudence: on the contrary, these qualities

are inbred in a nobleman, or else he learns them from his early youth. . . . Besides, the noble has more means than a peasant and these he can use to pay his subordinates, and reinforce the undermanned companies in his command. And if we may believe a current proverb, it would not do at all to set a peasant above a nobleman. In any case the peasant would become much too proud if he were suddenly to be dubbed 'Lord'; for you know it is commonly said:

'No one ever knows a sharper sword
Than that of a peasant become a great
  Lord.'

"If the peasants, by reason of long tradition or honest habit, held in their hands the charges or the commands of war, they would surely not allow the nobles a share in their honors. Why should we be more magnanimous? And then, however well disposed one may be towards you soldiers of fortune, however much one may wish to help you to conquer the highest ranks, you are, as a rule, already so decrepit when you are judged worthy of a better fate, that one necessarily thinks twice before promoting you. For then the ardor of youth is dead within you and you have only one thought in your head: To spare this sickly body that so many tribulations have used and which is no longer much good for war, and to care for it well. By then what do you care who fights and who gathers glory for himself? After all, doesn't a young dog go hunting more gaily than an old lion?"

The sergeant major answered:

"But who would be stupid enough to serve in the army and risk death all the time if he cannot hope to obtain promotion by his good conduct, and to see his loyal services rewarded? To hell with this kind of warfare! From this point of view it doesn't matter whether a soldier behaves well or badly; whether he advances bravely to the enemy's fire or runs away! I have often heard our old colonel say that he did not want any soldier in his regiment who did not firmly believe that he could become a general by his good conduct; all the world has to admit that the nations which favor the promotion of common, but loyal soldiers, and which reward their bravery, are generally victorious."

"When one sees real qualities in a brave man they certainly receive recognition," Adelhold answered. "Thus we find men today who, after having handled the plow, the needle, the shoemaker's last, have taken sword in hand, have shown themselves to be outstanding by their exemplary conduct, by their heroism, by their bravery, by their enormous intrepidity and, thus overtaking the common or garden nobles, have raised themselves to the dignity of counts and barons. After all, what were John de Werd, the Imperial general; and the Swedish general, Stallhans, and the Hessian colonel, Jacob Mercier, and Saint-André, who commanded the city of Lipstadt, and a lot of others whom I do not want to name in order to be brief? Thus it is no novelty in our times that humble men but brave ones can attain by war to the highest honors. And this was the case in olden times. Tamerlane was a powerful king, and he terrorized the whole world, even though he only started out by guarding pigs; Agathocles, the tyrant of Syracuse, was the son of a potter; the father of the Emperor Valentinian was a ropemaker; Hugues Capet, son of a butcher, later became king of France; Pizarro, who con-

quered Peru, also started out guarding pigs, but he became ruler of the Western Indies and handled gold by the hundredweight."

"All this is very well," rejoined the old soldier. "But what's the use! I see very clearly that the way to this or that honor is closed to men of my sort by the nobility. The squire and the gentleman can get a good job as soon as he leaves his shell, and they fill posts that we could never aspire to; even though we have done more than this or that nobleman who struts about today and calls himself a colonel.

"Among the peasants more than one good mind goes to waste because lack of means has kept it from any studies. In the same way more than one brave soldier grows old under the musket, who would do better, and would be more justly employed commanding a regiment; and in such a position would know how to render great services to his general."

I simply could not listen any longer to the grumbles of this old ass. His complaints sounded hollow, when you could see that he himself often struck the poor soldiers like dogs. I looked again towards the trees that covered the countryside, and I saw them move and charge each other. The soldiers on the branches were thrown to the ground, sometimes in bunches, and there they died at once. In the blink of an eye they passed from life to death; in less time than I need to say it, one lost an arm, another a leg, a third his very head. And, looking better, I thought I saw that all these trees before me were really only one tree, on top of which sat enthroned Mars, the god of War, and whose branches spread through the length and breadth of Europe. It seemed as if this tree could have covered the whole world with its shade. But envy and hatred, suspicion and injustice, pride, vanity and ambition, and other beautiful virtues of the same sort, blew hard upon it, as did the bitter northern winds, so that the great tree seemed rickety and threadbare, and almost transparent.

2. A NEW WORLD

With central Europe in the throes of war, another world was rising to its east, still barbarous, still in some eyes almost colonial territory, but offering vast opportunities for trade and for the skills of the west. Between 1633 and 1639, the Duke of Holstein sent two embassies to Muscovy and beyond it into Asia, to sound out the possibilities of these lands. The reports they brought back leave the impression of places whose evolution was several centuries behind that of the west, the language of the Holsteiners reminding one of that which we can find in the chronicles of nineteenth century African explorers and exploiters.

Even while the good Germans wrote, however, the lands which they had scouted out were being forged into a powerful state by the rulers of the Romanov family. Halting legal and administrative reforms would only begin to show after the accession of Peter I in 1689; but his predecessors already encouraged the westernization if not of the country, at least of its army and technology. Foreigners were encouraged to enter the service of the Tsar, not least officers like Patrick Gordon of Auchleuchries, whose memoirs suggest that Russian attitudes to visitors have not changed too much in 300 years.

Muscovy

Livonia is, in all parts, very fertile, and particularly in wheat. For though it hath suffered much by the *Muscovites,* yet it is now more and more reduc'd to tillage, by setting the Forests afire, and sowing in the ashes of the burnt Wood and Turf, which for three or four years produce excellent good Wheat, and with great increase, without any Dung. . . . There is also abundance of Cattel, and Fowl so cheap, that many times we bought a young Hare for four pence; a Heath-Cock for six, and accordingly others, so that it is much cheaper living there than in *Germany.*

The Inhabitants were a long time Heathens, it being in the 12 age that the rayes of the Sun of righteousness began to break in upon them, occasion'd by the frequentation of certain Merchants of *Bremen,* and the Commerce they were desirous to establish in those parts. About the year 1158 one of their Ships having been forc'd by a Tempest into the Gulf of *Riga,* which was not yet known, the Merchants agreed so well with the Inhabitants of the Country, that they resolv'd to continue their Traffick there, having withall, this satisfaction, that, the people being very simple, they thought it would be no hard matter to reduce them to Christianity. *Menard,* a Monk of *Segeberg,* was the first that preach'd the Gospel to them, and was made first Bishop of *Livonia,* by Pope *Alexander* III in the year 1170. *Menard* was suc-

From *The Voyages and Travells of the Ambassadors Sent by Frederick Duke of Holstein, to the Great Duke of Muscovy, and the King of Persia* (London, 1669).

ceeded in the Bishoprick of *Livonia*, by *Bertold*, a *Monk*, of the Order of white Friers; but he, thinking to reduce those people rather by Arms than the word of God, met with a success accordingly, for having incens'd them, they kill'd him in the year 1186 and with him 11000 Christians. *Albert*, a Canon of *Bremen*, succeeded *Bertold*, in the Bishoprick. He laid the first foundations of the City of *Riga*, and of the Order of the Friers of the *short sword*, by authority from Pope *Innocent* the third, and by vertue of a power he had given them, to allow them the third part of that they should Conquer from the *Barbarians*. . . . This new Religious Profession was . . . joyn'd to the Order of *St. Mary* of *Jerusalem*, in the person of *Herman Balk*, Grand-Master of *Prussia*, in the year 1238. And it is since that time that the Master of *Livonia* had a dependence on the Grand-Master of *Prussia*. . . .

All the Champain Countrey, of the two Provinces of *Letthie* and *Esthonie*, is to this day people with these *Barbarians*, who have nothing of their own, but are slaves, and serve the Nobility in the Countrey, and the Citizens in Cities. They are called *Unteutche*, that is, *not-Germans*, because their language was not understood by the *Germans*, who went to plant in those quarters; though that of *Letthie* hath nothing common with that of *Esthonie*, no more than there is between them, as to their Cloaths and manner of Life. The Women of *Esthonie* wear their Petticoats very narrow, and without any folds, like sacks, adorn'd above on their backs with many little brass Chains, having at the ends Counters of the same metal, and below set out with a certain lacing of yellow glass. Those who would express a greater bravery, have about their Necks a Necklace of plates of silver of the bigness of a Crown, or half-Crown, and upon the breast, one as big as a round Trencher, but not much thicker than the back of a knife.

Maids wear nought on their heads, Summer nor Winter, and cut their hair as the men do, letting it fall negligently down about the head. Both Men and Women are clad with a wretched stuff made of Wool, or a coarse Linnen. They are yet unacquainted with Tannage, so that, in Summer, they have barks of Trees about their feet, and in the Winter, raw Leather of a Cow's hide. Both Men and Women do ordinarily carry all the Wealth they have about them.

Their Ceremonies of marriage are very odd. When a Country fellow marries a Lass out of another Village, he goes a hors-back to fetch her, sets her behind him, and makes her embrace him with the right hand. He hath in his hand a stick cleft at the top, where he puts a piece of brass money, which he gives to him who opens the wicket, through which he is to pass. Before, rides a man that playes upon the Bag-pipe, as also two of his friends, who, having naked swords in their hands, give two stroaks therewith, cross the Door of the House, where the marriage is to be consummated, and then they thrust the point of one of the swords into a beam, over the Bridegroom's head, which is done to prevent Charms, which, they say, are ordinary in that Country. 'Tis to the same end that the Bride scatters little pieces of Cloath, or red Serge by the way, especially where cross-ways meet, near Crosses, and upon the Graves of little Children dead without baptism, whom they bury in the Highways. She hath a Veil over her face while she is at the Table, which is not long; for, as soon almost as the Guests are set down, the married couple rise, and go to bed. About two hours after they get up, and are brought to sit down at the Table. Having drunk and danc'd till such time as they are able to stand no longer, they fall down on the floor, and sleep altogether like so many Swine.

We said the Gospel was preach'd in *Livonia* in the 12 age; but the *Livonians* are never the better Christians for it. Most of them are only such in name, and can hardly yet abstain from their Heathenish Superstitions. For though they are *Lutherans,* by profession, and that there is hardly a Village but hath its Church and Minister; yet are they so poorly instructed, and so far from regeneration, that it may be said, Baptism excepted, they have not any Character of Christianity. They very seldom go to Sermons, and never almost Communicate. They excuse their backwardness in frequenting the Sacraments, by alleging the great slavery they are in, which, they say, is so insupportable, that they have not time to mind their Devotions. If they go at any time to Sermon, or to the Communion, it is by force, or upon some other particular accompt. . . . 'Tis true, the gross and inexcusable ignorance of most of the Pastors in those quarters, who might well come to be Catechiz'd themselves, hath contributed much to the obduration of those poor people: but the late King of Sueden hath taken order, therein enjoyning, by a severe Ordinance, the Bishop of the Province, who hath his residence in the Cathedral Church of *Reuel,* to convocate a Synod once a year, for the regulation of Church affairs, and then to examine, not only the *Recipiendaries,* but also the *Pastors* themselves, thereby to oblige them to apply themselves to the constant study of the Holy Scripture.

It must be acknowledg'd, the slavery these people are in is great, and indeed insupportable; but it is true withall; that upon the least liberty given them, they would break out into any extravagance. For being perswaded that the Predecessors have been Masters of the Country, and that only force hath enslav'd them to the *Germans,* they cannot forbear their resentments of it, and discovering, especially in their drink, if any opportunity of regaining their liberty should offer it self, a readiness to prosecute it. Of which they gave an evident example, when, upon the irruption of Colonel *Bot,* the Peasants would side with the Enemy, and head together, to secure their Masters and deliver them up to the *Polanders.*

They believe there is another life after this; but their imaginations of it are very extravagant. A *Livonian* woman, being present at her husband's burial, put a Needle and Thread into the Grave, giving this reason for it, that, her husband being to meet, in the other World, with persons of good Rank, she was asham'd he should be seen with his Cloaths rent. . . .

These customs favour of their antient Idolatry. The Ministers do all they can to weed it out of them by little and little; to which end we saw, at *Narva,* the Catechism, Epistles, and Gospels, with their explications, which *Henry Stahl,* Superintendent of Ecclesiastical affairs in those parts (a person much esteem'd for his Learning and pains in instructing those *Barbarians*) had caused to be translated and Printed in their Language, to give them some apprehentions of Christian Religion. But Idolatry and Superstition are too deeply rooted in them, and their stupidity and stubborness too great to give way to any hope, that they will ever be susceptible of instruction. They do their devotions commonly upon hills, or neer a tree they make choice of to that purpose, and in which they make several incisions, bind them up with some red stuff, and there say their prayers, wherein they desire only temporal blessings. Two leagues from *Kunda,* between *Reuel* and *Narva,* there is an old ruin'd Chapel, whither the Peasants go once a year on Pilgrimage, upon the day of our Lady's Visitation. Some put off their cloaths; and in that posture having kneel'd by a great stone that is in the midst of the Chapel, they afterwards leap about it, and offer it Fruits and Flesh, recommending the preservation of themselves and their Cattel to it for that year. This piece of devotion is concluded with eating and drinking, and all kind of licentiousness, which seldom end without quarrels, murthers, and the like disorders.

They have such an inclination to Sorcery, and think it so necessary for the preservation of their Cattel, that Fathers and Mothers teach it their Children, so that there is scarce any Peasant but is a Sorcerer. They all observe certain superstitious Ceremonies, by which they think to elude the affects of it, upon which accompt it is, that they never kill any Beast, but they cast somewhat of it away, nor never make a Brewing, but they spill some part of it, that the Sorcery may fall upon that. They have also a custome of rebaptizing their Children, when, during the first six weeks after their birth, they chance to be sick or troubled with fits, whereof they think the cause to be, that the name, given them at their baptism, is not proper for them. Wherefore they give them another; but in regard this is not only a sin, but a crime which the Magistrate severely punishes in that Country, they conceal it.

As they are stubborn in their superstitions, so are they no less in the exact observation of their Customs. To which purpose we had a very pleasant, but true, story, related to us at Colonel *de la Barr's,* concerning an old Country fellow. Being condemn'd, for faults enormous enough, to lye along upon the ground, to receive his punishment, and Madam *de la Barre,* pittying his almost decrepit age, having so far interceded for him, as that his corporal punishment should be chang'd into a pecuniary mulct of about 15. or 16. pence, he thank'd her for her kindness, and said, that, for his part, being an old man, he would not introduce any novelty, nor suffer the Customs of the Country to be alter'd, but was ready to receive the chastisement which his Predecessors had not thought much to undergo, put off his cloaths, layd himself upon the ground, and receiv'd the blows according to his condemnation.

This is accounted no punishment, but an ordinary chastisement in *Livonia.* For, the people, being of an incorrigible nature, must be treated with that severity, which would elsewhere be insupportable. They are not permitted to make any purchase, and to prevent their so doing, they have only so much ground to manage, as will afford them a subsistence. Yet will they venture to cut down wood in some places of the Forests, and, having order'd the ground, sow wheat in it, which they hide in pits under ground, to be secretly sold. When they are taken in this, or any other fault, they make them strip themselves naked down to the hips, and to lye down upon the ground, or are ty'd to a post, while one of their Camerades beats them with a Switch, or Hollywand, till the blood comes of all sides; especially when the Master says "Beat him till the skin falls from the flesh."

Nor are they suffer'd to have any money; for as soon as it is known they have any, the Gentlemen and their Officers, who are paid by the Peasantry, take it from them, nay force them to give what they have not. Which cruelty of the Masters puts these poor people many times into despair, whereof there happened a sad example. A Peasant press'd by his Officer to pay what he neither had, not ought, and being depriv'd of the means whereby he should maintain his Family, strangled his Wife and Children, and when he had done hung himself up by them. The Officer coming the next day to the house, thinking to receive the mony, struck his head against the man's feet that was hanging, and so perceiv'd the miserable execution, whereof he was the cause.

MOSCOW

But it were not handsome to leave *Moscou* without giving some account of that great City, the Metropolis of all Muscovy, to which it gives the name, as it takes its own from the River *Moska.* This River, which passes through, and divides all the rest of the City, from that quarter of it which is called *Strelitz a Slaueda,* rises out of the Province of *Tuere,* and having joyn'd its waters with those of the *Occa,* near *Columna,* it falls together with the other, about half a league thence, into the *Wolga.* The City is elevated 55 degr. 36 min. its longitude 66 degrees, in the midst of all the Country, and almost at an equal distance from all the Frontiers, which is above 120 *German* leagues. It is about three leagues about, and, no doubt, hath been heretofore bigger than it is now. *Mathius de Michou,* a Canon of *Cracovia,* who flourish'd at the beginning of the last age, says, that, in his time, it was twice as big as the City of *Prague.* The *Tartars* of *Crim* and *Precop,*

burnt it in the year 1571. and the Poles set it a-fire in the year 1611. so as that there was nothing left of it but the Castle; and yet now there are numbred in it above 40000 houses, and it is out of all controversie one of the greatest Cities in *Europe.*

'Tis true, that, the Palaces of great Lords, and the Houses of some rich Merchants excepted, which are of Brick or Stone, all the rest are of Wood, are made up of beams, and cross-pieces of Firr laid one upon another. They cover them with barks of trees, upon which they sometimes put another covering of Turfes. The carelesness of the *Muscovites,* and the disorders of their house-keeping are such, that there hardly passes a moneth, nay not a week, but some place or other takes fire, which, meeting with what is very combustible, does in a moment reduce many houses, nay, if the wind be any thing high, whole streets into ashes. Some few days before our arrival, the fire had consumed the third part of the City; and about 5 or 6 years since, the like accident had near destroy'd it all. To prevent this, the *Strelits* of the Guard, and the Watch, are enjoyn'd, in the night time to carry Pole-axes, wherewith they break down the houses adjoyning to those which are a-fire, by which means they hinder the progress of it, with much better success than if they attempted the quenching of it. And that it may not fasten on other more solid structures, the doors and windows are very narrow, having shutters of Lattin, to prevent the sparks and flashes from getting in. Those who have their houses burnt, have this comfort withall, that they may buy houses ready built, at a market for that purpose, without the white-Wall, at a very easy rate, and have them taken down, transported, and in a short time set up in the same place where the former stood.

The streets of *Moscou* are handsome, and very broad, but so dirty, after rain hath ever so little moisten'd the ground, that it were impossible to get out of the dirt, were it not for the great Posts, which set together make a kind of bridge, much like that of the *Rhin,* near *Strasbourg* which bridges, in foul weather, serve for a kind of pavement.

The City is divided into four quarters, or circuits, whereof the first is called *Cataygorod,* that is, the mid-City, as being in the midst of the others. This quarter is divided from the rest by a brick-wall, which the *Muscovites* call *crasne stenna,* that is, red stone. The *Moska* passes on the South-side of it, and the River *Neglina,* which joyns with the other behind the Castle, on the North side. The Great Duke's Palace, called *Cremelena,* and which is of greater extent than many other ordinary Cities, takes up almost one half of it, and is fortify'd with three strong walls, and a good ditch, and very well mounted with Canon. In the midst of the Castle are two Steeples, one very high, and cover'd with Copper gilt, as all the other Steeples of the Castle are. This Steeple is called *Juan Welike,* that is, the *Great John.* The other is considerable only for the Bell within it, made by the Great Duke *Boris Gudenou,* weighing 33600 pounds. It is not toll'd, but upon great Festivals, or to honour the entrance and audience of Ambassadors: but to stir it there must be 24 men, who pull it by a Rope that comes down into the Court, while some others are above to help it on by thrusting. The Great Duke's Palace stands towards the further side of the Castle, with that of the Patriarch, and appartements for several *Bojares,* who have places at

Court. There is also lately built a very fair Palace of stone, according to the *Italian* Architecture, for the young Prince; but the Great Duke continues still in his wooden Palace, as being more healthy than stone-structures. The Exchequer, and the Magazine of Powder and provisions are also within the Castle.

There are also within it two fair Monasteries, one for men, the other for women, and above fifty Churches and Chapels, all built of stone; among others, those of the *B. Trinity, St. Mary's, St. Michael's,* wherein are the Sepulchres of the Great Dukes, and *St. Nicholas's.*

At the Castle-Gate, but without the Walls, on the South-side, is a fair Church Dedicated to the *B. Trinity,* and commonly called *Jerusalem.* When it was finish'd, the Tyrant *John Basilouits,* thought it so magnificent a structure, that he caus'd the Architect's eyes to be put out, that he might not afterwards do any thing that should be comparable to that. Near this Church are two great pieces of Canon, with the mouths towards that street by which the *Tartars* were wont to make their irruptions; but these pieces are now dismounted, and useless.

In the spacious place, before the Castle, is the chief Market of the City kept; all day it is full of people, but especially slaves, and idle persons. All the Market-place is full of Shops, as also all the street abutting upon it: but every Trade hath a station by it self, so as the Mercers intermingle not with the Linnen or Wollen-Drapers, nor Goldsmiths with Sadlers, Shoemakers, Taylors, Furriers, and the like, but every Profession and Trade hath its proper street: which is so much the greater convenience, in that a man does, of a sudden, cast his eye on all he can desire. Sempstresses have their shops in the midst of the Market, where there is also another fort of Women Traders, who have Rings in their mouths, and, with their Rubies and Turquoises, put off another commodity which is not seen in the Market. There is a particular street where are sold the Images of their Saints. 'Tis true, these go not under the name of Merchandise, among the *Muscovites,* who would make some difficulty to say they had *bought* a Saint; but they say, they receive them by way of Exchange or Trucking, for money: and so when they buy, they make no bargain, but lay down what the Painter demands.

There is yet another place, in this quarter, called the *Hairmarket,* because the Inhabitants go thither to be trimm'd, by which means the place comes to be so cover'd with hair, that a man treads as softly as if it were on a Feather-bed. Most of the principal *Goses,* or Merchants, as also many *Knez* and *Muscovian* Lords have their houses in this first circuit.

The second quarter is called *Czaargorod,* that is, *Czaar's Citie,* or the *Citie-Royal,* and includes the former as it were in a Semi-circle. The little River *Neglina* passes through the midst of it, and it hath its particular Wall, called *Biola stenna,* that is, the *white Wall.* In this quarter is the *Arsenal,* and the place, where Guns and Bells are cast, which is called *Pogganabrut,* the management whereof the Great Duke hath bestow'd on a very able man, one *John Valk,* born at *Nuremberg,* whom he sent for out of *Holland,* for this reason, that he was the first who found a way to discharge a Bullet of sixteen pound weight with five pound of pouder. The *Muscovites* who have wrought under this man, have so well learnt the mystery of founding that now they are as expert at it as the most experienc'd *Germans.*

In this quarter also there live many *Knez,* Lords, *Sinbojares,* or Gentlemen, and a great number of Merchants, who drive a Trade all the Countrey over, and Trades-men, especially Bakers. There are also some Butchers shambles, and Tipling-houses, which sell Beer, Hydromel, and Strong-water, Store-Houses of Wheat, Meal shops, and the Great Duke's stables.

The third quarter is called *Skoradom,* and includes the quarter called *Czaargorod,* from the East, along the Northside, to the West. The *Muscovites* affirm, that this quarter was five *German* Leagues about, before the City was burnt by the *Tartars,* in the year 1571. The little River *Jagusas* passes through it, and in its way falls into the *Mosca.* In this quarter is the Market for Wood and Houses before mentioned; where you may have Houses ready made, which may be taken asunder, transported thence, and set up any where else, in a short time, and with little pains and charge, since they consist only of beams, and posts, set one upon the other, and the vacuities are fill'd up with Mosse.

The fourth quarter is called *Strelitz a Slauoda,* because of the *Strelits,* or Musketiers of the Great Duke's Guard, who live in it. It is situated towards the South of *Cataygorod,* on the other side of the *Mosca,* upon the Avenues of the *Tartars.* Its Ramparts and Bastions are of Wood. The Great Duke *Basili Juanouits,* father of *Basilouits,* who built this quarter, design'd it for the quarters of such Soldiers, as were strangers, as *Poles, Germans,* and others, naming that place *Naeilki,* or, the quarter of *Drunkards,* from the word *Nali,* which signifies, *powre out:* for, these strangers being more inclin'd to drunkenness than the *Muscovites,* he would not have his own people, who were apt enough to debauch themselves, to become so much the worse by the others bad example. Besides the Soldiery, the poorer sort of the people have their habitations in this quarter.

There is, in the City and Suburbs of *Moscou,* a very great number of Churches, Monasteries and Chapels. In the former Impression of these Travels, we said, there were above fifteen hundred; but whereas *John Lewis Godefrey,* Author of the *Archontologia Cosmica,* thinks that number so excessive, that he sticks not to speak of it as a thing not likely to be true, I must indeed needs acknowledge, that I was much mistaken, and, now affirm for certain, that where I said there were 1500 there are above 2000. No *Muscovite* that hath liv'd at *Moscou,* nay no stranger, any thing acquainted with that City, but will confirm this truth, as knowing, there is no Lord but hath his private Chapel, nor any Street but hath many of them. 'Tis true, they are most of them very small ones, and but fifteen foot square; nay, before the Patriarch commanded they should be built of Stone, they were all of Wood: but that hinders not, but that the number of them may amount to what we have said.

Passages from the Diary of General Patrick Gordon of Auchleuchries

September 9, 1661

On Monday, it was ordered that I should be enrolled for maior, Pawl Menezes for captaine, William Hay for lievtennant, and John Hamilton for ensignie, to foot, under the regiment of Colonell Daniell Crawfuird, and a gratuity for our comeing in or welcome to the countrey, being to me twenty fyve rubles in money, and as much in sables, foure ells of cloth, and eight ells of damask; the rest accordingly, and our monthly pay equall with others of these charges. But the chancellour, [That is, as Gordon immediately afterwards calls him, the *dyak,* or scribe.] being a most corrupt fellow, delayed us from day to day in expectation of a bribe, which is not only usuall here, but, as they think, due; whereof I haveing no information, after expostulateing with him twice or thrice, and receiving no satisfactory answers, I went to the Boyar and complained; who, with a light check, ordered him againe, which incensing the Diack more, he delayed us still. But when, after a second complaint and order wee received no satisfaction, I went a third tyme to the Boyar, and very confidently told him, I knew not whether he or the Diack had the greatest power, seeing he did not obey his so many orders. Whereat, the Boyar, being vexed, caused stop his coach (he being on his way out of the towne to his countrey house) and caused call the Diack; whom, being come, he tooke by the beard and shak'd him three or foure tymes, telling him, if I complained againe, he would cause knute him. The Boyar being gone, the Diack came to me, and began to scold; and I, without any respect (whereof they gett but ever too much here), payed him home in his owne coyne, telling him that I cared not whither they gave me any thing or no, if they would but permitt me to go out of the countrey againe. With which resolution I went to the

From *The Diary of General Patrick Gordon of Auchleuchries* (Aberdeen, 1859).

Slobod, and now began in good earnest to consider how I might ridd myself of this countrey, so farr short of my exspectation, and disagreeing with my humour. For, haveing served in such a countrey [Poland and Sweden] and amongst such people, where strangers had great respect and were in great reputation, and even more trust as the natives themselves; and where a free passage, for all deserving persons, lay open to all honour, military and civill; and where, in short tyme, by good husbandry and industry, an estate might be gained; and, in marrying, no scruple or difference was made betwixt the natives and strangers, whereby many have attained to great fortunes, governements, and other honourable and profitable commands; as indigenation, also, being usually conferred on well qualifyed and deserving persons; where a dejected countenance or submissive behaviour is noted for cowardice and faintheartednes, and a confident, majestick, yet unaffected, comportment for virtuous generosity; the peoples high mindednes being accompanied and qualifyed with courteousnes and affability, wherein, meeting with the lyke humours, they contend for transandency. Whereas, on the contrary, I perceived strangers to be looked upon as a company of hirelings, and, at the best (as they say of women) but *necessaria mala;* no honours or degrees of preferment to be exspected here but military, and that with a limited command, in the attaining whereof a good mediator or mediatrix, and a piece of money or other bribe, is more availeable as the merit or sufficiency of the person; a faint heart under faire plumes, and a cuckoe in gay cloths, being as ordinary here as a counterfeited or painted visage; no marrying with natives, strangers being looked upon by the best sort

as scarcely Christians, and by the plebeyans as meer pagans; no indigenation without ejeration of the former religion and embraceing theirs; the people being morose and niggard, and yet overweening and valuing themselves above all other nations; and the worst of all, the pay small, and in a base copper coyne, which passed at foure to one of silver, so that I foresaw an impossibility of subsistance, let be of enriching my self, as I was made beleeve I should, befor I came from Polland. These, and many other reasons were but too sufficient to setle my self for disengageing my self of this place. The only difficulty was, how to attaine to it, which troubled me very much; every one, of whom I asked advice, alleadging it impossible. However I resolved to try and not to take any of their money, albeit I had gotten at Plesko and Novogrod some for expenses on the way.

Hearing that the Boyar was to stay a weeke out of the citty, I resolved not to go to the prikase untill he should returne, and then give up a petition or request for my dismission; bringing in for my reasons, that the ambassadour Zamiaty Fiodorovits Leontiuf, with whom I capitulated in Polland, had promised me to be paid in silver or other equivalent coine, which I found farr otherwise now, and that I found the constitution of my body not agreeable with this climate. But the Diack, getting notice of my intentions, and fearing the wrath of the Boyar at his returne, colluded with my Colonell to entice me into the towne; so that I being come one morning to pay my respects to my Colonel, he desired me to accompany him to the towne, which after some tergiversation I did; and being come and takeing a walke on the piazza, a writer, with a couple of catch-poles with him, came to me and desired me to come into the prikase, which I refused. He told me, that he had order to force me, if I would not come fairely. Being come into the chieffe writer, Tichon Fiodorovits Motiakin received me very courteously, desireing me to sitt downe; and then, after some very civill discourse, presented me with orders to diverse offices for money, sables, damask, and cloth for me and those who came with me; which I absolutely refused, telling him that I would stay untill the Boyar returned, with whom I hoped to prevaile and procure my dismission out of the countrey. This writer, being a courteous person, began to reason with me very civilly, showing me many reasons to divert me from such resolutions; and haveing sent for my Colonell (who was not farr to seeke) they both tooke me aside, and among other reasons told me, that it would be my ruine to desire out of the countrey, because the Russe would presume that comeing from such a countrey, with which they were in open warr, and being a Roman Catholick, I was come to spy out their country only, and then returne; and that, if I mentioned any such thing, they would not only not dismiss me, but send me to Sibiria or some remote place, and that they would never trust me thereafter. This, indeed, did startle me, considering the nature of the people; so that, with great reluctancy, I consented to accept of the orders for our comeing into the countrey.

September 17.

I got orders to receive from a Russe seven hundred men, who were to be in our regiment, being runneway sojours out of severall regiments, and fetched back from diverse places. Haveing received these, I marched through the Sloboda of the strangers to Crasna Cella, [The German editors explain *cella* or *selo* to be a village with a church—what in Scotland, would have been known to Gordon as a *kirktown.*] where wee gott our quarters, and exercized these souldiers twice a day in fair weather. I received money, twenty fyve rubles, for my welcome; and the next day, sables, and two dayes thereafter, damask and cloth.

September 25

I received a months meanes, in cursed copper money, as did these who came along with me.

About thirty officers, most whereof I had bespoke in Riga, came to Mosko, most of them being our countreymen, as Walter Airth, William Guild, Georg Keith, Andrew Burnet, Andrew Calderwood, Robert Stuart, and others, most whereof were enrolled in our regiment.

October

I marched, by order, into the utmost great towne, and to the Sloboda Zagrodniky, and tooke up my quarters.

At the first, some contentions did fall out betwixt the officers and sojours, with the rich burgesses, who would not admitt them into their houses. Amongst the rest, a merchant, by whom my quarters were taken up, whilst my servants were cleansing the inner room, he breake downe the oven in the utter roome, which served to warme both, so that I was forced to go to another quarter. But, to teach him better manners, I sent the profos [Profos, that is, provost—the provost marshal.] to quarter by him, with twenty prisoners and a corporalship of sojours, who, by connivence, did grievously plague him a weeke; and it cost him near a hundred dollers, befor he could procure an order out of the right office to have them re-moved, and was well laught at besides for his uncivility and obstinacy.

3. MERCANTILISM AND OTHER NOVELTIES

With growing economic activity, the seventeenth century developed an intense and novel economic awareness. Trade was seen to play such an important part in the wealth—and hence the power—of all countries, that statesmen and publicists considered it with more attention than ever before. Repeated attempts were made to attract bullion, to secure the greatest possible share of the profits of the carrying trade, to attract craftsmen whose skills were expected to improve the country's industrial position. The economic ideal for a country was seen as self-sufficiency at home, combined with a vigorous export trade which would bring bullion (i.e., riches) into the country; and a great deal of legislation tried to implement the ideal. These mercantilistic ideas, as they are called, would alter and develop with time; but the economic activity with which they were connected also encouraged the growth of a numerous and increasingly self-confident bourgeoisie. The rising class would soon make its presence felt, and its down-to-earth rationalism would affect cultural attitudes in time to come.

Thomas Mun

The mercantilist theory of national wealth appears very clearly in the following passage from Thomas Mun's book, *England's Treasure by Foreign Trade* (1664). Mun (1571–1641), who was a director of the English East India Company, was not interested in the crude mercantilism that concentrated on getting as much gold and silver as possible and had no idea of the real meaning of a country's import-export balance. He believed that England's real wealth lay in trade, in the volume and the profits of her exports, and he put his ideas in the little book that was not published until some years after his death.

THE MEANS TO ENRICH THE KINGDOM, AND TO INCREASE OUR TREASURE

Although a Kingdom may be enriched by gifts received, or by purchase taken from some other Nations, yet these are things uncertain and of small consideration when they happen. The ordinary means therefore to increase our wealth and treasure is by Foreign Trade, wherein we must ever observe this rule: to sell more to strangers yearly than we consume of theirs in value. For suppose that when this Kingdom is plentifully served with the Cloth, Lead, Tin, Iron, Fish and other native commodities, we do yearly export the overplus to foreign Countries to the

From Thomas Mun, *England's Treasure by Foreign Trade* (New York, 1895), pp. 7–27.

value of twenty two hundred thousand pounds; by which means we are enabled beyond the Seas to buy and bring in foreign wares for our use and Consumptions, to the value of twenty hundred thousand pounds; by this order duly kept in our trading, we may rest assured that the Kingdom shall be enriched yearly two hundred thousand pounds, which must be brought to us in so much Treasure; because that part of our stock which is not returned to us in wares must necessarily be brought home in treasure.

For in this case it cometh to pass in the stock of a Kingdom, as in the estate of a private man; who is supposed to have one thousand pounds yearly revenue and two thousand pounds of ready money in his Chest: If such a man through excess shall spend one thousand five hundred pounds per annum, all his ready money will be gone in four years; and in the like time his said money will be doubled if he take a Frugal course to spend but five hundred pounds per annum; which rule never faileth likewise in the Commonwealth, but in some cases (of no great moment) which I will hereafter declare, when I shall shew by whom and in what manner this balance of the Kingdom's account ought to be drawn up yearly, or so often as it shall please the State to discover how much we gain or lose by trade with foreign Nations. But first I will say something concerning those ways and means which will increase our exportations and diminish our importations of wares; which being done, I will then set down some other arguments both affirmative and negative to strengthen that which is here declared, and thereby to shew that all the other means which are commonly supposed to enrich the Kingdom with Treasure are altogether insufficient and mere fallacies.

THE PARTICULAR WAYS AND MEANS TO INCREASE THE EXPORTATION OF OUR COMMODITIES, AND TO DECREASE OUR CONSUMPTION OF FOREIGN WARES

The revenue or stock of a Kingdom by which it is provided of foreign wares is either Natural or Artificial. The Natural wealth is so much only as can be spared from our own use and necessities to be exported unto strangers. The Artificial consists in our manufactures and industrious trading with foreign commodities, concerning which I will set down such particulars as may serve for the cause we have in hand.

1. First, although this Realm be already exceeding rich by nature, yet might it be much increased by laying the waste grounds (which are infinite) into such employments as should no way hinder the present revenues of other manured lands, but hereby to supply ourselves and prevent the importations of Hemp, Flax, Cordage, Tobacco, and divers other things which we fetch from strangers to our great impoverishing.

2. We may likewise diminish our importations, if we would soberly refrain from excessive consumption of foreign wares in our diet and rayment, with such often change of fashions as is used so much the more to increase the waste and charge; which vices at this present are more notorious amongst us than in former ages. Yet might they easily be amended by enforcing the observation of such good laws as are strictly practiced in other Countries against the said excesses; where likewise by commanding their own manufactures to be used, they prevent the coming in of others, without prohibition, or offense to strangers in their mutual commerce.

3. In our exportations we must not only regard our own superfluities, but also we must consider our neighbors' necessities, that so upon the wares which they cannot want, nor yet be furnished thereof elsewhere, we may (besides the vent of the Materials) gain so much of manufacture as we can, and also endeavor to sell them dear, so far forth as the high price cause not a less vent in the quantity. But the superfluity of our commodities which strangers use, and may also have the same from other Nations, or may abate their vent by the use of some such like wares from other places, and with little inconvenience; we must in this case strive to sell as cheap as possible we can, rather than to lose the utterance of such wares. For we have found of late years by good experience, that being able to sell our Cloth cheap in Turkey, we have greatly increased the vent thereof, and the Venetians have lost as much in the utterance of theirs in those Countrys, because it is dearer. And on the other side a few years past, when by the excessive price of Wools our Cloth was exceeding dear, we lost at the least half our clothing for foreign parts, which since is no otherwise (well near) recovered again than by the great fall of price for Wools and Cloth. We find that twenty five in the Hundred less in the price of these and some other wares, to the loss of private mens revenues, may raise above fifty upon the hundred in the quantity vented to the benefit of the publique. For when Cloth is dear, other Nations do presently practice clothing, and we know they want neither art nor materials to this performance. But when by cheapness we drive them from this employment, and so in time obtain our dear price again, then do they also use their former remedy. So that by these alterations we learn, that it is in

vain to expect a greater revenue of our wares than their condition will afford, but rather it concerns us to apply our endeavors to the times with care and diligence to help ourselves the best we may, by making our cloth and other manufactures without deceit, which will increase their estimation and use.

4. The value of our exportations likewise may be much advanced when we perform it ourselves in our own ships. For then we get not only the price of our wares as they are worth here, but also the Merchants gains, the charges of insurance, and freight to carry them beyond the seas. As for example, if the Italian Merchants should come hither in their own shipping to fetch our Corn, our red Herrings or the like, in this case the Kingdom should have ordinarily but 25 s. for a quarter of Wheat, and 20 s. for a barrel of red herrings, whereas if we carry there wares ourselves into Italy upon the said rates, it is likely that we shall obtain fifty shillings for the first, and forty shillings for the last, which is a great difference in the utterance or vent of the Kingdoms stock. And although it is true that the commerce ought to be free to strangers to bring in and carry out at their pleasure, yet nevertheless in many places the exportation of victuals and munition are either prohibited, or at least limited to be done only by the people and Shipping of those places where they abound.

5. The frugal expanding likewise of our own natural wealth might advance much yearly to be exported unto strangers; and if in our payment we will be prodigal, yet let this be done with our own materials and manufactures, as Cloth, Lace, Embroideries, Cutworks and the like, where the excess of the rich may be the employment of the poor, whose labours notwithstanding of this kind, would be more

profitable for the Commonwealth, if they were done to the use of Strangers.

6. The Fishing in his Majesties seas of England, Scotland, and Ireland is our natural wealth, and would cost nothing but labour, which the Dutch bestow willingly and thereby draw yearly a very great profit to themselves by serving many places of Christendom with our Fish, for which they return and supply their wants both of foreign Wares and Money, besides the multitudes of Mariners and Shipping, which hereby are maintain'd, whereof a long discourse might be made to shew the particular management of this important business. Our Fishing plantation likewise in New England, Virginia, Greenland, the Summer Islands and the Newfoundland, are of the like nature, affording much wealth and employments to maintain a great number of poor, and to increase our decaying trade.

7. A Staple or Magazine for foreign Corn, Indigo, Spices, Raw silks, Cotton, Wool or any other commodity whatsoever, to be imported will increase Shipping, Trade, Treasure, and the Kings customs, by exporting them again where need shall require, which course of Trading hath been the chief means to raise Venice, Genoa, the low Countrys, with some others; and for such a purpose England stands most commodiously, wanting nothing to this performance but our own diligence and endeavor.

8. Also we ought to esteem and cherish those trades which we have in remote or far Countrys, for besides the increase of Shipping and Mariners thereby, the wares also sent thither and receiv'd from thence are far more profitable unto the kingdom than by our trades neer at hand; As for example; suppose Pepper to be worth here two Shillings the pound constantly, if then it be brought from the Dutch at Amsterdam, the Merchant may give there twenty pence the pound and gain well by the bargain, but if he fetch this Pepper from the East Indies, he must not give above three pence the pound at the most, which is a mighty advantage, not only in that part which serveth for our own use, but also for the great quantity which (from hence) we transport yearly unto divers other Nations to be sold at a higher price: whereby it is plain, that we make a far greater stock by gain upon these Indian Commodities, than those Nations do where they grow, and to whom they properly appertain, being the natural wealth of their Countries. But for the better understanding of this particular, we must ever distinguish between the gain of the Kingdom, and the profit of the Merchant; for although the Kingdom payeth no more for this Pepper than is before supposed, nor for any other commodity bought in foreign parts more than the Stranger receiveth from us for the same, yet the Merchant payeth not only that price, but also the freight, insurance, customs, and other charges which are exceeding great in these long voyages; but yet all these in the Kingdoms accompt are but commutations among ourselves, and no privation of the Kingdoms stock, which being duly considered, together with the support also of our other trades in our best Shipping to Italy, France, Turkey, the East Countries and other places, by transporting and venting the wares which we bring yearly from the East Indies. It may well stire up our utmost endeavors to maintain and enlarge this great and noble business, so much importing the Publique wealth, Strength, and Happiness. Neither is there less honour and judgment by growing rich (in this manner) upon the stock of other Nations, than by an industrious increase of

our own means, especially when this later is advanced by the benefit of the former, as we have found in the East Indies by sale of much of our Tin, Cloth, Lead and other Commodities, the vent whereof doth daily increase in those Countries which formerly had no use of our wares.

9. It would be very beneficial to export money as well as wares, being done in trade only, it would increase our Treasure; but of this I write more largely in the next Chapter to prove it plainly.

10. It were policy and profit for the State to suffer manufactures made of foreign Materials to be exposed custom-free, as Velvets and all other wrought Silks, Fustians, thrown Silks and the like, it would employ very many poor people, and much increase the value of our stock yearly issued into other Countries, and it would (for this purpose) cause the more foreign Materials to be brought in, to the improvement of His Majesties Customes. I will here remember a notable increase in our manufacture of winding and twisting only of foreign raw Silk, which within 35 years to my knowledge did not employ more than 300 people in the City and suburbs of London, where at this present time it doth set on work above fourteen thousand souls, as upon diligent inquiry hath been credibly reported unto his Majesties Commissioners for Trade. And it is certain, that if the said foreign Commodities might be exported from hence, free of custome, this manufacture would yet increase very much, and decrease as fast in Italy and the Netherlands. But if any man allege the Dutch proverb, "Live and let others live"; I answer, that the Dutchmen notwithstanding their own Proverb, do not only in these Kingdoms, encroach upon our livings, but also in other foreign parts of our trade (where they have power)

they do hinder and destroy us in our lawful course of living, hereby taking the bread out of our mouth, which we shall never prevent by plucking the pot from their nose, as of late years too many of us do practice to the great hurt and dishonour of this famous Nation; We ought rather to imitate former times in taking sober and worthy courses more pleasing to God and suitable to our ancient reputation.

11. It is needful also not to charge the native commodities with too great customes, lest by indearing them to the strangers use, it hinder their vent. And especially foreign wares brought in to be transported again should be favoured, for otherwise that manner of trading (so much importing the good of the Commonwealth) cannot prosper nor subsist. But the consumption of such foreign wares in the Realm may be the more charged, which will turn to the profit of the Kingdom in the Balance of the Trade, and thereby also enable the King to lay up the more Treasure out of his yearly incomes. As of this particular I intend to write more fully in his proper place, where I shall shew how much money a Prince may conveniently lay up without the hurt of his subjects.

12. Lastly, in all things we must endeavour to make the most we can of our own, whether it be Natural or Artificial; And forasmuch as the people which live by the Arts are far more in number than they who are masters of the fruits, we ought the more carefully to maintain those endeavors of the multitude, in whom doth consist the greatest strength and riches both of King and Kingdom: for where the people are many, and the arts good, there the traffique must be great, and the Country rich. The Italians employ a greater number of people, and

get more money by their industry and manufactures of the raw Silks of the Kingdom of Cicilia, than the King of Spain and his Subjects have by the revenue of this rich commodity. But what need we fetch the example so far, when we know that our own natural wares do not yield us so much profit as our industry? For Iron ore in the Mines is of no great worth, when it is compared with the employment and advantage it yields being digged, tried, transported, bought, sold, cast into Ordnance, Muskets, and many other instruments of war for offense and defense, wrought into Anchors, bolts, spikes, Hayles and the like, for the use of Ships, Houses, Carts, Coaches, Ploughs, and other instruments for Tillage. Compare our Fleece-wools with our Cloth, which requires shearing, washing, carding, spinning, weaving, fulling, dying, dressing and other trimmings, and we shall find these Arts more profitable than the natural wealth, whereof 1 might instance other examples, but I will not be more tedious, for if I would amplify upon this and the other particulars before written, I might find matter sufficient to make a large volume, but my desire in all is only to prove what I propound with brevity and plainness.

THE EXPORTATION OF OUR MONEYS IN TRADE OF MERCHANDISE IS A MEANS TO INCREASE OUR TREASURE

This Position is so contrary to the common opinion, that it will require many and strong arguments to prove it before it can be accepted of the Multitude, who bitterly exclaim when they see any moneys carried out of the Realm; affirming thereupon that we have absolutely lost so much Treasure, and that this is an act directly against the long continued laws made and confirmed by the wisdom of this Kingdom in the High Court of Parliament, and that many places, nay Spain itself which is the Fountain of Money, forbids the exportation thereof, some cases only excepted. To all which I might answer that Venice, Florence, Genoa, the Low Countries and divers other places permit it, their people applaud it, and find great benefit by it; but all this makes a noise and proves nothing, we must therefore come to those reasons which concern the business in question.

First, I will take for granted which no man of judgment will deny, that we have no other means to get Treasure but by foreign trade, for Mines we have none which do afford it, and how this money is gotten in the managing of our said Trade I have already shewed, that it is done by making our commodities which are exported yearly to over balance in value the foreign wares which we consume; so that it resteth only to shew how our moneys may be added to our commodities, and being jointly exported may so much the more increase our Treasure.

We have already supposed our yearly consumptions of foreign wares to be for the value of twenty hundred thousand pounds, and our exportations to exceed that two hundred thousand pounds, which sum we have thereupon affirmed is brought to us in treasure to balance the accompt. But now if we add three hundred thousand pounds more in ready money unto our former exportations in wares, what profit can we have (will some men say) although by this means we should bring in so much ready money more than we did before, seeing that we have carried out the like value.

To this the answer is, that when we have prepared our exportations of wares, and sent out as much of everything as we can spare or vent abroad; It is not therefore said that then we should add our money thereunto to fetch in the more money immediately, but rather first to enlarge our trade by enabling us to bring in more foreign wares, which being sent out again will in due time much increase our Treasure.

For although in this manner we do yearly multiply our importations to the maintenance of more Shipping and Mariners, improvement of His Majesties Customs and other benefits; yet our consumption of those foreign wares is no more than it was before; so that all the said increase of commodities brought in by the means of our ready money sent out as afore written, doth in the end become an exportation unto us of far greater value than our said moneys were, which is proved by three several examples following.

1. For I suppose that 100,000 Pounds being sent in our Shipping to the East Countries, will buy there one hundred thousand quarters of wheat clear aboard the Ships, which after being brought into England and housed, to export the same at the best time for vent thereof in Spain or Italy, it cannot yield less in those parts than two hundred thousand pounds to make the Merchant but a saver, yet by this reckoning we see the Kingdom hath doubled that Treasure.

2. Again this profit will be far greater when we trade thus in remote Countries, as for example, if we send one hundred thousand pounds into the East Indies to buy Pepper there, and bring it hither, and from hence send it for Italy or Turkey, it must yield seven hundred thousand pounds at least in those places, in regard of the excessive charge which the Merchant disburseth in those long voyages in Shipping, Wages, Victuals, Insurance, Interest, Customes, Imposts, and the like, all which notwithstanding the King and the Kingdom gets.

3. But where the voyages are short and the wares rich, which therefore will not employ much Shipping, the profit will be far less. As when another hundred thousand pounds shall be employed in Turkey in raw Silks, and brought hither to be after transported from hence into France, the Low Countries, or Germany, the Merchant shall have good gain, although he sell it there but for one hundred and fifty thousand pounds: and thus take the voyages altogether in their Medium, the moneys exported will be returned unto us more than Trebled. But if any man will yet object, that these returns come to us in wares, and not really in money as they were issued out.

The answer is (keeping our first ground) that if our consumption of foreign wares be no more yearly than is already supposed, and that our exportations be so mightily increased by this manner of Trading with ready money as is before declared: it is not then possible but that all the over-balance or difference should return either in money or in such wares as we must export again, which, as is already plainly shewed will be still a greater means to increase our Treasure.

For it is in the stock of the Kingdom as in the estates of private men, who having store of ware, do not therefore say that they will not venture out or trade with their money (for this were ridiculous) but do also turn that into wares, whereby they multiply their Money, and so by a continual and orderly change of one into the other grow rich, and when they please turn all their estates into

Treasure; for they that have Wares cannot want money.

Neither is it said that Money is the Life of Trade, as if it could not subsist without the same; for we know that there was great trading by way of commutation or barter when there was little money stirring in the world. The Italians and some other Nations have such remedies against this want, that it can neither decay nor hinder their trade, for they transfer bills of debt, and have Banks both public and private, wherein they do assign their credits from one to another daily for very great sums with ease and satisfaction by writings only, whilst in the mean time the Mass of Treasure which gave foundation to these credits is employed in Foreign Trade as a Merchandise, and by the said means they have little other use of money in those countries more than for their ordinary expenses. It is not therefore the keeping of our money in the Kingdom; but the necessity and use of our wares in foreign Countries, and our want of their commodities which causeth the vent and consumption on all sides, which makes a quick and ample Trade. If we were once poor, and now having gained some store of money by trade with resolution to keep it still in the Realm; shall this cause other Nations to spend more of our commodities than formerly they have done, whereby we might say that our trade is Quickened and Enlarged? No verily it will produce no such good effect: but rather according to the alteration of times by their true causes we may expect the contrary; for all men do consent that plenty of money in a Kingdom doth make the native commodities dearer, which as it is to the profit of some private men in their revenues, so is it directly against the benefit of the Publique in the quantity of the trade; for

as plenty of money makes wares dearer, so dear wares decline their use and consumption as hath been already plainly shewed in the last Chapter upon that particular of our cloth; And although this is a very hard lesson for some great landed men to learn, yet I am sure it is a true lesson for all the land to observe, lest when we have gained some store of money by trade, we lose it again by not trading with our money. I knew a Prince in Italy (of famous memory) Ferdinando the first, great Duke of Tuscanie, who being very rich in Treasure, endevoured therewith to enlarge his trade by issuing out to his Merchants great sums of money for very small profit; I myself had forty thousand crowns of him gratis for a whole year, although he knew that I would presently send it away in Specie for the parts of Turkey to be employed in wares for his Countries, he being well assured that in this course of trade it would return again (according to the old saying) with a Duck in the mouth. This noble and industrious Prince by his care and diligence to countenance and favour Merchants in their affairs, did so increase the practice thereof, that there is scarce a Nobleman or Gentleman in all his dominions that doth not Merchandise either by himself or in partnership with others, whereby within these thirty years the trade to his port of Leghorn is so much increased, that of a poor little town (as I myself knew it) it is now become a fair and strong City, being one of the most famous places for trade in all Christendom. And yet it is worthy our observation, that the multitude of Ships and wares which come hither from England, the Low Countries, and other places, have little or no means to make their returns from thence but only in ready money, which they may and do carry away freely at all times, to the incredible advantage of the said great Duke of Tuscanie and his subjects, who are much enriched by the continual great concourse of Merchants from all the States of the neighbor Princes, bringing them plenty of money daily to supply their wants of the said wares. And thus we see that the current of Merchandise which carries away their Treasure, becomes a flowing stream to fill them again in a greater measure with money.

There is yet an objection or two as weak as all the rest: that is, if we trade with our Money we shall issue out the less wares; as if a man should say, those Countries which heretofore had occasion to consume our Cloth, Lead, Tin, Iron, Fish and the like, shall now make use of our moneys in the place of these necessaries, which were most absurd to affirm, or that the Merchant had not rather carry out wares by which there is ever some gains expected, than to export money which is still but the same without any increase.

But on the contrary there are many Countries which may yield us very profitable trade for our money, which otherwise afford us no trade at all, because they have no use of our wares, as namely the East Indies for one in the first beginning thereof, although since by industry in our commerce with those Nations we have brought them into the use of much of our Lead, Cloth, Tin, and other things, which is a good addition to the former vent of our commodities.

Again, some men have alleged that those Countries which permit money to be carried out, do it because they have few or no wares to trade withall: but we have great store of commodities, and therefore their action ought not to be our example.

To this the answer is briefly, that if we have such a quantity of wares as doth fully provide us of all things needful from beyond the seas: why should we then doubt that our moneys sent out in trade, must not necessarily come back again in treasure; together with the great gains which it may procure in such manner as is before set down? And on the other side, if those Nations which send out their moneys do it because they have but few wares of their own, how come they then have so much Treasure as we ever see in those places which suffer it freely to be exported at times and by whomsoever? I answer, even by trading with their Moneys; for by what other means can they get it, having no Mines of Gold or Silver?

Thus may we plainly see, that when this weighty business is duly considered in his end, as all our humane actions ought well to be weighed, it is found much contrary to that which most men esteem thereof, because they search no further than the beginning of the work, which mis-informs their judgments, and leads them into error: For if we only behold the actions of the husbandman in the seed-time when he casteth away much good corn into the ground, we will rather accompt him a mad man than a husbandman; but when we consider his labours in the harvest which is the end of his endeavors, we find the worth and plentiful increase of his actions. . . .

4. THE RISE OF THE BOURGEOISIE

Daniel Defoe (c. 1659–1731), novelist and political pamphleteer, has left us some excellent descriptions of the events of his time. In *The Complete English Tradesman,* however, he is concerned to show the respectability, indeed the prestige, of trade and its connection with England's strength and prosperity. Chapter 24 of the book gives a long list of intermarriages between nobles and bourgeois, purporting to show "how some families owe their rise to trade, and others their descent and fortunes to prudent alliances with the families of citizens." Chapter 25, given below, is more down to earth.

The instances which we have given in the last chapter, abundantly make for the honour of the British traders; and we may venture to say, at the same time, are very far from doing dishonour to the nobility who have from time to time entered into alliance with them; for it is very well known, that besides the benefit which we reap by being a trading nation, which is our principal glory, trade is a very different thing in England than it is in many other countries, and is carried on by persons who, both in their education and descent, are far from being the dregs of the people.

King Charles II, who was perhaps the prince of all the kings that ever reigned in England, who best understood the country and the people he governed, used to say, that the tradesmen were the only gentry in England. His majesty spoke it merrily, but it had a happy signification in it, such as was peculiar to the bright genius of that prince, who, though he was not the best governor, was the best acquainted with the world of all the princes of his age, if not of all the men in it; and I make no scruple to advance these three points in honour of our country; viz.—

1. That we are the greatest trading country in the world, because we have the greatest exportation of the growth and product of our land, and of the manufacture and labour of our people; and the greatest importation and consumption of the growth, product, and manufactures of other countries from abroad, of any nation in the world.

2. That our climate is the best and most agreeable to live in, because a man can be more out of doors in England than in other countries.

3. That our men are the stoutest and best, because, strip them naked from the waist upwards, and give them no weapons at all but their hands and heels, and turn them into a room or stage, and lock them in with the like number of other men of any nation, man for man, and they shall beat the best men you shall find in the world.

As so many of our noble and wealthy families, as we have shown, are raised by and derived from trade, so it is true, and indeed it cannot well be otherwise, that many of the younger branches of our gentry, and even of the nobility itself, have descended again into the spring from whence they flowed, and have become tradesmen; and thence it is that, as I said above, our tradesmen in England are not, as it generally is in other countries, always of the meanest of our people. Nor

From Daniel Defoe, *The Complete English Tradesman* (London, 1724), Chap. XXV.

is trade itself in England, as it generally is in other countries, the meanest thing the men can turn their hand to; but, on the contrary, trade is the readiest way for men to raise their fortunes and families; and therefore it is a field for men of figure and of good families to enter upon.

Having thus done a particular piece of justice to ourselves, in the value we put upon trade and tradesmen in England, it reflects very much upon the understandings of those refined heads who pretend to depreciate that part of the nation which is so infinitely superior in wealth to the families who call themselves gentry, and so infinitely more numerous.

As to the wealth of the nation, that undoubtedly lies chiefly among the trading part of the people; and though there are a great many families raised within few years, in the late war, by great employments and by great actions abroad, to the honour of the English gentry, yet how many more families among the tradesmen have been raised to immense estates, even during the same time, by the attending circumstances of the war; such as the clothing, the paying, the victualling and furnishing, &c., both army and navy. And by whom have the prodigious taxes been paid, the loans supplied, and money advanced upon all occasions? By whom are the banks and companies carried on, and on whom are the customs and excises levied? Have not the trade and tradesmen borne the burden of the war? And do they not still pay four millions a year interest for the public debts? On whom are the funds levied, and by whom the public credit supported? Is not trade the inexhausted fund of all funds, and upon which all the rest depend?

As is the trade, so in proportion are the tradesmen; and how wealthy are

tradesmen in almost all the several parts of England, as well as in London? How common is it to see a tradesman go off the stage, even but from mere shopkeeping, with from ten to forty thousand pounds' estate to divide among his family! When, on the contrary, take the gentry in England, from one end to the other, except a few here and there, what with excessive high living, which is of late grown so much into a disease, and the other ordinary circumstances of families, we find few families of the lower gentry, that is to say from six or seven hundred a year downwards, but they are in debt, and in necessitous circumstances, and a great many of greater estates also.

On the other hand, let any one who is acquainted with England, look but abroad into the several counties, especially near London, or within fifty miles of it; how are the ancient families worn out by time and family misfortunes, and the estates possessed by a new race of tradesmen, grown up into families of gentry, and established by the immense wealth gained, as I may say, behind the counter; that is, in the shop, the warehouse, and the counting-house.

How many noble seats, superior to the palaces of sovereign princes, in some countries, do we see erected within few miles of this city by tradesmen, or the sons of tradesmen, while the seats and castles of the ancient gentry, like their families, look worn out and fallen into decay!

Again; in how superior a port do our tradesmen live, to what the middling gentry either do or can support! An ordinary tradesman now, not in the city only, but in the country, shall spend more money by the year, than a gentleman of four or five hundred pounds a year too; whereas the gentleman shall at the best stand stock still just where he began, nay, perhaps, decline: and as for the lower gentry, from a hundred pounds a year to three hundred, or thereabouts, though they are often as proud and high in their appearance as the other; as to them, I say, a shoemaker in London shall keep a better house, spend more money, clothe his family better, and yet grow rich too. It is evident where the difference lies; an estate's a pond, but trade's a spring: the first, if it keeps full, and the water wholesome, by the ordinary supplies and drains from the neighbouring grounds, it is well, and it is all that is expected; but the other is an inexhausted current, which not only fills the pond, and keeps it full, but is continually running over, and fills all the lower ponds and places about it.

This being the case in England, and our trade being so vastly great, it is no wonder that the tradesmen in England fills the lists of our nobility and gentry; no wonder that the gentlemen of the best families marry tradesmen's daughters, and put their younger sons apprentices to tradesmen; and how often do these younger sons come to buy the elder sons' estates, and restore the family, when the elder and head of the house, proving rakish and extravagant, has wasted his patrimony, and is obliged to make out the blessing of Israel's family, where the younger son bought the birthright, and the elder was doomed to serve him!

Trade is so far here from being inconsistent with a gentleman, that, in short, trade in England makes gentlemen, and has peopled this nation with gentlemen; for, after a generation or two, the tradesman's children, or at least their grandchildren, come to be as good gentlemen, statesmen, parliamentmen, privy-counsellors, judges, bishops, and noblemen, as those of the highest birth and the most

ancient families; as we have shown. Nor do we find any defect either in the genius or capacities of the posterity of tradesmen, arising from any remains of mechanic blood, which, it is pretended, should influence them; but all the gallantry of spirit, greatness of soul, and all the generous principles that can be found in any of the ancient families, whose blood is the most untainted, as they call it, with the low mixtures of a mechanic race, are found in these; and, as is said before, they generally go beyond them in knowledge of the world, which is the best education.

We see the tradesmen of England, as they grow wealthy, coming every day to the herald's office to search for the coats of arms of their ancestors, in order to paint them upon their coaches, and grave them upon their plate, embroider them upon their furniture, or carve them upon the pediments of their new houses; and how often do we see them trace the registers of their families up to the prime nobility, or the most ancient gentry of the kingdom!

In this search we find them often qualified to raise new families, if they do not descend from old; as was said of a certain tradesman of London, that if he could not find the ancient race of gentlemen, from which he came, he would begin a new race, who should be as good gentlemen as any that went before him.

Thus, in the late wars between England and France, how was our army full of excellent officers, who went from the shop, and behind the counter, into the camp, and who distinguished themselves there by their merits and gallant behaviour! And several such came to command regiments, and even to be general officers, and to gain as much reputation in the service as any; as Colonel Pierce, Wood,

Richards, and several others that may be named.

All this confirms what I have said before, viz., that trade in England neither is or ought to be compared with what it is in other countries; or the tradesman depreciated as they are abroad, and as some of our gentry would pretend to do in England; but that as many of our best families rose from trade, so many branches of the best families in England, under the nobility, have stooped so low as to be put apprentices to tradesmen in London, and to set up and follow those trades when they have come out of their times, and have thought it no dishonour to their blood.

To bring this once more home to the ladies, who are scandalized at that mean step, which they call it, of marrying a tradesman, it may be told them, for their humiliation, that, however they think fit to act, sometimes those tradesmen come of better families than their own; and oftentimes, when they have refused them to their loss, those very tradesmen have married ladies of superior fortune to them, and have raised families of their own, who, in one generation, have been superior to those nice ladies both in dignity and estate; and have, to their great mortification, been ranked above them upon all public occasions.

The word "tradesmen," in England, does not sound so harsh as it does in other countries; and to say a gentleman-tradesman, is not so much nonsense as some people would persuade us to reckon it; and, indeed, the very name of an English tradesman, will and does already obtain in the world; and as our soldiers, by the late war, gained the reputation of being some of the best troops in the world; and our seamen are at this day, and very justly too, esteemed the best

sailors in the world; so the English tradesman may be allowed to rank with the best gentlemen in Europe.

And hence it is natural to ask, whence comes all this to be so? How is it produced? War has not done it; no, nor so much as helped or assisted to it; it is not by any martial exploits; we have made no conquests abroad, added no new kingdoms to the British empire, reduced no neighbouring nations, or extended the possession of our monarchs into the properties of others; we have gained nothing by war and encroachment; nay, we have lost all the dominions which our ancient kings for some hundreds of years held in France; and, instead of being enriched by war and victory, on the contrary, we have been torn in pieces by civil wars and rebellions, and that several times, to the ruin of our richest families, and the slaughter of our nobility and gentry.

These things prove abundantly that the greatness of the British nation is not owing to war and conquests, to enlarging its dominions by the sword, or subjecting the people of other countries to our power; but it is allowing to trade, to the increase of our commerce at home, and the extending it abroad.

It is owing to trade, that new discoveries have been made in lands unknown, and new settlements and plantations made, new colonies planted, and new governments formed, in the uninhabited islands, and the uncultivated continent of America; and those plantings and settlements have again enlarged and increased the trade, and thereby the wealth and power of the nation by whom they were discovered and planted; we have not increased our power, or the number of our subjects, by subduing the nations which possess those countries, and incorporating them into our own; but have entirely planted our colonies, and peopled the countries with our own subjects, natives of this island; and, excepting the negroes, which we transport from Africa to America as slaves to work in the sugar and tobacco plantations, all our colonies, as well in the islands as on the continent of America, are entirely peopled from Great Britain and Ireland, and chiefly the former; the natives having either removed further up into the country, or, by their own folly and treachery raising war against us, been destroyed and cut off.

As trade has thus extended our colonies abroad, so it has (except those colonies) kept our people at home, where they are multiplied to that prodigious degree, and do still continue to multiply in such a manner, that, if it goes on so, time may come that all the lands in England will do little more than serve for gardens for them and to feed their cows, and their corn and cattle be supplied from Scotland and Ireland.

What is the reason that we see numbers of French, and of Scots, and Germans, in all the foreign nations in Europe, and especially filling up their armies and courts, and that you see few or no English there?

What is the reason that, when we want to raise armies, or to man navies, in England, we are obliged to press the seamen, and to make laws, and empower the justices of peace and magistrates of towns, to force men to go for soldiers, and enter into the service, or allure them by giving bounty-money as an encouragement to men to list themselves; whereas the people of other nations, and even the Scots and Irish, travel abroad and run into all the neighbour-nations, to seek service and to be admitted into their pay?

What is it but trade, the increase of business at home, and the employment of the poor in the business and manufactures of this kingdom, by which the poor get so good wages, and live so well, that they will not list for soldiers; and have so good pay in the merchants' service, that they will not serve on board the ships of war, unless they are forced to do it?

What is the reason that, in order to supply our colonies and plantations with people, besides the encouragement given in those colonies to all people that will come hither to plant and to settle, we are obliged to send away thither all our petty offenders, and all the criminals that we think fit to spare from the gallows, besides that we formerly called the kidnapping trade, that is to say, the arts made use of to wheedle and draw away young, vagrant, and indigent people, and people of desperate fortunes, to sell themselves, that is, bind themselves for servants, the number of which are very great?

It is poverty fills armies, mans navies, and peoples colonies; in vain the drums beat for soldiers to serve in the armies for fivepence a day, and the king's captains invite seamen to serve in the royal navy for twenty-three shillings per month, in a country where the ordinary labourer can have nine shillings a week for his labour, and the manufacturers earn from twelve to sixteen shillings a week for their work; and while trade gives thirty shillings per month wages to the seamen on board merchant-ships, men will always stay or go, as the pay gives them encouragement; and this is the reason why it has been so much more difficult to raise and recruit armies in England, than it has been in Scotland and Ireland, France and Germany.

The same trade that keeps our people at home, is the cause of the well-living of the people here; for as frugality is not the national virtue of England, so the people that get much, spend much; and as they work hard, so they live well, eat and drink well, clothe warm, and lodge soft; in a word, the working manufacturing people of England, eat the fat, drink the sweet, live better, and fare better, than the working poor of any other nation in Europe; they make better wages of their work, and spend more of the money upon their backs and bellies than in any other country. This expense of the poor, as it causes a prodigious consumption both of the provisions and of the manufactures of our country at home, so two things are undeniably the consequence of that part.

1. The consumption of provisions increases the rent and value of the lands; and this raises the gentlemen's estates, and that again increases the employment of people, and consequently the numbers of them, as well those that are employed in the husbandry of land, breeding and feeding of cattle, &c., as of servants to the gentlemen's families, who as their estates increase in value, so they increase their families and equipages.

2. As the people get greater wages, so they, I mean the same poorer part of the people, clothe better, and furnish better; and this increases the consumption of the very manufactures they make; then that consumption increases the quantity made; and this creates what we call inland trade, by which innumerable families are employed, and the increase of the people maintained; and by which increase of trade and people the present growing prosperity of this nation is produced.

The whole glory and greatness of England then being thus raised by trade, it must be unaccountable folly and ignorance in us to lessen that one article in our own esteem, which is the only fountain from whence we all, take us as a nation, are raised, and by which we are enriched and maintained. The Scripture says, speaking of the riches and glory of the city of Tyre, which was indeed at that time the great port or emporium of the world for foreign commerce, from whence all the silks and fine manufactures of Persia and India were exported all over the western world, "that her merchants were princes," and in another place, "by thy traffic thou hast increased thy riches." Certain it is, that our traffic has increased our riches; and it is also certain, that the flourishing of our manufacture is the foundation of all our traffic, as well our merchandise as our inland trade.

5. THE NEW SCIENCE

The "scientific revolution" is usually associated with the sixteenth and seventeenth centuries, although, of course, its origins may be traced a long way back. But for a technique or an idea to be historically significant, mere existence is not enough: acceptance and practice are needed and success is, to some extent, measured quantitatively. This is why the seventeenth century seems crucial to that revolution which, in the words of Herbert Butterfield (*The Origins of Modern Science,* London, 1949), "overturned the authority in science not only of the middle ages but of the ancient world." To Professor Butterfield this change of techniques and attitudes is the most important event since the rise of Christianity, more important by far than Renaissance or Reformation: "Since it changed the character of men's habitual mental operations even in the conduct of the non-material sciences, while transforming the whole diagram of the physical universe and the very texture of human life itself, it looms so large as the real origin both of the modern world and of the modern mentality that our customary periodisation of European history has become an anachronism and an encumbrance."

Quite apart from the new interpretations and perspectives these words suggest, it is interesting to see that such tremendous changes came about in the first place and quite literally as changes of *mind*. In other words, not as a result of new discoveries, new facts, new observations, but of new ways of looking at evidence which had been available for quite some time. What we find in the work of Descartes or Newton, as in that of William Harvey or Galileo, is "the art of handling the same bundle of data as before, but placing them in a new system of relations with one another by giving them a new framework." It was a system that would prepare the minds of men for Darwin's *Origin of Species* two centuries later.

Descartes: from *The Discourse upon Method*

René Descartes (1596–1650) was a versatile French philosopher and mathematician. Not only did he crisscross Europe as a soldier during some of the campaigns connected with the Thirty Years' War, but we owe him several important scientific discoveries. His meditations ruined the medieval scholastic methods and founded modern philosophy by suggesting a new principle for the use of reason in metaphysical matters. This method, generally known as "Cartesianism," is summarized as follows: "In order to get at truth, we must at least once in a lifetime get rid of all received [accepted] opinions, and reconstruct completely afresh, from the ground up, all the systems of our knowledge."

Descartes' work reflects a newly critical attitude to evidence and to ideas. Doubt had existed before: a hundred years earlier, Montaigne had represented the amiable but unconstructive doubt of the worldly-wise skeptic. But now doubt was to be used rationally, according to critical rules of evidence which would serve as an instrument of knowledge. This was the time when scientific attitudes were born, with William Harvey in medicine, Richard Simon in Biblical exegesis, Mabillon in historical criticism, presenting the typical attitudes of the future.

PART FIRST

. . . My design is not to point out the method which everyone must follow for the right direction of his understanding, but merely to show how I have attempted to conduct my own. Those who take it upon themselves to give precepts to others must assume that they are themselves better instructed than those to whom they give them, and if they make the least error, they are answerable for it. But as I offer this production merely as a piece of personal history, or of fiction, if you please, in which, among some examples which may well be imitated, there

From *The Philosophy of Descartes*, tr. Henry A. P. Torrey (New York, 1892), pp. 37–49.

will be found, perhaps, many others also which one might reasonably decline to follow, I hope that it may prove useful to some and harmful to none, and that all will take my frankness kindly.

I was brought up to letters from my childhood, and because I was led to believe that by means of them clear and certain knowledge of all that was useful in life might be acquired, I had an extreme desire for learning. But no sooner had I completed the whole course of studies at the end of which it is customary for one to be received into the circle of the learned, than I changed my opinion entirely. For I found myself involved in so many doubts and errors, that it seemed to me that I had derived no other advantage from my endeavors to instruct myself but only to find out more and more how ignorant I was. And yet I was in one of the most celebrated schools in Europe, where I thought there must be learned men if there were any such in the world. I had acquired all that others learned there, and more than that, not being content with the sciences which were taught us, I ran through all the books I could get hold of which treated of matters considered most curious and rare. Moreover, I knew what others thought about me, and I did not perceive that they considered me inferior to my fellow-students, albeit there were among them some who were destined to fill the places of our masters. And finally, our time appeared to me to be as flourishing and as prolific of good minds as any preceding time had been. Such considerations emboldened me to judge all others by myself, and served to convince me that there did not exist in the world any such wisdom as I had been led to hope for. However, I did not cease to think well of scholastic pursuits. I knew that the languages taught in the schools

were indispensable for the understanding of the ancient books; that light and graceful stories stimulate the mind; that the memorable deeds of history exalt it, and that when read with discretion they help to form the judgment; that the reading of all good books is like conversation with the noble men of bygone times—a studied conversation, even, in which only their best thoughts are disclosed. . . . But I thought I had already given time enough to languages and to the literature of the ancients, to their histories and to their fables. To talk with men of other times is like traveling. It is well to know something of the manners of foreign peoples, in order that we may judge our own more wisely, and that we may not suppose that what is different from our own habits is ridiculous and contrary to reason, as those do who have not seen the world. But if one spends too much time in traveling in foreign countries, he becomes at last a stranger in his own; and when one is too curious to know what has been done in past ages, he is liable to remain ignorant of what is going on in his own time. Moreover, fiction represents many events as possible which are not so; and even the most faithful histories, if they do not deviate from truth nor dignify events to make them more impressive, at least they almost always omit the meaner and the less illustrious incidents, so that it comes about that the rest is not what it really was, and those who govern their conduct by the examples there furnished are liable to fall into the extravagances of the paladins of our romances, and to conceive designs which surpass their ability. . . .

Above all I was delighted with the mathematics, on account of the certainty and evidence of their demonstrations, but I had not as yet found out their true use, and although I supposed that they were of service only in the mechanic arts, I was surprised that upon foundations so solid and stable no loftier structure had been raised: while, on the other hand, I compared the writings of the ancient moralists to palaces very proud and very magnificent, but which are built on nothing but sand or mud. . . . I revered our theology, and, as much as anyone, I strove to gain heaven; but when I learned, as an assured fact, that the way is open no less to the most ignorant than to the most learned, and that the revealed truths which conduct us thither lie beyond the reach of our intelligence, I did not presume to submit them to the feebleness of my reasonings, and I thought that, to undertake the examination of them and succeed in the attempt, required extraordinary divine assistance and more than human gifts. I had nothing to say of philosophy, save that, seeing it had been cultivated by the best minds for many ages, and still there was nothing in it which might not be brought into dispute, and which was, therefore, not free from doubt, I had not the presumption to hope for better success therein than others; and considering how many diverse opinions may be held upon the same subject and defended by the learned, while not more than one of them can be true, I regarded as pretty nearly false all that was merely probable. Then, as to the other sciences which derive their principles from philosophy, I judged that nothing solid could be built upon foundations so unstable; and neither the fame nor the emolument they promised me were sufficient to induce me to acquire them; for, thanks to a kind Providence, I did not find myself in a condition of life which required me to make science a profession for the bettering of my estate; and although I did not profess to despise fame,

like a cynic, still I thought very little of that which I could not hope to acquire except on false pretenses. And finally, as for the pseudo-sciences, I thought I was already sufficiently acquainted with their value to be proof against the promises of the alchemist, the predictions of the astrologer, the impostures of the magician, the artifices and vain boasting of those who profess to know more than they actually do know.

For these reasons, so soon as I was old enough to be no longer subject to the control of my teachers, I abandoned literary pursuits altogether, and, being resolved to seek no other knowledge than that which I was able to find within myself or in the great book of the world, I spent the remainder of my youth in traveling, in seeing courts and armies, in mingling with people of various dispositions and conditions in life, in collecting a variety of experiences, putting myself to the proof in the crises of fortune, and reflecting on all occasions on whatever might present itself, so as to derive from it what profit I might. For it appeared to me that I might find a great deal more of truth in reasonings such as everyone carries on with reference to the affairs which immediately concern himself, and where the issue will bring speedy punishment if he make a mistake, than in those which a man of letters conducts in his private study with regard to speculations, which have no other effect and are of no further consequence to him than to tickle his vanity the less they are understood by common people, and the more they require wit and skill to make them seem probable. And I always had an extreme desire to learn how to distinguish the true from the false, so that I might see clearly and proceed with assurance in the affairs of this present life.

It is true that while I employed myself only in observing the manners of foreigners, I found very little to establish my mind, and saw as much diversity here as I had seen before in the opinions of philosophers. So that the principal benefit I derived from it was that, observing many things which, although they appear to us to be very extravagant and ridiculous, are yet commonly received and approved by other great peoples, I gradually became emancipated from many errors which tend to obscure the natural light within us, and make us less capable of listening to reason. But after I had spent some years thus in studying in the book of the world, and trying to gain some experience, I formed one day the resolution to study within myself, and to devote all the powers of my mind to choosing the paths which I must thereafter follow; a project attended with much greater success, as I think, than it would have been had I never left my country nor my books.

PART SECOND

I was then in Germany, whither the wars, which were not yet ended there, had summoned me; and when I was returning to the army, from the coronation of the emperor, the coming on of the winter detained me in a quarter where, finding no one I wished to talk with, and fortunately having no cares nor passions to trouble me, I spent the whole day shut up in a room heated by a stove, where I had all the leisure I desired to hold converse with my own thoughts. One of the first thoughts to occur to me was that there is often less completeness in works made up of many parts and by the hands of different masters than in those upon which only one has labored. Thus we see

that buildings which a single architect has undertaken and erected are usually much more beautiful and symmetrical than those which many have tried to reconstruct, using old walls which were built for other purposes.

. . . And so I thought that the sciences contained in books, at least those in which the proofs were merely probable and not demonstrations, being the gradual accumulation of opinions of many different persons, by no means come so near the truth as the plain reasoning of a man of good sense in regard to the matters which present themselves to him.

And I thought still further that, because we all have been children before we were men, and for a long time of necessity were under the control of our inclinations and our tutors, who were often of different minds, and none of whom perhaps gave us the best of counsels, it is almost impossible that our judgments should be as free from error and as solid as they would have been if we had had the entire use of our reason from the moment of our birth, and had always been guided by that alone. . . .

As for all the opinions which I had accepted up to that time, I was persuaded that I could do no better than get rid of them at once, in order to replace them afterward with better ones, or perhaps with the same, if I should succeed in making them square with reason. And I firmly believed that in this way I should have much greater success in the conduct of my life than if I should build only on the old foundations, and should rely only on the principles which I had allowed myself to be persuaded of in my youth, without ever having examined whether they were true. . . .

My design has never reached further than the attempt to reform my own opinions, and to build upon a foundation altogether my own. But although I am well enough pleased with my work to present you here a sketch of it, I would not on that account advise anyone to imitate me. . . . The simple resolution to strip one's self of all that he has hitherto believed is not an example for everyone to follow. . . .

But having discovered while at college that there is nothing whatever so strange or incredible that has not been said by some philosopher; and afterward, in my travels, having observed that not all those who cherish opinions quite contrary to our own are therefore barbarians or savages, but that many of these peoples use their reason as well or better than we do; and having considered how differently the same man, with the same mind, would turn out, if he were brought up from infancy among the French or the Germans, from what he would if he always lived among the Chinese or with cannibals; and observing how, even in fashions of dress, the same thing which pleased us ten years ago, and, it may be, will please us again ten years hence, appears to us now extravagant and ridiculous; so that it is rather custom and example than certain knowledge which persuades us; and yet a plurality of votes is no proof that a thing is true, especially where truths are difficult of discovery, in which case it is much more likely that a man left to himself will find them out sooner than people in general—taking all these things into consideration, and not being able to select anyone whose opinions seemed to me to be preferable to those of others, I found myself, as it were, compelled to take myself as my guide. But like a man who walks alone and in the dark, I resolved to go so slowly and to use so much caution in everything,

that, even if I did not get on very far, I should at least keep from falling. Likewise I was unwilling at the start to reject summarily any opinion which might have insinuated itself into my belief without having been introduced there by reason, but I would first spend time enough to draw up a plan of the work I was undertaking and to discover the true method for arriving at the knowledge of whatever my mind was capable of.

I had studied, in earlier years, of the branches of philosophy, logic, and in mathematics, geometrical analysis and algebra, three arts or sciences which seemed likely to afford some assistance to my design. But on examination of them I observed, in respect to logic, that its syllogisms and the greater part of its processes are of service principally in explaining to another what one already knows himself, or, like the art of Lully, they enable him to talk without judgment on matters in which he is ignorant, rather than help him to acquire knowledge of them; and while it contains in reality many very true and very excellent precepts, there are nevertheless mixed with these many others which are either harmful or superfluous, and which are almost as difficult to separate from the rest as to draw forth a Diana or a Minerva from a block of marble which is not yet rough-hewn. . . . For this reason I thought that some other method should be sought out which, comprising the advantages of these three, should be exempt from their defects. And as a multiplicity of laws often furnishes excuses for vices, so that a state is best governed which has but few and those strictly obeyed; in like manner, in place of the multitude of precepts of which logic is composed, I believed I should find the four following rules quite sufficient, provided I should firmly and steadfastly resolve not to fail of observing them in a single instance.

The first rule was never to receive anything as a truth which I did not clearly know to be such; that is, to avoid haste and prejudice, and not to comprehend anything more in my judgments than that which should present itself so clearly and so distinctly to my mind that I should have no occasion to entertain a doubt of it.

The second rule was to divide every difficulty which I should examine into as many parts as possible, or as might be required for resolving it.

The third rule was to conduct my thoughts in an orderly manner, beginning with objects the most simple and the easiest to understand, in order to ascend as it were by steps to the knowledge of the most composite, assuming some order to exist even in things which did not appear to be naturally connected.

The last rule was to make enumerations so complete, and reviews so comprehensive, that I should be certain of omitting nothing.

Those long chains of reasoning, quite simple and easy, which geometers are wont to employ in the accomplishment of their most difficult demonstrations, led me to think that everything which might fall under the cognizance of the human mind might be connected together in a similar manner, and that, provided only one should take care not to receive anything as true which was not so, and if one were always careful to preserve the order necessary for deducing one truth from another, there would be none so remote at which he might not at last arrive, nor so concealed which he might not discover. . . .

And I am free to say that the exact observance of these few rules which I had laid down gave me such facility in solving all the questions to which these two sciences apply, that in the two or three months which I spent in examining them, having begun with the simplest and most general, and each truth that I discovered being a rule which was of service to me afterward in the discovery of others, not only did I arrive at many which formerly I had considered very difficult, but it seemed to me, toward the end, that I was able to determine even in those matters where I was ignorant by what means and how far it would be possible to resolve them. In this I shall not appear to you to be very vain, perhaps, if you will only consider that there is, in respect to each case, but one truth, and that he who finds it knows as much about it as anyone can know; as, for example, a child, who has learned arithmetic, when he has made an addition according to the rules, can be assured that he has found out, in respect to the sum that he has computed, all that it is possible for the human mind to discover. Because, in a word, the method which shows one how to follow the true order, and to take account exactly of all the circumstances of the subject under investigation, contains all that which gives certitude to the rules of arithmetic. But that which pleased me most in this method was the fact that by means of it I was using my reason in everything, if not perfectly, yet in a manner the very best in my power. . . .

PART FOURTH

I am in doubt as to the propriety of making my first meditations in the place

From Descartes, *Discourse on Method,* tr. John Veitch (Edinburgh, 1850), pp. 74–82.

above mentioned a matter of discourse; for these are so metaphysical, and so uncommon, as not, perhaps, to be acceptable to every one. And yet, that it may be determined whether the foundations that I have laid are sufficiently secure, I find myself in a measure constrained to advert to them. I had long before remarked that, in relation to practice, it is sometimes necessary to adopt, as if above doubt, opinions which we discern to be highly uncertain, as had been already said; but as I then desired to give my attention solely to the search after truth, I thought that a procedure exactly the opposite was called for, and that I ought to reject as absolutely.false all opinions in regard to which I could suppose the least ground for doubt, in order to ascertain whether after that there remained aught in my belief that was wholly indubitable. Accordingly, seeing that our senses sometimes deceive us, I was willing to suppose that there existed nothing really such as they presented to us; and because some men err in reasoning, and fall into paralogisms, even on the simplest matters of Geometry, I, convinced that I was as open to error as any other, rejected as false all the reasonings I had hitherto taken for demonstrations; and finally, when I considered that the very same thoughts [presentations] which we experience when awake may also be experienced when we are asleep, while there is at that time not one of them true, I supposed that all the objects [presentations] that had ever entered into my mind when awake, had in them no more truth than the illusions of my dreams. But immediately upon this I observed that, whilst I thus wished to think that all was false, it was absolutely necessary that I, who thus thought, should be somewhat; and as I observed that this truth, *I think, hence I am,* was so certain

and of such evidence, that no ground of doubt, however extravagant, could be aleged by the Sceptics capable of shaking it, I concluded that I might, without scruple, accept it as the first principle of the Philosophy of which I was in search.

In the next place, I attentively examined what I was, and as I observed that I could suppose that I had no body, and that there was no world nor any place in which I might be; but that I could not therefore suppose that I was not; and that, on the contrary, from the very circumstance that I thought to doubt of the truth of other things, it most clearly and certainly followed that I was; while, on the other hand, if I had only ceased to think, although all the other objects which I had ever imagined had been in reality existent, I would have had no reason to believe thàt I existed; I thence concluded that I was a substance whose whole essence or nature consists only in thinking, and which, that it may exist, has need of no place, nor is dependent on any material thing; so that "I," that is to say, the mind by which I am what I am, is wholly distinct from the body, and is even more easily known than the latter, and is such, that although the latter were not, it would still continue to be all that it is.

After this I inquired in general into what is essential to the truth and certainty of a proposition; for since I had discovered one which I knew to be true, I thought that I must likewise be able to discover the ground of this certitude. And as I observed that in the words *I think, hence I am,* there is nothing at all which gives me assurance of their truth beyond this, that I see very clearly that in order to think it is necessary to exist, I concluded that I might take, as a general rule, the principle, that all the things which we very clearly and distinctly conceive are true, only observing, however, that there is some difficulty in rightly determining the objects which we distinctly conceive.

In the next place, from reflecting on the circumstance that I doubted, and that consequently my being was not wholly perfect, (for I clearly saw that it was a greater perfection to know than to doubt,) I was led to inquire whence I had learned to think of something more perfect than myself; and I clearly recognised that I must hold this notion from some Nature which in reality was more perfect. As for the thoughts of many other objects external to me, as of the sky, the earth, light, heat, and a thousand more, I was less at a loss to know whence these came; for since I remarked in them nothing which seemed to render them superior to myself, I could believe that, if these were true, they were dependencies on my own nature, in so far as it possessed a certain perfection, and, if they were false, that I held them from nothing, that is to say, that they were in me because of a certain imperfection of my nature. But this could not be the case with the idea of a Nature more perfect than myself; for to receive it from nothing was a thing manifestly impossible; and, because it is not less repugnant that the more perfect should be an effect of, and dependence on the less perfect, than that something should proceed from nothing, it was equally impossible that I could hold it from myself: accordingly, it but remained that it had been placed in me by a Nature which was in reality more perfect than mine, and which even possessed within itself all the perfections of which I could form any idea; that is to say, in a single word, which was God. And to this I added that, since I knew some perfections which I did not possess, I was not the only being in

existence, (I will here, with your permission, freely use the terms of the schools); but, on the contrary, that there was of necessity some other more perfect Being upon whom I was dependent, and from whom I had received all that I possessed; for if I had existed alone, and independently of every other being, so as to have had from myself all the perfection, however little, which I actually possessed, I should have been able, for the same reason, to have had from myself the whole remainder of perfection, of the want of which I was conscious, and thus could of myself have become infinite, eternal, immutable, omniscient, all-powerful, and, in fine, have possessed all the perfections which I could recognise in God. For in order to know the nature of God, (whose existence has been established by the preceding reasonings,) as far as my own nature permitted, I had only to consider in reference to all the properties of which I found in my mind some idea, whether their possession was a mark of perfection; and I was assured that no one which indicated any imperfection was in him, and that none of the rest was wanting. Thus I perceived that doubt, inconstancy, sadness, and such like, could not be found in God, since I myself would have been happy to be free from them. Besides, I had ideas of many sensible and corporeal things; for although I might suppose that I was dreaming, and that all which I saw or imagined was false, I could not, nevertheless, deny that the ideas were in reality in my thoughts. But, because I had already very clearly recognised in myself that the intelligent nature is distinct from the corporeal, and as I observed that all composition is an evidence of dependency, and that a state of dependency is manifestly a state of imperfection, I therefore determined that it could not be a perfection in God to be compounded of these two natures, and that consequently he was not so compounded; but that if there were any bodies in the world, or even any intelligences, or other natures that were not wholly perfect, their existence depended on his power in such a way that they could not subsist without him for a single moment.

I was disposed straightway to search for other truths; and when I had represented to myself the object of the geometers, which I conceived to be a continuous body, or a space indefinitely extended in length, breadth, and height or depth, divisible into divers parts which admit of different figures and sizes, and of being moved or transposed in all manner of ways, (for all this the geometers suppose to be in the object they contemplate,) I went over some of their simplest demonstrations. And, in the first place, I observed, that the great certitude which by common consent is accorded to these demonstrations, is founded solely upon this, that they are clearly conceived in accordance with the rules I have already laid down. In the next place, I perceived that there was nothing at all in these demonstrations which could assure me of the existence of their object: thus, for example, supposing a triangle to be given, I distinctly perceived that its three angles were necessarily equal to two right angles, but I did not on that account perceive anything which could assure me that any triangle existed: while, on the contrary, recurring to the examination of the idea of a Perfect Being, I found that the existence of the Being was comprised in the idea in the same way that the equality of its three angles to two right angles is comprised in the idea of a triangle, or as in the idea of a sphere, the equidistance of all points on its surface from the centre,

or even still more clearly; and that consequently it is at least as certain that God, who is this Perfect Being, is, or exists, as any demonstration of Geometry can be.

But the reason which leads many to persuade themselves that there is a difficulty in knowing this truth, and even also in knowing what their mind really is, is that they never raise their thoughts above sensible objects, and are so accustomed to consider nothing except by way of imagination, which is a mode of thinking limited to material objects, that all that is not imaginable seems to them not intelligible. The truth of this is sufficiently manifest from the single circumstance, that the philosophers of the Schools accept as a maxim that there is nothing in the Understanding which was not previously in the Senses, in which however it is certain that the ideas of God and of the soul have never been; and it appears to me that they who make use of their imagination to comprehend these ideas do exactly the same thing as if, in order to hear sounds or smell odours, they strove to avail themselves of their eyes; unless indeed that there is this difference, that the sense of sight does not afford us an inferior assurance to those of smell or hearing; in place of which, neither our imagination nor our senses can give us assurance of anything unless our Understanding intervene.

Finally, if there be still persons who are not sufficiently persuaded of the existence of God and of the soul, by the reasons I have adduced, I am desirous that they should know that all the other propositions, of the truth of which they deem themselves perhaps more assured, as that we have a body, and that there exist stars and an earth, and such like, are less certain; for, although we have a moral assurance of these things, which is so strong that there is an appearance of extravagance in doubting of their existence, yet at the same time no one, unless his intellect is impaired, can deny, when the question relates to a metaphysical certitude, that there is sufficient reason to exclude entire assurance, in the observation that when asleep we can in the same way imagine ourselves possessed of another body and that we see other stars and another earth, when there is nothing of the kind. For how do we know that the thoughts which occur in dreaming are false rather than those other which we experience when awake, since the former are often not less vivid and distinct than the latter? And though men of the highest genius study this question as long as they please, I do not believe that they will be able to give any reason which can be sufficient to remove this doubt, unless they presuppose the existence of God. For, in the first place, even the principle which I have already taken as a rule, viz., that all the things which we clearly and distinctly conceive are true, is certain only because God is or exists, and because he is a Perfect Being, and because all that we possess is derived from him: whence it follows that our ideas or notions, which to the extent of their clearness and distinctness are real, and proceed from God, must to that extent be true. Accordingly, whereas we not unfrequently have ideas or notions in which some falsity is contained, this can only be the case with such as are to some extent confused and obscure, and in this proceed from nothing, [participate of negation,] that is, exist in us thus confused because we are not wholly perfect. And it is evident that it is not less repugnant that falsity or imperfection, in so far as it is imperfection, should proceed from God, than that truth or perfection should proceed from nothing. But if we did not

know that all which we possess of real and true proceeds from a Perfect and Infinite Being, however clear and distinct our ideas might be, we should have no ground on that account for the assurance that they possessed the perfection of being true.

But after the knowledge of God and of the soul has rendered us certain of this rule, we can easily understand that the truth of the thoughts we experience when awake, ought not in the slightest degree to be called in question on account of the illusions of our dreams. For if it happened that an individual, even when asleep, had some very distinct idea, as, for example, if a geometer should discover some new demonstration, the circumstance of his being asleep would not militate against its truth; and as for the most ordinary error of our dreams, which consists in their representing various objects in the same way as our external senses, this is not prejudicial, since it leads us very properly to suspect the truth of the ideas of sense; for we are not unfrequently deceived in the same manner when awake; as when persons in the jaundice see all objects yellow, or when the stars or bodies at a great distance appear to us much smaller than they are. For, in fine, whether awake or asleep, we ought never to allow ourselves to be persuaded of the truth of anything unless on the evidence of our Reason. And it must be noted that I say of our *Reason,* and not of our imagination or of our senses: thus, for example, although we very clearly see the sun, we ought not therefore to determine that it is only of the size which our sense of sight presents; and we may very distinctly imagine the head of a lion joined to the body of a goat, without being therefore shut up to the conclusion that a chimæra exists; for it is not a dictate of

Reason that what we thus see or imagine is in reality existent; but it plainly tells us that all our ideas or notions contain in them some truth; for otherwise it could not be that God, who is wholly perfect and veracious, should have placed them in us. And because our reasonings are never so clear or so complete during sleep as when we are awake, although some-times the acts of our imagination are then as lively and distinct, if not more so than in our waking moments, Reason further dictates that, since all our thoughts cannot be true because of our partial imperfection, those possesing truth must infallibly be found in the experience of our waking moments rather than in that of our dreams.

Newton: from *The Mathematical Principles of Natural Philosophy*

Isaac Newton (1642–1727) was perhaps the most illustrious all-round man of the early eighteenth century. Mathematician, physicist, astronomer, philosopher, and amateur theologian, he discovered the laws of universal gravity and of the decomposition of light, and he disputed with Leibnitz the priority of the differential calculus. The prevailing veneration of the great scientist appears in Pope's couplet intended for Newton's tomb in Westminster Abbey:

Nature and Nature's laws lay hid in night;
God said, "Let Newton be," and all was light.

For our purpose, we can find no better brief expression of the new scientific approach than in the definition of scientific method that he laid down in the great *Philosophiae Naturalis Principia Mathematica* of 1687.

RULES OF REASONING IN PHILOSOPHY

Rule I

We are to admit no more causes of natural things than such as are both true and sufficient to explain their appearances.

To this purpose the philosophers say that Nature does nothing in vain, and more is in vain when less will serve; for Nature is pleased with simplicity, and affects not the pomp of superfluous causes.

Rule II

Therefore to the same natural effects we must, as far as possible, assign the same causes.

As to respiration in a man and in a beast; the descent of stones in Europe and in America; the light of our culinary fire and of the sun; the reflection of light on the earth, and in the planets.

Rule III

The qualities of bodies, which admit neither intension nor remission of degrees, and which are found to belong to all bodies within the reach of our experiments, are to be esteemed the universal qualities of all bodies whatsoever.

For since the qualities of bodies are only known to us by experiments, we are to hold for universal all such as universally agree with experiments and such as are not liable to diminution can never be

From Isaac Newton, *The Mathematical Principles of Natural Philosophy*, 2 vols. (London, 1803), II, 160–162.

quite taken away. We are certainly not to relinquish the evidence of experiments for the sake of dreams and vain fictions of our own devising; nor are we to recede from the analogy of Nature, which uses to be simple, and always consonant to itself. We no other way know the extension of bodies than by our senses, nor do these reach it in all bodies; but because we perceive extension in all that are sensible, therefore we ascribe it universally to all others also. That abundance of bodies are hard, we learn by experience; and because the hardness of the whole arises from the hardness of the parts, we therefore justly infer the hardness of the undivided particles not only of the bodies we feel but of all others. That all bodies are impenetrable, we gather not from reason, but from sensation. The bodies which we handle we find impenetrable, and thence conclude impenetrability to be an universal property of all bodies whatsoever. That all bodies are moveable, and endowed with certain powers (which we call the *vires inertiae*) of persevering in their motion, or in their rest, we only infer the like properties observed in the bodies which we have seen. The extension, hardness, impenetrability, mobility, and *vis inertiae* of the whole, result from the extension, hardness, impenetrability, mobility, and *vires inertiae* of the parts; and thence we conclude the least particles of all bodies to be also all extended, and hard, and impenetrable, and moveable, and endowed with their proper *vires inertiae*. And this is the foundation of all philosophy. Moreover, that the divided but contiguous particles of bodies may be separated from one another, is matter of observation; and, in the particles that remain undivided, our minds are able to distinguish yet lesser parts, as is mathematically demonstrated. But whether the parts so distinguished and not yet divided, may, by the powers of Nature, be actually divided and separated from one another, we cannot certainly determine. Yet had we the proof of but one experiment that any undivided particle, in breaking a hard and solid body, suffered a division, we might by virtue of this rule conclude that the undivided as well as the divided particles may be divided and actually separated to infinity.

Lastly, if it universally appears, by experiments and astronomical observations, that all bodies about the earth gravitate towards the earth, and that in proportion to the quantity of matter which they severally contain; that the moon likewise, according to the quantity of its matter, gravitates towards the earth; that, on the other hand, our sea gravitates towards the moon; and all the planets mutually one towards another; and the comets in like manner towards the sun; we must, in consequence of this rule, universally allow that all bodies whatsoever are endowed with a principle of mutual gravitation. For the argument from the appearances concludes with more force for the universal gravitation of all bodies than for their impenetrability; of which, among those in the celestial regions, we have no experiments, nor any manner of observation. Not that I affirm gravity to be essential to bodies: by their *vis infita* I mean nothing but their *vis inertiae*. This is immutable. Their gravity is diminished as they recede from the earth.

Rule IV

In experimental philosophy we are to look upon propositions collected by general induction from phaenomena as accurately or very nearly true, notwithstanding any contrary hypotheses that may be imagined, till such time as other phaenomena occur, by which they may either be made more accurate, or liable to exceptions.

This rule must follow, that the argument of induction may not be evaded by hypotheses.

Locke: from *An Essay Concerning Human Understanding*

John Locke (1632–1704) was not only a scholar but also a doctor, a civil servant, and an amateur diplomat. Attached to the powerful Ashley family (Lords Shaftesbury) he met some of the greatest men in contemporary English politics (Buckingham, Halifax) and was the tutor of the second and the third Lords Shaftesbury. At one time he produced a constitution for the newly founded American colony of Carolina. In exile with his patron in Holland from 1682 to 1688, he returned in the fleet of William of Orange and set himself to provide a philosophical explanation for the dispossession of James II. Two *Treatises on Government* resulted, and part of one is given on page 423 below. His fame, however, rests chiefly on his philosophical writings, chief of which is the *Essay Concerning Human Understanding*, published in 1690. It is divided into four books: the first discusses innate ideas and concludes that they do not exist, the second deals with the origin of ideas, the third with language, the fourth lays down the limits of human understanding. Only two brief passages from books one and four are given below.

OF IDEAS IN GENERAL, AND THEIR ORIGIN

1. Idea is the object of thinking.— Every man being conscious to himself, that he thinks, and that which his mind is applied about, whilst thinking, being the ideas that are there, it is past doubt that men have in their mind several ideas, such as are those expressed by the words, "whiteness, hardness, sweetness, thinking, motion, man, elephant, army, drunkenness," and others. It is in the first place then to be inquired, How he comes by them? I know it is a received doctrine, that men have native ideas and original characters stamped upon their minds in their very first being. This opinion I have at large examined already; and, I suppose, what I have shown whence the understanding may get all the ideas it has, and

by what ways and degrees they may come into the mind; for which I shall appeal to every one's own observation and experience.

2. All ideas come from sensation or reflection.—Let us then suppose the mind to be, as we say, white paper, void of all characters, without any ideas; how comes it to be furnished? Whence comes it by that vast store, which the busy and boundless fancy of man has painted on it with an almost endless variety? Whence has it all the materials of reason and knowledge? To this I answer, in one word, From experience: in that all our knowledge is founded, and from that it ultimately derives itself. Our observation, employed either about external sensible objects, or about the internal operations of our minds, perceived and reflected on by ourselves, is that which supplies our

From John Locke, *An Essay Concerning Human Understanding* (London, 1881), pp. 59–61; 424.

understandings with all the materials of thinking. These two are the fountains of knowledge, from whence all the ideas we have, or can naturally have, do spring.

3. *The object of sensation one source of ideas.*—First. Our senses, conversant about particular sensible objects, do convey into the mind several distinct perceptions of things, according to those various ways wherein those objects do affect them; and thus we come by those ideas we have of yellow, white heat, cold, soft, hard, bitter, sweet, and all those which we call sensible qualities; which when I say the senses convey into the mind, I mean they from external objects convey into the mind what produces there those perceptions. The great source of most of the ideas we have, depending wholly upon our senses, and derived by them to the understanding, I call "sensation."

4. *The operations of our minds the other source of them.*—Secondly. The other fountain, from which experience furnisheth the understanding with ideas, is the perception of the operations of our own minds within us, as it is employed about the ideas it has got; which operations, when the soul comes to reflect on and consider, do furnish the understanding with another set of ideas which could not be had from things without; and such are perception, thinking, doubting, believing, reasoning, knowing, willing, and all the different actings of our own minds; which we, being conscious of, and observing in ourselves, do from these receive into our understanding as distinct ideas, as we do from bodies affecting our senses. This source of ideas every man has wholly in himself; and though it be not sense as having nothing to do with external objects, yet it is very like it, and might properly enough be called "internal sense." But as I call the other "sensation," so I call this "reflection," the ideas it affords being such only as the mind gets by reflecting on its own operations within itself. By reflection, then, in the following part of this discourse, I would be understood to mean that notice which the mind takes of its own operations, and the manner of them, by reason whereof there come to be ideas of these operations in the understanding. These two, I say, viz., external material things as the objects of sensation, and the operations of our own minds within as the objects of reflection, are, to me, the only originals from whence all our ideas take their beginnings. The term "operations" here, I use in a large sense, as comprehending not barely the actions of the mind about its ideas, but some sort of passions arising sometimes from them, such as is the satisfaction or uneasiness arising from any thought.

5. *All our ideas are of the one or the other of these.*—The understanding seems to me not to have the least glimmering of any ideas which it doth not receive from one of these two. External objects furnish the mind with the ideas of sensible qualities, which are all those different perceptions they produce in us; and the mind furnishes the understanding with ideas of its own operations.

These, when we have taken a full survey of them, and their several modes, combinations, and relations, we shall find to contain all our whole stock of ideas; and that we have nothing in our minds which did not come in one of these two ways. Let any one examine his own thoughts, and thoroughly search into his understanding, and then let him tell me, whether all the original ideas he has there, are any other than of the objects of his senses, or of the operations of his mind considered as objects of his reflection; and how great a mass of knowledge soever he imagines to be lodged there, he will, upon taking a strict view, see that he has not any idea in his mind but what one of these two hath imprinted, though perhaps with infinite variety compounded and enlarged by the understanding, as we shall see hereafter. . . .

OF KNOWLEDGE IN GENERAL

1. Our knowledge conversant about our ideas.—Since the mind, in all its thoughts and reasonings, hath no other immediate object but its own ideas, which it alone does or can contemplate, it is evident that our knowledge is only conversant about them.

2. Knowledge is the perception of the agreement or disagreement of two ideas.—Knowledge then seems to me to be nothing but the perception of the connection and agreement or disagreement and

repugnancy, of any of our ideas. In this alone it consists. Where this perception is, there is knowledge; and where it is not, there, though we may fancy, guess, or believe, yet we always come short of knowledge. For, when we know that white is not black, what do we else but perceive that these two ideas do not agree? When we possess ourselves with the utmost security of the demonstration that the three angles of a triangle are equal to two right ones, what do we more but perceive that equality to two right ones does necessarily agree to, and is inseparable from the three angles of a triangle?

3. This agreement fourfold.—But to understand a little more distinctly, wherein this agreement or disagreement consists, I think we may reduce it all to these four sorts: (1.) Identity, or diversity. (2.) Relation. (3.) Co-existence, or necessary connection. (4.) Real existence. . . .

6. WITCH HUNTING

As mentioned earlier, the high intellectual caliber of the era did nothing to banish the prevalence of witches which seems to have troubled Europe since the high Middle Ages. Superstition was rife, but superstition was coterminous with faith. As the eminent seventeenth-century divine, Joseph Glanvill, had pointed out, if you do not believe in witches you do not believe in spirits; if you do not believe in spirits, you do not believe in angels; if you do not believe in angels, you do not believe in God. Since all believed in God, all believed in devils and their fellow-traveling witches. The persecution of the devil's fifth column on earth culminated in a series of semi-hysterical panics that terrorized western Europe from Scotland to Bohemia, and even impinged on the attention of Cardinal de Richelieu (see A. Huxley, *The Devils of Loudun*) and Louis XIV, one of whose mistresses, Mme. de Montespan, was involved in a lurid and complicated scandal.

Persecutions for witchcraft continued to take place through most of the eighteenth century too. In England the last execution for this crime seems to have been carried out in 1684, but in Scotland a woman was burnt for it as late as 1727. European countries were slower to lose the habit; in 1749, a high-born nun was executed for witchcraft at Würzburg; six years later a young adventurer called Casanova was imprisoned by the Inquisition at Venice on a charge of magic, but escaped. He was luckier than the two witches burnt at Glarus, Switzerland, in 1782 and the two who suffered a similar fate in Poland eleven years later, when the Revolution had already triumphed in France. But these were the last it would seem; witches and the fear of witches endured, but the growth of skepticism meant that the law and authorities no longer countenanced superstition. John Wesley had foreseen the dire consequences of such skeptical tolerance: "It is true," he noted in his *Journal* (Vol. V, p. 375, 1768), "that the English have given up all accounts of witches and apparitions as mere old wives' fables. I am sorry for it. . . . Infidels have hooted witchcraft out of the world. . . . They well know (whether Christians know it or not) that the giving up of witchcraft is in effect giving up the Bible." However, we know that such dangerous skepticism did not long endure and, like the poor, witches of one sort or another are always with us.

The first and briefest of the selections below relates to the witch hunts which took place in the second half of the sixteenth century in the Rhenish domains of the Elector-Archbishop of Trier. The subsequent selections are self-explanatory.

The Witch-Persecution at Trier

Inasmuch as it was popularly believed that the continued sterility of many years was caused by witches through the malice of the Devil, the whole country rose to exterminate the witches. This movement was promoted by many in office, who hoped for wealth from the persecution. And so, from court to court throughout the towns and villages of all the diocese, scurried special accusers, inquisitors, notaries, jurors, judges, constables, dragging to trial and torture human beings of both sexes and burning them in great numbers. Scarcely any of those who were accused escaped punishment. Nor were there spared even the leading men in the city of Trier. For the Judge, with two Burgomasters, several Councilors and Associate Judges, canons of sundry collegiate churches, parish-priests, rural deans, were swept away in this ruin. So far, at length, did the madness of the furious populace and of the courts go in this thirst for blood and booty that there was scarcely anybody who was not smirched by some suspicion of this crime.

Meanwhile notaries, copyists, and innkeepers grew rich. The executioner rode a blooded horse, like a noble of the court, and went clad in gold and silver; his wife vied with noble dames in the richness of her array. The children of those convicted and punished were sent into exile; their goods were confiscated; plowman and vintner failed—hence came sterility. A direr pestilence or a more ruthless invader could hardly have ravaged the territory of Trier than this inquisition and persecution without bounds: many were the reasons for doubting that all were really guilty. This persecution lasted for several years; and some of those who presided over the administration of justice gloried in the multitude of the stakes, at each of which a human being had been given to the flames.

At last, though the flames were still unsated, the people grew impoverished,

All of witch-hunting documents from *Translations and Reprints*, Vol. 3, No. 4, G. L. Burr, Ed.

rules were made and enforced restricting the fees and costs of examinations and examiners, and suddenly, as when in war funds fail, the zeal of the persecutors died out.

The Witch-Persecution at Bamberg

On Wednesday, June 28, 1628, was examined without torture, Johannes Junius, Burgomaster at Bamberg, on the charge of witchcraft: how and in what fashion he had fallen into that vice. Is fifty-five years old, and was born at Niederwaysich in the Wetterau. Says he is wholly innocent, knows nothing of the crime, has never in his life renounced God; says that he is wronged before God and the world, would like to hear of a single human being who has seen him at such gatherings [as the witch-sabbaths].

Confrontation of Dr. Georg Adam Haan. Tells him to his face he will stake his life on it [er wolle darauf leben und sterben], that he saw him, Junius, a year and a half ago at a witch-gathering in the electoral council-room, where they ate and drank. Accused denies the same wholly.

Confronted with Hopffens Elsse. Tells him likewise that he was on Haupts-moor at a witch-dance; but first the holy wafer was desecrated. Junius denies. Hereupon he was told that his accomplices had confessed against him and was given time for thought.

On Friday, June 30, 1628, the aforesaid Junius was again without torture exhorted to confess, but again confessed nothing, whereupon, . . . since he would confess nothing, he was put to the torture, and first the

Thumb-screws were applied. Says he has never denied God his Savior nor suffered himself to be otherwise baptized; will again stake his life on it; feels no pain in the thumb-screws.

Leg-screws. Will confess absolutely nothing; knows nothing about it. He has never renounced God; will never do such a thing; has never been guilty of this vice; feels likewise no pain.

Is stripped and examined; on his right side is found a bluish mark, like a clover leaf, is thrice pricked therein, but feels no pain and no blood flows out.

Strappado. He has never renounced God; God will not forsake him; if he were such a wretch he would not let himself be so tortured; God must show some token of his innocence. He knows nothing about witchcraft . . .

On July 5, the above named Junius is without torture, but with urgent persuasions, exhorted to confess, and at last begins and confesses:

When in the year 1624 his law-suit at Rothweil cost him some six hundred florins, he had gone out, in the month of August, into his orchard at Friedrichsbronnen; and, as he sat there in thought, there had come to him a woman like a grass-maid, who had asked him why he sat there so sorrowful; he had answered that he was not despondent, but she had led him by seductive speeches to yield him to her will. . . . And thereafter this wench had changed into the form of a goat, which bleated and said, "Now you see with whom you have had to do. You must be mine or I will forthwith break your neck." Thereupon he had been frightened, and trembled all over for fear. Then the transformed spirit had seized him by the throat and demanded that he should renounce God Almighty, where-upon Junius said, "God forbid," and there-upon the spirit vanished through the pow-er of these words. Yet it came straightway back, brought more people with it, and persistently demanded of him that he re-nounce God in Heaven and all the heav-enly host, by which terrible threatening he was obliged to speak this formula: "I renounce God in Heaven and his host, and will henceforward recognize the Devil as my God."

After the renunciation he was so far persuaded by those present and by the evil spirit that he suffered himself to be otherwise baptized in the evil spirit's name. The Morhauptin had given him a ducat as dower-gold, which afterward be-came only a potsherd.

He was then named Krix. His para-mour he had to call Vixen. Those present had congratulated him in Beelzebub's name and said that they were now all alike. At this baptism of his there were among others the aforesaid Christiana Morhauptin, the young Geiserlin, Paul Glaser, [and others]. After this they had dispersed.

At this time his paramour had prom-ised to provide him with money, and from time to time to take him to other witch-gatherings. . . . Whenever he wished to ride forth [to the witch-sabbath] a black dog had come before his bed, which said to him that he must go with him, whereupon he had seated himself upon the dog and the dog had raised himself in the Devil's name and so had fared forth.

About two years ago he was taken to the electoral council-room, at the left hand as one goes in. Above at a table were seated the Chancellor, the Burgomaster Neydekher, Dr. Georg Haan, (and many others). Since his eyes were not good, he could not recognize more persons.

More time for consideration was now given him. On July 7, the aforesaid Jun-ius was again examined, to know what further had occurred to him to confess. He confesses that about two months ago, on the day after an execution was held, he was at a witch-dance at the Black Cross, where Beelzebub had shown him-self to them all and said expressly to their faces that they must all be burned to-gether on this spot, and had ridiculed and taunted those present. . . .

Of crimes. His paramour had immedi-ately after his seduction demanded that he should make away with his youngest son Hans Georg, and had given him for this purpose a gray powder; this, how-ever, being too hard for him, he had made away with his horse, a brown, instead.

His paramour had also often spurred him on to kill his daughter. . . . and because he would not do this he had been maltreated with blows by the evil spirit.

Once at the suggestion of his paramour he had taken the holy wafer out of his mouth and given it to her. . . .

A week before his arrest as he was go-ing to St. Martin's church the Devil met him on the way in the form of a goat, and told him that he would soon be im-prisoned, but that he should not trouble himself—he would soon set him free. Besides this, by his soul's salvation, he knew nothing further; but what he had spoken was the pure truth; on that he would stake his life. On August 6, 1628, there was read to the aforesaid Junius this his confession, which he then wholly ratified and confirmed, and was willing to stake his life upon it. And afterward he voluntarily confirmed the same before the court.

So ended the trial of Junius, and he was accordingly burnt at the stake. But it so happens that there is also preserved in Bamberg a letter, in quivering hand, secretly written by him to his daughter while in the midst of his trial (July 24, 1628):

Many hundred thousand good nights, dearly beloved daughter Veronica. Innocent have I come into prison, innocent have I been tortured, innocent must I die. For whoever comes into the witch prison must become a witch or be tortured until he invents something out of his head—and God pity him—bethinks him of something. I will tell you how it has gone with me. When I was the first time put to the torture, Dr. Baum, Dr. Kotzendorffer, and two strange doctors were there. Then Dr. Braun asks me, "Kinsman, how come you here?" I answer, "Through falsehood, through misfortune." "Hear, you," he says, "You are a witch; will you confess it voluntarily? If not, we'll bring in witnesses and the executioner for you." I said, "I am no witch. I have a pure conscience in the matter; if there are a thousand witnesses, I am not anxious, but I'll gladly hear the witnesses." Now the Chancellor's son was set before me . . . and afterward Hopffens Elsse. She had seen me dance on Haupts-moor. . . . I answered: "I have never renounced God, and will never do it—God graciously keep me from it. I'll rather bear whatever I must." And then came also—God in highest Heaven have mercy—the executioner, and put the thumb-screws on me, both hands bound together, so that the blood ran out at the nails and everywhere, so that for four weeks I could not use my hands, as you can see from the writing. . . . Thereafter they first stripped me, bound my hands behind me, and drew me up in the torture. Then I thought heaven

and earth were at an end; eight times did they draw me up and let me fall again, so that I suffered terrible agony. . . .

And this happened on Friday, June 30, and with God's help I had to bear the torture. . . . When at last the executioner led me back into the prison, he said to me: "Sir, I beg you, for God's sake confess something, whether it be true or not. Invent something, for you cannot endure the torture which you will be put to; and, even if you bear it all, yet you will not escape, not even if you were an earl, but one torture will follow after another until you say you are a witch. Not before that," he said, "will they let you go, as you may see by all their trials, for one is just like another." . . .

And so I begged, since I was in wretched plight, to be given one day for thought and a priest. The priest was refused me, but the time for thought was given. Now, my dear child, see in what hazard I stood and still stand. I must say that I am a witch, though I am not,—must now renounce God, though I have never done it before. Day and night I was deeply troubled, but at last there came to me a new idea. I would not be anxious, but, since I had been given no priest with whom I could take counsel, I would myself think of something and say it. It were surely better that I just say it with mouth and words, even though I had not really done it; and afterwards I would confess it to the priest, and let those answer for it who compel me to do it. . . . And so I made my confession, as follows; but it was all a lie.

Now follows, dear child, what I confessed in order to escape the great anguish and bitter torture, which it was impossible for me longer to bear.

Here follows his confession, substantially as it is given in the minutes of his trial. But he adds:

Then I had to tell what people I had seen [at the witch-sabbath]. I said that I had not recognized them. "You old rascal, I must set the executioner at you. Say—was not the Chancellor there?" So I said yes. "Who besides?" I had not recognized anybody. So he said: "Take one street after another; begin at the market, go out on one street and back on the next." I had to name several persons there. Then came the long street. I knew nobody. Had to name eight persons there. Then the Zinkenwert—one person more. Then over the upper bridge to the Georgthor, on both sides. Knew nobody again. Did I know nobody in the castle—whoever it might be, I should speak without fear. And thus continuously they asked me on all the streets, though I could not and would not say more. So they gave me to the executioner, told him to strip me, shave me all over, and put me to the torture. "The rascal knows one on the market-place, is with him daily, and yet won't name him." By that they meant Dietmeyer: so I had to name him too.

Then I had to tell what crimes I had committed. I said nothing. . . . "Draw the rascal up!" So I said that I was to kill my children, but I had killed a horse instead. It did not help. I had also taken a sacred wafer, and had desecrated it. When I had said this, they left me in peace.

Now, dear child, here you have all my confession, for which I must die. And they are sheer lies and made-up things, so help me God. For all this I was forced to say through fear of the torture which was threatened beyond what I had already endured. For they never leave off with the torture till one confesses something; be he never so good, he must be a witch. Nobody escapes, though he were an earl. . . .

Dear child, keep this letter secret so that people do not find it, else I shall be tortured most piteously and the jailers will be beheaded. So strictly is it forbidden. . . . Dear child, pay this man a dollar. . . . I have taken several days to write this: my hands are both lame. I am in a sad plight.

Good night, for your father Johannes Junius will never see you more. July 24, 1628.

And on the margin of the letter he added:

Dear child, six have confessed against me at once: the Chancellor, his son, Neudecker, Zaner, Hoffmaisters Ursel, and Hopffens Elsse—all false, through compulsion, as they have all told me, and begged my forgiveness in God's name before they were executed. . . . They know nothing but good of me. They were forced to say it, just as I myself was. . . .

The Methods of the Witch-Persecutions

It was in Franconia, during the persecutions just above described, that the noble Jesuit poet, Friedrich von Spee, was made the confessor of those sentenced to death for witchcraft and was thus inspired to write (though anonymously) the book whose eloquent protest gave the persecution throughout Europe its first effective check. Not till long afterward did the philosopher Leibnitz reveal its authorship, on the authority of his friend Johann Philipp von Schonborn, Archbishop of Mainz, who as a boy at Würzburg had known and loved Father Spee and had learned from him the whole story in answer to a question as to the young father's whitened hair. The last of the fifty-one doubts into which Spee's *Cautio criminalis* (Rintein, 1631) is divided runs thus (Burr's note):

WHAT, NOW, IS THE OUTLINE AND METHOD OF THE TRIALS AGAINST WITCHES TO-DAY IN GENERAL USE? — A THING WORTHY OF GERMANY'S CONSIDERATION.

I answer: . . .

1. Incredible among us Germans and especially (I blush to say it) among Catholics are the popular superstition, envy, calumnies, backbitings, insinuations, and the like, which, being neither punished by the magistrates nor refuted by the pulpit, first stir up suspicion of witchcraft. All the divine judgments which God has threatened in Holy Writ are now ascribed to witches. No longer do God or nature do aught, but witches everything.

2. Hence it comes that all at once everybody is clamoring that the magistrates proceed against the witches—those witches whom only their own clamor has made seem so many.

3. Princes, therefore, bid their judges and counselors to begin proceedings against the witches.

4. These at first do not know where to begin, since they have no testimony or proofs, and since their conscience clearly tells them that they ought not to proceed in this rashly.

5. Meanwhile they are a second time and a third admonished to proceed. The multitude clamors that there is something suspicious in this delay; and the same suspicion is, by one busybody or another, instilled into the ear of the princes.

6. To offend these, however, and not to defer at once to their wishes, is in Germany a serious matter: most men, and even clergymen, approve with zeal whatever is but pleasing to the princes, not heeding by whom these (however good by nature) are often instigated.

7. At last, therefore, the judges yield to their wishes, and in some way contrive at length a starting-point for the trials.

8. Or, if they still hold out and dread to touch the ticklish matter, there is sent to them a commissioner [Inquisitor] especially deputed for this. And, even if he brings to his task something of inexperience or of ardor, as is wont to happen in things human, this takes on in this field another color and name, and is counted only zeal for justice. This zeal for justice is no whit diminished by the prospect of gain, especially in the case of a commissioner of slender means and avaricious, with a large family, when there is granted him as salary so many dollars per head for each witch burned.

besides the fees and assessments which he is allowed to extort at will from the peasants.

9. If now some utterance of a demoniac or some malign and idle rumor then current (for proof of the scandal is never asked) points especially to some poor and helpless Gaia, she is the first to suffer.

10. And yet, lest it appear that she is indicted on the basis of rumor alone, without other proofs, as the phrase goes, lo a certain presumption is at once obtained against her by posing the following dilemma: Either Gaia has led a bad and improper life, or she has led a good and proper one. If a bad one, then, say they, the proof is cogent against her; for from malice to malice the presumption is strong. If, however, she has led a good one, this also is none the less a proof; for thus, they say, are witches wont to cloak themselves and try to seem especially proper.

11. Therefore it is ordered that Gaia be haled away to prison. And lo now a new proof is gained against her by this other dilemma: Either she then shows fear or she does not show it. If she does show it (hearing forsooth of the grievous tortures wont to be used in this matter), this is of itself a proof; for conscience, they say accuses her. If she does not show it (trusting forsooth in her innocence), this too is a proof; for it is most characteristic of witches, they say, to pretend themselves peculiarly innocent and wear a bold front.

12. Lest, however, further proofs against her should be lacking, the Commissioner has his own creatures, often depraved and notorious, who question into all her past life. This, of course, cannot be done without coming upon some saying or doing of hers which evil-minded men can easily twist or distort into ground for suspicion of witchcraft.

13. If, too, there are any who have borne her ill will, these, having now a fine opportunity to do her harm, bring against her such charges as it may please them to devise; and on every side there is a clamor that the evidence is heavy against her.

14. And so, as soon as possible, she is hurried to the torture, if indeed she be not subjected to it on the very day of her arrest, as often happens.

15. For in these trials there is granted to nobody an advocate or any means of fair defense, for the cry is that the crime is an expected one, and whoever ventures to defend the prisoner is brought into suspicion of the crime—as are all those who dare to utter a protest in these cases and to urge the judges to caution; for they are forthwith dubbed patrons of the witches. Thus all mouths are closed and all pens blunted, lest they speak or write.

16. In general, however, that it may not seem that no opportunity of defense has been given to Gaia, she is brought out and the proofs are first read before her and examined—if examination it can be called.

17. But, even though she then denies these and satisfactorily makes answer to each, this is neither paid attention to nor even noted down: all the proofs retain their force and value, however perfect her answer to them. She is only ordered back into prison, there to bethink herself more carefully whether she will persist in her obstinacy—for, since she has denied her guilt, she is obstinate.

18. When she has bethought herself, she is next day brought out again, and there is read to her the sentence of torture —just as if she had before answered

nothing to the charges, and refuted nothing.

19. Before she is tortured, however, she is led aside by the executioner, and lest she may by magical means have fortified herself against pain, she is searched, her whole body being shaved, . . . although up to this time nothing of the sort was ever found. . . .

21. Then, when Gaia has thus been searched and shaved, she is tortured that she may confess the truth, that is to say, that she may simply declare herself guilty; for whatever else she may say will not be the truth and cannot be.

22. She is, however, tortured with the torture of the first degree, i.e., the less severe. This is to be understood thus: that, although in itself it is exceeding severe, yet, compared with others to follow, it is lighter. Wherefore, if she confesses, they say and noise it abroad that she has confessed without torture.

23. Now, what prince or other dignitary who hears this can doubt that she is most certainly guilty who thus voluntarily without torture confesses her guilt?

24. Without any scruples, therefore, after this confession she is executed. Yet she would have been executed, nevertheless, even though she had not confessed; for when once a beginning has been made with the torture, the die is already cast —she cannot escape, she must die.

25. So, whether she confesses or does not confess, the result is the same. If she confesses, the thing is clear, for, as I have said and as is self-evident, she is executed: all recantation is in vain, as I have shown above. If she does not confess, the torture is repeated—twice, thrice, four times: anything one pleases is permissible, for in an excepted crime there is no limit of duration or severity or repetition of the tortures. As to this, think the

judges, no sin is possible which can be brought up before the tribunal of conscience.

26. If now Gaia, no matter how many times tortured, has not yet broken silence, —if she contorts her features under the pain, if she loses consciousness, or the like, then they cry that she is laughing or has bewitched herself into taciturnity, and hence deserves to be burned alive, as lately has been done to some who though several times tortured would not confess.

27. And then they say—even clergymen and confessors—that she died obstinate and impenitent, that she would not be converted or desert her paramour, but kept rather her faith with him.

28. If, however, it chances that under so many tortures one dies, they say that her neck has been broken by the Devil.

29. Wherefore justly, forsooth, the corpse is dragged out by the executioner and buried under the gallows.

30. But if, on the other hand, Gaia does not die and some exceptionally scrupulous judge hesitates to torture her further without fresh proofs or to burn her without a confession, she is kept in prison and more harshly fettered, and there lies for perhaps an entire year to rot until she is subdued.

31. For it is never possible to clear herself by withstanding and thus to wash away the aspersion of crime, as is the intention of the laws. It would be a disgrace to her examiners if when once arrested she should thus go free. Guilty must she be, by fair means or foul, whom they have once but thrown into bonds.

32. Meanwhile, both then and earlier, they send to her ignorant and headstrong priests, more importunate than the executioners themselves. It is the business of these to harass in every wise the wretched

creature to such a degree that, whether truly or not, she will at last confess herself guilty; unless she does so, they declare, she simply cannot be saved, nor share in the sacraments.

33. The greatest care is taken lest there be admitted to her priests more thoughtful and learned, who have aught of insight or kindliness; as also that nobody visits her prison who might give her counsel or inform the ruling princes. For there is nothing so much dreaded by any of them as that in some way the innocence of any of the accused should be brought to light. . .

34. In the meantime, while Gaia, as I have said, is still held in prison, and is tormented by those whom it least behooves, there are not wanting to her industrious judges clever devices by which they not only find new proofs against Gaia, but by which moreover they so convict her to her face (an 't please the gods!) that by the advice of some university faculty she is then at last pronounced to deserve burning alive. . . . .

35. Some, however, to leave no stone unturned, order Gaia to be exorcised and transferred to a new place, and then to be tortured again, in the hope that by this exorcism and change of place the bewitchment of taciturnity may perhaps be broken. But, if not even this succeeds, then at last they commit her alive to the flames. Now in Heaven's name, I would like to know, since both she who confesses and she who does not, perish alike, what way of escape there is for any, however innocent? O unhappy Gaia, why hast thou rashly hoped? why hast thou not, at first entering prison, declared thyself guilty? why, O foolish woman and mad, wilt thou die so many times when thou mightst die but once? Follow my counsel, and before all pain declare thyself guilty

and die. Thou wilt not escape; for this were a disgrace to the zeal of Germany.

36. If, now, any under stress of pain has once falsely declared herself guilty, her wretched plight beggars description. For not only is there in general no door for her escape, but she is also compelled to accuse others, of whom she knows no ill, and whose names are not seldom suggested to her by her examiners or by the executioner, or of whom she has heard as suspected or accused or already once arrested and released. These in their turn are forced to accuse others, and these still others, and so it goes on: who can help seeing that it must go on without end?

37. Wherefore the judges themselves are obliged at last either to break off the trials and so condemn their own work or else to burn their own folk, aye themselves and everybody: for on all soon or late false accusations fall, and, if only followed by the torture, all are proved guilty.

38. And so at last those are brought in question who at the outset most loudly clamored for the constant feeding of the flames; for they rashly failed to foresee that their turn, too, must inevitably come —and by a just verdict of heaven, since with their pestilent tongues they created us so many witches and sent so many innocent to the flames.

39. But now gradually many of the wiser and more learned begin to take notice of it, and, as if aroused from deep sleep, to open their eyes and slowly and cautiously to bestir themselves. . . .

46. From all which there follows this corollary, worthy to be noted in red ink: that, if only the trials be steadily pushed on with, there is nobody in our day, of whatsoever sex, fortune, rank or dignity who is safe, if he have but an enemy and slanderer to bring him into suspicion of witchcraft. . .

V. The Political Debate

In the great orderly pattern of seventeenth-century thought, one thing still remained to be settled: the nature and justification of political authority. In the Middle Ages this had rested with God and been shared equally between God's representatives on earth—the Pope and the Prince. With the Reformation, this ideal equilibrium had been broken: where only one pope had reigned before, now there were several, each claiming ultimate religious authority for his version of God's will and revelation. The result of this was a growth in the power of princes at the expense of the Church. Where, once upon a time, religious authority had provided the sanction of political power, under the new dispensation political authority guaranteed and reinforced this or that form of religion. By a natural evolution, it came to be argued that the prince was the ultimately significant representative of God on earth, ruling his country by divine right and dispensation. This was the thesis of Bossuet, but it was challenged by a rival theory based on a justification more immediate and worldly than the will of God: the contract.

The contract theory of government, which appealed to the common sense of an increasingly businesslike public, presented society as the result of an agreement between its members, and the political form of society, its system of government, as arising out of a similar agreement. The contract theory was not necessarily more liberal than that of divine right: the king of Hobbes is a less restrained and probably a harsher ruler than that of Bossuet. But, in the hands of Locke, the logical implications of contractual relationships were carried to revolutionary conclusions: a contract was seen for what it had always been—an undertaking with mutual obligations binding on both parties and sanctions for failure to carry out its terms—and the new view severely shook the firm, unquestioned basis of monarchial power.

1. BOSSUET

Jacques Bénigne Bossuet (1627–1704), bishop of Meaux, was one of the great orators and polemicists of the reign of Louis XIV. Appointed tutor to the Dauphin, the King's heir, Bossuet wrote for his edification a series of works expounding the divine rights and God-appointed duties of kings. The following passages are taken from one of these, the *Treatise on Politics, Based on the Very Words of Holy Writ,* most of which was composed in 1678.

472

On the Nature and the Properties of Royal Authority

Firstly, royal authority is sacred; secondly, it is paternal; thirdly, it is absolute; fourthly, it is subject to reason.

God establishes kings as his ministers, and reigns through them over the peoples. We have already seen that all power comes from God. The Prince, adds Saint Paul, "is a minister of God to thee for good. But if thou do that which is evil, be afraid; for he beareth not the sword in vain: for he is a minister of God, an avenger for wrath to him that doeth evil." So princes act as ministers of God and his lieutenants on earth. It is through them that He rules His empire. This is why we have seen that the royal throne is not the throne of a man, but the throne of God Himself. Nor is it peculiar to the Jews alone to have kings appointed by God. . . . He governs all peoples, and gives kings to all.

It appears from all this that the person of the king is sacred, and that it is a sacrilege to attack him. God has His prophets anoint them with a sacred unction, as He has His pontiffs and His altars anointed. But, even without the external application of this unction, their charge renders them sacred, as being the representatives of the divine majesty, delegated by His providence to the execution of His designs. It is thus that God Himself speaks of Cyrus as His anointed— "his right hand I have holden to subdue nations before him." The title of Christ is given to kings; and everywhere we see them called the Christ, or the anointed of the Lord.

Translated by the editor.

Kings must be guarded as being sacred; and he who neglects to guard them deserves to die. He who guards the life of the prince, places his own in the safekeeping of God.

Saint Paul, after having said that the prince is the minister of God, concludes thus: "Wherefore Ye must needs be in subjection, not only because of the wrath, but also for conscience's sake." . . . And again, "servants, obey in all things your temporal masters and whatsoever Ye do, do it heartily as to the Lord, and not as unto men." If the apostle speaks thus of servitude, which is an unnatural condition; what should we think of legitimate subjection to princes and to the magistrates who are the protectors of public liberty? This is why Saint Peter says, "submit yourselves to every ordinance of man for the Lord's sake: whether it be to the king as supreme, or unto governors, as unto them that are sent by him for the punishment of evildoers and for the praise of them that do well." And, even if they did not carry out their duty, we must respect in them their charge and their ministry. "Servants, be subject to your masters with all fear; not only to the good and gentle, but also to the froward and unjust." There is thus a religious character about the respect we show to the prince. The service of God and the respect for kings are one; and Saint Peter puts these two duties together: "Fear God; honor the king." . . . Indeed, God has infused something of divinity into princes: "I have said Ye are Gods; and all of you are children of the Most High."

The kings must respect their own power and use it only to the public good.

Their power coming from above, as we have said, they must not believe that it belongs to them to be used as they please; but they must use it with fear and restraint, as a thing which comes from God and for which God will call them to account. Kings should therefore tremble when using the power that God has given them, and think how horrible is the sacrilege of misusing a power which comes from God.

THE ROYAL AUTHORITY IS PATERNAL, AND ITS INHERENT CHARACTER IS GOODNESS

We have seen that kings take the place of God, who is the true father of all mankind. We have also seen that the first idea of power arrived at by men is that of paternal power; and that kings have been made on the model of fathers. Also, everybody agrees that the obedience which is due to the public power is to be found, in the Ten Commandments, in the commandment which obliges men to honor their parents. From all this, it follows that the title of king is the title of a father, and that goodness is the most natural characteristic of kings.

Because God is great and sufficient unto Himself, He turns, so to speak, entirely towards doing good to men, according to the word: "As is His greatness, so is His compassion." He places an image of His greatness in kings in order to force them to imitate His goodness. He raises them to a level where they have nothing more to desire for themselves. We have heard David saying: "What can Your servant add to all the greatness with which You have clothed him?"

THE ROYAL AUTHORITY IS ABSOLUTE

In order to render this idea odious and unbearable, many pretend to confuse absolute government with arbitrary government. But there are no two more dissimilar things. . . . The prince need render no account to anyone for the orders he gives. "I counsel thee to keep the king's commandment and that in regard to the oath of God. Be not hasty to go out of his sight: stand not in an evil thing; for he does whatsoever pleases him. Where the word of a king is, there is power; and who may say unto him, What dost thou?" Without this absolute authority the king can do no good, nor punish evil; his power must be such that no one can hope to escape it.

Men must therefore obey princes as they obey justice itself, without which there can be no order or purpose in things. They are Gods, and share in a fashion the divine independence: "I have said Ye are Gods. . . ." There is only God who can judge their judgements and their persons. "God standeth in the congregation of the mighty; He judgeth among the Gods."

THE ROYAL AUTHORITY MUST BE INVINCIBLE

If there is in a State any authority which can stand in the path of public power and embarrass it in its exercise, no one is safe.

If the prince himself, who is the judge of judges, fears powerful men, what stability could there be in the State? It is therefore necessary that authority should be invincible, and that nothing should be able to breach the rampart behind which the public peace and private weal are safe.

OF MAJESTY

Majesty is the reflection of the greatness of God in the prince. God is infinite, God is all. The prince, as a prince, is not regarded as a private individual: he is a public figure, the whole State rests in him; the will of the whole people is comprehended in his. Just as all perfection and all virtue are concentrated in God, so all the power of private individuals is concentrated in the person of the prince. What greatness, that one man should carry so much! The power of God makes itself felt in an instant from one end of the world to the other: the royal power acts in the same way throughout the whole kingdom. It keeps the whole kingdom in being, as God keeps the whole world. If God were to withdraw His hand, the world would fall back into nothingness: if authority ceased in the kingdom, everything would be confusion.

Now, put together all the great and august things that we have said on the subject of royal authority. See a great people united in one person: see this sacred, paternal, and absolute power: see the secret purpose which governs the whole body of the State comprehended in one head: you see the image of God in the kings; and you get an idea of royal majesty. . . . God is holiness itself, goodness itself, power itself, reason itself. The majesty of God is in these things. The majesty of the prince is in the image of these things. This majesty is so great that its source cannot be in the prince; it is borrowed from God who gives it to him for the good of the peoples, for whom it is salutary that they should be held in by a superior power.

There is something divine about a prince, which inspires the peoples with fear.

Therefore, use your power boldly, oh, kings! For it is divine and salutary to mankind; but use it with humility. You are endowed with it from outside. Fundamentally, it leaves you weak; it leaves you mortal; it leaves you sinners; and burdens you with greater responsibility towards God.

ON THE OBEDIENCE DUE TO THE PRINCE

The subjects owe unlimited obedience to the prince. If the prince is not punctually obeyed, the public order is overthrown and there is no more unity, and consequently no more cooperation or peace in a State.

Open godlessness, and even persecution, do not absolve the subjects from the obedience they owe to princes. The character of royalty is holy and sacred, even in infidel princes; and we have seen that Isaiah calls Cyrus "the anointed of the Lord." Nebuchadnezzar was godless, and proud to the point of wanting to equal God and put to death those who refused him a sacrilegious worship; and nevertheless Daniel addresses him thus: "You are the king of kings: and the God of Heavens has given you the kingdom and the power and the empire and the glory."

The subjects may oppose to the violence of princes only respectful remonstrances, without murmurs or rebellion, and prayers for their conversion.

If God does not hearken to the prayers of His faithful; if in order to try and chasten His children He permits their persecution to grow worse, they must then remember that Jesus Christ has "sent them as lambs in the midst of wolves." Here is a truly holy doctrine, truly worthy of Jesus Christ and of His disciples.

ON THE DUTIES OF THE PRINCE

The purpose of government is the welfare and conservation of the State. . . .

The good constitution of the body of the State consists in two things: religion and justice. These are the internal and constitutive principles of States. By the one we render to God what is owed to Him, and by the other we render to men that which they deserve. . . . The prince must employ his authority to destroy false religion in his State.

The prince is the minister of God: "He beareth not the sword in vain: for he is a revenger to execute wrath upon him that doeth evil." He is the protector of the public peace which is based upon religion; and he must maintain his throne, of which, as we have seen, religion is the foundation. Those who will not suffer the prince to act strictly in religious matters, because religion should be free, make an impious error. Otherwise, one would have to tolerate in all the subjects and in all the country idolatry, mohammedanism, judaism, any false religions; blasphemy, even atheism, and the greatest crimes would be the least punished.

2. HOBBES: THE LEVIATHAN

Thomas Hobbes (1588–1679) was born and brought up an Elizabethan and died at ninety-one under the Restoration. As tutor to the noble Cavendish family and as a scholar in his own right, he traveled widely, meeting many of the greatest minds of his time. Friend of Ben Jonson, Bacon, and Galileo, he knew and argued with Descartes. The troubles of the Civil War drove him to Paris, where he lived from 1641 to 1652. In 1647 he was appointed tutor to the Prince of Wales, but the future Charles II had to break the relationship when the publication of *The Leviathan* in 1651 shocked too many people. It nevertheless remains one of the most thorough —and perhaps, therefore, thoroughly depressing—analyses of the motives and patterns of political behavior.

The extreme authoritarianism of Hobbes has been attributed to the natural timidity of a man whose mother may have been frightened by the Spanish Armada, and whom the Civil War persuaded that anything was better than disorder.

OF THE NATURAL CONDITION OF MANKIND AS CONCERNING THEIR FELICITY AND MISERY

Nature hath made men so equal, in the faculties of the body and mind; as that though there be found one man sometimes manifestly stronger in body, or of quicker mind than another, yet when all is reckoned together, the difference between man and man, is not so considerable, as that one man can thereupon

From Thomas Hobbes, *The Leviathan* (London, n. d.), pp. 63–65, 82–88.

claim to himself any benefit, to which another may not pretend, as well as he. For as to the strength of body, the weakest has strength enough to kill the strongest, either by secret machination, or by confederacy with others, that are in the same danger with himself.

And as to the faculties of the mind, setting aside the arts grounded upon words, and especially that skill of proceeding upon general and infallible rules, called science; which very few have, and but in few things; as being not a native faculty, born with us; nor attained, as prudence, while we look after somewhat else, I find yet a greater equality amongst men than that of strength. For prudence is but experience; which equal time equally bestows on all men, in those things they equally apply themselves unto. That which may perhaps make such equality incredible, is but a vain concept of one's own wisdom, which almost all men think they have in a greater degree than the vulgar; that is, than all men but themselves, and a few others, whom by fame or for concurring with themselves, they approve. For such is the nature of men, that howsoever they may acknowledge many others to be more witty, or more eloquent, or more learned; yet they will hardly believe there be many so wise as themselves; for they see their own wit at hand, and other men's at a distance. But this proveth rather that men are in that point equal, than unequal. For there is not ordinarily a greater sign of the equal distribution of anything, than that every man is contented with his share.

From this equality of ability, ariseth equality of hope in the attaining of our ends. And therefore if any two men desire the same thing, which nevertheless they cannot both enjoy, they become enemies; and in the way to their end,

which is principally their own conservation, and sometimes their delectation only, endeavour to destroy or subdue one another. And from hence it comes to pass, that where an invader hath no more to fear than another man's single power; if one plant, sow, build, or possess a convenient seat, others may probably be expected to come prepared with forces united, to dispossess and deprive him, not only of the fruit of his labour, but also of his life or liberty. And the invader again is in the like danger of another.

And from this diffidence of one another, there is no way for any man to secure himself, so reasonable, as anticipation; that is, by force, or wiles, to master the persons of all men he can, so long, till he see no other power great enough to endanger him: and this is no more than his own conservation requireth, and is generally allowed. Also because there be some, that taking pleasure in contemplating their own power in the acts of conquest, which they pursue farther than their security requires; if others, that otherwise would be glad to be at least within modest bounds, should not by invasion increase their power, they would not be able, long time, by standing only on their defence, to subsist. And by consequence, such augmentation of dominion over men being necessary to a man's conservation, it ought to be allowed him.

Again, men have no pleasure, but on the contrary, a great deal of grief, in keeping company, where there is no power able to overawe them all. For every man looketh that his companion should value him, at the same rate he sets upon himself: and upon all signs of contempt, or undervaluing, naturally endeavours, as far as he dares (which amongst them that have no common power to keep them in quiet, is far enough to make them destroy each other), to extort a greater value from his contemners, by damage; and from others, by the example.

So that in the nature of man we find three principal causes of quarrel. First, competition; second, diffidence; thirdly, glory.

The first maketh men invade for gain; the second, for safety; and the third, for reputation. The first use violence, to make themselves masters of other men's persons, wives, children, and cattle; the second, to defend them; the third, for trifles, as a word, a smile, a different opinion, and any other sign of undervalue, either direct in their persons, or by reflection in their kindred, their friends, their nation, their profession, or their name.

Hereby it is manifest, that during the time men live without a common power to keep them all in awe, they are in that condition which is called war; and such a war, as is of every man, against every man. For "war" consisteth not in battle only, or the act of fighting, but in a tract of time, wherein the will to contend by battle is sufficiently known; and therefore the notion of "time" is to be considered in the nature of war, as it is in the nature of weather. For as the nature of foul weather lieth not in a shower or two of rain, but in an inclination thereto of many days together; so the nature of war consisteth not in actual fighting, but in the known disposition thereto during all the time there is no assurance to the contrary. All other time is "peace."

Whatsoever therefore is consequent to a time of war, where every man is enemy to every man, the same is consequent to the time wherein men live without other security than what their own strength and their own invention shall furnish them withal. In such condition there is no place for industry, because the fruit thereof is uncertain, and consequently no culture of the earth; no navigation, nor use of the commodities that may be imported by sea; no commodious building; no instruments of moving and removing such things as require much force; no knowledge of the face of the earth; no account of time; no arts; no letters; no society; and, which is worst of all, continual fear and danger of violent death; and the life of man, solitary, poor, nasty, brutish, and short.

It may seem strange to some man, that has not well weighed these things, that Nature should thus dissociate, and render men apt to invade, and destroy one another; and he may therefore, not trusting to this inference made from the passions, desire perhaps to have the same confirmed by experience. Let him therefore consider with himself, when taking a journey, he arms himself, and seeks to go well accompanied; when going to sleep, he locks his doors; when even in his house, he locks his chests; and this when he knows there be laws, and public officers, armed, to revenge all injuries shall be done him; what opinion he has of his fellow-subjects, when he rides armed; of his fellow citizens, when he locks his doors; and of his children and servants, when he locks his chests. Does he not there as much accuse man's nature in it? The desires and other passions of man are in themselves no sin. No more are the actions that proceed from those passions, till they know a law that forbids them; which till laws be made they cannot know, nor can any law be made till they have agreed upon the person that shall make it.

It may peradventure be thought there was never such a time nor condition of war as this; and I believe it was never generally so, over all the world, but there are many places where they live so now. For the savage people in many places of America, except the government of small families, the concord whereof dependeth on natural lust, have no government at all, and live at this day in that brutish manner, as I said before. Howsoever, it may be perceived where there were no common power to fear, by the manner of life which men that have formerly lived under a peaceful government, use to degenerate into a civil war.

But though there had never been any time, wherein particular men were in a condition of war one against another; yet in all times, kings, and persons of sovereign authority, because of their independency, are in continual jealousies, and in the state and posture of gladiators; having their weapons pointing, and their eyes fixed on one another; that is, their forts, garrisons, and guns upon the frontiers of their kingdoms; and continual spies upon their neighbours; which is a posture of war. But because they uphold thereby the industry of their subjects; there does not follow from it that misery which accompanies the liberty of particular men.

To this war of every man, against every man, this also is consequent; that nothing can be unjust. The notions of right and wrong, justice and injustice, have there no place. Where there is no common power, there is no law: where no law, no injustice. Force and fraud are in war the two cardinal virtues. Justice and injustice are none of the faculties neither of the body nor mind. If they were, they might be in a man that were alone in the world, as well as his senses, and passions. They are qualities that relate to men in society, not in solitude. It is consequent also to the same condition, that there be no propriety, no dominion, no "mine" and

"thine" distinct; but only that to be every man's, that he can get; and for so long, as he can keep it. And thus much for the ill condition, which man by mere nature is actually placed in; though with a possibility to come out of it, consisting partly in the passions, partly in his reason.

The passions that incline men to peace, are fear of death; desire of such things as are necessary to commodious living; and a hope by their industry to obtain them. And reason suggesteth convenient articles of peace, upon which men may be drawn to agreement. These articles are they which otherwise are called the Laws of Nature. . . .

OF THE CAUSES, GENERATION AND DEFINITION OF A COMMONWEALTH

The final cause, end, or design of men, who naturally love liberty, and dominion over others, in the introduction of that restraint upon themselves, in which we see them live in commonwealths, is the foresight of their own preservation, and of a more contented life thereby; that is to say, of getting themselves out from that miserable condition of war, which is necessarily consequent, as hath been shown above to the natural passions of men, when there is no visible power to keep them in awe, and tie them by fear of punishment to the performance of their covenants, and observation of those laws of Nature. . . .

For the laws of Nature, as "justice," "equity," "modesty," "mercy," and in sum, "doing to others, as we would be done to," of themselves, without the terror of some power, to cause them to be observed are contrary to our natural passions, that carry us to partiality, pride, revenge, and the like. And covenants, without the sword, are but words, and of no strength to secure a man at all. Therefore notwithstanding the laws of Nature, which every one hath then kept, when he has the will to keep them, when he can do it safely, if there be no power erected, or not great enough for our security; every man will, and may lawfully rely on his own strength and art, for caution against all other men. And in all places, where men have lived by small families, to rob and spoil one another, has been a trade, and so far from being reputed against the law of Nature, that the greater spoils they gained, the greater was their honour; and men observed no other laws therein, but the laws of honour; that is, to abstain from cruelty, leaving to men their lives, and instruments of husbandry. And as small families did then; so now do cities and kingdoms, which are but greater families, for their own security, enlarge their dominions, upon all pretences of danger, and fear of invasion, or assistance that may be given to invaders, and endeavour as much as they can, to subdue, or weaken their neighbours, by open force and secret arts, for want of other caution, justly; and are remembered for it in after ages with honour.

Nor is it the joining together of a small number of men, that gives them this security; because in small numbers, small additions on the one side or the other, make the advantage of strength so great, as is sufficient to carry the victory; and therefore gives encouragement to an invasion. The multitude sufficient to confide in for our security, is not determined by any certain number, but by comparison with the enemy we fear; and is then sufficient, when the odds of the enemy is not of so visible and conspicuous mo-

ment, to determine the event of war, as to move him to attempt.

And be there never so great a multitude; yet if their actions be directed according to their particular judgments and particular appetites, they can expect thereby no defence, nor protection, neither against a common enemy, nor against the injuries of one another. For being distracted in opinions concerning the best use and application of their strength, they do not help but hinder one another; and reduce their strength by mutual opposition to nothing; whereby they are easily, not only subdued by a very few that agree together; but also when there is no common enemy, they also make war upon each other, for their particular interests. For if we could suppose a great multitude of men to consent in the observation of justice, and other laws of Nature, without a common power to keep them all in awe, we might as well suppose all mankind to do the same; and then there neither would be, nor need to be any civil government or commonwealth at all; because there would be peace without subjection.

Nor is it enough for the security, which men desire should last all the time of their life, that they be governed and directed by one judgment, for a limited time: as in one battle, or one war. For though they obtain a victory by their unanimous endeavour against a foreign enemy; yet afterwards, when either they have no common enemy, or he that by one part is held for an enemy, is by another part held for a friend, they must needs by the difference of their interests dissolve, and fall again into a war amongst themselves.

It is true that certain living creatures, as bees and ants, live sociably one with another, which are therefore by Aristotle numbered amongst political creatures;

and yet have no other direction than their particular judgments and appetites; nor speech, whereby one of them can signify to another, what he thinks expedient for the common benefit: and therefore some man may perhaps desire to know, why mankind cannot do the same. To which I answer,

First, that men are continually in competition for honour and dignity, which these creatures are not; and consequently amongst men there ariseth on that ground, envy and hatred, and finally war; but amongst these not so.

Secondly, that amongst these creatures, the common good differeth not from the private, and being by nature inclined to their private, they procure thereby the common benefit. But man, whose joy consisteth in comparing himself with other men, can relish nothing but what is eminent.

Thirdly, that these creatures, having not, as man, the use of reason, do not see, nor think they see any fault in the administration of their common business; whereas amongst men, there are very many that think themselves wiser, and abler to govern the public, better than the rest; and these strive to reform and innovate, one this way, another that way; and thereby bring it into distraction and civil war.

Fourthly, that these creatures, though they have some use of voice, in making known to one another their desires and other affections; yet they want that art of words, by which some men can represent to others that which is good in the likeness of evil; and evil in the likeness of good; and augment or diminish the apparent greatness of good and evil; discontenting men, and troubling their peace at their pleasure.

Fifthly, irrational creatures cannot distinguish between "injury" and "damage"; and therefore as long as they be at ease, they are not offended with their fellows, whereas man is then most troublesome, when he is most at ease; for then it is that he loves to show his wisdom, and control the actions of them that govern the commonwealth.

Lastly, the agreement of these creatures is natural; that of men is by covenant only, which is artificial: and therefore it is no wonder if there be somewhat else required, besides covenant, to make their agreement constant and lasting; which is a common power, to keep them in awe, and to direct their actions to the common benefit.

The only way to erect such a common power, as may be able to defend them from the invasion of foreigners, and the injuries of one another, and thereby to secure them in such sort, as that by their own industry, and by the fruits of the earth, they may nourish themselves and live contentedly, is, to confer all their power and strength upon one man, or upon one assembly of men, that may reduce all their wills, by plurality of voices, unto one will: which is as much as to say, to appoint one man, or assembly of men, to bear their person; and every one to own, and acknowledge himself to be author of whatsoever he that so beareth their person, shall act, or cause to be acted, in those things which concern the common peace and safety; and therein to submit their wills, every one to his will, and their judgments, to his judgment. This is more than consent, or concord; it is a real unity of them all, in one and the same person, made by covenant of every man, in such manner, as if every man should say to every man, "I authorize and give up my right of governing myself, to this man, or to this assembly of men, on this condition, that thou give up thy right to him, and authorize all his actions in like manner." This done, the multitude so united in one person is called a "commonwealth," in Latin *civitas*. This is the generation of that great LEVIATHAN, or rather, to speak more reverently, of that "mortal god," to which we owe under the "immortal God," our peace and defence. For by this authority, given him by every particular man in the commonwealth, he hath the use of so much power and strength conferred on him, that by terror thereof, he is enabled to perform the wills of them all, to peace at home, and mutual aid against their enemies abroad. And in him consisteth the essence of the commonwealth; which, to define it, is *one person of whose acts a great multitude, by mutual covenants one with another, have made themselves every one the author, to the end he may use the strength and means of them all, as he shall think expedient, for their peace and common defence.*

And he that carrieth this person is called "sovereign," and is said to have "sovereign power"; and every one besides, his "subject."

The attaining to this sovereign power is by two ways. One, by natural force; as when a man maketh his children to submit themselves and their children to his government, as being able to destroy them if they refuse; or by war subdueth his enemies to his will, giving them their lives on that condition. The other is, when men agree amongst themselves to submit to some man, or assembly of men, voluntarily, on confidence to be protected by him against all others. This latter may be called a political commonwealth, or commonwealth by "institution"; and the former, a commonwealth by "acquisition." And first, I shall speak of a commonwealth by institution.

OF THE RIGHTS OF SOVEREIGNS BY INSTITUTION

A "commonwealth" is said to be "insituted," when a "multitude" of men do agree, and "covenant, every one, with every one," that to whatsoever "man," or "assembly of men," shall be given by the major part, the "right" to "represent" the person of them all, that is to say, to be their "representative"; every one, as well he that "voted for it," as he that "voted against it," shall "authorize" all the actions and judgments, of that man, or assembly of men, in the same manner, as if they were his own, to the end, to live peaceably amongst themselves, and be protected against other men.

From this institution of a commonwealth are derived all the "rights" and "faculties" of him, or them, on whom sovereign power is conferred by the consent of the people assembled.

First, because they covenant, it is to be understood, they are not obliged by former covenant to anything repugnant hereunto. And consequently they that have already instituted a commonwealth, being thereby bound by covenant, to own the actions and judgments of one, cannot lawfully make a new covenant, amongst themselves, to be obedient to any other, in anything whatsoever, without his permission. And therefore, they that are subjects to a monarch, cannot without his leave cast off monarchy, and return to the confusion of a disunited multitude: nor transfer their person from him that beareth it, to another man, or other assembly of men: for they are bound, every man to every man, to own, and be reputed author of all, that he that already is their sovereign, shall do, and judge fit to be done; so that one man dissenting, all the rest should break their covenant made to that man, which is injustice: and they have also every man given the sovereignty to him that beareth their person; and therefore if they depose him, they take from him that which is his own, and so again it is injustice. Besides, if he that attempteth to depose his sovereign, be killed, or punished by him for such attempt, he is author of his own punishment, as being by the institution, author of all his sovereign shall do: and because it is injustice for a man to do anything for which he may be punished by his own authority, he is also upon that title unjust. And whereas some men have pretended for their disobedience to their sovereign, a new covenant, made not with men, but with God; this also is unjust: for there is no covenant with God but by mediation of somebody that representeth God's person; which none doth but God's lieutenant, who hath the sovereignty under God. But this pretence of covenant with God, is so evident a lie, even in the pretenders' own consciences, that it is not only an act of an unjust, but also of a vile and unmanly disposition.

Secondly, because the right of bearing the person of them all, is given to him they make sovereign, by covenant only of one to another, and not of him to any of them; there can happen no breach of covenant on the part of the sovereign: and consequently none of his subjects, by any pretence of forfeiture, can be freed from his subjection. That he which is made sovereign maketh no covenant with his subjects before hand, is manifest; because either he must make it with the whole multitude, or one party to the covenant; or he must make a several covenant with every man. With the whole, as one party, it is impossible; because as yet they are not one person and if he make so many several covenants as there be men, those

covenants after he hath the sovereignty are void; because what act soever can be pretended by any one of them for breach thereof, is the act both of himself and of all the rest, because done in the person and by the right of every one of them in particular. Besides, if any one or more of them pretend a breach of the covenant made by the sovereign at his institution; and others, or one other of his subjects, or himself alone, pretend there was no such breach, there is in this case no judge to decide the controversy; it returns therefore to the sword again; and every man recovereth the right of protecting himself by his own strength, contrary to the design they had in the institution. It is therefore in vain to grant sovereignty by way of precedent covenant. The opinion that any monarch receiveth his power by covenant, that is to say, on condition, proceedeth from want of understanding this easy truth, that covenants being but words and breath, have no force to oblige, contain, constrain, or protect any man, but what it has from the public sword; that is, from the united hands of that man, or assembly of men that hath the sovereignty, and whose actions are avouched by them all, and performed by the strength of them all, in him united. But when an assembly of men is made sovereign, then no man imagineth any such covenant to have passed in the institution; for no man is so dull as to say, for example, the people of Rome made a covenant with the Romans, to hold the sovereignty on such or such conditions; which not performed, the Romans might lawfully depose the Roman people. That men see not the reason to be alike in a monarchy, and in a popular government, proceedeth from the ambition of some, that are kinder to the government of an assembly, whereof they may hope to participate, than of monarchy, which they despair to enjoy.

Thirdly, because the major part hath by consenting voices declared a sovereign; he that dissented must now consent with the rest; that is, be contented to avow all the actions he shall do, or else justly be destroyed by the rest. For if he voluntarily entered into the congregation of them that were assembled, he sufficiently declared thereby his will, and therefore tacitly covenanted to stand to what the major part should ordain: and therefore if he refuse to stand thereto, or make protestation against any of their decrees, he does contrary to his covenant, and therefore unjustly. And whether he be of the congregation or not; and whether his consent be asked or not, he must either submit to their decrees, or be left in the condition of war he was in before; wherein he might without injustice be destroyed by any man whatsoever.

Fourthly, because every subject is by this institution author of all the actions and judgments of the sovereign instituted, it follows, that whatsoever he doth it can be no injury to any of his subjects, nor ought he to be by any of them accused of injustice. For he that doth anything by authority from another doth therein no injury to him by whose authority he acteth: but by this institution of a commonwealth every particular man is author of all the sovereign doth; and consequently, he that complaineth of injury from his sovereign complaineth of that whereof he himself is author, and therefore ought not to accuse any man but himself; no, nor himself of injury; because to do injury to one's self is impossible. It is true that they that have sovereign power may commit iniquity, but not injustice or injury in the proper signification.

Fifthly, and consequently to that which was said last, no man that hath sovereign power can justly be put to death, or otherwise in any manner by his subjects punished. For seeing every subject is author of the actions of his sovereign, he punisheth another for the actions committed by himself.

And because the end of this institution is the peace and defence of them all; and whosoever has right to the end has right to the means; it belongeth of right to whatsoever man or assembly that hath the sovereignty to be judge both of the means of peace and defence, and also of the hindrances and disturbances of the same, and to do whatsoever he shall think necessary to be done, both beforehand, for the preserving of peace and security, by prevention of discord at home and hostility from abroad; and, when peace and security are lost, for the recovery of the same. And therefore,

Sixthly, it is annexed to the sovereignty to be judge of what opinions and doctrines are averse and what conducing to peace; and consequently, on what occasions, how far, and what men are to be trusted withal, in speaking to multitudes of people, and who shall examine the doctrines of all books before they be published. For the actions of men proceed from their opinions, and in the well-governing of opinions consisteth the well-governing of men's actions, in order to their peace and concord. And though in matter of doctrine nothing ought to be regarded but the truth; yet this is not repugnant to regulating the same by peace. For doctrine repugnant to peace can be no more true than peace and concord can be against the law of Nature. It is true that in a commonwealth, where, by the negligence or unskilfulness of governors and teachers, false doctrines are by time generally received; the contrary truths may be generally offensive. Yet the most sudden and rough bursting in of a new truth that can be, does never break the peace, but only sometimes awakes the war. For those men that are so remissly governed, that they dare take up arms to defend or introduce an opinion, are still in war; and their condition not peace, but only a cessation of arms for fear of one another; and they live, as it were, in the precincts of battle continually. It belongeth therefore to him that hath the sovereign power to be judge, or constitute all judges of opinions and doctrines, as a thing necessary to peace, thereby to prevent discord and civil war.

Seventhly, is annexed to the sovereignty, the whole power of prescribing the rules, whereby every man may know what goods he may enjoy, and what actions he may do, without being molested by any of his fellow subjects; and this is it men call "propriety." For before constitution of sovereign power, as hath already been shown, all men had right to all things, which necessarily causeth war: and therefore this propriety, being necessary to peace, and depending on sovereign power, is the act of that power, in order to the public peace. These rules of propriety, or *meum* and *tuum,* and of "good," "evil," "lawful," and "unlawful" in the actions of subjects, are the civil laws; that is to say, the laws of each commonwealth in particular; though the name of civil law be now restricted to the ancient civil laws of the city of Rome, which being the head of a great part of the world, her laws at that time were in these parts the civil law.

Eighthly, is annexed to the sovereignty, the right of judicature; that is to say, of hearing and deciding all controversies, which may arise concerning law, either civil or natural, or concerning fact. For without the decision of controversies, there is no protection of one subject against the injuries of another; the laws concerning *meum* and *tuum* are in vain, and to every man remaineth, from the natural and necessary appetite of his conservation, the right of protecting himself by his private strength, which is the condition of war, and contrary to the end for which every commonwealth is instituted.

Ninthly, is annexed to the sovereignty, the right of making war and peace with other nations and commonwealths; that is to say, of judging when it is for the public good, and how great forces are to be assembled, armed, and paid for that end; and to levy money upon the subjects to defray the expenses thereof. For the power by which the people are to be defended consisteth in their armies, and the strength of an army, in the union of their strength under one command, which command the sovereign instituted, therefore hath; because the command of the "militia," without other institution, maketh him that hath it sovereign. And therefore whosoever is made general of an army, he that hath the sovereign power is always generalissimo.

Tenthly, is annexed to the sovereignty, the choosing of all counsellors, ministers, magistrates, and officers, both in peace and war. For seeing the sovereign is charged with the end, which is the common peace and defence, he is understood to have power to use such means as he shall think most fit for his discharge.

Eleventhly, to the sovereign is committed the power of rewarding with riches or honour, and of punishing with corporal or pecuniary punishment, or with ignominy, every subject according to the law he hath formerly made, or if there be no law made, according as he shall judge most to conduce to the encouraging of men to serve the commonwealth, or deterring of them from doing disservice to the same.

Lastly, considering what value men are naturally apt to set upon themselves; what respect they look for from others; and how little they value other men; from whence continually arise amongst them, emulation, quarrels, factions, and at last war, to the destroying of one another, and diminution of their strength against a common enemy; it is necessary that there be laws of honour, and a public rate of the worth of such men as have deserved, or are able to deserve well of the commonwealth; and that there be force in the hands of some or other, to put those laws in execution. But it hath already been shown, that not only the whole "militia," or forces of the commonwealth, but also the judicature of all controversies, is annexed to the sovereignty. To the sovereign therefore it belongeth also to give titles of honour; and to appoint what order of place and dignity each man shall hold; and what signs of respect, in public or private meetings, they shall give to one another. . . .

OF THE SEVERAL KINDS OF COMMONWEALTH BY INSTITUTION, AND OF SUCCESSION TO THE SOVEREIGN POWER

The difference of commonwealths consisteth in the difference of the sovereign, or the person representative of all and every one of the multitude. And because the sovereignty is either in one man, or in an assembly of more than one; and into that assembly either every man hath right to enter, or not every one, but certain men distinguished from the rest; it is manifest, there can be but three kinds of commonwealth. For the representative must needs be one man, or more: and if more, when it is the assembly of all that will come together, then it is a "democracy," or popular commonwealth: when an assembly of a part only, then it is called an "aristocracy." Other kind of commonwealth there can be none: for either one or more, or all, must have the sovereign power, which I have shown to be indivisible, entire.

There be other names of government in the histories and books of policy, as "tyranny," and "oligarchy": but they are not the names of other forms of government, but of the same forms misliked. For they that are discontented under "monarchy," call it "tyranny"; and they that are displeased with "aristocracy," call it "oligarchy": so also they which find themselves grieved under a "democracy," call it "anarchy," which signifies want of government; and yet I think no man believes that want of government is any new kind of government: nor by the same reason ought they to believe that the government is of one kind when they like it, and another when they dislike it, or are oppressed by the governors.

It is manifest, that men who are in absolute liberty may, if they please, give authority to one man to represent them every one; as well as give such authority to any assembly of men whatsoever; and consequently may subject themselves, if they think good, to a monarch as absolutely as to any other representative. Therefore, where there is already erected a sovereign power, there can be no other representative of the same people, but only to certain particular ends, by the sovereign limited. For that were to erect two sovereigns; and every man to have his person represented by two actors, that by opposing one another, must needs divide that power, which, if men will live in peace, is indivisible, and thereby reduce the multitude into the condition of war, contrary to the end for which all sovereignty is instituted. And therefore as it is absurd to think that a sovereign assembly, inviting the people of their dominion to send up their deputies, with power to make known their advice, or desires, should therefore hold such deputies rather than themselves, for the absolute representatives of the people; so it is absurd also to think the same in a monarchy. And I know not how this so manifest a truth should of late be so little observed; that in a monarchy, he that had the sovereignty from a descent of six hundred years, was alone called sovereign, had the title of Majesty from every one of his subjects, and was unquestionably taken by them for their king, was notwithstanding never considered as their representative; the name without contradiction passing for the title of those men, which at his command were sent up by the people to carry their petitions, and give him, if he permitted it, their advice. Which may serve as an admonition, for those that are the true and absolute representative of a people, to instruct men in the nature of that office, and to take heed how they admit of any other general representation upon any occasion whatsoever, if they mean to discharge the trust committed to them.

The difference between these three kinds of commonwealth, consisteth not in the difference of power; but in the difference of convenience, or aptitude to produce the peace and security of the people; for which end they were instituted. And to compare monarchy with the other two, we may observe; first, that whosoever beareth the person of the people, or is one of that assembly that bears it, beareth also his own natural person. And though he be careful in his politic person to procure the common interest; yet he is more or no less careful to procure the private good of himself, his family, kindred, and friends; and for the most part, if the public interest chance to cross the private, he prefers the private: for the passions of men are commonly more potent than their reason. From whence it follows, that where the public and private interest are most closely united, there is the public most advanced. Now in monarchy, the private interest is the same with the public. The riches, power, and honour of a monarch, arise only from the riches, strength, and reputation of his subjects. For no king can be rich, nor glorious, nor secure, whose subjects are either poor, or contemptible, or too weak through want or dissension, to maintain a war against their enemies: whereas in a democracy, or aristocracy, the public prosperity confers not so much to the private fortune of one that is corrupt, or ambitious, as doth many times a perfidious advice, a treacherous action, or a civil war.

Secondly, that a monarch receiveth counsel of whom, when, and where he pleaseth; and consequently may hear the opinion of men versed in the matter about which he deliberates, of what rank or quality soever, and as long before the time of action, and with as much secrecy, as he will. But when a sovereign assembly has need of counsel, none are admitted but such as have a right thereto from the beginning; which for the most part are of those who have been versed more in the acquisition of wealth than of knowledge; and are to give their advice in long discourses, which may and do commonly excite men to action, but not govern them in it. For the "understanding" is by the flame of the passions, never enlightened, but dazzled. Nor is there any place, or time, wherein an assembly can receive counsel with secrecy, because of their own multitude.

Thirdly, that the resolutions of a monarch are subject to no other inconstancy, than that of human nature; but in assemblies, besides that of Nature, there ariseth an inconstancy from the number. For the absence of a few, that would have the resolution once taken, continued firm, which may happen by security, negligence, or private impediments, or the diligent appearance of a few of the contrary opinion, undoes to-day all that was concluded yesterday.

Fourthly, that a monarch cannot disagree with himself, out of envy or interest; but an assembly may; and that to such a height, as may produce a civil war.

Fifthly, that in monarchy there is this inconvenience; that any subject, by the power of one man, for the enriching of a favorite or flatterer, may be deprived of all he possesseth; which I confess is a great and inevitable inconvenience.

But the same may as well happen, where the sovereign power is an assembly: for their power is the same; and they are as subject to evil counsel, and to be seduced by orators, as a monarch by flatterers; and becoming one another's flatterers, serve one another's covetousness and ambition by turns. And whereas the favorites of monarchs are few, and they have none else to advance but their own kindred; the favorites of an assembly are many; and the kindred much more numerous than of any monarch. Besides there is no favorite of a monarch, which cannot as well succour his friends as hurt his enemies; but orators, that is to say, favorites of sovereign assemblies, though they have great power to hurt, have little to save. For to accuse, requires less eloquence, such is man's nature, than to excuse; and condemnation, than absolution more resembles justice.

3. LOCKE

Locke's treatises on government have generally been considered as offered in justification of the English Revolution of 1688. Such justification is provided by the philosopher largely by arguing that government and society exist in order to preserve the individual's rights, and that a ruler's failure to abide by this fundamental stipulation calls for his removal. The assumptions of this theory that explains society in terms of individual interests were outlined in a description of the "state of nature" and conclusions drawn from its implications, which were quite different from those of Hobbes and far more influential.

From: *The Second Treatise on Government*

OF THE STATE OF NATURE

To understand political power aright, and derive it from its original, we must consider what estate all men are naturally in, and that is, a state of perfect freedom to order their actions, and dispose of their possessions and persons as they think fit,

From John Locke, *Treatise on Government* (London, 1690), Book 2.

within the bounds of the law of nature, without asking leave or depending upon the will of any other man.

A state also of equality, wherein all the power and jurisdiction is reciprocal, no one having more than another, there being nothing more evident than that creatures of the same species and rank, promiscuously born to all the same advantages of nature, and the use of the same faculties, should also be equal one amongst another without subordination or subjection, unless the lord and master of them all should, by any manifest declaration of his will, set one above another, and confer on him, by an evident and clear appointment, an undoubted right to dominion and sovereignty. . . .

But though this be a state of liberty, yet it is not a state of license; though man in that state have an uncontrollable liberty to dispose of his person or possessions, yet he has not liberty to destroy himself, or so much as any creature in his possession, but where some nobler use than its bare preservation calls for it. The state of nature has a law of nature to govern it, which obliges every one, and reason, which is that law, teaches all mankind who will but consult it, that being all equal and independent, no one ought to harm another in his life, health, liberty or possessions. For men being all the workmanship of one omnipotent and infinitely wise Maker—all the servants of one sovereign Master, sent into the world by his order and about his business—they are his property, whose workmanship they are, made to last during his, not one another's pleasure. And, being furnished with like faculties, sharing all in one community of nature, there cannot be supposed any such subordination among us that may authorize us to destroy one another, as if we were made for one an-

other's uses, as the inferior ranks of creatures are for ours. Every one as he is bound to preserve himself, and not to quit his station willfully, so by the like reason, when his own preservation comes not in competition, ought he as much as he can, to preserve the rest of mankind, and not unless it be to do justice on an offender, take away, or impair the life or what tends to be the preservation of the life, the liberty, health, limb, or goods of another. . . .

OF THE BEGINNINGS OF POLITICAL SOCIETIES

Men, being, as has been said, by nature all free, equal, and independent, no one can be put out of this estate and subjected to the political power of another without his own consent. The only way whereby anyone divests himself of his natural liberty and puts on the bonds of civil society, is by agreeing with other men, to join and unite into a community for their comfortable, .safe and peaceable living one amongst another, in a secure enjoyment of their properties, and a greater security against any that are not of it. This any number of men may do, because it injures not the freedom of the rest; they are left, as they were, in the liberty of the state of nature. When any number of men have so consented to make one community or government, they are thereby presently incorporated, and make one body politic, wherein the majority have a right to act and conclude the rest. . . .

And thus every man, by consenting with others to make one body politic under one government, puts himself under an obligation to every one of that society to submit to the determination of the majority, and to be concluded by it; or else this original compact whereby he with others incorporates into one society, would signify nothing. . . .

For if the consent of the majority shall not, in reason be received as the act of the whole, and conclude every individual; nothing but the consent of every individual can make anything to be the act of the whole; but such a consent is next to impossible ever to be had. . . .

OF THE ENDS OF POLITICAL SOCIETY AND GOVERNMENT

If man in the state of nature be so free as has been said, if he be absolute lord of his own person and possessions, equal to the greatest and subject to nobody, why will he part with his freedom? Why will he give up this empire, and subject himself to the dominion and control of any other power? To which it is obvious to answer, that though in the state of nature he hath such a right, yet the enjoyment of it is very uncertain and constantly exposed to the invasion of others; for all being kings as much as he, every man his equal, and the greater part no strict observers of equity and justice, the enjoyment of the property he has in this state is very unsafe, very insecure. This makes him willing to quit this condition which, however free, is full of fears and continual dangers; and it is not without reason that he seeks out and is willing to join in society with others who are already united, or have a mind to unite for the mutual preservation of their lives, liberties and estates, which I call by the general name —property.

The great and chief end, therefore, of men uniting into commonwealths, and putting themselves under government, is the preservation of their property; to

which in the state of nature there are many things wanting.

First, There wants an established, settled, known law, received and allowed by common consent to be the standard of right and wrong, and the common measure to decide all controversies between them. For though the law of nature be plain and intelligible to all rational creatures, yet men, being biased by their interest, as well as ignorant for want of study of it, are not apt to allow of it as a law binding to them in the application of it to their particular cases.

Secondly, In the state of nature there wants a known and indifferent judge, with authority to determine all differences according to the established law. For every one in that state, being both judge and executioner of the law of nature, men being partial to themselves, passion and revenge is very apt to carry them too far, and with too much heat in their own cases, as well as negligence and unconcernedness, make them too remiss in other men's.

Thirdly, In the state of nature there often wants power to back and support the sentence when right, and to give it due execution. They who by any injustice offend will seldom fail where they are able by force to make good their injustice. Such resistance many times makes the punishment dangerous, and frequently destructive to those who attempt it.

Thus mankind, notwithstanding all the privileges of the state of nature, being but in an ill condition while they remain in it, are quickly driven into society. Hence it comes to pass, that we seldom find any number of men live any time together in this state. The inconveniences that they are therein exposed to by the irregular and uncertain exercise of the power every man has of punishing the transgressions of others, make them take sanctuary under the established laws of government, and therein seek the preservation of their property. It is this makes them so willingly give up every one his single power of punishing to be exercised by such alone as shall be appointed to it amongst them, and by such rules as the community, or those authorized by them to that purpose, shall agree on. And in this we have the original right and rise of both the legislative and executive power as well as of the governments and societies themselves.

For in the state of nature, to omit the liberty he has of innocent delights, a man has two powers.

The first is to do whatsoever he thinks fit for the preservation of himself and others within the permission of the law of nature, by which law, common to them all, he and all the rest of mankind are of one community, make up one society, distinct from all other creatures. And were it not for the corruption and viciousness of degenerate men there would be no need of any other, no necessity that men should separate from this great and natural community, and associate into lesser combinations.

The other power a man has in the state of nature is the power to punish the crimes committed against that law. Both these he gives up when he joins in a private, if I may so call it, or particular political society, and incorporates into any commonwealth separate from the rest of mankind.

The first power—viz., of doing whatsoever he thought fit for the preservation of himself and the rest of mankind, he gives up to be regulated by laws made by the society, so far forth as the preservation of himself and the rest of that society shall require; which laws of the society

in many things confine the liberty he had by the law of nature.

Secondly, The power of punishing he wholly gives up, and engages his natural force (which he might before employ in the execution of the law of nature, by his own single authority, as he thought fit), to assist the executive power of the society as the law thereof shall require. For being now in a new state, wherein he is to enjoy many conveniences from the labor, assistance, and society of others in the same community, as well as protection from its whole strength, he is to part also with as much of his natural liberty, in providing for himself, as the good, prosperity, and safety of the society shall require, which is not only necessary but just, since the other members of the society do the like.

But though men when they enter into society give up the equality, liberty, and executive power they had in the state of nature into the hands of the society, to be so far disposed of by the legislative as the good of the society shall require, yet it being only with an intention in every one the better to preserve himself, his liberty and property (for no rational creature can be supposed to change his condition with an intention to be worse), the power of the society or legislative constituted by them can never be supposed to extend farther than the common good, but is obliged to secure every one's property by providing against those three defects above mentioned that made the state of nature so unsafe and uneasy. And so, whoever has the legislative or supreme power of any commonwealth, is bound to govern by established standing laws, promulgated and known to the people, and not by extemporary decrees; by indifferent and upright judges, who are to decide controversies by those laws; and to employ the force of the community at home only in the execution of such laws, or abroad to prevent or redress foreign injuries and secure the community from inroads and invasion. And all this to be directed to no other end, but the peace, safety, and public good of the people.

OF THE EXTENT OF THE
LEGISLATIVE POWER

The great end of men's entering into society being the enjoyment of their properties in peace and safety, and the great instrument and means of that being the laws established in that society, the first and fundamental positive law of all commonwealths is the establishing of the legislative power. . . . This legislative is not only the supreme power of the commonwealth, but sacred and unalterable in the hands where the community have once placed it. Nor can any edict of anybody else, in what form soever conceived, or by what power soever backed, have the force and obligation of a law which has not its sanction from that legislative which the public has chosen and appointed. . . .

Though the legislative . . . be the supreme power in every commonwealth; yet,

First, it is not, nor can possibly be, absolutely arbitrary over the lives and fortunes of the people. . . . For nobody can transfer to another more power than he has in himself, and nobody has an absolute arbitrary power over himself, or over any other, to destroy his own life, or take away the life or property of another. A man, as has been proved, cannot subject himself to the arbitrary power of another; and having, in the state of na-

ture, no arbitrary power over the life, liberty, or possession of another, but only so much as the law of nature gave him for the preservation of himself and the rest of mankind, this is all he doth, or can give up to the commonwealth, and by it to the legislative power, so that the legislative can have no more than this. Their power in the utmost bounds of it is limited to the public good of the society. It is a power that hath no other end but preservation, and therefore can never have a right to destroy, enslave, or designedly to impoverish the subjects. The obligations of the law of nature cease not in society, but only in many cases are drawn closer, and have, by human laws, known penalties annexed to them to enforce their observation. Thus the law of nature stands as an external rule to all men, legislators as well as others. The rules that they make for other men's actions must, as well as their own and other men's actions, be conformable to the law of nature—i.e., to the will of God, of which that is a declaration, and the fundamental law of nature, being the preservation of mankind, no human sanction can be good or valid against it.

Secondly, the legislative or supreme authority cannot assume to itself a power to rule by extemporary arbitrary decrees, but is bound to dispense justice and decide the rights of the subject by promulgated standing laws, and known authorized judges. For the law of nature being unwritten, and so nowhere to be found but in the minds of men, they who, through passion or interest, shall miscite or misapply it, cannot so easily be convinced of their mistake where there is no established judge. To avoid these inconveniences which disorder men's properties in the state of nature, men unite into societies that they may have the united strength of the whole society to secure and defend their properties, and may have standing rules to bound it by which every one may know what is his. To this end it is that men give up all their natural power to the society they enter into, and the community put the legislative power into such hands as they think fit, with this trust, that they shall be governed by declared laws, or else their peace, quiet, and property will still be at the same uncertainty as it was in the state of nature.

Absolute arbitrary power, or governing without settled standing laws, can neither of them consist with the ends of society and government. . . . And, therefore, whatever form the commonwealth is under, the ruling power ought to govern by declared and received laws, and not by extemporary dictates and undetermined resolutions. . . . For all the power the government has, being only for the good of the society, as it ought not to be arbitrary and at pleasure, so it ought to be exercised by established and promulgated laws, that both the people may know their duty, and be safe and secure within the limits of the law, and the rulers, too, kept within their due bounds, and not tempted by the power they have in their hands to employ it to purposes, and by such measures as they would not have known, and own not willingly.

Thirdly, the supreme power cannot take from any man any part of his property without his own consent. For the preservation of property being the end of government, and that for which men enter into society, it necessarily supposes and requires that the people should have property, without which they must be supposed to lose that by entering into society, which was the end for which they entered into it; too gross an absurdity for any man to own. Men, therefore, in so-

ciety having property, they have such a right to the goods, which by the law of the community are theirs, that nobody hath a right to take them, or any part of them, from them without their own consent; without this they have no property at all. For I have truly no property in that which another can by right take from me when he pleases against my consent. Hence it is a mistake to think that the supreme or legislative power of any commonwealth can do what it will, and dispose of the estates of the subject arbitrarily, or take any part of them at pleasure. This is not much to be feared in governments where the legislative consists wholly or in part in assemblies which are variable, whose members upon the dissolution of the assembly are subjects under the common laws of their country, equally with the rest. But in governments where the legislative is in one man as in absolute monarchies, there is danger still, that they will think themselves to have a distinct interest from the rest of the community, and so will be apt to increase their own riches and power by taking what they think fit from the people. For a man's property is not at all secure, though there be good and equitable laws to set the bounds of it between him and his fellow-subjects, if he who commands those subjects have power to take from any private man what part he pleases of his property, and use and dispose of it as he thinks good.

But government into whosesoever hands it is put, being as I have before showed, entrusted with this condition, and for this end, that men might have and secure their properties, the prince or senate, however it may have power to make laws for the regulating of property between the subjects one amongst another, yet can never have a power to take to themselves the whole, or any part of the subjects' property, without their own consent; for this would be in effect to leave them no property at all. And to let us see that even absolute power, where it is necessary, is not arbitrary by being absolute, but is still limited by that reason, and confined to those ends which required it in some cases to be absolute, we need look no farther than the common practice of martial discipline. For the preservation of the army, and in it of the whole commonwealth, requires an absolute obedience to the command of every superior officer, and it is justly death to disobey or dispute the most dangerous or unreasonable of them; but yet we see that neither the sergeant that could command a soldier to march up to the mouth of a cannon, or stand in a breach where he is almost sure to perish, can command that soldier to give him one penny of his money; nor the general that can condemn him to death for deserting his post, or not obeying the most desperate orders, cannot yet with all his absolute power of life and death dispose of one farthing of that soldier's estate, or seize one jot of his goods; whom yet he can command anything, and hang for the least disobedience. Because such a blind obedience is necessary to that end for which the commander has his power—viz., the preservation of the rest, but the disposing of his goods has nothing to do with it.

It is true governments cannot be supported without great charge, and it is fit every one who enjoys his share of the protection should pay out of his estate his proportion for the maintenance of it. But still it must be with his own consent—i.e., the consent of the majority, giving it either by themselves or their representatives chosen by them; for if any one shall claim a power to lay and levy taxes on the people by his own authority, and without such consent of the people, he thereby invades the fundamental law of property, and subverts the end of government. For what property have I in that which another may by right take when he pleases to himself?

Fourthly, The legislative cannot transfer the power of making laws to any other hands, for it being but a delegated power from the people, they who have it cannot pass it over to others. The people alone can appoint the form of the commonwealth, which is by constituting the legislative, and appointing in whose hands that shall be. And when the people have said, "We will submit, and be governed by laws made by such men, and in such forms," nobody else can say other men shall make laws for them; nor can they be bound by any laws but such as are enacted by those whom they have chosen and authorized to make laws for them. . . .

These are the bounds which the trust that is put in them by the society and the law of God and nature have set to the legislative power of every commonwealth, in all forms of government.

First: They are to govern by promulgated established laws, not to be varied in particular cases, nor to have one rule for rich and poor, for the favorite at court, and the countryman at plough.

Secondly: These laws also ought to be designed for no other end ultimately but the good of the people.

Thirdly: They must not raise taxes on the property of the people without the consent of the people given by themselves or their deputies. . . .

Fourthly: The legislative neither must nor can transfer the power of making laws to anybody else, or place it anywhere but where the people have.

OF THE SUBORDINATION OF THE POWERS OF THE COMMONWEALTH

Though in a constituted commonwealth . . . there can be but one supreme power, which is the legislative, to which all the rest are and must be subordinate, yet the legislative being only a fiduciary power to act for certain ends, there remains still in the people a supreme power to remove or alter the legislative, when they find the legislative act contrary to the trust reposed in them. For all power given with trust for the attaining an end being limited by that end; whenever that end is manifestly neglected or opposed, the trust must necessarily be forfeited, and the power devolve into the hands of those that gave it, who may place it anew where they shall think best for their safety and security. And thus the community perpetually retains a supreme power of saving themselves from the attempts and designs of anybody, even of their legislators, whenever they shall be so foolish or so wicked as to lay and carry on designs against the liberties and properties of the subject. For no man or society of men having a power to deliver up their preservation, or consequently the means of it, to the absolute will and arbitrary dominion of another, whenever any one shall go about to bring them into such a slavish condition, they will always have a right to preserve what they have not a power to part with, and to rid themselves of those who invade this fundamental, sacred, and unalterable law of self-preservation for which they entered into society. And thus the community may be said in this respect to be always the supreme power, but not as considered under any form of government, because this power of the people can never take place till the government be dissolved.

In all cases whilst the government subsists, the legislative is the supreme power. For what can give laws to another must needs be superior to him. . . .

It may be demanded here, what if the executive power, being possessed of the force of the commonwealth, shall make use of that force to hinder the meeting and acting of the legislative, when the original constitution or the public exigencies require it? I say, using force upon the people, without authority, and contrary to the trust put in him that does so, is a state of war with the people, who have a right to reinstate their legislative in the exercise of their power. . . . In all states and conditions the true remedy of force without authority is to oppose force to it. The use of force without authority always puts him that uses it into a state of war as the aggressor, and renders him liable to be treated accordingly. . . .

OF TYRANNY

As usurpation is the exercise of power which another hath a right to, so tyranny is the exercise of power beyond right, which nobody can have a right to; and this is making use of the power any one has in his hands, not for the good of those who are under it, but for his own private, separate advantage. When the governor, however entitled, makes not the law but his will the rule, and his commands and actions are not directed to the preservation of the properties of his people, but the satisfaction of his own ambition, revenge, covetousness, or any other irregular passion [that is tyranny]. . . .

It is a mistake to think this fault is proper only to monarchies. Other forms of government are liable to it as well as that; for wherever the power that is put in any hands for the government of the people and the preservation of their properties is applied to other ends, and made use of to impoverish, harass, or subdue them to the arbitrary and irregular commands of those that have it, there it presently becomes tyranny, whether those that thus use it are one or many. Thus we read of the thirty tyrants at Athens, as well as one at Syracuse; and the intolerable dominion of the Decemviri at Rome was nothing better.

Wherever law ends, tyranny begins, if the law be transgressed to another's harm; and whosoever in authority exceeds the power given him by the law, and makes use of the force he has under his command to compass that upon the subject which the law allows not, ceases in that to be a magistrate, and acting without authority may be opposed, as any other man who by force invades the right of another. This is acknowledged in subordinate magistrates. He that hath authority to seize my person in the street may be opposed as a thief and a robber if he endeavors to break into my house to execute a writ, notwithstanding that I know he has such a warrant and such a legal authority as will empower him to arrest me abroad. And why this should not hold in the highest, as well as in the most inferior magistrate, I would gladly be informed. Is it reasonable that the eldest brother, because he has the greatest part of his father's estate, should thereby have a right to take away any of his younger brothers' portions? Or, that a rich man, who possessed a whole country, should from thence have a right to seize, when he pleased, the cottage and garden of his poor neighbor? The being rightfully possessed of great power and riches, exceedingly beyond the greatest part of the sons of Adam, is so far from being an excuse,

much less a reason for rapine and oppression, which the endamaging another without authority is, that it is a great aggravation of it. For the exceeding the bounds of authority is no more a right in a great than a petty officer, no more justifiable in a king than a constable.

May the commands, then, of a prince be opposed? May he be opposed? May he be resisted, as often as any one shall find himself aggrieved, and but imagine he has not right done him? This will unhinge and overturn all politics, and instead of government and order, leave nothing but anarchy and confusion.

To this I answer: That force is to be opposed to nothing but to unjust and unlawful force. Whoever makes any opposition in any other case draws on himself a just condemnation, both from God and man, and no such danger or confusion will follow, as is often suggested.

OF THE DISSOLUTION OF GOVERNMENT

He that will, with any clearness, speak of the dissolution of government, ought in the first place to distinguish between the dissolution of the society and the dissolution of the government. That which makes the community, and brings men out of the loose state of nature into one politic society, is the agreement which everyone has with the rest to incorporate and act as one body, and so be one distinct commonwealth. The usual, and almost only way whereby this union is dissolved, is the inroad of foreign force making a conquest upon them. . . . The world is too well instructed in, and too forward to allow of this way of dissolving of governments, to need any more to be said of it. . . .

There is, therefore, secondly, another way whereby governments are dissolved, and that is, when the legislative, or the prince, either of them act contrary to their trust.

First: the legislative acts against the trust reposed in them when they endeavor to invade the property of the subject, and to make themselves, or any part of the community, masters or arbitrary disposers of the lives, liberties, or fortunes of the people.

. . . Whensoever, therefore, the legislative shall transgress this fundamental rule of society, and either by ambition, fear, folly, or corruption, endeavor to grasp themselves, or put into the hands of any other, an absolute power over the lives, liberties, and estates of the people; by this breach of trust they forfeit the power the people had put into their hands for quite contrary ends; and it devolves to the people, who have a right to resume their original liberty, and by the establishment of a new legislative (such as they shall think fit), provide for their own safety and security, which is the end for which they are in society. What I have said here concerning the legislative in general holds true also concerning the supreme executor, who having a double trust put in him, both to have a part in the legislative and the supreme execution of the law, acts against both, when he goes about to set up his own arbitrary will as the law of the society. He acts also contrary to his trust when he employs the force, treasure, and offices of the society to corrupt the representatives, and gain them to his purposes, when he openly preengages the electors, and prescribes, to their choice, such whom he has, by solicitation, threats, promises, or otherwise, won to his designs, and employs them to bring in such who have promised beforehand what to vote and what to enact. Thus to regulate candidates and electors, and new model the ways of election, what is it but to cut up the government by the roots, and poison the very fountain of public security?

To this, perhaps it will be said that the people being ignorant and always discontented, to lay the foundation of government in the unsteady opinion and uncertain humor of the people, is to expose it to certain ruin; and no government will be able long to subsist if the people may set up a new legislative whenever they take offense at the old one. To this I answer, quite the contrary. People are not so easily got out of their old forms as some are apt to suggest. They are hardly to be prevailed with to amend the acknowledged faults in the frame they have been accustomed to. And if there be any original defects, or adventitious ones introduced by time or corruption, it is not an easy thing to get them changed, even when all the world sees there is an opportunity for it. This slowness and aversion in the people to quit their old constitutions has in the many revolutions that have been seen in this kingdom, in this and former ages, still kept us to, or after some interval of fruitless attempts, still brought us back again to, our old legislative of kings, lords, and commons; and whatever provocations have made the crown be taken from some of our princes' heads, they never carried the people so far as to place it in another line.

But it will be said this hypothesis lays a ferment for further rebellion. To which I answer:

First: no more than any other hypothesis. For when the people are made miserable, and find themselves exposed to the ill usage or arbitrary power, cry up their governors as much as you will for sons of

Jupiter, let them be sacred and divine, descended or authorized from Heaven; give them out for whom or what you please, the same will happen. The people generally ill treated, and contrary to right, will be ready upon any occasion to ease themselves of a burden that sits heavy upon them. They will wish and seek for the opportunity, which in the change, weakness, and accidents of human affairs, seldom delays long to offer itself. He must have lived but a little while in the world, who has not seen examples of this in his time; and he must have read very little who cannot produce examples of it in all sorts of governments in the world.

Secondly: I answer, such revolutions happen not upon every little mismanagement in public affairs. Great mistakes in the ruling part, many wrong and inconvenient laws, and all the slips of human frailty will be borne by the people without mutiny or murmur. But if a long train of abuses, prevarications, and artifices, all tending the same way, make the design visible to the people, and they cannot but feel what they lie under, and see whither they are going, it is not to be wondered that they should then rouse themselves, and endeavor to put the rule into such hands which may secure to them the ends for which government was at first erected, and without which, ancient names and specious forms are so far from being better, that they are much worse than the state of nature or pure anarchy; the inconveniences being all as great and as near, but the remedy farther off and more difficult.

Thirdly: I answer, that this . . . power in the people of providing for their safety anew by a new legislative when their legislators have acted contrary to their trust by invading their property, is the best fence against rebellion, and the probablest means to hinder it. For rebellion being an opposition, not to persons, but authority, which is founded only in the constitutions and laws of the government; those, whoever they be, who by force break through, and by force justify their violation of them, are truly and properly rebels. For when men, by entering into society and civil government, have excluded force, and introduced laws for the preservation of property, peace, and unity amongst themselves, those who set up force again in opposition to the laws, do *rebellare*—that is, bring back again the state of war, and are properly rebels, which they who are in power (by the pretence they have to authority, the temptation of force they have in their hands, and the flattery of those about them), being likeliest to do, the properest way to prevent the evil is to show them the danger and injustice of it who are under the greatest temptation to run into it. . . .

But if they who say it lays a foundation for rebellion mean that it may occasion civil wars or intestine broils to tell the people they are absolved from obedience when illegal attempts are made upon their liberties or properties, and may oppose the unlawful violence of those who were their magistrates when they invade their properties, contrary to the trust put in them, and that, therefore, this doctrine is not to be allowed, being so destructive to the peace of the world; they may as well say, upon the same ground, that honest men may not oppose robbers or pirates, because this may occasion disorder or bloodshed. If any mischief come in such cases, it is not to be charged upon him who defends his own right, but on him that invades his neighbor's. If the innocent honest man must quietly quit all he has for peace's sake to him who will lay violent hands upon it, I desire it may be considered what a kind of peace there will be in the world which consists only in violence and rapine, and which is to be maintained only for the benefit of robbers and oppressors. Who would not think it an admirable peace betwixt the mighty and the mean, when the lamb, without resistance, yielded his throat to be torn by the imperious wolf?

The end of government is the good of mankind; and which is best for mankind, that the people should be always exposed to the boundless will of tyranny, or that the ruler should be sometimes liable to be opposed when they grow exorbitant in the use of their power, and employ it for the destruction, and not the preservation, of the properties of their people?

Nor let any one say that mischief can arise from hence as often as it shall please a busy head or turbulent spirit to desire the alteration of the government. It is true such men stir whenever they please, but it will be only to their own just ruin and perdition. For till the mischief be grown general, and the ill designs of the rulers become visible, or their attempts sensible to the greater part, the people who are more disposed to suffer than right themselves by resistance, are not apt to stir. The examples of particular injustice or oppression of here and there an unfortunate man moves them not. But if they universally have a persuasion grounded upon manifest evidence that designs are carrying on against their liberties, and the general course and tendency of things cannot but give them strong suspicions of the evil intention of their governors, who is to be blamed for it? Who can help it if they, who might avoid it, bring themselves into this suspicion? Are the people to be blamed if they have the sense of rational creatures, and can think of things

no otherwise than as they find and feel them? And is it not rather their fault who put things in such a posture that they would not have them thought as they are? I grant that the pride, ambition, and turbulency of private men have sometimes caused great disorders in commonwealths, and factions have been fatal to states and kingdoms. But whether the mischief hath oftener begun in the people's wantonness, and a desire to cast off the lawful authority of their rulers, or in the rulers' insolence and endeavors to get and exercise an arbitrary power over their people, whether oppression or disobedience gave the first rise to the disorder, I leave it to impartial history to determine. This I am sure, whoever, either ruler or subject, by force goes about to invade the rights of either prince or people, and lays the foundation for overturning the constitution and frame of any just government, he is guilty of the greatest crime I think a man is capable of, being to answer for all those mischiefs of blood, rapine, and desolation, which the breaking to pieces of governments brings on a country; and he who does it is justly to be esteemed the common enemy and pest of mankind; and is to be treated accordingly. . . .

Here it is like, the common question will be made, Who shall be judge whether the prince or legislative act contrary to their trust? . . . To this I reply, The people shall be judge; for who shall be judge whether his trustee or deputy acts well and according to the trust reposed in him, but he who deputes him and must, by having deputed him, have still a power to discard him when he fails in his trust? If this be reasonable in particular cases of private men, why should it be otherwise in that of the greatest moment, where the welfare of millions is concerned and also where the evil, if not prevented, is greater, and the redress very difficult, dear, and dangerous? . . .

If a controversy arise betwixt a prince and some of the people in a matter where the law is silent or doubtful, and the thing be of great consequence, I should think the proper umpire in such a case should be the body of the people. For in cases where the prince hath a trust reposed in him, and is dispensed from the common, ordinary rules of the law, there, if any men find themselves aggrieved, and think the prince acts contrary to, or beyond that trust, who so proper to judge as the body of the people (who at first lodged that trust in him) how far they meant it should extend? But if the prince, or whoever they be in the administration, decline that way of determination, the appeal then lies nowhere but to Heaven; force between either persons who have no known superior on earth, or which permits no appeal to a judge on earth, being properly a state of war, wherein the appeal lies only to Heaven; and in that state the injured party must judge for himself when he will think fit to make use of that appeal and put himself upon it.

To conclude: The power that every individual gave the society when he entered into it can never revert to the individuals again, as long as the society lasts, but will always remain in the community; because without this there can be no community —no commonwealth, which is contrary to the original agreement; so also when the society hath placed the legislative in any assembly of men, to continue in them and their successors, with direction and authority for providing such successors, the legislative can never revert to the people whilst that government lasts; because, having provided a legislative with power to continue forever, they have given up their political power to the legislative and cannot resume it. But if they have set limits to the duration of their legislative, and made this supreme power in any person or assembly only temporary; or else, when, by the miscarriages of those in authority it is forfeited; upon the forfeiture of their rules, or at the determination of the time set, it reverts to the society, and the people have a right to act as supreme, and continue the legislative in themselves or place it in a new form, or new hands, as they think good.

1 2 3 4 5 6 7 8 9 10